juin 2011

D1087470

Healthcare and the Effect of Technology:
Developments, Challenges and Advancements

Stefane M. Kabene
Ecole des Hautes Etudes en Santé Publique (EHESP), France

MEDICAL INFORMATION SCIENCE REFERENCE

Hershey · New York

Director of Editorial Content:	Kristin Klinger
Director of Book Publications:	Julia Mosemann
Acquisitions Editor:	Lindsay Johnston
Development Editor:	Christine Bufton
Publishing Assistant:	Sean Woznicki
Typesetter:	Myla Harty
Production Editor:	Jamie Snavely
Cover Design:	Lisa Tosheff
Printed at:	Yurchak Printing Inc.

Published in the United States of America by
Medical Information Science Reference (an imprint of IGI Global)
701 E. Chocolate Avenue
Hershey PA 17033
Tel: 717-533-8845
Fax: 717-533-8661
E-mail: cust@igi-global.com
Web site: http://www.igi-global.com/reference

Library of Congress Cataloging-in-Publication Data

Healthcare and the effect of technology : developments, challenges, and
advancements / Stefane M. Kabene, editor.
      p. ; cm.
  Includes bibliographical references and index.
  Summary: "This book examines current developments and challenges in the incorporation of ICT in the health system from the vantage point of patients, providers, and researchers. The authors take an objective, realistic view of the shift that will result for patients, providers, and the healthcare industry in general from the increased use of eHealth services"--Provided by publisher.
  ISBN 978-1-61520-733-6 (hardcover)
 1. Medical informatics. 2. Medical telematics. 3. Medical technology. I. Kabene, Stefane M., 1956- [DNLM: 1. Medical Informatics Applications. 2. Electronic Health Records. 3. Telemedicine. W 26.5 H43445 2010] R858.H37 2010
  610.285--dc22
                              2009054324

British Cataloguing in Publication Data
A Cataloguing in Publication record for this book is available from the British Library.

Table of Contents

Section 1
Introduction and Overview of Technology in Health Care

Section 2
The Use of Technology:
From the Individual to the Community

Section 3
Who will put it in Place?

Section 4
Challenges:
Privacy and Data Record Linkage

Section 5
Challenges: Ethics

Section 6
Future Uses of Technology

Detailed Table of Contents

Section 1
Introduction and Overview of Technology in Health Care

Chapter 1

    Kendall Ho, University of British Columbia, Canada

While information technologies, the Internet, and mobile technologies are introducing innovative approaches to knowledge exchange, communication, and new knowledge generation, the health system is comparatively slow in taking up these approaches towards healthcare service delivery. This chapter discusses the opportunities that information technology (IT) can offer to health care system innovation and improvement, highlights some key IT trends that will guide research and development, and highlights some current examples. Some action steps are suggested to accelerate the adoption of IT into routine health practices.

Chapter 2

    Francesco Paolucci, The Australian National University, Australia
    Henry Ergas, Concept Economics, Australia
    Terry Hannan, Australian College of Health Informatics, Australia
    Jos Aarts, Erasmus University, The Netherlands

Health care is complex and there are few sectors that can compare to it in complexity and in the need for almost instantaneous information management and access to knowledge resources during clinical decision-making. There is substantial evidence available of the actual, and potential, benefits of e-health tools that use computerized clinical decision support systems (CDSS) as a means for improving health care delivery. CDSS and associated technologies will not only lead to an improvement in health care but will also change the nature of what we call electronic health records (EHR) The technologies that "define" the EHR will change the nature of how we deliver care in the future. Significant challenges relating to the evaluation of these health information management systems relate to demonstrating their ongoing cost-benefit, cost-effectiveness, and effects on the quality of care and patient outcomes. However, health information technology is still mainly about the effectiveness of processes and process outcomes, and the technology is still not mature, which may lead to unintended consequences, but it remains promising and unavoidable in the long run.

Chapter 3
Malina Jordanova, Solar-Terrestrial Influences Institute, Bulgaria

Brought to life by contemporary changes of our world, e-health offers enormous possibilities. In the World Health Organization's World Health Assembly resolution on e-health, WHO has defined e-health as the cost-effective and secure use of information and communication technologies in support of health and health-related fields, including healthcare services, health surveillance, health literature, and health education (WHO, 2005). It is impossible to have a detailed view of its potential as e-health affects the entire health sector and is a viable tool to provide routine, as well as specialized, health services. It is able to improve both the access to, and the standard of, health care. The aim of the chapter is to focus on how e-health can help in closing one gap - optimizing patient care. The examples included and references provided are ready to be introduced in practice immediately. Special attention is dedicated to cost effectiveness of e-health applications.

Chapter 4
Stefane M. Kabene, Ecole des Hautes Etudes en Santé Publique (EHESP), France
Melody Wolfe, University of Western Ontario, Canada

The integration of technology into health care has created both advantages and disadvantages for patients, providers, and healthcare systems alike. This chapter examines the risks and benefits of technology in health care, with particular focus on electronic health records (EHRs), the availability of health information online, and how technology affects relationships within the healthcare setting. Overall, it seems the benefits of technology in health care outweigh the risks; however, it is imperative that proper measures are taken to ensure successful implementation and integration. Accuracy, validity, confidentiality, and privacy of health data and health information are key issues that must be addressed for successful implementation of technology.

Section 2
The Use of Technology:
From the Individual to the Community

Chapter 5
Aviv Shachak, University of Toronto, Canada
Shmuel Reis, Technion- Israel Institute of Technology, Israel

The implementation of electronic health records (EHRs) holds the promise to improve patient safety and quality of care, as well as opening new ways to educate patients and engage them in their own care. On the other hand, EHR use also changes clinicians' workflow, introduces new types of errors, and can distract the doctor's attention from the patient. The purpose of this chapter is to explore these issues from a micro-level perspective, focusing on the patient consultation. The chapter shows the fine balance between beneficial and unfavorable impacts of using the EHR during consultations on patient safety and patient-centered care. It demonstrates how the same features that contribute to greater efficiency may cause potential risk to the patient, and points to some of the strategies, best practices, and enabling factors that may be used to leverage the benefits of the EHR. In particular, the authors point to the role that medical education should play in preparing practitioners for the challenges of the new, computerized, environment of 21st century medicine.

This chapter provides a novel, unique, and reasonably broad set of perspectives on the human resources (HR) and information technology (IT) ramifications of the electronic patient record (EPR) as an integral component of the total hospital information system.

Providing quality healthcare services to geographically isolated communities remains a considerable challenge to health service providers throughout the world. The conventional approach of referring patients to specialists often requiring the patient to travel long distances still remains mainstream. Meanwhile, the advancements in information and communication technologies (ICT) have acted as a catalyst for substantial changes in human activities in areas such as communication, commerce, and education. Researchers are exploring the potential of ICT to improve health services for patients in rural and remote areas. This chapter provides an overview of telemedicine applications and the experience of a research and health service which has pioneered the delivery of specialist pediatric services at a distance (telepediatrics) in Queensland, Australia.

Chapter 8

This chapter investigates the provision of public health information, especially health service quality and cost information, to the general public in the United States. The authors first review the health system of the US from three aspects: its public policy, structure, and accreditation of health institutions. Then the complexity of health information provision and the challenges in its interpretation are identified and analyzed. "Comparison-shopping" is introduced as a new mode of decision support for individuals to select health services, and examples of its current applications are given. The comparison-shopping mechanism in the e-commerce industry and the health information industry are compared and the different driving forces in health information comparison-shopping are analyzed. Several directions for future research are provided for researchers and health practitioners.

Section 3
Who will put it in Place?

Healthcare organizations are struggling to provide safe and high quality care while reducing costs. Abundant data on various aspects of care delivery are collected and stored in large databases in different parts of the organization. Informatics, as an area of study with roots in computer science and information science, has grown and evolved to enable collection, storage, retrieval, and analysis of data, and reporting of useful information. Health informatics (HI) ranges from bioinformatics to public health informatics depending on the level of focus and applications. At the same time, systems engineering (SE), as an interdisciplinary field of engineering, has grown to encompass the design, analysis, and management of complex health systems to improve their quality and performance. HI and SE are complementary in their approach to identification of problems, methodology, and solution procedure for improvement. This combination brings forth implications for industry and education to address pressing issues of today's health care delivery.

Chapter 10

The revolution in information technology and in information and knowledge management contributed to the generation of actionable information and actionable knowledge required to address critical problems of national and global health care. Yet, despite expectations, e-based approaches are far from fulfilling the dream of equitable and universal access to health across the globe. A dramatically new approach is needed if health care is to be brought "among the people." Based on maximum integration of computer technology (CT), information technology (IT), information management (IM), and knowledge management (KM), and multidimensional human expertise, the concept of "Teams of Leaders" (ToL) provides a foundation for such an approach. Utilizing the entire spectrum of IT/IM/KM, irrespective of specific platforms, and harnessing globally distributed human expertise, Teams of Leaders transcend bureaucracies and politics, create "bottom-up" flows of ideas and knowledge, and generate horizontal and vertical collaboration among hitherto isolated actors. By empowering people rather than concentrating on technology-facilitated improvements of processes, ToL may prove to be one of the pivotal concepts behind the desperately needed healthcare revolution.

Section 4
Challenges:
Privacy and Data Record Linkage

Candace J. Gibson, The University of Western Ontario, Canada
Kelly J. Abrams, Canadian Health Information Management Association, Canada

The introduction of information technologies and the electronic record in health care is thought to be a key means of improving efficiencies and effectiveness of the health care system ; ensuring critical information is readily available at the point of care, decreasing unnecessary duplication of tests, increasing patient safety (particularly from adverse drug events) ,and linking providers and patients spatially and temporally across the continuum of care as health care moves out of the traditional hospital setting to the community and home. There is a steady movement in many countries towards e-health and a fully implemented, in some cases, pan-regional or pan-national electronic heath record. A number of barriers and challenges exist in EHR implementation. These include lack of resources (both capital and human resources), resistance to change and adoption of new technologies, and lack of standards to ensure interoperability across separate applications and systems. From the public's perspective, maintaining the security, privacy, and confidentiality of personal health information is a prominent concern and privacy of personal health information still looms as a potential stumbling block for the implementation of a comprehensive, shared electronic record. There are some steps that can be taken to increase the public's comfort level and to ensure that these new systems are designed and used with security and privacy in mind.

Gulzar H. Shah, National Association of County and City Health Officials, USA
Kaveepan Lertwachara, California Polytechnic State University, USA
Anteneh Ayanso, Brock University, Canada

In this chapter, the authors provide a review of recent developments in probabilistic record linkage and their implications in healthcare research and public health policies. Their primary objective is to pique the interest of researchers and practitioners in the healthcare and public health communities to take full advantage of record linkage technologies in completing a health care scenario where different pieces of patient records are collected and managed by different agencies. A brief overview of probabilistic record linkage, software available for such record linkage, and type of functions provided by probabilistic record linkage software is provided. Specific cases where probabilistic linkage has been used to bridge information gaps in informing public health policy and enhancing decision-making in healthcare delivery are described in this chapter. Issues and challenges of integrating medical records across distributed databases are also outlined, including technical considerations as well as concerns about patient privacy and confidentiality.

Section 5
Challenges: Ethics

Chapter 13

  Robert J. Barnet, Georgetown University, USA

It is important to recognize that the four "p"s - power, position, prestige and profit - too frequently drive science, business, academia, and the professions. This chapter is concerned with the importance of appropriate consent, the just distribution of the material benefits of scientific research, and the possible exploitation of research subjects. Informed consent and social consensus may not adequately address the related ethical issues involved in biobanking and other related research. Past experiences internationally, especially among the marginalized, are reviewed. The chapter explores whether benefits that accrue to those involved in research, and even the larger community, can rely on the concept of social consensus. Is there sufficient attention to transparency and adequate consideration of present and future harms and benefits to research subjects, their descendants and the broader community? Are conflicts of interest, real and potential, adequately acknowledged and addressed?

Chapter 14

  Nada Gligorov, Mount Sinai School of Medicine, USA
  Stephen C. Krieger, Mount Sinai School of Medicine, USA

Technological advances in neuroscience have made inroads on the localization of identifiable brain states, in some instances purporting the individuation of particular thoughts. Brain imaging technology has given rise to what seem to be novel ethical issues. This chapter will assess the current abilities and limitations of functional neuroimaging and examine its ethical implications. The authors argue that currently there are limitations of fMRI (functional magnetic resonance imaging) and its ability to capture ongoing brain processes. They also examine the impact of neuroimaging on free will and privacy. The degree of variability of brain function precludes drawing meaningful conclusions about an individual's thoughts solely from images of brain activity. They argue that neuroimaging does not raise novel challenges to privacy and free will, but is a recapitulation of traditional moral issues in a novel context.

Section 6
Future Uses of Technology

Chapter 15

  Dario Bottazzi, Guglielmo Marconi Labs, Italy
  Rebecca Montanari, University of Bologna, Italy
  Tarik Taleb, NEC Research Laboratories, Germany

The demographic compression, along with heightened life expectancy and decreases in fertility rates, is dramatically raising the number of older adults in society, thus putting many countries' healthcare systems under significant pressure. Eventual loss of physical and cognitive skills makes it quite difficult for elders to maintain autonomous life-styles and often forces them to move to assisted living environments, with severe emotional and social impacts. The main challenge for the years to come is, therefore, to identify more sustainable approaches to eldercare, capable of improving elders' independence in order to avoid, or at least to delay, hospitalization. Providing suitable support for elders is, indeed, a highly challenging problem. However, recent advancements in pervasive computing enable the development of advanced eldercare services. The main focus of eldercare research to date has been directed towards the development of smart environments capable of assisting elders, for example, in monitoring their psychophysical conditions, and of reminding and facilitating their routine activities. Few research efforts have been directed towards the investigation of solutions capable of improving social engagement for elders living alone, and of facilitating the coordination of care-giving efforts. The chapter provides an overview of the state-of-the-art technology in eldercare research and suggests the extension of available solutions by adopting integrated approaches that aim at addressing both assistance and social/coordination issues stemming from eldercare.

Chapter 16

Jinan Fiaidhi, Lakehead University, Canada
Sabah Mohammed, Lakehead University, Canada
Yuan Wei, Lakehead University, Canada

Now that the health and medical sector is slowly but surely beginning to embrace Web 2.0 technologies and tactics such as social networking, blogging, and sharing health information, such usage may become an everyday occurrence. This new trend is emerging under the Health 2.0 umbrella where it has important effects on the future of medicine. This chapter introduces some important Health 2.0 concepts and discusses their advantages for health care and medical practice. In addition, this chapter provides a case study for building a Semantic Blog for Gene Annotation and Searching (GAS) among social network users. The GAS Blog enables users to syndicate and aggregate gene case studies via the RSS protocol, annotate gene case studies with the ability to add new tags (folksonomy), and search for/navigate gene case studies among a group or cross-groups based on FOAF, GO, and SCORM metadata. The GAS Blog is built upon an open source toolkit (WordPress) and further programmed via PHP. The GAS Blog is found to be very effective for annotation and navigation when compared with the traditional gene annotation and navigation systems, as well as with traditional search engines such as XPath.

Chapter 17

Emmett Davis, More Information, USA

Information and knowledge technologies, both alone and embedded in other advancing technologies, will transform health care. These technologies become part of health care because they bring efficiencies until they reach a tipping point where health care cannot function without them. These technologies add to the complexity of health care further creating a complex adaptive system. They function as strange attractors, or focal points, for intense, persistent, and accelerating change, which transforms the culture and control mechanisms of health care. Such smart technologies as artificial intelligence combined with genomic and nanotechnologies may bring about such a radical change that we could not return to today's health care system. For the transformation to be optimal, health care needs to address such issues as quality improvement processes, more intelligent electronic security, new control mechanisms, redefinition of the boundaries of health care enterprises, and a change from operating in discrete to continuous information flows.

Preface

The prevalence and increasing pervasiveness of information technologies, the Internet, and new mobile technologies is resulting in far-reaching change in how nearly every healthcare organization and healthcare provider functions. While most sectors have embraced Information and Communication Technology (ICT) with open arms, taking advantage of its benefits to enhance customer service, connect with customers, reduce costs, and increase market share, the healthcare industry has been painstakingly slow in incorporating ICT to aid in the delivery of healthcare services and the collection, management, and use of health information. Although in recent years the health services sector has begun to move towards the use of ICT services to aid in providing patients with health care solutions, this shift has been slow and cautious, and much more can be done to improve current healthcare practices and add value to healthcare transactions.

The complexity of the healthcare industry and its need for nearly-instantaneous, accurate information means that the adoption of information technology to deliver health services poses many substantial benefits, but also numerous potential risks. ICT services show the potential to improve the quality of health services and to be more financially efficient than traditional paper-based practices. So far however, uncertainty about the effect on quality of patient-care and outcomes, its cost effectiveness and the long term financial benefits of e-health has significantly slowed the adoption of ICT in the health services industry. While it is impossible to have an exact and detailed view of how the health care industry will be affected in future years by the greater utilization of ICT services, there already exists substantial proof as to the potential benefits of health information technology. Throughout the book we outline areas where information technology can offer healthcare systems safe and superior solutions to existing problems, or simply improve system efficiency. Using concrete examples, key IT trends in health services, research and development are highlighted. The risks and benefits associated with the integration of information technology in the healthcare industry are examined, and means of doing this in a way that ensures IT is both cost-effective and advantageous to patients as long as certain safeguards are maintained, such as ensuring the accuracy, reliability, privacy and confidentiality of any health information that is transferred through ICT services.

The book also explores the flip side of the assimilation of ICT in the healthcare industry, looking at the risks and unintended consequences of using technology to deliver healthcare solutions. Such threats, such as the greater susceptibility of electronic health records to being accessed, lack of adequate training of practitioners, inadequate systems pose valid challenges to the use of health information technology services, and in some cases significantly contribute to the resistance to change that exists regarding the amalgamation and adoption of ICT services in the health care industry. If viable policies are put in place, for instance, to safeguard the reliability and confidentiality of health information obtained and transferred through ICT solutions, such risks can be mitigated and the availability of that health data provide benefits, to the individual and to society, that far outweigh the risks.

The integration of ICT in the health services sector is not something that can be attained overnight, or by simply expending resources to upgrade facilities and equipment. The successful utilization of eHealth solutions will result in fundamental changes to the very way the health services sector is set up and run. Adopting ICT in the health care industry will also require changes in the scope and focus of medical education concerning the role of technology and how to use it most effectively. Additionally, the use of these new technologies poses new ethical questions, particularly in the areas of bioinformatics and biobanking of human tissues and in the emerging field of neuroimaging. New technologies also offer opportunities not possible today and may help to assist in easing the lives of the increasing number of elderly in the society and in researching and searching for information across collaborative networks. Ten years down the road the landscape may look totally different and unrecognizable from what we are familiar with today, but there is no turning back in advancing down this path of new technologies and health care improvements.

The book, comprised of seventeen chapters divided into six broader sections, examines current developments and challenges in the incorporation of ICT in the health system from the vantage point of patients, providers, and researchers. The authors take an objective, realistic view of the shift that will result for patients, providers, and the healthcare industry in general from the increased use of eHealth services, summarizing both the beneficial and potentially detrimental changes, and outline ways to insure maximum benefit while ensuring that the integrity and quality of patient care is not sacrificed.

Section 1 gives the reader an introduction and overview to the use of information and communications technologies in healthcare. Kendall Ho's first chapter provides a brief overview of "health in the digital world" and outlines some of the key technologies that are, and will, make a difference in health care. He outlines four IT trends that will potentially transform health care: the ideas of personalization, increased connectivity, social networking, and co-creation of information and knowledge. Often at odds with the traditional values of a more sedate health system these trends have transformed our modern cultures and society and will have an impact on health and health care. A further, more detailed analysis is given by Paolucci and co-authors in Chapter 2 looking at the effectiveness of IT and health informatics and the great promise of clinical decision support tools put into the hands of health providers. They also look at reasons for why the adoption of electronic records and these technologies has been relatively slow and what challenges (e.g. lack of standards for the integration of disparate technologies and legacy systems, unintended adverse effects, inadequate methodology in determining cost effectiveness) may be holding it up implementation. These topics are explored further in Chapter 3 by Jordanova, particularly from an international and global focus and looking at which 'players' may best be able to advance eHealth adoption. Finally Kabene and Wolfe delineate the risks and benefits of technology in three specific applications: the use of electronic health records, the access to reliable online medical information, and how technology changes the relationship of patients and providers.

In Section 2, in four chapters looking at computer use form the individual to the community, we pick up on the latter aspects of changed relationships in Shachak and Reis's excellent discussion of how the computer alters the traditional patient-provider interaction. The introduction of the computer as a third party in the consulting room accentuates for many physicians both the good and bad aspects of communication and personal styles and emphasizes the need for training of physicians in how best to use this tool in communicating with their patients. Another practicing physician, Bircher turns his eye to the electronic patient record and health information system in the hospital and the potential for positive use in managing resources and activities of physicians and nurses in that clinical setting, but the down-side if that technology does not adequately address clinical needs and/or if clinicians are not provided with adequate training to use it effectively. Chapter 7 by Edirippulige and Smith explores the use of technology to extend healthcare services (telepediatrics) to indigenous children in Australia living in remote areas with limited infrastructure and accessibility. Within this section Wan and evans-Mueller also present and extend the trend of "comparison-shopping" as a means for health consumers to assess and select between health services and health providers – a decision support tool that may prove useful to consumers, providers, and payers within the health system.

Section 3, comprised of two chapters, asks who will put these systems in place. In the Chapter 9 Pasupathy presents a rather simple answer in the form of a new type of health professional or systems engineer – in the practice of health systems engineering. These individuals have some overlap with health informaticians in that they have extensive knowledge of not only information technologies and the health system, but also a 'world view' that takes a holistic view of needs and systems and considers all aspects of the implication behind implementation of health information technology within the health organization. And in an intriguing argument von Lubitz in Chapter 10 suggests we should think of the deployment of IT and advanced information and knowledge management tools in the same way we approach a military campaign – have the right governing triad - politics, the "military" in the form of the healthcare industry, and the recipients of healthcare services – the people. The approach is one that can work globally or locally to coordinate efforts to put advanced technologies in place. In this military inspired model the 'man on the ground' becomes a team of leaders – individuals who are flexible, adaptable, comfortable in operating in complex environments, and build on interactions and a shared foundation of skills, knowledge, and attitudes of similar leaders.

Section 4, encompassing two chapters, looks at further challenges facing the security of healthcare information and how best to link various sources of health data to preserve privacy and confidentiality. A patient's right to complete medical confidentiality is one of the cornerstones of our healthcare industry, and any ICT solutions for the future will need to ensure that this basic right is not violated. Gibson & Abrams review the public's concerns over privacy and examine practices and policies that will be required to ensure privacy and confidentiality of patient information, as well as examining the implications that new health technology will have on health service delivery and public health in general. The key to an effective and efficient health record in which this vital information is shared is the linkage of health data from separate databases and repositories. Shah and co-authors look at specific technical solutions to ensuring that data is linked properly and effectively.

Section 5, in its two chapters, deals with some additional ethical challenges for the future produced by the introduction of new technologies in the area of medical research and future medical care such as biobanking and bioinformatics and functional brain imaging. These new diagnostic and research methods also lead to new ethical dilemmas that previously never existed or existed in more understandable frameworks. Consequently, in this section in Chapters 13 and 14, respectively, we look at the importance of a code of ethics in health ICT and the need to discuss and develop agreement on informed consent, not just for individuals but for societies and marginalized groups of people, and re-examine the concept of the mind-body dualism and free will.

Finally, Section 6 made up of the last three chapters of the book, gives us a glimpse of the future, both in terms of how health technology can be used to support an aging society and used in research to provide new collaborations and better shared knowledge management tools. Botazzi and colleagues examine how demographics is creating unique problems with aging "baby boomers" that can be alleviated by technological solutions for eldercare, to assist them in continuing to live at home or in care. Fiaidhi, Mohammed and Wei present a prototype for a gene annotating system (GAS) blog that builds on the unique technologies of Web 2.0 and shared networking and connectivity to provide a more efficient system for locating and annotating gene ontologies. Finally we come full circle in Chapter 17 with Davis describing the transformation of health care by these various technologies and explains that we are in fact at the tipping point where it is no longer a question of whether these technologies will be adopted but when and how this will change our thinking, doing and actions.

The field of health care and medical research and development is one where the fast paced acquisition of accurate knowledge is of the utmost importance in improving the quality of patient care and in reducing and containing rising health care costs. ICT applications and services can facilitate advancements in medical research and care by providing reliable information where and when it is needed. If certain precautions are not taken however, the benefits of e-health may be outweighed by the possible negative ramifications for patients and healthcare providers alike. Mindful of the consequences, the pros and the cons, that ICT can have for the healthcare industry, all authors have done a noteworthy job in ensuring that the material has been presented in a balanced and objective way, and most eloquently with relevant examples that readers will find both informative and interesting, truly describing the developments, challenges and advancements in technology in health care.

Acknowledgment

I would like to thank:

Valerie, Milou, Vidocq and Tahira for their love and support through this exciting project.

Kabene Ahcene and Kabene Doula for believing in me.

Candace Gibson for her friendship and incredible editorial assistance. She truly helped make this book a great book. Her work and friendship are truly invaluable.

IGI Global and its incredible staff for having believed in us and for their continuous assistance.

The authors who worked hard to provide us with top quality papers, the reviewers who gave their time so generously to take on the difficult task to choose the best papers and help, through their suggestions make them even better. Finally, many thanks to the editorial advisory board members for their vision and guidance.

Thank you all,

Stefane M. Kabene

Section 1
Introduction and Overview of Technology in Health Care

Chapter 1
Health in the Digital World:
Transformational Trends

Kendall Ho
University of British Columbia, Canada

ABSTRACT

While information technologies, the Internet, and mobile technologies are introducing innovative approaches to knowledge exchange, communication, and new knowledge generation, the health system is comparatively slow in taking up these approaches towards healthcare service delivery. This chapter discusses the opportunities that information technology (IT) can offer to health care system innovation and improvement, highlights some key IT trends that will guide research and development, and highlights some current examples. Some action steps are suggested to accelerate the adoption of IT into routine health practices.

INTRODUCTION

Modern information technologies (IT) such as computers, portable devices, and smart phones have evolved rapidly over the last decade, fueled by rapid research and development in electronic technologies, their increasing affordability and portability, the ubiquitous connectivity through high speed and wireless connections, and the evolution of the market place to accommodate these technologies due to consumer demand and expectations. As a result, IT touches our everyday lives in many differ-

ent ways, from work-related usage, such as instant stock quotations or instant messaging, to relaxation activities, such as Web entertainment and online friendships. This 24/7 electronic presence bears an unmistakable and culturally transformational force on how individuals access and disseminate information, communicate with others, learn and exchange knowledge, and provide services (Tapscott & Williams, 2006, pp. 10-15).

Imagine the following activities that are done every day, seamlessly supported by IT:

DOI: 10.4018/978-1-61520-733-6.ch001

- Obtaining the latest news from Web news services such as CNN.com (http://www.cnn.com)
- Going to Youtube (http://www.Youtube.com) to watch the latest clips of shows that one missed on TV
- Using the Web to book travel such as Expedia (http://www.expedia.com), banking, and other daily routines.

None of this would have been possible without the Internet. In fact, one could easily argue that with the various information and services now available on line and easily accessible at our fingertips through the computer keyboard, our everyday lives have been completely transformed by the Internet.

What about our health system? Compared to other sectors, our health system is far from taking full advantage of the latest IT trends to carry out health services, education, and research. There are many sites on the Web providing health information to seekers, and there are even organizations offering on-line health services. However, very few integrate IT as part of the comprehensive and personalized health experience that health consumers are trying to find on line, such as offering on line scheduling and personalized health record access while offering them health advice. An exception to this general phenomenon is the United States Department of Veterans Affairs electronic approach to health care delivery - MyHealtheVet (http://www.myhealth.va.gov) – where personalized and trusted health information, a personal health journal, prescription refills, telemedicine, and links to benefits and resources can be found (Naditz, 2008; Nazi & Woods, 2008). Otherwise, very few organizations or health sites can claim this comprehensive approach to providing IT-enabled health connectivity and transactional services to their health clients.

Worse yet, there are Web sites created by health organizations, commercial entities, and individuals offering health services that are unreli-

able, inaccurate, and may be downright harmful to consumers. For example, when evaluating accuracy and quality of health information of 25 health sites, a panel of 34 physician experts found the coverage of key information to be poor and inconsistent (Berland et al., 2001). In another study, qualified specialists in spinal surgery scored 50 scoliosis Web sites based on a maximum quality score of 32 and found that information about scoliosis on the Internet was of limited quality, with a descending order of quality of sites created by academic institutions (12.6), by physicians (11.3), commercial entities (11), unidentified sources (7.6), and non-physician health professionals (7.0) (Mathur et al., 2005). Similarly, the accuracy score (out of a maximum of 12) reflected poor information, with a descending order created by academic sites (6.6), physicians (6.3), unidentified (6.0), non-physician professionals (5.5), and commercial sites (5.0).

In summary, our current health system in general is inconsistently and significantly under-utilizing the Web and IT for health transactions, and falling far short of the transformational role that the electronic milieu can play in revolutionizing health service delivery. For example, consider, if at present, whether the majority of our citizens:

- Can book and coordinate appointments for health services, similar to booking airline flights?
- Can check their own lab test results and health records anytime, anywhere they want, similar to Internet banking?
- Can inquire about personal health issues by reaching health professionals as we do with our online brokers or travel agents?

Although one might argue that, since health services are decidedly personal and need a high degree of security, carrying out highly personal health services over the Internet would not be wise. However, with many different industries adopting the Internet as one of their core business strategies, should we not identify and maximize the potential of the Web to evolve and offer some of our core health services, wherever possible? In fact, the younger generation now, and the next generation of health consumers, will surely expect the access and delivery of key health services on line, and so health professionals of this generation should better prepare themselves for this evolution to take place (Lupianez-Villanueva, Mayer & Torrent, 2009).

This chapter explores the current underlying trends that drive the IT revolution in our everyday lives, and how these trends clash with our current health system culture. Understanding these trends in action today will help us anticipate how they will influence the future evolution of health in the electronic age, thereby helping health professionals to prepare for the inevitable digitization of our health system tomorrow.

KEY INFORMATION TECHNOLOGY TRENDS DISSECTED

While new varieties of applications and approaches show up on the Internet every day, several underlying trends can be observed that drive the popularity and transformational power of the Internet.

Personalization

The Internet environment can be an overwhelming experience for the uninitiated. Various companies, vendors, or Internet enthusiasts create ways to personalize the experience to ensure that the users experience personal services over time. Two such examples include: Google's (http://www.google.com) and Bing's (http://www.bing.com) search engines' capability to display a range of sites that match the keyword searches with the closest matched displayed first; and Google finance (http://www.google.com/finance) Web site's flexibility for individuals to identify their specific

stocks and type of news that they would like to track and display it in a customized fashion. The enthusiasm for a "Semantic Web" (Berners-Lee & Hendler, 2001), where the Web can be tailored to understand the meaning behind what users are explicitly asking, resulting in the delivery of the specific information that the users want, is the extension of this personalization philosophy. For example, when a person is inquiring about plane fare to and hotels in a city, the semantic interpretation would be that this person desires to travel there and thus related information such as restaurants and entertainment venues in that location are automatically made available to the seeker.

Personalization of the Web experience can be conceptualized in three areas:

- *Just for me*: Creating an environment where the end users can manipulate the various settings, layouts, and information to be viewed or utilized based on the individuals' choices. For example, Facebook (http://www.facebook.com) gives the end user choices of entering their own information, but permits the information to be accessed by others in various levels of detail depending on the relationship to the user - from acquaintances to very close friends and relatives. Also, many Web sites allow individuals to change the front page to cater to the individuals' preferences.

- *Just in time*: End users are looking for immediacy in information and its access, and the Internet can deliver effectively not only through its own content, but also by harnessing similar content uploaded by a variety of users from the same or different perspectives. For example, while Youtube is created and maintained by the Webmaster, the Youtube content is actually uploaded by a vast number of individuals and companies around the world. Many Youtube clips are up-to-the-minute videos from recent television shows or the latest unusual or rare news clips. These clips are then rated by participants, with the highest-rated ones being featured on the front page. The Inaugural speech of the current US president, the latest outcome of reality shows, dramatic news footage of a recent earthquake become content that can be easily accessible to end users.

- *Just in case*: End users want not only to be able to find content on the Web when they need it, but also to have the comfort of knowing that the information is there at their keyboard fingertips in case they need it. Mobile computing through personal digital assistants or smart phones with 24/7 connectivity provides the end users with the possibility of urgency in access, thereby fueling the growth of both the Internet and mobile devices, such as the iPhone, the Blackberry, and other smart phones. Text messaging features of these devices further allow individuals to connect to each other in real time while mobile, leading to trends such as flash mobs (i.e., texting to get a group together spontaneously at a certain time and place), or a last minute rendezvous to give individuals maximum flexibility and mobility for meetings.

Considerations for health applications: The current implementation of electronic health records (EHRs) is focused on documentation of health information of individuals to be accessed primarily by health professionals. The promise of EHR in personalization is to permit patients and health professionals to jointly access the highly personalized information of the patient, providing both with 24/7, just-in-time access whenever and wherever they are, and in case they need the information during travel or unexpected illnesses (Mantas, 2002). From a population health point of view, EHR also holds great promise in customizing the health system tailored to population health

needs, such as tracking chronic disease trends or spread of infections over time (Platt, 2009). However, national levels of EHR adoption have been sluggish due to two major barriers, funding to support EHR roll out and the fear of change among end users, including health professionals and patients (Jarvis, 2009). As a result, further research and developments in EHR adoption and end user engagement are necessary to advance this nationally and internationally (Hayrinen, Saranto, & Nkykanen, 2008).

While the EHR is more helpful for health professionals to collaborate, while patients may passively access their own data, a very strong and parallel trend has been developing towards the establishment of the electronic Personal Health Record (PHR) in which patients actively input their own health perspectives and data into this record to complement data from their health professionals (Iakovidis, 1998). Health consumers' access to their own health information and records is not only the fundamental method for their engagement and empowerment (Wiljer et al., 2008), but also forms the all-important foundation for them to actively seek advice and opinions on line armed with their own information.

Connectivity

The Internet can cater to the need and desire of individuals to be connected to a community of people sharing similar interests, thereby creating a powerful addiction for individuals to use the medium repeatedly. Internet gaming or simulations such as Second Life (http://secondlife.com) or Club Penguin (http://www.clubpenguin.com) are exemplars. Gaming companies also exploit this trend to ensure that their proprietary gaming machines, such as Wii™, Playstation™ or Xbox™, facilitate online connectivity to encourage players to play with and against other players online and to extend the freshness and challenge of the video games beyond the programs themselves. In these cases, connectivity led to unplanned challenges and excitement put forth by the individuals in the gaming communities, without the need of the programmers to inject fresh content to extend the "playability" of the games. This connectivity mentality that leads to effective networking (Deshpande & Jadad, 2006) further extends to the workplace where online collaboration such as MySpace (http://www.myspace.com), Twitter (http://www.twitter.com), Wikipedia documents (http://www.wikipedia.com) or Gtalk (http://www.google.com/talk), facilitate online connectivity for project collaboration and building of virtual teams (Birnsteel, 2008 p. 5).

Considerations for health applications: Today, health professionals working in a common environment, such as an emergency department, freely consult each other informally through hallway dialogues, etc., because they are physically connected. In the future, how do we take advantage of mobile technologies so that health professionals working in different locations, or even working at different times, can connect and carry out these "virtual hallway consultations?" Some examples of good practices in this interprofessional electronic connectivity towards excellence in care include the intensive care environment to augment decision making (Sapirstein, Lone, Latif, Fackler, & Pronovost, 2009), and electronic remote consultations between emergency departments (Campana, Jarvis-Selinger, Ho, Evans, & Zwimpfer, 2007). The challenge is to broaden these local best practices into regional and even national routines.

Social Networking

The concept of Web 2.0 is the use of the Web environment to promote communication, interactivity, and networking of individuals to build virtual communities (Birnsteel, 2008; Deshpande & Jadad, 2006). This concept underpins the successful establishment and growth of Web phenomena such as Facebook, MySpace, blogs, Wikipedia, and Youtube (Boulos, Marimba, & Wheeler, 2006;

Boulos & Wheeler 2007). In these electronic environments, individuals connect with each other and build professional, social, or informal relationships to form self-organized communities to share and democratize and decentralize information (Deshpande & Jadad, 2006). These social networking approaches offer individuals mutual support and development of relationships otherwise not possible due to geographic or temporal separation. Often, because of these communities, great information content and even validated knowledge emerge, such as in the case with Wikipedia or Linux User groups (http://linux.org/groups) where self organizing groups take responsibility of peer review, leading to validation of knowledge to benefit all the community members (see Co-creation below). While personal biases and interests might potentially taint the information presented, a voluntary peer review process such as used in Wikipedia and the Linux user group significantly reduces the biases or, at least, present alternative perspectives to help the readers to evaluate the information presented.

Considerations for health applications: Health professionals are used to knowledge sharing both with (e.g. writing books and magazine articles for pay) and without financial compensation (e.g. writing peer-reviewed journal articles where no financial compensation or royalties are paid back to the authors). Most health professionals recognize that health knowledge is meant to be shared for the greater purpose of optimizing patient-centred care. The social networking nature of the Web is a perfect fit for health professionals to take advantage of optimizing knowledge exchange. How could health professionals apply this approach to team-based practice and patient-centred care? A meta-analysis by Li et al. (2009) has documented exemplars of social networking of health professionals in shared communities of practice where communication and knowledge exchange leads to new knowledge created and evidence of collaboration. Information technologies will surely be able to help consolidate these relationships and knowledge-building approaches towards effective health care delivery.

Co-Creation

While meaningful interactions and knowledge exchange bind individuals together, the generation of new ideas and content through inspirations from these interactions is highly powerful in sustaining the relationship. The ability of individuals in a virtual community to contribute content for fellow community members to consider and discuss, and the resultant refinement of the materials into high quality knowledge signifies the "co-creation" trend (Deshpande & Jadad, 2006; Li et al., 2009; Tapscott & Williams, 2006). For example, feeling that one's vote counts drives the trend of "American Idol" and other programs where audience members are invited to text in, often at their own cost, to vote and determine outcomes. Also, content in Youtube is voted on voluntarily by viewers, and the ratings determine how prominently the content will then be ranked and displayed. Similar types of rating also take place on Expedia.com or other hotel booking sites. Wikipedia gets its quality content based not only on individuals submitting materials, but also on volunteer peer reviewers who validate and refine the content. These knowledge co-creation efforts are vitally important, not only for readers who will return time and time again to the sites to find information, but also for the raters or creators so that they feel that they have contributed to the knowledge pool. This positively reinforcing dynamic among contributors, raters, and readers results in a healthy and organic sustainability of knowledge creation, maintenance, and amplification (Li et al., 2009). This is why sites such as Ratemydoctor.com (http://ratemydoctor. com) thrive, as contributors submit their ratings in hope that this will help others to locate the doctors with the best services as perceived by the patients themselves.

Considerations for health applications: While the medical journals and research publications count on voluntary peer review, the content is ultimately owned by journals and publication companies when authors sign over their rights. As a result, these journal articles are often restricted in distribution. How can we benefit from social networking to democratize the knowledge and make it more readily accessible, and organize peer reviews to ensure content is validated? The movement of open source journals, where authors retain their copyrights, while journals receive the right to distribute content so that the knowledge is accessible via the open access journals distributed freely or which authors can further distribute themselves, are helping us to achieve knowledge democratization (Albert, 2006; Shieber, 2009). Also, universities such as the Massachusetts Institute of Technology are making their course materials freely available online as one way of using knowledge sharing as the glue to attract and retain new members (http://ocw.mit.edu/ OcwWeb).

CULTURAL CLASH: INFORMATION TECHNOLOGY TRENDS VERSUS HEALTH SYSTEM TRADITIONS

The four aforementioned trends – personalization, connectivity, social networking, and co-creation – underpin the success of many of the IT advances witnessed and experienced today, and transform the Internet to become a core part of the fabric of our current and future everyday "e-lives".

Meanwhile, health care remains relatively traditional in service delivery and implementation over all, and one can easily argue that the health care system, in general, is far from taking advantage of the Internet and its digital culture to advance the health and wellness agenda. Specifically, if we were to examine the tradition of health care juxtaposed against these IT trends, we see some underlying cultural differences that pitch the two into diametric opposition. Some of the dominant health system forces at play in service to the health consumer include:

- **System driven**: Individuals entering the health system cannot personalize the experience, but rather have to cater to the system's timing and information flow. For example, rarely do individuals have control over appointment times with health care professionals, or access to their own laboratory information or health records.

- **Isolated experience**: Individual patients often see individual health professionals without the benefit of having other health professionals known to the patient accompany them or advocate for them during new visits. For example, when patients are referred by their family doctors to specialists, with very few exceptions, the family doctor would almost never accompany the patient to see the specialist. The patients would prefer having their own family physicians as advocates to explain to the specialists why they were referred for assessment. While the personalization of the health care experience occurs during the core, one-on-one interaction between the health consumer and the health professional, this experience for the health consumer is often fragmented from one health professional to another, and often it is the health consumer who has to organize and integrate information from all these encounters.

- **Professional silos**: Health professionals often work in isolation from each other, and the most common form of communication between them is paper-based, such as through consultation letters or the traditional paper-based health record. As a result, each health professional involved in the care of a patient might only get an incomplete view of the care that the patient receives, while the patient must integrate the experiences himself or herself with piecemeal advice from all his/her health professionals. For example, a patient sees a doctor for the diagnosis of diabetes, and then is referred to a dietician for a diet review. However, if there are conflicts between the advice of the doctor and the dietician, the onus is on the patient to either choose which advice to follow, or to bring the questions back to ask the two professionals involved, or to ask another trusted source for validation. As a result, the patient is rarely able to have a unified picture of care integrated and interpreted by all of the health professionals treating the patient. This is a far cry from the great potential of having social networking of professionals based around the patient, so that everyone involved in the patient's care, including all health professionals and the patient himself/herself, can see the complete picture and collaboratively bring unified recommendations to minimize conflict and maximize cohesion in management approaches.

- **Professional custodianship of knowledge**: Health professionals are currently considered to be the experts in having mastered health knowledge. The reality is, with the explosion of health evidence through research, it is impossible for any one individual to know the full spectrum of most up to date health care information and disease management (Davis & Taylor-Vaisey, 1997). Also, with the vast source of health information made available through the Internet, patients are increasingly sophisticated in hunting for health information and in seeking decision aids that are specific to their own health or illnesses (O'Connor et al., 2001). We are now at a tipping point where health professionals can, and should, optimally partner with patients to discuss health information that is relevant to the patients, and engage them in optimal self management through coaching and support. This partnership between health professionals and patients, through validated information and a just-for-the-patient management plan co-created by the patient and the health professionals, is ideal for promoting excellence in health care delivery and effective health outcome for patients (Akesson, Saveman, & Nilsson, 2007; Grant & Middleton, 2009).

While the health system as a whole has quite a long way to go to achieve the knowledge co-creation model of care for effective partnerships with patients to support their just-in-time, just-for-them, and just-in-case needs, happily there are pockets of innovation in the health care system where individual doctors, health clinics, or hospital systems are revolutionizing the patient experience by taking advantage of the IT trends. As mentioned before, the U.S. Department of Veterans Affairs' "My HealtheVet" is an exemplar, where patients can get access to their health records, obtain trusted health information, make appointments to see their health professionals, and have their experiences unified electronically in one place. Hopefully, wholesale integration of IT trends into the overall health system's routine operationalization is on the near horizon.

E-HEALTH TRANSFORMATION: ACTION STEPS TO TAKE ADVANTAGE OF INFORMATION TECHNOLOGY

In the forward of the document "Web 2.0 in the Health Sector", Sir Muir Gray, Chief Knowledge Officer of the United Kingdom National Health Services, highlighted eight problems of the health care system today (Birnsteel, 2008), including: errors, poor patient experience, failure to adopt high value interventions, uncritically adopting low value interventions, waste, poor quality of care, unknowing variations in policy and practice, failure to recognize uncertainty, and ignorance. In health system transformation, we need to address at least these eight problems, and simultaneously improve health care accessibility, efficiency, quality, and patient experience.

IT can be one important bundle of solutions to revolutionize and improve the health care system, in particular when we choose to take advantage of its strong trends towards changing our existing health care culture. To achieve this cultural transformation in future health care delivery excellence and in addressing the issues highlighted by Sir Gray, we may consider improving the following five areas as our tactical beachheads:

- **Patient oriented:** To improve patients' experience in interacting with the health care system, having the following services available at their fingertips would be a tremendous start: for example, booking appointments; seeing own laboratory results; access to personalized health advice based on own electronic personal health record online; checking one's own medication profiles. Also, helping health consumers to gain accurate and personalized knowledge and skills to promote self management, and systematically providing support and online advice for wellness and illness prevention would be both reassuring to the patients, and also improve overall health outcomes of the population (Akesson et al., 2007; Grant & Middleton, 2009).
- **Health professional support towards evidence based health care:** Health professionals can use the Web as the source of the latest knowledge and up-to-date decision support in patient management. The Web will support the health professionals in their own learning pace and style, from decision support tools such as InfoPOEMs (Grad et al., 2008), providing mini-lectures online and electronic clinical

practice guidelines (e.g. Canadian Medical Association on line CME) to case simulations (Wagner, Bear & Sander, 2009), and Web casting or podcasting for the latest developments in health news (Westwood, Flett, Riding, & Moon, 2009).

- **Interprofessional collaboration:** IT and the Web can support a team building experience where health professionals – doctors, nurses, pharmacists, physiotherapists, dieticians, etc. – learn and work together towards optimal patient care (Li et al., 2009). eHealth provides the gateway for seamless information exchange between health professionals for patient-centred care, and facilitates knowledge exchange between health professionals to optimally contribute to patient wellness. IT can help overcome distance between health professionals in the virtual team, and facilitate asynchronous communication between them so as to provide better coordination of patient care over time.

- **Health system improvement through prospective population health evidence:** Prospective evidence based medicine through better knowledge capture, population health data refinement, and system cost-effectiveness can help to ensure optimal treatment for the right population, and an efficient health system to respond to the burden of diseases in the population. For example, IT can help to efficiently track the sources of the latest *Listeria* or Avian influenza outbreaks and analyze what needs to be improved to prevent future recurrences. This knowledge can then be rapidly disseminated to all health professionals for increased vigilance to avoid similar errors and to plan better health services to anticipate future outbreaks (Platt, 2009). This population health informatics approach will lead not only to cost-effectiveness, but also to the prospective generation of

understanding of anticipated benefits and unanticipated outcomes that will guide future implementation.

- **Evolving the brave new world of eHealth through the Plan-Do-Study-Act cycle:** As we carry out improvement of our health system today through IT, we will discover new ways of approaching health services and knowledge capture that we can't anticipate today. The next generation of eHealth will surely be different from what we can predict based on our understanding today, in areas such as the use of nanotechnologies in medical therapies; genomics and proteomics in personalized medication manufacturing and distribution; and personalized mobile electronic health records to predict future wellness based on genetic and environmental information (Glaser, Henley, Downing & Brinner, 2008). The well proven continuous improvement model of plan-do-study-act (Langley, Nolan, Nolan, Norman, & Provost, 2009) will be an important approach to introduce and validate current practices to ensure progressive evolution without putting patients or health systems at risk of harm.

CONCLUSION

IT and the Web have given us wonderful approaches towards health system improvement and excellence (Ho, 2008), and current examples of optimal IT use are highly promising. The future of the semantic Web and the hype of Web 3.0 (Getting, 2007, p. 18), where artificial intelligence is to be coupled with social networking to provide an "electronic personalized service in communities," might well materialize in the near future. In order to move us from today's health system to tomorrow's robust and personalized health care, IT will play an increasingly important part.

Today's multifaceted use of the Internet has given us glimpses of what we can do in health. Thoughtful transformation of the IT and Web trends into our health system culture today will not only improve the health system experience, but also open up a new platform for us to continually evolve the health system towards better future systems and delivery of care. Human ingenuity is the foundation that has brought us imaginative technologies and innovations and to where we are today, and all indicators and evidence point to the fact that our ingenuity through IT and the Web will make our health system better, and bring new innovations in eHealth tomorrow that we can't even perceive of today.

REFERENCES

Akesson, K. M., Saveman, B. I., & Nilsson, G. (2007). Health care consumers' experiences of information communication technology- a summary of literature. *International Journal of Medical Informatics*, *76*(9), 633–645. doi:10.1016/j.ijmedinf.2006.07.001

Albert, K. M. (2006). Open access: implications for scholarly publishing and medical libraries. *Journal of the Medical Library Association*, *94*(3), 253–262.

Berland, G. K., Elliot, M. N., Morales, L. S., Algazy, J. I., Kravitz, R. L., & Broder, M. S. (2001). Health information on the Internet: accessibility, quality, and readability in English and Spanish. *Journal of the American Medical Association*, *285*, 2612–2621. doi:10.1001/jama.285.20.2612

Berners-Lee, T., & Hendler, J. (2001). Publishing on the semantic Web. *Nature*, *410*, 1023–1024. doi:10.1038/35074206

Birnsteel, L. (2008). *E-health 2.0: Web 2.0 in the health sector: Industry review with UK perspective. E-health Media Ltd*. Retrieved September 17, 2009 from http://www.e-health-insider.com/img/ehi_reports0332/EHI-ehealth_20_research_report_2008_Exec_Summary.pdf

Boulos, M. N., Marimba, I., & Wheeler, S. (2006). Wikis, blogs and podcasts: a new generation of Web-based tools for virtual collaborative clinical practice and education. *BMC Medical Education*, *6*, 41–49. doi:10.1186/1472-6920-6-41

Boulos, M. N. K., & Wheeler, S. (2007). The emerging Web 2.0 social software: an enabling suite of sociable technologies in health and health care education. *Health Information and Libraries Journal*, *24*, 2–23. doi:10.1111/j.1471-1842.2007.00701.x

Campana, B. A., Jarvis-Selinger, S., Ho, K., Evans, W. L., & Zwimpfer, T. J. (2004). Use of telemedicine for an emergency craniotomy in a pediatric trauma. *Canadian Medical Association Journal*, *171*, 444–446. doi:10.1503/cmaj.1040006

Davis, D. A., & Taylor-Vaisey, A. (1997). Translating guidelines into practice. A systematic review of theoretic concepts, practical experience and research evidence in the adoption of clinical practice guidelines. *Canadian Medical Association Journal*, *157*, 408–416.

Deshpande, A., & Jadad, A. R. (2006). Web 2.0: Could it help move the health system into the 21st century? *Journal of Men's Health & Gender*, *3*(4), 332–336. doi:10.1016/j.jmhg.2006.09.004

Getting, B. (2007). *Basic definitions: Web 1.0, Web 2.0, Web 3.0. Practical ecommerce: insights for online merchants*. Retrieved September 14, 2009 from http://www.practicalecommerce.com/articles/464-Basic-Definitions-Web-1-0-Web-2-0-Web-3-0

Glaser, J., Henley, D. E., Downing, G., & Brinner, K. M. (2008). Personalized Health Care Workgroup of the American Health Information Community. Advancing personalized health care through health information technology: an update from the American Health Information Community's Personalized Health Care Workgroup. *Journal of the American Medical Informatics Association, 15*, 391–396. doi:10.1197/jamia.M2718

Grad, R. M., Pluye, P., Mercer, J., Marlow, B., Beauchamp, M. E., & Shulha, M. (2008). Impact of research-based synopses delivered as daily e-mail: a prospective observational study. *Journal of the American Medical Informatics Association, 15*, 240–245. doi:10.1197/jamia.M2563

Grant, R. W., & Middleton, B. (2009). Improving primary care for patients with complex chronic diseases: can health information technology play a role? *Canadian Medical Association Journal, 181*, 17–18. doi:10.1503/cmaj.091101

Hayrinen, K., Saranto, K., & Nykanen, P. (2008). Definition, structure, use and impacts of electronic health records: a review of the research literature. *International Journal of Medical Informatics, 77*(5), 291–304. doi:10.1016/j.ijmedinf.2007.09.001

Ho, K. (2008). Technology enabled knowledge translation: Using information and communication technologies to accelerate evidence based health practices. In: A.W. Kushniruk, & E.M. Borycki, (Ed.) Human, Social, and Organizational Aspects of Health Information Systems, (pp. pp. 301-313). Hershey, PA: Medical Information Science Reference.

Iakovidis, I. (1998). From electronic medical record to personal health records: present situation and trends in European Union in the area of electronic healthcare records. *Studies in health technology and informatics, 52*(Pt 1: suppl), 18-22.

Jarvis, C. W. (2009). Investigate funding alternatives to support successful EHR implementation. *The Journal of Medical Practice Management, 24*(6), 335–338.

Langley, G. L., Nolan, K. M., Nolan, T. W., Norman, C. L., & Provost, L. P. (2009). The improvement guide: A practical approach to enhancing organizational performance (2nd edition). San Francisco: Jossey-Bass, A Wiley Imprint. Retrieved August 24, 2009 from http://www.ihi.org/IHI/Topics/Improvement/ImprovementMethods/HowToImprove/

Li, L. C., Grimshaw, J. M., Nielson, C., Judd, M., Coyte, P. C., & Graham, I. D. (2009). Use of communities of practice in business and health care sectors: a systematic review. *Implementation Science; IS, 17*(4), 27. doi:10.1186/1748-5908-4-27

Lupianez-Villanueva, F., Mayer, M. A., & Torrent, J. (•••). Opportunities and challenges of Web 2.0 within the health care systems: an empirical exploration. *Informatics for Health & Social Care, 34*(3), 117–126. doi:10.1080/17538150903102265

Mantas, J. (2002). Electronic health record. *Studies in Health Technology and Informatics, 65*, 250–257.

Mathur, S., Shanti, N., Brkaric, M., Sood, V., Kubeck, J., Paulino, C., & Merola, A. A. (2005). Surfing for scoliosis: the quality of information available on the Internet. *Spine, 30*, 2695–2700. doi:10.1097/01.brs.0000188266.22041.c2

MIT Open Courseware. (n.d.). Retrieved August 24, 2009 from http://ocw.mit.edu/OcwWeb/Web/home/home/index.htm

Naditz, A. (2005). Telemedicine at the VA: VistA, MyHealtheVet, and other VA programs. *Telemedicine Journal and e-Health, 14*(4), 330–332. doi:10.1089/tmj.2008.9973

Nazi, K. M., & Woods, S. S. (2008). MyHealtheVet PHR: A description of users and patient portal use. *American Medical Informatics Association Annual Symposium Proceedings, Nov 6*, 1182.

O'Connor, A.M., Bennett, C.L., Stacey, D., Barry, M., Col, N.F., Eden, K.B., et al. (2006). Decision aids for people facing health treatment or screening decisions. *Cochrane Database of Systematic Reviews, 3*. Retrieved from Art. No.: CD001431. DOI: 10.1002/14651858.CD001431.pub2

Platt, R. (2009). Opportunity knocks: the electronic (public health) medical record. *Epidemiology (Cambridge, Mass.), 20*(5), 662–663. doi:10.1097/EDE.0b013e3181b0fb78

Sapirstein, A., Lone, N., Latif, A., Fackler, J., & Pronovost, P.J. (2009). Best practice & research. *Clinical anaesthesiolog, 23*(1), 115-126.

Shieber, S. M. (2009). Equity for open-access journal publishing. *PLoS Biology, 7*(8), e1000165. doi:10.1371/journal.pbio.1000165

Tapscott, D., & Williams, A. D. (2006). *Wikinomics: How mass collaboration changes everything.* New York: Penguin Group Inc.

Wagner, D., Bear, M., & Sander, J. (2009). Turning simulation into reality: increasing student competence and confidence. *The Journal of Nursing Education, 48*(8), 465–467. doi:10.3928/01484834-20090518-07

Westwood, M. A., Flett, A. S., Riding, P., & Moon, J. C. (2009). How to Webcast lectures and conferences. *British Medical Journal, 338*, b31. doi:10.1136/bmj.b31

Wiljer, D., Urowitz, S., Apatu, E., DeLenardo, C., Eysenbach, G, Harth, et al. & Canadian Committee for Patient Accessible Health Records. (2008). Patient accessible electronic health records: Exploring recommendations for successful implementation strategies. *Journal of Medical Internet Research, 10*(4), Retrieved from e34. doi:10.2196/jmir.1061

Chapter 2
The Effectiveness of Health Informatics

Francesco Paolucci
The Australian National University, Australia

Henry Ergas
Concept Economics, Australia

Terry Hannan
Australian College of Health Informatics, Australia

Jos Aarts
Erasmus University, Rotterdam, The Netherlands

ABSTRACT

Health care is complex and there are few sectors that can compare to it in complexity and in the need for almost instantaneous information management and access to knowledge resources during clinical decision-making. There is substantial evidence available of the actual, and potential, benefits of e-health tools that use computerized clinical decision support systems (CDSS) as a means for improving health care delivery. CDSS and associated technologies will not only lead to an improvement in health care but will also change the nature of what we call electronic health records (EHR). The technologies that "define" the EHR will change the nature of how we deliver care in the future. Significant challenges relating to the evaluation of these health information management systems relate to demonstrating their ongoing cost-benefit, cost-effectiveness, and effects on the quality of care and patient outcomes. However, health information technology is still mainly about the effectiveness of processes and process outcomes, and the technology is still not mature, which may lead to unintended consequences, but it remains promising and unavoidable in the long run.

INTRODUCTION

The Institute of Medicine (IOM) report, *To Err is Human: Building a Safer Health System* provides

a landmark review of the functionality of modern health care delivery in the information and technology revolutions (Kohn, Corrigan & Donaldson, 2000). It concludes that health care is error-prone and costly, as a result of factors that include per-

DOI: 10.4018/978-1-61520-733-6.ch002

sistent major errors and delays in diagnosis and diagnostic accuracy, under/over-use of resources (e.g. excessive ordering or unnecessary laboratory tests), or inappropriate use of resources (e.g. use of outmoded tests or therapies) (Kohn, Corrigan & Donaldson, 2000). Health care is complex and there are few sectors that can compare to it in complexity as well as in the need for almost instantaneous information management and access to knowledge resources during clinical decision-making. An example of a comparable system of complex decision-making can be seen in air travel and is highlighted in the report on the factors contributing to the Tenerife air disaster on Sunday 17th, 1977. In the final summary on this disaster, Weick (1990) makes the following comments that could also be used to describe health care decision-making:

The Tenerife air disaster, in which a KLM 747 and a PanAm 747 collided with a loss of 583 lives, is examined as a prototype of system vulnerability to crisis. It is concluded that the combination of interruption of important routines among interdependent systems, interdependencies that become tighter, a loss of cognitive efficiency due to autonomic arousal, and a loss of communication accuracy due to increased hierarchical distortion, created a configuration that encouraged the occurrence and rapid diffusion of multiple small errors (Weick, 1990, pp. 593).

This major air disaster led to significant changes in air travel and reforms in the regulatory framework that have resulted in a higher level of safety and quality in this industry.

If we compare the changes that occurred in aviation to improvements in health care delivery following the *To Err Is Human* report (Kohn, Corrigan & Donaldson, 2000), which focused on documenting deaths due to medical errors in the U.S. health care system, then the changes have not been as significant. A number of studies have found evidence of a lack of improvement in health

care delivery in the U.S. despite major public and private investments in technology. In 2005, Leape and Berwick (2005) reviewed the U.S. health delivery system five years after the IOM report was released. They found significant deficiencies and faults in nearly all aspects of health care delivery. For example, in patient diagnoses there remained significant errors in accuracy and delays. In attempts to evaluate a given diagnosis there were failures to employ appropriate tests (underuse), the continued use of outmoded tests or therapies (inappropriate use), and the failure to act on the results of tests or monitoring (ignoring medical alerts and reminders). In treatment protocols they reported significant errors in operations, surgical procedures, and tests. They also found evidence in the administration of medication, the continued administration of the wrong drugs, doses, and medications given to patients with a known allergy to the drug (also in Evans et al., 1998). Bates et al.(1994; 1997) and Rothschild et al., (2002) found the persistence of a high incidence of adverse drug events (ADE) and their associated costs during care delivery, and demonstrated a close relationship between the incidence of preventable ADE, costs and medical malpractice claims. Preventive care is also considered to be a significant area of health care where costs savings and better health outcomes can be delivered. Fries (1994) has estimated that healthcare cost savings of up to 70% can be achieved through the implementation of more effective preventive care measures. Other areas of healthcare information management that continue to impair healthcare delivery include persistent failures in communication, equipment failure, and other information systems failures.

It is well known that human beings in all lines of work make errors, and available data show that the health care sector is complex and error-prone resulting in substantial harm (Leape & Berwick, 2005). We also know that current and emerging technologies have the potential to provide significant improvements in healthcare delivery systems. Similar trends have occurred in aviation, which has also provided a guide as to where the focus of change should lie (Coiera, 2003).

In this chapter, the following questions are addressed:

- Can information technology and health information management tools improve the health care process, quality and outcomes, while containing costs?
- How do we assess the cost-effectiveness of health information technology?

This chapter will provide a historical perspective with examples of how information technologies, designed around computerised Clinical Decision Support Systems (CDSS), can facilitate the more accurate measurement of the healthcare delivery process, and have provided reproducible solutions for cost savings, improved patient outcomes, and better quality of care.

BACKGROUND: HISTORICAL PERSPECTIVE

The importance of clinical decision making (CDM) and its effects on outcomes in care have been well documented since the 1970s (Dick, Steen & Detmer, 1997; Kohn, Corrigan & Donaldson, 2000; Osheroff et al., 2006). The care process is now understood to function across complex environments involving the patient, primary care, prevention, in-hospital care, and sub-specialisation care. The information management interrelationships extend beyond the direct care process to research, epidemiology, planning and management, health insurance, and medical indemnity.

In 1976, McDonald discussed the key limitations of CDM in complex health information-rich environments, in particular by showing the failure of CDM to meet pre-defined standards of care, and concluded that computerised (electronic) decision support (CDSS) was an essential "augmenting tool" for CDM (McDonald, 1976). McDonald's

research became a stimulus to the ongoing research in this domain of health care and revealed not only the benefits of CDSS in health care, but also how we can now begin to "measure the care processes" and evaluate what we do much more effectively.

In 2008 the importance of CDSS in health care was reconfirmed in a policy document prepared by the American Medical Informatics Association (AMIA) entitled *A Roadmap for National Action on Clinical Decision Support* (Osheroff et al., 2006). In the Executive Summary, the functions of CDSS in a modern health care system are clearly defined:

Clinical decision support provides clinicians, staff, patients or other individuals with knowledge and person-specific information, intelligently filtered or presented at appropriate times, to enhance health and health care. It encompasses a variety of tools and interventions such as computerized alerts and reminders, clinical guidelines, order sets, patient data reports and dashboards, documentation templates, diagnostic support, and clinical workflow tools. Clinical decision support has been effective in improving outcomes at some health care institutions and practice sites by making needed medical knowledge readily available to knowledge users (Osheroff et al., 2006, p.4).

Achieving desirable levels of patient safety, care quality, patient centeredness, and cost-effectiveness requires that the health system optimize its performance through consistent, systematic, and comprehensive application of available health-related knowledge – that is, through appropriate use of clinical decision support (Osheroff et al., 2006, p.4).

The knowledge we have from more than 25 years of research in clinical information management systems allows us to conclude that "information is care" (Leao, 2007). In the words of Tierney et al. (2007, p. 373), "although health care is considered a service profession, most of what clinicians do is manage information."

A number of studies support the centrality of CDSS in improving CMD and the overall health care delivery system. From the 1950s to 1970s the technology supporting medical laboratory procedures was evolving. There was a dramatic escalation in the number of procedures performed with a minimal change in the number of technical personnel to support the care process. During this time the number of personnel in hospitals numbered in the 100s or 1000s, yet the number of procedures was rising to the millions each year (Speicher, 1983). Even though the average cost of many of these laboratory procedures at that time (e.g. chest X-rays, full blood analysis) was less than $20 US, the overall decision making process was already very costly. The results of the study by Speicher (1983) provide supportive evidence to the earlier study by Johns and Blum (1979) that linked CDM to resource utilisation and ongoing data generation in clinical environments and found that within a set of four nursing units where the annual expenditure was $44 million U.S., there were, on average, 2.2 million clinical decisions per year, 6,000 per day, and six per patient per day.

A further example that linked CDM to compliance with care, clinical outcomes, and resource utilisation is that of immunization rates. In 1993 Gardner and Schaffner showed that vaccination rates for common illnesses such as influenza, pneumococcus, hepatitis B, and tetanus-diphtheria ranged from 10 to 40%. These are diseases where the vaccines have a clinical effectiveness ranging from 60 to 99% (Gardner & Schaffner, 1993). There are several cost and quality implications of these vaccination rates. From a quality perspective Gardner and Schaffner were able to correlate low vaccination rates with preventable deaths. A similar study by Tang, LaRosa, Newcomb, and Gorden (1999) demonstrated similar effects of immunisation rates on clinical outcomes.

Further historical evidence for the close relationship between CDM and outcomes of health care has been documented for a variety of parameters that measure healthcare processes. These include: the failure to comply with pre-defined standards of care, adverse drug event (ADE) detection, preventive healthcare procedures, health insurance claims management, and data acquisition for research (Bates et al., 1994; James, 1989; Tierney et al., 2007). To these factors can be added the significant cost inflation associated with the attempts to manage health care predominantly as a business or administrative organizational model. James (1989) analysed a range of common clinical scenarios for procedures such as cholecystectomy, prosthetic hip replacement, and transurethral resection of the prostate (TURP). He found a wide variation, not only in the care process amongst groups of clinicians within different health care institutions for standardised conditions, but also within each individual practitioner's activities. He also found that low quality leads directly to higher costs; he defines these costs that arise from an initial process failure and the resulting low quality output, as "quality waste" (i.e., resources that are consumed, in the form of scrap or repairs, when a unit of output fails to meet quality expectations - in clinical care this can represent death or short and long term morbidity). James also emphasises the importance of documentation in determining the quality of care. He states that fundamental elements for quality improvement are to eliminate inappropriate variation and document continuous improvement (i.e., measure what we do). This is not possible using essentially paper-based record systems for decision support. It has also been shown in the Harvard Medical Practice Study looking at negligence in medical care that paper-based record systems actually hide decision-making errors that promote poor clinical outcomes (Brennan et al., 1991).

ADE remains a significant reason for poor, and preventable, patient outcomes. In 1998,

Cook, Woods, and Miller documented that 50% of ADEs are preventable and that they represent the highest incidence of medical deaths compared to motor vehicle accidents, breast cancer, and AIDS. These preventable events represent a cost of $17 to $29 billion U.S. per year. Bates et al. (1994) also demonstrated the costly nature of ADEs at the Brigham and Women's Hospital. All ADEs at that hospital cost $5.6 million U.S. and of these, preventable ADEs represented $2.6 million U.S. These figures excluded costs of injuries to patients, malpractice costs, and the costs of admissions due to ADE (Bates et al., 1994). The close relationship between ADEs and malpractice claims (outcomes) was demonstrated by Rothschild et al. (2002) and Studdert et al. (2006). These studies show that many of the added costs of these events were related to litigation and administrative costs and approximately 50% of the events were preventable.

Another factor contributing to the current status of health care delivery is the ability of clinicians to comply with pre-defined standards of care. For the three decades from 1979 to 1990, several studies demonstrated that the overall rate of what is done in routine medical practice that is based on published scientific research remained steady at between 10 to 20% (Ferguson, 1991; Williamson, Goldschmidt, & Jillson, 1979). In 2003 a RAND Corporation review revealed that, on average, patients received recommended care in only 54.9% of instances. While this reflects an improvement in compliance with care standards, it also indicates that around 45% of patients do not receive standardised care (Farley, 2005).

A final example that discusses the core principles of CDSS implementation is the Academic Model for Prevention and Treatment of HIV (AMPATH) in resource-poor Kenya (Tierney et al., 2007). This project saw the successful implementation of health information technologies based on electronic medical record (EMR) functionalities in a resource poor nation. The successful partnership now sees this EMR as the largest e-health

system for developing nations and is implemented in more than 23 countries.

To obtain an extensive review of successes, difficulties, and an understanding of the complexity of information management in health, as well as how solutions can be found, we refer to the 25 year review of electronic medical record systems that focuses on CDSS in North America and Europe in the full issue of the International Journal of Medical Informatics in 1999 (see Editorial by Safran, 1999, pp. 155-156).

CLINICAL INFORMATION SYSTEMS AND CLINICAL DECISION SUPPORT SYSTEMS (CDSS) IN THE 21ST CENTURY: THE IMPACT ON HEALTH CARE QUALITY, COSTS, AND OUTCOMES

The statement "information (management) is care" (Tierney et al., 2007, p. 374) emphasises one of the core principals of health care, that is, everything a provider does with a patient involves the flow of information (e.g. clinical history, physical examination, orders for tests, instructions for care, follow-up). This process involves the collection, management, and reporting of data in readable formats to the provider, thereby facilitating the care process (Tierney et al., 2007).

Coiera (2003) also provides a clear description of where "clinical informaticians" fit into the care process:

Informaticians should understand that our first contribution is to see healthcare as a complex system, full of information flows and feedback loops, and we also should understand that our role is to help others 'see' the system, and re-conceive it in new ways (Coiera, 2003, p. xxii).

Any clinical decision support system(s) (CDSS) provides clinicians, staff, patients, or other individuals with knowledge and person-specific information, intelligently filtered or presented at appropriate times, to enhance health and health care (Coiera, 2003; Osheroff et al., 2006). CDSS encompass a variety of tools and interventions, such as computerized alerts and reminders, clinical guidelines, order sets, patient data reports and dashboards, documentation templates, diagnostic support, and clinical workflow tools.

The following four key functions have been defined for CDSS (Perreault & Metzger, 1999):

(1) **Administrative:** These systems provide support for clinical coding and documentation, authorization of procedures, and referrals.

(2) **Managing clinical complexity and details:** Keeping patients on research and chemotherapy protocols; tracking orders, referrals follow-up and preventive care. That is, complying with pre-defined standards of care.

(3) **Cost control:** This involves activities such as the monitoring of medication orders and avoiding duplicate or unnecessary tests.

(4) **Decision support:** These are complex information management systems that support clinical diagnosis and treatment plan processes; and that promote use of best practices, condition-specific guidelines, and population-based disease management.

Based on the existing evidence it is accepted that health information management systems centred on CDSS provide the most significant opportunity to improve health care delivery and management (Brennan et al., 2007). One could wonder why their use is not universal (Ford, Menachemi, Peterson & Huerta, 2009). A major barrier to CDSS implementation is clinician involvement in the development of the information management tools. We know that age, gender, and computer literacy are not significant factors in the use of computers in health care (Sands, 1999; Slack, 2001). Uptake of health information technologies is related to the efficiency and useability

of the information management tools that CDSS deliver through the total e-health system. The current focus to provide solutions to the problem of clinician involvement relates to Computerized Provider Order Entry (CPOE) (Brennan et al., 2007). It is believed that CPOE will facilitate safe, effective care for patients by insuring that clinical care directions are communicated in a timely, accurate, and complete manner. The integration of clinical decision support functions with CPOE systems provides functionality that incorporates contemporary knowledge and best practice recommendations into the clinical management process. Additionally, by ensuring the quality, accuracy, and relevance of the decision logic integrated within CPOE systems, a guaranteed method for creating safe and effective practice is ensured. Brennan emphasises that CPOE is not a technology, rather it is a design (or redesign) of clinical processes that integrates technology to optimize provider ordering of medications, laboratory tests, procedures, etc. CPOE is distinguished by the requirement that the provider is the primary user. It is not the "electronification" of the paper record system in existing formats.

In summary the evidence to date indicates that the beneficial effects of health information technology on quality, efficiency, and costs of care can be found in three major areas (Chaudhry et al., 2006):

- increased adherence to guideline-based care,
- enhanced surveillance and monitoring, and
- decreased medication errors.

A recent overview of health information technology studies by Orszag (2008) from the US Congressional Budget Office (CBO) suggests, albeit with some qualifications, that a more comprehensive list of potential benefits from the use of HIT would include the following:

- Eliminating paper medical records – however, the CBO notes that these savings might not apply in very small practices that have low but relatively fixed costs related to medical records;

- Avoiding duplicated or inappropriate diagnostic tests – according to the CBO, some studies (e.g. Bates et al., 1998; Bates et al., 1994) suggest that electronic health records with a notice of redundancy could reduce the number of laboratory tests by about 6%;

- Reducing the use of radiological services - though the CBO notes that the evidence on this is weak. While studies (e.g. Harpole, Khorasani, Fiskio, Kuperman & Bates, 1997) show that HIT may ease the job of monitoring the use of radiological services, there is little evidence that it helps control costs;

- Promoting the cost-effective use of prescription drugs, particularly through decision support software and computerized provider order entry which prompts providers to use generic alternatives, lower-cost therapies, and cost-effective drug management programs (Mullett, Evans, Christenson & Dean, 2001);

- Improving the productivity of nurses and physicians – This has to be qualified, as one study found that when HIT was in use, nurses in hospitals saw reductions in the time required to document the delivery of care, but physicians saw increases in documentation time (Poissant, Pereira, Tamblyn, & Kawasumi, 2005). However, the CBO notes that the latter effect may reflect a short-run learning phase for doctors. Few studies have measured effects on physicians' efficiency in outpatient settings, and those that have show mixed results (Pizziferri et al., 2005).

- Reducing the length of hospital stays – HIT may reduce the average length of a hospital stay by speeding up certain hospital functions and avoiding costly errors (Mekhjian et al., 2002);

- General improvements in the quality of care through avoiding adverse drug events[1]; expanding exchanges of health care information thus reducing duplication of diagnostic procedures, preventing medical errors and reducing administrative costs; expanding the practice of evidence-based medicine[2]; and generating data for research on comparative effectiveness and cost-effectiveness of treatments. This benefit is also consistent with the results of an older literature review which found that HIT increased adherence to guideline- or protocol-based care (Chaudry et al., 2006). This increased quality of care would also be manifest in an associated decrease in malpractice claims, another prediction which is confirmed by a recent study (Virapongse et al., 2008).

Given the need for establishing the existing and ongoing benefits from investments in clinical information management technologies, it has been demonstrated that there are long-term financial benefits, in the form of an acceptable return on investment (ROI), in computerised provider order entry systems (Kaushal et al., 2006).

Despite these established benefits there remain many barriers to the widespread successful implementation of CDSS. Most of these are not technical. They relate to the design of information management tools and their acceptance by clinicians who have a long history of autonomy in health care (Beresford, 2008).

By contrast, the costs associated with implementation of HIT are:

- the initial fixed cost of the hardware, software, and technical assistance necessary to install the system;
- licensing fees;

- the expense of maintaining the system; and
- the "opportunity cost" of the time that health care providers devote to learning how to use the new system and how to adjust their work practices accordingly Orszag (2008).

On the costs of installation or implementation, the CBO notes that these may vary widely among physicians and among hospitals, depending on the size and complexity of those providers' operations and the extent to which a system's users wish to perform their work electronically. For instance, smaller practices will pay more per physician than larger practices to implement an HIT (Orszag, 2008).

The estimation of these costs will also be complicated by the differences in the types and available features of the systems being sold and differences in the characteristics of the practices that are adopting them. The CBO notes that existing studies of costs have tended to make the mistake of not including estimates of indirect costs, such as the opportunity costs of time which providers dedicate to learn the new system and to adopt it in their work routines (Orszag, 2008). The initial opportunity costs in terms of learning time and adapting the operations of the practice around the implemented system can turn out to be quite significant, with one survey of health IT adoption finding that reported productivity in a practice may drop between 10 to 15 per cent for several months after implementation (Gans, Kralewski, Hammons & Dowd, 2005). One study of a sample of 14 small physicians' offices implementing an HIT estimated the average drop in revenue from loss of productivity at about $7,500 per physician over a year (Miller, West, Brown, Sim & Ganchoff, 2005).

PUTTING HEALTH INFORMATION TECHNOLOGY (HIT) TO USE

Health information technology (HIT) systems are basically a repository for patient data. The physician is able to retrieve information, often in a clinically meaningful way that may not necessarily have been entered by himself/herself in the electronic health record (EHR). The information might have been acquired and created, for instance, during the patient's course in the healthcare organization. Increasingly, EHR systems are connected to regional health information networks enabling access to patient data in disparate systems, such as primary care.

Overcoming the Limitations of Paper-Based Records

The electronic patient record has been introduced to overcome perceived limitations encountered with the use of the paper-based medical record and to allow planning that goes beyond a static view of events. Some of the limitations of the paper-based patient record that can be overcome include:

- *Accessibility*. Often the record is not accessible when it is needed. It may be stored elsewhere, or another professional may be seeking to use it concurrently. Electronic records are accessible independent of place and time, and can be rapidly retrieved using a patient identifier. It is exactly this that is most valued by clinicians. However, access is usually constrained because of data protection and privacy. Authorizations and passwords are required to allow a clinician to review patient information. Making information available both from within the hospital and from ambulatory systems is a key goal of most national efforts to implement HITs.

- *Completeness*. Not all patient data are written in the record. This can pose problems when other professionals reading the record try to make sense of a patient problem or when a doctor tries to recall what she has done after seeing the information again. Forcing the user to enter data in all fields can improve the completeness of a patient record.

- *Readability*. Handwriting is often hard to read. On a medication list, numbers and units of dosages can be misinterpreted and require attention of a pharmacist checking the prescription or a nurse translating and transcribing the order or trying to prepare the medication to be administered. Entering the data digitally, and even structuring the fields, can enhance readability.

- *Analysis*. Information written in the record is generally not suited for quantitative analysis. Test results may be entered in pre-structured forms and even plotted on a graph, which may reveal a trend, but comparison with baseline data is painstakingly difficult. Auditing past records to identify and analyze patterns in a group of patients is very labor intensive and time consuming. Digitized data are exceptionally suited for computer analysis.

Some Reasons for Limited Diffusion of Health Information Technology & Electronic Health Records

If the advantages are so obvious, why then is the electronic record not widely in use and why haven't electronic records replaced paper records? It is often argued that physicians resist innovation and do not like to give up familiar tools. The wide adoption of advanced technology in health care, and certainly in emergency medicine, defies this argument. Paper-based records have proved to be durable tools for medical practice and information technology specialists have only

recently become aware of this (Clarke, Hartswood, Procter, Rouncefield & Slack, 2003). As a cognitive artefact, the physician can examine the paper record easily. The layout and structure can guide the physician to find the most relevant information and ignore other items. Often the use of tabs, coloured paper, tables, and flowcharts facilitates navigation through a paper-based record. Within a short period of time a complete mental picture of the patient can be created. In contrast, using a computer, a user can be forced to page through a large number of screens in order to find the needed piece of information.

The paper-based record also allows the physician to judge the quality of the information. Handwriting or a signature can show who entered the information and inform the physician about the trustworthiness of the information. The absence of information does not necessarily imply that the record is incomplete; it often means that a particular item was considered not relevant for the case at hand (Berg, 1998). For example, if the patient has no known history of heart problems and is in good physical condition, blood pressure recordings or an electrocardiogram (ECG) may be missing from the record.

This is not to say that there are no compelling arguments to adopt electronic records; there is ample evidence that the efficiency and quality of care benefits from their use (Dick, Steen & Detmer, 1997). However, one must look carefully at the role of paper-based records in medical practice and avoid simply translating it into an electronic system.

Particular Features of Electronic Health Records That Offer Advantages over Paper Records

The two powerful and distinctive advantages that electronic records have over a paper record are summarized in the concepts of accumulating and coordinating (Berg, 1999). Accumulating refers to the fact that an EHR system allows for powerful analysis of data. For example, lab test outcome data can be accumulated to show time-dependent trends. When grouped for a large number of patients, the same data can be subjected to statistical analysis to reveal patterns. Combined with data from other sources, information can be used for planning, billing, and quality assessment. A most powerful application is the combination of patient data with decision support techniques that enable the physician to make decisions about patient care founded on accepted clinical rules stored in a database and patient data that is as complete as possible. The other concept of coordination provides the opportunity to plan and coordinate activities of healthcare professionals by allowing concurrent access to the electronic record. Access is no longer dependent on the physical location of the record, but possible from every computer that is connected to the system.

Standardization and Integration of Technologies

Many conditions have to be met in order to successfully implement HIT and the EHR, most importantly standardization of the underlying technologies and of the content and meaning of healthcare data. This may seem obvious, but it has been shown that the lack of standardization is a major impediment to the introduction of electronic records in medical practice. Technological standards are required to link systems in networks. The wide diffusion of the Internet would have been impossible without underlying standards for communicating (e.g. messages, texts, and graphics) and establishing links and pointers to other sources of information. Yet, this achievement was not possible without negotiating and consultation about what and how to standardize. Often proprietary rights and the perceived need to protect markets stand in the way.

In health care, standardization is much harder since it is not only about the underpinning rationale and scientific evidence for data standards, but also about the diverse social and cultural values within and across geographic communities that influence choice of data standards. We will not elaborate on the standards relevant for health care; they are explained elsewhere. Typical examples include TCP/IP that determines how information is communicated on the Internet, HL7 that determines how health care information can be represented and communicated between diverse applications in health care, and SNOMED CT that describes how medical concepts are defined and represented. Standardization can be effected through national and international bodies with legislative power, such as ASTM (originally American Society for Testing and Materials), ISO (International Standards Organization) and CEN (Comité Européen de Normalisation). Also standardization can be achieved through market power, e.g., Microsoft's Windows operating system accounts for about 90% of the personal computer market and can therefore be construed as a *de facto* standard for personal computer operating systems.

Implementing Health Information Technology

The traditional approach to implementing health information technology has been top-down. An important factor in this respect was the perception that health information technology is an expensive resource that usually exceeded the financial capabilities of individual physicians and physician groups. However, the advent of personal computers to some degree altered this situation, particularly in primary care. In countries such as the Netherlands, the United Kingdom and Australia, up to 90% of GPs have adopted electronic health record systems (Jha, Doolan, Grandt, Scott & Bates, 2008). However, adoption, in many cases, was helped by financial incentives given by their governments.

A key characteristic of implementing information systems is that organizational changes are an integral part of implementation. Unfortunately, however, the changes are not always for the better, and more often than not, the performance of organizations is worse after a system has been installed than before. The natural tendency is then to conclude that the system was somehow badly designed. In 1975, when the design and operation of information systems were considered primarily technical activities, Henry C. Lucas, Jr. wrote about failing systems. However, all our experience suggests that the primary cause for system failure has been organizational behavior problems (Lucas, 1975). Thirty years of research has increased our understanding of information systems in organizational contexts; yet, the record in terms of developing and implementing successful systems is still dismal (Ewusi-Mensah, 2003). HIT systems are particularly hard to implement because not only do they affect health care organizations as a whole, but also the work of health professionals who pride themselves on their professional autonomy. Implementing HIT is a social process (Aarts, Doorewaard & Berg, 2004). But the relevant organizational changes are not easily predictable.

This creates a predicament for an implementer. S/he might like to design a system according to blueprints and to plan systematically its deployment. But Ciborra (2002) advises making organizational improvisation part of the implementation process, to allow prospective users to tinker with the system and let them find ways of working that fit them best, to plan for the unexpected and value emerging practices, and to give up strict control (Ciborra, 2002).

Adverse Effects of Health Information Technology

Recent studies reveal that putting HIT to use, whatever its many advantages may be associated with unexpected outcomes. A study by Koppel et al. (2005) of one CPOE system documented 22 different error-enhancing aspects of that system. Another study reported a doubling of infant mortality after the introduction of a CPOE system, probably resulting from increased time to enter orders, reduced communication among nurses and doctors, and the loss of advance information previously radioed in from the transfer team before patients arrived at the hospital (Han et al., 2005). Nebeker, Hoffman, Weir, Bennett, and Hurdle (2005), likewise, found high rates of ADEs in the highly computerized Veterans Administration system. Shulman, Singer, Goldstone, and Bellingan (2005) found that, compared to paper-based systems, CPOE was associated with fewer inconsequential errors, but also with more serious errors. Ash, Berg, and Coiera (2004); Campbell, Sittig, Ash, Guappone, and Dykstra (2006); and Aarts, Ash, and Berg (2007) have found unintended consequences from CPOE systems to be the rule, rather than the exception. Nemeth and Cook (2005, p. 262), noting these systems' interactivity and complexity, add: "If [human error] exists, error is a consequence of interaction with IT systems. The core issue is to understand healthcare work and workers". And although "healthcare work seems to flow smoothly," the reality is "messy."

METHODS OF ASSESSING COST-EFFECTIVENESS

There have not been many rigorous studies of cost effectiveness of e-health measures in the literature. The most recent literature review of studies in this field concluded that there remained a "paucity of meaningful data on the cost-benefit calculation of actual IT implementation" (Goldzweig, Towfigh, Maglione & Shekelle, 2009, p. 292). The studies which this literature review collected, after a comprehensive selection process, can be broken into four different approaches.

One approach looks at the experience of a few large organizations that had implemented multifunctional, interoperable electronic health records (EHRs), computerized physician order entry (CPOE), decision-support systems, and other functions. However, these studies cannot be described as appropriate cost effectiveness or cost benefit analyses since they only evaluated the impacts in terms of clinical performance/quality improvement or potential benefit in terms of patient safety measures, but did not attempt to quantify the costs of these technologies or to then derive a net benefit calculation using some common measure (for instance, some imputed welfare gain in terms of dollars).

Among the individual studies in this category:

- Three studies looked at a quality improvement project related to blood product administration that used automated alert technology associated with CPOE; electronic clinical reminders related to coronary artery disease and diabetes mellitus; and patient-specific e-mail to providers regarding cholesterol levels, and found small improvements in quality of care. (Lester, Grant, Barnett & Chueh, 2006; Rothschild et al., 2007; Sequist et al., 2005)
- Roumie et al. (2006) evaluated the impact of electronic provider alerts and found they provided a modest, non–statistically significant improvement over provider education alone as measured in terms of improvements in blood pressure control.
- Dexter, Perkins, Maharry, Jones, and McDonald (2004) compared the impact on rates of influenza and pneumococcal vaccinations of computer generated standing orders for nurses versus computerized physician reminders and found that immunization rates were significantly higher with the nurse standing order.
- Murray et al. (2004) and Tierney et al. (2005) evaluated computer-generated treatment suggestions for hypertension, and for asthma and chronic obstructive pulmonary disease (COPD), and it was found that

neither of these technologies resulted in improvements in care.
- Potts, Barr, Gregory, Wright, and Patel (2004), Butler et al., (2006) and Ozdas et al., (2006) evaluated the potential benefits of CPOE. These studies arrived at mixed results but generally found improvements in patient safety with the introduction of CPOE, as well as modest improvements in quality of care when CPOE was tailored to the management of patients with acute myocardial infarction.

Insofar as there was a basis for comparison implicit in these studies, this involved comparing the refinement in existing systems, addition of new applications or enhancement of existing functionalities, against the resulting improvements. The general finding was one of modest or even no benefits from the new applications or changed functionalities (Goldzweig et al., 2009, p. 285).

A second approach found in the literature review was to look specifically at the experiences of commercial practices implementing commercially available or developed electronic health records. Among the individual studies in this category:

- Garrido, Jamieson, Zhou, Wiesenthal, and Liang (2005) compared outcomes before and after the implementation of a home-grown EHR at commercial hospitals and found that the number of ambulatory visits and radiology studies decreased after implementation, while telephone contacts nearly doubled. On the other hand, limited measures of quality (immunizations and cancer screening) did not change.
- O'Neill and Klepack, (2007) assessed the effect of implementing a commercial EHR in a rural family practice, looking specifically at financial impacts rather than quality of care measures. They found that

average monthly revenue increased 11 per cent in the first year and 20 per cent in the second year, and the charge-capture ratio increased 65 to 70 per cent, because of better billing practices.

- Asaro, Sheldahl, and Char (2006); Del Beccaro, Jeffries, Eisenberg, and Harry (2006); Feldstein et al. (2006); Galanter, Polikaitis, and DiDomenico (2004); Han et al. (2005); Palen, Raebel, Lyons, and Magid (2006); Smith et al. (2006); Steele et al. (2005); and Toth-Pal, Nilsson, and Furhoff (2004) studied the effect of adding new functionalities to existing EHRs. Some of these studies found modest benefits, some found no benefits, and a few found marked benefits.

A third group of approaches involved evaluations of stand- alone applications such as health systems that link patients with their care providers and are intended to improve the management of chronic diseases; computer/video decision aids for use by patients and providers; text messaging systems for appointment reminders; electronic devices for use by patients to improve care; and patient-directed applications for use outside traditional settings. The main findings here were also mixed, with some studies showing no or only modest effects, and many more studies providing insufficient descriptions to reach strong conclusions.

Among the individual studies in this category:

- McMahon et al. (2005) compared Web-based care management with usual care for patients with diabetes. Intervention patients had a statistically significant, modest improvement in their results for 2 out of 3 clinical measures.
- Cavanagh et al. (2006), Grime (2004), and Proudfoot et al. (2004) evaluated an interactive, multimedia, computerized cognitive behavioral therapy package. In two of the studies, statistically significant improvements of modest size were found for patients in the intervention groups compared to usual care, although the differences were no longer significant at three or six months.
- Cintron, Phillips, and Hamel (2006); Jacobi et al. (2007); and Wagner, Knaevelsrud, and Maercker (2006) looked at Internet applications that could be accessed directly by the patient with three involving randomized trials. Clinical improvements were found.

Another set of studies covered by the literature review that are not directly relevant to the issue of cost effectiveness or even general effectiveness of HIT, but nonetheless have implications for the likely costs of implementing HIT, looked at barriers to HIT adoption. One of these studies, which involved a survey of US paediatric practices found that the main barriers to HIT adoption were resistance from physicians (77 per cent of practices without an EHR reported this barrier), system downtime (72 per cent), increase in physicians' time (64 per cent), providers having inadequate computer skills (60 per cent), cost (94 per cent), and an inability to find an EHR that met the practice's requirements (81 per cent) (Kemper, Uren & Clark, 2006). A survey of the Connecticut State Medical Society Independent Practice Association found that the most commonly stated barrier was cost (72 per cent) and other barriers were time necessary to train staff (40 per cent), lack of proficiency among staff (26 per cent), and lack of an IT culture within the office (18 per cent) (Mattocks et al., 2007).

One methodological problem with demonstrating that there are particular positive associations between clinical outcomes and use of HIT is that these associations are not necessarily causal - hospitals that have more HIT tend to have greater resources and better performance. However, one

25

study that at least attempted to control for these confounders still found a statistically significant relationship. Amarasingham, Platinga, Diener-West, Gaskin, and Powe (2009) looked at the relationship between HIT and both costs and clinical outcomes in hospitals in Texas. A particular focus in this study was whether increased automation of hospital information was associated with decreased mortality, complication rates and costs, and length of stay. They found strong relationships between the presence of several technologies and complication and mortality rates and lower costs. For instance, use of order entry was associated with decreases in mortality rate for patients with myocardial infarction and coronary artery bypass surgery. Use of decision support software was associated with a decrease in the risk of complications. Automated notes were associated with a decrease in the risk of fatal hospitalizations. The researchers controlled for the fact that hospitals that have more HIT tend to have more resources and still found that the relationships persisted, though there were also some instances in which relationships in the opposite direction were found. For example, electronic documentation was associated with a 35% increase in the risk of complications in patients with heart failure, though this may have been because it was easier to find these events due to better documentation (Bates, 2009).

In short, there is a dearth of appropriate cost effectiveness studies and of useful data for conducting such studies. Although the review by Goldzweig et al. (2009, pp. 290-291) concluded on the basis of the individual studies surveyed that "there is some empirical evidence to support the positive economic value of an EHR;" they also found that the projections of large cost savings in previous literature assumed levels of health IT adoption and interoperability that had not been achieved anywhere.

A less comprehensive survey by the US Congressional Budget Office (Orszag, 2008) focused on two prominent studies that attempted to quantify the benefits of HITs. One was a study by the RAND Institute (Girosi, Meili, & Scoville, 2005) and the other a study by the Center for Information Technology Leadership (CITL) (Pan 2004). Both these studies had estimated annual net savings to the US health care sector of about $80 billion (in 2005 dollars) relative to total spending for health care of about $2 trillion per year, though they identified different sources of those savings. The RAND research had quantified savings that the use of health IT could generate by reducing costs in physicians' practices and hospitals. In contrast, the CITL study narrowed the focus to savings from achieving full interoperability of health IT, while excluding potential improvements in efficiency within practices and hospitals.

The approach adopted by both these studies did have in common the use of various extrapolations and these were a source of criticism by the CBO that found that they were inappropriate by the standards of a rigorous cost effectiveness analysis. In particular, according to the Orszag (2008), the RAND study had the following flaws:

- It assumed "appropriate changes in health care" from HIT rather than likely changes taking into account present-day payment incentives that would constrain the effective utilization of HIT.
- It drew solely on empirical studies from the literature that found positive effects for the implementation of health IT systems, thus creating a possible bias in the results.
- It ignored ways in which some cost reductions would be mitigated by cost shifting in other areas.
- Some of its assumptions about savings from eliminating or reducing the use of paper medical records were unrealistic for small practices.

Similarly, the CITL study came in for criticism by the CBO for, in particular, not fully considering the impact of financial incentives in the analysis, estimating savings against a baseline of little or no information technology use, and using over-optimistic assumptions.

While the CBO identified the numerous ways in which two prominent studies of HIT may have overestimated the benefits of HIT, its list of benefits does suggest that there are some areas in which the long-term benefits of HIT may be underestimated insofar as the scale of use has not reached a critical mass. In particular, we would conjecture that the possible improvements in quality of care through the expansion of health care information and generation of data for research may presuppose a base of participating health care providers and institutions that have implemented HIT and are able to share data over their networks. It is possible that these benefits may not be significant until use of HIT is diffused over a greater percentage of health care providers and institutions.

In other words, some of the benefits to be derived from health IT increase in value as the network of those using the technology expands, i.e. as other providers also purchase health IT systems. This phenomenon is known to economists as network effects and is not necessarily restricted to benefits arising from exchange of information for research purposes - providers who can perform functions electronically, such as sending and receiving medical records or ordering laboratory and imaging procedures, also gain when other providers develop similar electronic capabilities. For example, the cost to a general practitioner of sending medical data to a consulting specialist is potentially lower with an HIT system, but only so long as the consulting specialist has an interoperable system that can receive the data electronically.

As a general matter, economists distinguish between direct and indirect network effects, where the former refer to "technological" externalities while the latter refer to "pecuniary" externalities. The former involve situations where use of a technology by agent A directly affects the value agent B derives from that technology (for

instance, through increased inter-operability). In the latter, the effects are mediated through the price system, so adoption by agent A reduces the cost of the technology (for instance, through the achievement of greater economies of scale) and hence yields a benefit to agent B. Generally, it is assumed that the price system will take account of pecuniary externalities (although this is not always correct), but the technological externalities can drive a wedge between private and social costs at the margin. When that occurs, it is crucial that cost-benefit studies appropriately distinguish between private and social costs and benefits; this is not generally the case with the studies of HIT deployment that we have reviewed.

At the same time, when network effects are significant, there will typically be multiple equilibria; for example, private costs and benefits may be equalised at one, low level of adoption (with low net benefits), and at another, high level of adoption (with potentially higher net benefits). At the low level equilibrium, no individual non-adopter will face a private net gain from adopting. For example, in a telephone system with few customers, the marginal subscriber gains little by joining the network. A cost-benefit evaluation conducted at that low level of adoption will therefore find that the private benefits of adoption are less than the private costs. However, were adoption levels increased, joining the telephone system would allow the marginal user to communicate with a greater base of subscribers, so that the benefits of subscription (especially taking account of the gains made by those receiving the calls) exceed the private costs.

These issues of differences between private and social costs and benefits and of multiple equilibria can create biases. For example, what may seem like low benefits relative to costs may reflect an initial low level equilibrium and an associated coordination failure. In other words, if instead of looking at a decision by say, an individual practitioner or medical practice to adopt HIT, one evaluated the costs and benefits of adding a large number of practitioners or medical practices to the installed base of HIT, the balance of the costs and benefits might differ.

It is pertinent that according to a new analysis of HIT deployment in seven industrialized countries, US deployment lags well behind other countries (Davis, Doty, Shea, & Stramekis, 2009). Electronic medical records usage ranged from nearly all physicians in the Netherlands to 23 per cent in Canada and 28 per cent in the US. Incidentally, the same study also found that physicians with greater IT capacity were more likely to report feeling well-prepared to manage patients with chronic diseases. Insofar as the bulk of HIT studies have been from the US, the benefits documented from use of HIT in these studies may not be representative of benefits in countries with a higher deployment of HIT. However, this is not a hypothesis we are in a position to test.

One barrier to the achievement of the full magnitude of network effects that would maximize the benefits of using HIT may be legal restrictions. A recent US study found that privacy regulations impose costs that deter the diffusion of EMR technology (Miller & Tucker, 2009). These regulations may inhibit adoption by restricting the ability of hospitals to exchange patient information with each other, which may be particularly important for patients with chronic conditions who wish to see a new specialist, or emergency room patients whose records are stored elsewhere. The study calculated that the inhibition of network benefits from privacy regulations reduced hospital adoption of EMR by 25 per cent.

It is clear from the various literature reviews discussed so far, first, that there have been very few studies that have attempted to meet the rigorous standards of a cost effectiveness analysis, and second, that there are numerous pitfalls in conducting such analyses owing to the use of various assumptions and extrapolations in quantifying benefits or costs. Another issue which remains to be addressed with greater rigour in the literature is how to quantify the likely benefits of HIT taking

into account various projections of network effects associated with different uptake rates.

CONCLUSION

The picture that emerges from our overview has several dimensions. First of all, it is evident that little is known about the overall impact of health IT on the outcomes of health care. In this chapter we have reported a number of studies that showed positive outcomes on, for example, the reduction of adverse drug events, better resource utilization, and improved adherence to clinical guidelines. These studies are well bounded in scope and size, and are mainly about the effectiveness of processes. However, the findings do not always unequivocally point to positive outcomes. Reminders and alerts are an essential feature of decision support in computerized physician order entry systems. They warn users of potentially dangerously interacting medications. A systematic review showed that they are suppressed frequently, and this may prevent detection of ADEs and thus compromise patient safety (van der Sijs, Aarts, Vulto, & Berg, 2006). Yet, the positive outcomes are often extrapolated to a larger population to make a case for the wide scale implementation of health IT.

Equally, implementing health IT often entails significant organizational change, both at the level of practicing medicine and the structure of health care organizations. However, a study of organizational change in Australian hospitals by Braithwaite, Westbrook, Hindle, Iedema, and Black (2006) provides a sobering reminder that there can be a large gap between expectations and reality. The introduction of clinical directorates, in which clinical departments, wards, and units that best fitted conceptually were joined together, was seen to increase the effectiveness of health delivery. Using diachronic data the authors found that the introduction of clinical directorates had no effect. Unfortunately, we have no way of fully knowing the effectiveness of health IT unless it has been widely adopted and diachronic data become available for analysis.

There is growing awareness that health IT is far from mature. In a report to the Office of the National Coordinator of Health Information Technology (ONCHIT), the American Medical Informatics Association writes that some current clinical decision support systems often disrupt clinical workflow in a manner that interferes with efficient delivery (Osheroff et al., 2006). In our overview we already mentioned the adverse effects of health IT, indicating how difficult implementation in practice is. In another study Koppel, Wetterneck, Telles, and Karsh (2008) also found that bar-coded medication administration systems did not reduce dispensing errors substantially because they induced workaround to mitigate unintended effects. The main causes seem to be the technology itself and the generally poor understanding of how technology affects work practices, let alone how it can improve them by introducing notions of patient-centered care and a working collaborative of different providers. A telling example is how computerized provider order entry systems are designed and implemented on the model of an individual physician prescribing medication, instead of a collaborative model involving physicians, pharmacists, and nurses who are all involved in providing medication to patients (Niazkhani, Pirnejad, Berg, & Aarts, 2009).

Often expectations are overblown. In a Dutch hospital the implementers of a CPOE system expected that physicians would use the system, because the system that was being replaced was also about electronic order entry (Aarts et al., 2004). They did not realize that physicians were not at all accustomed to electronic order entry, and that the system requires a doctor to send electronic notes, but doctors don't send notes as other people do that for them. Implementation should begin by asking the question 'what organizational problem is going to be solved,' and what can be done to engage problem owners. There is also a serious lack of organizational learning when a system is designed and implemented (Edmondson, Winslow, Bohmer, & Pisano, 2003). This may be due to the fact that implementation teams are often dissolved after the project is considered finished, leading to a change in personnel who actually use the system.

To conclude, we find ourselves in a double bind. The effectiveness of health IT is anecdotal, and increasingly unintended consequences are being reported (Ash et al., 2004). Health IT is far from mature. Hard work is needed to get safe and reliable systems to work in practice. Yet, it is a dictum that without IT, health care will grind to a halt. We have become dependent on health IT, and yet its overall contribution to health care is hard to quantify. It is comparable to the productivity paradox that some economists pointed to in the early 1990s. Society has become dependent and intertwined with information technology, and yet its contribution didn't seem to show up in the productivity figures (Brynjolfsson, 1993; Landauer, 1995). While some of the positive macroeconomic impacts did become clearer over time, the situation with respect to health IT is still at the earlier stage. This leaves a need to identify proxies for health IT effectiveness and better capture longitudinal and diachronic data to assess its impact on process and outcome.

REFERENCES

Aarts, J., Ash, J., & Berg, M. (2007). Extending the understanding of computerized physician order entry: Implications for professional collaboration, workflow and quality of care. *International Journal of Medical Informatics*, *76*(Suppl 1), 4–13. doi:10.1016/j.ijmedinf.2006.05.009

Aarts, J., Doorewaard, H., & Berg, M. (2004). Understanding implementation: the case of a computerized physician order entry system in a large Dutch university medical center. *Journal of the American Medical Informatics Association*, *11*(3), 207–216. doi:10.1197/jamia.M1372

Amarasingham, R., Plantinga, L., Diener-West, M., Gaskin, D. J., & Powe, N. R. (2009). Clinical information technologies and inpatient outcomes: a multiple hospital study. *Archives of Internal Medicine, 169*(2), 108–114. doi:10.1001/archinternmed.2008.520

Asaro, P. V., Sheldahl, A. L., & Char, D. M. (2006). Embedded guideline information without patient specificity in a commercial emergency department computerized order-entry system. *Academic Emergency Medicine, 13*(4), 452–458. doi:10.1111/j.1553-2712.2006.tb00325.x

Ash, J. S., Berg, M., & Coiera, E. (2004). Some unintended consequences of information technology in health care: the nature of patient care information system-related errors. *Journal of the American Medical Informatics Association, 11*(2), 104–112. doi:10.1197/jamia.M1471

Bates, D. W. (2009). The effects of health information technology on inpatient care. *Archives of Internal Medicine, 169*(2), 105–107. doi:10.1001/archinternmed.2008.542

Bates, D. W., Boyle, D. L., Rittenberg, E., & Kuperman, G. J., Ma'Luf, N., Menkin, V. et al. (1998). What proportion of common diagnostic tests appear redundant? *The American Journal of Medicine, 104*(4), 361–368. doi:10.1016/S0002-9343(98)00063-1

Bates, D. W., O'Neil, A. C., Boyle, D., Teich, J., Chertow, G. M., Komaroff, A. L., & Brennan, T. A. (1994). Potential identifiability and preventability of adverse events using information systems. *Journal of the American Medical Informatics Association, 1*(5), 404–411.

Bates, D. W., Spell, N., Cullen, D. J., Burdick, E., Laird, N., & Petersen, L. A. (1997). The costs of adverse drug events in hospitalized patients. Adverse Drug Events Prevention Study Group. *Journal of the American Medical Association, 277*(4), 307–311. doi:10.1001/jama.277.4.307

Beresford, E. B. (1991, Jul. - Aug.). Uncertainty and the shaping of medical decisions. *The Hastings Center Report, 21*(4), 6–11. doi:10.2307/3562993

Berg, M. (1998). Medical work and the computer-based patient record: a sociological perspective. *Methods of Information in Medicine, 37*(3), 294–301.

Berg, M. (1999). Accumulation and coordinating: occasions for information technologies in medical work. *Computer Supported Cooperative Work, 8*, 373–401. doi:10.1023/A:1008757115404

Braithwaite, J., Westbrook, M. T., Hindle, D., Iedema, R. A., & Black, D. A. (2006). Does restructuring hospitals result in greater efficiency?--An empirical test using diachronic data. *Health Services Management Research, 19*(1), 1–12. doi:10.1258/095148406775322016

Brennan, P. F. (2007). CPOE: sufficient, but not perfect, evidence for taking action. *Journal of the American Medical Informatics Association, 14*(1), 130–131. doi:10.1197/jamia.M2303

Brennan, T. A., Leape, L. L., Laird, N. M., Hebert, L., Localio, A. R., & Lawthers, A. G. (1991). Incidence of adverse events and negligence in hospitalized patients. Results of the Harvard Medical Practice Study I. *The New England Journal of Medicine, 324*, 370–376.

Brynjolfsson, E. (1993). The productivity paradox of information technology. *Communications of the ACM, 36*(12), 67–77. doi:10.1145/163298.163309

Butler, J., Speroff, T., Arbogast, P. G., Newton, M., Waitman, L. R., & Stiles, R. (2006). Improved compliance with quality measures at hospital discharge with a computerized physician order entry system. *American Heart Journal, 151*(3), 643–653. doi:10.1016/j.ahj.2005.05.007

Campbell, E. M., Sittig, D. F., Ash, J. S., Guappone, K. P., & Dykstra, R. H. (2006). Types of unintended consequences related to computerized provider order entry. *Journal of the American Medical Informatics Association, 13*(5), 547–556. doi:10.1197/jamia.M2042

Cavanagh, K., Shapiro, D. A., Van Den Berg, S., Swain, S., Barkham, M., & Proudfoot, J. (2006). The effectiveness of computerized cognitive behavioural therapy in routine care. *The British Journal of Clinical Psychology, 45*(Pt 4), 499–514. doi:10.1348/014466505X84782

Chaudhry, B., Wang, J., Wu, S., Maglione, M., Mojica, W., & Roth, E. (2006). Systematic review: impact of health information technology on quality, efficiency, and costs of medical care. *Annals of Internal Medicine, 144*(10), 742–752.

Ciborra, C. (2002). *The labyrinths of information, challenging the wisdom of systems*. Oxford, UK: Oxford University Press.

Cintron, A., Phillips, R., & Hamel, M. B. (2006). The effect of a web-based, patient-directed intervention on knowledge, discussion, and completion of a health care proxy. *Journal of Palliative Medicine, 9*(6), 1320–1328. doi:10.1089/jpm.2006.9.1320

Clarke, K., Hartswood, M., Procter, R., Rouncefield, M., & Slack, R. (2003). Trusting the record. *Methods of Information in Medicine, 42*(4), 345–352.

Coiera, E. (2003). Guide to health informatics (2nd ed.). New York: Arnold; Distributed in the USA by Oxford University Press.

Cook, R. I., Woods, D. D., & Miller, C. (1998). *A tale of two stories: contrasting views of patient safety*. Chicago: National Patient Safety Foundation.

Crosson, J. C., Ohman-Strickland, P. A., Hahn, K. A., DiCicco-Bloom, B., Shaw, E., Orzano, A. J., & Crabtree, B. F. (2007). Electronic medical records and diabetes quality of care: results from a sample of family medicine practices. *Annals of Family Medicine, 5*(3), 209–215. doi:10.1370/afm.696

Davis, K., Doty, M. M., Shea, K., & Stremikis, K. (2009). Health information technology and physician perceptions of quality of care and satisfaction. *Health Policy (Amsterdam), 90*(2-3), 239–246. doi:10.1016/j.healthpol.2008.10.002

Del Beccaro, M. A., Jeffries, H. E., Eisenberg, M. A., & Harry, E. D. (2006). Computerized provider order entry implementation: no association with increased mortality rates in an intensive care unit. *Pediatrics, 118*(1), 290–295. doi:10.1542/peds.2006-0367

Dexter, P. R., Perkins, S. M., Maharry, K. S., Jones, K., & McDonald, C. J. (2004). Inpatient computer-based standing orders vs physician reminders to increase influenza and pneumococcal vaccination rates: a randomized trial. *Journal of the American Medical Association, 292*(19), 2366–2371. doi:10.1001/jama.292.19.2366

Dick, R. S., Steen, E. B., & Detmer, D. E. (Eds.). (1997). *The computer-based patient record* (Rev. ed.). Washington, DC: National Academy Press.

Edmondson, A. C., Winslow, A. B., Bohmer, R. M. J., & Pisano, G. P. (2003). Learning how and learning what: effects of tacit and codified knowledge on performance improvement following technology adoption. *Decision Sciences, 34*(2), 197–223. doi:10.1111/1540-5915.02316

Evans, R. S., Pestotnik, S. L., Classen, D. C., Clemmer, T. P., Weaver, L. K., & Orme, J. F. Jr,… Burke, J. P. (1998). A computer-assisted management program for antibiotics and other antiinfective agents. *The New England Journal of Medicine, 338*, 232–238. doi:10.1056/NEJM199801223380406

Ewusi-Mensah, K. (2003). *Software development failures*. Cambridge, MA: The MIT Press.

Farley, D., Damberg, C., Berry, S., Sorbero, M., Teleki, S., Ricc, K., & Pollock, N. (2005). *Assessment of the National patient Safety Initiative*. Context and Baseline Evaluation Report 1. Rand Corporation, United States. Agency for Healthcare Research and Quality.

Feldstein, A., Elmer, P. J., Smith, D. H., Herson, M., Orwoll, E., & Chen, C.,... Swain, M. C. (2006). Electronic medical record reminder improves osteoporosis management after a fracture: a randomized, controlled trial. *Journal of the American Geriatrics Society, 54*(3), 450–457. doi:10.1111/j.1532-5415.2005.00618.x

Ford, E. W., Menachemi, N., Peterson, L. T., & Huerta, T. R. (2009). Resistance is futile: but it is slowing the pace of EHR adoption nonetheless. *Journal of the American Medical Informatics Association, 16*(3), 274–281. doi:10.1197/jamia. M3042

Fries, J. F. (1994). Can prevention lower health costs by reducing demand? Yes. *Hospitals & Health Networks, 68*(3), 10.

Galanter, W. L., Polikaitis, A., & DiDomenico, R. J. (2004). A trial of automated safety alerts for inpatient digoxin use with computerized physician order entry. *Journal of the American Medical Informatics Association, 11*(4), 270–277. doi:10.1197/jamia.M1500

Gans, D., Kralewski, J., Hammons, T., & Dowd, B. (2005). Medical groups' adoption of electronic health records and information systems. *Health Affairs (Project Hope), 24*(5), 1323–1333. doi:10.1377/hlthaff.24.5.1323

Gardner, P., & Schaffner, W. (1993). Immunization of adults. *The New England Journal of Medicine, 328*, 1252–1258. doi:10.1056/NEJM199304293281708

Garg, A. X., Adhikari, N. K., McDonald, H., Rosas-Arellano, M. P., Devereaux, P. J., & Beyene, J. (2005). Effects of computerized clinical decision support systems on practitioner performance and patient outcomes: a systematic review. *Journal of the American Medical Association, 293*(10), 1223–1238. doi:10.1001/jama.293.10.1223

Garrido, T., Jamieson, L., Zhou, Y., Wiesenthal, A., & Liang, L. (2005). Effect of electronic health records in ambulatory care: retrospective, serial, cross sectional study. *British Medical Journal, 330*, 581–585. doi:10.1136/bmj.330.7491.581

Girosi, F., Meili, R., & Scoville, R. (2005). *Extrapolating evidence of health information technology and costs*. Santa Monica, CA: RAND Corporation.

Goldzweig, C. L., Towfigh, A., Maglione, M., & Shekelle, P. G. (2009). Costs and benefits of health information technology: new trends from the literature. *Health Affairs (Project Hope), 28*(2), w282–w293. doi:10.1377/hlthaff.28.2.w282

Grime, P. R. (2004). Computerized cognitive behavioural therapy at work: a randomized controlled trial in employees with recent stress-related absenteeism. *Occupational Medicine (Oxford, England), 54*(5), 353–359. doi:10.1093/occmed/kqh077

Han, Y. Y., Carcillo, J. A., Venkataraman, S. T., Clark, R. S., Watson, R. S., & Nguyen, T. C. (2005). Unexpected increased mortality after implementation of a commercially sold computerized physician order entry system. *Pediatrics, 116*(6), 1506–1512. doi:10.1542/peds.2005-1287

Harpole, L. H., Khorasani, R., Fiskio, J., Kuperman, G. J., & Bates, D. W. (1997). Automated evidence-based critiquing of orders for abdominal radiographs: impact on utilization and appropriateness. *Journal of the American Medical Informatics Association, 4*(6), 511–521.

Jacobi, C., Morris, L., Beckers, C., Bronisch-Holtze, J., Winter, J., Winzelberg, A. J., & Taylor, C. B. (2007). Maintenance of internet-based prevention: a randomized controlled trial. *The International Journal of Eating Disorders, 40*(2), 114–119. doi:10.1002/eat.20344

James, B.C. (1989). Improving quality can reduce costs. *QA Review: quality assurance and news, 1*(1), 4.

Jha, A. K., Doolan, D., Grandt, D., Scott, T., & Bates, D. W. (2008). The use of health information technology in seven nations. *International Journal of Medical Informatics, 77*(12), 848–854. doi:10.1016/j.ijmedinf.2008.06.007

Johns, R. J., & Blum, B. I. (1979). The use of clinical information systems to control cost as well as to improve care. *Transactions of the American Clinical and Climatological Association, 90*, 140–152.

Kaushal, R., Jha, A. K., Franz, C., Glaser, J., Shetty, K. D., & Jaggi, T. (2006). Return on investment for a computerized physician order entry system. *Journal of the American Medical Informatics Association, 13*(3), 261–266. doi:10.1197/jamia.M1984

Kemper, A. R., Uren, R. L., & Clark, S. J. (2006). Adoption of electronic health records in primary care pediatric practices. *Pediatrics, 118*(1), e20–e24. doi:10.1542/peds.2005-3000

Kohn, L. T., Corrigan, J. M., & Donaldson, M. S. (Eds.). (2000). *To err is human, building a safer health system*. Washington, DC: National Academy Press.

Koppel, R., Metlay, J. P., Cohen, A., Abaluck, B., Localio, A. R., Kimmel, S. E., & Strom, B. L. (2005). Role of computerized physician order entry systems in facilitating medication errors. *Journal of the American Medical Association, 293*(10), 1197–1203. doi:10.1001/jama.293.10.1197

Koppel, R., Wetterneck, T., Telles, J. L., & Karsh, B. T. (2008). Workarounds to barcode medication administration systems: their occurrences, causes, and threats to patient safety. *Journal of the American Medical Informatics Association, 15*(4), 408–423. doi:10.1197/jamia.M2616

Landauer, T. K. (1995). *The trouble with computers: usefulness, usability, and productivity*. Cambridge, MA: MIT Press.

Leape, L. L., & Berwick, D. M. (2005). Five years after *To Err Is Human*: What have we learned? *Journal of the American Medical Association, 293*(19), 2384–2390. doi:10.1001/jama.293.19.2384

Lester, W. T., Grant, R. W., Barnett, G. O., & Chueh, H. C. (2006). Randomized controlled trial of an informatics-based intervention to increase statin prescription for secondary prevention of coronary disease. *Journal of General Internal Medicine, 21*(1), 22–29. doi:10.1111/j.1525-1497.2005.00268.x

Linder, J. A., Ma, J., Bates, D. W., Middleton, B., & Stafford, R. S. (2007). Electronic health record use and the quality of ambulatory care in the United States. *Archives of Internal Medicine, 167*(13), 1400–1405. doi:10.1001/archinte.167.13.1400

Lucas, H. C. Jr. (1975). *Why information systems fail*. New York: Columbia University Press.

Mattocks, K., Lalime, K., Tate, J. P., Giannotti, T. E., Carr, K., & Carrabba, A. (2007). The state of physician office-based health information technology in Connecticut: current use, barriers and future plans. *Connecticut Medicine, 71*(1), 27–31.

McDonald, C. J. (1976). Protocol-based computer reminders, the quality of care and the non-perfectability of man. *The New England Journal of Medicine, 295*(24), 1351–1355.

McGlynn, E. A., Ash, S. M., Adams, J., Keesey, J., Hicks, J., DeCristoforo, A., & Kerr, E. A. (2003). The quality of health care delivered to adults in the United States. *The New England Journal of Medicine, 348,* 2635–2645. doi:10.1056/NEJMsa022615

McMahon, G. T., Gomes, H. E., Hickson Hohne, S., Hu, T. M., Levine, B. A., & Conlin, P. R. (2005). Web-based care management in patients with poorly controlled diabetes. *Diabetes Care, 28*(7), 1624–1629. doi:10.2337/diacare.28.7.1624

Mekhjian, H. S., Kumar, R. R., Kuehn, L., Bentley, T. D., Teater, P., & Thomas, A. (2002). Immediate benefits realized following implementation of physician order entry at an academic medical center. *Journal of the American Medical Informatics Association, 9*(5), 529–539. doi:10.1197/jamia.M1038

Miller, A. R., & Tucker, C. (2009). Privacy protection and technology diffusion: the case of electronic medical records. *Management Science, 55*(7), 1077–1093. doi:10.1287/mnsc.1090.1014

Miller, R. H., West, C., Brown, T. M., Sim, I., & Ganchoff, C. (2005). The value of electronic health records in solo or small group practices. *Health Affairs (Project Hope), 24*(5), 1127–1137. doi:10.1377/hlthaff.24.5.1127

Mullett, C. J., Evans, R. S., Christenson, J. C., & Dean, J. M. (2001). Development and impact of a computerized pediatric antiinfective decision support program. *Pediatrics, 108*(4), E75. doi:10.1542/peds.108.4.e75

Murray, M. D., Harris, L. E., Overhage, J. M., Zhou, X. H., Eckert, G. J., & Smith, F. E. (2004). Failure of computerized treatment suggestions to improve health outcomes of outpatients with uncomplicated hypertension: results of a randomized controlled trial. *Pharmacotherapy, 24*(3), 324–337. doi:10.1592/phco.24.4.324.33173

Nebeker, J. R., Hoffman, J. M., Weir, C. R., Bennett, C. L., & Hurdle, J. F. (2005). High rates of adverse drug events in a highly computerized hospital. *Archives of Internal Medicine, 165*(10), 1111–1116. doi:10.1001/archinte.165.10.1111

Nemeth, C., & Cook, R. (2005). Hiding in plain sight: What Koppel et al. tell us about healthcare IT. *Journal of Biomedical Informatics, 38*(4), 262-263. doi:10.1016/j.jbi.2005.05.010

Niazkhani, Z., Pirnejad, H., Berg, M., & Aarts, J. (2009). The impact of computerized provider order entry systems on inpatient clinical workflow: a literature review. *Journal of the American Medical Informatics Association, 16*(4), 539–549. doi:10.1197/jamia.M2419

O'Neill, L., & Klepack, W. (2007). Electronic medical records for a rural family practice: a case study in systems development. *Journal of Medical Systems, 31*(1), 25–33. doi:10.1007/s10916-006-9040-1

Orszag, P. R. (2008). *Evidence on the costs and benefits of health information technology.* Washington, DC: The Office of the National Coordinator of Health Information Technology.

Orszag, P. R., & Ellis, P. (2007). The challenge of rising health care costs--a view from the Congressional Budget Office. *The New England Journal of Medicine, 357*(18), 1793–1795. doi:10.1056/NEJMp078190

Osheroff, J. A., Teich, J. M., Middleton, B. F., Steen, E. B., Wright, A., & Detmer, D. E. (2006). A roadmap for national action on clinical decision support (No. HHSP233200500877P). Bethesda, MD.

Ozdas, A., Speroff, T., Waitman, L. R., Ozbolt, J., Butler, J., & Miller, R. A. (2006). Integrating "best of care" protocols into clinicians' workflow via care provider order entry: impact on quality-of-care indicators for acute myocardial infarction. *Journal of the American Medical Informatics Association, 13*(2), 188–196. doi:10.1197/jamia.M1656

Palen, T. E., Raebel, M., Lyons, E., & Magid, D. M. (2006). Evaluation of laboratory monitoring alerts within a computerized physician order entry system for medication orders. *The American Journal of Managed Care, 12*(7), 389–395.

Pan, W.T. (2004, November 18 - 19). *Health information technology 2004: improving chronic disease care in California. California HealthCare Foundation.* San Francisco, CA: SBC Park.

Perreault, L., & Metzger, J. (1993). A pragmatic framework for understanding clinical decision support. *Journal of Healthcare Information Management, 13*(2), 5–21.

Pizziferri, L., Kittler, A. F., Volk, L. A., Honour, M. M., Gupta, S., & Wang, S. (2005). Primary care physician time utilization before and after implementation of an electronic health record: a time-motion study. *Journal of Biomedical Informatics, 38*(3), 176–188. doi:10.1016/j.jbi.2004.11.009

Poissant, L., Pereira, J., Tamblyn, R., & Kawasumi, Y. (2005). The impact of electronic health records on time efficiency of physicians and nurses: a systematic review. *Journal of the American Medical Informatics Association, 12*(5), 505–516. doi:10.1197/jamia.M1700

Potts, A. L., Barr, F. E., Gregory, D. F., Wright, L., & Patel, N. R. (2004). Computerized physician order entry and medication errors in a pediatric critical care unit. *Pediatrics, 113*(Pt 1), 59–63. doi:10.1542/peds.113.1.59

Proudfoot, J., Ryden, C., Everitt, B., Shapiro, D. A., Goldberg, D., & Mann, A. (2004). Clinical efficacy of computerised cognitive-behavioural therapy for anxiety and depression in primary care: randomised controlled trial. *The British Journal of Psychiatry, 185*, 46–54. doi:10.1192/bjp.185.1.46

Rothschild, J. M., Federico, F. A., Gandhi, T. K., Kaushal, R., Williams, D. H., & Bates, D. W. (2002). Analysis of medication-related malpractice claims: causes, preventability, and costs. *Archives of Internal Medicine, 162*(21), 2414–2420. doi:10.1001/archinte.162.21.2414

Rothschild, J. M., McGurk, S., Honour, M., Lu, L., McClendon, A. A., & Srivastava, P. (2007). Assessment of education and computerized decision support interventions for improving transfusion practice. *Transfusion, 47*(2), 228–239. doi:10.1111/j.1537-2995.2007.01093.x

Roumie, C. L., Elasy, T. A., Greevy, R., Griffin, M. R., Liu, X., & Stone, W. J. (2006). Improving blood pressure control through provider education, provider alerts, and patient education: a cluster randomized trial. *Annals of Internal Medicine, 145*(3), 165–175.

Safran, C. (1999). Editorial. *International Journal of Medical Informatics, 54*(3), 155–156. doi:10.1016/S1386-5056(99)00003-9

Sands, D. Z. (1999). Electronic patient-centered communication: managing risks, managing opportunities, managing care. *The American Journal of Managed Care, 5*(12), 1569–1571.

Sequist, T. D., Gandhi, T. K., Karson, A. S., Fiskio, J. M., Bugbee, D., & Sperling, M. (2005). A randomized trial of electronic clinical reminders to improve quality of care for diabetes and coronary artery disease. *Journal of the American Medical Informatics Association, 12*(4), 431–437. doi:10.1197/jamia.M1788

Shulman, R., Singer, M., Goldstone, J., & Bellingan, G. (2005). Medication errors: a prospective cohort study of hand-written and computerised physician order entry in the intensive care unit. *Critical Care (London, England), 9*(5), R516–R521. doi:10.1186/cc3793

Slack, W. V. (2001). *Cybermedicine: how computing empowers doctors and patients for better care*. San Francisco, CA: Jossey-Bass.

Smith, D. H., Perrin, N., Feldstein, A., Yang, X., Kuang, D., & Simon, S. R. (2006). The impact of prescribing safety alerts for elderly persons in an electronic medical record: an interrupted time series evaluation. *Archives of Internal Medicine, 166*(10), 1098–1104. doi:10.1001/archinte.166.10.1098

Speicher, C. D. S.J.J. (1983). Choosing Effective Laboratory Tests, W.B. Saunders, (Ed.). Philadelphia, PA: W.B.Saunders.

Steele, A. W., Eisert, S., Witter, J., Lyons, P., Jones, M. A., Gabow, P., & Ortiz, E. (2005). The effect of automated alerts on provider ordering behavior in an outpatient setting. *PLoS Medicine, 2*(9), e255. Retrieved from Doi: 10.1371/journal.pmed.0020255

Studdert, D. M., Mello, M. M., Gawande, A. A., Gandhi, T. K., Kachalia, A, & Yoon, C.,... Brennan, T.A. (2006). Claims, errors, and compensation payments in medical malpractice litigation. *The New England Journal of Medicine, 354*, 2024–2033. doi:10.1056/NEJMsa054479

Tang, P. C., LaRosa, M. P., Newcomb, C., & Gorden, S. M. (1999). Measuring the effects of reminders for outpatient influenza immunizations at the point of clinical opportunity. *Journal of the American Medical Informatics Association, 6*, 115–121.

Tierney, W. M., Overhage, J. M., Murray, M. D., Harris, L. E., Zhou, X. H., & Eckert, G. J. (2005). Can computer-generated evidence-based care suggestions enhance evidence-based management of asthma and chronic obstructive pulmonary disease? A randomized, controlled trial. *Health Services Research, 40*(2), 477–497. doi:10.1111/j.1475-6773.2005.0t369.x

Tierney, W. M., Rotich, J. K., Hannan, T. J., Siika, A. M., Biondich, P. G., & Mamlin, B. W. (2007). The AMPATH medical record system: creating, implementing, and sustaining an electronic medical record system to support HIV/AIDS care in western Kenya. *Studies in Health Technology and Informatics, 129*(Pt 1), 372–376.

Toth-Pal, E., Nilsson, G. H., & Furhoff, A. K. (2004). Clinical effect of computer generated physician reminders in health screening in primary health care--a controlled clinical trial of preventive services among the elderly. *International Journal of Medical Informatics, 73*(9-10), 695–703. doi:10.1016/j.ijmedinf.2004.05.007

van der Sijs, H., Aarts, J., Vulto, A., & Berg, M. (2006). Overriding of drug safety alerts in computerized physician order entry. Journal of the American Medical Informatics Association, 13(2), 138-147. Virapongse, A., Bates, D. W., Shi, P., Jenter, C. A., Volk, L. A., Kleinman, K. et al. (2008). Electronic health records and malpractice claims in office practice. *Archives of Internal Medicine,168*(21), 2362-7.

Wagner, B., Knaevelsrud, C., & Maercker, A. (2006). Internet-based cognitive-behavioral therapy for complicated grief: a randomized controlled trial. *Death Studies, 30*(5), 429–453. doi:10.1080/07481180600614385

Walker, J., Pan, E., Johnston, D., Adler-Milstein, J., Bates, D. W., & Middleton, B. (2005). The value of health care information exchange and interoperability. *Health Affairs (Project Hope)*, (Suppl Web Exclusives), W5-10–W15-18.

Weick, K. E. (1990). The vulnerable system - an analysis of the Tenerife air disaster. *Journal of Management, 16*(3), 571–596. doi:10.1177/014920639001600304

Williamson, J. W., Goldschmidt, P. G., & Jillson, I. A. (1979). Medical Practice Information Demonstration Project: Final Report. Baltimore, MD: Policy Research Inc. Office of the Assistant Secretary of Health, Department of Health, Education, and Welfare, contract 28277-0068GS.

ENDNOTES

[1]   Some studies suggest potential reductions in error rates from the use of health IT of between 50 per cent and over 90 per cent (Evans et al., 1998; Potts, Barr, Gregory, Wright, & Patel, 2004).

[2]   A review of studies on clinical decision support found that most such functions improved the performance of practitioners – see Garg et al., 2005. On the other hand, other research finds no evidence of an increase in physicians' adherence to evidence-based standards of treatment for a wide variety of conditions – see for instance Crosson et al., 2007, and Linder, Ma, Bates, Middleton, & Stafford, 2007.

Chapter 3
Closing the Gap:
E-Health and Optimization of Patient Care

Malina Jordanova
Solar-Terrestrial Influences Institute, Bulgaria

ABSTRACT

Brought to life by contemporary changes of our world, e-health offers enormous possibilities. In the World Health Organization's World Health Assembly resolution on e-health, WHO has defined e-health as the cost-effective and secure use of information and communication technologies in support of health and health-related fields, including healthcare services, health surveillance, health literature, and health education (WHO, 2005). It is impossible to have a detailed view of its potential as e-health affects the entire health sector and is a viable tool to provide routine, as well as specialized, health services. It is able to improve both the access to, and the standard of, health care. The aim of the chapter is to focus on how e-health can help in closing one gap - optimizing patient care. The examples included and references provided are ready to be introduced in practice immediately. Special attention is dedicated to cost effectiveness of e-health applications.

INTRODUCTION

Over the past decade the interest in e-health has risen very quickly. E-health is the application and extensive use of information and communication technology in all areas of health care, from delivery of professional care to patients to the life-long education of citizens and medical professionals. In the World Health Assembly resolution on e-health in 2005, the World Health Organization (WHO) has defined e-health as the cost-effective and secure use of information and communication technologies in support of health and health-related fields, including healthcare services, health surveillance, health literature, and health education (WHO, 2005). Despite the fact that almost all recognize the WHO as a world leading authority, responsible for providing leadership on global health matters, setting norms and standards, etc., and all its members respect its decisions, the term e-health in not accepted world-

DOI: 10.4018/978-1-61520-733-6.ch003

wide. Thus, before we begin it is necessary to clarify the confusion in terminology.

Vocabulary

Until the end of the 90s the term telemedicine was widely used. This word is a combination of two Greek words τήλε = tele - meaning "at a distance" and "medicina" or "ars medicina" meaning "healing". The introduction of "telemedicine" is ascribed to Thomas Bird, who in the 1970s had used the term to illustrate healthcare delivery, where physicians examined distant patients through the use of telecommunications technologies (Strehle & Shabde, 2006). But it may be well forgotten that in 1906 Einthoven published a paper on telecardiology (Einthoven, 1906)!

In the 1980s and 1990s multiple working definitions of telemedicine were introduced. Some of them were very broad such as "something to do with computers, people and health", others – extremely narrow, e.g., "the healthcare industry's component of business over the Internet" (Pagliari, 2005, see slide 8). More on various telemedicine and e-health definitions may be found in Oh, Rizo, Enkin, and Jadad (2005).

With more involvement of electronic communication systems, the major international organizations – the World Health Organization (WHO), the European Union (EU) and the International Telecommunication Union (ITU) - have officially adopted the term "e-health". The definitions of e-health in the literature are also numerous. The reader may come across definitions as short as three words, i.e. Internet-related health activities or as long as 74 words (Eysenbach, 2001; HIMSS 2008; Oh et al., 2005; Silber, 2003; WHO, 2005). One of the best definitions, short but covering all aspects of e-health, is the one published on Gunther Eysenbach's homepage (2006), where e-health equals medicine plus communication plus information plus society (e-health = Medicine + Communication + Information + Society). This definition covers all – the application of informa-

tion and communication technology in all medical fields plus the influence that e-health has on society, as health care is a social service.

At the First High Level Ministerial Conference on e-health, May 22-23, 2003, the European Commission accepted that e-health is the use of modern information and communication technologies applied to meet the needs of citizens, patients, healthcare professionals, healthcare providers, as well as policy makers (Silber, 2003). This was done as an attempt to put order among the mass of definitions applied in this field, at least at the level of the European Union.

For many authors telemedicine and e-health are synonyms and are used as synonyms in this chapter, too. Others accept that e-health is a broader term and includes telemedicine. A third group of authors separate both expressions, acknowledging that telemedicine incorporates telecardiology, teleradiology, telepathology, teleophthalmology, teledermatology, telesurgery, telenursing, etc., while e-health comprises e-Santé, information and communication technologies in health (ICT-Health), all types of health communication services, patient information systems, e-education, e-prescription, etc. Those who are particularly interested in detailed semantics of the words telemedicine and e-health may refer to the TM Alliance (2004).

In the attempts to distinguish between various aspects of e-health, several other terms have also been introduced:

- mHealth or mobile health, i.e., efficient high-quality healthcare services for mobile citizens;
- uHealth or ubiquitous health care, focusing on e-health applications that provide health care to people anywhere at any time using broadband and wireless mobile technologies.

So, what is the correct term – e-health or telemedicine? The consensus now is for e-health.

Unfortunately, even e-health does not satisfy all players. Another term is applied in the EU – tele-health. It is accepted that tele-health has a broader meaning and includes also social aspects of health care. The difference in terminology may also reflect some distinctions as used in different countries, for example, in Canada "tele-health" has been the preferred term, while in the USA it is "telemedicine." This can be seen even in the names of the professional organizations – Society for Tele-health in Canada (CST, http://www.cst-sct.org/en/), the American Telemedicine Association (ATA, http://www.americantelemed.org/i4a/pages/index.cfm?pageid=1) and in Europe, the International Society for Telemedicine and e-health (ISfTeH, www.isft.net) – the latter trying to compromise between telemedicine and e-health. At the moment all terms - telemedicine, e-health and tele-health are often used as synonyms and this still creates lots of confusion.

One additional expression has been introduced and used lately as an even broader description for e-health, i.e., the modern communication health environment (Lievens & Jordanova, 2004). It combines all aspects of health care and ICT as well as the four aspects of e-health – eCare, eLearning, eSurveillance, and eAdministration.

Historical Overview

Generally, the flourishing of e-health is attributed to telecommunication advances and inexpensive computer solutions. It is easy to forget that the first successful experiments in e-health were performed more than a century ago.

In 1905 Willem Einthoven succeeded in transmitting ECG signals via telephone. A year later in 1906, the first publication in the field appeared: Einthoven W., "Le telecardiogramme", *Archives Internationales Physiologie, 4*,132. Einthoven's experiments were not exceptional. There had been attempts to transmit cardiology records via radio in the 1910s. Successful telephone transmission of heart beats date back to the 1920s, while

Morse code was officially introduced in Sweden in 1922 as a tool for distant consultations for mariners. Trials of transfers of radiology images and videophone experiments were performed in early 1950s (Jordanova, 2009).

When man first went to space, the practical development of e-health became a must. Space flight forced scientists to find out how well and for how long humans can survive in space, as well as how well they can readapt after a flight. For example, the necessity to keep a closer look at astronauts' physiological parameters led to the development of devices and programs for monitoring of body functions. The development of many now common technologies, such as heart pacemakers, magnetic resonance imaging, and computerized axial tomography depended, to some extent, on achievements in the space program (Space medicine, 2008).

Since the 1990s, many efforts have been dedicated to the development of e-health in nearly every area of health care, e.g. radiology, pathology, emergency care, cardiology, and surgery. Thousands of projects have been conducted all over the world (a few examples: Bujnowska-Fedak, Staniszewski, Steciwko, & Puchala, 2000; Cooke, 2001; Demartines et al., 2000; Deng, Poole, Brown, & Miller, 2005; Hudson, 2005; Martínez, Villarroel, Seoane, & del Pozo, 2004; Royall, van Schayk, Bennett, Kamau, & Alilio, 2005; Shea, 2007; Soyer et al., 2005). e-health is becoming an everyday reality, not a dream.

It is impossible to have a detailed and complete view of the potential of e-health, as it affects the entire health sector and is a tool to provide routine, as well as specialized, health services. The aim of this chapter is to focus on the current e-health potential in closing one gap - optimization of patient care. The examples included and references provided are ready to be introduced into practice immediately. Special attention is also dedicated to cost effectiveness of e-health applications.

E-HEALTH: A TOOL FOR OPTIMIZATION OF PATIENT CARE

Who Needs E-Health?

E-health has been brought to life by the contemporary changes of our world. Changing demographics and a rapidly aging population; globalization; changes in disease patterns; the necessity to be prepared for and respond to natural disasters and possible bio-terrorism; cheaper and affordable information and communication technology solutions, and the necessity to cut the costs of healthcare budgets spent worldwide are only some of the catalysts for e-health development.

Despite the uncertainties with the terminology, there is no doubt that e-health calls upon several essential components of the community. It involves an important input at the political level (governmental or community as is the case of the countries in the European Union and Commonwealth of Independent States), in health, communication and technology, education, and industry. As it is all part of eGovernment, both at the national and international levels, communication and cooperation between all ministries and all bodies (companies, agencies, etc.) owned or controlled wholly or partly by the government is essential. More voices are raised with the demand of creating in all countries "e-health Coordinating Standing Committees" for a better coordination of all possible actions in the field of e-health (Lievens & Jordanova, 2007).

But one must never forget that the ultimate beneficiary of e-health is the patient / citizen via the healthcare professionals. No matter whether the patients are living in remote areas or in a metropolis, they all could benefit from e-health applications. In remote islands or remote regions, e-health applications may solve the critical issue of access to health care and reporting the results, and in densely populated areas the situation is not much different. Management of chronically ill patients, hospice care, or receiving a second opinion for difficult cases are just some of the applications of e-health in densely populated regions. The reason that e-health is applicable everywhere is that it does not have the goal of changing the essence of healthcare service. It is just optimizing it, including currently available technology.

No doubt, we all need e-health. But are we ready to accept it? Success or failure of e-health is a question of acceptance by the patient. Numerous studies have revealed patients' satisfaction with e-health applications (Born et al., 2008; Mair & Whitten, 2000; McNeil, Wales, & Azarmina, 2008; Whitten, Bergman, Meese, Bridwell, & Jule, 2009). In connection with this, the European Commission (EC) has accepted that a self-assured patient is more demanding and expects a more user-friendly approach, needs more information, and is ready to participate in planning his/her healthcare procedures. In addition, active patients play the most important role in evaluating, developing, and spreading innovative medical solutions. This could be achieved through education. An example to follow is the effort of the EU to maintain the European Patient Forum - the umbrella group of pan-European patient groups - active in the field of European public health and health advocacy (http://www.eu-patient.eu/).

E-Health Acceptance

e-health has the potential to change our lives. A survey performed by International Business Machines Corporation (IBM) in 2006 asked 150,000 people from 104 countries the question: "Five years from now, which technologies are going to be the breakout hits?" The company narrowed the results down to the five innovations that were the "most impactful" and they are: the 3-D Internet; mind-reading cell phones; nanotechnology for energy and the environment; e-health (telemedicine); and real-time speech translation (Boyle, 2006). e-health is among the top five technologies!

Other studies also support the increasing acceptance of e-health applications in various areas of health care such as chronic heart failure (Clark, Inglis, McAlister, Cleland, & Stewart, 2007; Pare, Jaana, & Sicotte, 2007), wound care (Hofmann-Wellenhof et al., 2006), psychiatry (Mucic, 2007, 2008; Stojakovic, 2008), psychology (Jordanova, Vasileva, Rasheva, & Bojinova, 2008), surgery (Nayeemuddin, Majeed, Muneer, & Misra, 2007), chronic disease and care for elderly and house bound patients (von Niman, 2007).

The acceptance of e-health is high and is rising due to its promises. The ten "e"-s of e-health have been described by Eysenbach (2001) as: efficiency; enhancing quality of care; evidence based care; empowerment of citizens and patients; education of physicians and citizens; encouragement of a new relationship between the patient and health professional; enabling communication and information exchange; extending the scope of health care beyond its conventional boundaries; ethical health care; and equity of health care. No doubt e-health offers a number of golden opportunities and benefits by focusing its strength on ensuring better:

- everyday health care – including home monitoring and care for the elderly; personalization of healthcare services; and individual healthcare management;
- enhanced and lifelong health education of both citizens and medical staff;
- prevention of illness;
- management of chronic diseases;
- management of emergency situations and disasters.

In sum, e-health can be a fantastic tool for optimization of patient care. But how?

E-Health Resources for Optimization of Patient Care

What is optimization? This is to make something as perfect, effective, or functional as possible. In health care this means making patient care as

effective as possible. Of course optimising is a strategic goal of the healthcare system.

Who is in Charge of Introducing E-Health Applications?

It is necessary to keep in mind that e-health is developed, and is still developing on a "grass roots" basis, i.e. in most cases the ideas, projects, technologies, and products are developed and implemented from the bottom up rather than from the top down. Even the introduction of hospital information systems, which are often cited as examples of e-health applications, are, in most cases, a result of the activity of local managers or decision makers. Although such activities could be supported by the national ministries of health, the ideas come from the bottom; they often do not include all hospitals in the country. This is not unexpected as the top down approach means a reorganization of the entire healthcare system. There are few administrators or policy makers who will take the risk of starting such a complete reorganization, as the healthcare system needs to be operational all the time and to serve patients every minute. Of course, there are exceptions, national efforts to introduce "e-health" in a step-wise fashion such, as the pan-Canadian initiatives focus on electronic health records (see Canada Health Infoway, http://www.infoway-inforoute.ca/lang-en/about-ehr/ehr-progress-map) or the United Kingdom's "National Program for Information Technology" (see NHS Connecting for Health, http://www.connectingforhealth.nhs.uk/).

Of course, the picture is not strictly black and white. Analyzing the available data and carefully following the development of e-health during the last decade (Jordanova, 2005) it is clear that there are two tendencies in e-health implementation at the national level:

1. Worldwide, countries with a high health expenditure as a percentage of their GDP are very active in introducing various e-health

activities. Good examples are the USA, Canada, Australia, Germany, and Israel. In some countries this has been related to a national policy. In many cases, the reason for the active promotion and implementation of e-health is the need to decrease healthcare costs while providing high quality services. If total health expenditures as per cent of GDP are analyzed for a 6 year period (from 2000-2005), it is obvious that many countries continually increased their health spending. The database of the WHO (http://www.who.int) shows that for these 6 years, many developed countries (e.g., Canada, most European countries), have increased health spending by over 1% of their GDP. In the USA the increase has been 2%. If the trend continues, then governments would be forced to reduce other costs to maintain health budgets.

2. On the other end of the spectrum are countries with a relatively low percentage of health expenditure, such as India or Russia (total expenditure on health was 5% of GDP for India and 5.2% for Russia for 2005). For them, the introduction of e-health is the only way to secure affordable healthcare services for the vast majority of the population. In these countries (as in many others), e-health is close to becoming a governmental priority.

There are examples of the introduction of e-health services realized with a careful, top-down approach that have been incorporated into the existing traditional healthcare system and are working perfectly well. Such examples are the beginning of telepsychiatry (Resmini et al., 2008) and telecardiology (Haddad, Alkmim, Wen, & Roschkes, 2008) in Brazil and the development of eight hospital trains by the Russian railways. Hospital trains, also called "Modern Mobile Diagnostic Centers," are equipped with teleconsultation centers and satellite antennas and are constantly on the move in east to west and north to south directions in Russia, offering medical care for remote and isolated regions (Sel`kov, Stolyar, Sel'kova, & Chevae, 2007; Selkov, Stolyar, Selkova, Atkov, & Chueva, 2005). In rare cases when e-health implementation is a result of cooperation of central and local governments, private companies, and NGOs, even more amazing results are achieved. A perfect illustration is the river health program in Ecuador (Rodas et al., 2006a, 2006b). A motor powered canoe was built containing an operating room, recovery room, a consultation office, and living quarters. It is capable of negotiating the charted channels and serves the province of Morona-Santiago, the most isolated one in Ecuador, where the roads are water channels and rivers. The integral health program includes: health information gathering; immunization; monitoring growth and development and the prevalent diseases of infancy and school-aged children; sexual health and reproduction; geriatrics; oral and mental health; surgery; education for basic sanitation; and the compilation of traditional knowledge regarding medicinal plants and their application (Rodas et al., 2006 a, 2006b).

Thus, for the moment, implementation is a matter of decisions at various levels, but mainly at local ones, to introduce e-health services in the healthcare system. If this is accompanied by political support, it is even better.

How Can E-Health Optimize Patients' Care?

Existing e-health resources are not dedicated to optimization exclusively only in patient care. They go hand in hand with opportunities to optimize the work of healthcare professionals. The final result is not only better quality health care, but lower stress for both patients and healthcare professionals, and increased psychological comfort for all that also reflects on the quality and quantity of health services.

How does e-health support optimization of patients' care? This is done via increased access to services; improved availability of different types of services; timely and controlled care; cost effectiveness and investment return. Then comes the core question: Optimizing how? What is possible today?

If it is not possible to optimize the entire system, let's optimize the work organization. There are lots of examples of hospital management systems and electronic patient records that reduce paper work in hospitals and clinics and free more time to be dedicated to patients or to continued medical education (Botsis, Paraskeva, & Syrigos, 2006; Gertz, 2007; Gyertson, 2006). The latter itself result in better patient care. Let's introduce one example, the ANOTO digital pen and paper technology (Ericson, 2009). The technology captures and converts handwritten information from medical and social care forms into a digital format, eliminating the need to type up notes. The digital pen looks like a ballpoint pen but has a tiny infrared camera at its tip that tracks its movements relative to a grey dot pattern printed on the paper. Recorded and saved information is transferred to a personal computer via a USB link or a mobile phone. A system based on ANOTO technology was also introduced in the Jefferson County Division of Children, Youth, and Families, in Colorado, USA. The goal was to reduce the cost and time spent on data entry and paperwork, in order to maximize casework time spent with families, to meet government audit standards, and to improve overall job satisfaction. The analyses revealed that system introduction resulted in over 580 hours a week saved for 145 caseworkers, i.e. over 29,000 hours at $ 20 per hour or a total of $560,000 annual savings. The time savings created a greater sense of job satisfaction, enabling employees to focus on working with families instead of doing data entry. In addition to this, audit scores significantly improved one month after implementation (Anoto Group AB, 2009).

Similar savings could be achieved by introducing video or Internet connections with patients, if and when possible, or by guiding patients in the use of small "smart' devices for medication control as, for example, the HomMed MedPartner medication reminder (Honeywell HomMed, 2007). Other examples of optimization of work are robotic arms and remote-controlled instrumentation in operating rooms (Lanfranco, Castellanos, Desai, & Meyers, 2004; Shah et al., 2008).

New Trends

Some of the new trends in e-health are resulting in rapid and striking results and in optimization of care.

1. Telenursing is the e-health application within professional nursing practice. Telenursing has developed during the last ten years (Schlachta-Fairchild, 2008). A very good example is in the US, where despite the fact that most health care services are reimbursed on a "per visit" basis and the use of telecare has not been heavily embraced, there was a 600% increase in telenursing in less than five years. It is expected that telenursing will develop even more rapidly internationally, especially where socialized medicine provides a financial impetus for telecare. With the demanding requirement to deliver the best care at the least cost, the increase in telenursing applications will be even more evident in the years to come.

The International Tele-nursing Role Survey, performed in 2004-2005 (Grady & Schlachta-Fairchild, 2005; Sorrells-Jones et al., 2006), gives more information on telenursing. The goals of this survey were to identify where telenursing is developed, whether telenursing is accepted, whether it is effective and whether telenurses are satisfied in their work. Results from 39 countries revealed that the typical telenurse is white, female, married with children, and working full-time in telenursing. Telenurses experience less than average role stress, role ambiguity, and role conflict, and have the same work satisfaction as other hospital-based nurses. The most important factors contributing to telenurses' work satisfaction are autonomy and interaction. Telenurses are also happy with this less physically demanding situation. They are sure that they are able to deliver, manage, and provide better patient education, keep patients out of the hospital, provide better outcomes, decrease hospitalizations, and save time. Fifty nine per cent of telenurses emphasized that they are more satisfied with their telenursing position than with "regular" nursing positions they had before (Castelli, Schlacta-Fairchild & Pyke, 2008; Gundim & Padilha, 2008; Schlachta-Fairchild, Castelli, & Pyke, 2008).

2. Telepsychiatry refers to the use of tele-communication technologies for provision of psychiatric services from a distance, most often via videoconferencing in real-time. Thus the patient and the therapist can see and hear each other at the same time. Telepsychiatry connects patients and health professionals, permitting effective diagnosis, treatment, education, transfer of medical data, and other activities related to mental health care. Several studies have demonstrated high reliability and patients' acceptance of telepsychiatry (Mucic, 2007, 2008). Among numbers of potential applications of telepsychiatry, the treatment of asylum seekers, refugees, and migrants in their mother language is of great importance (Mucic, 2007). Telepsychiatry is extremely helpful in moving towards a community-based outpatient approach. An example is the project for tele-assistance for mental diseases in the city of Sao Lourenco do Sul, Brazil (Resmini et al., 2008). After the mental health staff overcame their initial skepticism, and the method was validated

through daily practice, the results became evident. Decisions about therapeutic interventions are adopted immediately avoiding unnecessary hospitalizations. The preliminary results showed that telepsychiatry can play a significant role in the management of mental diseases.

3. The organization of psychological services in a technology-assisted environment, including telephone, Internet media (written, voice, or digital pictures) and video conferencing is named telepsychology or e-psychology. No doubt this is the future of psychology due to two main reasons. One, the trend of increasing psychological disorders and the heavy burden that these kind of disorders place on individuals, families, and communities all over the world. And second, while many people suffer from a variety of psychological disorders, care is not available to all who may need it. A simple example is depression. According to the WHO's world health report (WHO, 2003) in the European Region alone, 33.4 million people suffered from severe depression. That is 58 out of every 1,000 adults! Of all the disability-adjusted life-years lost, depressive disorders account for the largest share. Care providers recognize the problem in less than 50% of all depressed patients seeking medical help and only about 18% of these patients received correct treatment. And this is in Europe, where the situation with human resources is much better than in other regions of the world. Europe is a leader with 3.0 psychologists and 2.4 social workers per 100,000 people. Telepsychology applies a modern communication infrastructure to offer psychological help and consultations to those who need it, no matter where they are and at what time of the day or night they need help.

4. The application of Short Message Services (SMS) for management of chronic diseases is another emerging area. Most mental and

behavioral disorders are associated with a considerable risk for relapse after reaching the state of recovery. Unfortunately, once finishing inpatient treatment, most patients never seek after-hospital help. Mobile technology in the form of SMS, GMS (global system for mobile communication), and the Internet offers easy and user-friendly ways to support these patients on their way back to everyday life. A winning strategy was developed at the Centre for Psychotherapy Research in Stuttgart, Germany, for after-treatment of patients with bulimia nervosa using SMS. The intervention consists of weekly messages from the patients about their bulimic symptomatology and corresponding weekly feedback that is a mixture of pre-programmed and individually tailored information. Results indicate that the program is technically feasible, well-accepted by patients, and helpful for patients with bulimia nervosa in readjusting to everyday life after finishing inpatient treatment (Bauer, Percevic, & Kordy, 2004). Another success story is the "On Cue" 2002 project in South Africa (Kwankam, 2008) sending SMS reminders to patients with tuberculosis for drug regimen compliance. SMS were sent out every half hour within a chosen time-frame to remind patients to take their medicine. As of January 2003, the city of Cape Town has paid only $16/patient/year for SMS reminders. In this pilot, only one patient out of 138 was non-compliant (an astonishing 99.3% compliance rate). This is something that is worth trying more widely. An SMS system was introduced in the Saratov Railway Clinic, Russia that has 534 beds and is the main hospital in the Volga Region serving an area of 250,000 km² with more than 6 million people. The SMS system was used to control the daily schedule of patients with chronic diseases, to remind them about appointments for preventive treatment in the rehabilitative center, and to schedule them for doctors' visits. In addition, nurses received information about patients' health status prior to patients' hospital visits (Kasimov, Karchenova, & Tuchin, 2009).

5. Sweden has gone even further, developing a project for 24-hour teledermatology consultations via MMS (Multimedia Message Services). Clients took a digital image of the area of the skin that was of concern, included text that could give more information, and sent the MMS to a given number. Within 24 hours they received a MMS with medical information: a probable diagnosis, short explanatory text, treatment advice and if necessary, were advised to consult a doctor face-to-face. The average time for answering a message ranged from 8 to 25 minutes and users were extremely satisfied (Börve & Molina-Martinez, 2009).

6. Management of chronic diseases, elearning, telerehabilitation, sharing e-health intellectual property, and fostering e-health security, are also in the pipeline. Development of electronic or e-textiles is another important trend. E-textiles contain computational functionality yet remain soft, flexible, wearable, and washable. E-textiles with embedded "fall" detectors could be useful for people with kinetic problems; electronic cloths, such as coats retaining constant temperature under varying climatic conditions, could be worn by those working or living at extreme conditions; while textiles monitoring vital parameters could monitor patients at risk, chronic disease patients, and athletes. (Paradiso, Belloc, Loriga, & Tacini, 2005; Sum, Zheng, & Mak, 2005; Vontetsianos et al., 2009).

Cultural Differences

E-health is an enabler and a tool to support health care. But when considering e-health applications for optimization of patient care it is always necessary to have in mind that there are cultural differences among communities. One and the same service may be accepted and interpreted in various ways depending on the cultural and religious background of the citizens. No matter how good a given e-health tool or service is, if it is not culturally acceptable, it will not work.

An example is the SMS/MMS application. As mentioned above, MMS service is applied in Sweden (Börve & Molina-Martinez, 2009) to receive virtual teledermatology consultations. MMS include pictures of the problematic body area including hands, face, chest, belly, etc. About 74% of Swedes are Christians and belonged to the Church of Sweden (Lutheran). The pictures of the naked body are acceptable and do not cause problems. The same service is not automatically applicable in regions with predominantly Muslim populations. Sending pictures of naked body parts to an unknown doctor is culturally un-acceptable. Yet, the Short Message Service is used, but in a way that will not hurt citizens' feelings or cultural sensitivities. For instance, in Asia SMS gives an opportunity to improve maternal care. A project including the Philippines, Pakistan, and Indonesia has started applying SMS services to increase the proportion of clients accessing health information and to provide remote consultation and education to women and local healthcare staff (Dashtseren et al., 2009; Saligumba et al., 2009). The project will have an enormous impact on healthcare services without overloading health budgets as it is focused on groups that do not have regular access to health care partially due to financial problems, partially due to the need to travel, and partially to cultural and/or religious restrictions. This is an example how, if carefully applied, the same solution may answer the needs of a specific culture.

Another point to consider is the geopolitical differences in healthcare resources and demands. The needs of Central African countries are different from the needs of Central European countries. Countries, where shortage of funds is severe or countries with a combination of a shortage of health providers and a high disease burden, have no use of telesurgery if there are no funds for basic medication. Such countries or communities may benefit from available virtual consultation services, for example the exchange of knowledge and second opinions through iPath that requires only a small annual fee (http://telemed.ipath.ch); the use of free libraries and educational resources such as the online support for antiretroviral therapy (ART) and AIDS care delivery at the Institute for Tropical Medicine in Antverp (http://www.itg.be/itg); Med-e-Tel's free online library searchable by year, country, or topic (http://www.medetel.eu); the sleep heart rate and stroke volume data bank (http://www.pri.kmu.lt/datbank/); digital ophthalmology resources (http://www.bmii.ktu.lt:8081/unrs/eyes); or learning tools for prosthetists (http://helseutdanning.no/cambodia/index.htm) – just to name a few. All of these databases could be used for education of students and continuous education of medical staff, as well as for research activities.

Cost Effectiveness

Optimization of patient care with e-health also concerns its cost effectiveness. Initial studies were definite – there is no good evidence that telemedicine is a cost effective way to deliver healthcare (Whitten et al., 2002). Some authors even underlined that the costs are greater for the virtual consultations than for conventional outpatient appointments, although they supported the hypothesis that losses in productivity are lower (Jacklin et al., 2003). Perhaps one of the reasons for these conclusions is that some of these analyses were based on literature reviews (Whitten et al., 2002). In addition, when costs or e-health acceptance are discussed, it is necessary that the reader be careful, as the majority of the studies are based on samples with fewer than 100 participants as Whitten and Buis (2007) have indicated. Plus, as the same authors point out, only 26% of the studies reported a time frame, which is an essential parameter in determining long-term cost benefits.

Data from more recent studies on cost effectiveness focusing on large scale studies (i.e., either based on a large number of consultations or years of experience) are just the opposite. A Greek study, performed in 2005, calculated that the cost for remote consultation is 203.5 € compared to 270 € for referrals. The results proved to be relatively robust after being tested with a sensitivity analysis (Tsitlakidis, Mylonakis, & Niakas, 2005). The benefits and cost savings are even greater in the case of islands or other remote communities where patients have to travel long distances either for hospitalization or for specialist consultations. However, it should be noted that the cost of e-health procedures also depends on the number of patients served in the remote area.

Another detailed survey revealed the outcome of a five year period of telepediatric consultations. The authors underlined that the total cost of providing 1,499 consultations was $ 955,996 (Australian dollars). The estimated potential cost of providing an outpatient service to the same number of patients at the Royal Children's Hospital in Brisbane was $ 1,553,264; thus, telepediatric services resulted in a net saving of approximately $ 600,000 to the health service provider (Smith, Scuffham, & Wootton, 2007).

The strongest evidence for the efficacy of e-health in clinical outcomes comes from home-based monitoring of chronic disease management, hypertension, diabetes, and AIDS. There is also reasonable evidence that e-health is cost saving and with a quality equal to face-to-face care in emergency medicine, and is beneficial in surgical and neonatal intensive care units, as well as patient transfer in neurosurgery (Al-Rousan, Al-Ali, & Eberlein, 2006; Bensink et al., 2007; Bryant & Colgrave, 2006).

When discussing e-health applications for distant consultations and decision making it is worth citing a two year study in the US evaluating the quality and cost effectiveness of health care provided in urban and rural elementary school telehealth centers, using plain old telephone system (POTS) technology (Young & Ireson, 2003). The project linked a full-time school nurse, half-time mental-health consultant, pediatric practice, and psychiatrist via POTS with an electronic stethoscope; ears, nose, and throat endoscope; and an otoscope. One rural and one urban center were evaluated. Providers, nurses, children, and parents completed satisfaction questionnaires. A total of 3,461 visits to school nurses at both centers were completed during the two-year project. Satisfaction of all - provider, nurse, child, and parent - was high. Providers' and nurses' decision confidence scores ranged from 4 to 4.8 on a 5-point scale. Average family savings per encounter were 3.4 hours of work time, and when travel was included, family savings ranged from US$ 101 to $ 224 per encounter. The POTS-based technology helps to make this service a cost-effective alternative for improving access to health care for underserved children.

Especially interesting and convincing are long duration studies performed in countries with large territories, such as Russia and Brazil. According to the estimates of West Siberian physicians, based on almost ten years of e-health practice, patients paid an approximately 40 times smaller fee for the virtual consultations rendered by a Moscow expert, than they would have paid if they'd had to make a trip to Moscow to consult this same expert. The quality of the service was the same (Sel'kov et al., 2007). The same authors (Sel'kov, Stolyar, Atkov, Sel'kova, & Chueva, 2008) have done a detailed analysis of return on investment cost in e-clinics and demonstrated that the return on investment starts after an initial period of 2.5 years. Although most of their publications are in Russian, it is interesting to follow at least those published in other languages or translated, as the return on investment is only one of 20 indexes that are applied in their telemedicine project economic analyses.

Another example is the telecardiology service in the State of Minas Gerais in Brazil. The State of Minas Gerais has a territory equivalent to the size of France and a population of 19,000,000 living in 853 cities. Telecardiology has been operating since June 2006 in 82 remote and isolated villages. Preliminary results of the evaluation of economical feasibility have shown that the savings resulting from a 1.5% reduction on the number of treatments outside the village are sufficient to cover the operational cost of the system (Figueira, Alkmim, Ribeiro, Pena, & Campos, 2008).

Wisely chosen e-health applications are beneficial everywhere. In a study from a comparatively "smaller" country, Italy, in 2001, a 24/7 toll-free telephone hotline service for children and adolescents with Type 1 diabetes was organized in the Parma region (Bernardini, Chiari, & Vanelli, 2008). An extensive survey, carried out from the beginning of 2001 until the end of 2006, showed that the total number of children receiving help was 421 (mean age of 10.8 yrs with a mean duration of diabetes of 4.5 years). Within the five year period 20,075 calls were recorded, or an average of 11 calls per day. Fifty two per cent of the calls were emergency calls. Thanks to the available service, the admission to hospital because of diabetic ketoacidosis fell from an average of 10 cases per 100 children per year to 3 cases per 100 children per year. Thus, the costs for admission decreased by 60% (Bernardini et al., 2008).

Since 1994, an e-health service has been offered in Nishiaizu Town, Japan (Tsuji, Akematsu, & Taoka, 2007). Vital physiology parameters are transmitted to a remote medical institution monitoring patients diagnosed with high blood pressure, cerebral infarction, strokes, diabetes, and in the elderly. In several papers Tsuji et al. (2007), Akematsu and Tsuji (2009) analyzed the cost effectiveness of the system. They outlined that medical expenditures for lifestyle-related diseases of e-health users have dropped by 20.7%. The authors also demonstrated that long-time e-health users had lower medical expenditure than those who used it for a shorter time, a result that once again proved that if we are looking for cost–effectiveness it is necessary to concentrate on large scale and long lasting studies.

Our results also proved that e-health applications can be cost effective. But it is always necessary to ask the question: cost benefits for whom? The results of implementation of telepsychology consultations in Bulgaria are promising. Based on almost 6,000 hours of virtual consultations over five years it is clear that clients are saving money (http://www.e-therapy.bg/prices.php). Virtual consultations are three to four times cheaper compared to face-to-face visits. Unfortunately, this is not the case for the licensed psychologist providing the consultations. As psychology support is not covered by insurance funds, these experts have to rely only on rewards from their clients. The general practice has become to prepay for virtual sessions one by one or to provide an initial payment for three to four sessions depending on the problem that is treated. Bank transfer or credit card payments ensure that the contacts between patient and psychologist remain virtual. Usually, the profit is not enough to cover the cost for office, equipment, personal expenses, etc., at least at the beginning. Virtual psychology counseling must either be part of a pre-financed project or be combined with clinical service in order to allow 24 hour telepsychology support. Clinics that can afford this, hire several psychologists who offer both virtual counseling and work as clinical psychologists.

E-Health International Players

When discussing optimization of e-health, an obvious question is: Who has to take the lead? Who are the main e-health players?

It is not easy to enumerate all the players at various levels as the group is quite dynamic. At the national level there are various associations and societies, institutions, governmental and non-governmental organizations and foundations, telecom and IT companies, and military structures.

Some of the most prominent international players are: WHO, ITU (International Telecommunication Union), the EU and EC, the United Nations Office for Outer Space Affairs (UNOOSA), the United Nations Educational Scientific and Cultural Organization (UNESCO), the United Nations Children's Fund (UNICEF), the North Atlantic Treaty Organization (NATO), peace keeping bodies, associations and societies, and international telecom and IT companies. In addition, let's not forget the unique role of science and research, as well as the impact of business structures, industries (e.g. producers of medical devices, imaging products, pharmaceutical, telecom equipment and services, satellite connections, providers of services such as insurance, legal assistance, financing) and administration players. The list is too long but it is necessary to underline that only WHO is fully dedicated to health issues while other organizations deal with health issues among several other activities. Therefore it is WHO that has the ultimate coordinating responsibilities for international efforts.

But the efforts towards optimization must come from all these different organizations with the help of healthcare and information technology professionals, healthcare managers, nurses, patient organizations, etc. The challenge is to make all these parties work together for the patient's benefit. Because whatever way you look at it - the patient is central! It must be our personal concern too, as we are all potential patients. How would we like to be treated when we become patients?

What are the E-Health Challenges?

Yet another closely connected question is: what are the challenges of e-health? Coordination is the main one, i.e., to make all the possible players coordinate their skills and efforts to achieve an optimal development within the health environment using modern communication systems. This

is a Sisyphean task. When this is achieved, the benefits will be for all of us, and citizens will rely on high quality affordable health care at anytime, anywhere.

Introducing e-health at primary health care levels is another challenge and is based on the knowledge of ecology of medical care. Put in other words, where do people look first for medical help? Despite the predictions and expectations for people seeking care primarily at tertiary level facilities (Dovey et al., 2003; Green, Fryer, Yawn, Lanier, & Dovey, 2001; White, Williams, & Greenberg, 1961), the dominant numbers reveal that first are visits at the primary care levels. Understanding and taking into account the ecology of health care, defines the choice of primary care as one of the main fields of e-health applications.

Wide application of e-health for management of chronic diseases is another important challenge. Chronic diseases are now the leading causes of death and disability worldwide (WHO, 2006). Disease rates from these conditions are accelerating globally, advancing across every region and pervading all socioeconomic classes. The WHO World Health Report (2006) indicates that the mortality, morbidity, and disability attributed to the major chronic diseases currently account for almost 60% of all deaths and 43% of the global burden of disease. By 2020 the contribution is expected to rise to 73% of all deaths and 60% of the global burden of disease (WHO, 2002). E-health has an enormous unused potential to decrease, at least partially, the burden of chronic disease worldwide.

When challenges are discussed, the problem of the most important "showstoppers" of e-health implementation cannot be avoided. In an attempt to reveal the core of the problem and to name the main obstacles for worldwide implementation of e-health solutions we interviewed 51 prominent e-health experts in April, 2005. Participants were asked to fill in a questionnaire and to indicate the main obstacles to wide implementation and acceptance of e-health. The leading principle in choosing survey participants was their experience in e-health operation. Many answers were identical, so we were able to group them into nine categories. The results revealed that the high cost of e-health equipment, poor business plans, personal resistance of both medical staff and patients, plus lack of sufficient knowledge, and inadequately developed infrastructure are the main showstoppers of e-health implementation (Jordanova, 2005). These five categories accounted for over 71% of existing problems and are the main obstacles when aiming at international e-health implementation. These obstacles should be handled with a top-down and bottom-up approach at both the national and international level. The survey was repeated in 2008 with 75 experts. Preliminary analyses revealed that the results do not differ. One more category appears in a prominent position – the lack of an adequate reimbursement policy. This is also pointed out as one of the problems in telemedicine deployment in the US (Whitten & Buis, 2007). Other authors have also confirmed that personal resistance and technical challenges plus lack of education of both medical staff and patients are among the main obstacles for wide implementation of e-health services (Hopp et al., 2006; Mair et al., 2006).

Providers' acceptance of e-health and their satisfaction from the service offered is another challenge. E-health providers are among those that communicate with the patient, they are the "gatekeepers" to new technology, and the way in which the service is presented and made user-friendly (Whitten et al., 2007). Without their help and active involvement in promoting e-health, most patients will not have access to the service (Whitten & Buis, 2007; Whitten & Mackert, 2005).

Networking as Prerequisite for Success

Within the world of e-health, it is crucial for all the players to be aware of what is going on globally and this may be done via international networking initiatives. Therefore, cooperation and networking are important factors. Two specific network-enabling initiatives are:

- The International Society for Telemedicine and e-health (ISfTeH, http://www.isft.net), a not-for-profit organization, is the international representative body of national and international telemedicine and e-health organizations, dedicated to broadly promoting telemedicine, telecare, tele-health, and e-health around the world. ISfTeH supports the start up of national associations or societies and facilitates their international contacts; disseminates knowledge, information and experience; and provides access to recognized e-health experts. As part of ISfTeH's educational activity, a Working Committee on "Education" is now functioning. The mission of this Committee is: listing existing programs in e-health; establishing basic e-health templates for fundamental training programs; coordinating e-health educational efforts around the globe; assisting the set up of new courses in e-health; and defining the needs of universities and specialists for basic and continued education.
- e-health science, practice, and industry need a meeting place. Such a place is Med-e-Tel (The International e-health, Telemedicine and Health ICT Forum for Education, Networking and Business – http://www.medetel.lu/index.php). Med-e-Tel is a highly specialized event that brings suppliers of specific equipment and service providers together with buyers, healthcare professionals, decision makers, and policy makers from many countries and provides them with hands-on experience and knowledge about currently available products, technologies, and applications. Med-e-Tel is a forum where state-of-the-art products, ideas, and projects are presented and

discussed. Year after year it becomes a nurturing place for new co-operation and partnerships between scientific groups and institutions, and small, medium and large size enterprises, from all over the world. Annual meetings call together participants from over 50 countries with WHO, EC, ESA, ITU, UNOOSA, among the major players taking part in the event.

Med-e-Tel provides educational opportunities through its extensive program of presentations, panel discussions, workshops, and satellite symposia. It is accredited by the European Accreditation Council for Continuing Medical Education (EACCME) to provide European external CME credits for medical specialists. EACCME credits are recognized by the American Medical Association as well as by some countries in Asia and the Middle East. This is the highest possible recognition of the value of Med-e-Tel's Educational program.

ISfTeH and Med-e-Tel work together; they are two sides of the same coin. They both lead the way from needs to practical applications, highlight quantitative numbers and results, and serve networking – meeting real people, real business, real achievements, real products, discussing real problems, and education for business, science, practitioners, and citizens. ISfTeH, and especially Med-e-Tel, are the perfect organizations for following what is going on globally and the new trends in the area of e-health. Of course there are many other events covering this field. In fact, there are hundreds each year!

CONCLUSION

E-health is no longer an optional choice. The technology solutions are available and ready to be implemented in the healthcare system. E-health services are advancing and are acceptable to both clients/patients and medical professionals.

Teleconsultations provide effective doctor-patient consultations in a variety of circumstances (Mair & Whitten, 2000). Multinational and multicultural studies have proven that the satisfaction from a distant care management service is high and it can enhance self-care, change health-related behaviors, and improve outcomes in patients with a number of chronic conditions (Beck, 2007; Born et al., 2008; Korb, 2008; McNeil et al., 2008).

As shown by the examples given, if carefully implemented, taking into account the needs of the community, e-health is able to improve both access to and the standard of healthcare, and thus to close the gap between the demand for affordable, high quality healthcare to everyone, at any time, everywhere, and the necessity to stop the increase in healthcare budgets worldwide.

E-health is already a must, a fantastic challenge for the future, but it requires cooperation and coordination at all possible levels. It requires networking and planning, readiness to learn from others, and no efforts to re-invent the wheel. The main challenge is to be sure that available options are used optimally and in a coordinated manner and to ascertain that the desired effects do come through and those resources are indeed not diverted away from basic needs.

REFERENCES

Akematsu, Y., & Tsuji, M. (2009). An empirical analysis of the reduction in medical expenditure by e-health users. *Journal of Telemedicine and Telecare*, 15, 109–111. doi:10.1258/jtt.2009.003001

Al-Rousan, M., Al-Ali, A. R., & Eberlein, A. (2006). Remote patient monitoring and information system. *International Journal of Electronic Healthcare*, 2(3), 231–249.

Alliance, T. M. (2004). *Telemedicine 2010: Visions for a personal medical network*. Retrieved January 14, 2009, from http://www.euro.who.int/eprise/main/who/progs/tme/about/20021009_1

Anoto Group AB. (2009). *Protecting children – Digital pen and paper enables caseworkers to spend more time in the field.* Retrieved August 11, 2009, from http://www.anoto.com/filearchive/1/14709/pendatasolutions_children_090626.pdf

Bauer, S., Percevic, R., & Kordy, H. (2004). *The use of short message service (SMS) in the aftercare treatment for patients with Bulimia Nervosa.* Paper presented at Med-e-Tel 2004, Luxembourg, D.G. of Luxembourg. Retrieved December 15, 2008 from http://www.medetel.lu/download/2004/parallel_sessions/abstract/0422/THE_USE_OF_SHORT_MESSAGE_SERVICE.doc

Beck, T. (2007). *Regional need analysis questionnaire survey for analyzing the acceptance & awareness of e-health in 5 European countries Germany, Sweden, Finland, Poland, Lithuania.* Presented at Cross-border e-health in the Baltic Sea region. Stockholm, Sweden. Retrieved December 15, 2008 from http://www.e-healthconference.info/Presentations/b_thorsten_beck.pdf

Bensink, M., Wootton, R., Irving, H., Hallahan, A., Theodoros, D., Russell, T., et al. (2007). Investigating the cost-effectiveness of video telephone based support for newly diagnosed paediatric oncology patients and their families: design of a randomized controlled trial. *BioMed Central Health Services Research, 7*(38). Retrieved January 3, 2009 from http://www.biomedcentral.com/1472-6963/7/38

Bernardini, A. L., Chiari, G., & Vanelli, M. (2008). Telephone hotline service (THS) for children and adolescents with type 1 diabetes as a strategy to reduce diabetes-related emergencies and costs for admittance. *Global Telemedicine / e-health Updates* []. Luxembourg: Publ. Luxexpo.]. *Knowledge Resources, 1*, 26–29.

Born, A. P., Sparenberg, A., Russomano, T., Timm, R., Soares, E., & Schaun, T. (2008). Eight years of a tele-ECG system in southern Brazil: a multidisciplinary analysis regarding the degree of satisfaction. In Jordanova, M., & Lievens, F. (Eds.), *Global Telemedicine / e-health Updates: Knowledge Resources* (*Vol. 1*, pp. 203–204). Luxembourg: Luxexpo.

Börve, A., & Molina-Martinez, R. (2008). 24-hour anonymous medical information service using the mobile telephone in Sweden: A pilot study during the summer of 2008. In Jordanova, M., & Lievens, F. (Eds.), *Global Telemedicine/e-health Updates: Knowledge Resources* (*Vol. 2*, pp. 181–185). Luxembourg: Luxexpo.

Botsis, T., Paraskeva, P., & Syrigos, K. N. (2006). *Implementation of computerized information systems in oncology unit.* Paper presented at Med-e-Tel 2006. Retrieved August 10, 2009 from http://www.medetel.eu/download/2006/parallel_sessions/presentation/0406/Botsis.pdf

Boyle, A. (2006). Five-tech forecast. *Cosmic Log, MSNBC.* Retrieved September 18, 2009 from http://cosmiclog.msnbc.msn.com/archive/2006/12/28/23418.aspx

Bryant, D., & Colgrave, O. (2006). Knowledge and informatics within home medicine (KIM): the role of a home health hub. *International Journal of Healthcare Technology and Management, 7*(5), 335–347.

Bujnowska-Fedak, M., Staniszewski, A., Steciwko, A., & Puchala, E. (2000). System of telemedicine services designed for family doctors' practices. *Telemedicine Journal and e-Health, 6*(4), 449–452. doi:10.1089/15305620050503933

Castelli; D., Schlachta-Fairchild, L. & Pyke, R. (2008). Telenursing panel: telenursing implementation strategies and success factors. In M. Jordanova & F. Lievens (Eds.), *Global telemedicine / e-health updates: Knowledge resources,* (Vol. 1, pp. 409-414). Luxembourg: Publ. Luxexpo.

Clark, R. A., Inglis, S. C., McAlister, F., Cleland, J. G. F., & Stewart, S. (2007). Telemonitoring or structured telephone support programmes for patients with chronic heart failure: systematic review and metaanalysis. *British Medical Journal, 334,* 942–953. doi:10.1136/bmj.39156.536968.55

Cooke, F. (2001). Email health support service is already operating in Africa. *British Medical Journal, 322,* 51. doi:10.1136/bmj.322.7277.51

Dashtseren, I. F. A., Saligumba, I., & Khoja, S. (2009). Improving maternal health care services by using ICTs for remote consultation and education. In Jordanova, M., & Lievens, F. (Eds.), *Global Telemedicine/e-health Updates: Knowledge Resources* (*Vol. 2*, pp. 505–507). Luxembourg: Luxexpo.

Demartines, N., Mutter, D., Vix, M., Leroy, J., Glatz, D., & Rösel, F. (2000). Assessment of telemedicine in surgical education and patient care. *Annals of Surgery, 231,* 282–291. doi:10.1097/00000658-200002000-00019

Deng, L., Poole, M., Brown, H., & Miller, C. (2005). Learning through telemedicine: Case study of a wound care network. *International Journal of Healthcare Technology and Management, 6,* 4–6. doi:10.1504/IJHTM.2005.007005

Dovey, S., Weitzman, M., Fryer, G., Green, L., Yawn, B., Lanier, D., & Phillips, R. (2003). The ecology of medical care for children in the United States. *Pediatrics, 111,* 1024–1029. doi:10.1542/peds.111.5.1024

Einthoven, W. (1906). Le telecardiogramme. *Archives Internationales de Physiologie, 4,* 132.

Ericson, P. (2009). *Improving patient care through real-time electronic data capture with digital pen and paper.* Paper Presented at Med-e-Tel 2009. Retrieved August 11, 2009 from http://www.medetel.eu/download/2009/parallel_sessions/presentation/day2/improving_patient_care.pdf

Eysenbach, G. (2001). What is e-health? *Journal of Medical Internet Research, 3*(2). Retrieved January 28, 2009, from http://www.jmir.org/2001/2/e20/

Eysenbach, G. (2006). *Home Page.* Retrieved August 10, 2008 from http://yi.com/home/EysenbachGunther/

Figueira, R. M., Alkmim, M. B. M., Ribeiro, A. L. P., Pena, M., & Campos, F. E. (2008). Implementation and maintenance costs for a tele-health system in Brazil. In Jordanova, M., & Lievens, F. (Eds.), *Global telemedicine / e-health updates: Knowledge resources* (*Vol. 1*, pp. 354–359). Luxembourg: Luxexpo.

Gertz, R. (2007). *An electronic health record for Scotland: Legal problems regarding access and maintenance.* Paper Presented at Med-e-Tel 2007. Retrieved August 11, 2009 from http://www.medetel.eu/download/2007/parallel_sessions/presentation/0420/An_Electronic_Health_Record.pdf

Grady, J. L., & Schlachta-Fairchild, L. (2005). *The 2004 international telenursing role survey executive summary.* Retrieved September 20, 2009 from http://www.mtaloy.edu/tele-health/educational_research/04_05survey/IntlTelenursingSurveyExecSummary.pdf

Green, L. A., Fryer, G. E., Yawn, B. P., Lanier, D., & Dovey, S. M. (2001). The ecology of medical care revisited. *The New England Journal of Medicine, 344,* 2021–2025. doi:10.1056/NEJM200106283442611

Gundim, R. S., & Padilha, R. Q. (2008). Research project: a remote oncology nursing support, hospital Sírio Libanês, São Paulo, Brazil. In Jordanova, M., & Lievens, F. (Eds.), *Global telemedicine / e-health updates: Knowledge resources* (*Vol. 1*, pp. 406–408). Luxembourg: Luxexpo.

Gyertson, K. (2006). *Doc@Hand - The answer to patient recruitment.* Paper Presented at Med-e-Tel 2006. Retrieved August 11, 2009 from http://www.medetel.eu/download/2006/parallel_sessions/presentation/0406/Doc@Hand_the_answer.pdf

Haddad, A. E., Alkmim, M. B. M., Wen, C. L., & Roschkes, S. (2008). The implementation experience of the National Tele-health Program in Brazil. In Jordanova, M., & Lievens, F. (Eds.), *Global telemedicine / e-health updates: Knowledge resources* (*Vol. 1*, pp. 365–369). Luxembourg: Luxexpo.

Health Information and Management Systems Society (HIMSS). (2008). E-Health SIG White Paper, *Health Information and Management Systems Society News, 13* (7: 12). Retrieved December 16, 2008 from www.himss.org/content/files/e-health_whitepaper.pdf

Hofmann-Wellenhof, R., Salmhofer, W., Binder, B., Okcu, A., Kerl, H., & Soyer, H. (2006). Feasibility and acceptance of telemedicine for wound care in patients with chronic leg ulcers. *Journal of Telemedicine and Telecare, 12*(1), 15–17. doi:10.1258/135763306777978407

Honeywell HomMed. (2007). *MedPartner Medication Reminder.* Retrieved August 11, 2009 from http://www.hommed.com/Products/MedPartner.asp

Hopp, F., Whitten, P., Subramanian, U., Woodbridge, P., Mackert, M., & Lowery, J. (2006). Perspectives from the Veterans Health Administration about opportunities and barriers in telemedicine. *Journal of Telemedicine and Telecare, 12,* 404–409. doi:10.1258/135763306779378717

Hudson, H. (2005). Rural telemedicine: Lessons from Alaska for developing regions. *Telemedicine and e-Health, 11*(4), 460 -467.

Jacklin, P., Roberts, J., Wallace, P., Haines, A., Harrison, R., & Barber, J. (2003). The virtual outreach project group: economic evaluation of joint teleconsultations for patients referred by their general practitioner for a specialist opinion. *British Medical Journal, 327,* 84. doi:10.1136/bmj.327.7406.84

Jordanova, M. (2005). e-health: From space medicine to civil healthcare. In *Proceedings of 2nd International Conference on Recent Advances in Space Technologies*, Turkey, (pp. 739-743).

Jordanova, M. (2009). Telemedicine or e-health. In M. Jordanova, L. Vasileva, M. Rasheva & R. Bojinova. Telepsychology as a part of e-health. (pp. 7-36). Bulgaria: Academic Publishing House "M. Drinov."

Jordanova, M., Vasileva, L., Rasheva, M., & Bojinova, R. (2008). Tele-psychology: Users' demands. In Jordanova, M., & Lievens, F. (Eds.), *Global telemedicine / e-health updates: Knowledge resources* (*Vol. 1*, pp. 266–269). Luxembourg: Luxexpo.

Kasimov, O., Karchenova, E., & Tuchin, V. (2009). Role of nurses in different directions of the telemedicine activity in Saratov Railway Clinic. In Jordanova, M., & Lievens, F. (Eds.), *Global Telemedicine/e-health Updates: Knowledge Resources* (*Vol. 2*, pp. 207–209). Luxembourg: Luxexpo.

Korb, H. (2008). Telemonitoring – the intelligent solution for chronic patient care. In Jordanova, M., & Lievens, F. (Eds.), *Electronic Proceedings Med-e-Tel: The international educational and networking forum for e-health, telemedicine and health ICT* (pp. 9–15). Luxembourg: Luxexpo.

Kwankam, Y. (2008). *e-health and health system development: WHO priority areas.* Paper presented at 11th STI Symposium, April 22, 2008, Basel, Switzerland. Retrieved September 18, 2009 from http://www.sti.ch/fileadmin/user_upload/Bilder/Symposium/Yunkap_Kwankam__11_STI_Sysmposium_2008_WHO_proirity_areas.pdf

Lanfranco, A. R., Castellanos, A. E., Desai, J. P., & Meyers, W. C. (2004). Robotic surgery: A current perspective. *Annals of Surgery, 239*(1), 14–21. doi:10.1097/01.sla.0000103020.19595.7d

Lievens, F., & Jordanova, M. (2004). *An approach to the global vision about telemedicine/e-health.* Keynote presentation at Med-e-Tel, Luxembourg, G. D. of Luxembourg. Retrieved December 20, 2008 from http://www.medetel.lu/index.php?rub=educational_program&page=opening_session_2004

Lievens, F., & Jordanova, M. (2007). Telemedicine and medical informatics: The global approach. *Proceedings of World Academy of Science. Engineering and Technology, 31,* 258–262.

Mair, F., Goldstein, P., Shiels, C., Roberts, C., Angus, R., & O'Connor, J. (2006). Recruitment difficulties in a home telecare trial. *Journal of Telemedicine and Telecare, 12*(Suppl 1), 26–28. doi:10.1258/135763306777978371

Mair, F., & Whitten, P. (2000). Systematic review of studies of patient satisfaction with telemedicine. *British Medical Journal, 320,* 1517–1520. doi:10.1136/bmj.320.7248.1517

Martínez, A., Villarroel, V., Seoane, J., & del Pozo, F. (2004). A study of a rural telemedicine system in the Amazon region of Peru. *Journal of Telemedicine and Telecare, 10*(4), 219–225. doi:10.1258/1357633041424412

McNeil, I., Wales, J., & Azarmina, P. (2008). Satisfaction: the effect of a telephone based care management service on patient outcomes in the UK. In Jordanova, M., & Lievens, F. (Eds.), *Electronic proceedings Med-e-Tel: The international educational and networking forum for e-health, telemedicine and health ICT* (pp. 415–420). Luxembourg: Luxexpo.

Mucic, D. (2007). Telepsychiatry in Denmark: Mental health care in rural and remote areas. *Journal of e-health Technology and Application, 5*(3), 277-282.

Mucic, D. (2008). International telepsychiatry, patient acceptability. In Jordanova, M., & Lievens, F. (Eds.), *Global telemedicine / e-health updates: Knowledge resources* (*Vol. 1,* pp. 383–384). Luxembourg: Luxexpo.

Nayeemuddin, M., Majeed, M. A., Muneer, A., & Misra, A. (2007). *An out-patient survey of plastic surgery patients.* Paper presented at Med-e-Tel 2007, Luxembourg, G.D. of Luxembourg. Retrieved January 21, 2009, from http://www.medetel.lu/download/2007/parallel_sessions/presentation/0418/An_Out-Patient_Survey.pdf

Oh, H., Rizo, C., Enkin, M., & Jadad, A. (2005). What is e-health (3): A systematic review of published definitions. *Journal of Medical Internet Research, 7*(1), e1. Retrieved February 24, 2008 from www.jmir.org/2005/1/e1/

Pagliari, C. (2005). *Welcome and introduction.* Retrieved December 8, 2008, from http://www.e-health.ed.ac.uk/presentations/may2005/Claudia%20Pagliari.ppt

Paradiso, R., Belloc, C., Loriga, G., & Taccini, N. (2005). Wearable healthcare systems, new frontiers of e-textile. In Nugent, C., McCullagh, P., McAdams, E., & Lymberis, A. (Eds.), *Personalised Health Management Systems: The Integration of Innovative Sensing, Textile, Information and Communication Technologies* (pp. 9–17). Amsterdam, The Netherlands: IOS Press.

Pare, G., Jaana, M., & Sicotte, C. (2007). Systematic review of home telemonitoring for chronic diseases the evidence base. *Journal of the American Medical Informatics Association, 14,* 269–277. doi:10.1197/jamia.M2270

Resmini, F., Tavares, A. P., Sparenberg, A., Russomano, T., Bainy, S., & Timm, R. (2008). Telepsychiatry: A new tool for remodeling mental health assistance in South Brazil. In Jordanova, M., & Lievens, F. (Eds.), *Global telemedicine / e-health updates: Knowledge resources* (*Vol. 1,* pp. 395–397). Luxembourg: Luxexpo.

Retrieved January 30, 2009 from http://www.biomedcentral.com/1472-6963/7/35

Rodas, E. B., & Mora, F. Tamariz, Vicuna, A., Merrell, R. C., & Rodas, E. (2006 a). Telemedicine applications in mobile surgery. In M. Jordanova & F. Lievens (Eds.), e-Health: Proceedings of Med-e-Tel 2006, The international trade event and conference for e-health, telemedicine and health ICT, (pp. 307-309). Luxembourg: Publ. Luxexpo.

Rodas, E. B., & Mora, F. Tamariz, Vicuna, A., Merrell, R. C., Rodas, E. (2006 b). River health: Description of an integral healthcare program in a remote river basin of Ecuador. In M. Jordanova & F. Lievens (Eds.), e-Health: Proceedings of Med-e-Tel 2006, The international trade event and conference for e-health, telemedicine and health ICT, (pp. 311-313). Luxembourg: Publ. Luxexpo.

Royall, J., van Schayk, I., Bennett, M., Kamau, N., & Alilio, M. (2005). Crossing the digital divide: The contribution of information technology to the professional performance of malaria researchers in Africa. *African Health Sciences*, 5(3), 246–254.

Saligumba, F., Raza, S., Soegijoko, S., & Khoja, S. (2009). Community based e-health promotion for safe motherhood: Linking community maternal health needs with health services system. In Jordanova, M., & Lievens, F. (Eds.), *Global Telemedicine/e-health Updates: Knowledge Resources* (*Vol. 2*, pp. 489–490). Luxembourg: Luxexpo.

Schlachta-Fairchild, L. (2008). *International telenursing: A strategic tool for nursing shortage and access to nursing care.* Paper presented at Med-e-Tel 2008, Luxembourg, G. D. of Luxembourg. Retrieved December 31, 2008 from www.medetel.lu/download/2008/parallel_sessions/presentation/day1/international_telenursing.pdf

Schlachta-Fairchild, L., Castelli, D., & Pyke, R. (2008). International telenursing: A strategic tool for nursing shortage and access to nursing care. In M. Jordanova & F. Lievens (Eds.), Global telemedicine / e-health updates: Knowledge resources (Vol. 1, pp. 399-405).Luxembourg: Publ. Luxexpo.

Sel`kov, A. I., Stolyar, V. L., Atkov, O. U., Sel`kova, E. A., & Chueva, N. V. (2008). Development conception of E-Diagnosis departments of small towns and villages clinics for developing regions and countries. In M. Jordanova & F. Lievens (Eds.), Electronic proceedings Med-e-Tel 2008: The international educational and networking forum for e-health, telemedicine and health ICT (pp. 395-414). Luxembourg: Publ. Luxexpo.

Sel`kov, A. I., Stolyar, V. L., Atkov, O. U., Sel`kova, E. A., & Chueva, N. V. (2007). Telemedicine experience to serve e-clinics. In M. Jordanova & F. Lievens (Eds.), Electronic proceedings Med-e-Tel 2007: The international educational and networking forum for e-health, telemedicine and health ICT, (pp. 211-217). Luxembourg: Publ. Luxexpo.

Selkov, A., Stolyar, V., Selkova, E., Atkov, O., & Chueva, N. (2005). Nine-years experience in telemedicine for rural & remote districts of Russia. *Ukrainian Journal of Telemedicine and Medical Telematics*, 3(2), 141–147.

Shah, S., Kapoor, A., Ding, J., Guion, P., Petrisor, P., & Karanian, J. (2008). Surgical robotics, instrumentation and navigation. *International Journal of Computer Assisted Radiology and Surgery*, 3(1), 119–125. doi:10.1007/s11548-008-0181-1

Shea, S. (2007). The informatics for diabetes and education telemedicine (IDEATel) project. *Transactions of the American Clinical and Climatological Association, 118*, 289–304.

Silber, D. (2003). *The case for e-health.* Paper presented at the European Commission's first high-level conference on e-health. Brussels, Belgium.

Smith, A., Scuffham, P., & Wootton, R. (2007). The costs and potential savings of a novel telepaediatric service in Queensland. *BioMed Central Health Services Research, 7,* 35..doi:10.1186/1472-6963-7-35

Sorrells-Jones, J., Tschirch, P., & Liong, M. (2006). Nursing and tele-health: Opportunities for nurse leaders to shape the future. *Nurse Leader, 4*(5), 42–58. doi:10.1016/j.mnl.2006.07.008

Soyer, H. P., Hofmann-Wellenhof, R., Massone, C., Gabler, G., Dong, H., Ozdemir, F., & Argenziano, G. (2005). telederm.org: Freely available online consultations in dermatology. *Public Library of Science Medicine (PLoS Med), 2*(4), e87. Retrieved January 5, 2009 from http://medicine.plosjournals.org/perlserv/?request=get-document&doi=10.1371%2Fjournal.pmed.0020087&ct=1

Space medicine. (2008). *The Columbia Encyclopedia,* (6th ed.). New York: Columbia University Press. Retrieved January 28, 2009, from http://www.encyclopedia.com/doc/1E1-spacemed.html

Stojakovic, M. (2008). Posttraumatic stress disorder and telepsychiatry. In Jordanova, M., & Lievens, F. (Eds.), *Global telemedicine / e-health updates: Knowledge resources* (*Vol. 1,* pp. 385–388). Luxembourg: Luxexpo.

Strehle, E. M., & Shabde, N. (2006). One hundred years of telemedicine: Does this new technology have a place in paediatrics? *Archives of Disease in Childhood, 91,* 956–959. doi:10.1136/adc.2006.099622

Sum, K., Zheng, Y. P., & Mak, A. F. (2005). In Nugent, C., McCullagh, P., McAdams, E., & Lymberis, A. (Eds.), *Personalised Health Management Systems: The Integration of Innovative Sensing, Textile, Information and Communication Technologies* (pp. 43–50). Amsterdam, The Netherlands: IOS Press.

Tsitlakidis, C., Mylonakis, J., & Niakas, D. (2005). Economic evaluation of telemedicine for a remotely located population: the case of two Greek islands. *International Journal of Electronic Healthcare, 1*(3), 243–260. doi:10.1504/IJEH.2005.006473

Tsuji, M., Akematsu, Y., & Taoka, F. (2007). *How much can e-health systems save medical expenditures?* Paper Presented at 21st Pacific Science Congress Okinawa, Asia Pacific telemedicine Initiative, June 15-16, Okinawa, 2007.

von Niman, B. (2007). *User experience guidelines for e-health telecare services - ETSI Industry consensus workshop.* Paper presented at Med-e-Tel 2007, Luxembourg, G.D. of Luxembourg. Retrieved January 21, 2009, from http://www.medetel.lu/download/2007/parallel_sessions/presentation/0418/ETSI.pdf

Vontetsianos, T., Giovas, P., Milsis, A., Katsaras, T., Rigopoulou, A., Mpofos, D., & Giaboudakis, P. (2009). Clinical use of wearable technologies for chronic patients' early hospital discharge. In Jordanova, M., & Lievens, F. (Eds.), *Global telemedicine / e-health updates: Knowledge resources* (*Vol. 2,* pp. 186–190). Luxembourg: Luxexpo.

White, K. L., Williams, T. F., & Greenberg, B. G. (1961). The ecology of medical care. *The New England Journal of Medicine, 265,* 885–892.

Whitten, P., & Buis, L. (2007). Private payer reimbursement for telemedicine services in the United States. *Telemedicine Journal and e-Health, 13,* 15–23. doi:10.1089/tmj.2006.0028

Whitten, P., Buis, L., & Mackert, M. (2007). Factors impacting providers' perceptions regarding a midwestern university-based EMR. *Telemedicine Journal and e-Health, 13*, 391–397. doi:10.1089/tmj.2006.0057

Whitten, P. S, Bergman, A., Meese, M., Bridwell, K., & Jule, K. (2009). St. Vincent's home tele-health for congestive heart failure patients. *Journal of Telemedicine and e-Health, 15*, 148-153.

Whitten, P. S., & Mackert, M. S. (2005). Addressing tele-health's foremost barrier: Provider as initial gatekeeper. *International Journal of Technology Assessment in Health Care, 21*, 517–521. doi:10.1017/S0266462305050725

Whitten, P. S., Mair, F. S., Haycox, A., May, C. R., Williams, T. L., & Hellmich, S. (2002). Systematic review of cost effectiveness studies of telemedicine interventions. *British Medical Journal, 324*, 1434–1437. doi:10.1136/bmj.324.7351.1434

Whitten. P., Johannessen, L.,K., Soerensen, T., Gammon, D., & Mackert, M. (2007). A systematic review of research methodology in telemedicine studies. *Journal of Telemedicine and Telecare, 13*, 230-235.

WHO. (2002). Integrated chronic disease prevention and control, Retrieved January 2, 2009, from http://www.who.int/chp/about/integrated_cd/en/index.html

WHO. (2003). Mental health in WHO's European Region 2001. Retrieved September 20, 2009 from http://www.euro.who.int/document/rc53/edoc07.pdf

WHO. (2005). World Health Assembly resolution on e-health, WHA 58. 28, May 2005, Retrieved August 10, 2009, from http://www.euro.who.int/telemed/20060713_1

WHO. (2006). Chronic diseases and their common risk factor. Retrieved August 10, 2009, from http://www.who.int/chp/chronic_disease_report/media/Factsheet1.pdf

Young, T., & Ireson, C. (2003). Effectiveness of school-based tele-health care in urban and rural elementary schools. *Pediatrics, 112*, 1088–1094. doi:10.1542/peds.112.5.1088

Chapter 4
Risks and Benefits of Technology in Health Care

Stefane M. Kabene
Ecole des Hautes Etudes en Santé Publique (EHESP), France

Melody Wolfe
University of Western Ontario, Canada

ABSTRACT

The integration of technology into health care has created both advantages and disadvantages for patients, providers, and health care systems alike. This chapter examines the risks and benefits of technology in health care, with particular focus on electronic health records (EHRs), the availability of health information online, and how technology affects relationships within the health care setting. Overall, it seems the benefits of technology in health care outweigh the risks; however, it is imperative that proper measures are taken to ensure successful implementation and integration. Accuracy, validity, confidentiality, and privacy of health data and health information are key issues that must be addressed for successful implementation of technology.

ELECTRONIC HEALTH RECORDS

Technological advances in information and communication technologies (ICT) and computing have made way for the implementation of electronic health records (EHRs), the comprehensive compilation of health care provided to an individual over their lifetime —an exciting and impressive accomplishment. Despite the vast possibilities and efficiencies that EHRs can potentially offer, their implementation into existing healthcare systems poses some potentially deterring and serious risks, such as confidentiality breaches, identity theft, and technological breakdowns and incompatibilities. Therefore, electronic records should be not hastily integrated into healthcare systems without proper precautions.

Advantages

Electronic records offer many advantages over conventional paper-based methods of recording patient data. The comprehensiveness of EHRs can help to bridge the geographic and temporal gaps

DOI: 10.4018/978-1-61520-733-6.ch004

that exist when several clinicians who are geographically dispersed treat the same patient. It is extremely important that all clinicians are aware of past and current medical histories when one patient is treated by several healthcare providers (Mandl, Szolovits, & Kohane, 2001). Since paper-based records are location specific, information contained in one record may differ substantially from records kept in another area or by another provider. When various specialists treat the same patient, patient communication is often hindered, as it can be extremely difficult and time consuming to share patient records between providers using conventional methods (for example, by phone, fax or mail, or physically transporting the record from location to location). Electronic health records, however, enable comprehensive databases of information to be viewed and used by authorized users when they need it and where they need it.

Greater efficiency in accessibility of patient information is thus made possible by the use of electronic records. Accessibility allows for a faster transfer of medical history in a medical emergency or when visiting a new doctor, and also allows researchers and public health authorities—with the permission and consent of the patient—to efficiently collect and analyze updated patient data. Such access is imperative in emergency situations, and also allows public health officials to easily conduct outbreak and incident investigations that may help control epidemics and pandemics, such as SARS, Listeriosis, or new strains of influenza. Accessibility also enables health care providers to reduce costs associated with duplicating tests, since providers have access to already performed test results (Myers, Frieden, Bherwani, & Henning, 2008). Additionally, clerical activities such as appointment reminders and notification of laboratory results can be handled electronically, resulting in greater efficiency and reduced human error.

EHRs can also be equipped with authentication systems, a major guard against security breaches. Patients may be especially wary of having their personal health information part of a comprehensive database because they are unsure as to who will have access to their medical records. Authentication systems allow for the imposition of various security levels, providing greater control over access to personal information such as immunization records and diagnostic test results. Conversely, paper-based medical records allow healthcare staff to access any part of a patient's medical records. By applying authentication and role-based access to EHRs, personnel such as secretaries and clerical staff will only have access to necessary information (such as that needed for scheduling appointments or providing reminders of scheduled visits) (Myers et al., 2008). In case of an emergency, however, it is possible to develop policies that allow medical professionals to override the protection barriers and gain immediate access to all medical information (Mandl et al., 2001). An additional security feature is accountability, which enables the system to track input sources and record changes. Accountability systems provide an audit trail that can help to eliminate security breaches and, at the very least, track user activities to ensure their appropriateness, authorization, and ethicality (Myers et al., 2008).

Despite the impressive advantages EHRs offer, one must recognize the trade off that exists between accessibility and confidentiality. As noted by Rind et al. (1997, p. 138) "It is not always possible to achieve both perfect confidentiality as well as perfect access to patient information, whether information is computerized or handwritten." Confidentiality, among other issues, must be considered in order to utilize the EHR system to its fullest potential.

Disadvantages

One potential deterrent to full implementation of the electronic health record is compatibility and interoperability across different health information systems. Electronic health records require a standardized system and technology to promote transfer, input and compilation of data from multiple sources; unfortunately, these standards are not easily achieved due to the complexity of linking disparate and often older legacy systems and the incumbent costs of doing so. Thus, despite the potential of EHRs to increase communication between practitioners, and practitioners and patients, the various already existing computer systems pose a major road block. Until a standard model for secure data transmission and linkage is efficiently in place, EHRs will remain fragmented and inconsistent.

Of course, the most serious danger in widespread EHR implementation is the potential for security breaches. Electronically-bound information always comes with the risk of being exposed to inappropriate parties; "No matter how sophisticated security systems become, people will always manage to defeat them" (Mandl et al., 2001, p. 285). Due to the wealth of information contained in the EHR, they are an obvious target to for hacking and identity theft. Additionally, because electronic theft can occur in a variety of contexts—including the comfort of one's home—electronic theft may be harder to track or detect and require less physical effort and planning. In contrast, physically stealing medical records from an office is difficult to accomplish successfully, since most medical offices implement effective security measures.

Aside from security breaches, there are core problems associated with using computers to house mass amounts of important and often sensitive information. Technological issues arise throughout the lifetime of a computer system. Not only are computer systems created and updated rapidly, there are few systems that last the entire lifespan of a person. Such technological issues raise questions regarding the safety of transferring medical information from system to system, as any breakdown may cause record loss, or pose a potential security breach (Mandl et al., 2001).

The reaction of patients to confidentiality and privacy issues pose a major concern as well. As previously mentioned, patients have expressed concerns about who is seeing their medical information and for what purpose it is being used. Concerns also arise when patients are unable to see their own records, but secondary sources can view these records in an unregulated manner. Consequently, it has been noted that "they might fail to disclose important medical data or even avoid seeking medical care because of concern over denial of insurance, loss of employment or housing, or stigmatisation and embarrassment" (Mandl et al., 2001, p. 284). The failure to disclose important medical information can affect patient health and increase the risk of misdiagnosis. Since privacy is important for most patients when it comes to their medical records and health history, one option is to allow patients the right to decide who can examine and alter specific parts of their records. Although this seems like a plausible solution, its complexity can create problems that may lead to inferior care and uninformed practitioners (e.g., if certain portions of the history are restricted). Thus, granting patients the right to monitor their own privacy is not a solution in and of itself.

Discussion

It is very likely that EHRs will be the key to linking disparate pieces of a patient's medical record into a unified database. The comprehensiveness and accessibility of EHRs will mend the gap in provider-provider communication that currently exists due to temporal and geographic differences in paper-based records. However, in order for these possibilities to actualize, proper precautions must be taken, and specific policies enforced. Authentication and audit trails of EHRs allow various health care professionals different levels of access to patient records, as well as a mechanism to track the use and changes of each patient's file. Aside from these security enhancing features, various preventative actions should be taken in order to eliminate the risks associated with EHR use. When an electronic record system is put in place, staff and healthcare providers must use the system properly to obtain beneficial outcomes. Accordingly, education and training are also necessary components in enabling individuals to understand and maximize EHR system abilities. As well, a "change agent," or expert on electronic record systems, could help successful implementation and adoption of digital medical records. This change manager would be in charge of training staff, monitoring security and confidentiality, and enforcing policy.

In addition to educating employees, several preventative measures should be embedded into EHR systems; for example, passwords allowing for authentication and limiting the access of each person on an individual, role-based basis. Since different information is needed by various personnel, these passwords would allow doctors to access a wider range of information than, for instance, a secretary. Encryption, or the process of making the data unreadable unless the user possesses suitable authorization, is another preventative measure which hinders hackers from obtaining confidential information. Furthermore, it should be noted that already existing policies aid the privacy of an individual's electronic health record. In Canada, federal privacy legislation under the Personal Information Protection and Electronic Documents Act (PIPEDA) ensures privacy via rules for the collection, use, and disclosure of personal information (Taylor, 2003). In using EHR systems, health care providers must ensure that they comply with the PIPED Act in order to eliminate the risks of confidentiality and privacy breaches.

With regards to the issue of authentication, access to a patients' medical record for reasons incongruent with the individual's health care should be a decision that only the patient themselves can make. Although public health and government research could significantly benefit from access to patient medical records, due to issues of privacy and confidentiality, it is advised that every patient should possess the right to deny access to

their medical records for public use. Additionally, patients who choose to provide personal health information to government and public health associations should have the ability to limit what information is exposed. A technology such as "time keys" could be utilized in alignment with electronic records in allowing patients to give an organization access to their records only for a specified amount of time (Mandl et al., 2001).

Since patients visit a number of healthcare service providers over the course of their life, each provider has a different computer system that encodes and stores patient data according to different levels and standards—which poses a great challenge when attempting to unify all patient information into a single database. It has not yet been fully understood how one system will capture all data from various physicians into a standard computer form or interface that shares the information with other computers (i.e. similar to the web browser and access to disparate web pages) or whether only a minimum data set will be captured in a central repository. In the future, universal coding and standardization of data must be implemented in order to manage fragmented pieces of patient data. Due to vast language barriers and numerous medical terminologies, universal coding is a challenge; however, it is hopeful that future advancements in technology can develop systems able to appropriately incorporate EHRs and shared data repositories (Mandl et al., 2001).

ONLINE MEDICAL INFORMATION

Demographics

Fifty two million adults have used the Internet to access health or medical information through an estimated 20, 000 to 100,000 health related websites (Diaz et al., 2002). In general, 62% of Internet users go online for medical advice, and most of these Internet users are women between the ages of 50 and 64 (Rice, 2006). Searching for health information increases with education, as well as with years of Internet experience and access to a broadband connection (Rice, 2006, p 10). In a survey conducted by Diaz et al., (2002) 54% of respondents revealed that they used the Internet for health information, and a higher proportion of patients who used the Internet were college educated with an annual household income greater than $50 000.

Advantages

Technological advancement—in particular, the use of Internet research for medical information—has a major influence on health care for both patients and providers alike. Because the Internet provides such accessible health information, individuals are often encouraged to seek out information regarding their own health, as well as about the health of others. Additionally, medical information on the Internet allows individuals to become exposed to a wide array of health information and become involved in their own personal health (Rice, 2006).

In North America, the use of Internet research is an increasingly popular strategy for obtaining diagnostic information. In October 2002, 73 million American adults used the Internet to find health care information, and by November of 2004, this number had risen to 95 million (Rice, 2006). There are many advantages associated with the use of the Internet for medical research, such as easy access to a wide array of information, personalized information that is uncontaminated by medical jargon, and anonymity while searching for health information (Rice, 2006). Additionally, online websites and support groups provide information, support, acceptance, and a sense of understanding to patients and their loved ones (Rice, 2006). Since the Internet allows for immediate access to an incredible amount of information directed at both health care providers and patients, it provides a sense of privacy, convenience, and perspective (Cotton & Gupta, 2004). The Internet also allows users to ask awkward, sensitive, or detailed questions without the risk of facing judgment, scrutiny, or stigma (Cotton & Gupta, 2004). Consequently, doctors are beginning to see a new type of patient: a patient with sharp intelligence and curiosity who knows how to utilize and benefit from information available online (Ferguson, 2000).

Perhaps the most significant benefit online medical information offers is its ability to prevent long hospital wait-times for minor issues. Patients suffering from trivial matters who are simply seeking reassurance from doctors can go online and seek information without going to the hospital. Additionally, patients can gain medical knowledge and insight that may teach them to distinguish between symptoms that seem minor, but are actually serious. The Internet allows for patients to consult various perspectives on illness and treatments rather than visiting several doctors for multiple opinions. For example, if a patient is given a type of medicine to treat a thyroid problem, they can go online and research it, which enables them to gain perspective on their own medical issue. Since online medical information is free, it is fairly accessible to patients in tough financial positions. This is especially advantageous for countries such as the United States, in which private health care is extremely expensive. Online health information provides citizens of the United States with immediate information about health problems; such knowledge may help citizens decide whether it is necessary to visit a doctor or hospital.

Disadvantages

Although there are many advantages associated with the ability to research health-related information online, such as increased patient medical knowledge, it is imperative to consider the various disadvantages associated with hastily researching medical information on anonymous databases. For example, accurate information on credible websites may be hidden behind complicated medical language, and the quality and authenticity of available information is often questionable. At times, the vast amount of online information can be confusing, making it difficult for a patient to filter out what is important. Studies of post-surgery patients revealed that 83% had difficulties understanding online health information, and one third felt that the retrieved information was overwhelming (Rice, 2006).

A major problem occurs when patients try to diagnose and treat a potentially serious medical condition without consulting a doctor. Research indicates that 11% of those using the Internet for medical information revealed that they did not discuss this information with their doctor (Diaz et al., 2002). According to Berland et al. (2001), less than one quarter of search engines' first pages of links lead to relevant content; therefore, accessing health information using search engines and simple search terms is not sufficient. Additionally, Internet usage is often hindered by navigational challenges due to poor design features such as disorganization, technical language, and lack of permanent websites (Cline & Haynes, 2001). Support groups may also be problematic as they may distribute misleading information. Considering support information is often based on personal experience, it may lack the knowledgeable and experienced perspective developed by health care professionals who are trained to distinguish among resources, determine information accuracy, and examine the quality of information (Cotton & Gupta, 2004).

As most of the information available online lacks peer review, it may be misleading and inaccurate (Rice, 2006). Researchers consistently identify problems with the quality of online health information (Rice, 2006), and very few sites pass through traditional editorial processes or display sources of authorship or origin (Diaz et al., 2002). Much of this uncontrolled information commonly strays from recognized safety standards, is not updated regularly, and presents limited advice on avoiding dangerous drug interactions (Rice, 2006).

Despite the existence of many reliable medical and health related websites, several reviews have demonstrated that patients may encounter potentially misleading or inaccurate information when navigating the Internet in search of them. Some health seekers even fear that confidentiality breaches will track their Internet searches and unfavorably reveal their private information to insurance companies and employers (Cotton & Gupta, 2004).

Unfortunately, there exists a digital divide or gap between those who can access online resources and those who cannot. Internet health information remains inaccessible to large and specific parts of the population (lower income, those in rural communities with limited Internet access), and physically impaired and disabled persons are often at a disadvantage in a networked society (Rice, 2006). Additionally, those individuals who often cannot access the tools to seek health information online are usually those with preventable health problems or without health insurance (Rice, 2006). Sadly, it seems as though individuals who would benefit the most from online medical information are the least likely to acquire it.

Discussion

As noted, there are a number of advantages and disadvantages associated with researching medical information online. The advantages include access to a wide array of information, personalized information that is easy to understand, and anonymous help. Help is provided by support groups, and allows for the maintenance of privacy and anonymity. The Internet also allows patients to remain current on information regarding their own health or the health of others. However, some disadvantages include medical language barriers on legitimate websites, unequal Internet access, self diagnosis, and inaccurate information (Rice, 2006). Support groups may rely too heavily on personal experience, and consequently distribute misleading information (Culver, Gerr, & Frumkin,

1997). The risk in researching medical knowledge online is that much available information lacks peer review and accuracy. Confidentiality of information searching online is also a risk to consider. With all issues in consideration, it is apparent that the benefits of researching medical information, if used with the proper discretion, can have an invaluable impact on the patient.

As indicated in the demographics summarized above, it is evident that the majority of individuals currently researching medical information are well educated. Thus most individuals/patients who seek information online have the ability to understand the information, know the disadvantages of online data, and can utilize the online information to help address their own medical needs. The Internet also allows patients to seek medical advice immediately, easily, and at their convenience. Because Internet usage is on the rise, it is anticipated that the digital divide will narrow in scope, and more individuals will gain access to the information available on the Internet. Individuals who have not previously been able to take advantage of online information will have the opportunity to do so. However, not all individuals who gain access to online health information have the understanding to apply it; therefore, medical information on the Internet should be correct and user friendly. It is evident that there is already an increasing trend in search engines providing more valid, accurate information. For example, "Google" has a more advanced search tool "Google Scholar," which provides scholarly articles published by credible sources. Additionally, many medical websites inform patients of serious symptoms by stating that if certain symptoms are present, patients should seek medical attention immediately.

If online medical information is credible and user-friendly, it can be extremely beneficial to patients and providers. Doctors are forced to stay up to date and well informed about all advances in medicine, and by using online medical information, can do so with ease. Patients become well versed in their medical issues, and can provide their doctors with insightful questions. Additionally, patients expect doctors to know about the information available online and answer their questions; they have the opportunity to print articles, bring information directly to their physicians, or email their doctor for a professional opinion. However, if the information online does not maintain a certain level of accuracy and validity, negative implications may occur. Overall, the Internet should be used as a supplementary tool. Professional opinions should always be used as the primary source.

TECHNOLOGY AND RELATIONSHIPS

Technological progressions impact all relationships within healthcare, including those between patients and healthcare providers, patients and other patients, as well as those between various healthcare providers, including doctors, nurses, and specialists. In other words, the presence of information technology in health care has had a profound effect on relationship dynamics within the health care system. The relationships that exist between physicians and patients are important and central to the quality and efficiency of patient care—information technology (IT) affects both aspects of this relationship significantly. With the emergence and growing prevalence of technology in health care, patients have been able take a more active role with regards to their health. Through increased access to information, the possibility of faster communication through e-mail beginning to emerge, and the existence of online patient portals, the presence of IT has had many positive effects on the patient-physician relationship (Wald, Dube, & Anthony, 2007).

Advantages

The empowerment patients acquire by having access to their medical records along with online health researching enables them to intelligently discuss health issues with their clinician. In doing so, patients become a *de facto* part of the healthcare team. When properly counseled and mentored by healthcare professionals, individuals can potentially become true "clinical assistants" in their own health; they have more knowledge of their own problems and changes that enable clearer, more effective, and more efficient patient-provider communication.

Technology can also aid patient decision making. For example, giving patients a visual "map" of the treatment options has been shown to help patients remember treatment options and their differential impacts with more accuracy, enabling patients to make faster, more appropriate decisions that increase the overall chances of a positive outcome (Panton et al. 2008). Along with the increase in online health resources, electronic communication via e-mail between patients and doctors is also increasing (Ferguson, 2002). For example, Weiner and Biondich (2006) found that 95% of surveyed patients who used e-mail communication (about 16.5% of the survey group) felt it was more efficient than the telephone, and that e-mail proved especially useful for patients with "sensitive issues" (Houston, Sands, Jenckes, & Ford, 2004; Weiner & Biondich, 2006).

The patient-patient relationship is also facilitated in a positive manner by technology, and is often accomplished through online patient helpers, who oversee medical communication between patients. Online patient helpers are individuals who provide help for other patients via the Internet (Ferguson, 2000). For example, blogs and online support groups provide an environment in which helpers can serve as a valuable resource by assisting patients with medical information, encouraging discussion, and facilitating support. It should be noted that these online resources are best used to supplement the patient-physician relationship by encouraging patient-patient relations, and should by no means be the sole source of health information for any patient (Ferguson, 2000).

Disadvantages

While the provision of online health information can strengthen the patient-physician relationship, it can also hinder it. Since much of the information online is not credible, physicians may be required to spend unnecessary amounts of time separating fact from fiction with their patients (Dugdale, Epstein & Pantilat, 1999). Consequently, patients are putting pressure on physicians to help sort through and clarify their online findings—which is a timely and effortful endeavor for many physicians (Ferguson, 2002). Implementation of electronic health records (EHRs), and the increased reliance on technological devices in general, may also hinder the patient-physician relationship, as time-consuming, and potentially distracting, data entry can take valuable time away from patient-provider relations. The increasing use of IT in health care may be so time consuming that it actually diminishes the patient-physician relationship (Weiner & Biondich, 2006).

Although patient helpers encourage and facilitate patient-patient relationships, many patients do not have the formal training to differentiate between credible and non-credible information. Without this knowledge, some patients put too much reliance on online helpers, which can jeopardize both their health and the patient-physician relationship (Ferguson, 2000). Because some online sources are certainly not credible, and many patients are insufficiently equipped to differentiate between accurate and bogus sources, many doctors discourage the use of such information.

Discussion

The increasing presence of IT in health has profound effects on patient-physician and patient-patient relationships. With the surplus of health information available online, patients are able to actively participate in the patient-physician relationship and provoke discussion that serves in the best case to help patients make more informed decisions when choosing medical options. The growing acceptance of e-mail communication between patients and health professionals is giving patients greater access to medical advice. Also, online patient helpers give patients a portal for communicating to others in cyberspace that increases knowledge, promotes coping, and forms patient-patient relationships. However, if online medical information is used irresponsibly, it can have detrimental effects on one's health, and the patient-physician relationship. The presence of IT can waste time, and increase patient acceptance of non-credible information. If one substitutes online information for professional, clinical advice, the patient-physician relationship deteriorates. Negligence to seek out physician care can result in unfortunate health consequences. Overall, if these disadvantages are lessened or alleviated, than the presence of IT on the patient-physician relationship will be beneficial.

The increasing prevalence of e-mail communication between patients and doctors allows for physicians to be more accessible to their patients and vice versa. If used correctly, e-mail communication allows the physician-patient relationship to be more efficient—an important factor given the time pressures placed on today's physicians. Rapid communication also allows patients who are experiencing extremely stressful medical issues to be in immediate contact with their physician. E-mail also helps to reduce the apprehension of a face-to-face interaction that is often experienced by many patients, and allows doctors to answer general inquiries that do not require face-to-face contact. This may make booking a doctor's appointment easier for those who really need it (Wald et al., 2007). However, the inappropriate use of online patient-provider communication can be wasteful. It may lead to e-mail overload; patients may ask very similar questions that physicians would have to answer repeatedly. As well, patients may take advantage of such constant contact and abuse communication privileges (Weiner & Biondich, 2006).

Technology has enabled the emergence of patient-patient relationships, and these relationships can offer patients much needed emotional and psychological support when dealing with various illnesses (Mandl et al., 2001). Although patient-patient relationships can be very beneficial, individuals should be cautious before entering a relationship for anything more than support. If a patient were taking specific medical advice from their patient-patient relationship, it should be discussed with their physician, as the credibility of the average Internet user to be giving medical advice is most likely questionable. It is also important to keep in mind that diseases can affect patients in many different ways, so a patient giving advice may not know what is best for someone else (Culver et al., 1997). Sometimes patients feel more comfortable conversing with patient helpers as opposed to doctors because there is a mutual understanding: each individual has experienced the same illness. Online patient-patient relationships can be especially helpful for patients who are dealing with sensitive issues, such as AIDS. Given the social stigma surrounding the disease, being able to do anonymous research and talk to others in the same situation can help to reduce the embarrassment that infected individuals may feel. Patients can offer personal experiences about the disease and give advice (Wald et al., 2007). It should be mentioned that individuals seeking medical advice online may feel the need for face-to-face communication in person from a professional as opposed to a cyber friend—especially when seeking treatment.

CONCLUSION

In order to combat issues threatening the successful integration of technology in health care, certain steps must be taken. One of the most important considerations when implementing electronic health records is the provision of proper training to all employees. For example, secretaries in medical offices must be extremely knowledgeable in all PIPEDA legislation, and must demonstrate proper system use to preserve privacy and confidentiality of patient information. Firewalls and other prevention measures must be developed and updated frequently to ensure that the records are private, confidential, and secure.

A number of important implementations should be undertaken if the availability of online medical information is to be used to its fullest potential. First, governments and credible medical institutions should combine efforts in creating a large, easily understandable database of medical information accessible to laypersons (e.g. the National Library of Medicine's Medline Plus web site, see http://www.nlm.nih.gov/medlineplus/). Such a database will provide credible information that is current and understandable from a reliable source. Second, doctors need to play a role in the information put forth on the Internet by researching it themselves and posting correct articles and information for their patients. Last, there should be a stamp or certification that ensures health information posted on various websites is legitimate (e.g. the HONcode certification now provided voluntarily by the Health on the Net Foundation, see http://www.hon.ch/). As well, more stringent efforts to monitor non-credible information should be taken. A potential way of reducing harmful, non-credible online information is to implement legislation that restricts the release of medical information from those without formal training or licensure to certain groups (i.e. registered support groups).

In addressing healthcare relationships affected by technology, it is important to consider the potential for patient e-mails to affect physician stress levels and time management; email overflow puts pressure on physicians. The creation of a "frequently asked questions" page would help solve the issue of redundant e-mails, whereas the establishment of guidelines for users may help reduce e-mail abuse. Additionally, doctors should inform patients about the potential harms online

patient helpers may present. Patients should be aware that much information provided by online helpers is subjective, and may not be credible or valuable in their particular case. As well, specific patient-helper sites should make their purpose known to all visitors.

Technology undoubtedly has the potential to benefit healthcare; the IT advances discussed above will improve the efficiency, accuracy, and effectiveness of health care systems. Although the benefits are shadowed by risks, EHRs allow for increased and more efficient patient care; researching medical information online, if used properly, can provide a wealth of invaluable information for patients; and technology has allowed patient-physician and patient-patient relationships to become more effective. If the negative effects on these relationships can be mitigated via proper precautions and responsibility, the benefits will be maximized. Although the medical system is able to function without advancements in technology, technology allows for innovation and efficiencies that can greatly improve and revamp the way health care systems work.

REFERENCES

Berland, G. K., Elliott, M. N., Morales, L. S., Algazy, J. I., Kravitz, R. L., & Broder, M. S. (2001). Health information on the Internet: Accessibility, quality, and readability in English and Spanish. *Journal of the American Medical Association, 285,* 2612–2621. doi:10.1001/jama.285.20.2612

Cline, R. J. W., & Haynes, K. M. (2001). Consumer health information seeking on the Internet: The state of the art. *Health Education Research, 16,* 671–692. doi:10.1093/her/16.6.671

Cotton, S. R., & Gupta, S. S. (2004). Characteristics of online and offline health information seekers and factors that discriminate between them. *Social Science & Medicine, 59,* 1795–1806. doi:10.1016/j.socscimed.2004.02.020

Culver, J. D., Gerr, F., & Frumkin, H. (1997). Medical information on the internet: A study of an electronic bulletin board. *Journal of General Internal Medicine, 12*(8), 466–470. doi:10.1046/j.1525-1497.1997.00084.x

Diaz, J. A., Griffith, R. A., Ng, J. J., Reinert, S. E., Friedmann, P. D., & Moulton, A. W. (2002). Patients' use of the Internet for medical information. *Journal of General Internal Medicine, 17*, 180–185. doi:10.1046/j.1525-1497.2002.10603.x

Dugdale, D. C., Epstein, R., & Pantilat, S. Z. (1999). Time and the patient-physician relationship. *Journal of General Internal Medicine, 14*(1), 34–40. doi:10.1046/j.1525-1497.1999.00263.x

Ferguson, T. (2000). Online patient-helpers and physicians working together: A new partnership for high quality health care. *British Medical Journal, 321*, 1129–1132. doi:10.1136/bmj.321.7269.1129

Ferguson, T. (2002). From patients to end users. *British Medical Journal, 324*, 555–556. doi:10.1136/bmj.324.7337.555

Houston, T. K., Sands, D. Z., Jenckes, M. W., & Ford, D. E. (2004). Experiences of patients who were early adopters of electronic communication with their physician: satisfaction, benefits, and concerns. *The American Journal of Managed Care, 10*, 601–608.

Mandl, D. K., Szolovits, P., & Kohane, S. I. (2001). Public standards and patients' control: How to keep electronic medical records accessible but private. *British Medical Journal, 322*, 283–287. doi:10.1136/bmj.322.7281.283

Myers, J., Frieden, T. R., Bherwani, K. M., & Henning, K. J. (2008). Ethics in public health research: Privacy and public health at risk: Public health confidentiality in the digital age. *American Journal of Public Health, 98*, 793–800. doi:10.2105/AJPH.2006.107706

Panton, R. L., Downie, R., Truong, T., Mackeen, L., Kabene, S., & Yi, Q. L. (2008). A visual approach to providing prognostic information to parents of children with retinoblastoma. *Psycho-Oncology, 18*(3), 300–304. doi:10.1002/pon.1397

Rice, R. E. (2006). Influences, usage and outcomes of Internet health information searching: Multivariate results from the pew surveys. *International Journal of Medical Informatics, 75*, 8–28. doi:10.1016/j.ijmedinf.2005.07.032

Rind, D. M., Kohane, I. S., Szolovits, P., Safran, C., Chueh, H. C., & Barnett, G. O. (1997). Maintaining the confidentiality of medical records shared over the Internet and the World Wide Web. *Annals of Internal Medicine, 127*, 138–141.

Smith, R. (2000). Getting closer to patients and their families. *British Medical Journal, 321*, •••. Retrieved from http://www.bmj.com.proxy1.lib.uwo.ca:2048/cgi/reprint/321/7275/0.

Taylor, S. (2003). Protecting privacy in Canada's private sector. *Information Management Journal, 37*, 33–39.

Wald, H. S., Dube, C. E., & Anthony, D. C. (2007). Untangling the web – the impact of Internet use on health care and the physician-patient relationship. *Patient Education and Counseling, 68*(3), 218–224. doi:10.1016/j.pec.2007.05.016

Weiner, M., & Biondich, P. (2006). The influence of information technology on patient-physician relationships. *Journal of General Internal Medicine, 21*(Suppl 1), S35–S39. doi:10.1111/j.1525-1497.2006.00307.x

Section 2
The Use of Technology:
From the Individual to the Community

Chapter 5
The Computer–Assisted Patient Consultation:
Promises and Challenges

Aviv Shachak
University of Toronto, Canada

Shmuel Reis
Technion- Israel Institute of Technology, Israel

ABSTRACT

The implementation of electronic health records (EHRs) holds the promise to improve patient safety and quality of care, as well as opening new ways to educate patients and engage them in their own care. On the other hand, EHR use also changes clinicians' workflow, introduces new types of errors, and can distract the doctor's attention from the patient. The purpose of this chapter is to explore these issues from a micro-level perspective, focusing on the patient consultation. The chapter shows the fine balance between beneficial and unfavorable impacts of using the EHR during consultations on patient safety and patient-centered care. It demonstrates how the same features that contribute to greater ef- ficiency may cause potential risk to the patient, and points to some of the strategies, best practices, and enabling factors that may be used to leverage the benefits of the EHR. In particular, the authors point to the role that medical education should play in preparing practitioners for the challenges of the new, computerized, environment of 21st century medicine.

INTRODUCTION

Mrs. Jones is a new patient to the practice who has come in for a certificate that the local gym requires for enrollment. She is 50 years old, married and mother of two, who works as a high school teacher.

DOI: 10.4018/978-1-61520-733-6.ch005

Dr. Smith introduces himself, welcoming her to the practice. He asks for her USB memory stick, and her cumulative electronic health record (EHR) pops-up on his screen, indicating no significant health con- cerns. Her family tree (genogram) is also generated and is displayed. Dr. Smith asks "anything else?" and she answers that she would like to be informed about needed health promotion advice. Her family history contains the existence of heart disease (coronary artery disease) and breast cancer. Her life style is generally healthy. Dr. Smith performs a focused physical examination, and hooks her up to the multi-task physiological monitor that gives, within 90 seconds, a reading of her blood pressure and pulse, electrocardiogram, and lung function (spirometry) - all are normal. Since she had laboratory tests three months ago as part of a woman's health program she follows, Dr Smith shares with her the results of her cholesterol test (hypercholesterolemia or a high cholesterol level). The EHR automatically generates the recommended screening and health promotion recommendations for her age and risk status, which he explains, and then goes over some patient education materials that appear on the screen that he shares with her. Finally, she asks his opinion about the future consequences of her ten year old infection of the abdomen's inner lining (peritonitis) and a subsequent surgical procedure to explore it (laparotomy). The doctor does not recall any, but he sends a query through the Inforetriever (a program for updated sound medical information retrieval) on his desktop. When the evidence-based answer arrives 15 seconds later, he is able to share it with her. All the generated materials are beamed to her cell phone and emailed to her, together with the certificate.

Throughout the encounter Dr. Smith has been applying the patient-doctor–computer communication skills he had trained in six months ago at the national simulation center. The subsequent results of her age and risk appropriate screening arrive at his desktop (and hers) automatically within the next week. Dr. Smith interprets the results for her and sends them over the encrypted office email. Mrs. Jones also shares her exercise and diet program data electronically, and he monitors those. Three months later, a new cholesterol screen indicates that she has much improved. A week later Dr. Smith receives the annual report of his performance: the clinical quality indicators and patient safety monitoring show another

5 point improvement. The patient satisfaction survey is at its usual high. When Dr. Smith sits to plan his next year needs-based goals for his continuous learning plan he chooses tropical and poverty medicine. The bonus he will receive will enable him to finally choose the medical relief to Africa he has been hoping to accomplish for some years now.

To some readers, the above scenario may seem imaginary. However, the technologies which enable it have already been, or are being, developed. As this scenario demonstrates, the application of information and communication technology (ICT) in health care holds the promise to improve quality of care, as well as opening new ways to educate patients and engage them in their own care. However, there are also many challenges involved. In this chapter, we will review the present literature on the benefits of the computerized consultation, as well as the challenges and problems associated with it. We will discuss the fine line between benefits and risks of using the EHR during consultations, and demonstrate how the same features that contribute to efficiency may pose a risk or interfere with patient centeredness. Finally, we will discuss some of the strategies, best practices, and enabling factors that could enhance realization of the vision. In particular, we will point to the role that medical education should play in preparing practitioners for the challenges of the new, computerized, environment of 21st century medicine.

BACKGROUND

The potential and actual outcomes of ICT in health care are often discussed at the systems level. In particular, impacts on quality of care and patient safety of ICTs such as the EHR, computerized provider order entry (CPOE) and clinical decision support systems (CDSS) have been examined. Table 1 describes these and some other commonly used clinical information systems. Although the

Table 1. Types of commonly used clinical information systems

Type of system	Description
Electronic Medical Record (EMR)	An electronic record of health-related information on an individual that can be created, gathered, managed, and consulted by authorized clinicians and staff within one health care organization. The National Alliance for Health Information Technology (NAHIT), 2008
Electronic Health Record (EHR)	An electronic record of health-related information on an individual that conforms to nationally recognized interoperability standards and that can be created, managed, and consulted by authorized clinicians and staff across more than one health care organization. The National Alliance for Health Information Technology (NAHIT), 2008). The terms EMR and EHR are sometimes used interchangeably.
Personal Health Record (PHR)	An electronic record of health-related information on an individual that conforms to nationally recognized interoperability standards and that can be drawn from multiple sources while being managed, shared, and controlled by the individual. The National Alliance for Health Information Technology (NAHIT), 2008.
Computerized Provider Order Entry (CPOE)	A system which allows providers to post and communicate medical orders and their application. CPOE can facilitate patient safety and quality of care by means of eliminating illegible handwriting and use of predefined, evidence-based, order sets for specific medical conditions.
Clinical Decision Support Systems (CDSS)	Computerized systems which are designed to assist health care professionals in making clinical decisions (e.g. about diagnosis, treatment or care management). CDSS may be characterized by their intended function, the mode by which they offer advice, style of consultation and the underlying decision making process (Musen, Shahar & Shortliffe, 2006)
Picture Archiving and Communication System (PACS)	Computerized information system which is used to acquire, store, retrieve and display digital images; in particular diagnostic images such as x-rays, Computerized Tomography (CT) and Magnetic Resonance Imaging (MRI) images.

majority of studies have emerged from a small number of large health care organizations such as the Department of Veterans Affairs (DVA) or Kaiser Permanente in the US, a recent systematic review has concluded that health information systems can indeed improve quality of care and patient safety. Preventive care was the primary domain of quality improvement reported. The main benefits were increased adherence to guidelines, enhanced surveillance, and monitoring, and decreased medication errors. The major efficiency improvement was decreased utilization of care (Chaudhry et al., 2006).

However, a growing number of studies - especially of CPOE systems - have drawn attention to some of the unintended consequences of ICT in health care that may be beneficial or adverse. Such unintended consequences include more or new work for clinicians, unfavorable changes in workflow, high system demands, problems related to paper persistence, untoward changes in communication patterns, negative emotions, new kinds of errors, unexpected changes in the power structure, and overdependence on the technology (Campbell, Guappone, Sittig, Dykstra, & Ash, 2009; Campbell, Sittig, Ash, Guappone, & Dykstra, 2006).

As system-level outcomes of information systems are thought to emerge from the combination of multiple individual impacts (DeLone & McLean, 1992; 2003), through the rest of this chapter we will explore the impact of ICT in health care at a micro-level, focusing on the patient consultation. In particular we argue that there is a fine balance between benefits and risks of using EHR during consultation, which is greatly influenced by cognitive factors, and that the computer has become a third actor in the clinical encounter and thus influences patient-doctor relationships.

THE COMPUTER ENABLED (OR DISABLED) CONSULTATION: AN IN-DEPTH LOOK

Efficiency vs. Risk

One of the most serious reported unintended consequences of CPOE systems is the generation of new kind of errors. It has been termed "e-iatrogenesis" (Weiner, Kfuri, Chan, & Fowles, 2007). A deeper look at how these new types of errors arise, demonstrates that the line between greater efficiency and error is often very thin, and that sometimes the same features and user characteristics that make work more efficient, and presumably safer, are those which generate computer-related errors.

For example, in the EHR there are often drop-down lists, e.g. for patients' names, diagnoses, or medications. Structuring data this way is very useful in that it enables data analysis for health management, administration, and research purposes. "Point and click" also eliminates the need to type in data, which is time consuming and may divert the doctor's attention from the patient. Finally, these lists may serve as a quick reminder and thus minimize memory load (Shachak, Hadas-Dayagi, Ziv, & Reis, 2009). However, the structured format of entering data into the EMR is very different from the narrative structure of the traditional patient record. It has been demonstrated that moving to an EMR system affected physicians' information gathering and reasoning processes, and could lead to potential loss of information (Patel, Kushniruk, Yang, & Yale, 2000). Furthermore, experienced users perform selection from lists very quickly, in a semi-automatic manner. This automaticity, the term used in cognitive science to describe skilled performance that requires little or no conscious

attention (Wheatley & Wegner, 2001), makes it very easy to accidentally select the wrong item. Two of the most commonly reported errors with a primary care electronic medical record (EMR) system—selecting the wrong medication and adding to the wrong patient's chart—were associated, fully or in part, with selection from lists (Shachak et al., 2009). Similar errors were also reported with hospital CPOE systems, suggesting this is a universal problem (Campbell et al., 2009).

Other examples are the use of copy-paste and user- (or system-) generated templates. The computer allows quick copying and pasting of data, e.g. from a previous to the present visit, or from one patient's chart to another. Undoubtedly, copy-paste and templates make an efficient use of computers; however, they raise ethical questions and concerns about data quality (Thielke, Hammond, & Helbig, 2007). Moreover, copying and pasting poses the risk of inducing errors by accidental failure to update data which should be modified. In a cross-sectional survey held at two medical centers that use computerized documentation systems physicians' overall attitude toward copying and pasting was positive. However, they noted that inconsistencies and outdated information were more common in copied notes (O'Donnell et al., 2009). Thielke et al. (2007) have reported a steep rate of copy-paste examination data in EHR, including notes copied from another author or from a document older than six months, which they defined as high risk.

Similarly, templates may be inserted into the patient chart using keyboard shortcuts or a mouse click. Templates make work more efficient as they eliminate the need for extensive typing. Furthermore, if comprehensive templates are prepared they may serve as checklists that help clinicians make sure they have collected all required information, performed the necessary tests, or provided recommended treatment. However, the use of templates, too, can become semi-automatic. As in copy-paste, it is very easy to approve a template without correcting wrong data - "clicking enter, enter, enter is a prescription for error" as one of the physician participants in our study described it (Shachak et al., 2009).

Finally, alerts of drug contraindications can be beneficial or detrimental. Clearly, notifying clinicians that the patient is allergic to the medication they had just prescribed, or that it interacts with another drug the patient takes, is important. A number of studies have attributed significant improvements in medication safety to the embedding of alerts in CPOE systems; these improvements include reduced numbers of medication errors and adverse drug events (Bates et al., 1999; Eslami, Keizer, & Abu-Hanna, 2007; Tamblyn et al., 2003). However, others have reported alert override rates greater than 80% in various systems and settings (Hsieh et al., 2004; Weingart et al., 2003).

Why are alerts being overridden? Prescribers provide various reasons such as poor quality and high volumes of alerts, patients already taking the drug in question, and the monitoring of patients (Grizzle et al., 2007; Hsieh et al., 2004; Lapane, Waring, Schneider, Dube, & Quilliam, 2008; van der Sijs, Aarts, Vulto, & Berg, 2006; Weingart et al., 2003). A recent study also suggests that some specified reasons for alert override typed into a CPOE system were, in fact, failed attempts to communicate important medical information which no one has read (Chused, Kuperman, & Stetson, 2008). In addition to causing interference or increasing cognitive load, we propose that poor quality and too high a volume of alerts may result in formation of an automatic behavior to instantly shut down alerts, similar to the way users attempt to immediately close pop-up ads on websites (McCoy, Galleta, Everard, & Polak, 2004). This automatic behavior—or "alert fatigue" as van der Sijs et al. (2006) describe it—may accidentally result in overriding crucial alerts.

How can the risk-benefit balance shift to the benefits side? A key component in systems improvement is usability and human factors engineering. User interfaces need to be designed and evaluated with an understanding of these cognitive elements, in an attempt to reduce effort on one hand and prevent automaticity-related errors on the other. Examples include drop-down lists with greater distance between items, or highlighting items on mouse-over just before selection. Alerts acceptance can be improved by tiering alerts on the basis of their severity, and designating only critical alerts as interruptive (Paterno et al., 2009; Shah et al., 2005). To some extent, the system itself can detect and prevent errors. For example, one of the systems we had checked accepted an input that a three year old patient had been smoking for 15 years. When a doctor makes this error, it is likely s/he is adding to the wrong chart. Such errors are preventable by better system design.

Another key factor is education or training. Our findings suggest that experts are aware of these potential errors and, therefore, may be more careful when performing risky actions (Shachak et al., 2009). Education that goes beyond the technical aspects of using the system to a broader view of the benefits, risks, and principles of high-quality use is required. Simulation-based training, in particular, may be highly effective.

The Computer as a Third Player in the Patient-Doctor Encounter

In our initial scenario, the computer is an active actor in the consultation. It triggers some of the discussion and information exchange, and acts as a colleague or advisor. Indeed, in computerized settings, the consultation cannot be viewed as dyadic patient-doctor interaction anymore. Rather, it is now triadic relationships of the patient, the doctor, and computer (Pearce, Dwan, Arnold, Phillips, & Trumble, 2009).

The computer influences the consultation in various ways, beginning with the physical location of the monitor, keyboard, mouse, and other ancillary devices such as printers. The space these hardware occupy, their location, and orientation have significant influence on the consultation. For example, large fixed monitors may narrow the doctor's or the patient's personal space and interfere with eye contact. Even when it does not, the monitor in some settings is oriented towards the doctor only, which excludes the patient from the doctor's interaction with the computer. For some patients, this may be disturbing (Frankel et al., 2005; Pearce, Walker, & O'Shea, 2008).

However, the other option of a monitor that can be viewed by both doctor and patient is also not optimal for everyone. In our opening scenario, both Dr. Smith and Mrs. Jones seem to be comfortable with technology, so the computer becomes a useful tool to facilitate their discussion, share information, and help with decision making. However, this is not the case for all doctors and patients. As Pearce and others have demonstrated, whether the monitor's position promotes information sharing or becomes distracting depends on both the doctor's and patient's styles (Pearce, Trumble, Arnold, Dwan, & Phillips, 2008). Perhaps an optimal solution is the use of flat LCD monitors on mobile arms, or using mobile hand-held devices, which allow greater flexibility.

A positive influence of the EMR is greater information exchange (Shachak & Reis, 2009). EMR use was positively related to biomedical discussion, including questions about therapeutic regimen, exchange of information about medications, and patient disclosure of health information to the physician. Physicians who used an EMR were able to accomplish information-related tasks such as checking and verifying patient history, encouraging patients to ask questions and ensuring completeness at the end of a visit to a greater extent than physicians who used paper records (Arar, Wen, McGrath, Steinbach, & Pugh, 2005; Hsu et al., 2005; Kuo, Mullen, McQueen, Swank, & Rogers, 2007; Makoul, Curry, & Tang, 2001; Margalit, Roter, Dunevant, Larson, & Reis, 2006).

On the negative side, it is very hard for physicians to divide attention between the patient and the EMR. It has been demonstrated, that even within the first minute of the consultation, much of the interaction is driven by the computer, not by the patient's agenda (Pearce et al., 2008). Physicians often walked straight to the monitor after only a short greeting. The average physician screen gaze was 24% to 55% of the visit time and it was inversely related to their engagement in psychosocial question asking and emotional responsiveness (Margalit et al., 2006; Shachak et al., 2009). The computer often caused physicians to lose rapport with patients; e.g. physicians typed in data or screen gazed while talking to patients or while the patient was talking. Our literature review also suggests that the computer's potential to assist in patient education is underutilized (Shachak & Reis, 2009).

How can we make the ideal future scenario come true, and overcome the negative influences of the computer on patient centeredness? Computer skills are important enablers. Blind typing, navigation skills, the use of templates and keyboard shortcuts, and the ability to organize and search for information were associated with physicians' ability to effectively communicate with patients in computerized settings (Frankel et al., 2005; Shachak et al., 2009; Shachak & Reis, 2009).

Similarly, physicians' styles as well as their basic communication skills are highly important. Both Ventres et al. and Booth et al. identified relatively similar styles and suggested the computer's impact on patient centeredness depended on them (Booth, Robinson, & Kohannejad, 2004; Ventres, Kooienga, Marlin, Vuckovic, & Stewart, 2005; Ventres et al., 2006). We have recently provided a unified classification of these styles (Shachak & Reis, 2009). The three styles in this unified classification are:

1. **Informational-ignoring style.** This style is characterized by extensive information gathering, that is often facilitated by the EMR, and focus on details of information. Physicians with this style often lost rapport with patients while engaged with the EMR, e.g. they frequently talked while gazing at the monitor, hardly faced the patients, and

often left them idle while engaging with the computer.

2. **Controlling-managerial style**, which is characterized by separating computer use from communication. Physicians with this style alternated their attention between the patient and the computer in defined intervals or stages of the encounter. While with the patient, they turned away from the computer and vice versa. Switches of attention were often indicated by these physicians using non-verbal cues such as turning body or gaze.

3. **Interpersonal style**. This style is characterized by its focus on the patient. Physicians of this style oriented themselves to the patient even when using the EMR, did not usually talk while using the computer, and utilized the computer to share and review information together with the patient. They spent less time on data entry and usually refrained from using the computer in the beginning of the encounter.

Along the same lines, Frankel et al. (2005) have suggested that the computer facilitates both negative and positive baseline communication skills. Some of the physicians we observed were able to compensate for their lack of computer mastery by excellent communication skills (Shachak et al., 2009). Additionally, strategies and best practices may be employed. The major strategy we have identified is dividing the encounter into patient- and computer-focused stages that are clearly distinctive and indicated by body language and focus of gaze. Another is keeping the patients engaged by sharing the screen with them or reading out loud while typing (Shachak et al., 2009).

FUTURE RESEARCH DIRECTIONS

As pointed out, education is important for enhancing safer use of computers during consultation. Education at all levels, from medical school to residency to continuing medical education, is also essential for acquiring and continuously improving computer and communication skills and learning effective strategies for integrating the computer into the patient-doctor relationships. Dr. Smith in our scenario was trained in using the EHR at the national simulation center. The training he received went well beyond the technical aspects of using the software, which are usually the scope of clinical information systems implementations. Rather, he learned how to avoid EHR-induced errors, accommodate for his own and various patient styles, employ strategies and best practices for patient-doctor-computer communication, and make optimal use of the computer for patient education and shared decision making.

The development and evaluation of such educational interventions is one area for future research. Ten tips for physicians on how to incorporate the EMR into consultation had been suggested by Ventres, Kooienga, and Marlin (2006), and have been recently modified by us (Shachak & Reis, 2009). These tips include suggestions regarding the computer skills required of the physician, encounter management practices, and ways to engage the patient. However, as far as we can detect from the literature, educational modules of patient-doctor communication have not yet included the computer. As of February, 2008, we were able to find only two examples of instructional modules supporting the introduction of computers to clinical care settings (Institute for Healthcare Communication, 2008; Simpson, Robinson, Fletcher, & Wilson, 2005). We are currently in the process of developing and evaluating a simulation-based training intervention aimed at qualifying Family Medicine residents in incorporating the use of EMRs into consultations. A number of scenarios have been developed for training participants to identify the potential pitfalls, learn various strategies and skills for using an EMR during consultations, and employ them flexibly depending on the situation and the patient and physician styles.

Technology also opens new ways to incorporate the computer into a seamless clinical encounter. Present systems rely heavily on text, but we can envision a multimedia EHR which combines image, text, sound, and video with technologies such as voice and handwriting recognition, automatic transcription, natural language processing, and automated tagging. These technologies can minimize the interference of data entry with communication, maintain a significant narrative component of the record in rich media that may reduce ambiguity (Daft, Lengel, & Trevino, 1987) and, therefore, support reasoning and decision making, while still enabling fast retrieval and data structuring for management and analysis.

Multiple challenges are involved in the development of such multimedia EHRs including spoken and medical natural language processing, assigning metadata to videotaped medical interviews, language standardization, and semantic information retrieval. Furthermore, even if these technological challenges are overcome, numerous factors such as legal issues, cost, usability, time required to review information, and potential users' perceptions of the system—especially concerns about privacy and confidentiality—may still hinder adoption of multimedia-EHRs. All of these challenges open multiple directions for future research.

In our scenario Dr. Smith is conscious of the service the data he generates render for the benefit of the larger population, and welcomes feedback on his data quality. However, we have not discussed the relationships between micro and macro levels, and particularly how the way that physicians document influences data quality and the use of data for clinical management, administration, and research. More research is required to better understand the micro-macro relationships.

Finally, Web 2.0 applications such as RSS feeds, social networking, blogs, wikis, and Twitter open new ways of communication and knowledge

exchange among patients and doctors. These applications can add a component of virtual consultation into the clinical practice. They also facilitate many-to-many instead of, or in addition to, the traditional one-to-one communication (Hawn, 2009; Jain, 2009; Kamel Boulos & Wheeler, 2007). In this chapter we have focused on the impact of integrating ICT into the traditional patient-doctor consultation. The effect of Web 2.0 applications on medical practice and consultations in particular, remains to be seen. As far as we can detect, there is a dearth in rigorous research with this focus. Most of the literature to date consists of opinions and personal reports from the field.

LIMITATIONS

As the scope of this chapter is the medical consultation, the majority of research discussed emerged from ambulatory or outpatient settings. Acute care presents different challenges and employs much different workflow processes, though some of the challenges discussed here also apply (e.g. new types of errors—Campbell et al., 2009).

CONCLUSION

The micro level perspective provided in this chapter reveals some of the processes that underlie the impacts of ICT on the health care system. Throughout this chapter we have demonstrated the thin line between beneficial and adverse consequences of using ICT during consultation. Human-centered design, medical education, as well as developing the technologies toward the multimedia-EHR have the potential to improve the individual-level impact of the computerized consultation.

REFERENCES

Arar, N. H., Wen, L., McGrath, J., Steinbach, R., & Pugh, J. A. (2005). Communicating about medications during primary care outpatient visits: the role of electronic medical records. *Informatics in Primary Care*, *13*(1), 13–22.

Bates, D. W., Teich, J. M., Lee, J., Seger, D., & Kuperman, G. J., Ma'Luf, N. et al. (1999). The impact of computerized physician order entry on medication error prevention. *Journal of the American Medical Informatics Association*, *6*(4), 313–321.

Booth, N., Robinson, P., & Kohannejad, J. (2004). Identification of high-quality consultation practice in primary care: the effects of computer use on doctor-patient rapport. *Informatics in Primary Care*, *12*(2), 75–83.

Campbell, E. M., Guappone, K. P., Sittig, D. F., Dykstra, R. H., & Ash, J. S. (2009). Computerized provider order entry adoption: implications for clinical workflow. *Journal of General Internal Medicine*, *24*(1), 21–26. doi:10.1007/s11606-008-0857-9

Campbell, E. M., Sittig, D. F., Ash, J. S., Guappone, K. P., & Dykstra, R. H. (2006). Types of unintended consequences related to computerized provider order entry. *Journal of the American Medical Informatics Association*, *13*(5), 547–556. doi:10.1197/jamia.M2042

Chaudhry, B., Wang, J., Wu, S., Maglione, M., Mojica, W., & Roth, E. (2006). Systematic review: impact of health information technology on quality, efficiency, and costs of medical care. *Annals of Internal Medicine*, *144*(10), 742–752.

Chused, A., Kuperman, G. J., & Stetson, P. D. (2008). Alert override reasons: a failure to communicate. *AMIA Annual Symposium Proceedings*, 111-115.

Daft, R. L., Lengel, R. H., & Trevino, L. K. (1987). Message Equivocality, Media Selection, and Manager Performance - Implications for Information-Systems. *Management Information Systems Quarterly*, *11*(3), 355–366. doi:10.2307/248682

DeLone, W. H., & McLean, E. R. (1992). Information systems success: the quest for the dependent variable. *Information Systems Research*, *3*(1), 60–95. doi:10.1287/isre.3.1.60

DeLone, W. H., & McLean, E. R. (2003). The DeLone and McLean model of information systems success: a ten-year update. *Journal of Management Information Systems*, *19*(4), 9–30.

Eslami, S., Keizer, N. F., & Abu-Hanna, A. (2007). The impact of computerized physician medication order entry in hospitalized patients-A systematic review. *International Journal of Medical Informatics*. doi:.doi:10.1016/j.ijmedinf.2007.10.001

Frankel, R., Altschuler, A., George, S., Kinsman, J., Jimison, H., Robertson, N. R., & Hsu, J. (2005). Effects of exam-room computing on clinician-patient communication: a longitudinal qualitative study. *Journal of General Internal Medicine*, *20*(8), 677–682. doi:10.1111/j.1525-1497.2005.0163.x

Grizzle, A. J., Mahmood, M. H., Ko, Y., Murphy, J. E., Armstrong, E. P., & Skrepnek, G. H. (2007). Reasons provided by prescribers when overriding drug-drug interaction alerts. *The American Journal of Managed Care*, *13*(10), 573–578.

Hawn, C. (2009). Take two aspirin and tweet me in the morning: How Twitter, Facebook and other social media are reshaping medicine. *Health Affairs*, *28*(2), 361–368. doi:10.1377/hlthaff.28.2.361

Hsieh, T. C., Kuperman, G. J., Jaggi, T., Hojnowski-Diaz, P., Fiskio, J., & Williams, D. H. (2004). Characteristics and consequences of drug allergy alert overrides in a computerized physician order entry system. *Journal of the American Medical Informatics Association*, *11*(6), 482–491. doi:10.1197/jamia.M1556

Hsu, J., Huang, J., Fung, V., Robertson, N., Jimison, H., & Frankel, R. (2005). Health information technology and physician-patient interactions: impact of computers on communication during outpatient primary care visits. *Journal of the American Medical Informatics Association, 12*(4), 474–480. doi:10.1197/jamia.M1741

Institute for Healthcare Communication. (2008). Retrieved August 11, 2009, from http://www.healthcarecomm.org/index.php?sec=courses&sub=faculty&course=3

Jain, S. H. (2009). Practicing medicine in the age of Facebook. *The New England Journal of Medicine, 361*(7), 649–651. doi:10.1056/NEJMp0901277

Kamel Boulos, M. N., & Wheeler, S. (2007). The emerging Web 2.0 social software: an enabling suite of sociable technologies in health and health care education. *Health Information and Libraries Journal, 24*(1), 2–23. doi:10.1111/j.1471-1842.2007.00701.x

Kuo, G. M., Mullen, P. D., McQueen, A., Swank, P. R., & Rogers, J. C. (2007). Cross-sectional comparison of electronic and paper medical records on medication counseling in primary care clinics: a Southern Primary-Care Urban Research Network (SPUR-Net) study. *Journal of the American Board of Family Medicine, 20*(2), 164–173. doi:10.3122/jabfm.2007.02.060113

Lapane, K. L., Waring, M. E., Schneider, K. L., Dube, C., & Quilliam, B. J. (2008). A mixed method study of the merits of e-prescribing drug alerts in primary care. *Journal of General Internal Medicine, 23*(4), 442–446. doi:10.1007/s11606-008-0505-4

Makoul, G., Curry, R. H., & Tang, P. C. (2001). The use of electronic medical records: communication patterns in outpatient encounters. *Journal of the American Medical Informatics Association, 8*(6), 610–615.

Margalit, R. S., Roter, D., Dunevant, M. A., Larson, S., & Reis, S. (2006). Electronic medical record use and physician-patient communication: An observational study of Israeli primary care encounters. *Patient Education and Counseling, 61*(1), 134–141. doi:10.1016/j.pec.2005.03.004

McCoy, S., Galleta, D., Everard, A., & Polak, P. (2004, December 10-11). *A study of the effects of online advertising: A focus on pop-up and in-line ads*. Paper presented at the Third Annual Workshop on HCI Research in MIS, Washington, D.C.

Musen, M. A., Shahar, Y., & Shortliffe, E. H. (2006). Clinical decision support systems. In Shortliffe, E. H., & Cimino, J. J. (Eds.), *Biomedical informatics: computer applications in health care and biomedicine* (3rd ed.). New York: Springer.

National Alliance for Health Information Technology (NAHIT). (2008). *Report to the Office of the National Coordinator for Health Information Technology on defining key health information technology terms*. Retrieved October 15, 2009 from http://healthit.hhs.gov/portal/server.pt/gateway/PTARGS_0_10741_848133_0_0_18/10_2_hit_terms.pdf

O'Donnell, H. C., Kaushal, R., Barron, Y., Callahan, M. A., Adelman, R. D., & Siegler, E. L. (2009). Physicians' attitudes towards copy and pasting in electronic note writing. *Journal of General Internal Medicine, 24*(1), 63–68. doi:10.1007/s11606-008-0843-2

Patel, V. L., Kushniruk, A. W., Yang, S., & Yale, J. F. (2000). Impact of a computer-based patient record system on data collection, knowledge organization, and reasoning. *Journal of the American Medical Informatics Association, 7*(6), 569–585.

Paterno, M. D., Maviglia, S. M., Gorman, P. N., Seger, D. L., Yoshida, E., & Seger, A. C. (2009). Tiering drug-drug interaction alerts by severity increases compliance rates. *Journal of the American Medical Informatics Association, 16*(1), 40–46. doi:10.1197/jamia.M2808

Pearce, C., Dwan, K., Arnold, M., Phillips, C., & Trumble, S. (2009). Doctor, patient and computer-a framework for the new consultation. *International Journal of Medical Informatics*, *78*(1), 32–38. doi:10.1016/j.ijmedinf.2008.07.002

Pearce, C., Trumble, S., Arnold, M., Dwan, K., & Phillips, C. (2008). Computers in the new consultation: within the first minute. *Family Practice*, *25*(3), 202–208. doi:10.1093/fampra/cmn018

Pearce, C., Walker, H., & O'Shea, C. (2008). A visual study of computers on doctors' desks. *Informatics in Primary Care*, *16*(2), 111–117.

Shachak, A., Hadas-Dayagi, M., Ziv, A., & Reis, S. (2009). Primary care physicians' use of an electronic medical record system: A cognitive task analysis. *Journal of General Internal Medicine*, *24*(3), 341–348. doi:10.1007/s11606-008-0892-6

Shachak, A., & Reis, S. (2009). The impact of electronic medical records on patient-doctor communication during consultation: a narrative literature review. *Journal of Evaluation in Clinical Practice*, *15*, 641–649. doi:10.1111/j.1365-2753.2008.01065.x

Shah, N. R., Seger, A. C., Seger, D. L., Fiskio, J. M., Kuperman, G. J., Blumenfeld, B., et al. (2005). Improving override rates for computerized prescribing alerts in ambulatory care. *AMIA Annual Symposium Proceedings*, (pp. 1110).

Simpson, L., Robinson, P., Fletcher, M., & Wilson, R. (2005). e-Communication skills. Oxford, UK: Radcliff.

Tamblyn, R., Huang, A., Perreault, R., Jacques, A., Roy, D., & Hanley, J. (2003). The medical office of the 21st century (MOXXI): effectiveness of computerized decision-making support in reducing inappropriate prescribing in primary care. *Canadian Medical Association Journal*, *169*(6), 549–556.

Thielke, S., Hammond, K., & Helbig, S. (2007). Copying and pasting of examinations within the electronic medical record. *International Journal of Medical Informatics*, *76*(Suppl 1), S122–S128. doi:10.1016/j.ijmedinf.2006.06.004

van der Sijs, H., Aarts, J., Vulto, A., & Berg, M. (2006). Overriding of drug safety alerts in computerized physician order entry. *Journal of the American Medical Informatics Association*, *13*(2), 138–147. doi:10.1197/jamia.M1809

Ventres, W., Kooienga, S., & Marlin, R. (2006). EHRs in the exam room: tips on patient-centered care. *Family Practice Management*, *13*(3), 45–47.

Ventres, W., Kooienga, S., Marlin, R., Vuckovic, N., & Stewart, V. (2005). Clinician style and examination room computers: a video ethnography. *Family Medicine*, *37*(4), 276–281.

Ventres, W., Kooienga, S., Vuckovic, N., Marlin, R., Nygren, P., & Stewart, V. (2006). Physicians, Patients, and the Electronic Health Record: An Ethnographic Analysis. *Annals of Family Medicine*, *4*(2), 124–131. doi:10.1370/afm.425

Weiner, J. P., Kfuri, T., Chan, K., & Fowles, J. B. (2007). "e-Iatrogenesis": the most critical unintended consequence of CPOE and other HIT. *Journal of the American Medical Informatics Association*, *14*(3), 387–388, discussion 389. doi:10.1197/jamia.M2338

Weingart, S. N., Toth, M., Sands, D. Z., Aronson, M. D., Davis, R. B., & Phillips, R. S. (2003). Physicians' decisions to override computerized drug alerts in primary care. *Archives of Internal Medicine*, *163*(21), 2625–2631. doi:10.1001/archinte.163.21.2625

Wheatley, T., & Wegner, D. M. (2001). Automaticity of action, psychology of. In Smelser, N. J., & Baltes, P. B. (Eds.), *International encyclopedia of the social & behavioral sciences* (pp. 991–993). Oxford, UK: Pergamon.

Chapter 6
The Electronic Patient Record:
A Practicing Physician's Perspective

Nicholas G. Bircher
University of Pittsburgh, USA

ABSTRACT

This chapter provides a novel, unique, and reasonably broad set of perspectives on the human resources (HR) and information technology (IT) ramifications of the electronic patient record (EPR) as an integral component of the total hospital information system.

INTRODUCTION

The medical record is one of the cornerstones of medical care, both in the in-patient and out-patient environment, and, ideally will be in the Emergency Medical Services (prehospital) environment as well. The potential of the electronic patient record (EPR), however, as a component of a hospital management information system is enormous, and unfortunately, as yet, only minimally realized.

A contributing factor to the unrealized potential is that the electronic patient record is perceived as only a tiny fraction of the total informatics job at a given hospital. It is therefore marginalized both in terms of capital investment and as a central priority in IT planning. In principle, any IT professional would

be able to list the steps in the design, construction, implementation, and optimal operation of a comprehensive and integrated health care information system. In practice, there is an essentially complete disconnect between information technology (IT) objectives, human resources (HR) objectives, and patient care objectives, owing in part to a lack of central strategy and reliance on a plethora of legacy systems and vendors.

Medical care carries the intrinsic risks of death or serious bodily harm. An electronic patient record (EPR), if well done, can help to reduce these risks. The EPR can not only serve as a repository for information from health care providers, it should serve as a decision support system, reminding physicians, nurses, and other health care providers of needed additional tests, medications, or diagnostic criteria, as well as issuing alarms/alerts regarding

DOI: 10.4018/978-1-61520-733-6.ch006

impending or present danger to the patient. For example, an alarm system should notify caretakers of abnormal constellations of symptoms or signs, or when the patient meets the diagnostic criteria for life-threatening conditions such as systemic inflammatory response syndrome (SIRS) or sepsis. Similarly, it should remind caretakers of the criteria to call for a medical emergency team when those criteria are met in an individual patient. The ideal medical record would be similar to modern combat avionics - full-speed, real-time decision support along with appropriate warning and response algorithms, as well as integration with a network-centric information system. End-users are similar to aircraft pilots in the following regard: we don't know how to build the plane, we don't know how to fix the plane, but we become very annoyed when the instruments quit in mid-flight! Also, the medical record should be configured as part of an object oriented database. While the limitations of object oriented database management are recognized, the ability to actually do structured queries as described below is essential to modern quantitative management.

If, however, the electronic patient record materially interferes with the practice of medicine or nursing, the record itself may increase risks. The argument that computerizing the medical record always makes things better is a beautiful hypothesis, but in rare instances has been slain by ugly facts. At the Children's Hospital of Pittsburgh, implementation of computerized physician order entry (CPOE) increased mortality from 2.80% to 6.57% in children referred there for specialized care (Han et al., 2005). While Han's study was not designed to establish causation, the authors speculate that (1) delays in the delivery of time sensitive therapies in critically ill patients (especially vasopressors for shock and antibiotics for sepsis) and (2) significant disruptions of ICU team function caused by superimposition of computer tasks (as detailed in the article) were major contributory factors. While the typical experience is more positive, the presumption of

uniform benefit from either an EPR or CPOE is not securely established.

MEDICAL ISSUES

The quality of medical decision making in general is dependent on (1) access to the available information, (2) the quality of the information, and (3) the quantity of relevant information. In any given medical note, specific physicians will want specific information. Thus, optimization of the signal (relevant information) to noise (irrelevant information) is a necessary property of structured notes. Simply because someone (usually not a person who is ever going to try to wade through one of these notes) thinks every item of information available for that day should be included, does not mean that is a good idea. The use of hyperlinks to laboratory and radiographic reports for example would be vastly preferable to automatic inclusion of the text in every single progress note by every service.

Monitoring: Evolution of the 747 Cockpit

Real human systems engineering should be done in a rational rather than on an ad hoc basis. For instance, in the transition from the analog version of the 747 cockpit, the number of lights, gauges and switches changed from 971 to 365. Both programmable displays and careful simplification of procedures also reduced workload, allowing the number of crew members to decrease from three to two (see http://www.boeing.com/news/feature/747evolution/thenvsnow.html).

These same engineering principles need to be applied to the EPR. End-users hypothesize that there is a hyperbolic relationship between total programmer work and end-user work per unit operation. While end-users understand budgetary constraints on programming in general terms, they are not willing to accept increased work for them simply because a vendor did not think through the operation clearly. IT professionals who use the term "click counters" to describe end-users who have actually measured the additional incremental work due to poor programming do so at their own political peril. Any system with a negative return on investment (ROI) due to poor programming has a very limited lifespan in a truly competitive marketplace. For example, software which cannot carry the patient's weight from one operation to the next, requiring that it be re-entered each time a weight-based dose is computed is an appalling software failure.

Mistrust is substantially reinforced by catastrophic system failures, in which all end-users are prevented from completing computer-based tasks. Further, blaming the end-user for operator error when in fact the actual problem is a software/hardware issue at best creates confusion and at worst creates profound and permanent distrust. One of the best ways to drive smart people out of any organization is to force them to use a stupid system that fails frequently, and then to tell them that they are stupid. Although there are no data yet as to the influence of the EPR, clearly the effect can be bidirectional, either (1) a major selling point for recruitment and retention, or (2) it can create an environment so fundamentally hostile or unacceptable to employees that it threatens the stability of the institution.

Recording Speed: IT Ramifications of the "Code Record"

A crucial circumstance in which high speed recording should be mandatory is during critical medical events, for which a rapid response team has been called. The ideal EPR would interface with a "smart room" which has full disclosure recording of vital signs from monitors, as well as sound and video recording capability for use in emergencies. These are critical management tools in precisely the same way aircraft black boxes are.

The Medical Record: What you Don't Know May be Lethal to the Patient

The archetypal instance of this kind of lethality is an anaphylactic allergic reaction to certain drugs that can be avoided altogether, in most cases, and the risk significantly reduced in the remainder by blunting the anaphylactic reaction. If, however, the allergy is not easily accessible in the EPR, it will be missed, and disaster may ensue. The information set, as well as its structure, is crucial to decision making particularly in a time-compressed situation. The absolute worst way to array information is a list in which every number and every word is on a separate line. This seems absurd on its face; however, there are systems in which this is the easiest to program and therefore the most common form of progress note.

Logic of Diagnosis

Medical diagnosis is not easy to program (Miller, Pople, & Myers, 1982). A high functioning EPR, however, would be able to formulate (or at least recall) simple recommendations in the form of medical order sets to follow certain diagnostic tests, and to issue warnings that additional tests are needed. Conversely, arcane order sets that require ten times as long to do with the computer, or that structurally preclude certain needed actions, carry the risk of materially interfering with medical care.

Training Physicians to Use New Software

The use of a simulated medical record with meaningful documentation and help functions is essential to adequate training. Turning physicians loose with complicated software and no training is analogous to putting them in the cockpit of a 747 and expecting them to fly it. Ideally, physicians could practice on a simulated medical record the same way that pilots do. The basic version of the simulation could be easily done on their office computer. If, however, real measurements regarding the function of the program are desired, the structure should mirror high-end aviation simulation.

Fatigue and Medical Error

Despite the imposition of duty hour limitations by the Accreditation Council on Graduate Medical Education (ACGME), medical trainees, physicians, nurses, and other health care professionals still work in excess of 12-hour shifts on occasion. One important function that could be incorporated into a high-functioning EPR is a measure of wakefulness. Simply measuring response time to simple tasks, and warning the user of extremely long response times may alert them to fatigue. Alternatively, an imbedded performance vigilance task (PVT) to test wakefulness can be available on demand for those who feel fatigued. This is a patient safety, as well as an HR, issue as chronic, deliberate short staffing can result in patient injury or death.

Other Benefits of the EPR to Patients and Providers

In principle, a sophisticated EPR enhances the performance of a given physician and could also be used to promote telemedicine for distant patients. Patient education, based on information from the medical record is an essential IT function, but must be well structured. Patients could request that web links be sent to them regarding their discharge diagnoses from the medical record. Protection of health care information is a crucial goal as is making that information immediately available to any provider who has a legitimate use for that information

NURSING ISSUES

Ultimately, nursing time is finite on any given shift. If we arbitrarily divide work into computer-based (i.e., must be done using the computer) and non-computer based, there is a substantial potential for computer-based work to expand to the exclusion of non-computer related patient care, such as physical assessment of the patient and actual administration of medications. Thus, the expansion in computer-related work has both patient care and cost implications. The nurse who does all of non-computer related work during a given shift may wind up staying to complete the computer-based portion of her work, thus generating overtime, or worse may just leave with portions of the documentation unfinished. Or the nurse who does all of the computer-based work during a given shift may leave behind a tremendous amount of clinical work undone for the next shift to do. A more insidious effect occurs when new nurses actually alter nursing practice (i.e., omit physical assessment or medication administration) to allow more time to be spent on the computer documenting things that they may not have even done (Hadley, Graham, & Flannery, 2005).

Labor costs comprise roughly 70% of costs of operation of a hospital. Nursing labor costs are a large component of overall labor cost in any hospital and return on investment for nursing time can be severely limited by many factors, not the least of which is a medical record which triples the time spent in documentation. On the other hand, an ideal EPR actually tracks and predicts both nursing time for an individual patient, as well as that patient's estimated length of stay (LOS). In this way, the medical record becomes not only a repository of documentation, but also a real management information system, as it would provide accurate and timely data with real-time analytics, thereby allowing organizations to optimize both daily and overall staffing, and to reduce overtime and external agency use.

Although there is no clear data yet, a good EPR can be a significant selling point for potential recruits. A widely published and notoriously bad EPR can become an HR nightmare as it impacts both recruitment and retention. With respect to training, for an EPR to be maximally effective, it must be used to its full potential. Training is essential to avoid an agonizing learning curve that predisposes the end-user to avoid the software at all costs.

Among the biggest complaints by nurses about software are:

- Disorganized array of information: a great deal of time can easily be wasted when the needed information is arrayed arcanely (RCN, 2008: Thede, 2008).
- With certain tasks, the number of steps to accomplish the same task was higher, which may result in the perception by the end user that the tool is more complex and therefore difficult to use (Rinkus & Chitwood, 2002).
- No pull-down menus to define terms in a precise way: as nursing shifts from hand charting to menu-based charting, subtle nuances in assessment may be lost as terms are used incorrectly simply because what is on the "menu" is poorly defined, or worse, poorly understood by the bedside nurse (Lundberg, 2008).
- Inadequate choices for documentation, i.e., menu too limited to actually describe what is happening Although neither nursing nor medical diagnosis is usually formulated in terms of set theory, diagnostic error can be forced simply by incomplete mapping, i.e., whatever the patient's key symptom happens to be is not on the list to be charted, and therefore that information is neither sought nor noted. (Lundberg et al., 2008)
- Nursing documentation is critically dependent on the particular group of patients. Thus a very detailed motor examination is

need after spinal surgery, while an assessment of speech may be needed following an ischemic stroke (Hadley et al., 2005).

- No or minimal free text capability: on occasion, what is happening with the patient is completely off the menu (Moody, Slocumb, Berg, & Jackson, 2004).
- Absence of field specific text editors which results in completely inane entries becoming part of the medical record. The most easy to fix are numerical values which are out of range.
- Redundant documentation: having to enter exactly the same information in multiple places is an inexcusable and deliberate waste of nursing time (Moody et al., 2004).

Nursing Standards of Care and Documentation

The orientation of new nurses is an excellent time to convey the required standard of documentation for a particular institution. It is crucial, however, that nursing administrators insure that the local standard for nursing documentation, especially when software driven, meets the national standards. In litigation, the definition of nursing standards of documentation will come from those meeting all eight evidentiary foundations of an expert witness (Imwinkelried, 2002, p. 353), rather than from a software vendor. If new nurses are taught an inadequate standard, particularly if reinforced by software that makes adequate charting difficult or impossible, it is very difficult to remediate poor initial training.

QUALITY ASSURANCE ISSUES

Real measurement of quality in health care necessarily involves assessment of both outcome and process. This means (1) direct quantitative comparison of the expected versus the observed outcome for each patient for a variety of outcomes (e.g., hospital mortality, incidence of various complications, LOS, direct costs of services provided) and (2) careful scrutiny for material deviations from both medical and nursing standards of care. The real measurement of outcome differs enormously from the maintenance of the illusion of regulatory compliance that is labelled quality assurance by some.

Risk Stratification in Quality Assurance: Why IT Support is Essential

The interface between the medical record and the QA software must allow automatic transfer of selected fields to use risk adjustment software such as APACHE. Systematic data collection and comparison of predicted versus observed mortality is entirely dependent on the quality of the co-morbidity data available from the medical record. Independent of the enterprise data architecture and the core transaction systems, all data elements from all transaction systems must be available for analysis. For example, having nurses re-enter data elements available in the EPR into APACHE or other reporting systems is a waste of nursing time. While it is not necessary for the EPR and other transaction systems to have embedded statistical sophistication that is comparable to SPSS or SAS, it is absolutely necessary that the EPR be capable of reasonably facile generation of the appropriate files for analysis. Adaptive trial, time series analysis, and longitudinal analysis of patient outcomes require IT support. Analysis with respect to the performance of individual bedside providers requires human resources IT support as well. In the worst case scenario, using statistical methods to find a nurse serial killer requires computational support well beyond that available to most healthcare providers (Finkelstein & Levin, 1990).

Quantitative methods for comparing best real economic outcomes against best patient outcomes require real, job-based, cost accounting rather than the inaccurate and imprecise patient charge system. The EPR should be configured to do (or at least facilitate) real time cost accounting.

Under the Health Insurance Portability and Accountability Act of 1996 (HIPAA, Title 45, Subchapter C, US Code of Federal Regulations section 160, et. seq.) legislation governing the use, collection, and disclosure of personal health information several exceptions are outlined that allow information to be disclosed to those who need it. Under section 45 CFR 164.512 of the law (see http://edocket.access.gpo.gov/cfr_2007/octqtr/pdf/45cfr164.512.pdf) the HIPAA exceptions include uses and:

- Disclosures required by law;
- Disclosures for public health activities;
- Disclosures about victims of abuse, neglect or domestic violence;
- Disclosures for health oversight activities;
- Disclosures for judicial and administrative proceedings;
- Disclosures for law enforcement purposes;
- Disclosures about decedents;
- Disclosures for cadaveric organ, eye or tissue donation purposes;
- Disclosures for research purposes;
- Disclosures to avert a serious threat to health or safety;
- Disclosures for specialized government functions.

While each of these has its own set of regulatory rules that define specific use, hiding behind HIPAA to avoid measuring hospital performance is an indefensible position. This is especially true under circumstances in which a physician is asked to correct a chart or fill in a QA form on a particular patient and they are given, for instance, only a date. With all due respect, it is irrational for our IT colleagues to expect us to search for patients, for whom we might have provided services, based on a date alone.

MANAGEMENT ISSUES

The effective and efficient operation of any business enterprise is largely determined by whether those in charge have ongoing collection and analysis of crucial data. i.e., their information systems have matured from mere archives to decision support tools.

"IT is Killing Us!"

Dismissiveness towards human resources (HR), management, and providers, by IT can cripple your organization. As noted above, an electronic record can itself materially worsen working conditions to the point that physicians and nurses will leave (Milisen, Abraham, Siebens, Darras, Dierckx de Casterle, 2006; O'Brien-Pallas, Tomblin Murphy, & Shamian, 2008; Unruh, 2008). Recruitment and retention both suffer as word travels. This impact on core operations is magnified when IT limits the use of business intelligence to analyze problems from a fiscal and HR point of view. For example, analysis of unit-specific staff turnover rates as compared to the frequency of medical emergencies per patient day should be a relatively easy key performance indicator to compute. In virtually all institutions, however, this analysis would certainly require data re-entry or manual data tabulation first then re-entry. This is often a consequence of HR and medical emergency databases being maintained entirely separately (see http://www.ischool.drexel.edu/faculty/ssilverstein/failurecases/?loc=home).

Nursing Time: Where Does it Really go?

Using the nursing component of the EPR to measure login time and activity time is essential to real operations research. This key piece of operational information is rarely assessed except by external "time and motion" consultants. Relatively simple modifications to the EPR could provide useful information for management. For example, if 30% of ICU nursing time is spent on the telephone to Pharmacy trying to get scheduled medications, this is a tremendous waste of nursing time, and could be easily tracked by adding that to an EPR.

Strategic Management is related to Business Intelligence by Quantitative Measures of Organizational Performance

In simple language, (1) pick what you want to do, (2) pick how to spend your money, and (3) measure whether it works or not. Meaningful health care reform cannot be engineered until both (1) real-time measurement of system performance with respect to meaningful outcomes becomes an industry standard, and (2) cost accounting is done for every patient rather than on a "best guess" or more typically a "total guess" methodology. No meaningful health care cost containment will ever occur until both hospitals and insurance companies are forced as a matter of federal law to account for the direct actual costs of providing care, in a job-based fashion for each episode of patient care. The current system, in which total hospital charges are more than three times the total cost of operation (for example, see the Annual Report on the Financial Health of Pennsylvania's hospitals, PHC4, 2008), would be called accounting fraud in any other industry. The initial impact of Medicare's use of DRGs (diagnosis related groups) led to a substantial reduction in payment as compared to conventional fee-for-service (FFS) commercial insurance. Eventually the Center for Medicare and Medicaid Services (CMS) recognized that a one size fits all DRG classification led to under-reimbursement for complicated admissions. This led to the severity-adjusted DRG (Wynn & Scott, 2007) which comes closer to actual cost for complicated admissions, but does not yet represent actual individual job-based costing (Flood, 2001). As a consequence, cost-shifting (to FFS and self-pay patients) remains a key strategy in US hospitals

(Fisher, Goodman, Skinner, & Bronner, 2009; Folland, Goodman, & Stano, 2004). This variety of "voodoo" accounting would never be tolerated in any other sector, and gives ample opportunity for fraud, waste, abuse, and extraction of profit. Until the problem is fixed, American health care costs will vastly exceed American health care results, and an EPR that allows job-based cost accounting is crucial to the solution. Current accounting systems make so called micro-costing (true job based accounting) extremely labor intensive (Clement, Ghali, Donaldson, & Manns, 2009), and incorporating this function into the EPR is one possible solution.

HUMAN RESOURCES ISSUES

A large human resources problem occurs when IT has either been cut in terms of head count or populated with cheap labor to the point that it can neither recognize problems nor has any idea how to fix them on a long term basis. Perfectly good software running on an inadequate backbone will predictably and repeatedly fail, and if the experts in-house cannot recognize a hardware problem beyond the label "glitch in the server," the end-users will develop predictable Calvinist righteous indignation. Caution must also be taken in rewarding those in the clinical arena with a job in healthcare IT. Jobs in which considerable IT knowledge and skills are required if filled by those with no meaningful expertise in these areas will cripple the IT function.

Return on Investment on Training: Making IT Actually Work

The medical record, in principle, can be an excellent teaching tool if it is made interactive, and designed to help people learn how to use it. The complete absence of training and a worthless HELP function are great ways to insure "failure of buy-in during rollout," i.e., to insure permanent distrust of IT and the software imposed on the rest of the hospital (Baba, 1999).

Train Like You are Going to Fight

This phrase refers to the training being exactly the same as the actual software that will be delivered. Training that occurs six months prior to rollout and/or on software that differs materially from that which will actually be used (or worse, training by individuals who have no working knowledge of the software at all), is counterproductive. The training also needs to be focussed on what the audience will actually be doing, i.e., teaching CPOE to nurses may be counter-productive, and teaching physicians how to do nursing charting is an absolute waste of time. On the positive side, the EPR can be used both to measure and to insure regulatory compliance by having mandatory field completion for a desired level of documentation complexity.

The Role of Simulation in Effective Health Care Team Training

Practice charting on a simulated medical record, with authentic human or electronic coaches (as opposed to minimally knowledgeable "super-users") or a comprehensive help function, is an important tool, as is measurement of actual chart completion in real time (Hetzel, 1993).

There are five crucial steps or necessary elements in effective training (Braslow et al., 1997):

1. **Clinical Algorithm:** The clinical algorithm is simply the set of tasks that the end-user should be able to accomplish.
2. **Reliable and valid instrument:** A mock medical record that provides direct feedback (coaching) to the end-user can be used very effectively as a reliable and valid method of measuring task completion for training purposes. The key feature is the educational

test must ultimately provide a reliable and valid measure of on-the-job performance. In a closed employment setting, however, such validation is only possible if the real EPR measures the efficiency of staff using it.

3. **Iteratively refined curriculum:** The curriculum is the set of educational interventions used to alter performance in the affective, cognitive, or psychomotor domain. A key use of a mock medical record as a testing device is to determine what works and what doesn't work in terms of training.

4. **Educational test:** Real software measurement includes both the performance of the software as well as the performance of the end-users. This is true both for training as well as actual performance.

5. **Real life test:** In a real medical record, the rate of task completion should be measured both as a function of the effectiveness of IT training and as a measure of the individual's performance on the job. Persistent errors by end-users should be recorded and remediated.

Perspectives on Shared Governance: Why IT Must Support Ongoing Analysis of Turnover for HR

If the institution has a serious commitment to limiting nursing turnover, one necessary component of this is the analysis of why nurses leave. As noted above, nursing workload is a major determinant of nursing turnover. It is an inherent HR function to measure why people leave if causes of job dissatisfaction are clearly identified. Under reasonable circumstances, HR will be asked to identify why staff, especially nursing staff leave, as well as the rate at which they leave. There is also abundant data that nursing turnover is costly as well as dangerous to patient safety. The relative roles of poor IT training, poor software, and software-system interface problems should be part

of the routine search for causes of the epidemic of nursing dissatisfaction.

INFORMATION TECHNOLOGY ISSUES

While the impact of health informatics in health care has enormous potential to improve health care, it is quite clearly a two-edged sword. Given that ROI on IT can be negative in health care the same way it is in any other industry, due diligence is required.

Bad Informatics: Why Poorly Structured Systems and Software Impede Health Care

Systems which fail totally or hang frequently create repeated Skinnerian conditioning of those forced to watch the little hourglass (or for Mac users, the spinning wheel of death). That is, technophobic behavior is produced by classical conditioning. The technical difference between a phobia (an irrational fear) and a realistic fear is whether or not the feared event is actually going to occur. The more often the feared event actually does occur, the more likely the end-user is to be belligerent when they call the help desk. In some institutions, the help desk becomes known as the "helpless" desk as the personnel manning the phone may know less about the software in question than the end-user does.

Information technology could play an enormous role in re-engineering health care. The unfortunate organizational reality is illustrated by the following one-liner: How many psychiatrists does it take to change a light bulb? Only one, but the light bulb has to want to change. Just as IT professionals lament the cultural intransigence of healthcare professionals, healthcare professionals are generally appalled by the inflexibility in IT circles, leading to the single biggest lie in IT: "We can't do that." (Incidentally, the second biggest lie is: "That will be easy.") IBM generated roughly 43 billion USD in consulting fees for 2008 (see ftp://ftp.software.ibm.com/annualreport/2008/2008_ibm_annual.pdf). To the spectator of the IT market, this makes it appear that large consulting firms derive substantial revenue from getting jobs done that local IT can't or won't. Contrary to popular belief, end-users do actually notice the number of times a given ceiling is removed to rewire a given system, and this physical manifestation of bad planning further fuels distrust in both vendors and local IT administrators.

Quite unfortunately, many hospital administrators lack the quantitative background to make optimum use of the medical record as a management tool, in the context of an overall hospital information system. The impending merger of IBM and SPSS to "provide clients predictive analytics capabilities" (see http://www-03.ibm.com/press/us/en/pressrelease/27936.wss) demonstrates the critical importance of analytics (Davenport & Harris, 2007), for which the EPR really should be the basis.

Health Informatics

Health informatics or medical informatics is the intersection of information science, computer science, and health care. It deals with the resources, devices, and methods required to optimize the acquisition, storage, retrieval, and use of information in health and biomedicine. Health informatics tools include not only computers but also clinical guidelines, formal medical terminologies, and information and communication systems (Health informatics, Wikipedia).

This simple Wikipedia definition encompasses most of the features in general terms that should be in the EPR. The reality is, however, that some, if not most EPRs, fall far short of this goal.

Using an analogy from the avionics industry, the four basic tenets of network-centric warfare (Alberts, Gartska, & Stein, 1999) form the theo-

retical foundation for developing transformational mission capability packages. These are:

1. A robustly networked force improves information sharing.
2. Information sharing and collaboration enhance the quality of information and shared situational awareness.
3. Shared situational awareness enables self-synchronization.
4. These, in turn, dramatically increase mission effectiveness.

These basic principles should be incorporated into the design of the EPR as well. For example, when a physician enters a new order, a message should be sent to the patient's nurse to notify him/her that there is a new order. When new, abnormal laboratory findings become available the physician should be notified and a hyperlink to the conventional set of orders to treat the abnormality should be provided.

LEGAL ISSUES

Criminal Liability

Criminal liability may accrue in an HR or IT context for running a hospital or healthcare facility in a fashion in which those responsible knew or should have known that death or serious bodily injury would be the direct consequence of their actions or omissions. While corporate prosecution for homicide by reckless conduct (the precise language for this varies somewhat from jurisdiction to jurisdiction; see Brickley, 1995, pp. 661-678; Orland, 1995, pp. 410-438) is a remote likelihood, the death of a patient under circumstances in which the hospital as a corporation and specific corporate agents knew or should have known that depriving a nurse of adequate training, workable software, adequate staffing, or adequate equipment (cf. Title 28 of the Pennsylvania Code [Health and Safety]

Chapter 101, section 172, see http://www.pacode.com/secure/data/028/chapter101/s101.172.html) would lead to acts or omissions on his or her part sufficiently egregious to cause the patient's death could give rise to criminal liability. There are several precedents for corporate criminal and civil liability for the deaths of individuals endangered by those corporations (Wells, 1999).

Hospitals and all of their agents would be well advised to be respectful of the acumen of attorneys in general, both the plaintiff's bar as well as the prosecutors, with respect to epidemiologic computation, and ultimately the ability to subpoena the appropriate records for analysis. Specific methods for computing ratios of adverse events down to the level of the individual nurse are well known in the legal community (Finkelstein & Levin, 1990). Electronic documents that obscure this information, or render it inaccessible inadvertently will eventually warrant judicial attention (Cosgrave, 2008).

Electronic documents that deliberately prevent law enforcement efforts are obstruction of justice per se. Although computer forensics is well developed in other sectors, forensics of the electronic patient record is in its infancy. Fueled by multi-million dollar fees for litigation, it can be reasonably expected to grow rapidly (Sidoti, Asfendis, & Etish, 2009).

The hospital has unequivocal liability for the actions of its agents (Aiken & Catalano, 1994, pp. 189-211; Creighton, 1986, pp. 66-76), particularly in those instances in which the hospital has directed its agents to violate a longstanding practice, such as charting in an inappropriate fashion for the patient in question or deliberate violation of a hospital policy, medical or nursing standard of care, regulation or statute. The ideal EPR would compel, rather than prevent, appropriate charting, and the hospital bears absolute liability for the selection of the EPR and training its personnel. A poorly-constructed EPR creates a gold mine for attorneys as it may preclude effective charting. Lack of charting, inadequate charting, or worse,

wrong charting may be a direct contributor in failure to recognize that a patient is deteriorating and requires intervention. As above, the EPR should provide alarms to promote situational awareness, rather than obscuring the worsening condition of the patient.

Civil Liability

Doctors respond with variable degrees of righteous indignation when hospitals or their agents behave in a manner that materially interferes with the practice of medicine, i.e., creates a situation in which the physician is actively prevented from meeting the medical standard of care. Operating rooms that lack the correct instruments, pharmacies that take hours to get antibiotics to patients in septic shock, delayed recognition of the onset of shock of any variety by the bedside nursing staff, and admission of a critically ill patient to a portion of the hospital inadequately staffed for that patient, all carry the risk of death or serious bodily harm. Unfortunately, all of these circumstances are conceivably the direct consequence of a flawed EPR. One example of a program which, in large part, ultimately failed because of inadequate IT management was Kaiser-Permanente's kidney transplant program (see "We really did screw up" - http://www.baselinemag.com/c/a/Intelligence/QTEWe-Really-Did-Screw-UpQTE/1/).

An EPR which slows physician order entry to the point that the EPR must be abandoned should be considered a catastrophic failure, and forced reversion to manual methods should not be regarded by IT professionals as a routine thing. The HIT landscape is already littered with the wreckage of failed systems, both in the US and abroad. In no other professional community would failure at this rate be considered acceptable. Unfortunately, most hospitals, unbeknownst to their health care providers, increase the civil liability of their providers by buying from vendors insisting on the use of "hold harmless/non-warranty" and "learned intermediary" clauses. This contractual language asserts that the vendor has no liability whatsoever for catastrophic malfunction of their software, and that the health care provider knew or should have known how to work around the failure (Koppel & Kreda, 2009). Fortunately, not all courts have found the learned intermediary doctrine persuasive when the vendor is sued directly (see http://www.cov.com/files/upload/Karl.pdf).

Another aspect of regulatory law which has become prominent is the use of civil monetary penalties (CMP) for inadequately documented care pursuant to the Medicare documentation requirements. The ideal EPR would compel physicians to review documentation as it is created with respect to the appropriate coding of the encounter for billing purposes, and insure real time correction, if needed. Poor EPR design has the potential to propagate fraud on a sizable scale if required elements of the documentation are always omitted for a particular billing/coding level.

REGULATORY ASPECTS

In some jurisdictions, statistical evaluation of both patient outcome and staff functions are required. For example, in Pennsylvania, ICU directors have the following regulatory mandate, under Title 28 of the Pennsylvania Code [Health and Safety] Chapter 133, section 5 (see http://www.pacode.com/secure/data/028/chapter133/s133.5.html):

(a) Special care units shall be under the direction of a physician who has a special interest in and, preferably, additional experience in providing the type of care supplied by the special care unit. If an experienced physician is not available, direction of the unit may be provided by a medical staff committee.

(b) The special care unit director or committee shall be responsible for the establishment and implementation of written policies governing the following:

(1) Proper utilization of the service.

(2) Staff participation in appropriate training programs for safe and effective use of diagnostic and therapeutic equipment, for cardiopulmonary resuscitation and for other aspects of intensive care.

(3) Supervision of the collection and analysis of clinical data needed for the retrospective evaluation of care provided in the unit.

While embedded statistical algorithms are one option, a more robust option is the simple creation of files that can be analyzed using major statistical packages, such as SPSS or SAS. Computation of the off-service population (patients in other ICUs who should be in a specialty ICU) and boarders (patients in a specialty ICU who should be in a different ICU) should be an automatic function of the EPR and not require a massive data collection exercise as presently done in some institutions.

Staff training also should be an automatically tracked function, as well as staff experience and performance derived from the medical record of the patients for whom they care, both in terms of outcome as well as process, including documentation. Clinical data for evaluation of outcomes should be directly available from the medical record of patients, rather than hand audited followed by re-entry. The medical record is a primary source for the detection and evaluation of critical incidents, although a well integrated information system would automatically tag charts for review based on hospital-wide medical emergency teams being summoned. Medical records are the best single basis for the risk-adjusted evaluation of doctors, nurses, and individual units' performance.

While APACHE and other risk-adjusted systems provide very useful benchmark data, it is not the only means of doing this analysis. Real resources, however, are required to process this data, and to provide meticulous ongoing monitoring of mortality and morbidity, particularly related to deviations from the nursing standard of care that are, for every instance, reportable as noted below. The EPR must be configured to allow seamless analysis, and would be better if the EPR system had intrinsic capability to create files for this analysis rather than require elaborate database translations, or worse attempt to add homegrown statistical algorithms.

Human Resources Policy Issues and Regulations

Generic orientation policies for staff make no provision for arbitrary and capricious abandonment of the orientation process, especially as it pertains to documentation or other nursing standards of care and expertise. As a matter of law in Pennsylvania, Title 28 of the Pennsylvania Code [Health and Safety] Chapter 109, section 52 (see http://www.pacode.com/secure/data/028/chapter109/s109.52.html) requires an orientation as well as continuing education. One key feature of this regulation is that it requires actual measurement of the effectiveness of orientation annually at the very least. A mock medical record can be the test of the immediate educational effect of orientation on documentation. The real life effect, however, should be evaluated using real charting in the EPR. This regulation refers explicitly to "new and expanding programs," and requires an effective training program. The introduction of new software clearly qualifies under this regulation. It also points out as well each nursing unit and special care area requires a specific orientation. Part of the specific orientation for each unit is a detailed explanation of the nursing standards of documentation specific to that unit. A one-size-fits-all orientation, even with regard to software, does not best serve the needs of the several patient populations in different specialty units.

HR and IT Ramifications of Nursing Scope of Practice

The Ohio State Board of Nursing has a very simple scope of practice algorithm detailing legality, competency, safety, and accountability issues (see http://www.nursing.ohio.gov/pdfs/Practice/Decmodel.pdf). Careful monitoring should be part of the EPR to insure that nurses and physicians are not engaged in activities beyond the scope of their practice. One example, soon to be prosecuted in LA, is the illegal administration of a general anesthetic by a non-anesthesia provider Obviously the regulations for a particular state and federal jurisdiction should be incorporated as far as possible in the EPR to promote regulatory compliance.

Differential mortality data (specialty service versus off-service as above) is also a crucial piece of longitudinal analysis. Subtle trends with respect to both process variables (e.g., time from a neurological change being charted to imaging completed) and important outcomes (e.g., mortality) will be missed if not sought over time to insure a statistically adequate sample size.

An inadequate orientation to new software is even more egregious in the face of the special requirements required in Title 28 of the Pennsylvania Code [Health and Safety] Chapter 133, section 12. (see http://www.pacode.com/secure/data/028/chapter133/s133.12.html) Specifically, these educational programs should prepare special care unit personnel both (1) to recognize, interpret and record appropriate signs and symptoms in the critically ill patients, and (2) to perform specialized nursing procedures peculiar to the needs of patients in the unit. Critically ill specialty ICU patients have subtle nuances to their symptoms that if missed lead to irreparable harm. These nuances are not part of ordinary ICU care, particularly in those institutions that recognized the need for specialized ICU care decades ago. Similarly, nursing maintenance of lumbar and external ventricular drains

(EVD), intra-aortic balloon pumps, extracorporeal membrane oxygenation (ECMO), left and right ventricular assist devices, as well as an array of other devices unique to specialty patients, make it exceptionally unwise and under the language of this regulation illegal to deliberately fail to provide adequate training in new documentation software as it pertains to these devices. The ideal EPR would also provide local decision support for complex devices as well as immediate notification of on call personnel when they are needed.

The fact that a few institutions simply "go live" and offer minimal or no training in the use of software is neither an industry standard nor a legal precedent. Blatant sham "orientation" does not fit the spirit or the letter of the law, and both nurses and patients suffer materially when nursing education is done by on-the-job trial and error rather than any organized educational process.

A patient whose chart is not accessed on a periodic basis during a shift may or may not be monitored adequately. This is a key interface between IT, HR, and risk management goals. If the nursing staffing is not adequate to allow frequent monitoring and charting, the hospital has direct liability (1) for not knowing as a consequence of not looking and (2) allowing inadequate staffing to continue. The ideal medical record should have both login frequency and duration components.

Consider, for example, Pennsylvania House Bill 1033, an amendment to the Health Care Facilities Act, (http://www.legis.state.pa.us/CFDOCS/Legis/PN/Public/btCheck.cfm?txtType=PDF&sessYr=2009&sessInd=0&billBody=H&billTyp=B&billNbr=1033&pn=1190) which details safe staffing standards for professional nurses and requires the creation of a Professional Nurse Safe Staffing Committee to evaluate the hospital's staffing plan by collecting nursing-sensitive indicators including: (1) patient falls, (2) pressure ulcers, (3) staff mix, (4) hours per patient day, (5) nursing staff satisfaction, (6) patient satisfaction with: (a) nursing care, (b) overall care, (c) pain management, (d) patient education, (7) turnover

and vacancy rates, (8) overtime use, (9) use of supplemental staffing, (10) musculoskeletal injuries, (11) flexibility of human resource policies and benefit packages, (12) evidence of compliance with federal, state and local regulations, and (13) levels of nurse staff satisfaction.

Under the proposed legislation, the institution and HR have affirmative duties to monitor and correct staffing inadequacies, as well as outcomes related to staffing. "The budget is the budget" is not a defense on the occasions that patients are harmed or killed as a direct consequence of inadequate staffing. With respect to "road trips" (patients being taken off the unit for diagnostic procedures, sometimes for hours) and staffing, the ideal EPR would tell all concerned not only where the patient is but where the patient's nurse is as well.

As a matter of law in Pennsylvania, nurses are prohibited from taking assignments that involve highly specialized practice, unless the nurse has had the training appropriate to that area of nursing practice. The administrative maneuver of "pulling" nurses, i.e., temporarily assigning a nurse to a unit on which he or she does not work regularly, creates potential liability both for the nurse, as well as for the institution if the nurse is not adequately trained for that assignment. EPR logins on units where the nurse does not ordinarily work are available data. The EPR should make this information available for both administrative and regulatory review.

Further, engaging in a specific practice (such as using new software or an assignment for which she has not been oriented) under circumstances where the nurse knowingly lacks "the necessary knowledge, preparation, experience and competency to properly execute the practice" is a violation of nursing regulations.

The EPR ideally would be of assistance regarding the assessment of the patient with respect to normative data. The EPR could provide not only data but active decision support with respect to level of acuity, need to move to a more intensive care environment, and active reminders of both mandatory and prudent circumstances for physician notification, if not issuing the message to the physician itself. Additional decision support and real time evaluation of nursing care with immediate feedback is also an important EPR function.

One especially bizarre feature of current EPRs is they do not provide an automatic means of providing a short summary of the patient's history and the events of that shift. This is generally known as "report" and involves either a face-to-face discussion or an electronic or voice mail communication between either nurses or physicians regarding the patients for whom the care is being passed from one shift to another. Most electronic patient records do excel, however, at documenting exactly when a chart annotation is made, when alterations to annotations have been made, and making sure clearly delayed entries are duly labeled.

CONCLUSION

The EPR has enormous potential beyond a mere repository of clinical information. The strategy to make it an integrated management information system, however, requires real strategic commitment on the part of both EPR vendors and health systems as purchasers. It will also require an inter-disciplinary approach; if each department perceives itself as operating in a vacuum, the shared products ultimately meet all of the needs poorly. Making optimum use of the best available hardware will require very high-end technical knowledge. Moving toward both locally and nationally based processing of quality assurance data will also require specific investment.

REFERENCES

Aiken, T. D., & Catalano, J. T. (1994). *Legal, ethical, and political issues in nursing*. Philadelphia: F.A. Davis.

Alberts, D. S., Gartska, J. J., & Stein, F. P. (1999). *Network centric warfare: Developing and leveraging information superiority* (pp. 193–197). Washington, DC: CCRP Publication Series.

Baba, M. L. (1999). Dangerous liaisons: Trust, distrust, and information technology in American work organizations. *Human Organization, 58*, 331–346. Retrieved from http://findarticles.com/p/articles/mi_qa3800/is_199910/ai_n8856547/?tag=content;col1.

Braslow, A., Brennan, R. T., Newman, M. M., Bircher, N. G., Batcheller, A. M., & Kaye, W. (1997). CPR training without an instructor: development and evaluation of a video self-instructional system for effective performance of cardiopulmonary resuscitation. *Resuscitation, 34*, 207–220. doi:10.1016/S0300-9572(97)01096-4

Brickley, K. F. (1995). *Corporate and white collar crime. Cases and materials* (2nd ed.). Boston: Little, Brown and Company.

Clement, F. M., Ghali, W. A., Donaldson, C., & Manns, B. J. (2009). The impact of using different costing methods on the results of an economic evaluation of cardiac care: Microcosting vs gross-costing approaches. *Health Economics, 18*, 377–388. doi:10.1002/hec.1363

Cosgrave, C. M. (2008, February). Preparing your organization for E-discovery, Part 2. *HHN's Most Wired online magazine*. February 13, 2008. Available at: http://www.hhnmostwired.com/hhnmostwired_app/jsp/articledisplay.jsp?dcrpath=HHNMOSTWIRED/Article/data/Winter2008/080213MW_Online_Cosgrave&domain=HHNMOSTWIRED

Creighton, H. (1986). *Law every nurse should know* (5th ed.). Philadelphia: W.B. Saunders.

Davenport, T. H., & Harris, J. C. (2007). *Competing on analytics: The new science of winning*. Boston: Harvard Business School Press.

Finkelstein, M. O., & Levin, B. (1990). *Statistics for lawyers* (pp. 153–155, 489–490). New York: Springer-Verlag.

Fisher, E., Goodman, D., Skinner, J., & Bronner, K. (2009). *Health care spending, quality, and outcomes: More isn't always better.* A Dartmouth Atlas Project Topic Brief. Available at: http://www.dartmouthatlas.org/atlases/Spending_Brief_022709.pdf

Flood, C. M. (2001). *Profiles of six health care systems: Canada, Australia, the Netherlands, New Zealand, the UK, and the US*. A Report for the Standing Senate Committee on Social Affairs, Science and Technology. Available at: http://www.parl.gc.ca/37/1/parlbus/commbus/senate/Com-e/soci-e/rep-e/volume3ver1-e.pdf

Folland, S., Goodman, A. C., & Stano, M. (2004). *The economics of health and health care* (4th ed., pp. 311–313). Upper Saddle River: Pearson Education, Inc.

Hadley, F., Graham, K., & Flannery, M. (2005). Workforce management objective A: Assess use, compliance and efficacy: Nursing workload measurement tools. Ottawa, ON: Canadian Nurses Association. Retrieved from http://www.cna-aiic.ca/CNA/documents/pdf/publications/Workload_Measurement_Tools_e.pdf

Han, Y. Y., Carcillo, J. A., Venkataraman, S. T., Clark, R. S. B., Watson, R. S., & Nguyen, T. C. (2005). Unexpected increased mortality after implementation of a commercially sold computerized physician order entry system. *Pediatrics, 116,* 1506–1512. doi:10.1542/peds.2005-1287

Health informatics (2009, November 13). In *Wikipedia, the free encyclopedia*. Retrieved November 22, 2009 from http://en.wikipedia.org/wiki/Health_informatics

Hetzel, B. (1993). *Making software measurement work: Building an effective measurement program.* Boston: QED Publishing Group.

Imwinkelried, E. J. (2002). *Evidentiary foundations* (5th ed.). Newark, NJ: LexisNexis.

Koppel, R., & Kreda, D. (2009). Health care information technology vendors' "hold harmless" clause: Implications for patients and clinicians. *Journal of the American Medical Association, 301,* 1276–1278. doi:10.1001/jama.2009.398

Lundberg, C., Warren, J., Brokel, J., Bulechek, G., Butcher, H., McCloskey Dochterman, J., et al. (2008). Selecting a standardized terminology for the electronic health record that reveals the impact of nursing on patient care. *Online Journal of Nursing Informatics (OJNI), 12*(2). Available at http://ojni.org/12_2/lundberg.pdf

McIntyre, K. M. (1983). Medicolegal aspects of cardiopulmonary resuscitation (CPR) and emergency cardiac care. In McIntrye, K. M., & Lewis, A. J. (Eds.), *Textbook of advanced cardiac life support.* Dallas, TX: American Heart Association.

Milisen, K., Abraham, I., Siebens, K., Darras, E., & Dierckx de Casterle, B. (representing the BELIMAGE group). (2006). Work environment and workforce problems: A cross-sectional questionnaire survey of hospital nurses in Belgium. *International Journal of Nursing Studies, 43,* 745-754. Available at: http://www.scribd.com/doc/15107961/Autonomy-in-Nurses

Miller, R. A., Pople, H. E., & Myers, J. D. (1982). INTERNIST-1, an experimental computer-based diagnostic consultant for general internal medicine. *The New England Journal of Medicine, 307,* 468–476.

Moody, L. E., Slocumb, E., Berg, B., & Jackson, D. (2004). Electronic health records documentation in nursing: Nurses' perceptions, attitudes, and preferences. *Computers, informatics, nursing. CIN, 22*(6), 337–344.

O'Brien-Pallas, L., Tomblin Murphy, G., & Shamian, J. (2008 September). *Final report. Understanding the costs and outcomes of nurses' turnover in Canadian hospitals.* Nursing Health Services Research Unit. Available at: http://www. hhrchair.ca/images/CMSImages/TOS_Final%20 Report.pdf

Orland, L. (1995). *Corporate and white collar crime: An anthology.* Newark, NJ: LexisNexis Anderson Publishing.

Pennsylvania Health Care Cost Containment Council (PHC4). (June 2009). *An Annual Report on the Financial Health of Pennsylvania's Hospitals.* Financial Analysis: Volume One General Acute Care Hospitals. Available at: http://www. phc4.org/reports/fin/08/docs/fin2008report_volumeone.pdf

Rinkus, S. M., & Chitwood, A. (2002). Cognitive analyses of a paper medical record and electronic medical record on the documentation of two nursing tasks: patient education and adherence assessment of insulin administration. In *AMIA 2002 Annual Symposium Proceedings, Proc AMIA Symp*, (pp. 657-661).

Royal College of Nursing (RCN). (2008). *RCN e-Health Programme Policy Statement. Nursing content of electronic patient /client records.* Retrieved from http://www.rcn.org.uk/__data/assets/pdf_file/0010/176860/ndc_Briefing_June_08.pdf

Sidoti, M. S., Asfendis, P. E., & Etish, S. J. (2009). *Case Law Update: A discussion of key federal court decisions involving electronic discovery from 2008 to present.* Available at http://www. gibbonslaw.com/news_publications/articles. php?action=display_publication&publication_id=2718&practice_id=76

Thede, L. (2008 August). Informatics: The electronic health record: Will nursing be on board when the ship leaves? *Online Journal of Nursing Informatics, 13* (3). Available at www.nursingworld. org/MainMenuCategories/ANAMarketplace/ ANAPeriodicals/OJIN/Columns/Informatics/ ElectronicHealthRecord.aspx

Unruh, L. (2008). Nurse staffing: Key to good patient, nurse, and financial outcomes. Presentation at *136 Annual APHA Meeting*, San Diego, CA, October 26-29, 2008. Available at http:// www.dpeaflcio.org/programs/DPE_and_Professional_Associations/docs/APHA_2008_Nurse_ staffing_and_outcomes.pdf

Wells, C. (1999). The millennium bug and corporate criminal liability. *The Journal of Information, Law and Technology (JILT), 2.* Available at http://www2.warwick.ac.uk/fac/soc/law/elj/ jilt/1999_2/wells

Wynn, B. O., & Scott, M. (2007). *Evaluation of severity-adjusted DRG systems. Addendum to the Interim Report.* Santa Monica, CA: RAND Health. Available at http://www.rand.org/pubs/ working_papers/2007/RAND_WR434.1.pdf

Chapter 7
Extending Health Services to Rural Communities:
Telepediatrics in Queensland

Anthony C Smith
University of Queensland, Australia

Sisira Edirippulige
University of Queensland, Australia

ABSTRACT

Providing quality healthcare services to geographically isolated communities remains a considerable challenge to health service providers throughout the world. The conventional approach of referring patients to specialists often requiring the patient to travel long distances still remains mainstream. Meanwhile, the advancements in information and communication technologies (ICT) have acted as a catalyst for substantial changes in human activities in areas such as communication, commerce, and education. Researchers are exploring the potential of ICT to improve health services for patients in rural and remote areas. This chapter provides an overview of telemedicine applications and the experience of a research and health service which has pioneered the delivery of specialist pediatric services at a distance (telepediatrics) in Queensland, Australia.

INTRODUCTION

New technology has helped overcome barriers in distant communication and improve delivery of services in various fields of human activity. However, the impact of information and communication technologies (ICT) in health delivery has been somewhat slower than predicted – but its potential remains. This chapter provides an overview of telemedicine services that have been established in Queensland,

Australia by the Centre for Online Health (COH). Important factors related to the design and development of these services are explained.

BACKGROUND

Geographic isolation and restricted access to specialist health services are main contributing factors to the inequality of health care around the world. Remote communities often have limited health facilities and access to health care, particularly spe-

DOI: 10.4018/978-1-61520-733-6.ch007

cialist care, compared to their urban counterparts. Consequently health status of rural and remote populations is generally inferior. This is evident in both developed and developing counties. Rural communities are generally characterized with high rates of poverty, mortality, and limited access to primary health care services.

Recruitment and retention of health workers in rural areas is a problem characteristic of both developed and developing countries. For example, a US report indicated that there were only 55 primary care physicians per 100,000 residents in rural areas compared to 72 per 100,000 in urban areas. This number was significantly lower (36 per 100,000) in isolated and smaller rural areas (Fordyce, Chen, Doescher, & Hart, 2007). According to the same study, the number of specialists per 100,000 residents in rural areas was less than half that compared to urban areas, while the number of psychiatrists was three times less (Fordyce et al., 2007). Various studies have shown the disparity of specialist care in rural and urban communities. For example, studies have revealed that 25% of Americans living in rural areas receive suboptimal stroke care due to lack of facilities, specialists, and funding (Callison & Leira, 2008; Leira, Hess, Torner, & Adams, 2008). Another study has shown that people living in medically underserved areas have higher rates of cardiovascular morbidity and mortality (Colleran, Richards, & Shafer, 2007). Reports on rural America show that the level of care for patients with diseases such as diabetes is noticeably lower compared to their urban counterparts (Health Care in Urban and Rural Areas, Combined Years 2004-2006).

The situation in the developing world is even more daunting. The majority of the population in developing countries lives in rural areas where health facilities are significantly scarce. Lack of funding and low socio-economic development, coupled with difficult geography and topography, can be identified as some of the reasons for the poor health care in developing countries (Chou & Wang, 2009; Joshipura, 2008).

Thus, providing services to rural communities remains a serious challenge for health systems around the world. The conventional method is patient transfer from rural areas to urban centers. In some countries, systems are in place to refer patients from rural areas to urban tertiary centers and in some cases, governments provide subsidies to cover transport and other expenses of patients. The Royal Flying Doctor Service in Australia is an example of governments making special arrangements to transfer patients from rural locations (http://www.flyingdoctor.org.au/). Typically in developing countries patients voluntarily travel to urban hospitals to seek specialist care. Outreach services are another way to provide specialist care to rural areas; occasional visits of specialist health professionals to rural areas are arranged to meet the needs of local communities. Many of these methods involve long distance travel for patients, families, and/or health professionals. These methods are also costly, time consuming, and usually a major inconvenience.

THE AUSTRALIAN CONTEXT

In Australia, there are small townships which are located thousands of kilometers away from metropolitan regions. Access to health services and health facilities in such distant locations is often restricted. The difficulty of accessing health and medical services (particularly specialist care) in rural Australia is well documented (Humphreys, 1990; Judd & Humphreys, 2001). Consequently, rural communities often have poor health outcomes compared to their urban counterparts. The report published by the Australian Institute of Health and Welfare (AIHW) suggested that people living in remote communities have a higher mortality rate due to burns, fall, stroke, asthma, diabetes, homicide, suicide, and cancers (AIHW, 2008). There is also a significant increase in injury, mortality, hospital separation, and socio-economic disadvantages in rural and remote locations compared to capital cities (AIHW, 2008). The problems related to health status of indigenous communities - one of the main population-segments living in rural locations – have also been reported (Ring & Brown, 2003; WHO, 2008).

Queensland is the second largest state in Australia with a population of about 4.2 million. While two-thirds of the population is situated in the south-east region of the state, the remainder lives in major towns along the east coast (18%) or in remote townships (15%). The distances separating these communities from urban centers are vast. Because most specialist health centers are located in Brisbane, patients living in rural and remote communities usually have to travel to see the specialist if a referral is made.

In Queensland, the health department helps by subsidizing the travel costs incurred by regional patients through a Patient Travel Subsidy Scheme (PTSS) funded by the tate government. This is the conventional model of delivering specialist health services to patients living in non-metropolitan areas. Doctors in regional areas are able to refer patients to a specialist, which then makes them eligible for support through the scheme. In 2007, the travel scheme cost the Queensland health department approximately $32 million (Queensland Health, 2008).

Specialist outreach clinics are also arranged for groups of patients in selected rural and remote communities. These clinics involve specialist teams that travel out to communities to see patients periodically throughout the year. These clinics are well received in these areas and offer specialist staff valuable insight into the needs and resources available within these communities.

Efficient and cost effective ways of providing high quality health care to rural and remote communities is the only way to address the issue in these communities. Many alternative methods are being tested. The advancements in information and communication technologies (ICT) and the integration of these technologies in many

other human activities have prompted their use in health care.

Telemedicine

The use of ICT to deliver health services at a distance is known as telemedicine (Edirippulige & Wootton, 2006). The prefix 'tele' which derived from the Greek language, means 'at a distance'. A number of different terms such as telemedicine, telehealth, online health, and e-health are often used interchangeably. In this chapter, the term telemedicine is used.

Telemedicine applications can be used for clinical, administrative, education, or research purposes. Telemedicine can involve a wide range of participants and the exchange of information may take place locally within a hospital or internationally between hospitals or practitioners.

The communication involving telemedicine can be:

- Patient with health practitioners
- Practitioners with practitioners
- Patients with other patients
- Practitioner or patient accessing education material.

Telemedicine services may be further categorised according to the method of transmission used, i.e. either real-time (synchronous) or store-and-forward (asynchronous). Parties involved in a real-time telemedicine consultation communicate synchronously via a telecommunication network. Telephone discussions or videoconferencing sessions are examples of real-time applications. The primary advantage of real-time telemedicine is that there is usually no detectable time delay between the information being transmitted and received, that is, the parties concerned can interact as though they were present in the same room.

Store-and-forward telemedicine involves the transmission of stored information from one site to another over a period of time. Store-and-forward telemedicine, also referred to as asynchronous or pre-recorded, involves information being captured and then transmitted to the other party (for instance, a radiologic image for examination by a specialist). Common examples include communication via email or facsimile. The main advantage of this method of working is that the parties involved can work independently from one another, i.e., they do not have to be present at a pre-arranged time. The choice between real-time or store-and-forward telemedicine is often dependent on the type of information that is being shared, the facilities/telecommunications available, and the urgency of the response for continued health care (Edirippulige & Wootton, 2006).

Whether the telemedicine interaction is real time or store-and-forward, the technology required comprises three main components:

1. Equipment to capture the information
2. Telecommunications to transmit this information between sites
3. Equipment to display the information at the relevant sites.

It is important to understand that videoconferencing is just one of many different modalities used for telemedicine. The choice of communication technique will depend on the information that has to be transmitted, available telecommunications, urgency, and cost.

There are four types of information transfer common in telemedicine:

1. Audio: the most common form involves the transmission of speech using telecommunications. The telephone is the most common example to date. It is also possible to transmit heart or breath/lung sounds using an electronic stethoscope.
2. Text: messages can be transmitted by using fax machine for instance. However, better quality transmission can be achieved if

documents are transmitted in digital form. This is easy if the information already exists as a computer file. Alternatively, printed documents can be digitized using a flatbed scanner or a digital camera and then transmitted as still images.

3. Still images: still images may be transmitted for various health purposes such as diagnosis, management, and education. Low cost digital cameras are capable of capturing good quality images that can be transmitted to specialists for consultation. A flatbed scanner can be used to produce digital images or charts such as ECG traces. X-ray films can also be digitised this way, although when high quality diagnostic images are required, the equipment involved can be costly.
4. Moving images: high quality moving images can provide a better opportunity to communicate live. The use of commercial videoconferencing equipment for health related consultations is gaining popularity. Experiments have been conducted to examine the feasibility and effectiveness of various low cost video streaming techniques for health purposes including clinical, administration, education, and research (Lemaire, Boudrias, & Greene, 2001; Mulholland et al., 1999; Norris et al., 2002). Although videoconferencing techniques do not allow aspects such as touch, smell, and physical feeling, studies have shown the effectiveness of this tool in disciplines such as dermatology, neurology, and psychiatry.

Telemedicine applications in countries such as Australia, where there are significant distances, make sense in dealing with a widespread population dispersed over a large land area. The Queensland Telepediatric Service (QTS) was developed as an alternative method of delivering health services to regional and remote area of the state.

TELEPEDIATRICS

In November 2000, a telemedicine trial was initiated by the Centre for Online Health (COH) in close partnership with the Royal Children's Hospital (RCH) in Brisbane and selected regional hospitals in Queensland. Given that the conventional method of sending patients to the specialist was well established, a central referral center for telemedicine referrals was developed. The basic tenet of this initiative was to try to make telemedicine a convenient option, rather than a burden for the referring clinician.

The QTS gives regional clinicians a single point of contact for referring patients for a specialist consultation. A dedicated 1-800 toll-free telephone number is available that connects the referrer with a telepediatric coordinator who collects referral information and arranges a response by an appropriate specialist. The telepediatric coordinator plays an important role making sure all requests are managed with a minimal waiting time; all referrals have a guaranteed response time of 24 hours.

Since the QTS began, over 9,000 consultations have been conducted for thousands of children in Queensland. The COH currently delivers telepediatric services to 97 regional hospitals in Queensland and several health centers in northern New South Wales. The communication modes used are email, telephone, and videoconferencing. The majority, approximately 90%, of all referrals made to the telepediatric service result in a videoconference. The COH have installed a number of dedicated videoconference systems at selected sites for pediatric work but predominantly relies on the large network of videoconferencing systems available in public hospitals and health centers throughout Queensland. To date, more than 650 videoconferencing units have been installed and are managed by the Queensland Health department.

The QTS, which is based centrally within the RCH in Brisbane, has two specially equipped videoconference studios which are used routinely for the delivery of telepediatric services.

The studios contain commercial videoconferencing equipment including a video document camera, a laptop computer, and DVD recorder. ISDN and IP connectivity allows the COH to connect to other videoconference systems when required. Depending on the type of consultation

Figure 1. Specialist consultation via videoconferencing (centre for online health)

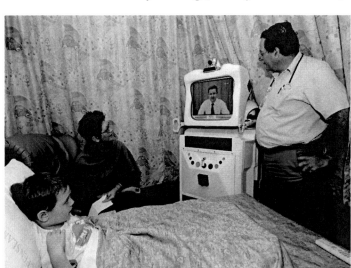

and the information which is being transmitted, the majority of connections are performed using a transmission speed of at least 384 kbit/s. However, in some regional areas, access to telecommunications is restricted to just 128 kbit/s.

Since the trial began in 2000, the telepediatric service has grown into a routine service at the RCH. Most of the telepediatric clinics are scheduled 12 months in advance in much the same way as the specialist outpatient department at the RCH. The telepediatric services cover 37 different subspecialist areas and involve more than 240 medical, nursing, and allied health staff (Smith & Gray, 2009). Some of the sub-specialties include cardiology, dermatology, diabetes, general pediatrics, neurology, oncology, orthopedics, post-acute burns care, psychiatry, and surgery (Justo et al., 2004; Smith, Batch, Lang, & Wootton, 2003; Smith, Youngberry, Mill, Kimble, & Wootton, 2004).

Mobile Telemedicine

In 2004, the COH introduced a mobile and wireless telemedicine unit at a regional hospital as an extension of services offered by the QTS. The mobile telemedicine unit gave regional clinicians the opportunity to consult with RCH specialists during virtual ward rounds at the bedside. The first mobile unit was stationed at a regional hospital in Gladstone (approximately 500 km north from Brisbane) where there has been no pediatrician for some years. To ensure that the videoconference facilities were child-friendly, the COH developed a mobile videoconference system in the shape of a robot (Smith, Coulthard, Clark, Armfield, Taylor, Goffe, et al., 2005). During ward rounds the unit was wheeled to the patient's bedside for the consultation.

The specialist in Brisbane is able to communicate directly with the local staff, patient, and family. Once the feasibility of these systems was demonstrated further funding was obtained to expand the network of mobile robot systems to five regional hospitals in Queensland.

One important feature of the mobile units is the remote management capability. These systems are fully maintained by QTS coordinators in Brisbane. All connections to the mobile systems are managed remotely, including call connections and daily quality tests.

Indigenous Health Screening

A combination of factors has led to the need for more innovative methods of providing specialist

Figure 2. Robot videoconference consultation at the bedside

health services to Indigenous children in central and far north Queensland. These factors include the large distances, the logistics of sending specialists to remote regions, and the high incidence of chronic disease, such as *otitis media,* amongst patients in these areas (Leach, 1999).

In 2008, the COH commenced a research trial of a mobile health screening service (http://www.healthescreen4kids.org) that will allow health workers to travel to surrounding communities and provide routine screening of children.

Regardless of where screening takes place, health workers will collect patient information and digital images of the patient's eyes and ears, together with a clinical history, hearing assessment, and a health risk questionnaire. This information is stored on a computer and transmitted via the Internet to a secure database which is routinely monitored by a team of specialists based in Brisbane. For example, children with suspected ear disease or hearing loss will have their records reviewed by an ENT specialist in Brisbane who will be able to view the images and data for diagnostic purposes and provide a recommended treatment plan for the primary care provider in the rural or remote community. If surgery is required, patients will be categorized according to urgency and scheduled for the next available clinic.

The need to address critical health issues of indigenous communities in Australia has been widely discussed (WHO, 2008). Improving the health status of Aboriginal children has been one of the priority areas of the Australian government. There is potential for this community-based telemedicine screening program to be expanded to other Aboriginal and Torres Strait Islander communities throughout the country that face similar challenges.

EVIDENCE FOR FEASIBILITY, QUALITY IMPROVEMENT, AND COST-SAVINGS

The COH has been responsible for examining the feasibility, clinical, and economic benefits of telemedicine services compared to traditional models of care available. In the context of telepediatrics, had the service not been available, many of these children and their families would have had to travel hundreds or thousands of kilometers to see the pediatric specialist in Brisbane. In addition to the reduced travel costs, families may be spared the stress, expense, and inconvenience of a journey to Brisbane. Telemedicine links also allow the local clinicians to play a significant role

Figure 3. Mobile health screening service for indigenous children

in the consultation process by interacting (real-time) with the specialist during the consultation (Smith et al., 2004).

User satisfaction from the patient and clinician has been shown to be consistently high (Smith et al., 2005). For many pediatric specialists who have provided their expertise to patients in remote areas, telemedicine has been integrated as an alternative method of consulting with their patients. Evidence shows that a substantial proportion of outpatient appointments can be performed at a distance; for example, 17% of all burns outpatient appointments at the RCH are done by telemedicine (Smith et al., 2004).

Clinicians from both sides (i.e., consultants at tertiary hospitals and clinicians in regional locations) have valued the opportunity that telemedicine offers for collegial communication. One of the major problems encountered by rural and regional health workers is the professional isolation. The QTS has offered an opportunity for the regional staff to develop closer contacts with urban counterparts and specialists. Regional staff has also found the telepediatric consultations to be of educational value. Meanwhile, the ability to discuss patients' conditions, treatment, and management plans with the specialist has been identified as a key benefit for regional staff (Justo et al., 2004).

The COH has also undertaken several economic analyses of the telemedicine programs. The studies have demonstrated that telemedicine programs provide significant cost savings for the health services due to reduced travel costs. For example, a cost minimization analysis of the QTS for two hospitals over a 5-year period showed that the costs of providing telepediatric services were about $1 million, compared to the potential cost of $1.6 million had all patients travelled to see the specialist in person (Smith, Scuffham, & Wootton, 2007).

Another study that compared the costs reported by families who travelled to see the specialist in person, to those families who had a videoconfer-ence appointment showed significant differences in time spent attending the appointment and out-of-pocket expenses (Smith, Youngberry et al., 2003).

BARRIERS TO EXPANSION OF TELEMEDICINE

One may question why new advancements in ICT have not had a major impact on the way that specialist health services are delivered. Although the potential of ICT in health care seems straightforward, the ability to seamlessly integrate ICT, here in the context of telemedicine, has been slow and fragmented. While there are examples of successful telemedicine services reported in the literature, we still unfortunately see failed and expensive attempts that are mainly the result of poor planning, consultation, and enquiry (Wootton & Tahir, 2004).

One common mistake made by telemedicine designers is giving priority to technology. This over-emphasis on the technology can often be misleading. While designing a telemedicine service, it is extremely important to undertake a thorough needs analysis. One should carefully examine the pros and cons of existing health services, if applicable, with consideration of how telemedicine might be useful. The selection of all other components in the telemedicine program, including the technology, must then be determined in alliance with these goals.

Telemedicine programs developed at the COH are not primarily technology-focused but instead are tailored to the clinical needs and operational requirements identified by the clinicians. It is important that telemedicine systems are easy to use, present no hindrance to the clinicians, and are conveniently accessible. It is also important that telemedicine services complement existing services, such as hospital outpatient services and travelling outreach clinics, provided by specialists (Smith & Gray, 2009).

This insight essentially comes as a result of the close interaction with clinicians who consequently use telemedicine. Successful telemedicine services cannot be developed in isolation from the clinicians. Understanding the needs of the clinicians and accommodating them is the key to a sustainable telemedicine service. It is also vital to give clinicians the opportunity to play a leading role in designing, developing, and running telemedicine projects (Yellowlees, 2006).

CONCLUSION

Telemedicine has tremendous potential for the delivery of health services to underserved areas. This chapter presents a brief overview of our experience with telepediatrics in Queensland, Australia, providing a range of services that have demonstrated promising results. The models of care developed for telepediatrics in Queensland should be just as useful for other medical disciplines where the need is likely to be as important.

REFERENCES

Australian Institute of Health and Welfare (AIHW). (2008). *Rural, regional and remote health: Indicators of health status and determinants of health, (cat. no. PHE 97)*. Canberra, Australia: Australian Institute of Health and Welfare.

Callison, R. C., & Leira, E. C. (2008). Strategies to improve acute stroke care of patients in rural and other geographically dispersed areas. *Current Treatment Options in Neurology, 10*(6), 450–454. doi:10.1007/s11940-008-0047-4

Chou, W. L., & Wang, Z. (2009). Regional inequality in China's health care expenditure. *Health Economics, 18*(Suppl 2), S137–S146.

Colleran, K. M., Richards, A., & Shafer, K. (2007). Disparities in cardiovascular disease risk and treatment: demographic comparison. *Journal of Investigative Medicine, 55*(8), 415–422. doi:10.2310/6650.2007.00028

Edirippulige, S., & Wootton, R. (2006). Telehealth and communication. In Conrick, M. (Ed.), *Health informatics, transforming health care with technology* (pp. 266–278). Melbourne, Australia: Thomson.

Fordyce, A. M., Chen, F. M., Doescher, M. P., & Hart, L. G. (2007). 2005 physician supply and distribution in rural areas of the United States. *Final Report #116*. Seattle, WA: WWAMI Rural Health Research Center, University of Washington.

Health Care in Urban and Rural Areas. Combined Years 2004-2006. (2006). *Update of Content in MEPS Chart-book No. 13*. Rockville, MD: Agency for Health Care Policy and Research. Retrieved from http://www.ahrq.gov/data/meps/chbook13up.htm

Humphreys, J. S. (1990). Super-clinics or a country practice? Contrasts in rural life and health service provision in northern NSW. In D.J. Walmsley (Ed.), Change and adjustment in Northern NSW, (pp. 73-84). Armidale: University of New England.

Joshipura, M. K. (2008). Trauma care in India: current scenario. *World Journal of Surgery, 32*(8), 1613–1617. doi:10.1007/s00268-008-9634-5

Judd, F., & Humphreys, J. (2001). Mental health issues for rural and remote Australia. *The Australian Journal of Rural Health, 6*(5), 254–258. doi:10.1046/j.1440-1584.2001.00417.x

Justo, R., Smith, A. C., Williams, M., Westhuyzen, J. V., & der, ., Murray, J., Sciuto, G., & Wootton, R. (2004). Paediatric telecardiology services in Queensland: a review of three years' experience. *Journal of Telemedicine and Telecare, 10*(Suppl 1), 57–60. doi:10.1258/1357633042614258

Leach, A. J. (1999). Otitis media in Australian Aboriginal children: An overview. *International Journal of Otorhinolaryngology, 49*(Suppl 1), S173–S178. doi:10.1016/S0165-5876(99)00156-1

Leira, E. C., Hess, D. C., Torner, J. C., & Adams, H. P. Jr. (2008). Rural-urban differences in acute stroke management practices: a modifiable disparity. *Archives of Neurology, 65*(7), 887–891. doi:10.1001/archneur.65.7.887

Lemaire, E. D., Boudrias, Y., & Greene, G. (2001). Low-bandwidth Internet-based videoconferencing for physical rehabilitation consultations. *Journal of Telemedicine and Telecare, 7*(2), 82–89. doi:10.1258/1357633011936200

Mulholland, H. C., Casey, F., Brown, D., Corrigan, N., & Quinn, M., McCord, B.et al. (1999). Application of a low cost telemedicine link to the diagnosis of neonatal congenital heart defects by remote consultation. *Heart (British Cardiac Society), 82*, 217–221.

Norris, T. E., Hart, G. L., Larson, E. H., Tarczy-Hornoch, P., Masuda, D. L., & Fuller, S. S. (2002). Low-bandwidth, low-cost telemedicine consultations in rural family practice. *The Journal of the American Board of Family Practice, 15*(2), 123–127.

Queensland Health. (2008). *Queensland Health Annual Report 2007-2008.* Brisbane, Australia: Queensland Government. Available at http://www.health.qld.gov.au/publications/corporate/annual_reports/annualreport2008/default.asp

Ring, I., & Brown, N. (2003). The health status of indigenous peoples and others. *British Medical Journal, 327*, 404–405. doi:10.1136/bmj.327.7412.404

Smith, A. C., Batch, J., Lang, E., & Wootton, R. (2003). The use of online health techniques to assist with the delivery of specialist paediatric diabetes services in Queensland. *Journal of Telemedicine and Telecare, 9*(Suppl 2), 54–57. doi:10.1258/135763303322596273

Smith, A. C., Coulthard, M., Clark, R., Armfield, N., Taylor, S., & Goffe, R. (2005). Wireless telemedicine for the delivery of specialist paediatric services to the bedside. *Journal of Telemedicine and Telecare, 11*(Suppl. 2), 81–85. doi:10.1258/135763305775124669

Smith, A. C., & Gray, L. (2009). Telemedicine across the ages. *The Medical Journal of Australia, 190*(1), 15–19.

Smith, A. C., Scuffham, P., & Wootton, R. (2007). The cost and potential savings of a novel telepaediatric service in Queensland. *BMC Health Services Research, 7*, 35. doi:10.1186/1472-6963-7-35

Smith, A. C., Youngberry, K., Christie, F., Isles, A., McCrossin, R., & Williams, M. (2003). The family costs of attending hospital outpatient appointments via videoconference and in person. *Journal of Telemedicine and Telecare, 9*(Suppl 2), 58–61. doi:10.1258/135763303322596282

Smith, A. C., Youngberry, K., Mill, J., Kimble, R., & Wootton, R. (2004). A review of three years experience using email and videoconferencing for delivery of post-acute burns care to children in Queensland. *Burns, 30*(3), 248–252. doi:10.1016/j.burns.2003.11.003

Wootton, R., & Tahir, M. S. M. (2004). Challenges in launching a Malaysian teleconsulting network. In Whitten, P., & Cook, D. (Eds.), *Understanding health communication technologies* (1st ed., pp. 11–18). San Francisco: John Wiley and Sons, Inc.

World Health Organisation (WHO). (2008). Australia's disturbing health disparities set Aboriginals apart. *Bulletin of the WHO, 86*(4), 241-320. Retrieved December 15, 2008, from http://www.who.int/bulletin/volumes/86/4/08-020408/en/index.html

Yellowlees, P. (2006). Successfully developing a telemedicine system. In Wootton, R., Craig, J., & Patterson, V. (Eds.), *Introduction to telemedicine*. London: Royal Society of Medicine Press.

Chapter 8
Health Service Quality Information Comparison:
A Preliminary Investigation

Yun Wan
University of Houston, USA

Susan Evans-Mueller
HCA Shared Services Group, USA

ABSTRACT

This chapter investigates the provision of public health information, especially health service quality and cost information, to the general public in the United States. The authors first review the health system of the US from three aspects: its public policy, structure, and accreditation of health institutions. Then the complexity of health information provision and the challenges in its interpretation are identified and analyzed. "Comparison-shopping" is introduced as a new mode of decision support for individuals to select health services, and examples of its current applications are given. The comparison-shopping mechanism in the e-commerce industry and the health information industry are compared and the different driving forces in health information comparison-shopping are analyzed. Several directions for future research are provided for researchers and health practitioners.

INTRODUCTION

Health service information includes service provider information, service cost information, and service quality information. They are three integral parts of quality health care for consumers. Service provider information allows consumers to find the health service they need. Service cost information provides consumers with the price of different care and allows consumers to compare and select commensurate support for their health needs. Finally, service quality information allows consumers to compare and pick the quality health services and providers from an otherwise seemingly identical set of them, thus making informed decisions.

With the popularity of the Web, there is increasingly easy access to service provider information and insurance information by the general public, however, most health service quality information is not accessible or easily accessed by the public. Thus in this chapter, we will focus on a discussion of health service quality information.

DOI: 10.4018/978-1-61520-733-6.ch008

Service quality information such as the service ratings of hospitals, doctors, dentists, and other specialists is critical for the general welfare of the society, because it makes it easier for patients to evaluate and compare different providers and make informed decisions. Though in the United States there are many efforts being spent by the government and independent organizations on improving the *quality* and *accessibility* of such information, the *effective and efficient use* of such information by the general public is not receiving equal attention. American society is a highly mobile society and people relocate frequently, thus there is a constant need for individuals and families to find new health services. Efficient and effective access to health service quality information would not only improve the quality of health services offered by service providers due to the pressure of comparisons among providers, but also bring benefit to consumers. The outcome is an overall increase in the quality of health services.

Recently, the "comparison-shopping" model has emerged as an innovative way to increase the efficacy of health service information provision especially quality information. Though still in its nascent stage of development, now a consumer could conduct comparison-shopping on health service information ranging from selection of health insurance provider, hospitals, or physicians, to prescription drugs. These services are still in a very primitive stage compared with a commodity comparison-shopping market such as shopping.com. But with a simple comparison list of service ratings of local dentists, for instance, a couple moved-in to a new neighborhood, could choose a quality dentist instead of taking a random chance.

This new way of obtaining health services information has important social consequences. If such a practice is widely used, it will increase service quality of health providers through competition. It could also reduce the cost of health care in general because cost is one aspect of comparison attributes valued by consumers. Take the example of insurance, Brown and Goolsbee (2002) provided empirical evidence on how Internet comparison shopping sites affected the price of life insurance in the 1990s. They found that growth of the Internet and comparison-shopping sites have reduced term life insurance cost by 8 to 15 per cent and increased consumer surpluses by $115 to $215 million per year and perhaps more. Though term life insurance is a relatively simple insurance compared with health insurance, we can reasonably expect that consumers will be able to compare health insurance and health insurance providers and coverage more effectively with more advanced decision support technology and get comparable benefits as those seen with term life insurance.

Currently, comparison-shopping on health-related information is provided by various entities, such as commercial enterprises, non-profit organizations, and government agencies. An analysis of this topic needs to address the complex structures of the U.S. health system. This complexity makes the underlying mechanisms of comparison-shopping in the health industry significantly different from its counterpart in the electronic commerce market. For instance, in the healthcare industry, public policy rules, while in the e-commerce industry, the invisible hand of the market rules.

Thus, we have to explore this topic from the structure of the U.S. health system including its public policy, the major stakeholders, as well as accreditation of the health system. Then we have analyzed the underlying mechanism of comparison-shopping in the health industry for different health-related categories such as insurance, service providers, and prescriptions. These were compared with those in the electronic commerce industry by identifying the driving forces in each category. Finally, we propose some future research directions.

AN OVERVIEW OF HEALTH ISSUES IN THE UNITED STATES

The Overall Health System

An essential foundation for our understanding the complexity of health information provision is the overall structure of the health system in the U.S. that can be illustrated by looking at the three basic groups of stakeholders: the *patients*, the *providers,* and the *payers*.

The patient population consists of the general public seeking health services. The health providers include physicians, nurses, clinical technicians, pharmacists, nurse practitioners, allied health specialists, and many other health professionals. Most provide health service via physicians' offices or in health facilities or clinics. The payers include self-pay patients, private insurance companies, indemnity plans, employers, and government payers (such as Medicare and Medicaid). The majority of the stakeholders are connected via three basic organizational forms: HMOs (Health Maintenance Organizations), PPOs (Preferred Provider Organizations), and (POS) Point of Service Plans.

There is a variety of health services available to patients. They include acute care, ambulatory care, assisted living, behavioral health care, home care, and hospice care. Home care includes home medical equipment services, home health professional services, personal care and support services, pharmaceutical services, etc. Hospice programs provide support for terminally ill patients and their families. There are also long term care services, such as nursing homes, skilled nursing facilities, or extended care services that provide 24-hour nursing or rehabilitative care to both young and old.

The hospital system in the U.S. is very complex. Overall, there are over 6,500 hospitals in the United States. The majority of them are general hospitals set up to deal with the full range of medical conditions for which most people require treatment. More than 1,000 hospitals specialize in a particular disease or condition (e.g. cancer, rehabilitation, psychiatric illness) or in one type of patient (e.g. children, the elderly).

Among these hospitals, some are teaching or community hospitals that are affiliated with medical schools. Patients in such hospitals have access to highly skilled specialists who teach medical students and residents and are usually familiar with new medical treatments. Some are voluntary hospitals or non-profit, community facilities operating under religious or other voluntary charitable auspices. In such hospitals, a board of trustees selected from the community's business and professional people are responsible for the appointment of a manager for administration of the daily operations. There are also for-profit commercial hospitals or proprietary hospitals owned by corporations or, less often, by individuals such as doctors who practice at the hospital. Hospital corporations usually own many facilities located in several states, and they often own nursing homes or other types of health care facilities as well. There are also government-supported hospitals, which are government owned facilities and can include facilities such as the VA (Veterans Administration) health facilities (Rosenberg, 1995).

The different origins and operation styles of these hospitals mean that their provision of service quality information to the public is also varied. For example, teaching hospitals/academic health centers, are usually in the position of providing cutting-edge health services, so they have the motivation to provide and compare their service to others. Proprietary hospitals might also wish to compare their quality of service information, because they want to attract more patients.

In addition, patients often travel from one facility to another for different health care needs. A patient may need acute care for a heart attack in one hospital, and rehabilitation services afterwards in another facility, home care for follow-up or

Table 1. Classification of health information

Health Information	Availability[1]	Comparability[2]	Protected or not
Patients			
- health conditions	High	n/a	Protected by HIPAA
- medical history	High	n/a	Protected by HIPAA
Health Service			
- general health information	High	Medium	Public
- service availability	High	Medium	Public
- service quality	Low	Low	Public
Pharmacy			
- pharmacy information	High	Low	Public
- pharmacy cost	Medium	Low	Public
Insurance			
- coverage and cost	High	High	Public
- credibility	Low	Low	Public

Note:

1. The accessibility of such type of information to the public and to what extent (low, medium, and high).

2. Whether the general public could benefit from the comparison of such type of information and to what extent (low, medium, and high).

with problems, visits to the primary care physician, etc – which makes it more complex on an individual user basis.

Some health information, particularly that related to general descriptions of medical or health conditions and diseases is readily available to health consumers (see Table 1), while specific, individual personal health information is limited in accessibility. As we can see, the federal HIPAA or the Health Insurance Portability and Accountability Act legislation of 1996 regulates and protects an individual's personal health information. Note that availability of specific medical histories and personal health information is "high" to those who need to access it for provision of health care, but is not available to the general public. HIPAA provides little guidance on the review, analysis, and release of health service information, including health service quality, medical costs including prescription drugs, as well as health insurance costs.

The lack of governance on public health information on the Internet poses serious concerns in both the health care community and among patients/consumers. For example, there is little control over the publication of general health information on the Internet, and health professionals have already voiced concerns that anyone can publish non-validated information on the Internet (Purcell, Wilson & Delamothe, 2002).

Consequently, the individual must be able to ascertain what information is accurate and legitimate, which, in many cases, is beyond their ability. So they often choose the popularity of a web site as the measure of accuracy of the information. However, research has found that the popularity of a health information web site only related to the type of information it contained, not to the quality of that information (Meric et al., 2002).

Compared with the relatively chaotic regulation of general health information on the Web, the information on service availability, quality, insurance, as well as pharmacy information and costs, are more accurate and objective. However, these three categories of information are provided by different organizations and companies, thus we have to examine them separately.

Health insurance information is provided by insurance companies and is subject to the general regulation of the government on the insurance industry, as well as specific regulations related to health policy clauses. Pharmacy information and costs are provided by pharmaceutical companies and drug vendors, respectively. This is objective information, but economic motivations create a lot of variations in the cost. Thus, comparison-shopping technologies could be introduced to potentially reduce the average cost of pharmaceuticals and bring more benefit to patients. Service availability information is generally available on the Web through web sites of clinics, hospitals, and other medical facilities. Information aggregation technology also makes the search of these services much easier nowadays. Service *quality* information is more difficult to access by the general public because its provision is largely undertaken by the accreditation organizations of the health industry as described in the next section.

THE ACCREDITATION SYSTEM FOR HEALTH SERVICES

Service quality information is mainly collected by accreditation organizations in the U.S. These accreditation bodies also play a role in regulating the quality of health services. The Joint Commission, formerly, the Joint Commission on Accreditation of Health Organizations (JCAHO), is a private sector US-based, non-profit organization. It is one of the best known primary accreditation bodies in the U.S. (more information about this organization can be obtained from their official website: http://www.jointcommission.org/). It evaluates and accredits approximately 16,000 health care organizations in the United States. The information collected in the Joint Commission surveys is of benefit to the healthcare facility, and is especially beneficial to patients considering utilizing a healthcare facility.

The Joint Commission survey teams, composed of health professionals, gather information by visiting health facilities, interviewing staff and patients, and examining records and procedures. The assessed performance is compared to the Joint Commission's standards and quality expectations. Hospitals must meet or exceed the requirements in order to achieve or maintain accreditation. Accreditation decisions are assigned in different categories based on the level of compliance, ranging from fully accredited, provisional accreditation and conditional accreditation, to denial of accreditation.

Another important evaluation survey is conducted by the Center for Medicare and Medicaid Services (CMS). In order for a health care organization to participate in, and receive payment from, Medicare or Medicaid programs, it must be certified as complying with the standards set forth in federal regulations, based on a survey conducted by a state agency on behalf of the CMS (JCAHO, 2006).

Organizations seeking Medicare approval may also choose to be surveyed by the Joint Commission or other accrediting organization. In this case, CMS may grant the accrediting organization "deeming" authority and deem each accredited health care organization as meeting Medicare and Medicaid certification requirements. For the time being, the deemed status options are available for ambulatory surgical centers, clinical laboratories, critical access hospitals, HMOs and PPOs, home health care, hospices, and hospitals.

To monitor the quality of health service, CMS conducts random validation surveys and complaint investigations of organizations with deemed status through Joint Commission accreditation. In addition, the Joint Commission is obliged to provide CMS with a listing of, and related documentation for, organizations receiving conditional accreditation, preliminary denial of accreditation, and accreditation denied. The Joint Commission also provides CMS with accreditation decision reports for hospitals involved in CMS validation surveys and any other survey report CMS requests (JCAHO, 2005).

HEALTH INFORMATION PROVISION TO THE GENERAL PUBLIC

The Challenge of Health Information Provision

As described in the previous section, there is considerable complexity in terms of challenges and opportunities of regulation, collection, dissemination, and utilization of health information because of the complexity of categories and variation in the interests of stakeholders.

From the patients' perspective, the first challenge comes from the difficulty of obtaining the specific service quality information about providers, such as doctors or hospitals. Even if patients can find such information as provided by accreditation organizations or government agencies, these evaluation surveys are only targeting the minimum level/bottom line of service quality and, beyond that, there is no information to make a more informed decision, especially when a patient wants to compare two similar health providers.

The second challenge is finding appropriate insurance plans and buying prescription drugs with a reasonable cost. Because most patients have to find service providers from their insurance plans, it is still difficult to find which insurance plan includes a good provider whom the patient identifies with a reasonable cost. This is especially true with the spiraling cost of health insurance (Baker, Wagner, Singer, & Bundorf, 2003).

The third challenge is the maintenance cost for their medical conditions, mainly the cost of prescription drugs, which has risen significantly in the last few years.

Use Comparison-Shopping for Health Information Provision

Comparison-shopping is not a new concept; the abundance of consumer products within the U.S. market economy has made it easier for consumers to compare products across a number of key factors. When consumers have to choose among several products to serve their needs, comparison-shopping assists them in comparing products via price, quality, and outlook.

In recent years, with the popularity of electronic commerce especially business-to-consumer (B2C) electronic commerce, comparison-shopping quickly shifted into its current online mode by pulling product information from online retailers and aggregating it for online shoppers to make shopping decisions. The Internet provides an ideal infrastructure for such a service to thrive.

As early as 1995, we witnessed the first online comparison-shopping service, BargainFinder, developed by Andersen Consulting. When a consumer provided a singer or band name, for instance, as a query to its search engine, BargainFinder could search up to nine online music stores and retrieve the price of CDs for the query. BargainFinder became a "killer app" and gained public attention almost instantly (Krulwich, 1996).

The success of BargainFinder stimulated more sophisticated comparison-shopping services such as mySimon.com and Pricescan.com in the late 90s. Most of these first generation comparison-shopping services were acquired by established e-commerce portals or major IT players such as Amazon.com and Microsoft.

Comparison-shopping entered the mainstream B2C market when the second generation services such as shopping.com and pricegrabber.com came onto the stage after 2000. More and more consumers were familiar with this new mode of online shopping and visited these comparison-shopping sites first, instead of exploring individual online vendors. Recent survey statistics indicate comparison-shopping sites ranked Yahoo, eBay, and Amazon as among the most visited websites (Nielsen//Netratings, 2004).

When we look into the health information field, we find that comparison-shopping is as important for patients for health services searching, if not more than for any other purchase a consumer could make. Actually, patients will be as comfortable conducting comparison-shopping on health services such as selecting hospital services, doctors, dentists, insurance plans, as well as prescription drugs, as if they were comparison-shopping on commodities, where they can utilize different decision heuristics and strategies that they have developed in online shopping, in the selection of health services.

Sensing this demand, businesses in the medical insurance field became pioneers in the U.S. health system to provide comparison-shopping services. This is a natural move for insurance agents since they already have various insurance company data on hand and all they need is to make it available online for the general public. Such a move could improve their reach to potential customers, and reduce their operation costs in hiring fewer agents and employees in customer services. Thus, comparison-shopping services such as insurable. com, healthinsurance.com, and ehealthinsurance. com, emerged quickly in the late 90s.

The next emerging fields in health service for comparison-shopping are the selection of prescription drugs, hospitals, and physicians. We attribute this lagging behind to three factors: the lack of commercial motivations from comparison-shopping service providers, relatively scant data available for comparison compared with the health insurance field, and concerns of copyright violation when the comparison-shopping service providers have to retrieve data collected by non-profit and private organizations (such as the Joint Commission).

Due to the same factors, the current comparison-shopping service providers in these emerging fields are mainly non-profit organizations that own the data or and those federal or state government agencies that have the power to regulate the price of prescription drugs. Specifically, we found that the comparison of hospital services is mainly provided by government agencies and accreditation organizations. For example:

1. The US Department of Health and Human Services provides comparison information on hospitals. (http://www.hospitalcompare. hhs.gov/)
2. The Joint Commission provides information on hospitals as well as other health care service providers (http://www.jcaho.org)

Some state governments have begun to provide state specific hospital information for their resident patients. Massachusetts Health Quality Partners (MHQP), for example, is an independent state agency that monitors the quality of health services in Massachusetts. It provides side-by-side comparisons on clinic data via different search criteria based on different information needs. MHQP also looks at the quality of health service through patient experiences. Patients complete surveys and rate what it is like to work with their doctors. This information is then used to compare patient experiences across the state via a tabular comparison-shopping format for easy comparison on the Web This service is available from their official site: http://www.mhqp.org/quality/clinical/cqSearch.asp?nav=032400.

Comparison-shopping on physician services is provided by some state governments. For example, New York State provides such a service and allows individuals to review a physician's profile that includes their medical education, legal actions taken against the doctor, translation services available at the doctor's office, and so forth (see http://www. nydoctorprofile.com/welcome.jsp).

Probably, the most widely available comparison-shopping services are on prescription drugs, prompted by increasing costs in recent years. These are mainly provided by state governments. For example, the Connecticut attorney general's office provides a comparison-shopping service on prescription drugs and allows patients to compare pharmacy prescription drug prices across the state of Connecticut (http://www.dir.ct.gov/ag/ DrugSearchGIS.asp). The State of Illinois makes similar comparison-shopping information available to its residents (http://www.consumeraffairs. com/news04/2006/01/il_drug_shop.html).

The Potential Challenges of Comparison-Shopping for Health Services

Though there are many emerging online comparison-shopping services available for health service selection as noted above, we identified a few challenges that could hinder the movement in this direction.

First, unlike comparison-shopping in the e-commerce industry, health information provision, especially information on hospitals, physicians, and prescription drug prices, does not have similar commercial motivations behind them to support their development. In the e-commerce industry, the product information providers (i.e., the online retailers) actually pay to participate in comparison-shopping because of the potential revenue it could return. The more online retailers join the comparison-shopping, the more the remaining online retailers also have to join to maintain their competitiveness – as a result, it forms a positive feedback loop and establishes the prosperity of comparison-shopping service providers.

In health service information provision, such commercial motivation is not strong, though some private hospitals, HMOs, or doctors who own their own clinic may be interested in such comparisons. In addition, the ways that a health service provider (usually non-profit in nature) operates to attract patients are traditionally different from those in the business world. The sophistication and breadth of comparison-shopping for health services may not develop as fast as its counterpart in the e-commerce industry.

Second, intertwined with the first challenge, intellectual property rights, especially copyright issues, for information on the Web are still pending in many aspects. The efforts in comparison-shopping over a wider category of health services may be delayed by copyright issues (Lindberg & Humphreys, 1998). In the e-commerce field, comparison-shopping service providers also experienced copyright issues initially when they retrieved data from different online vendors for comparison. However, when online vendors found comparison-shopping could actually increase their revenues, they changed their attitude and began to pay to participate (Plitch, 2002). In the health service industry, this change is unlikely, due to the non-profit nature of many parts of the system. Privately-owned accreditation organizations may want to retain their monopoly power on these data. For government agencies, though copyright is not an issue, bureaucratic procedures often discourage initiatives by small startups that want to make data more accessible to the public.

On the other hand, since government agencies are supported by tax revenue, they do have the motivation of public accountability for provision of health information to the tax payers, which explains the availability of current comparison-shopping services, though with a different model from e-commerce. However, more explicit public policies are still needed, not only to further improve such services, but also to sustain such efforts and avoid undermining pressure from interest groups. For example, Illinois enacted a law in 2005, the Prescription Price Disclosure Act that ensures consumers can comparison-shop to find the lowest price for their prescription medications. It requires pharmacists to disclose the current retail price of any brand or generic prescription drug or medical device which the pharmacy offers for sale. As can be seen from this case, we need either the market to encourage voluntary participation as in the e-commerce industry, or a strong legislation from government to force compliance. We expect more public policies and regulations will have to be enacted to promote the services to compensate for the lack of commercial motivation for comparison-shopping by health service providers.

FUTURE RESEARCH DIRECTIONS

Comparison-shopping on health information is a brand new tool and application to explore. We think the first priority in research is to establish a proper framework for the classification of health information as needed by patients. This framework should include all aspects of health information that a patient needs to make health care decisions. We also need research on how to standardize health information so as to make the electronic retrieval of information and aggregation by comparison-shopping search engines easier to perform. A related project that has been underway for quite some time is the concept of regional health exchanges (Havenstein, 2005). In this plan, the U.S. government hopes to provide a backbone for a national health information infrastructure where all hospitals will be connected and patient information is stored electronically in real-time. With such a backbone network, the government could easily implement, collect, and publish service quality information.

Another topic in future research might be a detailed analysis of the impact of public policies on health information provision in the comparison-shopping mode. As explained in previous sections, in the e-commerce market, the driving force for the cooperation of online vendors in comparison-shopping is the commercial benefit. However, in the case of health information provision, the motivation of providing comparison information is dominantly non-commercial. So the impact of public policy regulations as the shaping force on this market needs to be investigated in detail.

CONCLUSION

In this chapter, we give a brief description of health service information and its provision to the public. We identified the problems of current health information provision, especially service quality evaluation information to patients. We introduced the emerging field of comparison-shopping and its application in several aspects of health information provision such as health insurance, hospital, physician, and prescription drug selection.

We identified the challenges of the development of this field by contrasting it with the comparison-shopping industry in the electronic commerce world, where a more efficient mechanism is driving the sophistication and maturity of this new mode of decision support. We argue that public policy is the most effective way to influence the development of comparison-shopping for health services. Finally, we have proposed several future research directions in this new field.

REFERENCES

Baker, L., Wagner, T. H., Singer, S., & Bundorf, M. K. (2003). Use of the Internet and e-mail for health care information: Results from a national survey. *Journal of the American Medical Association, 289*, 2400–2406. doi:10.1001/jama.289.18.2400

Bishop, L., Holmes, B. J., & Kelley, C. M. (2005). *National Consumer Health Privacy Survey 2005 California HealthCare Foundation*. CHCF.

Brown, J. R., & Goolsbee, A. (2002). Does the Internet make markets more competitive? Evidence from the life insurance industry. *The Journal of Political Economy, 110*, 481–507. doi:10.1086/339714

Havenstein, H. (2005, October). Regional health exchanges slowly start to share data. *Computerworld*. Retrieved from http://www.computerworld.com

Joint Commission on Accreditation of Healthcare Organizations (JCAHO). (2005). *2004 General public quality report user guide*. Retrieved from http://www.jointcommission.org.

Joint Commission on Accreditation of Healthcare Organizations (JCAHO). (2009). *Federal deemed status and state recognition: Facts about federal deemed status and state recognition*. Retrieved on October 12, 2009 from http://www.jointcommission.org/StateFederal/deemed_status.htm

Krulwich, B. (1996). The BargainFinder agent: Comparison price shopping on the Internet. In Williams, J. (Ed.), *Bots, and Other Internet Beasties*. Indianapolis, IN: Macmillan Computer Publishing.

Lindberg, D. A. B., & Humphreys, B. L. (1998). Medicine and health on the Internet: The good, the bad, and the ugly. *Journal of the American Medical Association, 280*, 1303–1304. doi:10.1001/jama.280.15.1303

Meric, F., Bernstam, E. V., Mirza, N. Q., Hunt, K. K., Ames, F. C., & Ross, M. I. (2002). Breast cancer on the World Wide Web: Cross sectional survey of quality of information and popularity of websites. *British Medical Journal, 324*, 577–581. doi:10.1136/bmj.324.7337.577

Nielsen//Netratings. (2004). *Web surfers comparison shop online for Mother's Day gifts, according to Nielson//NetRatings, Inc.* Retrieved from http://www.nielsen-online.com/pr/pr_040507.pdf

Plitch, P. (2002, September 16). E-Commerce (A special report): The rules --- Law: Are bots legal? --- Comparison-shopping sites say they make the Web manageable; Critics say they trespass. *Wall Street Journal*, p. R13.

Purcell, G. P., Wilson, P., & Delamothe, T. (2002). The quality of health information on the Internet. *British Medical Journal, 324*, 557–558. doi:10.1136/bmj.324.7337.557

Rosenberg, C. E. (1995). *The care of strangers: the rise of America's hospital system*. Baltimore, MD: The John Hopkins University Press.

Section 3
Who will put it in Place?

Chapter 9
Systems Engineering and Health Informatics:
Context, Content, and Implementation

Kalyan Sunder Pasupathy
University of Missouri, USA

ABSTRACT

Healthcare organizations are struggling to provide safe and high quality care while reducing costs. Abundant data on various aspects of the care delivery process (both clinical and non-clinical) are collected and stored in large databases in different parts of the organization. Informatics, as an area of study with roots in computer science and information science, has grown and evolved to enable collection, storage, retrieval, and analysis of data, and reporting of useful information. Health informatics (HI) ranges from bioinformatics to public health informatics depending on the level of focus and applications. At the same time, systems engineering (SE), as an interdisciplinary field of engineering, has grown to encompass the design, analysis, and management of complex health systems to improve their quality and performance. HI and SE are complementary in their approach to identification of problems, methodology, and solution procedure for improvement. This combination brings forth implications for industry and education to address pressing issues of today's health care delivery.

INTRODUCTION

With advances in clinical sciences and medical technology, people are living longer and there is a greater demand for healthcare services. The Institute of Medicine's report *To Err is Human* (Kohn et al., 2000) describes serious concerns in health care owing to undesirable outcomes related to safety and quality issues. These issues have been attributed to breakdowns in processes embedded in the service delivery structure (Institute of Medicine, 2001). Healthcare delivery systems have two major goals – *doing things right* and *doing the right things*. These are known as *efficiency* and *effectiveness*, respectively, in systems theory. With rising costs, efficiency is an important goal for all systems, including health care and this can be ensured through proper allocation of resources. Effectiveness and

DOI: 10.4018/978-1-61520-733-6.ch009

obtaining the desired outcomes, on the other hand, is all the more important in health care, considering the dire consequences of errors and process breakdowns that may lead to harm and even death. Yet, healthcare organizations are struggling to provide safe and high quality care, while reducing costs. Healthcare expenditure has been on the rise, for example, the United States spent nearly two trillion dollars in 2005. This amount accounted for 16% of its GDP, a proportion which is higher than any other country in the world (England, 2007; OECD, 2009). Hence, healthcare providers, insurance companies, and health care policymakers are striving to find more cost-effective methods to deliver health care. Providers are increasingly looking at methods that would help them reduce costs without compromising on the quality of care.

The Institute of Medicine (IOM) identified a four-level, patient-centered conceptual model as the unifying framework and guiding principle for redesigning and improving the healthcare system, to achieve better performance goals (Reid et al., 2005, p. 20). This IOM report proposes using information technology and systems-engineering tools to provide safe and high quality care that is efficient, effective, and patient-centered.

In today's healthcare organization, data is collected every day and stored in large databases. Intuitively, when data are abundant and no other sources of expert knowledge exist, one could expect that knowledge could be gathered from the data that are available. Informatics is the science of collecting, storing, retrieving, analyzing, and reporting information acquired from health data (Coiera, 2003; Protti, 1995). Given the abundant information on clinical, financial, human resources, care delivery, quality, patient satisfaction and outcomes, data mining tools are needed for decision-making. These tools extract hidden information from large databases so that organizations are able to identify important patterns, predict future behaviors, and make proactive, knowledge-driven decisions (Medina-Borja

& Pasupathy, 2007). Such decisions (both clinical and managerial) will not be effective, unless they are based on true representations of processes that transcend any of the individual areas above, within a health system (e.g. clinical, financial). If no one within the organization has a holistic understanding of the system, finding an expert who will clarify the relationships or finding enough organizational documentation to point in the right direction is a challenging task. To be able to have a holistic representation of the processes within a hospital, an understanding of the broader systems, including the clinical system, hospital organizational system, etc. is necessary. Further, how can the relationships "mined" and the resulting patterns be validated against the real-world behavior of health systems? Several systems engineering tools classified under system-design, system-analysis, and system-control tools can come to the rescue. These are proposed by the Institute of Medicine report in 2005 under the umbrella of systems engineering (Reid et al., 2005).

The goal of this chapter is to accomplish the following,

- Provide an introduction to health informatics
- Establish the need for systems engineering in the health system
- Discuss the impact of the integration of health informatics and systems engineering for healthcare organizations.

This chapter is organized into three major sections - context, content, and implementation - followed by consideration of future directions before providing concluding remarks. The context section describes data usage for decision making, introduces health informatics, and describes the need for models. The content section describes systems engineering concepts and tools. And finally, the implementation section describes the use of health informatics and systems engineering for healthcare improvement.

CONTEXT

Decision Making

Decision making is the process of implementing an action within a system to solve a problem or improve the system. The goal is to accomplish some change. Decision making involves understanding of the system under consideration, understanding facts and/or data from the existing system, and knowledge of the science to determine the change needed (Dinkelbach, 1990). The action can range from a minor intervention to a total redesign of the system. A patient opting to undergo a certain procedure, a physician ordering a specific medication for a patient, the pharmacy manager adding a technician to a shift, administrators adding a new care delivery process, or an insurance firm determining the amount of payment for a certain treatment are a few examples of decisions made. They are similar because they all go through the same process of fact gathering, analysis of existing facts, understanding the domain (e.g. care delivery team, pharmacy), and then implementing the action. They are different because they range in terms of the specific context, the level of aggregation within the healthcare sector (see Figure 1), the time horizon, effort (or money) involved in both conducting the analysis and implementing the change. The patient's decision is at the individual (or patient) level. The physician's and the pharmacist's decisions are at the care team level. The administrator's decision is at the organizational (or hospital) level. Based on the level at which the decision is made, it can be task-oriented, operational, tactical, or strategic in nature. Typically, strategic decisions are at the highest level ranging over long time periods (say, three years or more), involve organizational leaders, transcend various departments, and require maximum effort (time and money). Tactical decisions are one step lower for medium term decisions and consume lesser effort. Operational decisions are further down, followed by task-oriented decisions. And finally,

the insurance decision is at the environment (or outside the hospital) level. The people who make the decisions are physicians, nurses, pharmacists, administrators such as the Chief Executive Officer, Chief Operating Officer, Chief Financial Officer, Chief Information Officer, operational managers, insurance analysts, community health experts, etc.

The person who makes the decision, the decision maker is posed with certain needs and preferences and at least two options. Considering these, the decision maker makes a choice to satisfy his/her needs. All of the needs, the preferences, and the options available constitute a decision problem. To arrive at a decision, certain analyses need to be done. For this purpose, the real-life decision problem should be represented in a mathematical framework called a decision model (Dinkelbach, 1990; Glaser, 2002).

Data for Decision Making

Data are vital pieces of evidence in the decision making process and data are collected at all levels. Data help in better understanding the system being studied. Large quantities of data are collected day after day, at various levels within the hospital

Figure 1. Four levels of the healthcare system

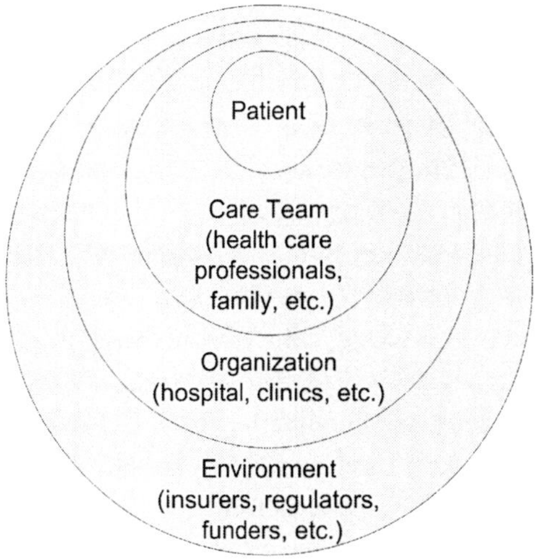

– daily staff logs, prescription orders, medical records, patient satisfaction, human resources, billing and financial data – and are stored in various systems. The quantity of data stored by organizations doubles every three years (Lyman & Varian, 2003). For example, prescriptions ordered by the physician are captured in a computerized order entry system; pharmacy orders are stored in an electronic pharmacy system, medication administration to the patient in electronic medical record systems, and others (Lehmann & Shortliffe, 2003). Non-clinical data is captured and stored in other systems, such as for human resources, financial electronic systems for expenses, reimbursement, etc. There is tremendous enthusiasm in recent years to automate medical records and create a complete health information infrastructure (Shortliffe, 2005). How can such information be used to make effective decisions?

To understand this better, let us consider the case of a nursing unit manager, and her system – the nursing unit domain. Nursing unit managers supervise a team of nurses and are key decision makers, and often receive reports on their units from multiple sources. They make decisions primarily at the tactical and operational levels focusing on a time horizon ranging from a few weeks to a few years. To improve operations and thereby improve safety, quality, and value, managers need to be pointed in the right direction, and the information should guide them and provide action items to make interventions and changes. Because of the existence of data sets in separate departments in a de-compartmentalized manner, often reports end up being aggregations or summaries of granular data. This fails to provide the necessary linkage to process items where actual interventions can be made. For instance, patients provide a wealth of data describing their experience during the stay at the hospital through satisfaction questionnaires. These data are rarely coupled with, and analyzed against, processes within the delivery structure that have an impact on perceptions of the patient. Certain data items

are highly sensitive. Databases such as prescription orders and medical records may be stored in departments exclusively for security reasons. There are strict legislative regulations such as those of the Health Insurance Portability and Accountability Act (HIPAA) set forth by the Centers for Medicare and Medicaid Services (CMS) available at http://www.cms.hhs.gov/HIPAAGenInfo/ and institutional guidelines for storage, accessibility, and dissemination of such data for the purpose of security. But this does not necessarily preclude analyzing data and providing useful information, while still ensuring confidentiality of individuals and key identifiable data.

The analysis of such data can range from a simple statistical analysis to building relationships and identifying hidden patterns. Such advanced tools of "mining" data are referred to as data mining and a related concept of knowledge discovery in databases (KDD) (Fayyad, Piatetsky-Shapiro, & Smyth, 1996). Data mining is performed using several types of models and algorithms such as neural networks and genetic programming. Data mining includes two major tasks – knowledge discovery and prediction. The first step is used to gather knowledge out of the data set, and the second step is used to determine what the future might look like, and make predictions based on the results. For example, data mining can be used to discover patterns and identify opportunities for improvement in quality of care and patient satisfaction (Hebbar, Pasupathy & Williamson, 2008). Hospitals send out satisfaction questionnaires to patients to gather their perceptions on the care that was provided. These survey data give the hospital an evaluation of the quality as perceived by the patient, along with their level of satisfaction that is required for reporting purposes by the Centers for Medicare and Medicaid Services. However, more important than the rating is the analysis of the data, where relationships can be built between the process-related data and quality measures, impact on outcomes such as referrals can be understood, and decisions for interventions can be made (Pasupathy & Triantis, 2007a). Even though perceived quality and satisfaction are the result, such as in a rating, mining of the data can give areas within the process where change can be effected.

CONTENT

Data mining is one component of a broader field of study called informatics. Informatics is the science of collecting, storing, retrieving, and analyzing data, and presenting the information to make decisions. The term *informatika* was originally coined by Mikhailov, Chernyl, and Gilyarevskii (1966). Informatics is different from information technology and information management. According to the Information Technology Association of America, information technology deals with the design, development, and maintenance of hardware including computers and networks to provide the underlying infrastructure to support the processing of information. Information management deals with the day-to-day operations necessary to process information (Wigand, Picot, & Reichwald, 1997). Informatics is a much broader area of study. Informatics is not restricted to just the computational aspects, but also concerns itself with the study of cognitive and social/organizational aspects of information analysis and use. This includes enabling an individual's interaction with information technology, as well as interaction with other individuals who are part of teams and work groups. The data stores are mined, analyzed, patterns discovered, and decisions are made for change to improve quality and performance (Friedman et al., 2004; Hersh 2002; Hersh 2006). Health informatics narrows down the study of information science to applications within the healthcare sector (Hersh, 2008a; 2008b). Specifically, health informatics can range from bioinformatics to public health informatics depending on the level of focus and applications (Coiera, 2003; Friedman et al., 2004). The major sub-specialties in health informatics along with the level of focus and some application areas of study are highlighted in Table 1.

To better understand informatics, it is important to understand the data-information-knowledge hierarchy which was originally proposed by Blum (1986) and wisdom was added by Nelson and Joos (1989). Information occurs along the learning path from data to wisdom (see Figure 2). As we move from data to wisdom, both complexity and learning increase, with data being at the lower end in Figure 2. Data are comprised of numbers and

Table 1. Sub-specialties in health informatics

Sub-specialty in Health Informatics	Level of Focus	Application Area
Bioinformatics	Micro-level	Molecular biology, protein sequence analysis, gene expression, etc.
Imaging informatics	Tissue or organ level	Radiology, diagnostic imaging, scanning, cancer treatment, etc.
Consumer informatics	Individual level (patient)	Methods for analyzing patient's need for information and making it available.
Medical/Clinical informatics	Care team level (physicians, nurses, pharmacists, therapists, patient's family, etc.)	Patient's diagnosis, treatment, care delivery, teamwork, etc.
Organizational/Health management informatics	Organizational level (departments, operating units, suppliers, insurance firms, etc.)	Organization's capacity and capability, performance, operations, process integration, adaptive systems, etc.
Public health informatics	Community level	Public health policy, behavioral risk analysis, emergency response, etc.

Figure 2. The data to wisdom hierarchy

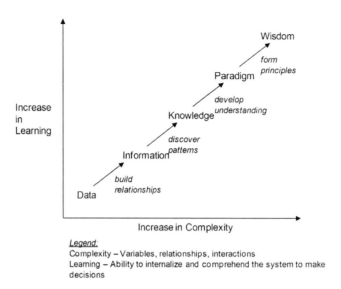

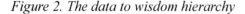

symbols without the awareness of any structure. It is the lowest level in the hierarchy and carries no meaning. Information is one step higher and has some meaning attributed to it because of organization, and processing of data by building relationships between data items. Knowledge is still higher and emerges as patterns are discovered in the information that is available. Knowledge is useful in decision making. Further learning provides understanding of systems that leads to people forming mental models or paradigms. Paradigms are frameworks and mindsets that people form based on what they have seen, heard, and felt. It is the sum total of all their life's experiences. This forms reference points in their minds that they use for comparison purposes when they come across situations. These can also be conceived of as filters that are formed, through which the individual views and analyzes the world. The whole process of learning is to broaden this mindset. The final step in the hierarchy is principle generation which is formed from paradigms. Principles cannot be proven right or wrong, they just exist. These principles give rise to wisdom. Wisdom is the highest level in the hierarchy and to achieve this level, one has to go through the other levels from bottom-up.

Let us look at a simple example in public health (similar examples can be found in other areas). Analyzing the impact of demographic variables on say, the incidence of cancer in a community is important for designing interventions. A composition of 75% African Americans, and 33% cancer incidence rate separately are examples of data. If we were to build a relationship between these two data items to say that African Americans beyond a certain age have a 33% incidence rate of cancer becomes a piece of information. When the analyst is able to discover a pattern, and say that African Americans have a higher incidence rate than the general population with a rate of 25%, then that is knowledge. Several such patterns help develop an understanding of how various demographic variables affect cancer incidence rate, and hence a paradigm of the system can be formed. And finally, these paradigms help to form principles of what kinds of interventions (ways to educate and change behaviors, increase screening, along with others) can be made to improve diagnosis and treatment, and transfer concepts from one application area to another.

To be able to make sensible decisions with systems, one ought to have knowledge, as well as a thorough understanding, and move farther from data, and closer to wisdom on the hierarchy. Thus, even though the complexity increases, learning also increases along the way. Often, the decisions need to be evaluated for their impact in the real world. Further, paradigms may inhibit the individual from seeing the big picture. At this juncture, a model can be helpful to compare one's paradigms with the real world to change and/or better understand the real world system. Hence, models are necessary. A model is an abstraction of the real world, where a replica is created that can be manipulated for scenario analysis, without having to deal with the consequences in the real world. Models can be statistical, optimization-based, or simulation-based. Models represent a given system in the form of any combination of variables, equations, relationships, etc. Models replicate the real world and enable the analyst to study 'what-if' scenarios and predict future behavior of the system (Neelamkavil, 1987). Such models have to be validated to ensure that they succinctly and sufficiently capture the real world system. Models should be large and detailed enough to capture necessary complexities in the real world, so that they are useful for understanding and decision making. However, no one model that is developed can be comprehensive enough to capture every aspect of the real world, because the model itself, is being built, and is restricted by assumptions and paradigms (Silvert, 2001). Even if such a comprehensive model can be built, we

are restricted by available computing power to be able to simulate and/or analyze such a model. Computing power is growing by the day and more powerful computers are able to handle ever larger models. More discussions on this topic are presented in the implementation section.

The modeling process is shown in Figure 3. The process involves building a model based on the real world system. This is done based on the modeler's understanding of the real world. The modeler gathers information from the real world and processes it forming the paradigm. Based on this paradigm, the modeler then "acts" to build the model. Once the model is built, the information gathered from running the model and additional information from the real world help change the paradigm. This feedback helps the modeler to go back and make changes to (act on) the model. This is repeated until the model sufficiently represents the real world. Then the model is run to analyze various scenarios and based on the results, decision is made to act in the real world.

Systems Engineering and Health Care

So far we have discussed the context of health informatics and informatics used for decision making. The modeling described in the latter part of the previous section is a component of an area of study called systems engineering. Systems engineering is an interdisciplinary field of engineering concerned with the design, analysis, and management of complex systems (Blanchard & Fabrycky, 2005). Traditional engineering disciplines such as civil, mechanical, electrical, and so forth, are all content-intensive and focus on natural laws, fundamental principles, and specific processes (Kurstedt, 2000). Systems engineering is a different discipline based on the systems process(es) and approaches involved in solving a problem based on "engineering" (transforming or (re)designing) any system.

Figure 3. The modeling process

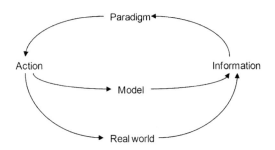

Systems engineering is being referred to with various names, some based on the tools used, and others based on the potential impact on outcomes. Most common references are listed in Table 2 with a prefix followed by a suffix to describe the area of focus and interest.

Some of the other terms include Management Systems Engineering, and the well-known Industrial Engineering. When the systems engineering focus is on health care, then it is called health systems engineering.

Health (or Healthcare) Systems Engineering (HSE) refers to a focus area related to industrial engineering that is applied within a healthcare setting. It is a harmonious and robust blend of the systems approach and the engineering process as applied to the healthcare system. It is a new field of engineering that takes a comprehensive approach to health systems, and is increasingly becoming popular in the healthcare industry as a method for improving quality and safety of care, while bringing down costs. It refers to the process of using the disciplines, practices, and methods of engineering analysis and design, to systematically diagnose and correct problems in processes. HSE professionals, unlike clinical professionals, act or operate behind the scenes. They rarely have contact, if any at all, with a patient. They may not directly impact the outcomes in health care as physicians and nurses do, but work on improving the embedded processes in the delivery of care (Arveson, 1998).

Table 2. Alternative terms for systems engineering

Prefix	Suffix
Process	Management
Operations	Engineering
Quality	Improvement
Management	Reengineering
Performance	
Health Systems	
Healthcare Systems	
Business Process	
Operational Performance	

Health systems engineering involves identifying the problem areas, prioritizing changes, getting feedback on decisions, and using the data to improve processes. It uses practices that are accepted in other engineering fields, such as measurements, testing, feedback, control loops, work breakdown structures, and risk mitigation, and applies them appropriately to a healthcare organization. Each health systems engineering project includes five basic steps, (1) problem identification; (2) data collection; (3) analysis; (4) solution; and (5) design and/or intervention. Along with these steps, it is important that health systems engineers foster an environment of continuous learning and improvement in the organization. As can be seen with the steps, there is an overlap between informatics and systems engineering. The modeling approaches can be used in a wide range of systems in terms of aggregation, from the micro level through community level, as shown in Table 1 (Friedman et al., 2004). Health management engineering is a subset of health systems engineering that focuses on the management aspects within the health system. In recent times, health systems engineering has also been referred to as health management engineering (Belson, 2007).

Health systems engineering involves using a set of tools to design, analyze, and control health systems and evaluate performance for improvement. Several such tools have been identified by the Institute of Medicine and the National Academy of Engineering report (Reid et al., 2005, pp. 28, 35, 46). Each of these tools requires additional skills to be able to accomplish the systems engineering process. The various tools are listed in Table 3 along with more specific skills necessary to be able to use the respective tools.

These tools could be used in isolation or in conjunction with one another. For instance, productivity measuring and monitoring can be used in conjunction with the balanced scorecard concept to analyze a system (Medina-Borja, Pasupathy, & Triantis, 2007). Here, the balanced scorecard gives a broad framework, including various perspec-

Table 3. Systems engineering tools

	Specific Tool	**Skills Required**
System Design	Concurrent engineering (Winner et al., 1988) and quality function deployment (Sullivan 1986, 1988; Hauser & Clausing, 1988; Chaplin et al., 1999)	Structured and detailed analysis of stakeholder requirements, Stakeholder perceptions and benchmarking against competitors, Translation of stakeholder wants into care delivery system concept, Identification of detailed processes within delivery system, Deployment of service delivery
	Human-factor engineering, cognitive-systems engineering, computer-supported cooperative work and resilience engineering (Cook et al., 1989; Klein & Isaacson, 2003; Klein & Meininger, 2004; Patterson et al., 2004)	Activity analysis, Ethnographic analysis, Focus groups, Meta analysis, Persona, Subjects in tandem, User as analyst, Questionnaire, Think aloud, Prototyping, Wizard of Oz, Usability lab, Observations, Interviews, Failure analysis, Failure-mode effects analysis, Fault tree analysis, Root-cause analysis, Creation of interdisciplinary team, Data collection, Data analysis to determine how and why an event occurred, Identification of clinical and administrative processes to be redesigned
System Analysis	Modeling and Simulation (Queuing methods, Discrete-event simulation) (Murray & Berwick, 2003; Brandeau 2004; Schaefer et al., 2004)	Flowchart or Process map, Data collection, Fitting arrival and service distributions, Model in simulation software, Quantitative analysis for staffing/capacity planning
	Enterprise-Management Tools Supply-chain management (Feistritzer & Keck, 2000; Thomas et al., 2000) Game theory (Tsay & Nahmias, 1998) Systems-dynamics models (Sterman, 2000; Lattimer et al., 2004; Taylor & Dangerfield, 2005) Productivity measuring and monitoring (Ness et al., 2003; O'Neill & Dexter, 2004; Ozcan et al., 2004)	Demand forecasting, Inventory tracking, Inventory modeling, Enterprise Resource Planning, Network optimization, Transportation strategy, Procurement and Vendor Relationship Management Microeconomics, Mathematical modeling Systemic thinking, Cause-and-effect formulation, Data collection, Stock-and-flow modeling, Model in simulation software, Analysis for policy making Process mapping, Input-output-outcome relationships, Production economics
	Financial Engineering and Risk Analysis Tools Stochastic analysis and Value-at-risk (Jorion 1997) Optimization tools for decision making Distributed decision making and agency theory	Risk prediction and quantification, Credit assessments, Pricing of services, Valuation of combined risks for engaging in multiple markets Stochastic programming, Revenue management and pricing Agent-based modeling
	Knowledge Discovery in Databases (Data mining, Predictive modeling and Neural networks) (Eich et al., 1997; Mitchell 1997, McCarthy, 1997; Friman et al., 2002; Ray et al., 2004; Wei et al., 2004)	Data warehousing, Probability and statistics, Data mining
System Control	Statistical process control	Control charts
	Scheduling (Hershey et al., 1981; O'Keefe, 1985; Mullinax & Lawley, 2002; Green 2004)	Demand forecasting, Setting service standards, Optimization
Other Performance and Quality Improvement	The Baldrige National Quality Program (NIST 2009)	Organizational profile, Strategic planning, Process management, Measurement, analysis, knowledge management
	Six Sigma Method (Harry 1988; Chassin 1998; Batalden et al., 2003; Godfrey et al., 2003)	Process Map, Cause and Effects matrix, Failure Mode and Effects Analysis
	Toyota Production System/ Lean Enterprise (Monden 1983; Spear & Bowen 1999)	Waste definition, Kaizen, Value stream mapping, Spaghetti diagramming
	Balanced Scorecard (Kaplan & Norton 1992, 1996a, 1996b)	Various perspectives, Cause-effect relationships, Leading and lagging indicator identification

tives (customer, financial, internal business, and innovation, learning and growth) from a systems standpoint. Productivity monitoring can be done using tools such as data envelopment analysis that is based on systems theory and production economics. Another example is the combination of system dynamics modeling with productivity monitoring (Pasupathy & Triantis, 2007b).

Simulation is another tool used by management engineers to improve an existing process. Computer-based modeling and simulation are used to practice tasks in life-like circumstances using digital models, with feedback from observers, peers, and video cameras (Noor, 2007). Using simulation, management engineers see whether a particular decision can be implemented by an organization and predict its consequences, given the organization's structure, resources, and processes. Various alternatives could be experimented with, to see which one would improve efficiency and capacity management of the organization. To avoid duplication of services, management engineers apply dynamic modeling of healthcare delivery and analyze the system as a supply chain (Noor, 2007). They use artificial intelligence-based decision support and risk management systems to help health care organizations make clinical decisions under uncertainties.

IMPLEMENTATION

Several of the tools listed in Table 3 are data and computation-intensive. This means that they require significant investments in computing resources. Availability of computing resources has been on the increase. Several healthcare organizations are investing in large information technology systems to house clinical, business operations, and financial data (Curry & Knowles, 2005; Feld & Stoddard, 2004; McDermott, 1999; Pare, 2002). Firms such as 3M, Cerner Corporation, Eclipsys, General Electric Systems, MediTech, are pioneers in designing and developing large-scale systems

with multiple modules for specific operations in pharmacy, radiology, surgery, etc. Organizations should also be in a position to have the capability to extract data from multiple sources relating to care delivery processes and conduct analyses. Computer technology is required for advanced modeling and analysis (Pasupathy et al., 2008). Organizations can develop such capabilities in-house and implement data mining and systems modeling (Medina-Borja, Pasupathy, & Triantis, 2007; Pasupathy & Medina-Borja, 2008; Pasupathy, Medina-Borja, & Triantis, 2008).

Based on the qualifications of systems engineers and health informaticians (Friedman et al., 2004), there is a lot of overlap in their capabilities and competencies, and their responsibilities in the workplace. These professionals who perform such work may be required to serve as in-house consultants. Systems engineers and health informaticians are required to perform projects involving process improvement, staffing analysis, scheduling, etc. Others may provide internal consultation, facilitation, and analytic services throughout a medical center using principles of continuous improvement, systems analysis, and change management. Activities may include productivity monitoring, systems improvement, operational analysis, work process design, information system development and implementation, facility planning, and other process improvement efforts. These professionals can work at various levels within a healthcare setting ranging from entry level through intermediate positions to leadership positions. As an individual at the entry level, those with such training may work as Health Management Engineer, Decision Analyst, Decision Support Analyst, Quality/Performance Improvement Analyst, Project Management Analyst, or Financial Analyst. These typically require less than two years of experience. At the intermediate level, they may work as managers or supervisors overseeing analysts and/or engineers and require two to five years of experience. Those with seven or more years of experience can be recruited for leadership positions such as Director of Management Engineering or Quality Improvement, Vice President of Operations, Chief Operating Officer, Chief Information Officer, or Chief Financial Officer.

Systems Engineering: Health Informatics within the Organizational Structure

Systems engineering-health informatics cannot be successful without a suitable organizational setting where the culture promotes learning and growth and is conducive for employees to voice their thoughts and concerns. For such professionals to be successful in a hospital/health facility, it is critical that health systems engineers have easy access to important information and high-level executives. According to the Healthcare Information and Management Systems Society (HIMSS), factors that such positions require for effectiveness in the organization include full visibility throughout all functions and levels; authorization to directly observe or work with any/all levels of the organization; access or response to executive-level decision makers; direct reporting lines to executive management and their support; high-level recognition of process improvement activities to drive and facilitate interdisciplinary teams; Chief Executive Officer alignment for support of the organization's vision; Chief Operating Officer alignment for support of operational optimization; and Chief Information Officer alignment to meet the challenges involved in collecting, utilizing, and maintaining information.

As Crane (2007) points out, factors that are imperative for systems engineering-health informatics to succeed in a hospital environment include, (1) backing of the hospital's top-level management, and (2) cooperation from physicians, clinical staff, and non-clinical staff. Strong backing of the management is necessary for health systems engineers to coordinate activities from one department to another, solve problems, and be effective on a system wide basis. Cooperation of clinical and non-clinical staff is necessary for any intervention to be successfully implemented.

While dealing with healthcare data and especially those involving patient information, Institutional/Ethics Review Board and Health Insurance Portability and Accountability Act (HIPAA) aspects need to be considered. According to HIMSS, around 20% of healthcare organizations have not implemented the necessary technology and processes to comply with HIPAA, and remain non-compliant due to issues ranging from regulation misinterpretation to lack of employee competence with technology (Fogarty 2006). Johnson and Warkentin (2008) demonstrate the importance of factors both at the organizational and the individual professional levels for privacy and information security. Specifically, the authors show the importance of organizational support and self-efficacy for compliance.

Integration of systems engineering with health informatics and successful implementation of improvement interventions cannot happen without strong involvement of the executive level in change management, as shown in Figure 4. This requires a deep and renewed understanding of the healthcare sector, expertise in organizational design, organizational change, and intervention methodology (Buchan 2004; Hempel 2004). As Melville, Kraemer, and Gurbaxani (2004) point out, although it is possible to apply information systems/technology for improved organizational performance with minimal changes, successful implementation can only happen with significant changes in organizational policies, rules, structure, workplace practices, and culture.

In Figure 4, a need is identified by the President/Chief Executive Officer in conjunction with the Chief Medical Officer/Chief Nurse where clinical effectiveness is evaluated, and errors, for instance, are reported. This triggers a plan to improve quality by the Chief Operating Officer. The Chief Human Resources Officer is involved in developing mechanisms to enable behavior change and the Chief Information Officer is responsible for

Figure 4. Integration of systems engineering-health informatics within the organizational setting (an example)

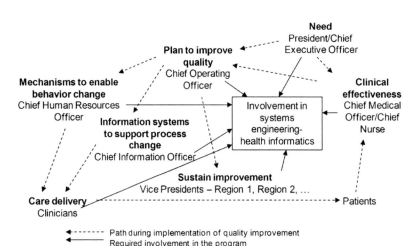

providing information systems support for process change. These mechanisms and support systems are provided to the clinicians and others involved in the delivery of care. The Vice Presidents of the various regions are responsible for sustaining the improvements obtained. This shows an example of a quality improvement initiative involving all senior leaders. The illustration is the application of theory of change to a specific clinical example and can be modified to other quality improvement initiatives. Also, the need does not necessarily arise from the CEO-level and can start at any position within the organization.

At the University of Missouri Hospital, systems engineering-health informatics capability and involvement to perform process and quality improvement is coordinated through the Office of Clinical Effectiveness (OCE). The hospital is a 307-bed hospital with 527 active medical staff admitting more than 20,000 patients per year. The Office is led by a director and staffed with physicians, nurses, and health services researchers. OCE promotes and facilitates high-quality clinical operations and works on initiatives throughout the health system. The office is positioned within the executive team in the organization with direct

reporting lines to the Chief Executive Officer and access to strategic planners and key decision-makers. Table 4 shows the working relationships maintained by the Office of Clinical Effectiveness (OCE) with key hospital executive offices.

The office and the hospital take advantage of the close working relationship with the university to leverage expertise in systems engineering-health informatics through two associations. The first association involves OCE's close working relationship with the Center for Healthcare Systems Engineering to gain access to engineering experts at the university. OCE charters several process improvement projects (e.g., seven in 2007-2008) for industrial engineering students directed by faculty experts in the Industrial & Manufacturing Systems Engineering Department. These projects vary from the design of improvements in managing insulin orders to analysis of patient transport systems and redesign of hospitality coordinator roles. The other association is with the Department of Health Management & Informatics and other departments within the Schools of Medicine, Nursing, and Health Professions through the Center for Health Care Quality. The hospital also has ties with the University of Missouri Informatics

Table 4. Working relationships of OCE with key hospital executive officers

Executive Office led by	Working relationship
Chief Executive Officer (CEO)	Alignment with vision and mission of the organization
Chief Operating Officer (COO)	Interventions and improvement in operations
Chief Information Officer (CIO)	Collection, storage, retrieval and analysis of clinical process data
Chief Medical Officer (CMO)	Culture change in clinical services and performance improvement of physician practices
Chief Financial Officer (CFO)	Access to budget to fund process improvement projects, programs and initiatives
Chief Human Resources Officer (CHRO)	Ability to involve and facilitate interdisciplinary teams

Institute (MUII). The hospital recruits expertise in health systems engineering, for analyzing and improving processes within inpatient pharmacy to reduce medication errors and improve capacity utilization (Silver, Zhang and Pasupathy, 2010; Zhang and Pasupathy, 2009). Some of the other projects include analyzing human-computer interaction and building better decision support systems (Gong et al., 2008; Gong 2009).

OCE works closely with other offices and departments to lead and direct quality improvement initiatives. According to the University of Missouri Health Care System's 2007 Annual Report, in December 2006, an interdisciplinary team was organized to develop detection procedures for impending cardiac arrest or other medical emergencies before hospital patients experienced deterioration that led to a drop of cardiac and respiratory arrest rates by about 33 per cent. Another initiative also reported in the annual report involved combining skills of five physician services, nurses, case management, and physical therapy to develop innovative care models and protocols for hip fracture care to reduce process variability. This reduced the mortality rate, while also reducing the length of stay by more than 30% and the cost of care by about 40%.

Data mining has been used to analyze large groups of data sets on patients, to predict relationships between variables. Mitchell (1997) used data mining to identify groups of symptoms that exhibited high risk of women requiring emergency C-sections. Merck-Medco Managed Care used data mining to discover patterns and identify drugs and treatments that are less expensive without compromising the effectiveness of the treatment (McCarthy, 1997). Medicare databases have been mined to discover risk of cardiac arrest when commonly prescribed antibiotics are used in combination with other drugs that have drug interactions with the antibiotics (Ray et al., 2004).

Systems Engineers, Health Informaticians: Education and Training

Health Informaticians (HI) are professionals that develop and deploy systems and methods based on information and communication technologies within the healthcare sector (Covvey et al., 2001; 2002). They require a knowledge base in the health system, computer science, and information systems. Together, systems engineering and health informatics are complementary. The need for systems engineering and health informatics capability also has implications for curriculum design in programs at both the baccalaureate and graduate degree levels. Health systems engineering tools should be introduced early in the curriculum and students should be required to work on problems and case studies to gain hands-on exercises and experience. Systems engineering enables the integration of informatics with modeling and analysis using the systems methodologies and enable decision making. Students need to use the wealth of data to identify meaningful information for decision-making purposes (Molina & Medina-Borja, 2006; Sterman, 2002; Sweeney & Sterman, 2000). Competency in systems engineering-health informatics will provide the required orientation and enable graduates to perform and succeed in today's complex healthcare system. Based on the needs in the healthcare sector, a National Science Foundation-funded curriculum design project was conducted and evaluated at the University of Missouri (Columbia, MO). Table 5 describes a curriculum that was designed at the undergraduate level and offered as a specialization in industrial engineering in conjunction with Health Management and Informatics (Wu et al., 2007).

FUTURE RESEARCH DIRECTIONS

There has been a major influx of capital by healthcare organizations and funding by government agencies to acquire and research information technology infrastructure. While this direction is necessary for healthcare delivery systems to move forward, it is not sufficient to deliver efficient and effective care. Information technology should be more than just a tool that automates existing processes. It should enable organizational capability and elevate the processes for streamlining and improvement, in present day complex adaptive systems – delivery systems that can adapt to variations and day-to-day complexities and evolve on a continuous basis. Organizational learning will be embedded in the system and not in individual experts or consultants. Systems engineering concepts can make the link in terms of enabling the organization by the engineering approach.

The National Science Foundation and the National Institutes of Health in the United States are in the forefront with specific programs targeted towards funding research along these lines. The National Science Foundation has a Service Enterprise Systems program that funds research in the optimization of healthcare delivery systems. The National Institutes of Health, through the Office of Behavioral and Social Sciences Research, funds projects that use systems science, including system dynamics modeling, agent-based modeling, and network modeling, for health care problems. These research endeavors will pave the way for an increased focus on systems engineering-health informatics.

Table 5. Content of an undergraduate curriculum emphasizing systems engineering-health informatics

Content	Title of course	Knowledge and/or Skills Developed
Systems concepts	Systems theory	Systems theory, systems perspective, systems structure, systems processes, systems communication, systems hierarchy and control, systems operation.
Health care context	Introduction to healthcare systems, structure and operations	Basic understanding of the structure and functions of the US healthcare system. Emphasis is placed on the various components within the system.
Systems engineering	Methodologies and tools of systems engineering and health informatics	Systems engineering methodologies, tools and techniques; use of data; informatics
Healthcare systems	Healthcare systems analysis and design	Application of analytical methodologies, quantitative tools and techniques including optimization, simulation, data mining, etc. to healthcare
Application of learning	Capstone project	Real-life problems, teamwork, problem situation, holistic and systems-orientation, use of tools and techniques.

Through the American Recovery and Reinvestment Act of 2009, the National Institutes of Health has designated at least 200 million USD for a new initiative called the Challenge Grants in Health and Science Research. A major component has been designated toward informatics-related research for processing healthcare data in various realms such as clinical, public health, biological, genetic, etc. Some examples under the cyber-infrastructure research potential include building technologies to support data coordination and computational thinking; analytic approaches to obtain large scale observational data and actionable information from electronic health records; post-marketing surveillance; and decision support for complex clinical decisions.

Health systems informatics is emerging as an area of study that brings together the strength of health informatics and systems engineering. It combines the power of informatics to build patterns and systems engineering to model, validate, simulate, and analyze the processes within the healthcare system, be it at the gene or protein level or at the public health or community level, and anywhere in-between.

CONCLUSION

Systems engineering or health informatics cannot sufficiently improve quality of healthcare delivery in isolation. Together the power that they can bring to care delivery and knowledge management can go far to transform the existing organization. As Reid et al. (2005) point out, the lack of adequate use of systems engineering and informatics in the healthcare sector is a challenge and an opportunity for improvement. Organizations should focus on information technology innovation that goes beyond supporting day-to-day procedural operations with a short-term focus, to enabling and elevating the organization as a whole onto a path of continuous learning and growth. Such a transformation cannot be done individually within functional areas, be it operations, or clinical or information technology. Systems engineering-health informatics should acquire an in-depth understanding of the clinical and managerial aspects of the organization.

Systems engineering-health informatics should also be involved in, for instance, clinical and inter-professional efforts to foster and grow collaboration and teamwork. Such capability can enable health professionals to breakdown process barriers and organizational silos to see the broader picture of the process, the entire breadth of the service encounter between the patient and various clinicians. This starts to create organizational learning and accumulates knowledge within the organization (Khatri, 2006a; Hansen & Thompson, 2002; Pearlson, 2001).

Knowledge thus acquired cannot be easily captured and stored, to be transferred over time. In the past, experts experienced the organization in different capacities, and gathered knowledge over time. We are living in changing times, when there is greater specialization and functional separation, and knowledge does not exist in one person or place within the organization. Data can be stored easily in the form of databases, and information in the form of reports. But, it is hard to capture and store knowledge, since knowledge tends to exist in a tacit form. Here is where systems engineering and informatics can step up to the challenge. Traditional information technology systems end up just supporting existing operations and automating manual data collection. Information technology projects and implementation initiatives should be better coordinated and well aligned to go above and beyond strategic initiatives on an organizational scorecard. Systems should be developed to not only collect and store information, but also to place a greater emphasis on analysis and synthesis. These systems should challenge existing organizational mindsets and paradigms. Systems engineering modeling tools and techniques, such as system dynamics and agent-based modeling, can be used to model the organization's underlying structure. These models demonstrate the behavior of the organization as a system. The fundamental principle is that the structure of the system predicts behavior. Thus, systems engineering and informatics together, exhibit tremendous opportunity for extracting information from the wealth of data that are stored within health facilities and the health system. This information thus generated, can be used to test if the existing paradigms modeled hold, or inform the organization for a paradigm shift, thus creating a knowledge-intensive learning organization.

REFERENCES

Ackoff, R. L. (1989). From data to wisdom. *Journal of Applied Statistics, 16*, 3–9.

Arveson, P. (1998). *The emerging field of management engineering.* Retrieved March 31, 2008, from http://www.balancedscorecard.org/ManagementEngineering/tabid/134/Default.aspx

Batalden, P. B., Nelson, E. C., Edwards, W. H., Godfrey, M. M., & Mohr, J. J. (2003). Microsystems in health care, Part 9. Developing small clinical units to attain peak performance. *Joint Commission Journal on Quality and Safety, 29*(11), 575–585.

Belson, D. (2007). *Improving efficiency, management engineering comes to the safety net.* Retrieved March 30, 2008, from http://www.chcf.org/documents/hospitals/ManagementEngineering.pdf

Blanchard, B. S., & Fabrycky, W. J. (2005). *Systems engineering and analysis.* Upper Saddle River, NJ: Prentice Hall.

Blum, B. J. (1986). *Clinical Information Systems.* New York: Springer-Verlag.

Brandeau, M. L. (2004). Allocating resources to control infectious diseases. In Brandeau, M. L., Sainfort, F., & Pierskalla, W. P. (Eds.), *Operations research and health care, A handbook of methods and applications* (pp. 443–464). Boston: Kluwer Academic Publishers.

Buchan, J. (2004). What difference does ("good") HRM make? *Human Resources for Health, 2*, 1–7. doi:10.1186/1478-4491-2-6

Chaplin: E., Mailey, M., Crosby, R., Gorman, D., Holland, X., Hippe, C. et al. (1999). Using quality function deployment to capture the voice of the customer and translate it into the voice of the provider. *Joint Commission Journal on Quality Improvement, 25(6),* 300–315.

Chassin: M. (1998). Is healthcare ready for Six Sigma quality? *The Milbank Quarterly, 76*(4), 565–591.

Coiera, E. (2003). *Guide to Health Informatics* (2nd ed.). New York: Oxford University Press.

Cook, R. I., & McDonald, J. S. R. & Smalhout, R. (1989). Human error in the operating room, Identifying cognitive lock up. *Cognitive Systems Engineering Laboratory Technical Report 89-TR-07.* Columbus, OH: Department of Industrial and Systems Engineering, Ohio State University.

Covvey, H. D., Zitner, D., Bernstein, R., & MacNeill, J. E. (2001). The development of model curricula for health informatics. In V.L. Patel, R. Rogers, & R. Haux (Eds.), *Medinfo 2001, Proceedings of the 10th World Congress on Medical Informatics,* (pp. 1009-1113). Amsterdam: IOS Press.

Covvey, H. D., Zitner, D., & Bernstein, R. M. (2001, March). Pointing the way: Competencies and curricula in health informatics. *H/IT Advisors.* Available online at http://www.informatics-review.com/thoughts/pointing.html

Crane, A. B. (2007). Management engineers: A scientific approach to pinpoint a hospital's problems and find common-sense solutions. *Hospitals & Health Networks, 4,* 50–54.

Curry, A., & Knowles, G. (2005). Strategic information management in health care – myth or reality? *Health Services Management Research, 18*(1), 53–62. doi:10.1258/0951484053051942

Dinkelbach, W. (1990). Operational research modeling. In Grochla, E. V. (Ed.), *Handbook of German Business Management* (pp. 1564–1575). Stuttgart, Germany: Poeschel/Springer.

Eich, H. P., Ohmann, C., & Lang, K. (1997). Decision support in acute abdominal pain using an expert system for different knowledge bases. In *Proceedings of 10th IEEE Symposium on Computer-Based Medical Systems (CBMS'97).* Available online at http://csdl2.computer.org/persagen/DLAbsToc.jsp?resourcePath=/dl/proceedings/cbms/&toc=http://csdl2.computer.org/comp/proceedings/cbms/1997/7928/00/7928toc.xml&DOI=10.1109/CBMS.1997.596400

England, R. S. (2007). *The physician's role in rising health care costs: Perspectives on the high and rising cost of physician compensation.* Retrieved March 17, 2008, from http://64.233.167.104/search?q=cache,p9wh2ciGLA8J,www.age-usa.org/docs/Robert_England_Paper_on_MDs_and_Health_Costs.doc%3FPHPSESSID%3D6219d b4f036f9151c3b77607dd56eb85+The+Physici an%E2%80%99s+Role+in+Rising+Health+Ca re+Costs&hl=en&ct=clnk&cd=1&gl=us&clien t=firefox-a

Fayyad, U., Piatetsky-Shapiro, G., & Smyth, P. (1996, Fall). From data mining to knowledge discovery in dDatabases. *AI Magazine,* (pp. 37-54). Retrieved on December 17, 2008 from http://borg.cs.bilgi.edu.tr/aimag-kdd-overview-1996-Fayyad.pdf

Feistritzer, N. R., & Keck, B. R. (2000). Perioperative supply chain management. *Seminars for Nurse Managers, 8*(3), 151–157.

Feld, C. S., & Stoddard, D. B. (2004). Getting IT right. *Harvard Business Review, 82*(2), 72–79.

Fogarty, K. (2006). Stitching up health records, privacy compliance lags. *eWeek.* Retrieved August 10, 2009 from http://www.eweek.com/article2/0,1896,1949646,00.asp

Friedman, C. P., Altman, R. B., Kohane, I. S., McCormick, K. A., Miller, P. L., & Ozbolt, J. O. (2004). Training the next generation of informaticians: The impact of "BISTI" and bioinformatics – A report from the American College of Medical Informatics. *Journal of the American Medical Informatics Association, 11*(3), 167–172. doi:10.1197/jamia.M1520

Friman, O., Borga, M., Lundberg, M., Tylén, U., & Knutsson, H. (2002, August). Recognizing emphysema: A neural network approach. In *ICPR'02 Proceedings of 16th International Conference on Pattern Recognition.* Available online at http://www.imt.liu.se/mi/Publications/Publications/PaperInfo/fbltk02.html

Glaser, B. (2002). *Efficiency versus sustainability in dynamic decision making, Advances in intertemporal compromising.* New York: Springer-Verlag.

Godfrey, M. M., Nelson, E. C., Wasson, J. H., Mohr, J. J., & Batalden, P. B. (2003). Microsystems in health care, Part 3. Planning patient-centered services. *Joint Commission Journal on Quality and Safety, 29*(4), 159–170.

Gong, Y. (2009). An Intelligent Medical Incident Reporting System [Kuala Lumpur.]. *HiMSS Asia-Pac, 09*(Feb), 24–27.

Gong, Y., Richardson, J., Luan, Z., Alafaireet, P., & Yoo, I. (2008). *Analyzing Voluntary Medical Incident Reports,* AMIA Annual Symposium.

Green, L. V. (2004). Hospital capacity planning and management. In Brandeau, M. L., Sainfort, F., & Pierskalla, W. P. (Eds.), *Operations Research and Health Care: A Handbook of Methods and Applications* (pp. 15–42). Boston: Kluwer Academic Publishers.

Hansen, J. I., & Thompson, C. A. (2002). Knowledge management: When people, process, and technology converge. *LIMRA's MarketFacts Quarterly, 21*(2), 14–21.

Harry, M. J. (1988). *The nature of six sigma quality.* Schaumburg, IL: Motorola University Press.

Hauser, J. R., & Clausing, D. (1988). The house of quality. *Harvard Business Review, 3,* 63–73.

Healthcare Information and Management Systems Society (HIMSS). (2007). *Management engineering and process improvement.* Retrieved March 28, 2008 from http://www.himss.org/ASP/topics_managementProcess.asp

Hebbar, S., Pasupathy, K., & Williamson, M. (2008). Determinants of patient satisfaction. In *Proceedings of the 3rd INFORMS Workshop on Data Mining and Health Informatics,* Washington, DC.

Hempel, P. S. (2004). Preparing the HR profession for technology and information work. *Human Resource Management, 43*(2/3), 163–177. doi:10.1002/hrm.20013

Hersh, W. (2002). Medical informatics – improving health care through information. *Journal of the American Medical Association, 288,* 1955–1958. doi:10.1001/jama.288.16.1955

Hersh, W. (2006). Who are the informaticians? What we know and should know. *Journal of the American Medical Informatics Association, 13,* 166–170. doi:10.1197/jamia.M1912

Hersh, W. (2008a). Health and biomedical informatics: Opportunities and challenges for a twenty-first century profession and its education. In Geissbuhler, A., & Kulikowski, C. (Eds.), *IMIA Yearbook of Medical Informatics 2008* (pp. 138–145). Stuttgart, Germany: Schattauer.

Hersh, W. (2008b). *Information retrieval: A health and biomedical perspective* (3rd ed.). New York: Springer.

Hershey, J., Pierskalla, W., & Wandel, S. (1981). Nurse staffing management. In Boldy, D. (Ed.), *Operational research applied to health services* (pp. 189–220). London: Croom-Helm Ltd.

Institute of Medicine. (2001). *Crossing the quality chasm: A new health system for the 21st century.* Washington, DC: National Academy Press.

Johnson, A. C., & Warkentin, M. (2008). Information privacy compliance in the healthcare industry. *Information Management & Computer Security, 16*(1), 5–19. doi:10.1108/09685220810862715

Kachhal, S. K., & Schramm, W. R. (1995). Changing roles of IEs in healthcare. *IIE Solutions, 27*(9), 26–30.

Kaplan, R. S., & Norton, D. P. (1992). The balanced scorecard – measures that drive performance. *Harvard Business Review, 70,* 71–79.

Kaplan, R. S., & Norton, D. P. (1996a). *The balanced scorecard-translating strategy into action.* Boston: Harvard Business School Press.

Kaplan, R. S., & Norton, D. P. (1996b, Fall). Linking the balanced scorecard to strategy. *California Management Review, 4,* 53–79.

Khatri, N. (2006a). Building HR capability in health care organizations. *Health Care Management Review, 31*(1), 45–54.

Khatri, N. (2006b). Building IT capability in health care organizations. *Health Services Management Research, 19*(2), 73–79. doi:10.1258/095148406776829095

Klein, H. A., & Isaacson, J. J. (2003). Making medication instructions usable. *Ergonomics in Design, 11*, 7–11.

Klein, H. A., & Meininger, A. R. (2004). Self-management of medication and diabetes, cognitive control. *IEEE Transactions on Systems, Man, and Cybernetics. Part A, Systems and Humans, 34*(6), 718–725. doi:10.1109/TSMCA.2004.836791

Kohn, L. T., Corrigan, J. M., & Donaldson, M. S. (Eds.). (2000). *To err is human: building a safer health system. Committee on Quality of Health Care in America, Institute of Medicine.* Washington, DC: National Academy Press.

Kurstedt, H. A. (2000). *Management systems theory, applications, and design.* Blacksburg, VA: Manuscript, Virginia Tech.

Lattimer, V., Brailsford, S., Turnbull, J., Tarnaras, P., Smith, H., & George, S. (2004). Reviewing emergency care systems. I: Insights from system dynamics modeling. *Emergency Medicine Journal, 21*, 685–691. doi:10.1136/emj.2002.003673

Lehmann, H. P., & Shortliffe, E. H. (2003). Information technology support of clinical research: An introduction. *Information Systems Frontiers, 5*(4), 415–419. doi:10.1023/B:ISFI.0000005654.91278.5a

Lyman, P., & Varian, H. R. (2003). *How much information.* Retrieved on December 17, 2008 from http://www.sims.berkeley.edu/how-much-info-2003

McCarthy, V. (1997). Strike it rich! *Datamation, 43*(2), 44–50.

McDermott, R. (1999). Why information technology inspired but cannot deliver knowledge management. *California Management Review, 41*(4), 103–117.

McLaughlin. D. B. & Hays, J. M. (2008). Health-care operations management. Chicago: Health Administration Press.

Medina-Borja, A., & Pasupathy, K. (2007, August). Uncovering complex relationships in system dynamics modeling: Exploring the use of CHAID and CART. In *Proceedings of the System Dynamics Conference,* Boston.

Medina-Borja, A., Pasupathy, K., & Triantis, K. (2007). Large scale data envelopment analysis (DEA) implementation: A strategic performance management approach. *The Journal of the Operational Research Society, 58*(8), 1084–1098. doi:10.1057/palgrave.jors.2602200

Melville, N., Kraemer, K., & Gurbaxani, V. (2004). Information technology and organizational performance: An integrative model of IT business value. *Management Information Systems Quarterly, 28*(2), 283–322.

Mikhailov, A.I., Chernyl, A.I., & Gilyarevskii, R.S. (1966). Informatika – novoe nazvanie teorii naučnoj informacii. *Naučno tehničeskaja informacija, 12,* 35–39.

Mitchell, T. M. (1997). Does machine learning really work? *AI Magazine, 18*(3), 11–20.

Molina, G., & Medina-Borja, A. (2006). Are we teaching our students to think systematically? Systems thinking in engineering education. *International Conference on Engineering Education,* San Juan, PR.

Monden, Y. (1983). *Toyota production system, practical approach to production management.* Norcross, GA: Industrial Engineering and Management Press, Institute of Industrial Engineers.

Mullinax, C., & Lawley, M. (2002). Assigning patients to nurses in neonatal intensive care. *The Journal of the Operational Research Society, 53*(1), 25–35. doi:10.1057/palgrave/jors/2601265

Murray, M., & Berwick, D. M. (2003). Advanced access, reducing waiting and delays in primary care. *Journal of the American Medical Association, 289*(8), 1035–1040. doi:10.1001/jama.289.8.1035

National Institute of Standards and Technology (NIST). (2009). *Baldrige National Quality Program.* Available online at: http://www.quality.nist.gov

Neelamkavil, F. (1987). *Computer simulation and modelling.* New York: Wiley.

Nelson, R. & Joos, I. (1989). On language in nursing: From data to wisdom. *PLN Visions, 6.*

Ness, R. M., Klein, R. W., & Dittus, R. S. (2003). The cost-effectiveness of fecal DNA testing for colorectal cancer. *Gastrointestinal Endoscopy, 57*(5), AB94–AB94.

Noor, A. K. (2007). Re-engineering healthcare. *Mechanical Engineering (New York, N.Y.), 11,* 22–27.

O'Keefe, R. M. (1985). Investigating outpatient departments, implementable policies and qualitative approaches. *The Journal of the Operational Research Society, 36*(8), 705–712.

O'Neill, L., & Dexter, F. (2004). Evaluating the efficiency of hospitals' perioperative services using DEA. In Brandeau, M. L., Sainfort, F., & Pierskalla, W. P. (Eds.), *Operations research and health care: A handbook of methods and applications* (pp. 147–168). Boston: Kluwer Academic Publishers.

OECD. (2009). *OECD Health Data 2009.* Accessed on August 7, 2009 from http://www.oecd.org/dataoecd/46/2/38980580.pdf

Ozcan, Y. A. Merwln: E., Lee, K., & Morrissey, J. P. (2004). State of the art applications in benchmarking using DEA: The case of mental health organizations. In M.L. Brandeau (Ed.), Operations Research and Health Care: A Handbook of Methods and Applications, (pp. 169–190). Boston: Kluwer Academic Publishers.

Pare, G. (2002). Implementing clinical information systems: a multiple-case study within a US Hospital. *Health Services Management Research, 15,* 71–92. doi:10.1258/0951484021912851

Pasupathy, K., Gong, Y., Vest, S., Cole, N., & Jackson-Thompson, J. (2008). Quality-oriented establishment of characteristics for central cancer registry software systems. *Journal of Registry Management, 35*(2), 81–89.

Pasupathy, K., & Medina-Borja, A. (2008). Integrating Excel, Access, and Visual BASIC to deploy performance measurement and evaluation at the American Red Cross. *Interfaces, 38*(4), 324–337. doi:10.1287/inte.1080.0366

Pasupathy, K., Medina-Borja, A., & Triantis, K. (2008). Performance Measurement and Evaluation System, Intellectual Property, VTIP09-034, http://vtip.org/availableTech/technology.php?id=284982.

Pasupathy, K., & Triantis, K. (2007a). A framework to evaluate service operations: Dynamic service-profit chain. *Quality Management Journal, 14*(3), 36–49.

Pasupathy, K., & Triantis, K. (2007b). Investments in operational attributes and impact on outcomes in training services. In *Proceedings of the System Dynamics Conference,* Boston.

Patterson, E. S., Cook, R. I., Woods, D. D., Chow, R., & Gomes, J. O. (2004). Hand-off strategies in settings with high consequences for failure: lessons for health care operations. *International Journal for Quality in Health Care, 16*(2), 125–132. doi:10.1093/intqhc/mzh026

Pearlson, K. E. (2001). *Managing and using information systems: A strategic approach.* New York: Wiley.

Protti, D. J. (1995). The synergism of health/medical informatics revisited. *Methods of Information in Medicine, 34,* 441–445.

Ray, W. A., Murray, K. T., Meredith, S., Narasimhulu, S. S., Hall, K., & Stein, C. M. (2004). Oral erythromycin and the risk of sudden death from cardiac causes. *The New England Journal of Medicine, 351*, 1089–1096. doi:10.1056/NEJMoa040582

Reid, P. P., Compton, W. D., Grossman, J. H., & Fanjiang, G. (Eds.). (2005). *Building a better delivery system: a new engineering/health care partnership. Committee on Engineering and the Health Care System, Institute of Medicine and National Academy of Engineering.* Washington, DC: National Academy Press.

Schaefer, A. J., Bailey, M. D., Shechter, S. M., & Roberts, M. S. (2004). Medical treatment decisions using Markov decision processes. In Brandeau, M. L., Sainfort, F., & Pierskalla, W. P. (Eds.), *Operations research and health care: A handbook of methods and applications* (pp. 595–614). Boston: Kluwer Academic Publishers.

Shortliffe, E. H. (2005). Strategic action in health information technology: Why the obvious has taken so long. *Health Affairs, 24*(5), 1222–1233. doi:10.1377/hlthaff.24.5.1222

Silipec, S. (1988). Making the switch from manufacturing to health care. *Industrial Engineering (American Institute of Industrial Engineers), 20*(10), 76–77.

Silver, J., Zhang, B., & Pasupathy, K. (2010) Interruptions in Pharmacy: Classification and Error Estimation. *Proceedings of the 2010 Industrial Engineering Research Conference*, Cancun, Mexico.

Silvert, W. (2001). Modeling as a discipline. *International Journal of General Systems, 30*(3), 261–282. doi:10.1080/03081070108960709

Smalley, H. E. (1982). *Hospital management engineering.* New Jersey: Prentice-Hall, Inc.

Spear, S. J., & Bowen, H. K. (1999). Decoding the DNA of the Toyota production system. *Harvard Business Review, 77*(5), 96–106.

Sterman, J. D. (2000). *Business dynamics, system thinking and modeling for a complex world.* New York: Irwin McGraw-Hill.

Sterman, J. D. (2002). All models are wrong: reflections on becoming a systems scientist. *System Dynamics Review, 18*, 501–531. doi:10.1002/sdr.261

Sullivan, L. P. (1986). Quality function deployment. *Quality Progress, 19*(6), 39–50.

Sullivan, L. P. (1988). Policy management through quality function deployment. *Quality Progress, 21*(6), 18–20.

Sweeney, L. B., & Sterman, J. D. (2000, Winter). Bathtub dynamics, initial results of a systems thinking inventory. *System Dynamics Review, 16*, 249–286. doi:10.1002/sdr.198

Taylor, K., & Dangerfield, B. (2005). Modelling the feedback effects of reconfiguring health services. *The Journal of the Operational Research Society, 56*, 659–675. doi:10.1057/palgrave.jors.2601862

Thomas, J. A., Martin, V., & Frank, S. (2000). Improving pharmacy supplychain management in the operating room. *Healthcare Financial Management, 54*(12), 58–61.

Tsay, A. A., & Nahmias, S. (1998). Modeling supply chain contracts: A review. In Tayur, S., Magazine, M., & Ganeshan, R. (Eds.), *Quantitative models for supply chain management* (pp. 299–336). Boston: Kluwer Academic Publishers.

Wei, J. S., Greer, B. T., Westermann, F., Steinberg, S. M., Son, C. G., & Chen, Q. R. (2004). Prediction of clinical outcome using gene expression profiling and artificial neural networks for patients with neuroblastoma. *Cancer Research, 64*(19), 6883–6891. doi:10.1158/0008-5472.CAN-04-0695

Wigand, R. T., Picot, A., & Reichwald, R. (1997). *Information, organization and management: Expanding markets and corporate boundaries.* Hoboken, NJ: Wiley & Sons.

Winner, R. I., Pennell, J. P., Bertrand, H. E., & Slusarczuk, M. M. G. (1988). *The role of concurrent engineering in weapons system acquisition.* IDA Report R-338. Alexandria, VA: Institute for Defense Analysis.

Wu, B., Hicks, L., Jang, W., Savage, G., Pasupathy, K., Klein, C., et al. (2007). Conceptual framework of healthcare systems engineering and pilot curriculum development. In *Conference of American Society of Engineering Education*, Hawaii.

Zhang, B., & Pasupathy, K. (2009). *Pharmacy System Informatics: Data Mining using Data Envelopment Analysis to Improve Performance.* San Diego, CA: Data Mining System Informatics Workshop.

Chapter 10

Healthcare among the People:
Teams of Leaders Concept (ToL) and the World of Technology–Oriented Global Healthcare

Dag von Lubitz
MedSMART Inc, FUSA

ABSTRACT

The revolution in information technology and in information and knowledge management contributed to the generation of actionable information and actionable knowledge required to address critical problems of national and global health care. Yet, despite expectations, e-based approaches are far from fulfilling the dream of equitable and universal access to health across the globe. A dramatically new approach is needed if health care is to be brought "among the people." Based on maximum integration of computer technology (CT), information technology (IT), information management (IM), and knowledge management (KM), and multidimensional human expertise, the concept of "Teams of Leaders" (ToL) provides a foundation for such an approach. Utilizing the entire spectrum of IT/IM/KM, irrespective of specific platforms, and harnessing globally distributed human expertise, Teams of Leaders transcend bureaucracies and politics, create "bottom-up" flows of ideas and knowledge, and generate horizontal and vertical collaboration among hitherto isolated actors. By empowering people rather than concentrating on technology-facilitated improvements of processes, ToL may prove to be one of the pivotal concepts behind the desperately needed healthcare revolution.

INTRODUCTION

The past 20 years have been characterized by the unprecedented alteration of the world's political structure. The initially slow changes induced by the collapse of the Soviet Union combined with the

explosive growth of information and telecommunication technologies, has led to a global avalanche of new thought, structure, and action. The rapidly developing and enthusiastically embraced spirit of mondialism has been instrumental in shifting international relations from polarization to a meshwork of political and economical alliances spanning the entire globe and most of its peoples. While the

DOI: 10.4018/978-1-61520-733-6.ch010

growing popularity of the Internet and electronic means of conducting business across the boundaries of time and space provided impetus for the rapid change of seemingly immutable attitudes in the West, the new means of communication among individuals and groups facilitated the coalescence of previously isolated isles of social and political dissatisfaction into larger, more structured entities. Unified, their concerted action rapidly transformed into the growing application of historically unprecedented, worldwide pressures applied by militant, non-nation state actors. With ever increasing speed, power started to move from access and possession of money to the level of connectivity and unfettered access to the expanse of global networks (Rothkopf, 2008; Slaughter, 2009).

The striking change of global political and economic frameworks was inevitably accompanied by the emergence of several new destabilizing societal factors. Among the most telling indicators of the growing complexity of factors contributing to worldwide stress is the inclusion of resources, environment, and demographics as elements critically impacting the level of national and global security (Tuchman Mathews, 1989). Despite this awareness, the ongoing globalization of economic and social relations introduced and facilitated by the progress of information and telecommunication technologies (Rifkin, 2001) has done little to assuage problems of the less developed world (Adato & Meinzen-Dick, 2002; Hussain, 2001; but also see Mishra, 2003; Sharma 2005). Despite increasingly frequent warnings of violent consequences (Priest, 2004; Smith, 2007), the process of destabilization appears unstoppable: the gap between the rich and the poor widens.

There is no more doubt that health care has a powerful impact on regional, or even global, stability and security (Associated Press, 2006; Carter, 2008; Garrett, 2007a). Yet, even if equitable access and delivery of healthcare services is a frequent subject of national and international debates (e.g., WHO, 2008), there is a pronounced

lack of a coherent strategy leading to a rapid and efficient implementation of sustainable health care in poverty stricken parts of the world (Bazell, 2007; Garrett, 2007a, 2007b; Sachs, 2007; see also Medscape Today Editorial, 2008).

The West entered the period of "technology rapture" and the belief that the IT/IM/KM trinity will solve most of the dilemmas of its ailing and ageing populations. The "Rest" chafes under pressures generated by the scarcity of providers, modern medicaments, adequate training, and the ponderous and bureaucratic methods of their affluent counterparts (Carr 2004; Colgan, 2002; Stuckler et al., 2008). Yet, it is from precisely those regions where healthcare services are at their worst that globally threatening diseases emerge (Bhargava & Chatterjee, 2007; Durbak & Straus, 2005; Fonkwo, 2008; Garrett, 2007 a, 2007b). E-health care, explosively developing among the affluent countries of the world, seems not to make any difference in regions where threats emerge, and whose populations are most exposed to their impact. What is good for the goose is still the distant dream of the gander (von Lubitz, Levine, & Wolf, 2002). Meanwhile, the issue of health care for the world's most impoverished silently crept from a subject occasionally pricking the collective Western conscience to the forefront of global security (Heymann, 2003; US National Security Council, 2008; Zilinskas & Chapman, 2007).

GLOBAL HEALTH CARE IN CRISIS

The Missing Doctor

Health and its maintenance are considered a basic human right (Gruskin & Tarantola, 2002; WHO, 2006), and the Western nations make continuous efforts to assure the widest access of all their citizens to the highest possible quality of health care (European Institute of Medicine, 2003; National Coalition on Healthcare, 2004). Among developing and less developed nations the situation is far worse: in several regions of the globe even rudimentary healthcare services are often unavailable or even non-existent (Akhtar, 1991; Gesler & Webb, 1983). Statistically, in 1983 the number of physicians per 10,000 people in several African countries was less than one (Gesler & Webb, 1983). Twenty years later, the situation has not improved (Chen et al., 2004; Scheffler, Liu, Kinfu, & Dal Poz, 2008; World Health Statistics, 2008). The scarcity of physicians is matched by the lack of nurses, healthcare technical personnel, inadequate facilities, and the increasing "brain-drain" (Social Watch, 2008; von Lubitz et al., 2002; WHO, 2008). Unsurprisingly, in several countries of the Third World the level of deliverable health care stagnates, or even retreats, rather than advances (Social Watch, 2008).

The Missing Money

Although the EU's healthcare expenditure is about 50% that of the US, Europeans appear to receive an equal, if not better quality of care, compared to US patients (World Health Organization, 2004, 2006, 2008). It seems, therefore, that neither gross nor per capita expenditure on health care provides the best indicator of the actual effect of money spent on maintenance of health. While the United States spent in 2001 nearly $ 4,900 per person, and Mexico, its closest southern neighbor, disbursed $ 370, Mali could afford only $ 12 per person (World Health Organization Report, 2004, 2008; see also Abel Smith, 1989). Mali may have vastly lower administrative burdens, its salary levels may be significantly less, and its population altogether vastly healthier than that of the US. However, the significance of the healthcare expenditure figures becomes deeply alarming when seen in the context of mortality rates caused by "common illnesses" such as cardiovascular disease (CVD). For a very long time CVD has been considered the "malady of Westerners." Yet, a recent study showed that in India and South Africa, CVD mortality rates are now vastly higher than in the West, and nearly

identical to those seen in the US thirty years ago, i.e., prior to the development of effective means of treatment (Leeder, Raymond, Greenberg, Liu, & Esson, 2004). Both India and South Africa are approximately at the middle of the healthcare expenditure list. The situation is similar in other developing and underdeveloped countries (World Health Organization, 2004; World Health Statistics, 2008). Hart's observation made in 1995 (Hart, 1995) that increasing demand for health care is accompanied by proportionately fewer resources available to provide such care, holds as true today as when it was made. Moreover, there is rapidly growing evidence that indicates that diseases affect nations not only by forcing them to spend money on their elimination, but also by reducing productivity, and consequently, their gross national product (Hart, 1995; Leeder et al., 2004; Sachs, 2001; World Health Organization, 2004, 2008). The effect of this trend is felt most strongly among the countries with middle to low per capita incomes, i.e., where the incidence of preventable diseases is also the highest (World Health Organization, 2008).

The Price of New Arrivals

Recent outbreaks of potentially pandemic diseases such as SARS or avian influenza demonstrated that in addition to AIDS, malaria, or tuberculosis, there is a growing potential for the emergence of new infectious diseases whose consequences may have a crippling effect on national, or even global, economies (Economist, 2003; Fonkwo, 2008; Garrett, 2007a, 2007b; Lee et al., 2003; Lee & McKibbin, 2003; Zilinskas & Chapman, 2007). The close relationship between disease and economy has also been recognized by the members of the World Economic Forum who stressed that health will not only have a major impact on the future of business, but also on global security (Evans, 1993; Sachs, 2001; US National Intelligence Council, 2008; World Economic Forum, 2002). Moreover, the extent of cumulative consequences related to the new pandemics appears to be far greater than the regional social and economic destabilization caused by HIV/AIDS (Zilinskas & Chapman, 2007).

Many of the diseases considered major bioterrorism candidates (such as hemorrhagic fevers, anthrax, plague) are endemic to countries within the "non-integrating gap" of Barnett (2004) where a combination of poverty, poor health care, and politico/economical instability serve as the natural breeding grounds for regional conflicts and terrorism (Barnett, 2004; Garrett, 2001; Smith, 2007; US National Intelligence Council, 2008). Addressing problems posed by inadequacy of health care in these critical regions is greatly complicated by Western commercial interests (Bissio, 2008), contributing to the drain of resources spread already thin by the need to rebuild the *entire* social, economic, and political fabric of societies slowly emerging from devastating conflicts (Fukuyama, 2004; Priest, 2004). Based on strategies that lack clarity and precision, the efforts to establish acceptable levels of basic healthcare services in the destitute parts of the world are poorly coordinated, and the outpouring of fiscal resources produces only a minimal ground effect (Garrett, 2007a; Social Watch, 2008; World Health Statistics, 2008).

HEALTH CARE AND ADVANCED INFORMATION AND KNOWLEDGE MANAGEMENT TECHNOLOGIES

Health care is an information rich and knowledge intensive environment. In order to treat and diagnose even a simple condition a physician must integrate and synthesize data from a large number of clinical and administrative sources to allow medically appropriate management of the disease. Medical care must be backed up by efficient administrative systems assuring efficient use of resources. Finally, the overall healthcare structure needs to be supervised and supported by legisla-

tive foundations that in turn reflect directly on the manner in which health care is provided. Given the need to combine massive amounts of data and information into a coherent whole and disseminate these findings to practitioners, administrators, and political decision makers in a timely fashion, the benefits of ICT to support healthcare operations are indisputable (Ball & Lillis, 2000; Ellingsen & Monteiro, 2008; Hagland, 2008; Korukonda & Korukonda, 2006; Wu, Huang, Hisa, & Tsai, 2006; Yee, 2007).

Big Problems of the Small, but Vital

Unsurprisingly, the combination of the last decade's development in advanced telecommunications, information technology (IT), and information and knowledge management (IM and KM) resulted in proliferation of healthcare-oriented electronic platforms such as EHRs (electronic health records), PACS (picture archiving and communication systems), CDSS (clinical decision support systems), etc. (Dols, 2001; Wen & Tan, 2005). Paradoxically, the investment in ICT may have also resulted in unforeseen frustrations, elevated rather than reduced operational costs, or even in confusion, with the potential to endanger patient safety (Ash & Bates, 2005; Boaden & Joyce, 2006; Charette, 2008; Joshi, 2008; Miller, West, Martin Brown, Sim, & Ganchoff, 2005; Sidorov, 2006). Until very recently, one of the principal reasons behind these difficulties was the platform-centric application of ICT (Bates, 2005; Binns, 2004; Blobel, 2004; Iakovidis, 1998; von Lubitz, in press; von Lubitz & Wickramasinghe, 2006a). Despite these problems at the micro-operational level, where interoperating single-vendor systems are utilized, implementation of electronic healthcare technologies brought significant benefits. At the macro level however (e.g., national or global) major difficulties emerged (Brewin, 2008; Ellingsen & Monteiro, 2008; Mandl, Szlovitts, & Kohane, 2001): a combination of islands of automation, information silos, and incompatible data/

information and knowledge bases significantly increased the potential for chaos. Consequently, instead of enabling and facilitating smooth and seamless flow of relevant information across the entire spectrum of involved actors, inappropriately employed e-based methods may add to the already existing problems (von Lubitz, in press; von Lubitz & Wickramasinghe, 2006a, 2006b; see also Haux, 2006).

The issue of compatibility and interoperability of platforms and platform systems is not trivial. Health care represents a unique, ultra-complex environment that can be characterized as the *domain of domains* (von Lubitz, in press). As indicated in the Introduction, at the level of large scale operations (national, multinational, and global), the efficient delivery of health care is contingent on a number of seemingly unrelated factors, while simultaneously affecting these factors with equal and reciprocal intensity. Economy, political stability, social structure, infrastructure development and quality within the region, even cultural characteristics of the target population, may have an important bearing on the combined effectiveness of the overall effort. Compounding these difficulties is the fact that the increase in efficiency and quality of the delivered health care does not depend solely on the efficient business models or clinical approaches: translation of research results into clinical practice, development of new drugs, personnel training at all level of their involvement in the process of delivery, and even patient education play an increasingly important role. Implementation of error-free and safe national or international EHR systems is clearly only a single aspect of the very complex territory. It is, therefore, at the level of utmost complexity, where individual domains intersect into a unified field of *healthcare operations* rather than the narrowly defined health care itself that both the major benefits and equally major difficulties of implementing advanced information/communications/computing technologies (IC^2T)

become apparent (Joshi, 2008; von Lubitz & Wickramasinghe, 2006a).

Big Headaches of the "Big Hitters"

Grid computing, cloud computing, and network-centric operations have been suggested as the operational platforms capable of sustaining the rapidly increasing demand for information and knowledge processing in health care (Kladiashvili, in press; Sujith, 2008; von Lubitz, in press; von Lubitz & Wickramasinghe, 2006a). Problems of system compatibility and interoperability are particularly acute at this high end of e-operations in health care, and the need for "adapters, shims, and glue" is urgent (Radetzky et al., 2006). Paradoxically, although effective solutions are eagerly sought, (BioMoby Consortium, 2008; Oliveira et al, 2005; Oster et al., 2008; Radetzky et al., 2006; Saltz et al., 2008), the number of different approaches that have been chosen increases uncertainty; it is entirely unknown what will emerge as the universal standard. If, as in the past, purely commercial considerations prevail, there is a strong likelihood that the individual healthcare sub-fields will once again select what is most suitable to the demands and peculiarities of each individual discipline with disregard, or only cursory attention, to the needs of others. In the current commercially driven platform-centric mentality of health care, free market forces and the resulting competition may suppress the overall requirements of the healthcare system as a whole (von Lubitz & Wickramasinghe, 2006a) leading to the renewed fragmentation and solidification of platform-centric philosophy. Consequently, any form of integrative, multi-platform work will demand the development of new middleware that will contribute another layer of problems of reliability, adaptability, and conformity with both the future and legacy platforms. Unsurprisingly, several authors continue to draw attention to the persistently retarding impact of these factors on the implementation of cross-domain grid computing as a tool in collaborative, broad-scope approaches to national and international health care (Bartocci et al., 2007; Hubbard, 2002; Karasawas, Baldock, & Burger, 2004).

One More Chasm: The Cognitive Gap

Probably the least recognized and yet quite significant concern associated with cloud and grid computing, and network-centric operations is the level of practical user comfort (particularly among healthcare providers). The general level of computer literacy among healthcare practitioners (be it on the delivery or administrative side of the field) is average, and may be the source of significant practical difficulties in interactions with the increasingly complex operational environment of the grid or multilayered nets (Kalawsky, O'Brien, & Coveney, 2005; Shefter, 2006; von Lubitz et al., 2008a; Ward, Stevens, Brentnall, & Briddon, 2008). Although implementation of user-transparent portals has been proposed (Aloisio et al., 2005; Andronico et al., 2005; Ichikawa, Date, Kaishima, & Shimojo, 2005; Neerincx & Leunissen, 2005; von Lubitz & Wickramasinghe, 2006b), in view of the continuing deficiencies in advanced computer literacy and skills among healthcare personnel both in the UK and US (Devitt & Murphy, 2004; Lacher, Nelson, Bylsma, & Spena, 2000), even among those nations characterized by the world's most advanced health care and computer environments, the state of intimacy between healthcare practitioners and "mesh of grids" may still be quite far away (von Lubitz, in press). Consequently, a new class of professionals – the human "grid/net-user interfaces" – may need to be created. Neither the problem nor the solution is new to health care: the analysis and interpretation of complex clinical trials or administrative data relies heavily on professional statisticians. Nonetheless, the need to educate a new generation of specialists familiar with advanced computing methods, and their application in handling extensive IM/KM demands

created by the wide range of healthcare-related disciplines will slow down the emergence of grid computing/network-centric operations as an inter-domain collaborative platform even further.

Paradoxically, despite the significant operational impact that e-methods of increasingly greater potency may have, the notions of applying sophisticated, Western style technology to alleviate the health care plight of the poorer nations is unrealistic; in very many LDCs computer-based solutions are simply a secondary issue to the continuous scarcity of the necessary tools, i.e., computers themselves (Bello et al., 2004; Blignaut, 1999; Callen, Buyankhishig,& McIntosh, 2008; Eddirippulige et al., 2007; Social Watch, 2008; UNESCO, 2005). Providing only a partial solution, the use of Personal Digital Assistant interfaces as the entry point to the health care grids and networks of networks (meshes) has been recently suggested (Kalawsky, Nee, Homes, & Coveney, 2005). The combination of the relatively simple functionality of PDAs, ASP (Application Software Provider) philosophy, and wireless access to the Internet may be of particular suitability to providers in the remote/underdeveloped regions where, even with continuing "computer starvation" (UNESCO, 2005), the penetration by information technology and wireless networks continues to improve (von Lubitz & Patricelli, 2006. 2008; von Lubitz et al., 2006; see also Figure 1).

Is it Simply a Matter of Strategy?

Despite the extraordinarily broad scope of current and potential uses, one must bear in mind that the concept of e-health centers on a large-scale adoption of technology platforms, rather than of philosophies that will assure equitable access to health across the globe. Currently, all such platforms are associated with a number of limitations, e.g., standardization, interoperability, and the need for technical expertise to provide maximum utility and functionality. The latter is particularly acute in regions affected by pervasive

Figure 1. Table of worldwide status and evolutionary trend in information science and technology (left arrow: decline, right arrow: improvement. The size of the arrow indicates magnitude of the trend; numbers – number of countries affected) *

	⬅	⬅	No change	➡	➡	Total
Worse	0	0	6[a]	50	3	59
Below average	0	0	4	38[b]	13	55
Above average	0	0	0	6	18	24
Better	0	0	0	6	21[c]	27
Total	0	0	10	100	55	165

[a] Note, however, that two out of three countries in Sub-Saharan Africa experience situations worse than average

[b] Although the situation continues to be below average in South America and the Caribbean significant progress has been made between 2007 and 2008 (Social Watch 2007, 2008)

[c] Principal beneficiaries are Europe and North America

and persistent poverty where the lack of technical expertise and often rudimentary technology infrastructure combines with the paralyzing scarcity of personnel trained in even elementary aspects of healthcare delivery (Social Watch, 2008; World Health Report, 2008; World Health Statistics, 2008; see also UNESCO, 2005).

E-health appears to have a dual nature: it is embraced enthusiastically (and understandably) by the developed societies, yet it may ultimately widen the global gap in access to the "basic human right" - health (WHO, 2006). One must also realize that even among the Western-minded societies, permeation of grid computing and network-centric IM/KM operations in health care is restricted to the most obvious, and, for the most part, domain-specific activities (e.g., bioinformatics, drug discovery, insurance industries) (von Lubitz, in press). Unsurprisingly, due to the commercial potential of such applications, the thrust of development appears to concentrate on these areas as well. In consequence, and contrary to the best intentions, the collaborative, interdisciplinary efforts based on grid computing and network-centricity (Olive, Rahmouni, & Solmonides, 2008 a; Olive et al., 2008b; von Lubitz & Wickramasinghe, 2006a)

are predominantly domain-centered as well (von Lubitz, in press).

As the result of these trends, and despite increasingly wider availability and access to facilitating technologies, much of the information of significance to the broader healthcare community continues to be disseminated in the traditional form of publications, lectures, and university level training. Viewed from the perspective of health care as a "domain of domains" (which is emphatically different from a *healthcare-relevant discipline* perspective – von Lubitz, in press), grid computing is an extraordinarily powerful information management, but only a relatively weak knowledge management, tool. Network-centric operations (or network-enabled capabilities – NEC) (von Lubitz et al., 2008a) are, on the other hand, an excellent tool supporting both knowledge management and generation of new knowledge. However, the output is limited to the exceedingly rich *actionable knowledge* (von Lubitz et al., 2008b) that, as necessary as it may be, is largely inadequate as the substrate for a meaningful, cohesive action on a broad and complex front (von Lubitz, in press).

Altogether, the progress of IT/IM and KM in health care contributed to an unprecedented expansion of knowledge, methods of delivery, and facilitation of provider-recipient interactions. It led to simplification, unification, and potentially a global range of administrative methods that may, ultimately, improve delivery of health care in the worldwide context. At the same time, however, the impact of technology on health care appears as a largely chaotic series of forays, each with a narrowly defined set of goals, none intended as part of a clearly defined, cohesive action executed by national and multinational entities, and intended to transform the existing chaos into a structured, coordinated global effort. Having the extraordinarily potent weapon made available – technology – we seem not to have the strategy that would allow us to use it effectively, efficiently, and with a definitive purpose in mind. At present, however, the concept of e-health simply does not translate into "effect based operations" on the ground.

MATTERS MILITARY

In 2007 a book appeared in which a British general, Sir Rupert Smith, argued that state-on-state war became the concept of the past, and the classical military conflict transited into the state of "war among the people" (Smith, 2007). One may wonder about the connection between war and health care other than the most obvious: en masse generation by the former of the subjects, in all richness and variety of their broken bodies and minds, to be tended by the latter. However, a closer inspection of Smith's arguments reveals a striking applicability of the classical military tenets to the creation of concepts that should serve as the foundation for the efficient and effective approach to global health care (see Table 1).

The "Healthcare Governing Triad" and the Importance of Strategy

Traditionally, the conduct of affairs among nation-states has been directed by the overarching triad of politics, military, and people (von Clausewitz, 1976; see also Gray, 2006). The interplay among the three results in national policies on which subsequent strategies are built. Oddly enough, parallels exist in the arena of health care whose national and international exercise is the result of push-pull forces governing the interaction of politics, the "military" in the form of the healthcare industry (i.e., the entire spectrum of professionals involved in delivery and administration of health care), and the recipients of healthcare services – the people.

Shifts in the balance of power among the constituents of the "governing triad" are mirrored in the ensuing policies and the subsequent strategies employed in fulfillment of goals defined by those policies. Problems emerge when one of the elements of the triad becomes dominant, and the subsequent policies begin to support interests of only one actor. In the US, vacillating political stances combined with the relative apathy of the citizenry led to a vacuum filled by the health care industry. Until recently the latter played the dominant role in defining the strategy which served its own interests, but also significantly contributed to the present dilemmas faced by politicians (i.e., fiscal chaos, uncertainty about future directions, etc.) and health care recipients that is the public (i.e., lack of universal healthcare coverage, inequity of access, uncertainty about the future) (Carr, 2004). However, the balance within the US healthcare governing triad may yet be restored: following the conclusion of the hotly contested healthcare debate in the US. Whether promises Mr. Obama made during his election campaign are realized fully or only in part, and what will be the nature of that "part" when translated into legislation remains yet to be seen. The seesaw of polarization among US lawmakers combined with the intensity of public sentiment on the future course of US health care may provide powerful counterpoints or impetus multipliers to industrial influences and only time will tell what impact the present turbulence and uncertainty will have on clearly defined strategies

Table 1. Critical factors determining operational success of global health care operations*

FORMING	Physical creation of forces that are coherent, adequate, and appropriately structured to deal with the specific theater tasks set forth by the predefined strategy. During the process, personnel, materiel, and all resources required to support deployed forces, including political and economical elements, are amassed, their mutual relationships and dependencies defined, and command structure clarified. In multi-organization, multinational operations the process may be complex and subject to individual actor policies and regulations. Fulfillment of prior national commitments or conference-declared intent, subordination of national interests to operational needs, and to the objectives defined strategy may be the most difficult goal to attain at the force formation stage. Forming of forces in health care operations involves both local (e.g., administrative centers, healthcare facilities, policies, local personnel) and external elements (e.g., outside training personnel, outside delivery personnel, distributed technologies, fiscal resources provided by international entities). In environments where possibility of violence exists adequate security elements must be incorporated into the overall force and their security functions approved both by the local governments and at the international level.
DEPLOYING	Actual movement and placement of forces in preparation for operations. Following placement, command structure is tested, and the rule of unity of theater command enacted. Final pre-operations adjustments are made, essential physical constituents (e.g., technology, supply trains, facilities) are checked for operational adequacy. Personnel readiness and adequacy are confirmed.
DIRECTING	The most difficult element of multi-organization/ international/multinational operations in health care. WHO has advisory and coordinating capacity but does not have command authority. Since execution of strategy at the theater and tactical level of operations demands unity of effort and consequent unity of command, these must be defined by the participating actors and declared binding at the force-forming stage. If theater strategy is to succeed, a similar entity to WW2 SHAEF needs to be created and endowed with similar powers of operational theater command. Fragmented command structure typical of current global health care operations creates, sustains, and amplifies chaos.
SUSTAINING	International healthcare operations are characterized by long duration, intensity of effort, and demand for a very wide range of resources. Unless these factors are clearly recognized, and the price of their sustenance accepted and codified by all involved actors, the ground effort assumes characteristics of an offensive running out of momentum. The effort stalls, efficiency is lost, and the goal is never reached. Sustaining global health care operations demands continuous and unwavering support of people, nations, and international bodies.
RECOVERING	Don't send out a force that you can't get back. And don't deploy a force unless, at the end of the deployment, the effort can be managed locally, sustained locally (eventually only with outside fiscal assistance decreasing over time), and further developed through committed actions of local governments/authorities. The overriding philosophy of international healthcare operations must be the development of independence and sustainability rather than transition from inadequacy to subjugation.

* Modified after Smith, 2007

and subsequent actions, and on the ultimate form of the US healthcare ssytem.

In the EU, healthcare coverage is either universal or near-universal, but significant differences among individual member states exist, and center on the inequity of access, cost containment, and divergent philosophies of delivery (European Policy Center, 2008; Jakubowski & Busse, 1998; WHO, 2008). The balance within the European healthcare governing triad has increasingly shifted toward the political element which imposes regulatory pressures that hamper industry's initiative, and also leads to demonstrable problems in the attainment of stated objectives. With multinational bureaucracies of the European Union laboriously grinding toward goals predetermined by both the EU Parliament and the individual member legislatures, the best, albeit slightly sardonic, indicator of the present and future difficulties of European health care is provided by the EU itself - "The whole European health-care System is very complicated." (See para. 2, Council of Occupational Therapists for the European Union - http://www.cotec-europe.org/eng/22/).

Considering difficulties the richest countries of the world have in grappling with their essentially surmountable problems, a firm global approach to health care appears to be unattainable. The complexity of issues that need to be addressed collides with the vast number of principal and peripheral actors, each with their own, often narrowly defined, agenda that is often not only incompatible with the agendas of others, but also not subordinated to the interests of the whole (Garrett, 2007 a; 2007b; see also World Health Organization and its Reports and other publications at http://www. who.int/ publications/en/.) Coherence, which is the critical aspect of complex, large operations (Smith, 2007) is entirely missing. There is no "governing triad", no checks and balances, and virtually no strategies. Hence, the advocated implementation of e-solutions is not the answer to the existing problems, and simpler concepts must be employed before advanced technology can facilitate further progress.

The Concept of Deployment and Employment of a "Healthcare Force"

It borders on being painfully banal when stating that the development of globally adequate, accessible, and efficient health care is a complex task that badly needs to be addressed. The fact has been obvious to most for several years. What is less obvious is that such development is broadly similar to the creation, deployment, and employment of military force. Rules involved in that process can be adapted then adopted in the civilian reality of health care operations.

Ideally, whether at the national or international level, the existing policies determine what constitutes "adequate healthcare," the strategy directing its development, implementation, and sustainment through allocation of suitable fiscal resources (Figure 2). The process of implementing these policies, be it at the regional, national, multinational, or global level, is contingent on a coherent, highly coordinated application of several mutually interdependent elements. First of all, the adequate number of a wide range of professionals responsible for direct delivery and administration of healthcare services is needed.

Sufficient and activity-relevant materiel required for the delivery of these services (from syringes to clinics) needs to be available wherever the services are delivered, and the continuous flow of that materiel to wherever it is consumed must be assured by the efficient logistics system. Administrative services must exist to support and assure overall coordination of all elements involved in the intended activities. In essence, the equivalent of a military *force* needs to be created (Smith, 2007; see Table 1).

Following its creation, the force is *deployed*, i.e., all its constituent elements are made physically available for the forthcoming *employment*. *Strategic needs* cause the created force to be deployed to the *theater* of operations, where they are employed in order to reach strategically determined objectives (e.g., increase of access to healthcare delivery professionals, reduction of regional morbidity or mortality, or increase in the number of service access points). Attainment of these objectives leads to the fulfillment of the goals defined by the national/international

Figure 2. The ideal environment and activities of a healthcare force

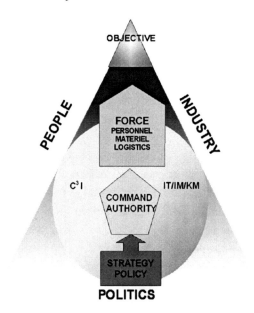

policies. In the context of health care "theater of operations" consists not only of the physical space in which actual operations are conducted (e.g., Sub-Saharan Africa or South-East Asia) but of *all* elements that affect these operations: political realities affecting all participants, economies, social structures, logistics, infrastructure and its availability, presence or absence of moral and political support afforded the employed force by the local population, etc. Health care "theater of operations" may be also represented by a broad concept, e.g., the worldwide reduction of mortality caused by cardiovascular diseases. In that case, physical regions in which relevant operations are conducted become part of the mosaic factors characterizing the conceptual theater rather than its dominant elements. In either case, a thorough understanding all involved nuances is critical: in its absence the effort fails.

Similarities

Factors affecting major health care operations are similar to those governing deployment and employment of military force as the instrument of national strategy. In both cases the implementation is contingent on national policies and on strategies derived from these policies. Operations implementing the chosen strategy are conducted within a theatre of national, international, and progressively more global dimensions. All operations within the theater are inevitably subject to influences caused by the interaction among unpredictable yet tightly inter-related elements. The outcome of these interactions causes "friction" which retards progress, alters its direction, and introduces uncertainty and hesitation (von Clausewitz, 1976). In similarity to military or complex business activities, the entity commanding and controlling health care operations cannot ignore either the "external confounders" or their direct and indirect consequences without risking collapse of the entire effort (Sachs 2001; Sachs, 2007; WHO, 2008). Not surprisingly, national

healthcare crises, such as the outbreak of SARS or the threat posed by avian influenza, are managed using approaches that are ideologically nearly identical to those employed by the military: mobilization of forces that are suitable and adequate to countering the crisis, professionalism of the involved personnel, and support of their effort by technological development (Smith, 2007; see also Figure 2).

Coherence of Effort: Problems of Command and Control in Global Health Care Operations

Similar to the military, the efficiency of healthcare operations is contingent on coherence of effort. Its absence, whether in purpose or due to the divergence between the purpose and resources applied toward its attainment, is the most common and consistent source of failure (Smith, 2007). Current dilemmas of both national and global health care can be tracked to the lack of such coherence. In the US, for example, little is being done to reduce the persistent association between poverty, lack of healthcare insurance, and poor health (Dubay, Holahan, & Cook, 2006; Kaiser Family Foundation, 2008; US Census Bureau, 2008). Largely similar problems are found among other affluent nations (WHO, 2008). Despite billions of dollars spent on healthcare efforts in poor and destitute regions of the world, the missing coherence of effort results in unchanged conditions on the ground (Garrett, 2007a; 2007b; WHO, 2008.)

Lack of coherence among the international efforts to assure access to health care in poverty stricken regions is largely the result of the deficient or non-existent unified command and control. In multinational, highly intricate environments of global healthcare operations, issues of command and control are vastly more complicated and critical than at the national level. Contrary to the national legislative bodies, WHO does not have the mandate either to command or control, but merely to encourage and appeal. Command

and control are therefore reduced to a mosaic implemented by individual actors concentrating on their own segment of the entire effort. Coherence is hopelessly lost, and each involved component of global health care operations, be it a national or international agency (e.g., a national ministry of health or a WHO or UN element), a non-governmental organization (NGO) (such as Red Cross or Red Crescent), or a private or volunteer organization (faith-affiliated groups, private foundations, etc.) conducts its activities at its own tempo, adheres to its own guidelines and policy-dictated schedules, but with little or no coordination with other participating entities. "Global healthcare strategy" emerges as nothing but relatively loosely stitched and independently created plans, intentions, and ideas, all freely interpreted by the participating actors, but formally binding none. Instead of an orderly progression of effect-oriented actions leading toward clearly identified objectives, a chaotic series of forays emerges, all of them costly, most of them ineffective, only a few leading to even partly desirable outcomes, and most eroding the remaining vestiges of trust (Taylor-Goby, 2006). Meanwhile, the spill-over affects adversely non-health care elements such as regional economies, societal and political stability, etc. (Fonkowo, 2008; Garrett 2007a; Sachs, 2001; World Economic Forum, 2002).

In armed conflict, the failure to adhere to some of these fundamental principles and practices of warfare results in the inevitable rout. In health care, the failure to adopt, adapt, and follow similar practices either because they are "military" in nature and therefore evoke hesitation in many, or due to the unawareness that such principles may apply to the non-military setting, results in consequences that are much more subtle: one billion people worldwide have no access to health care (Carr, 2004), over 17 million people die from preventable cardiovascular disease (WHO, 2008), and more than 190,000 worldwide fatalities are caused by measles (mostly in non-immunized children). The latter, despite the existence of a very cheap vaccine

(approximately USD 0.4) that has been available for the past 40 years (WHO, 2008).

The global span of e-based methods that transcend space and time was expected to change all that. However, in the environment characterized by the lack of coherence, implementation of technology both as a "force multiplier" and the creator of cohesion is subject to the influences of the environment in which e-based approaches are to be implemented. In the Third World, poor understanding of the nature of individual theaters of operations, inadequacy of personnel and materiel, uneven nature of support that largely depends on the good will of others contribute to the lacking cohesion of effort, and often lead to mediocre outcomes, simply because the underlying philosophies represent those who promote e-based solutions with the greatest vigor – the developed nations (Akhtar, 1991; Fernandez, 2002; Social Watch, 2008; World Health Report, 2008). Thus, while e-methods that could and should provide the matrix within which the military concept of C^3I (Command, Control, Communications, Intelligence, see Table 2) is executed in order to enhance coherence and health care relevance of all actions, the principal applications of technology concentrate on predominantly commercial tasks that are not always aligned with the health care needs of target populations (UNESCO, 2005; WHO, 2008).

Health Care among the People

In parallel to Smith's observation about war, access, and delivery of health care at the global level became the matter of "healthcare among the people." Realization of this fact is best reflected in the latest World Health Report (WHO, 2008) where, for the first time, the emphasis has been placed on the people, their perception of needs, and the essential role of primary health care as the fundamental platform on which to build the future of global health. Contrary to the past focus on internationalism, collaboration among often

Table 2. Ideal and real role of advanced IT/IM/KM and e- based technologies in C³I framework of large scale health care operations*

ROLE	IDEAL FUNCTION	REALITY
COMMAND	Facilitation of strategic/theater level supervision of the overall effort assuring uniformity and coherence of all actions, their conformity to and alignment with the political goals.	None in the context of the overall effort.
CONTROL	Facilitation of coordination of effort through the determination and implementation of "who, where, when, how." Important in development of "just-in-time work-arounds" in times of increased friction.	None in the context of the overall effort.
COMMUNICATIONS	Backbone of unfettered information and knowledge exchange among hierarchical (vertical), peer (lateral) chains of actors. Network-centric/network-enabled principles particularly useful in assuring reliability of dissemination. Platform-independent implementation utilizing all forms of methods (from legacy to most advanced).	Extensive and highly efficient in the developed and some parts of the developing world; flexible utilization of all platforms and technologies, often in "fused" packages. Badly faltering in the underdeveloped world despite marked increase in web-based communications and wireless telephony
INTELLIGENCE	Collection of all strategic and theater relevant information (including non-healthcare sources) through all means available, e.g., grid/cloud computing, network-centric and network-enabled channels, social networks, and conversion into pertinent actionable knowledge.	Among developed countries extensive and productive within healthcare domain, moderate to poor in assimilation of relevant intelligence from health care unrelated domains. Collection often platform-centric with little cross-over/exchange capability with other platforms. In the developing and underdeveloped countries all aspects sporadic to nonexistent. The exception is growing collection of public health data, where efficiency increases rapidly

*⁾ Note that in the civilian (health care) context, the role of each function is distinctly different from that commonly seen in the military environment: roles may be identical, the functions and significance are not.

gigantic blocks of nations, corporations, and NGOs, the 2008 report places global health care among the people and emphasizes the critical role of the bottom of the health care pyramid – primary care - while underlining the complex vertical and horizontal interactions among the host of issues impacting the establishment of adequate healthcare services at that level (WHO, 2008).

Difficulties notwithstanding, there is a lot of hope that advanced technology may greatly improve all aspects of healthcare access, delivery, and administration and help to eliminate the North-South cleft. Yet, the enthusiastic acceptance of IT, IM, and KM by healthcare professions and all healthcare-related disciplines led also to a paradox where the definition of "continuum of care" offered by the National Cancer

Institute (http://ncim.nci.nih.gov/ncimbrowser/ConceptReport.jsp?dictionary= NCI%20 MetaThesaurus&code=C0009853) sounds similar to the definition of supply chain management (http://jpfarrell.blogspot.com/2008/08/glossary-of-terms-used-on-site.html).

While the implementation of already proven business methods may be both sensible and justifiable (Wickramasinghe & Schaffer, 2006), the uncritical acceptance of business precepts in healthcare practice may lead to the undesired effect of transforming healthcare delivery into an increasingly mechanized and commoditized process, where the ultimate goal of "people" will be swept aside by "technology and processes" of bureaucracy. In the end, although the present use of IT/IM and KM generated a vast amount of healthcare-relevant, domain-specific "actionable knowledge" (von Lubitz et al., 2008a; 2008b) the cardinal transforming element is missing. The presence of this element has been shown to provide a catalyst transforming the wealth of pre-existing actionable knowledge into a clear strategy and coherent, effect-based theater and tactical operations aimed at the strategy-defined objectives (Bradford & Brown, 2008). Ultimately, it is the element that may transform global "healthcare operations" into the reality of "healthcare among the people."

THE CONCEPT OF "TEAMS OF LEADERS" (ToL)

The concept of *"actionable understanding"* was introduced several years ago by the US Army general Frederic Brown to denote the final "product" of all actions and activities performed within the broad realm of the "Teams of Leaders" (ToL) environment (Bradford & Brown, 2008; Brown, 2002). ToL is the direct outcome of the requirements faced by the US Army following the end of the Cold War when the expanded range and character of missions, spanning from combat to peace keeping and nation building, demanded introduction of a completely new readiness model. The new model, based on a clear understanding that in the new environment of global range operations the performance of an individual soldier could lead to strategic consequences, stressed flexibility and deployment readiness.

Today, decisions made by the "man on the spot" have the potential to influence national interests, the fate of alliances, and the difference between rebuilding broken societies and perpetuation of armed conflict. To fulfill such historically unprecedented demands a new breed of soldier-leaders was needed: flexible, adaptable, versatile, and comfortable in operating within the complex setting of Joint Interagency, Inter-government, Multinational (JIIM) operations in which military

and civilian concepts intertwined into a tightly woven mesh (Bradford & Brown, 2008; Brown, 2002; Brown, 2008a, 2008b). In several aspects, the issues affecting the US Army were nearly identical to those still hampering large-scale health care operations today: organizational complexity; wide mission spectrum; the need for mission-centered cooperation of numerous local, national, and international agencies; and the need to adapt in order to address increasingly larger host of rapidly diversifying issues, while continuing simultaneous engagement in routine activities (Brown, 2008a). Overriding all that is the often critical role of the individual healthcare worker whose knowledge, intellectual agility, and the ability to make swift decisions may, indeed, decide the future of the world. SARS and avian influenza outbreaks have clearly indicated that.

WHAT IS ToL?

Conceptually, ToL centers on the active, platform independent fusion of advanced IM, KM and High Performing Leader Teams (HPLT; see Bradford &Brown, 2008; von Lubitz, in press; von Lubitz & Beakley, 2009; also see Figure 3). What distinguishes ToL from a specialized social network is the essential prerequisite for the development and functions of HPLT: the shared foundation of *skills, knowledge,* and *attitudes* (SKA) based on the previously acquired appropriate and universally high-quality professional preparation of individual team members. The preparation demands intensive training to *task, condition, and standard,* and the ability to demonstrate complete, practical mastery of performance.

The details of the required civilian training standards in health care and other fields of operations, and the broad availability of civilian training organizations that satisfy the unprecedentedly high demands have been extensively described elsewhere (von Lubitz, in press; von Lubitz & Beakley, 2009). In the present context it is however

Figure 3. A high performing leader team (HPLT) may consist of individuals (I), teams of individuals (TJ), organizations (O), and virtual organizations (VO)

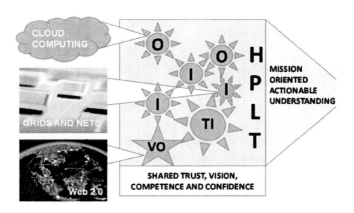

necessary to underline the essential role of rigorous professional training that satisfies strictly defined metrics-based performance standards. Such training assures not only the general uniformity of education/training outcomes that are concomitant with the high professional capability of the participants, but also serves as the chief promoter in the development of shared confidence in mutual professionalism and ability to act appropriately under a very wide range of conditions both as individuals and teams of individuals.

Training alone is not sufficient: it must have roots in active learning which, in the context of leader team development, requires collaborative learning shown to significantly improve critical thinking and task performance (Cavalier & Klein, 1998; Gokhale, 1995; Lou, 2001). To assure the required task performance to a predetermined standard, the learning process is experiential rather than didactic. It also involves routine exposure to sudden, unpredictable scenario changes (confounders) necessary to develop the required mental flexibility and adaptability by individuals within the team and the entire team (Bradford & Brown, 2008; Brown 2002; von Lubitz, 2008). The training approach used in preparation of HPLT members has been pioneered and traditionally used as the cornerstone of professional education

in medicine, nursing, etc. (Kyle & Murray, 2008; Wong, 1996) resulting in mastery of essential skills, knowledge, and the related mental and physical attributes that are employed as easily under routine circumstances as in the environments of maximum stress, uncertainty, and tempo.

Performance assessment under rigorous and highly demanding conditions constitutes the essential part of High Performing Leader Team development. Consequently, training turns into self-evaluation, and evaluation promotes further training: the teams attain pitch efficiency. Due to the standardized approach used in HPLT development, teams can be inserted as "modular elements" whenever and wherever required, and the standardized training/testing regimen assures that organizations, whether real or virtual, which co-opt HPLTs as part of their operational profile will have full confidence and trust in their capabilities. The latter is of possibly the greatest significance in the development of efficiency and cohesion that, in turn, serves as the critical lubricant in multi-organizational efforts (Smith, 2007). Conversely, it has been demonstrated on several occasions (Buck, Trainor, & Aguirre, 2006; McEntire, 1999; Perry 2006; van Rooyen, Hansch, Curtis, & Burnham, 2001) that absence of such trust and acceptance are among the primary reasons for failures during complex humanitarian relief operations in which healthcare activities nearly always play a major role (Brennan & Nandy, 2001; Noji, 2005; Silenas, Waller, D'Amore, & Carlton, 2008; van Rooyen et al., 2001).

ToL as Knowledge Generator and Evidence-Based, Best Practices Generator

Continuing limitations in the use of sophisticated, technology-based methods in the process of generating actionable knowledge (see above, and von Lubitz, in press) may lead to inadvertent "stove-piping." Implementation of ToL avoids this issue through the horizontal spread attained by means of platform-independent, peer-to-peer exchanges, social and professional networks, text- and visual blogs, avatars, etc., whose increasing functionality, reach, and practicality of use are supported and expanded by the rapidly growing impact of Web 2.0 (Anderson, 2007). Combined with the enterprise-wide access to primary information and knowledge sources (e.g., WebMD, BMJ Portal, MDChoice, or CDC Portal or WHO Portal and the professional fora (e.g., NetDoc, DocGuide, or GlobalMedNet), the resulting pervasive, system-wide use of IT promotes generation of ad hoc collaborative entities (teams) needed to address common problems or develop just-in-time solutions. In the process of such interactions, and by fusing expertise of team members and teams with all available e-based resources and analytic tools, both new knowledge and best practices are created. Technology frees individual team members, and teams themselves, from the constraints of time, space, organizational/inter-organizational cultures, and – most importantly – the destructive influence of organizational status and rank. ToL and its inherent processes of action and interaction have been employed with great success by the US Army in a wide range of pilot projects involving both military and civilian affairs (Bradford & Brown, 2008; Brown, 2008a, 2008b; Dixon,

Allen, Burgess, Kilner, & Schweitzer, 2005). Based on the already well-proven methods and techniques ToL is now vigorously implemented on the national and international/multinational scale by the organization of great complexity involved in a wide range of support and nation building missions that demand the closest possible cooperation with other, equally complex, organizations of national, international, multi-national, or even global level (e.g., EU, UN, WHO; see Bradford & Brown. 2008; Brown 2008a).

ToL as an "Action Swarm" Builder

The extensive use of IT, IM, and KM as the means of sharing information and knowledge serves as a powerful promoter of rapid development of shared vision, competence, confidence, and trust (Bradford & Brown, 2008) which, cumulatively, constitute the critical attribute of High Performing Leader Teams. The close relationship of team members to each other, and to members of other teams, is the chief mechanism transforming previously top-down bureaucratic and organizational structures into a bottom-up/lateral knowledge and "best practices" generator. Due to the pervasive nature of the exchanges within the lattice of the rapidly forming relationships, the process of transformation helps to demolish the existing organizational barriers. Instead, close socialization ensues, and fosters further growth of mutual confidence and trust among members of leader teams. The process becomes a chain reaction: professional and social relationships based on universal trust and confidence expand rapidly and freely, and teams of Teams of Leaders begin to emerge. Individuals and groups who have been isolated physically and/or organizationally now convert into "swarms" that converge whenever needed and whose constitution matches exactly the requirements of the task and mission at hand (see Figure 4). Such swarms are essential when addressing problems affecting performance at the level of "domain of domains," and the activities of Teams of Leaders have been shown to restore coherence to disorganized multi-organizational efforts (Bradford & Brown, 2008; Brown 2008a), and help in aligning them with the underlying strategies. Indeed, ToL has reached such a level of maturity and broad utility that its implementation and applications manual has been developed and disseminated by the US Army (Lipnack, Stamps, Prevou, & Hannah, 2010).

ToL as the Generator of "Actionable Knowledge"

Throughout the transition from HPLT to ToL a less tangible but critical advantage emerges: people who previously had no knowledge of each other, who might have been separated by distance, institutional or specialty barriers begin to rapidly form a network of close social relationships. Consequently, the development of collaborative spirit that often characterizes interactions between the local ambulance company and the countryside hospital can now emerge between physicians and first responders residing in different continents. The collaboration-building attribute of ToL is strengthened by the fact that teams can change

their status from informal to formal depending on circumstances. Also, because of the intensity of the existing interactions, team members cooperate as readily and effectively in distributed environments as when the contact is based either on the mix of physical and distributed, or direct interactions. Actionable knowledge generated through network-centric activities that might have been shared between the two isolated groups (von Lubitz et al., 2008a) transforms through ToL-based interaction into a broad based *"actionable understanding"* which unifies several groups (Bradford & Brown, 2008).

Actionable understanding constitutes the most essential prerogative for operational efficiency in the environments of uncertainty and rapid, unpredictable change (Bradford & Brown, 2008) seen, for example, during responses to major disasters or rapidly escalating healthcare threats such as pandemics or incidents of bioterrorism (von Lubitz & Beakley, 2009; von Lubitz & Wickramasinghe, 2006a). Circumstantial evidence also indicates that the lack of such understanding was among the chief sources of errors in the response of national healthcare systems to such catastrophic events as the European heat wave of 2003 or

Figure 4. Operations of teams of leaders

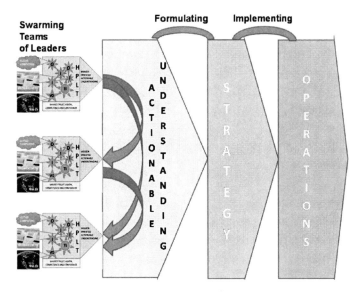

Hurricane Katrina in 2005 (Ballester, Michelozzi, & Iniguez, 2003; Bouchama, 2003; Cooper & Block, 2006; Honore, 2009; Michelon, Magne, & Simon-Delavell, 2005).

Why ToL?

Global population growth, increasing poverty, large scale migrations, climate change, pollution, to name but a few of the host of other emerging issues, all pose new health care problems and risks whose solution, or its absence, may influence the stability of nations, regions, and even the entire globe (Garrett, 1994; Lewis, 2006; von Lubitz et al., 2002). These are issues that cannot be solved by mere per capita increase in the number of healthcare workers in the underdeveloped countries, improved immunization programs, or by promoting maternal health. Today, health care has become tightly intertwined with economy, politics, urban development, industrialization, military operations, and international travel. Suddenly, it became an integral part of the global societal mesh: from a simple concept of assuring health to a manageable number of patients, health care became one of the cornerstones of nearly everything we do. In truth, the efficiency of global healthcare networks may determine the future of the human race. Unless timely contained, an outbreak of a potentially pandemic disease will have a worldwide, destabilizing impact whose consequences are not only grim, but entirely unpredictable (Economist, 2003; Garrett, 1994; Osterholm & Branswell, 2005; PandemicfluGov; Vallat, 2007).

Dissemination and Synthesis of Multidisciplinary Knowledge

Modern health care is a "domain of domains." It is intensely complex, involves disciplines that, until recently, seemed to be entirely unrelated to health care (e.g., military operations or advanced computer technologies and methods, see Kulkarni & Nathanson, 2005; Kun, 2001; Silenas et al., 2009): it represents probably the only field outside military operations where success of missions (particularly when conducted on a national, international, or global scale) demands extraordinarily close cooperation of vast numbers of individuals, agencies, and nations.

Implementation of ToL throughout the entire spectrum of health care operations will have both an immediate and long-lasting effect (see Table 4) chiefly due to the nature in which information and knowledge are gathered, handled, and disseminated.

At peer-to-peer level, ToL promotes lateral spread and sharing of information and knowledge greatly extending beyond one's own professional specialty. Likewise, ToL supports downward migration of knowledge from more experienced/senior professionals within teams to the more junior ones. The direct advantage of such spread is the enhancement of distributed socialization across unrelated, but mutually relevant, intra- and inter-domain professional specialties. In similarity to within-profession trends, on-line communities of practice will form. However, from the outset, ToL promotes and consolidates interdisciplinary and trans-domain communities of practice. The latter facilitate/amplify innovation, contribute to the lateral/vertical dissemination of knowledge, and to the dissemination and development of evidence-based practices (Auf der Heide, 2006; McClure Wasko & Faraj, 2000; Seely Brown & Duguid, 1991; see also Ho, Peterson, & Masoudi, 2008; Kersten, Thompson, & Frohnal, 2008, Nash & Quigley, 2008; Seers, 2007).

ToL as a "Force-Multiplier"

The need for the closest possible cooperation among national and international entities in global health care efforts is evident: operational costs increase at a staggering rate, the access gap widens alarmingly, and almost uncontrollable human bioincursion into new habitats enhances chances

Table 3. Organizational and personal impact of ToL-based activities (after von Lubitz, in press)

TYPE OF ACTIVITY	IMPACT
OPERATIONS	Generates actionable understanding Supports strategy development Promotes mission definition Promotes actor cooperation and collaboration across disciplines and domains Speeds OODA Loop (for observe, orient, decide, and act) cycles Increases OODA Loop operational space and reach Promotes extraction and analysis of mission-relevant intelligence Promotes generation of alternative approaches ("workarounds") Serves as force multiplier Maximizes mission support through the employment of shared skills, knowledge and attitudes
RESOURCES	Promotes strategy-relevant resource assembly Promotes mission-centered, parallel use of intellectual and material resources Maximizes optimal resource exploitation Utilizes legacy and future IT/IM/KM platforms Maximizes resource deployment speed Promotes mission-relevant resource concentration Maximizes utilization of platform-independent CT/IT/IM/KM resources
ORGANIZATION	Promotes creation of collaborative actor grids Promotes ad hoc creation of collaborative virtual organizations and communities of practice Maximizes mission-centered utilization of actionable information and actionable knowledge Supports hierarchical and peer-to-peer interaction Maximizes information and knowledge sharing among all actors of the mission grid Generates bottom-up actionable knowledge generation and top-bottom actionable information flows Promotes interdisciplinary and inter-domain information and knowledge distribution and use
SOCIAL	Maximizes generation of trust and understanding among all actors Enhances mentoring Maximizes personal contacts Enhances personal knowledge and competence beyond boundaries of own discipline/specialization (promotes "generalist" education) Maximizes development of shared skills, knowledge, and attitudes

*The impact of ToL is made clearer by comparison with factors listed in figure 1

of the exposure to pathogens for which we are entirely unprepared (although HIV and Ebola are the best known examples, several other diseases and pathogens have been described in the past decade alone, e.g. Fonkwo, 2008; GAO, 2004; also see Garrett, 1994). Since September 2001 bioterrorism became an ever-present threat, while disasters such as the Tsunami of 2004, Hurricane Katrina, or the Myanmar Cyclone of 2008 showed that we are unable to deal adequately with catastrophic events. At present, the entire healthcare system of the world labors painfully, inefficiently, and very expensively under constraints imposed by conflicting bureaucracies, national politics, and divergent philosophies (Coulter & Ham, 2000; Fernandez, 2002; von Lubitz et al., 2002).

The absence of a clearly defined global strategy and foresight among the Western nations, and our failure to incorporate into future plans anything beyond the most obvious, are not typical of health care alone. The inability of the West to detect, analyze, and counteract the growing dissatisfaction with its policies is among the principal causes underlying the explosive emergence of anti-Western sentiment, religious extremism, and – ultimately – international terrorism as the sole means available to the populations of the "gap" to attain emotional if not economical "parity" with the developed countries (Barnett, 2004; Onen, 2004). In turn, the political destabilization that typically accompanies these extreme forms of protest weakens the economies in the underdeveloped

163

regions, promotes escalation of poverty, and leads to an even greater decline of their already meager (or practically nonexistent) healthcare systems (Akhtar, 1991). Consequently, despite substantial funds provided by multinational Western sources (Garrett, 2007a; Li & Eastman, 2003; Ma'ayeh, 1999; US Mission to the UN, 2002), attempts to establish comprehensive solutions to health care needs of the developing and underdeveloped world continue to fail (Afford, 2003; Attaran, 2004; Pal & Mittal, 2004; Zupan, 2003).

ToL may change all that. It brings to the forefront the fact that technology (such as grid or cloud computing), no matter how powerful it might be, serves nothing but the solution of tactical tasks whether simple or unimaginably complex. Processes (such as IM and KM) or their combination (network-centric operations) lead to the formulation and operational implementation of actionable knowledge, typically also in a very task specific (i.e., narrow) context. By bringing together people able to maximally exploit their mutual talents and expertise, able to efficiently implement technology and processes, and by rooting their activities in the maximum, platform-independent use of all tools and methods and processes offered by ITC, ToL

permits to develop the strategy which serves as the guide and rationale of all subsequent theater operations (Figure 5).

Such strategy cannot be devised by even the most intense application of either technology or processes alone. ToL provides the needed catalyst and force multiplier. It is in that context that ToL, contrary to "within the profession" approaches, supports the development of both evidence-based methods and of best practices among a much wider range of professionals, disciplines, and agencies than has been possible previously. Creation of such best practices binds isolated bureaucracies, their agencies, and personnel into a coherent force operating under uniform "rules of engagement" that the jointly-created best practices represent.

Most importantly, however, ToL brings people to the forefront: it facilitates generation of locally appropriate solutions by the people on the ground. It transforms grand but unrealistic international schemes into a coordinated bottom-up effort whose ground effect becomes measurable, lasting, and aligned with the overall strategy - strategy that is devised on the basis of vertical inputs generated within the realm of ToL operations. All that relates directly to the manner in which e-tools,

Figure 5. Interactions within the ToL environment

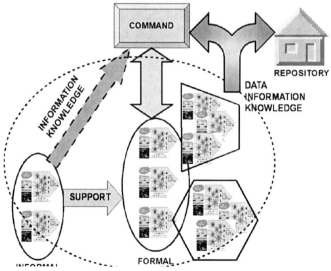
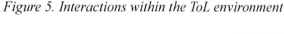

methods, and processes are used in the operational environment of ToL-based healthcare operations: ToL transforms advanced technology from a Ferrari accessible only to a few into a hammer available to all.

ToL as a Builder of Flexible Strategies

In the ToL environment, results are generated at the practitioner level rather than at the level of executive policies (von Lubitz & Beakley, 2009). What emerges is the bottom-up spread of knowledge developed through consensus of practitioners, supported by joint practical experience and accepted by the involved professions far more willingly than directives descending from the executive level of bureaucracies (Tierney, 2006; Ward & Wamsley, 2007). Once thoroughly analyzed and tested within practitioners' communities, the generated best practices can be converted via a hierarchical process into a flexible and practical strategy with clear and attainable objectives. As such, it is a strategy that is acceptable and understandable to all involved actors at the horizontal and hierarchical levels of administration and operations. Continuous up-down-lateral interactions keep the strategy attuned to changes in the operational environment; knowledge ceases to be confined to vertical and often entirely separated channels of profession and bureaucracy, and spreads laterally. Strategy becomes actionable rather than bureaucratic (von Lubitz et al., 2008a). With the development of mutual confidence and trust, it turns into *actionable understanding* (Bradford & Brown, 2008) – the catalyst that transforms individual, often seemingly incompatible, components into a functional entity capable of effective action.

By promoting mutual trust, ToL furthers rapid development and coalescence of shared attitudes among all actors. It is a process of critical significance in international and multinational operations in any arena, be it civilian or military (Bradford & Brown, 2008; Brown, 2008a; Smith, 2007). It has

been said that, in the context of issues facing health care at the global scale, mutual trust has eroded since the policies of the developed nations are rooted within their mono-cultural, ethno-centric concepts, and the remedies proposed by the rich may therefore be beyond the reach and without any relevance to the present and future problems of the poor (Fernandez, 2002). ToL not only allows for fully empowered inclusion and interaction of all affected groups – in order to be effective, the concept of ToL *demands* such inclusion since only then can problems be addressed effectively and efficiently. By its very nature, ToL brings health care among the people.

CONCLUSION

It would be exceedingly naïve to expect that consequent implementation of ToL practices will offer a dilemma-solving panacea. Nonetheless, in the realm of health care it may provide the launch pad for the needed remedies. ToL is endowed with a number of distinct and unique advantages. First of all, the essential physical constituents already exist, several of which have been discussed in this chapter. Furthermore, the ToL concept is already implemented with significant success and on a large scale by the US European Command (EUCOM) as part of its extensive interaction with the civilian authorities of several European and non-European countries (that also include health care issues, e.g., Bradford & Brown, 2008). Hence, "lessons learned" can be readily adopted into the purely civilian environment. Most importantly, however, ToL unifies the currently disconnected fields of health care and its technology support and fosters rapid development of actionable understanding rather than actionable knowledge. As argued in the preceding sections, it is actionable understanding rather than actionable knowledge that serves both as the prerequisite and the *essential* prelude to creating a solid foundation for the development of the badly-needed collaboration and cooperation among all involved health care actors. Without such understanding, all efforts to relieve the mounting pressures of conflicting demands, inequities, and deficiencies will ultimately fail. The signs of the approaching collapse are clearly visible already, and the currently favored erratic application of ever larger amounts of money or increasingly complex, technology-based solutions to avert the inevitable is, equally clearly, utterly inadequate. ToL may be an important contributor in changing all that.

ACKNOWLEDGMENT

Lieutenant General Frederic J Brown, Ph.D., US Army (Ret.) is gratefully acknowledged for stimulating discussions with the author of ToL, its operational and theoretical nuances, and for providing access to the unpublished sources showing the extent of the practical use of ToL. I am also grateful to Claire Rubin, critic extraordinaire and the Editor at Journal of Homeland Security and Emergency Management (JHSEM) who kindly agreed to review the manuscript: her unsparing remarks were instrumental in making it palatable to the reader.

REFERENCES

Abel-Smith, B. (1989). Health economies in developing countries. *The Journal of Tropical Medicine and Hygiene, 92*, 229–241.

Adato, M., & Meinzen-Dick, R. (2002). Assessing the impact of agricultural research on poverty using the sustainable livelihoods framework. *International Food Policy Research Institute (IFPRI)*. Retrieved from http://www.ifpri.org/sites/default/files/publications/eptdp89.pdf

Afford, C. W. (2003). *Corrosive reform: failing health systems in Eastern Europe*. Geneva: International Labour Office. Available at http://www.ilo.org/public/english/protection/ses/download/docs/corrosive.pdf

Akhtar, R. (1991). *Health care patterns and planning in developing countries*. New York: Greenwood Press.

Aloisio, G., Barba, M. C., Biasi, E., Cafaro, M., Fiore, S., & Mirto, M. (2005). A web service-based Grid portal for Edgebreaker compression. *Methods of Information in Medicine, 44*(2), 233–238.

Anderson, P. (2007). *What is Web 2.0? Ideas, technologies and implications for education*. Retrieved from http://www.jisc.ac.uk/media/documents/techwatch/tsw0701b.pdf

Andronico, G., Barbera, R., Falzone, A., Lo Re, G., Pulvirenti, A., & Rodolico, A. (2005). The GENIUS web portal – an easy way to access the Grid. *Methods of Information in Medicine, 44*(2), 215–220.

Ash, J. S., & Bates, D. W. (2005). Factors and forces affecting EHR adoption: Report of a 2004 ACMI discussion. *Journal of the American Medical Informatics Association, 12*(1), 8–12. doi:10.1197/jamia.M1684

Associated Press. (2006). Global warming causing disease to rise: Malaria, dengue fever increasing as temperature heats up, experts warn. *MSNBC*. Retrieved from http://www.msnbc.msn.com/id/15717706/

Attaran, A. (2004). Where did it go wrong? *Nature, 430*, 2–3. doi:10.1038/430932a

Auf der Heide, E. (2006). The importance of evidence-based disaster planning. *Annals of Emergency Medicine, 1*, 34–49. doi:10.1016/j.annemergmed.2005.05.009

Βελλο, Ι.Σ., Αρογυνδαδε, Φ.Α., Σανυσι, Α.Α., Εζεομα, Ι.Τ., Αβιοψε–Κυτεψι, Ε.Α., & Ακινσολα, Α. (2004). Κνοωλεδγε ανδ υτιλιζατιον οφ Ινφορματιον Τεχνολογψ αμονγ ηεαλτη χαρε προφεσσιοναλσ ανδ στυδεντσ ιν Ιλε–Ιφε, Νιγερια: α χασε στυδψ οφ α υνιωερσιτψ τεαχηινγ ηοσπιταλ. *ϑουρναλ οφ Μεδιχαλ Ιντερνετ Ρεσεαρχη, 6* (4), ε45.

Βιομοβψ Χονσορτιυμ. (2008). Ιντεροπεραβιλιτψ ωιτη Μοβψ 1.0 ιτσ βεττερ τηαν σηαρινγ ψουρ τοοτηβρυση. *Βριεφινγσ ιν Βιοινφορματιχσ, 9* (3), 220–231.

Ball, M. J., & Lillis, J. C. (2000). Health information systems: challenges for 21ˢᵗ century. *AACN Clinical Issues, 11*(3), 386–395. doi:10.1097/00044067-200008000-00006

Ballester, F., Michelozzi, P., & Iñiguez, C. (2003). Editorial: Weather, climate, and public health. *Journal of Epidemiology and Community Health, 57*, 759–760. doi:10.1136/jech.57.10.759

Barnett, T. P. M. (2004). *The Pentagon's new map.* New York: Putnam & Sons. Βαρτοχχι, Ε., Χαχχιαγρανο, Δ., Χαννατα, Ν., Χορραδινι, Φ., Μερελλι, Ε., Μιλανεσι, Λ., & Ρομανο, Π. (2007). Αν αγεντ–βασεδ μυλτιλαψερ αρχηιτεχτυρε φορ βιομεδιχαλ γριδσ. *IEEE Network, 6*(2), 142–148.

Bates, D. W. (2005). Physicians and ambulatory electronic health records. *Health Affairs, 24*(5), 1180–1189. doi:10.1377/hlthaff.24.5.1180

Bazell, R. (2007). Global healthcare is fashionable, but falls short. *MSNBC.* Retrieved from http://www.msnbc.msn.com/id/18274808/

Bhargava, A., & Chatterjee, B. (2007). Chikungunya fever, falciparum malaria, dengue fever, Japanese encephalitis...are we listening to the warning signs for public health in India? *Indian Journal of Medical Ethics, 4*(1), 18–23.

Binns, P. (2004). The impact of the electronic health record on patient safety: an Alberta perspective. *Healthcare Papers, 5*(3), 47–51.

Bissio, R. (2008). Rights in the time of crisis. In *Rights is the answer. Social Watch Report 2008,* (pp. 1-3). Retrieved from http://www.socialwatch.org/sites/default/files/pdf/en/bangladeshoverview2008_eng.pdf

Blignaut, P. J. (1999). Software for primary healthcare in a developing country: Background and problem statement. *Computers in Nursing, 17*(6), 291–296.

Blobel, B. (2004). Advanced EHR architectures – promises or reality. In B. Blobel, G. Gell, C. Hildebrand, & R. Engelbrecht, (Eds.), *Contribution of Medical Informatics to Health, Proceedings of MIE 2004 Special Topics Conference,* (pp. 73-78). Amsterdam: IOS Press.

Boaden, R., & Joyce, P. (2006). Developing the electronic record: what about patient safety. *Health Services Management Research, 19*(2), 94–104. doi:10.1258/095148406776829103

Bouchama, A. (2005). The 2003 European heat wave. *Intensive Care Medicine, 30*(1), 1–3. doi:10.1007/s00134-003-2062-y

Bradford, Z. B., & Brown, F. J. (2008). America's army: A model for interagency effectiveness. Westport, CN: Praeger Security International.

Brennan, R. J., & Nandy, R. (2001). Complex humanitarian emergencies: a major global challenge. *Emergency Medicine, 13*(2), 147–156.

Brewin, B. (2008, November 13). Adoption of e-health records depends on consolidation of systems. *NextGov.* Retrieved from http://www.nextgov.com/nextgov/ng_20081113_1406.php

Brown, F. J. (2002). Imperatives for tomorrow. *Military Review, 85*, 81–91.

Brown, F.J. (2008a). *Institutionalizing EUR ToL*. Unpublished working document (author's permission 12/31/08).

Brown, F.J. (2008b). *Designing of ToL pilots*. Unpublished working document (author's permission 12/31/08).

Buck, D. A., Trainor, J. E., & Aguirre, B. E. (2006). A critical evaluation of Incident Command System and NIMS. *Journal of Homeland Security and Emergency Management, 3*(3), 1–27. doi:10.2202/1547-7355.1252

Callen, J. L., Buyankhishig, B., & McIntosh, J. H. (2008). Clinical information sources used by hospital doctors in Mongolia. *International Journal of Medical Informatics, 77*(4), 249–255. doi:10.1016/j.ijmedinf.2007.06.003

Carr, D. (2004). Improving the health of the world's poorest people. [Washington, DC: Population Reference Bureau. Retrieved from http://www.prb.org/pdf/ImprovingtheHealthWorld_Eng.pdf]. *Health Bulletin, 1*.

Carter, M. J. (2008, December 30). Global agenda increasingly disease driven. *Inter Press Service (IPS)*. Retrieved from http://www.ipsnews.net/news.asp?idnews=43619

Cavalier, J. C., & Klein, J. D. (1998). Effects of cooperative versus individual learning and orienting activities during computer-based instruction. *Educational Technology Research and Development, 46*(1), 5–17. doi:10.1007/BF02299826

Charette, R. (2008, May 19). E-health needs better design. *NextGov*. Retrieved from http://techinsider.nextgov.com/2008/05/ehealth_needs_better_design.php

Chen, L., Evans, T., Anand, S., Boufford, J. I., Brown, H., & Chowdhury, M. (2004). Human resources for health: overcoming the crisis. *Lancet, 364*, 1984–1990. doi:10.1016/S0140-6736(04)17482-5

Colgan, A. L. (2002). Hazardous health: the World Bank and IMF in Africa: Africa Action position paper. *Africa Action*. Retrieved from http://www.africaaction.org/action/sap0204.htm

Cooper, C., & Block, R. (2006). *Disaster: Hurricane Katrina and the failure of homeland security*. New York: Times Books/Henry Holt and Company.

Coulter, A., & Ham, C. (2002). *The global challenge of health care rationing*. Buckingham, UK: Open University Press.

Devitt, N., & Murphy, J. (2004). A survey of the information management and technology training needs of doctors in an acute NHS trust in the United Kingdom. *Health Information and Libraries Journal, 21*(3), 164–172. doi:10.1111/j.1471-1842.2004.00492.x

Dixon, N. M., Allen, N., Burgess, T., Kilner, P., & Schweitzer, S. (2005). *CompanyCommand: Unleashing the power of the army profession*. West Point, NY: Center for the Advancement of Leader Development & Organizational Learning.

Dols, V. (2001). Challenges faced by e-health comparative data warehouses. *Journal of Healthcare Information Management, 15*(2), 183–188.

Dubay, L., Holahan, J., & Cook, A. (2006). The uninsured and the affordability of health insurance coverage. *Health Affairs, 26*(1), w22–w30. .doi:10.1377/hlthaff.26.1.w22

Durbak, C. K., & Strauss, C. M. (2005). Securing a healthier world. In Dodds, F., & Pippard, T. (Eds.), *Human and environmental security: An agenda for change*. London: Earthscan.

Economist. (2003, April 5). After the outbreak; SARS. *The Economist*. Retrieved from http://www.economist.com/world/asia/displaystory.cfm?story_id=E1_TGRPRNP

Eddrippulige, S., Marasinghe, R. B., Smith, A. C., Fujisawa, Y., Herath, W. B., Jiffry, M. T., & Wootton, R. (2007). Medical students' knowledge and perception of e-health: results of a study in Sri Lanka. *Medinfo, 12*(Pt.2), 1406–1409.

Ellingsen, G., & Monteiro, E. (2008). The organizing vision of integrated health information systems. *Health Informatics Journal, 14*(3), 223–236. doi:10.1177/1081180X08093333

European Institute of Medicine. (2003). *Health is wealth: Strategic Vision for European healthcare at the beginning of the 21st century*. Salzburg, Austria: European Academy of Arts and Sciences.

European Ministers of Education. (1999). *Bologna Declaration*. Retrieved from http://www.bologna-bergen2005.no/Docs/00-Main_doc/990719BOLOGNA_DECLARATION.PDF

European Policy Center. (2008). *International Perspective Report*. Retrieved from http://www.epc.eu/en/er.asp?AI=439&LV= 293&PG= ER/ EN/ detail&TYP=ER&see=y&t=2

Evans, G. (1993). Health and security in the global village. *World Health Forum, 14*, 133–135.

Fernandez, I. (2002). Global battle cry: Health is a right, not a commodity. *Canadian HIV/AIDS Policy & Law Review, 7*, 80–84.

Fonkwo, P. N. (2008, July). Pricing infectious disease. The economic and health implications of infectious diseases. *EMBO Reports, 9*(Suppl 1), S13–S17. doi:10.1038/embor.2008.110

Fukuyama, F. (2004). Nation Building 101. *Atlantic Monthly, 293*(1), 159–162. Retrieved from http://www.esiweb.org/pdf/esi_europeanraj_reactions_id_27.pdf.

GAO. (2004). *Emerging infectious diseases: Review of state and federal disease surveillance efforts (GAO 04-877), I-IV* (pp. 1–64). Washington, DC: Government Accounting Office.

Garrett, L. (1994). *The coming plague: newly emerging diseases in the world out of balance*. New York: Penguin.

Garrett, L. (2001, Winter). Responding to the nightmare of bioterrorism. *The Responsive Community, 12*(1), 88–93.

Garrett, L. (2007a, January/February). The challenge of global health. *Foreign Affairs*. Retrieved from http://www.foreignaffairs.org/20070101faessay86103/laurie-garrett/the-challenge-of-global-health.html?mode=print

Garrett, L. (2007b, January/February). Midway in the journey. From "marvelous momentum" to healthcare for all: success is possible with the right programs. *Foreign Affairs*. Retrieved from

Gesler, W. M., & Webb, J. L. (1983). Patterns of mortality in Freetown, Sierra Leone. *Singapore Journal of Tropical Geography, 4*(2), 99–118. doi:10.1111/j.1467-9493.1983.tb00136.x

Gokhale, A. A. (1995). Collaborative learning enhances critical thinking. *Journal of Technology Education, 7*(1), 22–30.

Gray, C. S. (2006). Clausewitz, history, and the future strategic world. In Murray, W., & Sinnreich, R. H. (Eds.), *The past as prologue: the importance of history to the military profession* (pp. 111–132). Cambridge, UK: Cambridge University Press.

Gruskin, S., & Tarantola, D. (2002). Health and human rights. In Detels, R., McEwan, J., Beaglehole, R., & Tanaka, H. (Eds.), *The Oxford textbook of public health* (pp. 311–336). New York: Oxford University Press.

Hagland, M. (2008). Turning data into improved care: a number of healthcare facilities are working to transform terabytes of raw data into a guide for better care. *Healthcare Informatics, 25*(8), 58–66.

Hart, J. T. (1995). Clinical and economical consequences of patients as producers. *Journal of Public Health, 17*, 383–386.

Haux, R. (2006). Health information systems – past, present, and future. *International Journal of Medical Informatics, 75*(3), 268–281. doi:10.1016/j.ijmedinf.2005.08.002

Heymann, D. (2003). Evolving infectious disease threats to national and global security. In Chen, L., Leaning, J., Narasimhan, V., & de Waal, A. (Eds.), *Global health challenges for human security.* Cambridge, MA: Harvard University Press.

Ho, P. M., Peterson, P. N., & Masoudi, F. A. (2008). Evaluating the evidence: Is there a hierarchy. *Circulation, 118*(16), 1675–1684. doi:10.1161/CIRCULATIONAHA.107.721357

Honoré, R. (2009). *Survival: How a culture of preparedness can save you and your family from disaster.* New York: Simon and Schuster.

http://www.foreignaffairs.com/articles/62458/paul-farmer-and-laurie-garrett/from-marvelous-momentum-to-health-care-for-all-success-is-possib

Hubbard, T. (2002). Biological information: making it accessible and integrated (and trying to make sense of it). *Bioinformatics (Oxford, England), 18*(Suppl. 2), S140.

Hussain, I. (2001). Impact of globalization on poverty in Pakistan. *Mahbub ul Haq Human. Developmental Review, 1*, 23–31. Retrieved from http://www.sbp.org.pk/about/speech/2001/Impact_of_globalization_Mahboobul_Haq.pdf.

Iakovidis, I. (1998). From electronic medical record to personal health records: present situation and trends in European Union in the area of electronic healthcare records. *Studies in Health Technology and Informatics, 52*(Pt. 1 Suppl.), 18–22.

Ichikawa, K., Date, S., Kaishima, T., & Shimojo, S. (2005). A framework supporting the development of a Grid portal for analysis based on ROI. *Methods of Information in Medicine, 44*(2), 265–269.

Jakubowski, E., & Busse, R. (1998). *European Parliament Report: Healthcare systems in the EU: A comparative study.* Luxembourg: European Parliament. Retrieved from http://www.europarl.europa.eu/workingpapers/saco/pdf/101_en.pdf

Joshi, S. (2008). HIPPA, HIPPA, Hooray? Current challenges and initiatives in health informatics in the United States. *Medical Informatics Insights, 1*, 45-56. Retrieved from http://www.la-press.com/hipaa-hipaa-hooray-current-challenges-and-initiatives-in-health-i-a1198

Kaiser Family Foundation. (2008). *The uninsured: A primer. Key facts about Americans without health insurance.* Washington, DC: Kaiser Family Foundation. Retrieved from http://www.kff.org/uninsured/upload/7451-04.pdf

Kalawsky, R.S., Nee, S.P., Holmes, I., & Coveney, P.V. (2005) A grid-enabled lightweight computational steering client: a .NET PDA implementation. *Philosophical transactions. Series A, Mathematical, physical, and engineering sciences, 363*(1833), 1885-1894.

Kalawsky, R.S., O'Brien, J. & Coveney, P.V. (2005) Improving scientists' interaction with complex computational-visualization environments based on a distributed grid infrastructure. *Philosophical transactions. Series A, Mathematical, physical, and engineering sciences, 363*(1833), 1867-1884.

Karasawas, K. A., Baldock, R., & Burger, A. (2004). Bioinformaticsatics integration and agent technology. *Journal of Biomedical Informatics, 37*(3), 205–219. doi:10.1016/j.jbi.2004.04.003

Kersten, H. B., Thompson, E. D., & Frohna, J. G. (2008). The use of evidence-based medicine in pediatrics: Past, present, and future. *Current Opinion in Pediatrics, 20*(3), 326–331. doi:10.1097/MOP.0b013e3283005843

Kladiashvili, E. (in press). *Grid Technologies for eHealth: Applications for Telemedicine Services and Delivery*. Hershey, PA. *IGI Press*.

Korukonda, A. R., & Korukonda, S. (2006). From buzzword to business strategy. *International Journal of Electronic Healthcare, 2*(4), 362–377.

Kulkarni, R., & Nathanson, L. A. (2005). Medical informatics in medicine. *E-Medicine*. Retrieved from http://www.emedicine.com/emerg/topic879.htm

Kun, L. G. (2001). Telehealth and the global health network in the 21st century: From homecare to public health informatics. *Computer Methods and Programs in Biomedicine, 64*(3), 155–167. doi:10.1016/S0169-2607(00)00135-8

Kyle, R., & Murray, B. (2008). *Clinical simulation: Operations, engineering, and management*. Amsterdam: Elsevier Press.

Lacher, D., Nelson, E., Bylsma, W., & Spena, R. (2000). Computer use needs of internists: A survey of members of the American College of Physicians-American Society of Internal Medicine. In *Proceedings of the AMIA Symposium,* (pp. 453-456). Philadelphia, PA: American College of Physicians-American Society of Internal Medicine.

Lee, J. W., & McKibbin, W. J. (2003). Globalization and disease: The case of SARS. *The Brookings Institution*. Retrieved from http://www.brookings.edu/dybdocroot/views/papers/mckibbin/20030520.pdf

Lee, M. Y., Albright, S. A., Alkasab, T., Damassa, D. A., Wang, P. J., & Eaton, E. K. (2003). Tufts Health Sciences Database: lessons, issues, and opportunities. *Academic Medicine, 78*, 254–264.

Leeder, S., Raymond, S., Greenberg, H., Liu, H., & Esson, K. (2004). A race against time: The challenge of cardiovascular disease in developing countries. *The Earth Institute at Columbia University, May 2004*. Retrieved from http://www.earthinstitute.columbia.edu/news/2004/images/raceagainsttime_FINAL_051104.pdf

Lewis, W. W. (2006). *The power of productivity: Wealth, poverty, and the threat to global stability*. Chicago, IL: Chicago University Press.

Li, M., & Eastman, C. J. (2003). Working with funding agencies in the delivery of healthcare in the Asia Pacific region. *The Medical Journal of Australia, 178*, 13–16.

Lipnack, J., Stamps, J., Prevou, M., & Hannah, M. (2010). *Teams of Leaders Handbook*. Leavenworth, KS: Battle Command Knowledge System Combined Arms Center - Knowledge.

Lou, Y. (2001). Small group and individual learning with technology. *Review of Educational Research, 71*(3), 449–521. doi:10.3102/00346543071003449

Ma'ayeh, S. (1999, October 26) US-funded $ 40m primary healthcare initiative gets under way. *Jordan Times*. Retrieved from http://www.jordanembassyus.org/102699005.htm

Mandl, K. D., Szolovits, P., & Kohane, I. S. (2001). Public standards and patients' control: how to keep electronic medical records accessible but private. *British Medical Journal, 322*, 283–287. doi:10.1136/bmj.322.7281.283

McClure Wasko, M., & Faraj, S. (2000). "It is what one does": why people help others in electronic communities of practice. *The Journal of Strategic Information Systems, 9*(2-3), 155–173. doi:10.1016/S0963-8687(00)00045-7

McEntire, D. A. (1999). Issues in disaster relief: progress, perpetual problems and prospective solutions. *Disaster Prevention and Management, 8*(5), 351–361. doi:10.1108/09653569910298279

Medscape Today. (2008). Editorial: Rotavirus Surveillance – Worldwide, 2002 – 2008. *Medscape*. Retrieved from http://www.medscape.com/viewarticle/584676_1

Michelon, T., Magne, P., & Simon-Delavell, F. (2005). Lessons of the 2003 heat-wave in France and action taken to limit the effects of future heat waves. In Kirch, W., Bertollini, R., & Menne, B. (Eds.), *Extreme weather events and public health response* (pp. 131–140). Berlin, Heidelberg: Springer. doi:10.1007/3-540-28862-7_13

Miller, R. H., West, C., Martin Brown, T., Sim, I., & Ganchoff, C. (2005). The value of electronic health records in solo and small group practices. *Health Affairs*, *24*(5), 1127–1137. doi:10.1377/hlthaff.24.5.1127

Mishra, R. C. (2003). *Information technology and poverty reduction in South Asia*. Delhi, India: Authors Press.

Nash, D. B., & Quigley, G. D. (2008). Looking forward to the end of autonomy. *Headache*, *48*(5), 719–726. doi:10.1111/j.1526-4610.2008.01113.x

National Coalition on Healthcare. (2004). *Building a better health: Specifications for reform*. Washington DC: National Coalition on Healthcare. Accessed 11/14/2009 at http://www.kaisernetwork.org/health_cast/uploaded_files/072004_nchc_health-care_transcript.pdf

Neerincx, P. B. T., & Leunissen, J. A. M. (2005). Evolution of web services in bioinformatics. *Briefings in Bioinformatics*, *6*(2), 178–188. doi:10.1093/bib/6.2.178

Noji, E. K. (2005). Disasters: introduction and state of the art. *Epidemiologic Reviews*, *27*(1), 3–8. doi:10.1093/epirev/mxi007

Nunn, S., & Hamburg, M. (2003, May 26). Op-ed: Diseases gaining ground: SARS exposes gaps in system that should be addressed. *Atlanta Journal-Constitution*. Retrieved from http://www.nti.org/c_press/ oped_sars_052603.pdf

OECD (Organization for Economic Co-operation and Development). (2004). *OECD Health Data 2004*. OECD. Retrieved from www.oecd.org/health/healthdata

Olive, M., Rahmouni, H., & Solomonides, T. (2008). SHARE the journey: a European Health-grid Roadmap. *EU Commission: Information Society and Media*. Retrieved from http://ec.europa.eu/information_society/activities/health/docs/publications/200810share-roadmap.pdf

Olive, M., Rahmouni, H., Solomonides, T., Breton, V., Legré, Y., Blanquer, I., & Hernandez, V. (2008). SHARE, from vision to road map: technical steps. *Studies in Health Technology and Informatics*, *129*(Pt.2), 1149–1153.

Oliveira, I. C., Oliveira, J. L., Lopéz-Alonso, V., Martin-Sanchez, F., Maojo, V., & Sousa Pereira, A. (2005). Grid requirements for the integration of biomedical information resources for health applications. *Methods of Information in Medicine*, *44*(2), 161–167.

Onen, C. L. (2004). Medicine in resource-poor settings: time for a paradigm shift? *Clinical Medicine*, *4*, 355–360.

Oster, S., Langella, S., Hastings, S., Ervin, D., Madduri, R., Phillips, J. … Saltz, J. (2008). caGrid 1.0: An enterprise grid infrastructure for biomedical research. *Journal of the American Medical Informatics Association, 15*(2), 138-149.

Osterholm, M., & Branswell, H. (2005). Emerging pandemic: Costs and consequences of an avian influenza outbreak. *Global Health Initiative/Woodrow Wilson International Center for Scholars*. Retrieved from http://www.wilsoncenter.org/index.cfm?event_id=142787&fuseaction=topics.event_summary&topic_id=116811

ςαν Ροοψεν, Μ.ϑ., Ηανσχη, Σ., Χυρτισ, Δ., & Βυρνηαμ, Γ. (2001). Εμεργινγ ισσυεσ ανδ φυτυρε νεεδσ ιν ηυμανιταριαν ασσιστανχε. *Πρεηοσπιταλ ανδ δισαστερ μεδιχινε, 16*(4), 216–222.

Pal, S. K., & Mittal, B. (2004). Fight against cancer in countries with limited resources: The post the post genomic era scenario. *Asian Pacific Journal of Cancer Prevention, 5*, 328–333.

PandemicFlu.gov. (n.d.). Retrieved from http://www.pandemicflu.gov/global/index.html

Perry, M. (2006). Humanitarian relief challenges in the wake of South East Asian tsunami disaster. *Department of Management Working Paper Series, Monash University.* Retrieved from http://www.buseco.monash.edu.au/mgt/research/working-papers/2006/wp16-06.pdf

Priest, D. (2004). *The mission: waging war and keeping peace with American military.* New York: Norton.

Radetzky, U., Leser, U., Schultze-Rauschenbach, S. C., Zimmermann, J., Lüssem, J., Bode, T., & Cremers, A. B. (2006). Adapters, shims, and glue – services interoperability for in silico experiments. *Bioinformatics (Oxford, England), 22*(9), 1137–1143. doi:10.1093/bioinformatics/btl054

Retrieved from http://www.scielosp.org/scielo.php?script=sci_arttext&pid=S0042-96862008000700011&lng=en&nrm=iso

Rifkin, J. (2001). *The age of access.* New York: Tarcher/Putnam.

Rothkopf, D. (2008). *Superclass: The global power elite and the world they are making.* New York: Farrar, Straus and Giroux.

Sachs, J. D. (2001). *Microeconomics and health: Investing in health for economic development.* Geneva: WHO.

Sachs, J. D. (2007, January). Beware false tradeoffs. *Foreign Affairs.* Retrieved from http://www.foreignaffairs.org/special/global_health/sachs

Saltz, J., Hastings, S., Langella, S., Oster, S., Kurc, T., & Payne, P. (2008). The roadmap for caGrid, an enterprise Grid architecture for biomedical research. *Studies in Health Technology and Informatics, 138*, 224–237.

Scheffler, R. M., Liu, J. X., Kinfu, J., & Dal Poz, M. L. (2008). Forecasting the global shortage of physicians: an economic- and needs-based approach. *Bulletin of the World Health Organization, 86*(7), 516–523. .doi:10.2471/BLT.07.046474

Seely Brown, J., & Duguid, P. (1991). Organizational learning and communities of practice: toward a unified view of working, learning, and innovation [Special Issue]. *Organization Science, 2*(1), 40–57. doi:10.1287/orsc.2.1.40

Seers, K. (2007). Evaluating complex interventions. *Worldviews on Evidence-Based Nursing, 4*(2), 67–68. doi:10.1111/j.1741-6787.2007.00083.x

Sharma, M. (2005). Information and communication technology for poverty reduction. *Turkish On-Line Journal of Distance Education, 6*(2). Retrieved from http://tojde.anadolu.edu.tr/tojde18/notes_for_editor/note2.htm

Shefter, S. M. (2006). Workflow technology: the new frontier. How to overcome the barriers and join the future. *Lippincott's Case Management, 11*(1), 25–34.

Sidorov, J. (2006). It ain't necessarily so: the electronic health record and the unlikely prospect of reducing healthcare costs. *Health Affairs, 25*(4), 1079–1085. doi:10.1377/hlthaff.25.4.1079

Silenas, R., Waller, S.G., D'Amore, A.R., & Carlton, P.K. (2008). US Armed Forces medical operations other than war. *International journal of risk assessment and management, 9*(4), 367-375.

Slaughter, A. M. (2009, January-February). America's edge: power in the networked century. *Foreign Affairs.* Retrieved from http://www.foreignaffairs.org/20090101faessay88107-p0/anne-marie-slaughter/america-s-edge.html

Smith, P. (2007). *The utility of force: The art of war in the modern world*. New York: Knopf.

Social Watch. (2007). *In Dignity and Rights.* Uruguay: Montevideo. Retrieved from http://www.socialwatch.org/en/informeImpreso/overview2007.htm

Social Watch. (2008). *Rights is the Answer.* Uruguay: Montevideo. Retrieved from http://www.socialwatch.org/en/informeImpreso/index.htm

Stuckler, D., King, L. P., & Basu, S. (2008). International monetary fund programs and tuberculosis outcomes in post-communist countries. *PLoS Medicine, 5*(7), e143. .doi:10.1371/journal.pmed.0050143

Sujith, E. (2008, June 24). Cloud computing in healthcare. *Frost & Sullivan.* Retrieved from http://www.frost.com/prod/servlet/market-insight-top.pag?docid=135578323

Taylor-Gooby, P. (2006). Trust, risk, and healthcare reform. *Health Risk & Society, 8*(2), 97–103. doi:10.1080/13698570600677092

Tierney, K. J. (2006). Testimony on needed emergency management reforms. *Journal of Homeland Security and Disaster Management, 4*(3), 15.

Tuchman Matthews, J. (1989 Spring). Redefining security. *Foreign Affairs.* Retrieved from http://www.foreignaffairs.org/19890301faessay5953/jessica-tuchman-mathews/redefining-security.html

UNESCO. (2005). *Towards knowledge societies.* Paris: UNESCO Publishing. Retrieved from http://unesdoc.unesco.org/images/0014/001418/141843e.pdf

US Census Bureau. (2008). *Income, poverty, and health insurance coverage in the United States: 2007.* Washington, DC: US Census Bureau. Retrieved from http://www.census.gov/prod/2008pubs/p60-235.pdf

US Government. (2008). *Federal guidance to assist states in improving state-level pandemic influenza operating plans.* Washington, DC: US Government: Retrieved from http://www.flu.gov/news/guidance031108.pdf

US Mission to the UN. (2002). *Release 65: USAI leads public and private partners to improve health and save lives through food fortification.* New York: USUN. Retrieved from http://www.un.int.usa/02_065.htm

US National Intelligence Council. (2008). *Strategic implications of global health.* Washington, DC: Office of the Director of National Intelligence.

Vallat, B. (2007, July 11). *Avian influenza epizootie: where do we stand in 2007.* [Snowdon Lecture]. Retrieved from http://www.csiro.au/multimedia/SnowdonLecture2007Ch2.html

Von Clausewitz, C. (1976). On War (M. Howard & P. Paret Trans.). In Howard, M., & Paret, P. (Eds.), *On War.* New York: Knopf.

von Lubitz, D. K. J. E. (2008). Medical readiness for operations other than war: Boyd's OODA Loop and training using advanced distributed simulation technology. *International Journal of Risk Assessment and Management, 9*(4), 409–432. doi:10.1504/IJRAM.2008.020417

von Lubitz, D. K. J. E. (in press). The Teams of Leaders (ToL) concept: the grid, the mesh, and the people in the world of information and knowledge-based global healthcare. In Kladiashvili, E. (Ed.), *Grid Technologies for eHealth: Applications for Telemedicine Services and Delivery.* Hershey, PA: IGI Press.

von Lubitz, D. K. J. E., & Beakley, J. (2009). "Teams of Leaders" concept in homeland security and disaster management operations. *International Journal of Homeland Security and Emergency Management, 5*(1), 25. doi:.doi:10.2202/1547-7355.1458 von Lubitz, D. K. J. E., Beakley, J., & Patricelli, F. (2008a). "All hazards approach" to network-centric disaster management: the role of information and knowledge management, and Boyd's OODA Loop in disaster leadership. *The Journal of Disaster Study, Policy and Management*. DOI:10.1111/j.0361-3666.2008.01060.x Retrieved from http://www.blackwell-synergy.com/ toc/disa/0/0

von Lubitz, D. K. J. E., Beakley, J., & Patricelli, F. (2008b). Disaster management: The structure, function, and significance of network-centric operations. *Journal of Homeland Security and Emergency Management*, *11*(5). Retrieved from http://www.bepress.com/jhsem/vol5/iss1/1.

von Lubitz, D. K. J. E., Levine, H., Patricelli, F., & Richir, S. (2008). Distributed simulation-based medical training: Going beyond the obvious. In Kyle, R., & Murray, B. (Eds.), *Clinical Simulation: Operations, Engineering, and Management* (pp. 591–625). Amsterdam: Elsevier Press.

von Lubitz, D. K. J. E., Levine, H., & Wolf, E. (2002). The goose, the gander, or the Strasbourg paté for all: Medical education, world, and the Internet. In Chin, W., Patricelli, F., & Milutinovic, V. (Eds.), *Electronic business and education: Recent advances in Internet infrastructures* (pp. 189–210). Boston: Kluwer Academic Publishers.

von Lubitz, D. K. J. E., & Patricelli, F. (2006). Networkcentric healthcare operations; Data warehousing and the associated telecommunication platforms. *International Journal of Services and Standards*, *3*(1), 97–119. doi:10.1504/IJSS.2007.011830

von Lubitz, D. K. J. E., & Patricelli, F. (2008). Telecommunications infrastructure for worldwide network-centric healthcare operations and the associated information system. *The International Journal of Business and Systems Research*, *2*(1), 34–51. doi:10.1504/IJBSR.2008.018119

von Lubitz, D. K. J. E., & Wickramasinghe, N. (2006a). Healthcare and technology: the doctrine of network-centric healthcare. *International Journal of Electronic Healthcare*, *4*, 322–344.

von Lubitz, D. K. J. E., & Wickramasinghe, N. (2006b). Networkcentric healthcare: outline of entry portal concept. *International Journal of Electronic Business Management*, *4*(1), 16–28.

von Lubitz, D. K. J. E., Wickramasinghe, N., & Yanovsky, G. (2006). Networkcentric healthcare operations: the telecommunications structure. *International Journal of Networking and Virtual Organisations*, *3*(1), 60–85. doi:10.1504/IJNVO.2006.008785

Ward, R., Stevens, C., Brentnall, P., & Briddon, J. (2008). The attitudes of health care staff to information technology: a comprehensive review of the research literature. *Health Information and Libraries Journal*, *25*(2), 81–97. doi:10.1111/j.1471-1842.2008.00777.x

Ward, R., & Wamsley, G. (2007). From a painful past to an uncertain future. In Rubin, C. (Ed.), *Emergency management: The American experience 1900-2005* (pp. 207–242). Fairfax, VA: PERI.

Wen, H. J., & Tan, J. (2005). Mapping e-health strategies: Thinking outside the traditional healthcare box. *International Journal of Electronic Healthcare*, *1*(3), 261–276. doi:10.1504/IJEH.2005.006474

Wickramasinghe, N., & Schaffer, J. L. (2006). Creating knowledge-driven healthcare processes with the Intelligence Continuum. *International Journal of Electronic Healthcare*, *2*(2), 164–174.

Wong, J. G. (1996). Efficiency and effectiveness in the urgent care clinic. *Postgraduate Medicine*, *99*(4), 161–166.

World Economic Forum. (2002). *Eurasia economic summit 2002: health and the future of business.* The Global Health Initiative of the World Economic Forum, 8 August.

World Health Organization (WHO). (2004). *The World Health Report: Changing history.* Geneva: World Health Organization.

World Health Organization (WHO). (2006). *Constitution of the World Health Organization.* Retrieved from http://www.who.int/governance/eb/who_constitution_en.pdf

World Health Organization (WHO). (2008). *Closing the gap in a generation: Health equity through action on the social determinants of health. Commission on Social Determinants of Health Final Report.* Geneva: World Health Organization.

World Health Statistics. (2008). *World Health Statistics Report.* Geneva: World Health Organization. Retrieved from http://www.who.int/whosis/whostat/en

Wu, J. H., Huang, A. S., Hisa, T. L., & Tsai, H. T. (2006). Revolution or evolution? An analysis of E-health innovation and impact using a hypercube model. *International Journal of Electronic Healthcare, 2*(1), 12–34. doi:10.1504/IJEH.2006.008688

Yee, K. C. (2007). Bermuda Triangle or three to tango: generation Y, e-health and knowledge management. *Studies in Health Technology and Informatics, 129*(Pt.2), 1184–1188.

Zilinskas, R. A., & Chapman, R. C. (2007, January). *Security and public health: how and why do public health emergencies affect the security of a country.* Available as an NTI: Issue Brief at http://www.nti.org/e_research/e3_84.html

Zupan, J. (2003). Perinatal mortality and morbidity in developing countries: A global view. *Medecine Tropicale, 63*, 366–368.

Section 4
Challenges:
Privacy and Data Record Linkage

Chapter 11

Will Privacy Concerns Derail the Electronic Health Record?
Balancing the Risks and Benefits

Candace J. Gibson
The University of Western Ontario, Canada

Kelly J. Abrams
Canadian Health Information Management Association, Canada

ABSTRACT

The introduction of information technologies and the electronic record in health care is thought to be a key means of improving efficiencies and effectiveness of the health care system; ensuring critical information is readily available at the point of care, decreasing unnecessary duplication of tests, increasing patient safety (particularly from adverse drug events), and linking providers and patients spatially and temporally across the continuum of care as health care moves out of the traditional hospital setting to the community and home. There is a steady movement in many countries towards eHealth and a fully implemented, in some cases, pan-regional or pan-national electronic heath record. A number of barriers and challenges exist in EHR implementation. These include lack of resources (both capital and human resources), resistance to change and adoption of new technologies, and lack of standards to ensure interoperability across separate applications and systems. From the public's perspective, maintaining the security, privacy, and confidentiality of personal health information is a prominent concern and privacy of personal health information still looms as a potential stumbling block for the implementation of a comprehensive, shared electronic record. There are some steps that can be taken to increase the public's comfort level and to ensure that these new systems are designed and used with security and privacy in mind.

INTRODUCTION

The introduction of information and communication technologies (ICT) and the electronic record in health care is touted by most as a key means of improving efficiencies and effectiveness of the health care system; ensuring critical information is readily available at the point of care, decreasing unnecessary duplication of tests, increasing patient safety (particularly from adverse drug events),

DOI: 10.4018/978-1-61520-733-6.ch011

and linking providers and patients spatially and temporally across the continuum of care as health care moves out of the traditional hospital setting to the community and home (Bates & Gawande, 2003; Health Canada, 2001; IOM, 2001). Whether these benefits are realized remains to be seen, but there is a steady movement in many countries towards eHealth and a fully implemented, in some cases, pan-regional or pan-national electronic heath record.

A number of barriers and challenges exist in the implementation of such an ambitious project. These include lack of resources (both capital and human resources), resistance to change and adoption of new technologies, and lack of standards to ensure interoperability across separate applications and systems, to name a few. From the public's perspective, maintaining the security, privacy, and confidentiality of personal health information is a prominent concern. A recent survey of Canadians indicated that they would support the development of an electronic health record but not at the expense of personal privacy (EKOS, 2007). The National Health Service (NHS) in the UK has just completed an extensive public consultation on privacy after backtracking on its opt-out policy for electronic records[1]. President Barack Obama's economic stimulus package to build new infrastructure included $20 billion for plans to link doctors and hospitals with new information technology but was attacked in a bitter dispute over how to protect the privacy of electronic medical records. Consumer groups and patient privacy advocates, the health care industry and lawmakers have been unable to agree on privacy safeguards that would allow individuals to control the use of their medical records for both primary care and secondary uses (e.g. planning and management of services; research and statistical analysis; and fundraising)[2]. Similar concerns over privacy and the adequacy of security measures for electronic records are echoed in other countries across the world (e.g. New Zealand, see Chhanabhai & Holt, 2007).

Thus privacy of personal health information still looms as a potential stumbling block for the implementation of a comprehensive, shared electronic record. There are some steps that can be taken to increase the public's 'comfort' level and to ensure that systems are designed and used with security and privacy in mind.

DEFINITIONS

To set the stage for this discussion a few definitions are necessary.

The *electronic health record* represents the longitudinal lifetime record of an individual's encounters with the health care system and various health care providers, residing within a computerized architecture. It includes information in different formats, for example, text, voice, and digital images. This information, such as, demographic data, clinical data and diagnostic results, alerts, reminders, and evidence-based decision-making support is accessible to authorized users based on the user's role and relationship with the patient. Other terms may refer to an *electronic patient record*, the institutional record of patient encounters, or the *electronic medical record*, the physician's office record of care. The electronic health record is seen as the linked multi-user, multi-facility, multi-purpose record connecting the institutional (the EPR) and provider level (the EMR) records to provide the comprehensive lifetime record (Nagle, 2007).

Personal health information is information collected on the physical and mental health of an individual and the health services they receive. Within the Health Insurance Portability and Accountability Act legislation (HIPAA 1996) in the United States the term "protected health information" is used to designate all "individually identifiable health information"[3] held or transmitted by covered entities under the Act, in any form or media, whether electronic, paper, or oral. This is in distinction to "de-identified health information"[4] on which it places no restrictions on use or disclosure.

Privacy is the right to control information about ourselves, including the collection, use, and disclosure of that information, while *confidentiality* is the obligation on the part of health providers to protect someone else's personal information, to maintain its secrecy and not misuse or wrongfully disclose it. *Security* is the process of assessing and countering threats and risks to information, primarily the technical and administrative safeguards necessary to protect personal information. Technical safeguards include mechanisms for data back-up (hardware and software), anti-virus protection, intruder alerts, secure networks and the means of providing safe and secure remote and wireless access and transmission of data, the layout and location of workstations, authentication (that may include level of access determined by the user's role), and audit trails that can provide transaction logs and track inappropriate use. Administratively, facilities should have clearly defined policies and procedures for confidentiality that set out and define access rights (for example by professional status or the relation between the user and patient, by type of data, and/or intended action) and for privacy that are consistent with current legislation or policies of professional organizations.

INFORMATION GOVERNANCE

Issues of privacy and confidentiality of personal health information fall under what has been termed "information governance" (Cayton, 2006; CHI, 2007; NHS: Systems and Services: Information Governance - http://www.connectingforhealth.nhs.uk/systemsandservices/infogov). Information governance addresses "those matters involved in handling personal health information in a confidential and secure manner and in compliance with appropriate legal, ethical and quality standards" (CHI, 2007, p. iv). Within the UK's National Health Service definition, information governance also includes ensuring "confidentiality and security of all records, and especially patient records, and to enable the ethical use of them *for the benefit of individual patients and the public good*" (italics added) (Cayton, 2006). Although many of these issues are also of concern and have been addressed in the paper record, the use of an electronic record, particularly an individual's lifetime health history and integrated health records across institutions and health providers, presents an unprecedented access to large volumes of sensitive data or potential risks for breaches of privacy and confidentiality. While in many cases technical issues have been addressed to allow role-based, authorized access to patient and provider directories and repositories of clinical data (laboratory test results, diagnostic images, medication histories), questions regarding who will be responsible for whatever data will be made available in a regional or national electronic record across multiple jurisdictions with different privacy laws has yet to be determined. The question and the necessary safeguards become increasingly more complex if data is to be made available on an international or global scale.

Beyond the individual record of health care, electronic records may also have extraordinary value in providing information on public health and disease surveillance; research opportunities provided by data mining; and the planning, management, and deployment of scarce resources. These secondary uses of health data, which may indeed provide benefits to the health system as a whole, must be balanced against the individual's right to keep their information private and secure.

Principles of Fair Information Practices

Across all provinces in Canada the protection of all data collected during health care is covered by the federal *Personal Information Protection and Electronic Documents Act* (2000). In many provinces this legislation has been superseded by specific provincial health information privacy laws (e.g. British Columbia, Alberta, Manitoba, Saskatchewan and Ontario have introduced their own health information privacy laws). In general all of these acts have been based on the ten fair information principles set out in the Canadian Standards Association's Model Code for the Protection of Personal Information (CAN/CSA-Q830-96) which in turn are based on internationally accepted fair information practice principles[5]. Briefly summarized these include:

- *Accountability*: An organization (a health care facility or health care provider) is responsible for personal information under their control and shall designate an individual(s) who is/are accountable for compliance with the principles.
- *Identifying*: Purposes The purpose(s) for which personal information is collected is to be identified by the organization at or before the time the information is collected.
- *Consent*: The knowledge and consent of the individual are required for the collection, use, or disclosure of personal information, except where inappropriate.
- *Limiting Collection*: The collection of personal information should be limited to that which is necessary for the purposes that were identified by the organization (see above) and this information must be collected by fair and lawful means.
- *Limiting Use, Disclosure, and Retention*: Personal information should not be used or disclosed for purposes other than those for which it was collected, except with the consent of the individual or as required by law. Personal information should be retained only as long as necessary to fulfill those purposes.
- *Accuracy*: Personal information should be as accurate, complete, and up-to-date as

necessary for the purposes for which it is to be used.
- *Safeguards*: Personal information should be protected by security safeguards appropriate to the sensitivity of the information.
- *Openness*: An organization should make readily available to individuals specific information about its policies and practices relating to the management of personal information.
- *Individual Access*: Upon request, an individual should be informed of the existence, use, and disclosure of his/ her personal information and be given access to that information. An individual should be able to challenge the accuracy and completeness of the information and have it amended as appropriate.
- *Challenging Compliance*: An individual should be able to address a challenge concerning compliance with these principles to the designated individual (s) accountable for the organization's compliance.

In addition national health professional associations, e.g. the Canadian Medical Association (CMA), the Canadian Health Information Management Association (CHIMA, 2004), Canada's Health Informatics Association (COACH, 2007), have produced codes of conduct and privacy guidelines whose provisions may exceed those of the federal and provincial laws currently in place in the Canadian health care system.

Although a patchwork of laws across Canada permit or require health information collection, use, disclosure and access without patient consent, or even knowledge, this Code would require that all of these laws and any proposed laws be reviewed for consistency with its provisions. Moreover, existing practices and initiatives concerning health information collection, use, disclosure and access, including health information systems or networks, may be contrary to patient expectations and the physician's duty of confidentiality. These practices and initiatives must also be reviewed for consistency with this Code. Many laws, practices and initiatives may not withstand the kind of scrutiny deemed necessary and reasonable for the protection of privacy and the trust and integrity of the therapeutic relationship (CMA, 1998).

These ten principles and codes of conduct have been instituted (by law) within individual practices or institutions (either single or integrated health care facilities), but have not yet been fully operationalized within a multijurisdictional, interoperable EHR framework. Within Canada's health system in which the ten provinces and three territories are responsible for delivery of health care, each jurisdiction has slight variations in legal requirements and practice. As data move from one jurisdiction to another (for example as an individual may require care outside of their home province or across the border in the USA) the designated information custodian will change and laws and regulations regarding use and disclosure of data may change from jurisdiction to jurisdiction. How do we manage information coming from multiple institutions or jurisdictions – in which consent may have been obtained in one jurisdiction but not in another? Does it mean having to obtain consent each time that information crosses a border where the laws may be more or less strict in protecting patient privacy? Can this consent be circumvented in some cases if medically necessary for treatment? Which laws should be followed if one jurisdiction allows data to be used for research purposes without prior explicit consent and another jurisdiction does not?

Public Perceptions of Privacy and Confidentiality

The Public's Concerns

Frequent media reports of health information security breaches have led to public distrust and fear that the current mechanisms in place to safeguard personal health information are inadequate and lead Canadians to state that they would like to see electronic health records, but only if privacy is protected (EKOS, 2007). Almost nine in 10 Canadians (88%) support the development of EHRs, with nearly two-thirds of Canadians believing there are few types of personal information that are more important for privacy law protection than personal health information. While advanced encryption and security technologies have increased comfort levels with sharing and accessing personal information online, privacy is highly valued. Opposition to the development of EHRs is centred almost entirely on concerns for the security and confidentiality of personal health information (only 39% of Canadians think health information is safe and secure). EHRs are seen as superior to paper-based records in providing physicians and other health providers with ready access to patient information to make faster and more accurate diagnoses, to reduce the number of repeated tests and redundancies in the health system, and for reducing errors in prescriptions and treatments. Among those who have or will have access to an electronic record, Canadians hold the greatest trust in their family doctor to preserve the safety and security of their health record (46% have a "great deal of trust"), other health care providers less so and, interestingly, researchers (11-14%) and the information technology specialists who run the computer systems (11%) little at all. The ability to access a summary of their own health status is appealing to most Canadians (84%). One in three Canadians reported experience with an EHR and this group expresses stronger support for an electronic record, greater comfort about safety and security of their personal health information, and greater awareness of the laws and institutions that regulate privacy. Few Canadians think that a system of EHRs would be too costly to implement (64% disagreed it would cost too much).

To allay their fears over security, specific initiatives would make them more comfortable with an EHR – top of the list was the ability to find out who accessed the health record and when. Other options included making unauthorized access a serious offence, privacy assurances (such as being informed of breaches, knowing how breaches are responded to, being provided with an accessible privacy policy, and oversight by government or privacy agency), access to their record to make corrections or to hide/mask sensitive information, and endorsement for an EHR from their physician. Close to three in four Canadians expressed relatively high comfort levels with, and strong support for, the secondary use of data within the EHR (such as public health surveillance; planning, monitoring, and evaluating the health care system). Support for using EHRs in health research exists but only if personal details are not shared or linked to other records (84% support it, if details such as name and address are not known to the researcher). If personal details are not removed from the record, support for research drops dramatically (to 50%). If consent is obtained ahead of time there is support (66%) for linking personal health information to other records that may be related to health outcomes (e.g. education or income).

A survey of 300 respondents across four major cities in New Zealand presents a similar picture of support for electronic records but concern about the security and privacy of their health records (73% highly concerned) (Chhanabhai & Holt, 2007). Most believed that the EHR would lead to their medical information being shared easily, with 40% fearing this would lead to sensitive medical information leaking out, and 42% that it would allow sharing of their medical information without their knowledge. Overall half (53%) believed that the EHR would have an inherent weakness in its security system. Participants were primarily worried about unauthorized access to their record by hackers (79%), vendor access (73%) or malicious software (68%). Eighty per cent of survey respondents agreed that the addition of security measures such as anti-virus protection, firewalls,

restricted system access, audit trails, and encryption would make the EHR more secure.

These general concerns have shown little change in survey responses over the past decade. In 1999, the California HealthCare Foundation (CHCF) released a study of Americans' attitudes and behaviors concerning health privacy. The study found that nearly three out of four Americans had significant concerns about the privacy and confidentiality of their medical records. In 2005, following implementation of national privacy protections under the Health Insurance Portability and Accountability Act (HIPAA 1996) and a national initiative to adopt electronic medical records, a second survey revealed that, despite federal protections under HIPAA, two in three Americans are still concerned about the confidentiality of their personal health information and are largely unaware of their privacy rights (CHCF, 2005).

These studies also point out a lack of public awareness about privacy rules and regulations, how health information is stored and accessed, what their rights are as patients/consumers, and heightened and/or unrealistic fears of security or privacy breaches. For example, studies find that hackers are responsible for less than 20% of improper releases of medical information; by far the highest number of inappropriate access occurs due to insiders or inadequate personnel or operational privacy and security policies (Chhanabhai & Holt, 2007).

Privacy Protective Behaviour

By far the most serious consequence of the public concern about privacy and security of health information is the possibility that patients will withhold medical information. Surveys tend to show that is true. An estimated 1.2 million Canadians have withheld personal information from a health care provider because of concerns over with whom the information would be shared, or how it might be used (EKOS, 2007). One in eight Americans, or roughly 50 million people, engages in privacy-protective behavior to shield themselves from misuse of their information. These behaviors included asking a physician not to report a health problem or to record a less serious (or less embarrassing) diagnosis, avoiding their regular physician for certain health conditions, avoiding certain diagnostic tests due to anxiety that others might find out about the results, or paying out of pocket for procedures to avoid submitting a claim (CHCF, 2005). In the US, these behaviors may be related to concerns that claims information provided to an insurer might be seen by an employer and used to limit job opportunities.

Locking Away Information

The Personal Health Information Protection Act of Ontario (PHIPA 2004) allows for the provision of a "lock box" for information that a patient does not want shared with other stakeholders. A lock box refers to the right to withhold or withdraw consent for the collection, use, or disclosure of personal health information. The inclusion of a lock box provision is an attempt to strike a balance between the right to privacy and security of personal health information and the need for timely access to that information for health care provision. Both Saskatchewan and Manitoba have legislation that allows for the withholding or withdrawal of consent to access personal health information. Newfoundland has targeted 2010 for implementation of their privacy legislation, the Personal Health Information Act of NL, and it will also include a lock box provision (http://www.assembly.nl.ca/Legislation/sr/statutes/p07-01.htm).

Current privacy legislation allows for implied consent to collect, use, and disclose health information during care and for those within the "circle of care" (i.e. those providing services after the initial collection of information). Dissemination of information to those within the circle of care is allowed unless the health information custodian (the person/facility responsible for maintaining the personal health information at the initial point of collection) is aware that consent has been revoked or withheld. If a patient decides to withhold access to clinically relevant information, the health practitioner must get specific consent from the patient to allow for the disclosure. There are a few instances where a lock box provision can be overridden including a significant risk to the patient's health or safety, or risk to the health and safety of a third party (Government of Ontario: PHIPA, 2004). The question remains however, what constitutes a "significant" risk.

How does the lock box provision work in an electronic health record? Most EHR systems were not developed with this provision in mind. Older legacy information systems do not have the capability to "lock" at an individual field or datum level – the lock box provision must be placed on the entire record if it is available at all. If the lock box must be removed for patient care, this unlocks the entire record. Future systems will be developed to include alerts and warnings such as drug interactions and condition alerts and will be "intelligent" enough to provide a warning to physicians that there is a drug interaction with a new drug prescribed in conflict with one previously subscribed but in the lock box. It is hoped these new systems will allow the lock box provision to function in a more seamless and efficient manner (Government of Ontario 2004).

It is important that the patient understands the full consequences of requesting a lock box provision. A privacy officer should be available to discuss the role of the lock box as well as the benefits and problems associated. The patient should have a clear understanding of the limits of the current health record systems – paper, hybrid (some paper and electronic), and electronic. The lock box provision is often misunderstood and patients request a lock box provision when the reasons for the request are already included within existing legislation (for example, patient signed consent must be provided prior to release of any personal health information to an employer).

The National Health Service in the UK has done a remarkable job of connecting its health providers in health care facilities, primary care trusts, and physician's offices to a national networked IT infrastructure over the past decade through its Connecting for Health program, but not without a few bumps along the road (Hendy et al, 2005). A local electronic record is maintained through the NHS Care Record Service on the national high speed backbone. Despite cost overruns, delays in rolling out services, and privacy gaffes, by mid-December 2008, more than half of UK general practices were electronically interconnected and able to exchange and access patient information[6]. A subset of essential demographic and medical information (allergies, current medications, adverse drug reactions) – the Summary Care Record – will be extracted and reside on the national network (the "Spine") and be available to authorized health care professionals treating patients anywhere at any time in the NHS in England. Along the way it has become apparent that communication with patients was essential and informing consumers of what was being done with their data and their options was absolutely paramount in getting the public to fully participate in a national EHR. Communications via the Internet, pamphlets, brochures, and public consultations on various options are now being made through an extensive public information program. The information program will precede the uploading of any clinical data to the Spine in a summary care record, to allow patients to express their preferences. In addition a National Information Governance Board[7] regularly reviews the Care Record Guarantee detailing how the record will be protected and used. Privacy guardians known as the Caldicott Guardians[8] play a strategic and advisory role in every organization to ensure that the principles of limited use, restricted access on a 'need to know' basis, and compliance with the law are adhered to (Greenough & Graham, 2004).

The national roll out of the SCR is taking place gradually with information coming from their GP's record initially. Later, it will come from other parts of the NHS as well, so that details about any current health problems, summaries of care, and clinicians providing care, may be added.

The information within the health records is confidential and protected by several system access controls such as the use of a smartcard and password for access that defines role-based access, limiting what people can do on the system according to their job role (e.g. the physician can see all of the medical information, while a clerk/receptionist can see only relevant demographic and scheduling information) and defining a legitimate relationship that prevents those who are not directly involved in the care of the patient from gaining access to sensitive personal information. The public information program ensures that patients are given enough information to make an informed choice, particularly with regard to limiting participation in the care records service, and are asked to consider the health benefits and any risks to their privacy and the confidentiality of information about their health.

Patients have at least four options for their health information:

1. *Consent/dissent to share*: The individual can choose to prevent confidential information from being shared between organizations such as a GP's practice, local hospital, and primary care trust. Information would still flow as part of normal clinical communications between organizations, but it would prevent the information recorded by one NHS organization from being accessible by another NHS organization without explicit consent (except under exceptional circumstances where allowed by law).

2. *Sealing*: Provides an "electronic envelope" or the ability to seal sensitive patient information that can only be seen by the original physician or health care team or released only with an individual's consent (similar to Ontario's lock box provision). In this case

an icon is displayed in the record to show that some information has been withheld. A second treating physician could ask for permission to see that hidden information but can do so only with the patient's consent. In this situation an information alert is also raised with the information governance officer in the hospital indicating that this user has accessed the data. (The NHS is also experimenting with a form of personal health record – HealthSpace – in which information in the SCR is stored and, if the patient has a HealthSpace account, they are also sent notification of this access).

3. *Sealing and locking*: A stronger version of the previous option in which this sensitive information can never be accessed outside of the sealing team. On the record itself there is no indicator that any information has been sealed.

4. *Consent/dissent to store*: Under the normal course of treatment a Summary Care Record is automatically created for each patient unless they explicitly object (or "opt-out").

Opting Out

The latter option was provided after a severe backlash of public opinion and the discovery that health data was automatically being transferred to the Summary Care Record on the NHS Spine. Patients can now opt out entirely from this option – data still flows from their health care providers, but will not be available in emergency circumstances, for example, in which the individual may need care outside of their own region/trust/authority. Some patients have complained that although this option is allowed the NHS makes it exceedingly difficult to do so. The fears on the part of providers are that in the latter two options vital information about allergies or contraindicated medications will not be available in emergencies, after hours, or when patients are travelling.

SECONDARY USES OF HEALTH DATA

So far we have dealt with the primary use of data for clinical care (i.e. for diagnosis and treatment of illness), but often health data is used for secondary purposes related to research, education, disease surveillance, public health, planning, management and evaluation of resources. Primary health data is identifiable and refers to a specific person, whereas secondary health data is often aggregate or de-identified data in which personal identification has been stripped and the collected data is used only for analysis and summarization. This also has implications legally under current privacy legislation that gives physicians and health care facilities the right to collect data for clinical purposes, but insists that individuals must be informed of any secondary uses of that data and give their consent for its use for these other purposes at the time of collection. This has often meant a fine balancing act between ensuring that privacy and confidentiality of personal health data is maintained, while not hampering the beneficial and necessary aspects of planning, management and deployment of resources or the use for research and educational purposes.

A strict definition of primary use of health data is "the use of personal health information by the organization or entity [health facility or health provider] that produced or acquired the data in the process of providing real-time, direct care of an individual" (Safran et al, 2007). As such, this data is person-identifiable. Secondary use of health data refers to the non-direct care use of personal health information that includes its use for quality or safety measurement; outcomes analysis; clinical and health services research or epidemiological studies; costing and funding; public health surveillance; policy development; provider or institution certification and/or accreditation; and marketing or other business or commercial activities (Safran et al, 2007). In these latter examples, data may be person-identifiable or anonymized, aggregate data depending on its use and needs.

Health research can increase our understanding of the causes, patterns, and outcomes of disease, help to assess the effectiveness of strategies for improving prevention, diagnosis and treatment of disease, and guide the development and evaluation of policies for increasing the effectiveness and efficiency of health services (CIHR, 2002, p. 5). This data can be derived from health surveys, hospital and/or physician-based health records, provincial and federal billing and registration data, vital statistics (e.g. birth and death records), socio-demographic data, cancer registry data, and employment records (CIHR, 2002, p. 5).

While the secondary use of health data may be desired to achieve a number of socially relevant goals, the privacy and confidentiality of this health data must also be protected and preserved. In many cases the focus of analysis or research is on aggregate trends and can be conducted with information that has been made completely anonymous or de-identified in a way to remove as many identifiers as possible and replaced with encrypted codes. In some cases, for example, data collected in some disease registries, data collected for public health surveillance, data collected in long-term studies of exposure to risk factors and potential disease outcomes, it may be necessary to link that de-identified data to potentially identifying personal information. Data may also be collected across provincial or territorial boundaries and different legislative requirements for data protection may apply in each jurisdiction.

Several of the major Canadian grant funding agencies have elicited commentary and input from a number of stakeholders and developed a set of ethical guidelines for the secondary use of health data (CIHR, 2002; 2005) and best practices that can be adapted for use by agencies or individuals who need to use health data (CIHR, 2006)[9]. The Canadian Health Information Management Association has also developed a set of guidelines for "Health Data Access, Use, and Control for Secondary Uses" that builds on these principles and extends the concept of data stewardship at the local level to ensure the responsible handling of health information and to see that the benefits of use are balanced against the possible risks to individual privacy and security of health data (CHIMA, PPB-0003.07).

With regard to the secondary use of data for research or other purposes, the principles of limiting use and disclosure, and consent, require that individuals provide consent prior to any use of their health data. In many instances this can be done at the time of patient admission or registration (e.g. for inclusion of data in a cancer registry), but in some cases it is not possible to determine beforehand what may be needed for future research.

Recall that the public supports the use of de-identified data for health research (but have somewhat limited trust in researchers!), but would insist on informed consent prior to use if personal health information was to be used (EKOS, 2007). A recent US survey commissioned by the Institute of Medicine explored health privacy and health research issues to try to understand just what troubles some consumers about health researchers using their medical records, even where protection of the consumer's identity is promised. They found "a U.S. public divided right down the middle on this matter": 50% agree that they would still worry about such researcher access (12% strongly and 38% somewhat) and 50% disagree and would not be worried (15% strongly and 35% somewhat) (Westin, 2007). About 8% of Americans had declined to participate in health research in which their personal health information would be used and concern about confidentiality was the most frequently chosen reason for not participating (expressed by almost a third of this group and representing about 5 million adults). Further probing into what kind of patient/consumer consent would be necessary to obtain personal health information for use in research indicated that 57% would agree to have their PHI used in a health research project if privacy-oriented conditions were met (that included 38% requiring notice and express consent case-by-case and 19% with advance agreement only if assured that their identity was protected and the project was supervised by an institutional review board) (Westin, 2007, p. 19-20).

SOLUTIONS - OVERCOMING THE PRIVACY BARRIER

Experiences in the UK and the US in building robust health information privacy and security systems that are premised upon a rights-based approach to patient privacy can provide insight into building health information systems that facilitate the sharing of information between jurisdictions in a cost-effective manner. It is important that health care providers and administrators stay current with changing legal, technological, and administrative frameworks.

Privacy by Design

This approach advocated by both the organization charged with implementing the pan-Canadian electronic health record (CHI, 2006) and a provincial privacy commissioner (see Cavoukian, 2009) emphasizes building privacy into the design specifications and architecture of the technology itself to ensure that the ten fair information practice principles are incorporated (e.g. with technical safeguards, audit trails, authentication and user identity management with definition of roles and subsequent role-based or work-group based access). As these principles state, it is essential to keep data collection to only that which is needed for identified purposes, to minimize the routine collection and use of personally identifiable information, and to use encrypted or coded information whenever possible. In all introductions of new services or technologies risks to privacy should be assessed (by conducting a privacy impact assessment and follow up with annual privacy audits – see

below). Privacy-enhancing technologies (PETs), such as encryption, public key infrastructures, smart cards or secure password protection, should be used where possible, and individuals should be given maximum control over their own data (Rindfleisch, 1997).

Data Stewards – The Health Information Management Professional

The Health Information Management (HIM) professional is uniquely trained to oversee the privacy, confidentiality, and security of the health record. They are already familiar with the principles and practices of records management, data quality, and data stewardship, and the HIM professional has traditionally held the role of custodian of the health record (AHIMA, 2003; CHIMA, PPB-0003.07, 2007).

After definitions and processes have been standardized, the greatest protections related to access, use, and control of protected health information will be based on administrative handling and responsible human intervention. Any assurances will be vested in organizational philosophy and due diligence manifesting in policies, procedures, practices, and consistent enforcement and follow-through (CHIMA, PPB-0003.07, p. 6).

The introduction of privacy legislation has changed the way health providers think about ownership of health records and the information it contains. While most understand the patient owns their health information and the individual health care provider or health facility owns the physical record, there is confusion or a lack of understanding by some practitioners about the ability to use personal health information for secondary purposes. At the time of data collection, all uses of the data must be clearly identified and consent received for the stated uses. Simple physical ownership of the record doesn't allow for data use for purposes other than those originally identified and for which consent was granted. The responsibility for the protection of personal health information goes beyond legislation – it is an ethical, moral, and legal responsibility. Legislation dictates only the minimum standards for protection of personal health information, and the use and sharing of the data, particularly with linked and shared data, have grown faster than the legislation (CHIMA, 2004).

The ability to use data for secondary purposes becomes even more confusing in a multijurisdictional health record. Data collection at one site may include consent to use the information for secondary purposes such as research or marketing, while data collected at another site may include consent for use for direct patient care only. As the data is incorporated into a multijurisdictional record, it may no longer be clear which data was collected for what purpose. The further away from the original site and use of the collected data, the greater the risk for the inappropriate use of data.

Health data is collected and held by a number of other agencies beside those involved in direct patient care – government, health insurers, vendors, and employers, to name a few. Without a clear definition of stakeholder rights and responsibilities, consumer trust in the exchange of such information will be further eroded. Thus, data stewardship becomes more important as we move forward with electronic, multijurisdictional health records.

The HIM professional has traditionally been responsible for the dissemination of health information post-care – this is especially true in the acute and community care settings. Information is disseminated to family physicians, consultants, other care agencies, insurance companies, and employers. The role of the HIM professional is to act as an advocate for the patient as well as to ensure the timely provision of health information for continuing care, payment provision, and other uses. While technology can build in safeguards for role-based access and provide an audit trail, the majority of breaches in confidentiality and privacy occur due to improper or inadequate policies and procedures or through lack of education/knowledge regarding legislation and facility policy and procedures (Chhanabhai & Holt, 2007; EKOS, 2007). As an example, most people sign blanket consent forms for insurance companies, not realizing that they have consented to the release of *any and all information*, not just the episode of care that may be related to a specific accident or injury. Guardianship of personal health information requires an evaluation of the appropriateness of the request, not just the confirmation of a signed consent.

An excerpt from the American Health Information Management Association's policy statement on the privacy, confidentiality, and security of health information summarizes the necessary conditions for achieving a secure record and defines the role of the HIM professional as the primary data custodian (AHIMA, 2003).

Privacy, Confidentiality, and Security of Health Information will be achieved when:

- *Privacy and confidentiality protections are uniform and set the high standard throughout the country through federal preemptive law(s) that establish fair, reasonable, and uniform health information practices, across all states, which understand and respect the rights of the individual and the public and apply to the medium in which such information is stored, transferred, or accessed.*
- *An individual will have the right to:*
  - *Access his or her health information in any setting (with minimal limits);*
  - *Have an understanding of his or her privacy rights and options;*
  - *Be notified about all information practices concerning his or her information;*
  - *Appropriately challenge the accuracy of his or her health information; and*

○ *Have the right, in certain electronic or Internet situations, to opt-in or authorize the collection or use of information beyond what is originally authorized by the individual or law.*

- *The collection and use of health information will be permitted only for legitimate purposes, and only as provided by law, and will be uniform across all jurisdictions and entities and for all individuals.*

- *Credentialed HIM professionals, given their training and education in privacy and information release and HIM, are considered the primary custodians of health information and principal experts in maintaining the privacy, confidentiality, and security of information in the healthcare industry.*

- *Laws, practices, and technologies are put in place to provide protections required to maintain appropriate privacy, confidentiality, security, and integrity of health information.*

The Need for Privacy Impact Assessments /Risk Assessments

Safeguards are necessary to eliminate or reduce the risk of an information security breach. Three types of threats can be identified – agents, targets, and events. An agent is the person willing and able to carry out the threat. The target is the object of the security threat such as data confidentiality. The event is the occurrence, the breach itself. There are four general types of events specific to information security including a breach in confidentiality, a threat to data integrity, data unavailability, and data accountability (CHIMA, 2009). A privacy risk assessment (PRA) is a tool used to identify potential threats to privacy, confidentiality, and the security of personal health information. A PRA identifies the extent to which a facility is in compliance with PIPEDA and identifies the areas that need improvement. A PRA is also a frame-

work to ensure privacy is considered throughout the design and implementation of services and programs within a facility. There are two parts to a PRA – a Threat and Risk Assessment (TRA) and a Privacy Impact Assessment (PIA).

The TRA includes a threat and risk analysis and an assessment of current safeguards. The assessment can be performed by an internal information security team or by an external team. A TRA focuses on the management of the systems and processes used to collect, use, and disclose information rather than on the systems themselves. There is an assessment and analysis of the threats and vulnerabilities. The risks and threats are managed by implementing administrative, technical, physical, and operational controls and safeguards. There are three main sections within a TRA – the assessment, analysis, and management of identified risks and threats. The risks can be addressed in three general categories although a combination of each is usually necessary to mitigate the risk.

1. *Management*: the management of the information security programs throughout the organization including the implementation or revision of security policies and procedures that include the incorporation of privacy legislation.

2. *Operational*: this includes contingency planning; increasing user awareness, education and training; ensuring physical and environmental protections are in place; implementing IT support and operations; and managing security breaches.

3. *Technical*: technical security as executed by the information systems. These controls include audit trails; user identification and authentication protocols; access control; encryption and firewall protection. (CHIMA, 2004).

A PIA is used in the evaluation and assessment of the privacy impacts of a new or revised program or service. It should be completed any time that personal information is collected, used, or disclosed whether the information was originally collected by the program itself or by a different department or facility[10].

A PIA is completed to assess current information practices; identify the areas requiring improvements or further development; to ensure due diligence in the implementation of a new system or program or during a major revision to a program or service; and to respond to public concerns about privacy. The completion of a PIA whenever information systems are implemented or revised is simply good practice (CHIMA, 2004).

THE FUTURE

The Personal Health Record

As the patient-centred hub of medical care the consumer controlled "personal health record" (PHR) represents a shift in both the traditional view of the provider-patient relationship and of who controls medical information. This technology is still in its infancy and many forms of personal health records exist with little standardization in what they contain, where they reside, and how they exchange information. Currently personal health records encompass a wide variety of applications that allow individuals to collect, view, manage or share copies of their health information or transactions electronically. Fundamental to the PHR is the idea of health information as a *personal* commodity, not an institutional asset – a shift in the emphasis from clinician to patient (who is now seen as a consumer of health services) and in the health information custodian from the organization to the individual (Gearon et al., 2007; Tang et al., 2006). In Canada there has been limited deployment, most in the form of 'patient portals' or 'tethered PHRs' provided by health facilities or physicians. These portals provide limited access to personal health information (e.g. test results, radiology images) and are usually targeted to

specific disease groups (e.g. those with diabetes, chronic renal failure, hypertension, breast cancer for display of laboratory results, monitoring of weight, blood pressure, blood glucose, access to decision support tools) (Nagle, 2007). They also provide links to quality health information and patient education materials, links to support groups (through chat rooms or social networking sites such as Facebook), personal diaries, links to providers, and other services. The future, 'untethered' or stand-alone personal health record represents a comprehensive tool to manage personal health information from a variety of health care providers and facilities that is managed and coordinated by the individual (Gearon et al., 2007; Tang et al., 2006).

The benefits of a personal health record include better communication between patient/consumer and provider (secured email messaging, automated scheduling) and shared decision making, complete and longitudinal information about previous and present health status and use of health services (as with the EHR), greater access to customized, credible health information and knowledge, easy access to test results, the inclusion of patient preferences for services or treatments including advanced directives, dietary and lifestyle practices, records of allergies and immunizations, alerts and reminders for preventative examinations, and information from home monitoring devices. As with the EHR, many of the same barriers to adoption apply – the lack of interoperability and standards to allow for sharing of data and information, determination of who will pay (the consumer or provider or payer), and privacy and security of health information. PHRs again raise the possibility of information storage in multiple places with different institutional policies or legal restrictions on collection and use and authorized access. These PHRs will change the way data are acquired, exchanged, and used during health encounters - the decision over what data are collected and chosen to become part of the electronic record will be determined when the individual decides what is important to include and from whom and from where. This also means that consumers must now control permissions for access, remember all of the places their records reside, and take greater responsibility for their health and the care they receive (Gearon et al., 2007; Nagle, 2007; Tang et al, 2006).

Information technology and search engine companies Microsoft and Google have entered the personal health record market with their own offerings of HealthVault (http://www.healthvault.com/Personal/index.html) and Google Health (http://www.google.com/intl/en-US/health/tour/index.html) respectively. Uptake of these personal health organizers has been minimal. Microsoft requires a user name and password for login, uses encryption to upload your health information (but it is stored on a Microsoft central server), allows you to designate with whom data can be shared and add additional custodians, but it also allows access to other third party programs and software applications for use in the HealthVault system that have their own privacy rules and standards. Microsoft also uses aggregate data to inform potential advertisers of, for instance, how many users live in the United States. Google Health has a similar privacy policy with access open to third party applications and use of aggregate data to publish trend statistics and associations[11].

Some believe that the barriers and possibilities for a fragmented and incomplete record with the stand-alone PHR are too great and an integrated personal health record, built on an existing health facility or provider record represents the best solution (Ball &Gold, 2006; Tang et al, 2006). This year the UK has started to offer a form of a personal record, HealthSpace, a "free secure online personal health organizer" to users of the NHS (http://www.connectingforhealth.nhs.uk/systemsandservices/healthspace). Individuals will be able to access and view their Summary Care Record (provided through their GP's system) as well as store and keep track of measures of blood pressure, blood sugar levels, weight, etc.

The user's HealthSpace account is designed to be viewed online from anywhere in the world and shared with those who have been given consent to share that information (a secure login card is not issued until the user has registered with a local HealthSpace Registration office and presented personal identification).

The implementation of the electronic record, in one form or another, is inevitable. The potential benefits and value-added resources for creating efficiencies in the health care system are far too great to abandon its eventual deployment. The final shape of the electronic record and who will 'own' it or act as the custodian is still uncertain, but the need for security, privacy, and confidentiality of the data held within it will transform the role of health providers and health consumers alike and both will need to be far more cognizant of the rights, regulations, and policies concerning the collection, use, and disclosure of health information.

WEB RESOURCES

- Canada Health Infoway – http://www.info-way-inforoute.ca/lang-en/
- Office of the Privacy Commissioner of Canada - http://www.privcom.gc.ca/index_e.asp
- National Health Service, Connecting for Health – http://www.connectingforhealth.nhs.uk/
  - Also see Information Governance section – http://www.connectingfor-health.nhs.uk/systemsandservices/infogov
- Information Commissioner's Office (UK) - http://www.ico.gov.uk/
- U.S. Department of Health and Human Services
  - Office for Civil Rights - http://www.hhs.gov/ocr/office/index.html
  - Health Information Privacy - http://www.hhs.gov/ocr/privacy/index.html

- ◦ Health Information Technology - http://www.hhs.gov/healthit/
- ◦ Health Information Technology: The Nationwide Privacy and Security Framework for Electronic Exchange of Individually Identifiable Health Information - http://www.hhs.gov/healthit/privacy/framework.html

REFERENCES

AHIMA. (2003, July 10). *American Health Information Management Association (AHIMA) Statement on the Privacy, Confidentiality, and Security of Health Records.* Available at http://library.ahima.org/xpedio/groups/public/documents/ahima/bok1_019923.hcsp?dDocName=bok1_019923

Ball, M. J., & Gold, J. (2006). Banking on health: Personal records and information exchange. *Journal of Healthcare Information Management, 20*(2), 71–83.

Bates, D. W., & Gawande, A. A. (2003). Improving safety with information technology. *The New England Journal of Medicine, 348,* 2526–2534. doi:10.1056/NEJMsa020847

California HealthCare Foundation. (1999, January). *Medical privacy and confidentiality survey.* CHCF Organization. Available at http://www.chcf.org/topics/view.cfm?itemID=12500

California HealthCare Foundation. (2005, November). *National consumer health privacy survey 2005.* CHCF Organization. Available at: http://www.chcf.org/topics/view.cfm?itemID=115694

Canada Health Infoway. (2006). *Electronic health record privacy and security: conceptual architecture.* Ottawa, Canada: CHI.

Canada Health Infoway. (2007, March). *White paper on information governance of the interoperable electronic health record (EHR).* Ottawa, Canada: CHI.

Canadian Health Information Management Association. (2004). *A toolkit for privacy and access & disclosure of personal & health information.* London, Canada: CHIMA.

Canadian Health Information Management Association. (2007). Health data access, use, and control for secondary uses. *Professional Practice Brief: PPB – 0003.07.*

Canadian Health Information Management Association. (2009). *Fundamentals in health information management.* Ottawa, Canada: CHA Press.

Canadian Institutes of Health Research (CIHR). (2002, November). *Secondary use of personal information in health research: case studies.* Available at http://www.cihr-irsc.gc.ca/e/6827.html

Canadian Institutes of Health Research (CIHR). (2005). *CIHR best practices for protecting privacy in health research - September 2005.* Ottawa, Canada: Public Works and Government Services Canada. Available at http://www.cihr-irsc.gc.ca/e/documents/et_pbp_nov05_sept2005_e.pdf

Canadian Institutes of Health Research (CIHR). (2006). *Harmonizing research & privacy: Standards for a collaborative future. Executive Summary: Privacy Best Practices for Secondary Data Use (SDU).* Ottawa, ON: CIHR.

Canadian Medical Association. (1998). *CMA health information privacy code.* Available online at http://www.cma.ca/index.cfm/ci_id/3216/la_id/1.htm

Canadian Standards Association. (1996). *Model code for the protection of personal health information.* Can be accessed online at http://www.csa.ca/standards/privacy/code/Default.asp?language=english

Cavoukian, A. (2009). *Privacy by design: The 7 foundational principles.* Toronto, ON: Office of the Information and Privacy Commissioner of Ontario. Available at http://www.ipc.on.ca/images/Resources/7foundationalprinciples.pdf

Cayton, H. (2006). Information governance in the Department of Health and the NHS. UK: National Health Service (No. 3349).

Chhanabhai, P., & Holt, A. (2007). Consumers are ready to accept the transition to online and electronic records if they can be assured of the security measures. *Medscape General Medicine*, *9*(1), 8.

COACH. (2009). *Guidelines for the protection of health information*. COACH (Canada's Health Informatics Association). Available through http://coachorg.com

EKOS Research Associates. (2007, August). *Electronic health information and privacy survey: What Canadians think — 2007*. Submitted to Canada Health Infoway, Health Canada, and the Office of the Privacy Commissioner of Canada, Ottawa.

Gearon, C.J., Barrett, M., Flatley Brennan, P., Kibbe, D., Lansky, D., Nobel, J., & Sands, D. (2007, June). Perspective on the future of the personal health record. *California Health Care Foundation iHealth Report*.

Government of Newfoundland and Labrador. (2007). *New legislation to protect personal health information*. Retrieved February 1, 2009 from http://www.releases.gov.nl.ca/releases/2008/health/0520n03.htm

Government of Ontario. (2004). *Personal Health Information Protection Act (PHIPA)*, 2004. Retrieved February 1, 2009 from http://www.e-laws.gov.on.ca/html/statutes/english/elaws_statutes_04p03_e.htm

Greenough, A., & Graham, H. (2004). Protecting and using patient information: the role of the Caldicott Guardian. *Clinical Medicine*, *4*(3), 246–249.

Health Canada. (January 2001). *Toward electronic health records*. Ottawa: Office of Health and the Information Highway, Health Canada.

Hendy, J., Reeves, B. C., Fulop, N., Hutchings, A., & Masseria, C. (2005). Challenges to implementing the national programme for information technology (NPfIT): a qualitative study. *British Medical Journal*, *331*, 331–336. doi:10.1136/bmj.331.7512.331

HIPAA. (1996, August). *Public Law 104-191: Health Insurance Portability and Accountability Act of 1996*. Available in brief at Administration Simplification, Department of Health and Human Services at http://aspe.hhs.gov/admnsimp/pl104191.htm. Full content available at http://frwebgate.access.gpo.gov/cgi-bin/getdoc.cgi?dbname=104_cong_public_laws&docid=f:publ191.104.pdf

Institute of Medicine. (2001). *Crossing the quality chasm: A new health system for the 21st Century*. Washington, DC: National Academy Press.

Nagle, L. M. (2007). Informatics: Emerging concepts and issues. *Electronic Healthcare*, *5*(4), 1–2.

Office of the Privacy Commissioner of Canada. (n.d.). *Fact Sheet: Privacy Impact Assessments*. Retrieved January 26, 2009 from http://www.privcom.gc.ca/pia-efvp/index_e.asp

PIPED Act (2000, update 2006). *Personal Information Protection and Electronic Documents Act*. Department of Justice, Canada. Full text available at http://laws.justice.gc.ca/en/P-8.6/text.html

Rindfleisch, T. C. (1997). Privacy, information technology, and health care. *Communications of the ACM*, *40*(8), 92–100. doi:10.1145/257874.257896

Safran, C., Bloomrosen, M., Hammond, E., Labkoff, S., Markel-Fox, S., Tang, P. C., & Detmer, D. E. (2007). Toward a national framework for the secondary use of health data: An American Medical Informatics Association White Paper. *Journal of the American Medical Informatics Association, 14*, 1–9. doi:10.1197/jamia.M2273

Tang, P. C., Ash, J. W., Bates, D. W., Overhage, M., & Sands, D. Z. (2006). Personal health records: Definitions, benefits, and strategies for overcoming barriers to adoption. *Journal of the American Medical Informatics Association, 13*, 121–126. doi:10.1197/jamia.M2025

Westin, A. F. (2007). *How the public views privacy and health research*. Washington, DC: National Academy of Sciences.

ENDNOTES

[1] See "Consultation on the wider use of patient information" – NHS Connecting for Health – http://www.connectingforhealth.nhs.uk/systemsandservices/research/consultation.

[2] See NYTimes, January 18, 2009 "Privacy Issue Complicates Push to Link Medical Data" – The stimulus package was later passed by the Congress with few changes (nursing homes and long term care facilities were added as covered entities, but no changes were made to the current privacy stipulations).

[3] The term "individually identifiable health information" means any information, including demographic information collected from an individual, that-(A) is created or received by a health care provider, health plan, employer, or health care clearinghouse; and (B) relates to the past, present, or future physical or mental health or condition of an individual, the provision of health care to an individual, or the past, present, or future payment for the provision of health care to an individual, and (i) identifies the individual; or (ii) with respect to which there is a reasonable basis to believe that the information can be used to identify the individual. From the OCR-HHS.

[4] The term "de-identified information" is that from which all potentially identifying information has been removed.

[5] OECD – OECD Guidelines on the Protection of Privacy and Transborder Flows of Personal Data adopted in September 1980 represent international consensus on general guidance on the collection and management of personal information. See http://www.oecd.org/document/18/0,3343,en_2649_34255_1815186_1_1_1_1,00.html

[6] News release, NHS Connecting for Health: 5,000 practices now live with GP2GP. GP2GP is a national system in the UK that enables patients' electronic health records to be transferred directly and securely from one GP practice to another. See http://www.connectingforhealth.nhs.uk/newsroom/news-stories/5-000-practices-now-live-with-gp2gp

[7] The National Information Governance Board for Health and Social Care (NIGB) provides leadership and promotes consistent standards for information governance across health and social care. It considers ethical issues; the interpretation and application of the law and policies; and provides advice on information governance matters at a national level. The Board reports annually to the Secretary of State for Health and is responsible for the NHS Care Record Guarantee for England. Members of the Board are either members of the public appointed by the Appointments Commission or represent stakeholders in health and social care. The Chair, Harry Cayton, was appointed by the Appointments Commission on behalf of the Secretary of State for Health and is the Chief Executive

of the Council for Healthcare Regulatory Excellence and author of the Review of Information Governance which called for the establishment of such a national oversight body (Cayton, 2006).

[8]   A Caldicott Guardian is a senior person responsible for protecting the confidentiality of patient and service-user information and enabling appropriate information-sharing. The Guardian plays a key role in ensuring that the NHS and its partner organisations satisfy the highest practical standards for handling patient identifiable information. The Guardian actively supports work to facilitate and enable information sharing and advise on options for lawful and ethical processing of information as required. A UK Council of elected Caldicott Guardians meets four times a year.

[9]   The Inter-Agency Advisory Panel on Research Ethics (PRE) has officially launched the draft 2nd edition of the Tri-Council Policy Statement: Ethical Conduct for Research Involving Humans (TCPS) for comment from researchers across Canada. The draft 2nd edition includes a new set of core principles, clarified definitions, simplified articles and new chapters on qualitative research and research involving Aboriginal peoples.

[10]   The Office of the Privacy Commissioner of Canada website provides a list of resources for developing and completing a PIA (http://www.privcom.gc.ca/pia-efvp/index_e.asp, accessed January 26, 2009).

[11]   A new Web tool from Google.org may be able to detect regional outbreaks of the flu a week to 10 days before they are reported by the Centers for Disease Control and Prevention (reported in NYTimes - http://www.nytimes.com/2008/11/12/technology/internet/12flu.html?_r=1&ref=health). In early February the CDC reported that flu cases had recently spiked in the mid-Atlantic states; Google's search data show a spike in queries about flu symptoms two weeks before that report was released. Its new service at google.org/flutrends analyzes those searches as they come in, creating graphs and maps of the country that, ideally, will show where the flu is spreading. Some public health experts say the Google data could help accelerate the response of doctors, hospitals and public health officials to the flu, reducing the spread of the disease and, potentially, saving lives, but concerns over privacy or search histories that might reveal personal information prompted patient privacy advocacy groups to write to the CEO of Google for assurances that none of the search data would be able to be traced back to individual users (Google Flu Trends and Privacy - http://epic.org/privacy/flutrends/).

Chapter 12

New Technology and Implications for Healthcare and Public Health:
The Case of Probabilistic Record Linkage

Gulzar H. Shah
National Association of County and City Health Officials, USA

Kaveepan Lertwachara
California Polytechnic State University, USA

Anteneh Ayanso
Brock University, Canada

ABSTRACT

In this chapter, the authors provide a review of recent developments in probabilistic record linkage and their implications in healthcare research and public health policies. Their primary objective is to pique the interest of researchers and practitioners in the healthcare and public health communities to take full advantage of record linkage technologies in completing a health care scenario where different pieces of patient records are collected and managed by different agencies. A brief overview of probabilistic record linkage, software available for such record linkage, and type of functions provided by probabilistic record linkage software is provided. Specific cases where probabilistic linkage has been used to bridge information gaps in informing public health policy and enhancing decision-making in healthcare delivery are described in this chapter. Issues and challenges of integrating medical records across distributed databases are also outlined, including technical considerations as well as concerns about patient privacy and confidentiality.

INTRODUCTION

The necessity for comparing and matching data records from multiple sources in order to determine which sets of records belong to the same person, object, or event can arise in many contexts. Scholarly interests in this area span several academic disciplines (e.g., statistics, information systems, management sciences) as well as communities

DOI: 10.4018/978-1-61520-733-6.ch012

of practitioners (e.g., in electronic commerce, public health, vital records, welfare fraud detection, e-government). As computerized databases have now become ubiquitous in business sectors, the possibility of extensive analysis using these databases relies on the ability to integrate heterogeneous databases across organizations and functional units. Such data integration requires the presence of an error-free unique identifier or *key* attribute common among the data sets being matched. Unfortunately, in most real-world situations, this common key attribute across data sets is rarely available. Consequently, instead of relying upon a deterministic approach using unique identifiers, past research studies have proposed probabilistic algorithms to achieve the goal of record matching across heterogeneous databases. Among these early studies, seminal work by Newcombe, Kennedy, Axford, and James (1959) and Fellegi and Sunter (1969) provide theoretical frameworks for computer-aided record linkage operations. Other more recent scholarly studies on this topic include Dey, Sarkar, and De (1998); Bell and Sethi (2001); Sarathy and Muralidhar (2006); and Jiang, Sarkar, De, and Dey (2007). Although the algorithmic procedures to match data records suggested in these studies may vary, they share a common objective of linking records that belong to the same entity while minimizing the likelihood of erroneous matching (i.e., ensuring sensitivity and specificity).

Statistical theory used in record linkage was developed in the 1950s and was further refined in the 1970s and 1980s (Jaro, 1989; Newcombe et al., 1959). Until the early1980s, no commercial record linkage software was marketed, and those with a need for record linkage had to develop their own software (e.g., the Generalized Record Linkage System (GRLS) developed at Statistics Canada). They often faced the choice of using less accurate methods or expending considerable staff time to create proprietary systems. For example, in the late 1970s, the U.S. National Agricultural Statistics Service spent what is conservatively

estimated as 50 staff-years to develop a state-of-the-art system (Day, 1997).

OVERVIEW OF RECORD LINKAGE CONCEPTS AND TECHNIQUES

Record linkage is a computer-based process to match records from different and often heterogeneous sources of data that refer to the same entities such as persons, events, or other objects of interest. However record linkage is sometimes performed within a single data set when multiple records are present in a single database for a person or other entity (e.g., records for multiple hospitalizations in a hospital discharge data set for a 12-month period). Record linkage within a single data set is also performed to remove duplicate records, referred to as "deduplication" (Winkler, 1999).

There are many applications of record linkage in both public and private sectors and its use has become even more significant with advances in the underlying techniques and the implementation tools. Detailed technical descriptions of record linkage are available elsewhere (see, for example, Fair, 1995, 1997; Newcombe, 1994). In addition to applications in health care and public health, record linkage is widely employed in other fields. For example, Probert, Semenciw, Mao, and Gentleman (1997) described how record linkage was used to integrate immigration and mortality databases in Canada. Quass and Starkey (2003), White (1997), and NeSmith (1997) provided examples on how record linkage could be used to consolidate genealogical data. Other examples of record linkage applications in public sectors include consolidating tax return records (Czajka, 1997; Harville & Moore, 1999; Steel & Konschnik 1997; Wahl, 1997); verifying housing mortgage applications (Herzog & Eilerman, 1997; Herzog, Scheuren, & Winkler, 2007); tracking academic progress in public schools (Miller, 1997); and public safety (Scheetz, Zhang, Kolassa, Allen, & Allen, 2008; Utter, 1997). In the private sector, companies can also use record linkage to improve their marketing and advertising efforts (Fair, 1997; Fellegi, 1997; Lyon, 1994); to evaluate customer credit ratings (Fellegi, 1997); and to determine a patient's insurance eligibility (Fellegi, 1997).

In general, when record linkage techniques are employed, they are used to integrate data and improve quality. Record linkage has several other uses (Fair, 1995, 1997; Newcombe, 1994). Record linkage can be used to eliminate duplicate records and identify missing records from data sources, for example, by linking births and deaths with census records. In addition, by combining results from several data sources, record linkage can provide improved estimates for key variables that, otherwise, demand significant data collection efforts (Herzog et al., 2007). The use of population-based record linkage can help avoid selection bias in situations such as case-control studies because participants are not self-selected in population-based studies (see, for example, Kisely, Smith, Lawrence, & Maaten, 2005). Record linkage data can also be used to improve data coverage by identifying possible underreporting of special cases, thus providing enhanced data representation. Another important use of record linkage is in following-up individuals, such as an individual's vital status or mobility patterns for different administrative and resource allocation purposes. When building new data sources/databases, for example, new registries can be created by using record linkage to combine a variety of relevant data sources.

RELEVANCE OF RECORD LINKAGE IN HEALTH CARE

The importance of linking medical and vital statistics records was recognized long before computers and electronic health records (EHRs) became widely available (Dunn, 1946). Registrars of vital records, health, welfare, and other types of organizations continuously maintained complete and accurate records in order to carry out their primary responsibilities.

The restructuring and amalgamation of hospitals have meant that existing records in two or more facilities need to be merged or linked to create an integrated health information system. In addition, a change in health care patterns (i.e., more care that occurs outside of the hospital) has created the need for linking records across the continuum of care. The need for reconciled and accurate records became more critical as governments moved towards regional and national health care that necessitated regional and national EHRs.

Computerization of healthcare records during the last three decades has revolutionized the way a patient's medical history is stored, retrieved, and shared among scientific communities and healthcare practitioners interested in health care research, policy, and practice. Many providers, public health agencies, and insurance companies have switched from paper-based records (that in most cases are eventually converted into digital formats) to paperless electronic health records (EHRs). EHRs have a potential to be instrumental in improving quality and efficiency in health care as they are a rich source of information on patient demographics and medical histories (Flegel, 2008; Jha et al., 2006). EHRs can also lead to reducing medical and administrative costs associated with lack of timely care, inappropriate care, and adverse results from poor quality care (Sidorov, 2006). Moreover, EHRs are appealing to researchers and practitioners due to their accessibility, timeliness, searchability, and ease of analysis.

Many of these promises, however, hinge upon the assumption that EHRs can be integrated across completely separate databases maintained by different agencies (Bradley et al., 2008; Shah, Clarkson-Freemna, Ahmad, Varner, & Xu, 2008; Shah, Greenway & Yang, 2007). Yet, the lack of unique patient identifiers, such as social security numbers or a universal patient identification number; errors and omissions in data; and state and federal regulations, such as HIPAA in the US (the

Health Insurance Portability and Accountability Act), make such integration of EHRs extremely difficult. As an alternative to deterministic record linkage that relies on unique patient identifiers, probabilistic linkage uses information from a variety of attributes such as patient name, date of birth, and street address in order to enable effective record linkage (Blakeley & Salmond, 2002).

DIFFERENT APPROACHES TO RECORD LINKAGE

Generally, there are three key methods in record linkage. Among the three methods, probabilistic linkage is the focus of our chapter and is currently the most commonly used method in record linkage applications.

Deterministic (Direct/ Exact) Record Linkage

This method requires a common unique *key* across data sets in order to match records. The key attribute is a unique identifier that allows records from different data sets to be reconciled. Examples of key attributes include social security numbers, tax identification numbers, and national identification numbers. This method is the simplest and most efficient way to link records across heterogeneous data sets and can be done using most standard database management and statistical applications such as Microsoft Access, Oracle, SPSS, or SAS.

However, common unique identifiers could be incomplete, inaccurate, or even absent in large healthcare databases. In such cases, a more advanced deterministic matching approach is used. For example, instead of relying upon a single *key* variable, a database administrator may create a truth table that utilizes several variables to determine the match (see, for example, Meyer, 1997). For instance, if a social security number is not present in the databases, a deterministic matching

program may examine whether last names, first names, and date of births on the records can help determine a match.

In addition, deterministic record linkage that relies solely upon a single key attribute can prove problematic in large healthcare databases due to concerns over confidentiality and patient privacy. In the US, HIPAA regulations and state data privacy laws generally prohibit sharing information on unique identifiers such as social security numbers. In Europe, the 2002 Directive on Privacy and Electronic Communications outlined a number of confidentiality and security requirements for electronic data sharing. The coverage of this directive also included electronic health records and other electronic exchange of consumer-specific information.

Names, when combined with other potentially identifiable variables, such as date of birth or street address, can be successfully used for deterministic linkage. Nonetheless, a multiple variable approach to deterministic linkage may not be effective for several reasons. First, a patient's name could be recorded differently across data repositories (e.g., when nicknames such as Bill or Nick are used, instead of William or Nicholas in one data set, but not in the others). Another potential problem is when first names and last names are erroneously swapped in one of the data sets. Moreover, the date values such as date of birth or death could cause a problem in deterministic linkage, such as when the date values are missing or inaccurate, or when the month and date values are accidentally switched. Due to such potential problems, the idea of creating standardized patient identification numbers was proposed in 1998 by the Department of Health and Human Services (HHS) and the Health Care Financing Administration (HCFA). However, the proposal received very little public support and thus far has not been implemented. The European Union (EU) has also sought to enhance the interoperability among its members' electronic health record systems. In July 2008, the EU issued a set of recommendations on cross-border interoperability of electronic health records. However, these recommendations will be implemented only as a demonstration project and not a mandate among its member states.

Probabilistic Record Linkage

Generally, probabilistic linkage aims to match records across heterogeneous data sets through the calculation of probability that the records belong to the same entity, while adjusting for incomplete and missing data. Seminal works by Newcombe et al. (1959) and Fellegi and Sunter (1969) provide theoretical foundations for most of the current probabilistic linkage software. A brief overview of probabilistic linkage based on these two studies is described here.

The probability calculation includes observed agreements and disagreements on all data attributes applicable for the linkage. In other words, two records may be a positive match even though they present different (or even conflicting) information in some attributes. For this reason, probabilistic linkage techniques usually require human intervention (e.g., to set linkage parameters and thresholds, to manually classify a possible match of two records where computer software is unable to make a decision, or to provide examples of matched and non-matched records).

When common data attributes in the two records in question are considered, there is a number of factors that influence probabilistic linkage algorithms. First, we consider the probability that values in a given attribute between the two records would agree if the two records are in fact a match, as well as the probability that values in a given attribute would agree if the two records are not a match. For example, an agreement between two records on a relatively rare last name such as "Micklon" could be an indicator of a good match, although the two records may present conflicting information in other attributes. On the other hand, an agreement on a very common last name such as "Johnson" would likely require

additional matches in other attributes in order to determine whether or not the two records belong to the same person. Second, a probabilistic linkage algorithm also takes into account the number of expected matches that could occur randomly. These factors then are used to calculate the so-called *linkage weight* which is a measure of how the data presented in the two records in question improve our ability to match the records.

In general, when comparing records from different databases, comparison of most records would be concluded as non-matching, while a small number of records will be deemed a positive match. An approximate distribution of matching and non-matching pairs is presented in Figure 1. The records that fall into the area where user intervention is needed can lead to erroneous linkage (i.e., Type I (false positive) error or linked when they are not a match and Type II (false negative) error or not linked when they are a match), especially if left to computer software to decide. Thus, the accuracy of the linkage of these records depends upon the expertise of the human users.

In large data sets, comparing each and every record to determine a match would be impractical, if not impossible. As a result, in order to reduce the number of records that are considered likely candidates for matching, most practitioners would perform a process called blocking during which data records are divided into blocks based on similarity of data values in certain attributes.

Students of record linkage often ask what are the minimum required variables for efficient linkage when using probabilistic record linkage? According to Scott Schumacher, Chief Scientist, Initiate Systems, it largely depends upon problem size (or false-positive rate). It also depends upon attribute information or native strength (i.e., discriminatory power of a variable) and frequency (or uniqueness of variable attributes). Problems with good data quality can be answered with basic attributes such as first and last name, date of birth, zip code, and specially social security number, if

Figure 1. Approximate distribution of matching and non-matching pairs of records

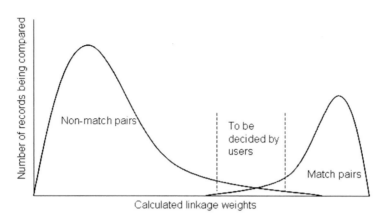

available. As data quality decreases or problem size increases, more information is required to achieve acceptable matching rates. The problem size and data quality can be determined through simple modeling, informing a situation as to whether a workable system is available for a set of databases (Schumacher, 2007).

Deterministic and probabilistic approaches, the two most commonly used methods, to record linkage have their respective strengths and weaknesses, but the latter is clearly superior in precision. Simplicity and operational ease are among the obvious strengths of the deterministic approach. The probabilistic approach is relatively more resource intensive, yet it is superior in performing linkages when there are errors and omissions in data, and common unique identifiers are either available only for a subset of the cases or are not available at all, a situation frequently encountered by practitioners in most large healthcare databases. A recent study indicates that because common patient identifiers are often missing, incomplete, or inaccurate, the deterministic approach clearly has very low sensitivity or ability to correctly identify the highest proportion of actual matches. In other words, deterministic matching is likely to miss a large proportion of actual matches. The deterministic approach has only slightly better positive predictive value (PPV), or precision rate, (97%) than the probabilistic approach (96%).

That is, of those matches that are identified as matches (though many may be missed), a high proportion are true matches. probabilistic record linkage, however, has higher sensitivity (97%) than the deterministic algorithm (79%) with minimal sacrifice to PPV (Campbell, 2008). In many situations, probabilistic, deterministic, and clerical techniques are combined to meet research needs (Clark, 2004).

Unsupervised Record Linkage

As mentioned above, probabilistic linkage is very effective when a common key attribute is not present among the data sets being linked. However, probabilistic linkage requires a certain level of human intervention. As illustrated in Figure 1, users need to manually classify at least a small number of records that the probabilistic algorithms cannot decide. Since the 1990s, scientists and engineers have experimented with artificial intelligence in order to create a record linkage tool that does not require human intervention. This category of "unsupervised" or "automated" linkage techniques usually involve artificial intelligence algorithms such as machine learning, cluster analysis, and rule-based data mining. Examples include machine learning algorithms that employ Bayesian networks to classify text into different groups, and information retrieval in Web search engines (Winkler, 1999). In addition to applications in healthcare and public health, record linkage techniques of this type can be found in business applications such as data warehousing, customer relationship management, and fraud detection.

Many of these techniques, however, have been tested or experimented on a relatively small data set (Goiser & Christen, 2006). In addition, some of the techniques require a "training" data set for the software to learn to recognize the decision patterns in order to link subsequent data records. Thus, in order for the linkage software of this type to work effectively, the training data set must adequately reflect the actual data that the software will eventually process. Unfortunately, such training data sets may not be readily available (Goiser & Christen, 2006). For these reasons, unsupervised record linkage is not yet as widely used as traditional probabilistic linkage. As mentioned above, algorithms used in most commercial linkage software remain largely based on at least one of the probabilistic linkage techniques.

APPLICATIONS AND BENEFITS OF PROBABILISTIC RECORD LINKAGE IN HEALTH CARE

Probabilistic record linkage plays a pivotal role in completing a healthcare scenario where different pieces of the patient records are collected and managed by different agencies (see, for example, Love, Rudolph, & Shah, 2008; Scheetz et al., 2008). Record linkage has been harnessed in bringing together individual healthcare records from a variety of sources for a variety of purposes. For instance, children's healthcare information systems such as clinical care records, public health administrative records, and emergency medical systems are linked with their school records and other socio-demographic information to support scientific research, public health surveillance, and a variety of other purposes. A recent study

by Hinman and Davidson (2009) has summarized such data integration efforts.

One of the most powerful uses of probabilistic record linkage in health care has been in the arena of linkage of genealogical records with morbidity and mortality records to determine genetic bases of disease and to generate understanding of how persons with different genetic predispositions respond to certain pharmacotherapy (Emery & Hayflick, 2001; Emery, Lucassen & Murphy, 2001; Kim, Labkoff, & Holliday, 2008; Lusignan & Weel, 2006). For instance, Teerlink, Hegewald, and Cannon-Albright (2007) studied heritable aspects of asthma-related mortality using Utah death certificates linked to a genealogical database of Utahans. Data linkages have also been performed for assessing variation in risk of diseases and death due to genetic predispositions (Deirdre et al., 2003; Mili, Khoury, Flanders, & Greenberg, 1993). Effective injury surveillance or trauma system evaluation also requires integration of data from multiple sources, often necessitating the use of probabilistic linkage (Clark, 2004; Goldacre, Abisgold, Yeates, & Seagroatt, 2006).

Examples involving probabilistic linkage between public health data and medical data abound. In 2007, a Web-based survey of agencies involved in linkage of healthcare administrative data sets and other public health data sets examined the purposes for which record linkage is performed, the data sets used in record linkage projects, and strengths, weaknesses, functionalities, and pricing of record linkage software available in the market (Shah, 2007a ; Shah, Fatima & McBride, 2007). Based on a large number of Listserv groups maintained by the National Association of Health Data Organizations (NAHDO), practitioners involved in data linkage efforts in their respective agencies were identified for this study, and a survey questionnaire was administered to those individuals, resulting in 36 completed questionnaires (72% response rate).

The survey findings suggested that probabilistic record linkage is used in health care and public health for a wide variety of purposes. Identifying duplicates within a large (single) data file is one of the simplest uses. Individual healthcare providers contribute data to state or national data repositories. A large data file may contain duplicate records on the same episode of care (e.g., same hospital discharge), but with different levels of detail. Probabilistic record linkage is used to consolidate these duplicate records. Perhaps the most frequent objective of record linkage is to bring together information from two or more databases, often maintained by different agencies, so that analyses of records on the same entity or person can be performed.

There are many situations where more sophisticated new analyses are only possible through probabilistic record linkage. Record linkage is also used for cleaning and standardizing data files. As mentioned elsewhere, completion of health records for purposes such as immunization records, disease registries, and resource utilization was among the use of record linkage mentioned by survey respondents (Shah, Fatima, & McBride, 2007). Augmenting data through linkage, to reduce data collection burden is used by many agencies to achieve a more efficient use of resources. For example, rather than collecting information on hospital characteristics as part of hospital discharge data, state agencies responsible for compiling discharge data mostly obtain hospital profiles from some other sources, such as the American Hospital Association (AHA). Then the state agencies would link the two data sources, using identifiable attributes such as hospital names or addresses. Many agencies also augment such administrative data with geographic characteristics such as average household income for the county or zip code of patients' residence or hospital location (Shah, Fatima & McBride, 2007).

Other specific uses included the following:

- Tracking episodes of care or health outcomes, morbidities and other risk factors

that are associated with a specific health outcome;
- Determining general and condition-specific readmission rates (Shah, 2007b);
- Determining completion rates for registries;
- Research on complications and readmission resulting from shorter stay in hospital;
- Cost of certain events of interest (e.g., cost of deliveries with complications);
- Program evaluation and disease surveillance;
- Disease prevalence research (e.g., to identify cancer diagnoses among a particular study cohort by linking with a Cancer Registry); and
- For informing evaluation, performance monitoring, and needs assessment.

In addition, the survey respondents indicated the following specific uses of probabilistic record linkage:

Health immunization: It is not uncommon that an individual infant or child can receive different vaccinations from different sources and their immunization records may be stored with different agencies including health insurance providers, public health clinics, and individual providers' clinics. Health providers and public health officials can take advantage of probabilistic record linkage in combining immunization records of individual children. In fact, several state agencies have utilized probabilistic record linkage to combine immunization records from various sources, to enable the assessment of completion (e.g., Utah Statewide Immunization Information System or USIIS). The linked immunization file in such cases is then maintained and owned by the government public health agencies.

Motor vehicle accidents: Currently involving 33 states, the Crash Outcome Data Evaluation System (CODES) is the largest system using probabilistic linkage of healthcare data sets with

Figure 2. Data sets linked by healthcare and public health agencies

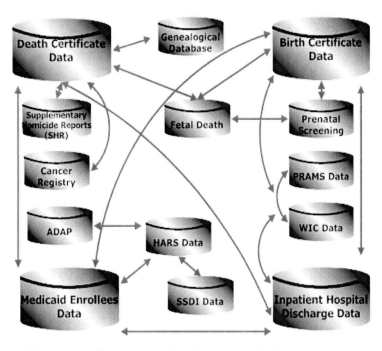

PRAMS: Pregnancy Risk Assessment and Management System
HARS: HIV/AIDS Reporting System ; SSDI: Social Security Disability Insurance
WIC: Women, Infant, Children; ADAP: AIDS Drug Assistance Program

other important data sets (Love et al., 2008; Scheetz et al., 2008). For patients involved in motor vehicle crashes, information on motor vehicle crash scene is collected by the EMS; data on treatment in the emergency room are collected by the emergency department; and inpatient records are captured in the inpatient hospital discharge abstract by the hospital. In addition, data on crash-related deaths are recorded on the death certificate. Additional data on driver characteristics and vehicle characteristics are obtained from driver's license and motor vehicle divisions. Using probabilistic linkage, each state's CODES projects combine individual patient's records from different sources to create a real-world crash outcome statewide data system to support traffic safety decisions, by examining their impact on deaths, injury type and severity, and healthcare resource utilization and cost. These CODES data are unique resources on vehicle characteristics, characteristics of the occupants, responsiveness of the trauma system, and outcomes of the crashes. In addition to guiding policies on drivers' safety, effective response to crash sites, and variety of healthcare systems decisions, CODES projects also lead to improvement in quality of data systems contributing to these projects.

Complication and hospital re-admission: Probabilistic record linkage is frequently used to detect hospital readmission at a national or state level because of the implications for both cost and quality of hospital care, and the additional burden for patients and families (Anderson & Steinberg, 1984; Benbassat & Taragin, 2000; Daly, Douglas, Kelley, O'Toole, & Montenegro, 2005). Tracking hospital readmissions within the same hospital system is often done using the unique patient identification number assigned by the hospital, but such a unique identification number is not present when readmissions occur across hospital systems. Readmissions can be tracked in other ways, including through retrospective interviews, longitudinal surveys of cohorts and panels, and through chart reviews; but typically, probabilistic linkage of hospital discharge data file is performed to track readmissions.

Application of probabilistic record linkage in study of hospital readmissions is more relevant now than ever before, due to the skyrocketing cost of care, and technological advances in hardware and software that facilitate easy tracking of readmissions, more timely data availability, and greater consumer awareness and concern about quality of care. It is also more important to track readmissions because readmission rates have been found to be on the rise, at least in some states (Goldstein, 2006). Hospital readmissions are tracked in health care for a variety of reasons, including assessment of quality of care, risk adjustment in healthcare outcome studies, maternal and child health outcomes, post-surgical follow-ups, and for disease management (Cook, Depares, Singh, & McElduff, 2006; Datar & Sood, 2006; Escobar et al., 2005; Jiang et al., 2005; Kemper, Kennedy, Dechert, & Saint, 2005; Liu et al., 2005; Oddie, Hammal, Richmond, & Parker, 2005; VanSuch, Naessens, Stroebel, Huddleston, & Williams, 2006).

A VALUE CONFLICT: INFORMATION PRIVACY VERSUS UTILITY AND FLOW

There is a paradoxical relationship between patients' rights to **privacy** and anonymity/confidentiality, and the scientific community's desire to improve the delivery of medical care and to promote public health. Integrating individual medical records from multiple sources fuels scientific research to improve better disease prevention, prognosis, and intervention. On the other hand, there are increasing concerns about protection of the privacy of the patient information contained within medical records (McClanahan, 2008). In

some cases such linkages are performed on data collected by hospital systems for quality improvement and resource management purposes, which federal and state regulations generally cover as legitimate uses of data without requiring additional permissions from patients. HMOs, insurance companies, and large healthcare systems often link data for research purposes, and the patient permission in such cases is obtained at the time of care to cover these uses.

Having a unique patient identifier can revolutionize the integration of healthcare records. Discussion about the importance of developing a unique patient identifier has been on the horizon since the 1990s. A recent study by the Rand Corporation lists reduction in medical errors and promotion of patient safety among the chief advantages of the unique patient identifier, but the cost for developing such an identifier is estimated to be around $11 billion. The return on such investment is likely to be higher than the cost (Hillestad et al., 2008). Many are resistant to its development due to concerns that individuals will be under a microscope of scrutiny. Before the Health Insurance Portability and Accountability Act of 1996 was implemented, a patient's social security number was used widely in record linkage. Since most healthcare data sets are large, there were problems with the use of social security numbers for linkage, including errors, omissions, filler values (e.g., 999 99 9999), and use of other family members' social security numbers (e.g., a hospital may use a mother's social security number for her newborn child's record). While privacy concerns are relevant in probabilistic linkage, they are less so compared to deterministic linkage, in that probabilistic linkage can be performed without unique identifiers, relying primarily on semi-unique identifiers such as date of birth, first name, last name, gender, race, and ethnicity.

One of the important privacy concerns is based on the possibility that someone can acquire individual data sets not sufficient to identify individual patients, but can create identifiable records through probabilistic linkage of several data sets. Privacy concerns are based on the possibility that revealing the identity of patients with sensitive conditions such as HIV infection can cause serious implications for patients in terms of social stigma. Reconstitution of patient identity through linkage can also reveal pre-existing medical conditions and therefore may affect a patient's eligibility for health insurance. The issue is further complicated due to a potential risk of identity theft for purposes of getting a "healthy" record. The principle of a right to privacy and no uses of data that haven't been consented to may be violated in such reconstruction of patient identity.

Data owners are often aware of such threats. Therefore, they are genuinely reluctant to share, thus limiting the data utility. Rather than erring toward restricting data access to legitimate users due to these concerns, a practical approach is that data owners should use strict data use agreements with serious penalties for data misuse, before releasing patients' medical records and other data.

FUNCTIONALITY AND PRICES OF RECORD LINKAGE SOFTWARE

According to the 2007 survey by the National Association of Health Data Organizations (NAHDO), frequently used data linkage software are Link Plus, AutoMatch, Link King (available free of cost at http://www.the-link-king.com/), Link Pro, and Initiate Identity Hub. Others include CHOICEMAKER, OX-LINK, LINKAGEWIZ, GRLS, FEBRL, and GDRIVER. It is not surprising that the most frequently used linkage programs are the ones that are either free or in the lowest price bracket. Of these, AutoMatch, developed originally by Matchware Technologies, is no longer available with the same name (and price). It was enhanced and repackaged as Integrity by Vality Inc., for a price that is several times its original price. However those who have Automatch, can still use it for most of their data

linkage needs (Shah, 2007a; Shah et al., 2007). The 2007 NAHDO Survey sheds light on which features of the probabilistic linkage software are important to users (Shah, 2007a; Shah, Fatima & McBride, 2007). Among the most important features was user control.

Ability to Designate Blocking Variables

Most users placed a high premium on having the ability to designate the blocking variables. blocking refers to the process of sorting out records according to certain variables and comparing records for possible matches within similar blocks. For instance, if the user specifies blocking variables as first name and year of birth, only those records having the same first name and year of births are compared for matching. This is one of the most important features of probabilistic linkage in increasing the efficiency of linkage.

Ability to Standardize Addresses and Names

Ability of probabilistic record linkage software to standardize the address and names is another highly desirable feature. One way to standardize names is by indexing the names by their pronunciation. The most common approach to achieve this indexing is the Soundex phonetic algorithm. The reason for importance of this functionality is that a cross-cutting feature of most public health and healthcare data sets is their imperfection in terms of completion and incompatibility of data formats. This necessitates using all possible variables in matching. While name and address are among the most important matching variables, their use is limited, if they are not standardized.

Price

The evaluation of software packages used in healthcare and public health shows that there is not much variation among software regarding the control over match specifications, including the ability to designate the matching and blocking variables. With some slight variation, the same is true about their ability to standardize names and addresses. There is a large variation though in the prices of the available commercial record linkage software, ranging from "free" to over $200,000. Of the surveyed respondents, a large portion uses software packages that are free or less than $5,000. This trend may suggest that there is a relative availability of well-functioning free linkage software, mostly through the Centers for Disease Control and Prevention (CDC) and other government agencies or from non-profit organizations for individuals/agencies.

CONCLUSION

This chapter sought to update the readers about 'what', 'how', 'who' and 'why' questions regarding probabilistic record linkage in health care, and emphasize the impact of this important development on the healthcare industry, to underscore the value of its use. A review of the recent developments in probabilistic record linkage and its impact on assessment of various dimensions of health care including surveillance, quality, disparities, access, cost, and resource allocation has been provided. By documenting the dimensions of this important, yet underutilized, technological development, we aim to trigger healthcare researchers' and practitioners' interest in exploiting it to its full potential in serving the research and decision making needs of the healthcare community.

Complete and accurate information is increasingly acknowledged as the foundation of healthcare policy and planning to promote understanding of barriers to access, quality, and safety of care. To help improve quality of health information systems, probabilistic record linkage has gradually become an important data integration and quality improvement tool in health care and public health.

It not only allows linkage of information from multiple data sources in the absence of a common unique identifier, but it can also help standardize and verify data.

Several commercial software packages have become available in the last ten years. There is a wide variation in their cost, but some are totally free (e.g., Link King), and easily downloadable from the Internet. In the current uncertain economy, most users are better off using free or inexpensive software, particularly because studies have shown that the functions offered by these software packages are sufficient for most practical purposes. For complex data design and for tasks requiring unsupervised probabilistic linkage or artificial intelligence, consumers can select advanced and relatively pricier software packages (e.g., Initiate Identity Hub or Choice Maker).

Probabilistic and deterministic approaches to record linkage have their respective strengths and weaknesses but the former is clearly superior in precision. While simplicity is an obvious strength of the deterministic approach, the probabilistic approach is superior when linking data with errors and omissions and those without unique identifiers. Deterministic matching is likely to miss a large proportion of actual matches but, once identified as matches, a high proportion are true matches.

In general, probabilistic record linkage is used in health care and public health to integrate data and improve their quality; to eliminate duplicate records; for data augmentation; and to build new data sources such as new disease registries. Probabilistic record linkage has numerous specific applications in health care and public health, particularly linkage of hospital discharge data with a large number of administrative and health services databases. It is frequently used to detect hospital readmissions at a national or state level because of the implications for both cost and quality of hospital care, and the additional economic burden and suffering for patients. Probabilistic linkage plays a pivotal role in public health agencies' ability to monitor injuries from motor vehicle crashes as a large number of states link a large number of data sets, including ambulatory care data, hospital discharge data, emergency room data and inpatient discharge data, as part of their Crash Outcomes Data Evaluation System (CODES).

Probabilistic record linkage can help researchers answer questions not possible to pursue from individual data bases. For instance, information from previous surveys (e.g., from 1998) on health status, risk behaviors, et cetera, can be linked with death certificate data that allows the assessment of risk factors for mortality (e.g., using Cox's Proportional Hazards Model).

With greater evidence of the utility of record linkage, an increasing number of state and federal agencies, hospital associations, hospital care systems, and pharmaceutical research organizations are beginning to prepare linked data sets for research and evaluation of care, that were previously not possible. An impressive number of linked data sets are being made available by the National Center for Health Statistics (NCHS). For instance, through probabilistic record linkage, NCHS links their population-based surveys with many sources of data, including National Hospital Discharge and Ambulatory Surgery Data, National Vital Records (mortality) Data, and Birth Certificate Data. These data are available as public use files to researchers for appropriate research use. NCHS is currently in the process of linking their Survey Data with Medicare enrollment and claims records collected by the Centers for Medicare and Medicaid Services (CMS). These data will be available to researchers in the near future. These data sets will allow the study of changes in health status, healthcare utilization, and expenditures in elderly and disabled people.

Record linkage is one of the most substantive technical developments pertaining to improvement and uses of patient information systems. Several developments, particularly in the last decade, created an enabling environment to trigger a focus on probabilistic record linkage. Those developments include technological developments allowing healthcare information systems to collect patient information into large computer-based databases; expansion of the role of government in creating administrative data files (e.g., national level collection of hospital discharge, emergency department, and ambulatory care data by state health departments and federal agencies such as the Agency for Healthcare Research and Quality –AHRQ); increasing demand by healthcare consumers for quality of care; and the escalating interest of government agencies and consumer advocates in measuring and improving patient safety and the quality of healthcare.

REFERENCES

Anderson, G. F., & Steinberg, E. P. (1984). Hospital readmissions in the Medicare population. *The New England Journal of Medicine, 311*(21), 1349–1353.

Bell, G. B., & Sethi, A. (2001). Matching Records in a National Medical Patient Index. *Communications of the ACM, 44*(9), 83–88. doi:10.1145/383694.383711

Benbassat, J., & Taragin, M. (2000). Hospital readmissions as a measure of quality of health care: advantages and limitations. *Archives of Internal Medicine, 160*(8), 1074–1081. doi:10.1001/archinte.160.8.1074

Blakely, T., & Salmond, C. (2002). Probabilistic record linkage and a method to calculate the positive predictive value. *International Journal of Epidemiology, 31*(6), 1246–1252. doi:10.1093/ije/31.6.1246

Bradley, C. J., Given, C. W., Luo, Z., Roberts, C., Copel, G., & Virnig, B. A. (2007). Medicaid, Medicare, and the Michigan tumor registry: A linkage strategy. *Medical Decision Making, 27*(4), 352–363. doi:10.1177/0272989X07302129

Campbell, K. M. (2008). Record linkage software in the public domain: a comparison of Link Plus, the Link King, and a `basic' deterministic algorithm. *Health Informatics Journal, 14*(1), 5–15. doi:10.1177/1460458208088855

Clark, D. E. (2004). Practical introduction to record linkage for injury research. *Injury Prevention, 10*(3), 186–191. doi:10.1136/ip.2003.004580

Cook, G., Depares, J., Singh, M., & McElduff, P. (2006). Readmission after hysterectomy and prophylactic low molecular weight heparin: retrospective case-control study. *British Medical Journal, 332,* 819–820. doi:10.1136/bmj.38783.624444.55

Czajka, J. L. (1997, March 20-21) Linking administrative records over time: Lessons from the panels of tax returns. In Record Linkage Techniques - 1997: Proceedings of an International Workshop and Exposition (pp. 49-56), Arlington, VA. Washington, DC: National Academy Press.

Daly, B. J., Douglas, S. L., Kelley, C. G., O'Toole, E., & Montenegro, H. (2005). Trial of a disease management program to reduce hospital readmissions of the chronically critically ill. *Chest, 128*(2), 507–517. doi:10.1378/chest.128.2.507

Datar, A., & Sood, N. (2006). Impact of postpartum hospital-stay legislation on newborn length of stay, readmission, and mortality in California. *Pediatrics, 118,* 63–72. doi:10.1542/peds.2005-3044

Day, C. (1997). A checklist for evaluating record linkage software. In: Record Linkage Techniques - 1997: Proceedings of an International Workshop and Exposition (pp. 483-488). Arlington, VA. March 20-21, 1997. Washington, DC: National Academy Press.

Deirdre, H. A., Gloria, G., Sven, C., Lene, M., Martha, L., & Hans-Olof, A. (2003). Mortality and cancer incidence among individuals with Down Syndrome. *Archives of Internal Medicine, 163*(6), 705–711. doi:10.1001/archinte.163.6.705

Dey, D., Sarkar, S., & De, P. (1998). A probabilistic decision model for entity matching in heterogeneous databases. *Management Science, 44*(10), 1379–1395. doi:10.1287/mnsc.44.10.1379

Dunn, H. L. (1946). Record linkage. *American Journal of Public Health, 36*(12), 1412–1416. doi:10.2105/AJPH.36.12.1412

Emery, J., & Hayflick, S. (2001). The challenge of integrating genetic medicine into primary care. *British Medical Journal, 322,* 1027–1030. doi:10.1136/bmj.322.7293.1027

Emery, J., Lucassen, A., & Murphy, M. (2001). Common hereditary cancers and implications for primary care. *Lancet, 358,* 56–63. doi:10.1016/S0140-6736(00)05257-0

Escobar, G., Greene, J., Hulac, P., Kincannon, E., Bischoff, K., & Gardner, M. (2005). Rehospitalization after birth hospitalization: patterns among infants of all gestations. *Archives of Disease in Childhood, 90,* 125–131. doi:10.1136/adc.2003.039974

Fair, M. E. (1995). An overview of record linkage in Canada. In *Proceedings of the Social Statistics Section of the American Statistical Association,* (pp.25-33), Alexandria, VA.

Fair, M. E. (1997, March 20-21). Record linkage in an information age society. In Proceedings of an International Workshop and Exposition (pp. 427-441), Arlington, VA. Washington, DC: National Academy Press.

Federal Committee on Statistical Methodology. (n.d.). Retrieved January 29, 2009, from http://www.fcsm.gov/working-papers/charlesday.pdf

Fellegi, I. P. (1997, March 20-21). Record linkage and public policy – A dynamic evolution. In: Record Linkage Techniques - 1997: Proceedings of an International Workshop and Exposition (pp. 3-12), Arlington, VA. Washington, DC: National Academy Press.

Fellegi, I. P., & Sunter, A. B. (1969). A theory for record linkage. *Journal of the American Statistical Association, 69*(6), 1183–1210. doi:10.2307/2286061

Flegel, K. (2008). Getting to the electronic medical record. *Canadian Medical Association Journal, 178*(5), 531. doi:10.1503/cmaj.080139

Goiser, K., & Christen, P. (2006). Towards automated record linkage. In *Proceedings of the Fifth Australasian Conference on Data Mining and Analytics,* (pp. 23-31).

Goldacre, M. J., Abisgold, J. D., Yeates, D. G. R., & Seagroatt, V. (2006). Risk of multiple sclerosis after head injury: record linkage study. *Journal of Neurology, Neurosurgery, and Psychiatry, 77,* 351–353. doi:10.1136/jnnp.2005.077693

Goldstein, J. (2006, September 29). Readmissions up, but deaths down. *Philadelphia Inquirer,* (pp. A01).

Harville, D. S., & Moore, R. A. (1999). Determining record linkage parameters using an iterative logistic regression approach. In *Proceedings of the Survey Research Methods Section of the American Statistical Association* (pp. 689-694), Alexandria, VA.

Herzog, T. N., & Eilerman, W. J. (1997). Linking records on federal housing administration single-family mortgages. In Record Linkage Techniques - 1997: Proceedings of an International Workshop and Exposition (pp. 279-291). Arlington, VA. March 20-21, 1997. Washington, DC: National Academy Press.

Herzog, T. N., Scheuren, F. J., & Winkler, W. E. (2007). *Data quality and record linkage techniques.* Washington, DC: Springer.

Hillestad, R., Bigelow, J. H., Chaudhry, B., Dreyer, P., Greenberg, M. D., & Meili, R. C. (2008). *Identity crisis: An examination of the costs and benefits of a unique patient identifier for the U.S. health care system.* Santa Monica, CA: RAND Corporation.

Hinman, A. R., & Davidson, A. J. (2009). Linking children's health information systems: Clinical care, public health, emergency medical systems, and schools. *Pediatrics, 123,* S67–S73. doi:10.1542/peds.2008-1755D

Jaro, M. A. (1989). Advances in record-linkage methodology as applied to matching the 1985 census of Tampa, Florida. *Journal of the American Statistical Society, 84*(406), 414–420.

Jha, A. K., Ferris, T. G., Donelan, K., DesRoches, C., Shields, A., Rosenbaum, S., & Blumenthal, D. (2006). How common are electronic health records in the United States? A summary of the evidence. *Health Affairs, 25*(6), w496–w507. doi:10.1377/hlthaff.25.w496

Jiang, H. J., Andrews, R., Stryer, D., & Friedman, B. (2005). Racial/ethnic disparities in potentially preventable readmissions: The case of diabetes. *American Journal of Public Health, 95,* 1561–1567. doi:10.2105/AJPH.2004.044222

Jiang, Z., Sarkar, S., De, P., & Dey, D. (2007). A framework for reconciling attribute values from multiple data sources. *Management Science, 53*(12), 1946–1963. doi:10.1287/mnsc.1070.0745

Kemper, A. R., Kennedy, E. J., Dechert, R. E., & Saint, S. (2005). Hospital readmission for bronchiolitis. *Clinical Pediatrics, 44,* 509–513. doi:10.1177/000992280504400607

Kim, D., Labkoff, S., & Holliday, S. H. (2008). Opportunities for electronic health record data to support business functions in the pharmaceutical industry—A case study from Pfizer, Inc. *Journal of the American Medical Informatics Association, 15*(5), 581–584. doi:10.1197/jamia.M2605

Kisely, S., Smith, M., Lawrence, D., & Maaten, S. (2005). Mortality in individuals who have had psychiatric treatment - Population-based study in Nova Scotia. *The British Journal of Psychiatry, 18*(6), 552–558. doi:10.1192/bjp.187.6.552

Liu, S., Heaman, M., Joseph, K.S., Liston, R.M., Huang, L., Sauve, R., & Kramer, M.S. (for the Maternal Health Study Group of the Canadian Perinatal Surveillance System). (2005). Risk of maternal postpartum readmission associated with mode of delivery. *Obstetrics and Gynecology*, *105*, 836–842.

Love, D., Rudolph, B., & Shah, G. H. (2008). Lessons learned in using hospital discharge data for state and national public health surveillance: Implications for Centers for Disease Control and Prevention tracking program. *Journal of Public Health Management and Practice*, *14*(6), 533–542.

Lusignan, S., & Weel, C. (2006). The use of routinely collected computer data for research in primary care: opportunities and challenges. *Family Practice*, *23*(2), 253–263. doi:10.1093/fampra/cmi106

Lyon, D. (1994). *The electronic eye: The rise of surveillance society*. Minneapolis, MN: University of Minnesota Press.

McClanahan, K. (2008). Balancing good intentions: Protecting the privacy of electronic health information. *Bulletin of Science, Technology & Society*, *28*(1), 69–79. doi:10.1177/0270467607311485

Meyer, S. (1997, March 20-21) Using MS Access to perform exact record linkages. In: Record Linkage Techniques - 1997: Proceedings of an International Workshop and Exposition (pp. 280-286), Arlington, VA. Washington, DC: National Academy Press.

Mili, F., Khoury, M. J., Flanders, D. W., & Greenberg, R. S. (1993). Risk of childhood cancer for infants with birth defects: A record linkage study. Atlanta, Georgia, 1968-1988. *American Journal of Epidemiology*, *137*(6), 629–638.

Miller, E. (1997, March 20-21). Record linkage of progress towards meeting the New Jersey high school proficiency testing requirements. In: Record Linkage Techniques - 1997: Proceedings of an International Workshop and Exposition, (pp. 227-234), Arlington, VA. Washington, DC: National Academy Press.

NeSmith. N.P. (1997). Record linkage and genealogical files. In: Record Linkage Techniques - 1997: Proceedings of an International Workshop and Exposition (pp. 358-361). Arlington, VA. March 20-21, 1997. Washington, DC: National Academy Press.

Newcombe, H. B. (1994). Cohorts and privacy. *Cancer Causes & Control*, *5*, 287–292. doi:10.1007/BF01830251

Newcombe, H. B., Kennedy, J. M., Axford, S. L., & James, A. P. (1959). Automatic linkage of vital records. *Science*, *130*, 954–959. doi:10.1126/science.130.3381.954

Oddie, S. J., Hammal, D., Richmond, S., & Parker, L. (2005). Early discharge and readmission to hospital in the first month of life in the Northern Region of the UK during 1998: a case cohort study. *Archives of Disease in Childhood*, *90*(2), 119–124. doi:10.1136/adc.2003.040766

Probert, A., Semenciw, R., Mao, Y., & Gentleman, J. F. (1997, March 20-21). Analysis of immigration data: 1980-1994. In Record Linkage Techniques - 1997: Proceedings of an International Workshop and Exposition (pp. 287-291), Arlington, VA. Washington, DC: National Academy Press.

Quass, D., & Starkey, P. (2003, August 24-27). Record linkage for genealogical databases. In *ACM SIGKDD 03 Workshop on Data Cleaning, Record Linkage, and Object Consolidation*, (pp. 40-42), Washington, DC.

Sarathy, R., & Muralidhar, K. (2006). Secure and useful data sharing. *Decision Support Systems*, *42*, 204–220. doi:10.1016/j.dss.2004.10.013

Scheetz, L. J., Zhang, J., Kolassa, J. E., Allen, P., & Allen, M. (2008). Evaluation of injury databases as a preliminary step to developing a triage decision rule. *Journal of Nursing Scholarship, 40*(2), 144–150. doi:10.1111/j.1547-5069.2008.00219.x

Schumacher, S. (2007, August). Probabilistic record linkage. Paper presented at *2007 CDC Assessment Initiative Annual Conference*, Atlanta, GA.

Shah, G. H. (2007a). *Application of record linkage in public health: A review of software packages and purposes of linkage*. Poster presented at National Association of Health Data Organizations' Annual Meeting, October 18 – 20, 2007, San Diego, CA.

Shah, G. H. (2007b). *Tracking hospital readmissions: Business case, and future directions*. Presented at 2007 CDC Assessment Initiative Annual Conference, Atlanta, GA.

Shah, G. H., Clarkson-Freeman, P. A., Ahmad, S. R., Varner, M., & Xu, W. (2008). Episiotomy and obstetric trauma in Utah: Evidence from linked hospital discharge and birth data. *Utah's Health. An Annual Review, 13*, 44–52.

Shah, G. H., Clarkson-Freeman, P. A., Cofrin, K., & Xu, W. (2007). Cesarean deliveries and newborn injuries: Evidence from linked Utah birth certificate and inpatient discharge data. *Utah's Health. An Annual Review, 12*, 10–24.

Shah, G. H., Fatima, F., & McBride, S. (2007). A *critical assessment of record linkage software used in public health*. National Association of Health Data Organizations (NAHDO) White Paper, 2008. Retrieved Jan 28, 2009 from http://nahdo.org/cs/media/p/124/download.aspx

Shah, G. H., Greenway, J. A., & Yang, W. (2007). Episiotomy and obstetric trauma in Nevada: Evidence from linked hospital discharge and birth data. *Nevada Public Health Association Journal, 4*(1), 1–10.

Sidorov, J. (2006). It ain't necessarily so: The electronic health record and the unlikely prospect of reducing health care costs. *Health Affairs, 25*(4), 1079–1085. doi:10.1377/hlthaff.25.4.1079

Steel, P. M., & Konschnik, C. A. (1997, March 20-21). Post-matching administrative record linkage between sole proprietorship tax returns and the standard statistical establishment list. In Record Linkage Techniques - 1997: Proceedings of an International Workshop and Exposition (pp. 179-189). Arlington, VA. Washington, DC: National Academy Press.

Teerlink, C. C., Hegewald, M. J., & Cannon-Albright, L. A. (2007). A genealogical assessment of heritable predisposition to asthma mortality. *American Journal of Respiratory and Critical Care Medicine, 176*, 865–870. doi:10.1164/rccm.200703-448OC

Utter, D. (1997, March 20-21). Use of probabilistic linkage for an analysis of the effectiveness of safety belts and helmets. In: Record Linkage Techniques - 1997: Proceedings of an International Workshop and Exposition (pp. 67-70), Arlington, VA. Washington, DC: National Academy Press.

VanSuch, M., Naessens, J. M., Stroebel, R. J., Huddleston, J. M., & Williams, A. R. (2006). Effect of discharge instructions on readmission of hospitalised patients with heart failure: Do all of the Joint Commission on Accreditation of Healthcare Organizations heart failure core measures reflect better care? *Quality & Safety in Health Care, 15*, 414–417. doi:10.1136/qshc.2005.017640

Wahl, J. B. (1997 March 20-21). Linking federal estate tax records. In: Record Linkage Techniques - 1997: Proceedings of an International Workshop and Exposition (pp. 171-178), Arlington, VA. Washington, DC: National Academy Press.

White, D. A. (1997, March 20-21). Review of the statistics of record linkage for genealogical research, record linkage techniques. In Record Linkage Techniques - 1997: Proceedings of an International Workshop and Exposition (pp. 362-373), Arlington, VA. Washington, DC: National Academy Press.

Winkler, W. E. (1999). *The state of record linkage and current research problems. Technical report, Statistical Research Division, U.* Washington, DC: S. Census Bureau.

Section 5
Challenges:
Ethics

Chapter 13
Biobanking:
Justice, Social Consensus, and the Marginalized

Robert J. Barnet
Georgetown University, USA

ABSTRACT

It is important to recognize that the four "p"s - power, position, prestige and profit - too frequently drive science, business, academia, and the professions. This chapter is concerned with the importance of appropriate consent, the just distribution of the material benefits of scientific research, and the possible exploitation of research subjects. Informed consent and social consensus may not adequately address the related ethical issues involved in biobanking and other related research. Past experiences internationally, especially among the marginalized, are reviewed. The chapter explores whether benefits that accrue to those involved in research, and even the larger community, can rely on the concept of social consensus. Is there sufficient attention to transparency and adequate consideration of present and future harms and benefits to research subjects, their descendants and the broader community? Are conflicts of interest, real and potential, adequately acknowledged and addressed?

INTRODUCTION

There may be unsolvable dilemmas when "modern science" and its associated technologies have unanticipated or undesired social and economic impacts. It is possible that, although there may be benefits to individuals because of scientific and technological advancement, unanticipated, and even unrecognized, harm may result to those who

DOI: 10.4018/978-1-61520-733-6.ch013

are initially benefited and their off spring. There may also be adverse effects on others, including contemporary more distant peoples, as well as future generations. Especially when genetic studies are undertaken, what should be considered are not just the potential benefits and harms, but also the belief systems, values, basic needs, and priorities of all affected parties. There are times when, because of the values and priorities of those involved, what may seem to be "scientifically appropriate" may not be ethically correct when all the individuals involved are considered. This concern extends not just to the measurable benefits, but also to outcomes that may be in conflict with, and disruptive to, alternative and traditional values and belief systems. Because something can be done does not mean it should be done.

It may be that the most *efficient* policy is to obtain a broad consent that anticipates and authorizes future scientific research and development. It is not at all clear that a policy of broad consent without adequate justification is the most *ethical* policy. At what point can the rights of the research subject trump potential benefits of research, especially when there is no feasible way to review the consent process? It can be argued, for example, that participants should maintain their right to request destruction of the material and to opt out, in advance, of any secondary research. Although it may be time consuming, a clear provision at the time of initial consent for possible future use of the material and results of the study is essential. Although it may not be possible to anticipate all potential uses and benefits, does the consent process consider the issue of possible future material benefit and financial gain?

Biobanking refers to the practice of creating a repository for biological material or data. The associated activities include the collection, storage, analysis, and distribution of the biological material or data. Although material or data may be included from animals, bacteria, or the environment, the material is typically from human sources and includes tissue and blood samples as well as relevant clinical data or records. A common goal of biotechnology firms is to obtain data that may result in marketable developments that will improve the health and well being of both the studied population and society in general. From the perspective of the biotech industry, indigenous peoples, for example, may offer valuable information about the treatment of certain diseases because of their genetic homogeneity, disease prevalence, diet, etc. Technology companies have at least two financial incentives to be involved in, and supportive

of, biobanking. By obtaining patents that secure the commercial rights over genetic material, any profits from pharmaceutical and other products developed typically go to the holder of the patent. In addition, future researchers who make use of the data must typically pay a fee.

Although the indigenous peoples represent only a relatively small portion of the population --or *because* they represent a small percentage of the population-- they should be of special concern. There are, in fact, several hundred million indigenous peoples throughout the world. The issues raised are relevant whether the studies are designed for ethnic studies, disease research, or both.

There are several reasons for geneticists to give special attention to indigenous populations. DNA from the indigenous populations is of particular interest to researchers because it may demonstrate genetic markers that have remained unaltered for many centuries. It is presumed that these groups have a more homogenous biographical ancestry than more diverse societies and that there is a higher probability of obtaining archetypal blood samples. This is of special interest to those interested in understanding the origin, migration, and history of humankind.

Another justification is the possibility that, through adaptation, indigenous groups may have developed specific genetic patterns that influence either their susceptibility or resistance to certain diseases. In addition their experiences with traditional medications may give clues to possible therapeutic interventions and associated pharmacological inquiries. The indigenous people may, and often do, actively resist involvement because of their history of past experiences, their fear of future exploitation, their sense of a low probability of benefits for them, and their different world views.

On the subject of the future use of specimens the World Health Organization (WHO) in its 1998 proposed international guidelines on ethical issues in medical genetics and genetic services stated that "specimens that could be useful to concerned families in the future should be saved and should be available" (World Health Organization, 1997, p. 13). In 2003 the WHO allowed anonymized information and samples to be used (World Health Organization, 2003). The Council for International Organizations of Medical Sciences (CIOMS, 2002) in its ethical guidelines effectively allowed for the use of samples with conditions, but included a review by an ethical committee. These guidelines, which concentrate on the protection of identity and the use of a committee with broad powers, do not guarantee freedom from abuse. In 2003 UNESCO deferred to domestic legislatures (UNESCO, 2003).

SOCIAL CONSENSUS AS THE BASIS OF SOUND PUBLIC POLICY

The conviction that access to data is necessary for the "common good" and the benefit of future generations may be proffered as ethical justification for innovative methods of obtaining consent. These include "community consent," presumed consent, broad consent, and the broader concept of social consent. In the case of biobanking, those intending to move the science and its applications forward may too quickly embrace social consensus as a consent strategy—without fully appreciating its limitations.

Social consensus may be a condition for a policy to be introduced and implemented effectively. Public policies on organ transplantation, definition of death, euthanasia, genetic screening and diagnosis, and human stem cell research are recent examples. The concept of social consensus, however, is elusive, along with the measures to secure it. Technocratic decision making, as a paternalistic activity frequently led by experts, sometimes poses a challenge to democratic decision making, presumably based on a well-informed and rational public. It remains to be proven whether public involvement in policymaking can be a solution to ethical value conflicts in society. Some argue

that group or blanket consent is necessary to allow biobank development to move forward given the difficulties of attaining individual consent. This chapter explores why that may not be so.

Mats G. Hansson, of Uppsala University and the Bioethics Center at the Karolinska Institute in Sweden, a proponent of social consensus, believes that submission of informed consent is an act of trust on the part of the patient or research subject. He qualifies that with the concern that "a strict application of the rule of informed consent may not be sensitive to the multiplicity of patient interests at stake, and could thus be detrimental to trust" (2005, pp. 415-418). However, even with concern that "regulations for patient consent that are too strict... might hinder progress" Hansson et al. subsequently concluded that "broad consent and consent for future research are valid ethically and should be recommended for biobank research" (Hansson, Dillner, Bartram, Carlson, & Helgesson, 2006, pp. 266-269).

Trust between research subjects and patients and the researchers is necessary for the success of biobank research. Hansson seems to presume that there has been full and open disclosure of, not only the benefits to science and the researchers, but also that information obtained will be used appropriately. In both the clinical and research setting significant time is required to obtain meaningful understanding and consent. The assent is often obtained because of the "trusting relationship."

Steinmann argues, correctly in my judgment, that biobanking and "research on large-scale tissue collections are simply too complex for the application in the full sense of understanding, judgment and choice. They allow only for the negative use of autonomy" (2009, pp. 282). Steinman alleges that "truly informed consent" is impossible, optional models "tend to overwhelm donors" and that there is a tendency to place the value of research over the autonomy of donors. Blanket consent and consent established by social consensus both transfer the choice to others (Steinmann, p. 285). Although samples may be provided with an understanding that the donation will help scientists and benefit others this is not the only result. The challenge is to ensure that the researchers, or their associates, will not receive benefits disproportionate to their time, talent, and resources. According to Steinmann it should be recognized that the "interest of the individual is somehow diminishing against the enormous benefits of research, and so does the capacity of the individual to make an informed well-founded decision" (Steinmann, p. 287).

Hajime Sato has pointed out that, while social consensus is considered to be a necessary condition for a policy to be introduced and implemented effectively, such as with the policies on organ transplantation, definition of death, euthanasia, genetic screening and diagnosis, and human stem cell research, the concept of consensus is, in fact, "elusive along with the measures to achieve it." Sato continues:

Technocratic decision making, as a paternalistic activity frequently led by experts, sometimes poses a challenge to democratic decision making, supposedly based on a well-informed and rational public. It. ... remains to be proved whether public involvement in policymaking can be a solution to ethical value conflicts in society. It may be expedient but it is unclear whether the rights of individuals, or even of the community, are protected (Sato, 2004, pp. 12-22).

The danger of policy built on broad consensus alone is that some individual values and priorities may not be recognized, identified, and respected. This is particularly critical if a country seeks to earn the public trust of all its members, including the most disenfranchised. In a study published in Science (Gaskell et al., 2005, pp. 1908-1909) four groups were queried about how decisions should be made involving biotechnology. Options offered were to decide on the basis of expert scientific advice or on moral criteria. "Scientific elitists," as well as "scientific populists," who constitute

about two thirds of the population studied, not surprisingly, opted for scientific evidence. Both moral elitists and moral populists favored decisions "based on the average citizen's views of the moral and ethical issues." Based on this study a policy decision on the advice of scientific experts, involves the risk that not only will the views and concerns of a significant minority be excluded, but also that the range of views of minorities will be obscured by reliance on the average.

It is anticipated that any biobanking initiative will begin by identifying, understanding, and respecting the diverse values and priorities of any society's entire population. Critical to establishing a genuine consensus within any community is early and continued involvement of all elements of the community. Any policy introduced should benefit, or at least not harm, all individuals within a community. The involvement of all elements of the population as early as possible is important first of all to avoid any perception of exclusion and to, in fact, integrate all perspectives. Not only should the involvement be early and meaningful but it should be ongoing. Experience with marginalized, non-dominant, and minority populations suggest that there is a tendency among these groups to perceive the undertakings of those in control as actions that are often self serving and exclusionary. These fears, in light of past experiences, are not groundless. On the other hand, one of the ironies that may result is that, because of the complexity of the human genetic makeup, virtually everyone in the end may be classified within small segments of the population.

The caution an experienced genetics researcher, Eric Juengst, voices about community engagement should be noted.

"Community engagement" has recently become an ethical watchword for population-based studies of human genetic variation. The theoretical aims of community engagement are to allow human populations who are the subjects of genetic variation research some meaningful control over

the initiation and conduct of that research. This goal echoes the clear obligation to secure the informed consent from any human individuals being recruited for research... Conducting community engagements for genetic variation research is a delicate and hazardous business: issues of representativeness, social identity, internal politics, and cross-cultural differences abound (Juengst, 2003, p. 182).

Juengst concludes that there is a basic contradiction between the theoretical aims of the exercise [of community engagement] and the actual goals it is capable of achieving. He argues that "it is time to recognize that genetic populations cannot always have a voice in, or be protected from, the recruitment of their members into genetic variation studies, and to face and make explicit decisions about when to forgo efforts to involve them" (Juengst, 2003, p. 182).

POLICY CRITERIA FOR A JUST SOCIETY

How should we judge whether a society and the decisions it makes are moral? How any benefits or related harms that might accrue are distributed is an important consideration. Although public policy is often established on the basis of meeting the needs of the largest number of the population there is reason for concern, from an ethical perspective, that certain segments of the population, as well as certain individuals, will either receive special benefits, no benefit, or will be exploited.

John Rawls (1971) has emphasized the importance of social policy that ensures that every one should have access to those resources that meet their basic needs. Rawls' two principles of justice follow:

First: Each person is to have an equal right to the most extensive basic liberty compatible with a similar liberty for others.

Second: Social and economic inequalities are to be arranged so that they are both (a) reasonably expected to be to everyone's advantage, and (b) attached to positions and offices open to all.

...The second principle applies, in the first approximation, to the distribution of income and wealth and to the design of organizations that make use of income and wealth and to the design of organizations that make use of differences in authority and responsibility, or chains of command. While the distribution of wealth and income need not be equal, it must be to everyone's advantage. And at the same time, positions of authority and offices of command must be accessible to all (Rawls, 1971, pp. 60-61).

Rawl's theory of justice depends upon his theory of society in which liberty and opportunity, income and wealth, and the bases of self-respect are to be distributed equally unless an unequal distribution of any, or all, of these values is to everyone's advantage. Injustice then, is, for Rawls, simply the presence of inequalities that do not bring benefit to everyone (1971, p. 62).

Feminist thought challenges patterns of oppression. Suzanne Holland's essay on a feminist appraisal of the embryonic stem cell debate in the United States is relevant to biobanking proposals:

What is so compelling about moving forward with research on hES [human embryonic stem cells] and EG [embryonic germ] cell research is the promise that it contains the potential for therapies that "will serve to relieve human suffering" as the NBAC [National Bioethics Advisory Commission] put it. But a feminist ethical analysis has to ask, whose suffering? And at whose expense? (Holland, 2001, pp. 73-86).

Holland is concerned that women, the poor, who are largely female, and most persons of color will be excluded from these therapies, even as it is possible that their eggs are commercialized downstream for profit. Further, she raises not just the justice issues of exclusion and possible exploitation, but also the issue of the appropriate allocation of resources by asking if "we *ought* to expend precious resources in this arena while daily; the numbers of persons without access to basic health care grows" (Holland, 2001, pp. 73-86).

Holland has suggested criteria for assessing whether a social policy is appropriate and demonstrates an appropriate social and ethical commitment to each and every person. Recognizing that every individual has an inherent dignity and worth, I propose the following guidelines based on her criteria:

- First, social policy should reflect a fundamental trust in the moral agency of each person and recognize that all persons deserve the opportunity to make legitimate choices about what effects their lives and to be respected when they exercise those choices.
- Second, social policy should aim to provide the means to meet the basic needs for all members of society.
- Third, social policy should honor the inherent dignity of all human persons independent of all accidentals.

Unfortunately, although public funding can focus attention on the health needs of persons on the margin, the private sector has neither the obligation, nor normally the incentive to do so. Their research and marketing is typically targeted at those with the ability to pay. They will undoubtedly anticipate at least an adequate return on investment from genetic technologies as they have from past biotech and pharmaceutical products. This is the legacy of the "free market."

THE UNITED KINGDOM MODEL

The Wellcome Trust and the United Kingdom Medical Research Council (MRC), in cooperation with the United Kingdom Biobank, commissioned a research project in order to develop a model that may provide the basis for a governance framework for biobanks. It was anticipated that the legal foundation would be modified later to suit a "more comprehensive…full fledged biobank." (Wellcome Trust Statement on Biobanks, 2002, p. 1) The UK project involved consultation with the public implemented through general practitioners.

The "key findings" of the related qualitative research commissioned by the Wellcome Trust to explore the views of the public and particular interest groups about the proposed UK Biobank concluded:

- Medical research as a whole had a broadly positive image among the general public.
- The use of biologic samples in research was not a well-known practice among the general public, but was considered acceptable in principle if consent was obtained.
- The purpose of the UK Biobank—to increase understanding of and provide information to combat diseases—was considered admirable, particularly by those with experience of illness in their family.
- While the full range of potential implications was often not immediately apparent and such implications sometimes caused initial concern, once they had been discussed and explained, positive views of the collection were restored.
- The majority also considered that, provided such essential conditions as informed consent and confidentiality were integral features of the project, they would be prepared to donate samples to the study.

- Most people felt that it would be important for donors to receive feedback about the progress of the research.

Several facts should be noted. Although the findings indicated a "broadly positive image" of the program to collect blood samples, there was not universal acceptance (The Wellcome Trust, 2003, p. 8). "Signs emerged that trust was starting to erode: some younger and ethnic minority respondents felt cynical or wary about GPs." Individuals at two specific hospitals had "coloured perceptions of medicine in general." Attitudes toward pharmaceutical companies, although it was acknowledged that their products were beneficial, were "ambivalent" and the companies were criticized as "profit driven" (2003, p. 6).

Professor Alastair Campbell of Bristol University was appointed chair of the Ethics and Governance Council of the United Kingdom Biobank in October 2006. What influence this Council has had and will have on policy is uncertain. The challenge is to replicate any successes of the UK model while at the same time remaining open on how to improve the process and avoiding any of its failings.

LEARNING FROM THE EXPERIENCES OF COUNTRIES ENGAGED IN SIMILAR PROJECTS

North America

The study of the history of the peopling of the Americas offers an opportunity for extensive scientific and cultural investigation. In the scientific realm, genetic and archeological evidence suggest that the ancestors of the Native Americans crossed from Siberia between 13,000 and 17,000 years ago. Most Native American tribes have different stories of their creation or origin. The Havasupai, for example, believe that their ancestors emerged from beneath the earth of the Grand Canyon. These indigenous peoples have a world view that is different from most of us. Yet it is one that should be acknowledged and respected. Memory, for example, is the most important intellectual resource among most of these indigenous cultures (Toledo, 2006). In addressing the difference Francis Romero, an Indian health researcher, has noted:

The fear is that the [genetic] research is going to cast doubts on, not only, who they are but also their relationship to their environment. But I still rely on my traditional beliefs. The two are complementary for me. One hundred years from now, what we know about science will change too (Wheelwright, 2005, p. 3).

There are a series of North American projects that raise relevant issues.

Genetic Studies among Native Americans in North America

The results of the experience with genetic research among North American Native Americans have been mixed. There has been some cooperation by Native American groups. The Navaho, the largest group of Native Americans in the United States of approximately 300,000, has ruled out participation in genetic studies. Other groups, such as the Northern Plains tribes have devised stiff protections and very detailed protocols. Researchers are required to list not only what benefits might occur but also what harms might result (Wheelwright, 2005). There is an ongoing study being conducted by the National Institutes of Health investigating genetic factors in cardiac disease among Native Americans entitled *Strong Heart*. One source suggests that this has proceeded, to this point, without controversy, but then notes that Robert Williams, an anthropological geneticist at Arizona State University abruptly halted his analysis of

12 tribal groups after he found that the amount of European heritage varied widely among the groups (Wheelwright, 2005).

The Salt River Tribe

The Salt River Pima-Maricopa Tribe of Arizona held discussions in 2006 about cooperating in genetic studies. The concern of Native Americans (and undoubtedly other indigenous peoples) is exemplified in a statement from Jacob Moore, a representative of the Salt-River tribe: "Tribes, in general, have been taken advantage of for so long that there is distrust. The attitude is, 'the mainstream society has taken every thing else. Once they have our genetic code, there isn't anything else they can take from us" (Wheelwright, 2005, p. 6).

The Nuu-Chah-Nulth of British Columbia

In the 1980s a researcher, Ryk Ward at the University of British Columbia collected blood samples for an arthritis study from the Nuu-chah-nulth. Ward took his samples to the University of Utah and then the University of Oxford where they were used by Ward and others for unrelated studies without consent or authorization (Dalton, 2002).

The Havasupai Tribe of Arizona

The Havasupai tribe of Arizona is an isolated group of Native Americans who live in a remote area of the Grand Canyon accessible only by helicopter, by an eight hour hike, or horseback ride. It is alleged that the Havasupai are vulnerable because of their isolation. The Havasupai submitted samples to Arizona State University in the 1990s for a project on diabetes but another researcher, without informing the subjects and without obtaining their permission, used the material to do studies on human migration and schizophrenia. The second researcher is alleged to have obtained the material on the pretense of helping the first researcher with nutritional studies on diabetes. It is alleged the samples were mishandled and the consent of the research participants was abused. In 2004 both the tribe and tribal members filed a legal action alleging ethical violations including breach of trust, fraud, and violation of tribal members civil rights (Minard, 2005).

The National Geographic Genomic Project in Alaska

The National Geographic Society in conjunction with IBM has undertaken the Genographic Project, which involves the collection of genetic data from around the world with specific emphasis on indigenous populations. One of the ten sites is at Fudan University, Shanghai, under the directorship of Professor Li Jin. The plan is to collect DNA samples and oral history from 100,000 individuals. Among those included in the study are the Native Americans in Alaska. Resistance has developed to this project. The International Treaty Council which works for the rights of indigenous peoples is opposing the project as exploitive and unethical. The Indigenous Peoples Council on Biocolonialism is "alarmed" by the project (2005a, p.1). In May of this year, the United Nations Permanent Forum on Indigenous Issues recommended that the project be investigated by the World Health Organization and The Human Rights Commission that the project be suspended. It appears the concept of "free, prior and informed consent" was at issue (International Indian Treaty Council, 2008).

The Indigenous Peoples Council on Biocolonialism has expressed its concern about the National Geographic because it is similar to the Human Genome Diversity Project and believes it is an attempt to escape legal and public judgment by utilizing private funding.

It is quite likely this project will advance new theories of origins that may contradict our own knowledge of ourselves. There is no claim as to which understanding is correct, and will result in a clash of knowledge systems. Moreover, there could be serious implications that result from so called "scientific assertion that indigenous peoples are not "indigenous" to their territories but instead are recent immigrants... .This cuts at the right of self-determination as peoples, under international human rights law (2005b, p. 2).

There is concern, for example, about whether the 20 minutes allotted to each participant is sufficient to obtain a valid consent. The consent form indicates that, "It is possible that some of the findings that result may contradict an oral, written or other tradition" (Indigenous Peoples Council on Biocolonialism, 2006, p. 4). Even among more sophisticated populations it is unclear if democratic decision making, presumably based on responses obtained from a well-informed and rational public can be a solution to ethical value conflicts in society (Sato, 2004).

It will be difficult enough to obtain meaningful consent from certain groups, such as the indigenous peoples, but to ensure that there have been valid decisions that involve more sophisticated understanding will be even more difficult.

There is a perception that the Project is trying to induce the indigenous people to participate by establishing a "Legacy Fund" (Indigenous Peoples Council on Biocolonialism, 2006). That fund proposes to donate money to indigenous peoples' preservation projects. Opponents counter that their blood is "sacred, inalienable and not for sale" (2005a, p. 7). Mention is made, not only of concern over collection of DNA from the current inhabitants, but also material from "the sacred ancestors." Although the institution of such a fund may be perceived by the researchers as offering a benefit it is not clear that the potential subjects concur. Immediately apparent here is the problem of determining what counts as a benefit. Researchers, drawing upon their own values and experience, may sincerely believe that what they are proposing will benefit the targeted population.

Without sufficient time devoted to listening to the experience and values of the people they propose to study, they may instead do irreparable harm.

The project is characterized as being "reminiscent of the 'failed Human Genome Diversity Project' which was found to be unsuitable for United States government funding because of "intractable bioethical problems." This project, since it is funded by private funds (from the Waitt Family Foundation of Gateway Computer) is not subject to the same scrutiny (Harry & Kanche, 2006).

OTHER COUNTRIES AND REGIONS

Australia

The Australian government has recently established responsibility agreements with various aboriginal communities including the Mulan community of Western Australia. In an agreement which might be conceived of, at best, as paternalistic, the government is to provide petrol pumps in exchange for the acceptance of behavior modification such as washing and showering. The goal is to reduce the incidence of trachoma infection. These agreements have been characterized as being based on "mutual obligation and reciprocity" (Boddington & Raisden, 2006). The inherent power imbalance is apparent. Beyond this, not only issues involving substitution of the values of the majority but also the creation of dependence need to be examined.

South America

Although there are significant numbers of indigenous populations in various regions of South America there are special concerns about incidents involving the indigenous peoples in the Amazon region of Brazil and Argentina. It is not uncommon to hear the conventional wisdom that there are no indigenous people in Argentina. The

International Work Group for Indigenous Affairs (2007), however, estimates that there are 15 or 20 groups constituting at least 400,000 individuals. The total number in Brazil is probably comparable although there are a larger number of tribal groups. There have been significant genetic studies done in various parts of the continent. Although the economic exploitation of these individuals and their environment has been publicized they are a group that is ripe for exploitation by biotechnology interests because of their genetic makeup and because they may have had unique exposure to, and experience with, local disease and medicinals.

China

In November 1993 the Chinese Human Genome Project (HGP) undertook the collection of DNA samples with emphasis on ethnic minorities in the Yunnan Province. Samples were collected from 25 ethnic groups characterized by relative isolation and the practice of marrying within their own ethnic group. Recognizing that there were unique opportunities in relatively isolated and homogenous areas of China this early work was followed by a more intense involvement by Harvard investigators and their associated commercial entities.

As the project developed, the scientific goals became complicated by the political and social reality of China. This was intertwined with the goals of entrepreneurial interest, both domestic and international, and academic prestige and integrity (Harvard and NIH). Multiple ethical concerns, that had typically been isolated in other situations, were present here in the aggregate. Issues related to the "one child" policy, that sought to insure optimal genetic outcome were also raised. The specters of mandatory sterilization or abortion, as well as genetic manipulation were raised.

In the mid 1990s, a Harvard professor, Geoffrey Duyk, enlisted the services of Xu Xiping, a research associate at Harvard University. Xu Xiping was from the relatively isolated Anhui

Province of China, an area with a high illiteracy rate. The population of Anhui Province was of special interest to researchers because of its homogeneity and the fact that the population had been stable for a thousand years.

The collection and export of blood samples was accomplished with the cooperation of Xu Xiping. Issues raised include whether the rights of the people of Anhui have been violated and whether there was (both in China and the United States) appropriate research protocols that had been followed. Populations, in real or relative poverty, with limited or no formal education are undoubtedly vulnerable to the solicitations of investigators who offer, or promise, rewards. In addition, the possibility has been raised that political pressure by Communist party members may have coerced cooperation (Pomfret & Nelson, 2000).

A November 2000 report (US Embassy Beijing, 2000) from the United States Embassy indicates that collaborative research projects depend on poorly paid health workers who receive poor supervision. The report further states that while provincial health departments are nominally subordinate to the Minister of Health they concentrate on maintaining ties to local leaders and that "honesty and effectiveness" varies widely. The Embassy Report recommends that that research be performed in "the more prosperous parts of the country" which is not the areas in which the genetic studies will be most rewarding. They point out that "local officials have such great arbitrary power that a farmer may not want to say no" (2000, p. 27).

Both Dr. Duyk and Xu Xiping subsequently formed commercial companies. Dr. Duyk's company, Millennium, reportedly contributed 3 million USD to support the collection of DNA by a consortium including Harvard and Anhui University. Margaret Sleeboom, after extensive research, details the concerns this saga involves including "the promise of pharmaceutical profits and advances in medical knowledge" and "the story of how an American exploited the vulnerability of a backward population of mountainous Anhui province" (Sleeboom, 2005, p. 61).

What is undisputed is that Xu Xiping transferred, without permission, a large number of samples to the United States. It appears that there was, in all probability, a lack of informed decision making on the part of the subjects. Although there was no measurable harm to the subjects documented, it is unclear whether they were treated unfairly and exploited. It is alleged that they were promised medical benefits that were never received.

Sleeboom, evaluating who was interested in the project and what perspective they might have had, lists four groups of "actors" involved in the project and its aftermath:.

- Nation States (USA and China) working in the interest of the people themselves
- Pharmaceutical companies and their clients (shareholders)
- University researchers claiming to work in the interest of science and
- Patients who want to get better.

Sleeboom follows with seven perspectives she identified based on the "interests and ideals" of those who critique the situation: national interest; scientific knowledge; human health; developing medicine; human rights; academic interest; and money (Sleeboom, 2005, p. 58)

Political issues, commercial interests, paternalistic attitudes towards the vulnerable Chinese research subjects and the lack of transparency were part of the reality. It is critical to understand that those cultures, in which individual autonomy is not a strong determinant, may be more accepting of family or community based decision making. However, it is apparent that trust and transparency remain critical, not just for ethical reasons but so that the reported scientific results are valid.

Qiu Renzong, a Chinese ethicist of stature, has argued that although the findings of the genome project may benefit some individuals, there is a danger of violation of human rights. Qiu holds that it is ethically justified to utilize the findings of genetic studies "to better understand disease and to advance the treatment and prevention of illness." However, he argues that human genome research "should not be used for genetic selectivity and for the advancement of eugenics" (Qui, Personal communication, 2008). Although Qiu has noted the difficulties in obtaining meaningful informed consent in the populations under discussion, it is clear that he does not oppose increased efforts directed at obtaining more valid informed consent, improved decision making, and promotion of greater transparency. Sleeboom cites statements that were attributed to Qui in 1993 and 2001 (Sleeboom, 2005, pp. 69). Qui, in a report to UNESCO in 1999, acknowledged that "concern for the collective good has at times led geneticists and others in China to infringe upon individual autonomy" (1999, p. 4). The social and cultural reality in China is now far different than it was at that time. However, the earlier experiences, the continued practices involving limited meaningful communication, the residual collective-orientation and paternalism, especially, but not only, in the isolated rural areas, and the continued political reality complicated by domestic entrepreneurial elements dictate a need for both greater transparency and continued caution.

Taiwan

Various countries have undertaken projects involving the construction of a national biomedical database. One of the acknowledged purposes of such projects is entrepreneurial. Taiwan, for example, has undertaken such a program with the goal of the commercial development of genomic medicinal research and the promotion of Taiwan as an "island of biomedical and related industries" (ELSI Symposium, 2006). The plan was to collect blood samples and health data from 200,000 people over a ten year period. As proposed, this project is limited to the biobanking of blood samples and does not include the collection of tissues and organs during the pilot stage.

The aboriginal groups in Taiwan make up less than 2% of the total population. The 12 tribes, with their own unique culture and customs, have roots that can be traced back 6,000 years. They have felt marginalized by mainstream society and complained in the past that they have been stereotyped and that important issues which affect their lives have been ignored (Gluck, 2005). In considering the initiation of such projects in the past there has been special concern about the accuracy of the data and an ethical emphasis on consent and confidentiality. Relevant to that issue it is apparent that in Taiwan there has been concern about the method and motivation of the manner in which scientists have collected blood samples (Pollack, 2006).

There are aspects of the Taiwan Biobanking project that raise significant ethical issues. The fact that the motivation for the Taiwan project involves a desire to commercialize biotechnology should give pause to those who have as a primary concern the rights and welfare of the indigenous peoples. Power, position, prestige, and profit are dominant forces in virtually all contemporary countries, developed or undeveloped. This is not unique to Taiwan. In Taiwan there is a "strong governmental tendency to count on industrial policy in driving the industrialization of biotechnology." This tendency in any government, it is acknowledged, "attracts the human rights infringement concern" (ELSI Symposium, 2006, p. 2).

The Taiwan project was especially attractive to biobank researchers because Taiwan has a very extensive computerized registry of the Taiwanese population that provided both a genealogical database and the mechanism to follow the participants. The Taiwanese National Health Care system covers all residents. The medical records are all computerized and centralized in a national data base. The medical and genetic information is not anonymized or "de-identified" but can only be "coded" or "encrypted."

Liu (2009) reported that the because of pressure from the media and human right groups, sample collection was postponed until December 2008. The criticism focused on "invasion of privacy, possible exploitation of the indigenous peoples, lack of transparency, lack of prior public consultation, lack of monitoring, lack of IRB approval and the use of 'free health checks' as an enticement (Liu, 2009, slide 20). As of August 2009, samples from only approximately 1,000 individuals had been collected (2009, slide 16).

Liu indicates that the claim that the UK Biobank model was followed in Taiwan was not justified by the facts. He states that there was no independent governance council until after sample collection was started. In addition, Liu reports that two members of the current governance council are co-principal investigators. In his conclusion Liu pleads for "accountability, accessibility, transparency and "bottom up" participation.

OTHER PROGRAMS AND POLICIES THAT RAISE ISSUES RELATED TO BIOBANKING

Some of the above examples have dealt not only with exploitation and issues related to identity and culture, but also with values and priorities. Findings that develop from genetic studies may challenge some of the traditional beliefs and values that are cherished by any population group but especially by indigenous peoples. There may be psychological sequelae as well. In addition there are other relevant concerns that are related to genetic engineering. Although they may not be directly related to the collection and use of human genetic information, they underline concerns about contemporary research and its interrelationship to commercial ventures in contemporary society. The following topics raise issues that are central to the concerns and emphasize the unanticipated, and typically long term, consequences of genetic alteration.

Genetic Engineering of Crops

Traditional crops have adapted to the soil and climatic conditions over centuries. With the perceived need to increase yield, the genetic modification of traditional seeds has been encouraged (Pollack, 2006). The introduction of genetically engineered crops can create problems in at least two ways. The seeds produced by these crops are typically sterile. The farmer, especially the small scale farmer, may be trapped in a dependent relationship because of the need for fertilizer and the need to purchase new seeds for each crop. In addition, it is not possible to control the spread of genetically controlled crops. It was reported that a genetically engineered grass was found growing in the wild in the State of Oregon. This grass had been tested for its resistance to an herbicide (developed with the involvement of the Monsanto Corporation) used to eliminate undesirable weeds. It was noted that Monsanto had acquired the largest supplier of cotton seeds in the United States which would add to its "commanding position in the business of biotechnology crops" (Pollack, 2006).

There are lessons to be learned from this that have a direct implication for genetic modification done to treat disease. First, genetic engineering may create unanticipated economic dependencies. Second, the genetic modification directed at the elimination of one undesirable characteristic may make manifest and propagate other characteristics, some of which may have been latent. On balance it is possible that other unintended and less desirable characteristics may emerge. From these perspectives the need for caution is apparent. Again full disclosure, transparency, and a relationship rooted in mutual trust are critical.

The Unanticipated Effects of the Biofuel Initiatives

The economic impact of the shift of arable land to food production should also be of concern. The goal of the production of fuel from agricultural crops cannot be considered independent of the impact on the cost of food and subsequent availability of basic food products to major segments of the world's population. As land use is altered it can be anticipated that genetic enhancement will be utilized to increase the yield of the most economically desired crops as well, perhaps, of the "orphaned" crops.

Iceland's Database of Medical Records

The Iceland experience underlines further the caution with which the partnership in research of government with private industry should be viewed. In 2000 the Icelandic Government gave a private firm, DeCode Genetics, access to the database containing the entire country's medical records with the anticipation that this data would be cross-referenced with genetic and genealogical information. DeCode has proceeded to drug development. The Iceland Supreme Court has since ruled that the law creating the database violated the country's privacy protection (Overby, 2004).

The International Economic Crisis of 2008-2009 and Health Care in the United States

The Clinton Health Care proposal of 1993 was an attempt to address the need for health care reform and specifically to provide access to basic health care for some 35 million who did not have health care coverage. Part of the motivation was the economic impact of health care costs on American business and a resultant competitive disadvantage in world markets. As part of this plan the development of for-profit managed health care involving competition was promoted.

The Clinton proposal failed to be passed into law. One result of the failure of the Clinton proposal was the legitimization and expansion of entrepreneurial, for-profit managed health care. At least in part due to the expansion of entrepreneurial managed care, there has been a rise in the cost of health care (Harrington, 2003). At the same time the number of individuals without health care insurance has increased. The claim that private industry, at least in health care, will benefit the general public has not been proven.

At the time of this writing (2009), the United States is again in the midst of a vigorous debate on health care. The discussion is driven by commercial interest, including the insurance, biotechnology, and pharmacological industries, as well as the health care professions. It is unclear to what extent the commercialization of genetic information will be any different.

THE ETHICAL CHALLENGES

If the global experience has taught us anything it is the need for there to be meaningful external oversight of biomedical industries. Issues that have been raised include whether the projects are designed for ethnic studies, disease research, or both. A provision for the anticipation of possible future ownership, use, and control of the material and results of the study is essential. Obviously critical is how best to secure the necessary oversight, not only by achieving a legal clearance to proceed, but also to set in place monitoring processes to ensure that the initiative proceeds in a manner that is both ethical *and* legal.

There are questions that underline the potential ethical issues and concerns which should be asked and answered by the leadership of these projects.

Lori Andrews (2005) describes in detail the multiple problems that exist in critiquing the issues that are present in biobanking. Tissues that are banked vary in biological type and source. There are multiple commercial interests numbering in the thousands internationally. The potential financial gain is in the billions of dollars. Ideally the information should be coded and anonymized.

This alone is insufficient to control abuse. The examples cited earlier in this chapter underline how easily abuse and misuse can occur.

Andrews has proposed a series of six basic questions involving such issues as adequate informed consent and ownership of the data:

1. What type of information, if any, should the source of tissue be given before tissue is entered into a biobank?
2. What should be done with the genetic information?
3. Under what circumstances is commercialization of biobank samples and information appropriate?
4. How can people protect themselves from unauthorized and unwarranted use of, or commercialization of, their tissue samples?
5. What new institutional policies and legal regulations might be necessary to govern the emerging biobank economy?
6. How should the fruits of biobanking be distributed?

What may be most important is Andrews' sixth question. There are also other questions that are fundamental and should precede the implementation of biobanking. Are there other priorities that are more important to the people of a given society at this time? Will the gains be allocated for health benefits, for economic benefit, or for both? Will the benefits be distributed broadly or narrowly? It is conventional wisdom that such projects will lead to improved health and well being for everyone. If the current structures are not set up to distribute health care benefits equitably what guarantee will society have that anticipated benefits from this project will be distributed equitably?

Left open is the issue of whether any set of rules can ensure that the material benefits from information technology, including biobanking, will be distributed equitably. It should also be asked if any benefits accrued will be helpful to the subjects of the research in a way that is consistent with their culture, values, and priorities. That will require not only legal and institutional guidelines, but also transparency and honesty. A formal legal regulation of information technology is not sufficient. A moral or ethical commitment is also required.

In Washington, DC, there is a powerful reminder of the criterion for an attempt to create a moral society. Located along the famous Cherry Tree Walk on the Western edge of the Tidal Basin near the National Mall, is the Franklin Delano Roosevelt Memorial, a memorial not only to FDR, but also to the era he represents. The memorial traces twelve years of American history through a sequence of four garden areas, each one devoted to one of FDR's terms of office. Into the beautiful pink granite, framed by waterfalls, are carved memorable extracts from Roosevelt's speeches. My favorite is taken from the wisdom Franklin Delano Roosevelt offered in his Second Inaugural Address (1937): "The test of our progress is not whether we add more to the abundance of those who have much; it is whether we provide enough for those who have too little." Such a stance requires not only a moral stance but moral courage.

However, it is not just the indigenous and marginalized that can be exploited. It may well be that the benefits of many genetic advances will be limited to a fortunate few. It may well be that a greater emphasis on basic health care, better nutrition, prevention of disease, clean water and improved sanitation, and better housing with better community planning that leaves us less dependent on both fossil and alternative fuels, will provide for the basic needs of more. A just and compassionate society should carefully consider how it allocates its resources between scientific advancement and meeting the basic needs of its members.

REFERENCES

Andrews, L. (2005). Harnessing the benefits of biobanks. *The Journal of Law, Medicine & Ethics*, *33*, 22–30. doi:10.1111/j.1748-720X.2005. tb00207.x

Boddington, P. & Räisänen, U. (2006, August 24). *Attributions of responsibility within health care policy: Sharing our responsibility within a situation of inequality.* Presented at European Society of Philosophy and Medicine, Helsinki, Finland.

Council for International Organizations of Medical Sciences. (2002). *International ethical guidelines for biomedical research involving human subjects.* Retrieved from CIOMS Web Site http://www. cioms.ch/frame_guidelines_nov_2002.htm

Dalton, R. (2002). Tribe blasts 'exploitation' of blood samples. *Nature*, *420*, 111. .doi:10.1038/420111a

Ethical, Legal and Social Issues [ELSI] Symposium on Biobanking. (2006). *Reexamining the ELSI implications of biobanking: A cross cultural perspective.* Presented at ELSI Symposium, Taiwan, September 17-18, 2006.

Gaskell, G., Einsiedel, E., Hallman, W., Hornig Priest, S., Jackson, J., & Olsthoorn, J. (2005). Social values and the governance of science. *Science*, *310*, 1908–1909. doi:10.1126/science.1119444

Gluck, C. (2005, July 4). Taiwan's aborigines find new voice. *BBC News*. Retrieved from http://news. bbc.co.uk/2/hi/asia-pacific/4649257.stm

Hansson, M. (2005). Building on relationships of trust in biobank research. *Journal of Medical Ethics*, *31*(7), 415–418. doi:10.1136/ jme.2004.009456

Hansson, M., Dillner, J., Bartram, C., Carlson, J., & Helgesson, C. (2006). Should donors be allowed to give broad consent to future biobank research? *The Lancet Oncology*, *7*, 266–269. doi:10.1016/ S1470-2045(06)70618-0

Harrington, C. (2003, May). Health care costs on the rise. *Journal of Accountancy, 195*(5), 59–63.

Harry, D., & Kanehe, L. (2005, Winter). Genetic research: Collecting blood to preserve culture? *Cultural Survival Quarterly, 29*(4). Retrieved from http://www.culturalsurvival.org/ourpublications/csq/article/genetic-research-collecting-blood-preserve-culture.

Holland, S. (2001). Beyond the embryo: A feminist appraisal of the embryonic stem cell debate. In Holland, S., Lebacqz, K., & Zoloth, L. (Eds.), *The human embryonic stem cell debate* (pp. 73–86). Cambridge, MA: The MIT Press.

Indigenous Peoples Council on Biocolonialism. (2005a, April 13). *Indigenous peoples oppose National Geographic & IBM genetic research project that seeks indigenous peoples' DNA.* Retrieved from http://www.ipcb.org/issues/human_genetics/htmls/geno_pr.html

Indigenous Peoples Council on Biocolonialism. (2005b, April 13). *IPCB action alert to oppose the genographic project.* Retrieved from http://www.ipcb.org/issues/human_genetics/htmls/action_geno.html

Indigenous Peoples Council on Biocolonialism. (2006, May 15). *Collective statement of indigenous organizations opposing "The Genographic Project" Agenda Item 4.* Retrieved from http://www.ipcb.org/issues/human_genetics/htmls/unpf5_collstate.html

International Indian Treaty Council. (9 March 2008). *The UN declaration on the rights of indigenous peoples, treaties and the right to free, prior, and informed consent: The framework for a new mechanism for reparations, restitution and redress.* Retrieved from http://www.treatycouncil.org/PDFs/FPIC%20Treaties%20and%20the%20UN%20Dec%20UNPFII%203508.pdf

International Work Group for Indigenous Affairs. (2007, July). *Indigenous peoples in Argentina.* Retrieved from http://www.iwgia.org/sw17294.asp

Juengst, E. (2003). Community engagement in genetic research: The "slow code" of research ethics? In Knopper, B. (Ed.), *Populations and genetics: Legal and socio-ethical perspectives* (p. 182). Leiden, The Netherlands: Brill Academic Publishers.

Liu, H. (2009, August). *In the name of "UK Biobank Model"—The myth of the governance of Taiwan Biobank.* Powerpoint presented at European Society of Philosophy and Medicine, Helsinki, Finland.

Minard, A. (2005, March 24). UA scientist named in two suits by Havasupai tribe members. *Arizona Daily Star.* Retrieved from: http://www.nathpo.org

Overby, S. (2004). *Iceland court ruling stalls medical database.* Retrieved from http://www.mis-asia.com

Pollack, A. (2006, August 16). Monsanto buys delta and pine land, top supplier of cotton seeds in America. *The New York Times.* Retrieved from http://www.nytimes.com/2006/08/16/business/16seed.html

Pomfret, J., & Nelson, D. (2000, December 20). An isolated region's genetic mother lode. *Washington Post*, A1.

Qiu, R. (1992, February). Asian perspectives: Tension between modern values and Chinese culture. In Z. Bankowski, & R. J. Levine (Eds.), *Ethics and research on human subjects: International Guidelines,* (pp. 188-197). Presented at The XXVIth CIOMS Conference, Geneva, Switzerland.

Qiu, R. (1999, September). A concern for the collective good. From *Is China's law eugenic?* Retrieved from: http://www.unesco.org/courier/1999_09/uk/dossier/txt07.htm

Qiu, R. (2001, April). *Protecting human genome and safeguarding human rights.* Presented at UNESCO's Workshop related to Ethical Issues on Biotechnology and Biosafety, Hangzhou, Peoples Republic of China.

Qui, R. (2008, March). Personal communication.

Rawls, J. (1971). *A theory of justice.* Cambridge, MA: The Belknap Press of Harvard University.

Roosevelt, F. (1937, January). *Second inaugural address.* Retrieved from: http://www.bartleby.com/124/pres50.html

Sato, H. (2004). Social consensus on medical technology policy; ethical issues and citizen participation. *Eiseigaku Zasshi Nippon,* (. *Japanese Journal of Hygiene, 59*(1), 12–22.

Shao-hua, L. (29 August 2000). Genes, ethics, and Aborigines. *Taipei Times.* Retrieved from http://www.taipeitimes.com/news/2000/08/29/print/0000050974

Sleeboom, M. (2005). The Harvard case of Xu Xiping: Exploitation of the people, scientific advance, or genetic theft? *New Genetics & Society, 24*(1), 57–78. doi:10.1080/14636770500037776

Steinman, M. (2009). Under the pretence of autonomy: Contradictions in the guidelines for human tissue donation. *Medicine, Health Care, and Philosophy, 12,* 281–28. doi:10.1007/s11019-009-9181-3

The Wellcome Trust. (2000, July 23). *Ethical aspects and public consultation. Public perceptions of the collection of human biological samples.* Retrieved from http://www.wellcome.ac.uk/en/1/biovenpopethepub.html

Toledo, V. (2006). Indigenous peoples and biodiversity. In Levin, S. (Ed.), *Encyclopedia of biodiversity.* Princeton, NJ: Academic Press.

United Nations Educational, Scientific and Cultural Organization (UNESCO). (2003). *International declaration on human genetic data.* Retrieved from http://portal.unesco.org/en/ev.php-URL_ID=17720&URL_DO=DO_TOPIC&URL_SECTION=201.html

United States Embassy Beijing. (2000). *Human research subject protection in China: Implications for U.S. collaborators.*

Wheelwright, J. (2005). Native America's alleles. *Discover, 26*(5), 3. Retrieved from http://discovermagazine.com/2005/may/native-americas-alleles.

World Health Organization (WHO). (1998). *Proposed international guidelines on ethical issues in medical genetics and genetic services.* Retrieved from http://whqlibdoc.who.int/hq/1998/WHO_HGN_GL_ETH_98.1.pdf

World Health Organization (WHO). (2003). *Guideline for obtaining informed consent for the procurement and use of human tissues, cells, and fluids in research.* Retrieved from http://www.who.int/reproductivehealth/topics/ethics/human_tissue_use.pdf

Chapter 14
Functional Neuroimaging, Free Will, and Privacy

Nada Gligorov
Mount Sinai School of Medicine, USA

Stephen C. Krieger
Mount Sinai School of Medicine, USA

ABSTRACT

Technological advances in neuroscience have made inroads on the localization of identifiable brain states, in some instances purporting the individuation of particular thoughts. Brain imaging technology has given rise to what seem to be novel ethical issues. This chapter will assess the current abilities and limitations of functional neuroimaging and examine its ethical implications. The authors argue that currently there are limitations of fMRI (functional magnetic resonance imaging) and its ability to capture ongoing brain processes. They also examine the impact of neuroimaging on free will and privacy. The degree of variability of brain function precludes drawing meaningful conclusions about an individual's thoughts solely from images of brain activity. The authors argue that neuroimaging does not raise novel challenges to privacy and free will, but is a recapitulation of traditional moral issues in a novel context.

INTRODUCTION

The development of brain imaging technology in neuroscience has given rise to a new domain in ethics: neuroethics. This fledgling new branch of philosophy is interdisciplinary. Neuroethics covers areas of medicine, cognitive science, and philosophy of mind, and aims to produce systematic reflections about the ethical issues stemming from the rapid development of brain imaging technology in neuroscience.

For clinicians, neuroscience promises to provide new diagnostic and therapeutic tools to treat neurological and psychiatric disorders. For philosophers and cognitive scientists, brain science helps lead the way towards the reduction of mental, or psychological states, to physical, or brain states. Traditionally, philosophers have tried to answer questions about free will, personhood and personal identity, and consciousness and other purportedly unique aspects

DOI: 10.4018/978-1-61520-733-6.ch014

of mental states. Cognitive scientists aim to explain even broader psychological phenomena, including memory, learning, and attention, by combining methods of psychology and neuroscience. Both fields are mostly focused on achieving the scientific explanation of psychological states.

Neuroscience has had a similar goal. Its aim is to uncover the structure and function of the nervous system and ultimately provide physical explanations, in terms of neurological function, of all psychological states. The growing ability of science to uncover the workings of the brain raises numerous ethical issues. If refined enough, brain imaging technology could be used to identify particular mental states, thereby breaking one of the last frontiers of absolute privacy. Already, brain imaging is being utilized in commercial applications for lie detection.

Biomedical sciences have always promised to uncover the nature of life in general and the human body in particular. In the doctor's office or hospital, the vast knowledge that can be obtained using diagnostic tests has often made large encroachments on our bodily privacy, and has made the commitment to doctor-patient confidentiality one of the primary principles in bioethics. It seems, however, that brain technology provides physicians and all other interested parties with a new resource to gain information about our minds. Although most accept some compromise when it comes to their bodily privacy when needed for medical treatment, the possible erosion of the privacy of mental states seems potentially unwarranted.

Our commonsense idea about mental states defines them as inherently private. The origin of this commonsense conception of the mind is unclear, but it is easy to assume that part of it stems from Cartesian dualism (Descartes, 1992). Rene Descartes, the 17th century French philosopher, cleaved what for many years seemed to be an unbridgeable gap between the mind and the body. He argued that the world is made of two distinct substances, *res extensa*, the body, and *res cogitas*, the mind. He argued further that we know our minds first

and our bodies second, and that this primacy of access confirms the intimate link between the self and the mind. Descartes essentially argues that mental states are tied to our conscious access to them, which means that mental states can be accessed only by the person experiencing them. Conscious access to mental states reveals their properties to the person experiencing the state and in a veridical way. In Descartes' view, we cannot be wrong about the content of conscious states and that the nature of those states is determined by how they seem to us. Mental states, according to Descartes, are inherently private.

Technological advances in brain science seem to contradict the Cartesian conception of the mind. Brain imaging permits the localization of mental states in the brain, and the study of their nature independent of the person having those states, thereby permitting others, at least in principle, to access our mental states. Neuroscience has often yielded results which run contrary to commonsense ideas about psychology, revealing, for example, that many psychological states are not conscious states (see Merikle & Daneman, 2000). This result puts into question our ability to provide truthful reports of our mental states. The cited scientific evidence not only runs contrary to Descartes original argument that we know our minds better than our bodies, but it also promises to close the gap between mind and body.

For bioethicists, technological advances in neuroscience raise what seem to be novel ethical issues, including the moral permissibility of the further erosion of privacy. Is it morally permissible to use brain imaging in court proceedings? There are, however, further more complex ethical issues connected to the human ability to be moral. We tend to identify our selves with our minds. Our ability to be moral has often been supported by mental phenomena such as free will. If free will is nothing but a brain process, determined by natural laws, our ability to make voluntary choices becomes questionable, and our ability to hold people responsible for their actions is diminished. Questions in the field of neuroethics are not just ethical questions connected to the use of brain imaging technology, but deeper moral questions about our ability to be moral, rational, to define ourselves in terms of our mental processes as distinct from our bodies. Even further, brain imaging theoretically has the potential to localize and define the function of consciousness (Fins et al., 2008), which has been considered one of the last bastions of subjectivity. If successful, the identification of our conscious states with brain states might make it possible to define not just how I am thinking, but what I am thinking about. Neuroscience threatens to objectify the subjective experience of mental states.

In the first section of this chapter, we present and assess the current state of functional brain imaging and its potential uses in clinical neurology and research. The second section of this chapter presents the philosophical background necessary to frame the discussion of the ethical implications of brain imaging technology. The third section will address two of the major ethical implications of functional neuroimaging. First we will discuss the impact of neuroimaging on how we conceive of free will, moral deliberation, and moral action. We will then consider issues of mind reading and the use of fMRI in lie detection. We will argue that brain imaging technology will not raise unique ethical issues, but will expand the realm within which ethical issues arise.

OVERVIEW OF FUNCTIONAL NEUROIMAGING

The Role of Structural and Functional Imaging

In medicine, magnetic resonance imaging (MRI) is primarily used to produce structural images of organs, including the central nervous system (Logothetis, 2008). In clinical neurology, the principle of localization is paramount: i.e., that

from an examination of the patient intended to reveal particular neurological deficits, the location of the injury or damage to the nervous system can be deduced. This paradigm rests on the vast knowledge base of functional neuroanatomy that has been elucidated over the past two centuries, and in clinical practice the results of a meticulous neurological examination remain the focal point of localizing and diagnosing disorders affecting the nervous system. Structural neuroimaging has added confirmatory tests of considerable importance to the process of locating clinical pathology within the nervous system, but these have traditionally been static images. While the neurologic examination demonstrates the location of pathology based on distorted function, for instance, the sudden right-sided weakness and loss of language ability from a left-hemisphere stroke affecting speech-production areas and motor cortex, conventional structural imaging provides a picture of the affected area and does not provide direct information about its functional ability. As applied to medical diagnosis, for example, in diagnosing a stroke or brain tumor, a brain scan is similar in principle to a mammogram: it is a way of visualizing what is inside the body, without having to physically open it (Crawford, 2008). Over the past 20 years, MRI has become the methodology of choice for imaging the brain, and allows neuroanatomy to be demonstrated in immaculate detail. In practice, the clinical neurological examination provides the gauge of the function or dysfunction of the nervous system, and the MRI provides the picture of its structure and damage.

Functional neuroimaging, however, as typified by fMRI (functional MRI), departs from this paradigm. Here the imaging methodology is no longer simply static and structural, but attempts to capture real-time information about the function of the brain. Because of its conceptual potential to capture or explain behavior in strictly neuroanatomical terms, fMRI has grabbed the imagination of scientists, policy makers, and the general public. It is a nascent technology, co-evolving in its capabilities and its applications. The following sections will provide an overview of the technique, its clinical and research applications, and a description of the limitations of the current technology as they pertain to its current and potential applications in clinical neurology and neuroscience.

Overview of Clinical and Research Applications of fMRI

Functional neuroimaging is utilized in both research and, to a lesser degree, clinical settings. fMRI is used routinely not just to study sensory processing or control of action, but also to draw conclusions about the neural mechanisms of cognitive capacities (Logothetis, 2008). In the clinical setting, fMRI is used for purposes of evaluating precise functional areas, for instance, in patients with potentially operable brain tumors. The main use of fMRI in tumor imaging is the pre-operative localization of eloquent cortical regions – areas of precise functional purpose, such as language ability – that may have been displaced, distorted, or compressed by the tumor. Functional imaging paradigms using motor tasks, language and speech production, and memory are able to show activation of relevant cortical areas. In this way, using fMRI, a neurosurgeon will be able to characterize the brain's functional anatomy so as to avoid and spare these eloquent areas of the brain during surgical resection (Fenton, Meynell, & Baylis, 2009).

In the research setting, fMRI is utilized for several distinct purposes in clinical neuroscience: to understand aspects of how the normal brain produces mental and cognitive functions; to obtain a window into the mechanisms of disease states; and more recently, to utilize knowledge gained from these paradigms to make conclusions about the neural functioning of individual patients. One example of the use of fMRI to elucidate the neural mechanisms that underlie particular mental func-

tions or experiences is a study by Eisenberger, Lieberman, and Williams (2003), in which an experimental paradigm was developed to expose individuals to social rejection while undergoing an fMRI. Participants were scanned while playing a virtual ball-tossing game, in which they were ultimately excluded. This study tested the hypothesis that the brain regions of social pain are similar to those of physical pain, whose neural substrates have been extensively elucidated. The authors measured the fMRI activity in 13 individuals at the same time as the actual rejection took place, and later obtained a self-report measure of how much distress the subject had experienced. Distress was found to be correlated with activity in the anterior cingulate cortex (ACC), which is an important mediator of the physical pain response.

Functional imaging is also utilized to garner a better understanding of neurologic disease, as a review of fMRI studies in Parkinson disease illustrates (Nandhagopal, McKeown, & Stoessl, 2008). Parkinson disease is a common adult-onset neurodegenerative disease that results in a characteristic tremor, rigidity and slowness of movement, and is classically localized to a small region of dopamine-releasing cells termed the substantia nigra. Through fMRI studies, substantially broader involvement of diffuse neural networks and brain regions has been implicated in the disease process, with significant potential consequences for the management of this condition. Building on this type of disease-state fMRI research, functional imaging could ultimately be useful in the pre-symptomatic diagnosis of diseases of the brain, such as childhood-onset schizophrenia, as abnormalities in intrinsic neuronal networks have been shown in adults using fMRI techniques (Fenton et al., 2009).

The promise of functional neuroimaging is to further build on the understanding of the activity patterns in the normal brain and in categories of disease states, and to use this framework to make meaningful conclusions about individuals. A fine example of fMRI research in clinical neurology is a paper by Owen et al., "Detecting awareness in the vegetative state," published in *Science* in 2006. They describe a 23-year-old woman in a persistent vegetative state for over a year after a motor vehicle crash, whom they studied using fMRI to elucidate her degree of conscious awareness. In their experimental paradigm, the patient was instructed to perform two mental imagery tasks during the scan – to imagine playing a game of tennis, and to imagine visiting all of the rooms of her house. During the tennis task, she showed activity in regions of motor action and planning, and during the task where she envisioned her house she showed activity in brain regions of memory and visual association. Her neural responses were indistinguishable from those observed in healthy volunteers performing the same imagery tasks in the scanner. It was concluded that despite her apparent vegetative state, the patient had evidence of consciousness on her fMRI, and that her decision to cooperate by imagining particular tasks when asked to do so represented a clear act of intention (Owen et al., 2006). This study garnered significant national attention in the scientific and popular media, and we will discuss implications of this study in a later section examining the potential role of functional neuroimaging on mind-reading and privacy.

Overview of the fMRI Technique

In the popular consciousness, the results of functional neuroimaging are tantamount to a direct envisioning of thought. In fact the beautiful graphics that both MRI and fMRI produce, and the excitement about what they imply, often mask the immense complexity of the mechanical, physical, and analytic procedures utilized in creating them (Logothetis, 2008). It must be stated first that fMRI is in fact not a direct measure of neural activity, but rather a technology that functionally maps the working brain by tracking changes in oxygenation in particular brain regions. This, in turn, is accomplished through measurements of regional blood supply in the brain, and correlating these regions with various behavioral functions and cognitive tasks (Fenton et al., 2009). Functional MRI signals are presumed to result from changes in the activity of the neuronal populations responsible for the functions in question (Logothetis, 2008). When neurons are active they consume oxygen, carried by hemoglobin in red blood cells from local blood vessels and capillaries. The local response to this increased oxygen demand is an increase in blood flow to regions of increased neural activity, occurring after a delay of several seconds. Although active neurons consume oxygen and thus increase the amount of deoxygenated hemoglobin in the blood, the increased supply of oxygenated blood results in a net increase in the concentration of oxygenated hemoglobin (Roskies, 2008).

Oxygenated and deoxygenated blood yield different magnetic signals, which can be detected using the MRI scanner. The magnetic resonance (MR) signal of blood therefore varies depending on its level of oxygenation. The blood-oxygen-level dependent (BOLD) signal is the fMRI measure of blood deoxyhemoglobin, and thus the BOLD MR signal uses the blood oxygenation level as a surrogate marker for increased neural activity. Increased levels of deoxyhemoglobin reduce the BOLD signal; reduced concentrations increase it. Almost all fMRI research uses BOLD as the method for determining where activity occurs in the brain. BOLD effects are measured using rapid acquisition of images, which can capture moderately good spatial and temporal resolution; images are usually taken every 1 to 4 seconds, and the voxels (three-dimensional pixels, or volumetric pixels) in the resulting image typically represent cubes of tissue about 2 to 4 millimeters on each side in humans. Once this data is acquired, it is statistically analyzed to generate an analyzable "image" that is used to visualize the location of discrete brain areas from which activity is recorded.

Practical and Theoretical Limitations of fMRI

Like any technique, fMRI has advantages and disadvantages, and in order to be useful, the experiments that employ it must be carefully designed and conducted to maximize its strengths and minimize its weaknesses. The limitations of fMRI pertain to both *how* it identifies brain function, and *what* it identifies as brain function. The following section will examine the technique of fMRI through the perspective of what it fails to capture.

In terms of *how* fMRI identifies regions of brain activity, critical factors determining the utility of fMRI for drawing conclusions in brain research are spatial and temporal resolution (Logothetis, 2008). The spatial resolution of fMR imaging is not as refined as that of traditional structural MRI. While neuroimaging allows visualization at the millimeter scale, the incremental building blocks of regional neural activity are those that occur on a cellular and subcellular level. Although these may ultimately be the most elemental and important phenomena that generate brain function as we know it, fMRI is not able to resolve events occurring on this microscopic scale. Since functional neuroimaging is intended to identify regions responsible for the generation of behaviors, attempting to study dynamic interactions at the level of single neurons would probably make little sense, even if it were technically feasible, particularly considering there are 10^{10} neurons in the cortex alone (Logothetis, 2008). However, given that the size of an fMRI voxel is on the order of several cubic millimeters, each voxel comprises approximately 5 million neurons. Is this degree of spatial resolution sufficient to draw meaningful conclusions about the nature of neural activity? The degree of spatial resolution an imaging modality must possess in order to be useful necessarily depends on the question being addressed – "it makes no sense to read a newspaper with a microscope", as neuroanatomist

Valentino Braitenberg once pointed out (as quoted in Logothetis, 2008). Systems for recording individual nerve firings necessarily miss the "big picture," just as neuroimaging that captures the whole brain neglects the small. It bears mentioning that one would similarly fail to read a newspaper using the Hubble telescope; the scale at which one examines needs to be gauged just right – neither too great nor too small.

Similarly, neural function is necessarily a real-time process, and the temporal resolution at which fMRI captures brain activity is limiting as well. Traditional fMRI experimental paradigms have excellent functional contrast-to-noise ratio (they can identify the signal recorded during a behavioral test from the "quiet" during between-test periods), but they are usually long intervals, lasting from 20 to 60 seconds, and may be confounded by the general state of arousal of the subject. High-speed fMRI methods, capable of whole-brain imaging with a temporal resolution of a few seconds, enabled the employment of more modern experimental designs. The time course of the response in such experiments is closer to the underlying neural activity (Logothetis, 2008). Brain scans are nonetheless not images of cognition in process, as the neural activity on a cellular level occurs on a time scale orders of magnitude faster than the BOLD response can measure. Neuroscience here is limited, not only by the practical limitations of the fMRI technique, but on the incomplete understanding of how the fleeting, oscillatory electrophysiology at the cellular level gives rise to the large-scale patterns of brain activity that we can recognize. The limitations of fMRI as an abstracted, large-scale surrogate for actual microscopic neural activity render it similar to any other physiological correlate of mental function, such as the electrodermal response used in a conventional lie detector (Uttal, 2001).

A further factor regarding *how* fMRI is utilized to identify local areas of brain activity is the use of subtraction analysis. Experimental fMRI paradigms require a "task state" designed to place specific experimental demands on the brain, as compared with a "control" state. A number of theoretical assumptions are required for this methodology; in particular that by subtracting the brain activity recorded in the control state from that recorded during the task state, the "difference" between the two states can be identified and correlated with the specific cognitive demands of the task. This paradigm requires that the task and control states differ in a single cognitive process, which is often difficult to prove. Furthermore, it presumes a somewhat linear form of brain processing, such that serial subtractions would identify, rather than obfuscate, the neural mechanisms of the cognitive processes under investigation. Functional MR imaging may fail to distinguish other physiologically relevant parameters, such as large changes in the firing rate of a few neurons, small changes in the firing rates of many neurons, or changes in temporal pattern of nerve cell activity in the absence of changes in mean firing rates (Roskies, 2008). Distinguishing "background noise" from important, yet subtle, signals is as yet an imperfect science. Without a coherent unifying theory of brain function, it is difficult to know what data are being subtracted that shouldn't be, and what data aren't being subtracted that should.

An additional issue pertaining to subtraction analysis is the conceptual failure to take into account aspects of brain function that are not discretely localizable. In an attempt to make a controlled experimental environment to identify a single brain function, the subtraction method eliminates from the picture the fact that, as in real life, the entire brain is active in both conditions. This can yield an artificial impression of neat functional localization, which subtracts out all the distributed functions (Crawford, 2008). Although more modern imaging protocols have attempted to correct this issue, overlapping networks of neurons subserving different functions are likely to go unnoticed owing to the spatial averaging that characterizes the subtraction paradigms (Logothetis, 2008).

As described above, fMRI uses oxygenated blood flow as a surrogate marker for cell nerve functions. This however, reveals limitations of *what* fMRI identifies as "brain activity." Neuronal firing can be both excitatory and inhibitory, and the vast networks of neural impulses that ultimately yield brain function rely on a complex interplay between excitation and inhibition. Indeed, shifting the balance from one of excitation to inhibition (or the reverse) is the mechanism behind myriad neurological conditions from seizures to migraines to mood disorders. Dynamic alterations in this balance, whether they lead to net excitation or inhibition, inevitably and strongly affect the regional metabolic energy demands, and thus the regulation of oxygenated cerebral blood flow (Logothetis, 2008). This is what the BOLD fMRI records as "activity". Although the functional implications of excitatory and inhibitory synaptic transmission are quite different, BOLD fMRI fails to distinguish between them (Roskies, 2008), and indicates only that "something" is happening in a region of increased oxygenated blood flow in the brain. In this way, *what* an fMRI records is limited to the process, but not the content of brain activity.

Issues Pertaining to fMRI Data Analysis

Functional neuroimaging studies result in enormous data sets that must first be parsed into what is and is not valuable. This requires setting thresholds on the raw data, which is a process that is inherently somewhat arbitrary, as well as hypothesis-driven. It is not just threshold-limited data from one scan that is typically analyzed in order to make claims about neural activity, but rather pooled and processed data from multiple trials, and often, multiple subjects. Although this inserts a further layer of abstraction, this pooling is necessary because the signal-to-noise ratio for neuroimaging is quite low; data from multiple scans is averaged in an attempt to maximize the signal being studied (Roskies, 2008).

There are numerous debates regarding the proper statistical and data analysis techniques that should be used in fMRI studies, ranging from questions about how to correct for multiple comparisons to whether analysis should be hypothesis-driven or whether brute-force statistics suffice (Roskies, 2008). A provocatively-titled 2009 paper by Vul, Harris, Winkielman, and Pashler, "Voodoo Correlations in Social Neuroscience" caught the attention of the national media with the assertion that many significant fMRI studies in the cognitive neurosciences literature utilized flawed statistical designs that artificially boosted the strength of the results, potentially even elevating spurious findings into statistical significance. The group found that studies that linked brain regions to behaviors and feelings, including social rejection, neuroticism, and jealousy, had selected fMRI voxels for analysis across subjects *because* they correlated highly with the behavioral measure in question. They argue that such an analysis will inflate the observed across-subject correlations, and can even produce significant measures out of pure noise. This is referred to as nonindependence error, roughly the experimental equivalent of a tautology.

Unsurprisingly, the Vul et al. article incited considerable backlash in the cognitive neuroscience field, including from authors of studies critiqued in the paper. Jabbi, Keysers, Singer, and Stephan (in press) argued that, because fMRI research entails adjusting significance thresholds for multiple comparisons, (the thousands of voxels in a brain image), their statistical methods don't have the problems that Vul et al. claimed. Correcting for multiple comparisons (that is, running numerous statistical tests looking for a positive correlation) ensures that the correlations exhibited by the selected voxels do not exceed a certain probability of having occurred by chance alone.

Issues Pertaining to the fMRI Image

Up to this point, we have considered issues in the experimental design, neuroimaging technique, and data analysis of fMRI. All of these degrees of abstraction from the actual neurological substrate happen before the generation of the colorful fMRI brain image with which the reader may be familiar. The fMRI data are not originally in the format of an image, but rather in data structures that encode numerical values, MRI signal intensity collected in an abstract framework called "k-space". Visual representations of data in k-space bear no visual resemblance to images of brains (Roskies, 2008). These data are transformed to a spatial format through a Fourier transform, resulting in an image that can be color-coded and presented atop a typical greyscale MRI image of the corresponding brain. The design decisions are made by convention, but a number of analytic decisions are employed in the creation of fMRI images, including setting thresholds, smoothing out of the voxels, and choosing colors to indicate particular findings of the study in question. Some experimenters use color gradations to indicate relative levels of activity, while others use color gradations to indicate relative levels of statistical significance.

These particulars might not be of importance were it not for the filtering of fMRI images into the mainstream media and the public consciousness. As these studies become more common, these "pictures of brain function" have become incorporated into the lay public's common sense notions of what constitutes brain activity and our understanding thereof (Roskies, 2008, as cited in Fenton et al., 2009). As we consider the potential ethical and societal implications of advanced functional neuroimaging, the results of a recent study at Yale are striking: in a paper entitled "The Seductive Allure of Neuroscience Explanations." Weisberg, Keil, Goodstein, Rawson, and Gray (2008) describe giving their subjects various explanations for certain psychological phenomena that are familiar to everyday experience. Some of these explanations were designed to be of notably poor quality. Their subjects consisted of three groups: neuroscientists, neuroscience students, and lay adults. The study found that all three groups did well at identifying the poor explanations, except when those explanations were preceded with the words, "Brain scans indicate…." Although this did not sway the neuroscientists, the students and lay adults were more likely to accept the bad explanation (Weisberg et al., 2008).

In another set of experiments by McCabe and Castel published in the journal *Cognition*, readers were shown to infer more scientific value for articles that included brain images than those that do not, regardless of whether the article included reasoning errors. These data demonstrate that some of the impact of brain imaging research lies not in the robustness of the study design, but in the persuasive power of the brain images themselves. The authors argue that brain images are influential because they appeal to people's affinity for reductionist explanations of cognitive phenomena (McCabe & Castel, 2008).

OVERVIEW OF NATURALISTIC VIEWS OF THE MIND

Issues regarding the subjectivity of consciousness, personal identity, personhood, and morality have often been sequestered in philosophical quarters. In addition, some see a clear division between philosophical and scientific problems. Although there are issues in philosophy that might remain untouched by the trends in science, philosophy in the 20th century has often seen itself in continuity with scientific projects. The developments in neuroscience are seen as relevant in the resolution of some of the most perennial philosophical problems. Philosophers who are working in the area of philosophy of mind acknowledge the relevance of the developments in neuroscience because they see themselves as working on different aspects of

the same problem. Philosophers endorsing views contrary to Descartes have made efforts to explain the workings of the mind in ways that are coherent with the scientific approach to the brain. Most of those ways are meant to deflate the distinction between mind and body. Descartes claimed that there were two substances, but most modern approaches to mind agree that there is only one physical substance that underlies both mental and physical phenomena (Descartes, 1992).

Within the contemporary approaches to the mind there are various explanatory factions. There are approaches that are reductive, aiming to reduce the mind to the brain. Among those there are the type-type identity theorists, which argue that each type of mental state is identical to a type of physical state (Place, 1956). For example, pain as a type of mental state is identical to a physical type, such as activation of a particular area in the brain. The resulting claim is each time a person is in pain, a particular area in the brain is active. This approach diminishes some of the mystery associated with the subjectivity of mental states. If our mental states can be explained in terms of brain states, then our mind can be explained using a scientific theory. One of the major criticisms of this view is that it fails to account for crucial features of our mental states. Mental states make fine discriminations; consider for example the various kinds of pain: sharp, dull, weak, and strong. Our mental states also are said to be *about* something, and have semantic properties. Brain states have none of those properties, thus a theory about brain states cannot account for all the complexities of the mind. A variant of the identity view is the token-token identity theory. In this view each instance of pain state is identical with a physical state, but the physical states need not be the same for all kinds of pain states (Davidson, 1970).

Another major explanatory approach to mental states that is in continuity with a physical explanation of brain state is functionalism. Functionalism defines mental states in terms of their functional role. Just like one could provide a definition of the heart by listing all of its functions in the body, mental states can be implicitly defined by their function. Functionalists argue that mental states can be explained in terms of inputs, specified as the environmental effects on the body, their interaction with other types of mental states, and outputs, which is the resulting behavior. A pain state can be explained by bodily trauma (input), it causes fear, distress, and thoughts about how to avoid further pain, and results in withdrawal behavior including outward expressions of pain such as wincing and screaming, "Ouch!" (Putnam, 1960).

The functional explanation of mental states is sometimes favored because it allows for multiple realizations. It allows for an explanation for why both humans and animals can experience pain without being physically identical. Furthermore, it supports developments of artificial intelligence because it allows for the instantiation of the mind in a machine. Functionalism does not contrast mental features to physical features like dualism; rather they provide an explanation of psychology in a way that could blend in with physical accounts of brain and behavior. One of the flaws of functionalism is that it seems to explain mental states in relation to inputs, outputs, and relations to other mental states, failing to account for intrinsic properties of those states. Some therefore argue that two sensational states could have the same functional definition, but very different internal qualities (Block, 1978).

Both functionalism and identity theory address the issue of reconciling the existence of mental states with physical states. Each position proposes the explanation of the former in terms of the latter. Eliminative Materialism (EM) is the view that our common sense psychology featuring pains, beliefs, and emotions, constitutes a false theory and needs to be replaced by a scientific explanation of brain states (Churchland, 1981). EM does not attempt to reduce mental states to brain states because they argue that mental states do not exist. Moreover, eliminativists argue that our folk-psychology

stands in the way of scientific progress because it binds scientists to a faulty framework. It is illusory to attempt localization of mental states in the brain if they do not exist. Although this position does not seem to have intuitive appeal, the virtues of this view, although not conspicuous, exist but are beyond the scope of the chapter.

All of the positions cited thus far about the mind provide a theoretical framework for the explanation of mental states in terms of brain science, but are waiting for scientific discoveries that could confirm a physicalist view of the mind. It is clearer, then, why philosophers are interested in the developments of brain imaging technology.

We have thus far listed the position of dualism, identity theory, functionalism, and EM. All the views, with the exception of dualism, are compatible with the assumption that science about the brain ought to have a significant impact on our conception of the mind. Philosophical conceptions of the mental are also relevant for the neuroscientist. Some theoretical conceptions underlie the usefulness of brain imaging technology. Scientists must rely on working hypotheses about the brain in order to support their empirical work. The idea that fMRI can help uncover features of mental states rests on the idea that mental states have features that can be "observed" by looking at an fMRI. Such a stance already depends on the assumption that brain states are in some sense instantiating mental states. Contrary to that view, one could argue that the essential features are subjective; they are bound in our subjective access of them, and cannot be reduced by definition (Nagel, 1974). The subjectivist definition of mental states would therefore deny that fMRI is a way of accessing mental features.

Another assumption is that the brain is modular. "The premise is that mental processes can be analyzed into separate and distinct faculties, components, or modules, and further that these modules are instantiated, or realized, in localized brain regions" (Crawford, 2008, p.66). Modularity requires that there are discrete functions in the brain, which can be identified in isolation from all other processes in the brain. That assumption is necessary to support the notion that fMRI can picture a particular brain process. The localization of various psychological processes, such as memory, emotion, perception, and consciousness are supported by the assumption of their modularity. The upshot is that empirical research of the brain is supported by these particular theoretical views, and it can be seen as evidence of the reduction of mind to the brain only within certain theoretical frameworks.

But there are problems with the assumption of modularity. "The difficulty lies in arriving at a specific taxonomy of the mental" (Crawford, 2008, p. 66). The localization of brain processes is done in terms of other scientific frameworks, which are themselves still in development. "The discipline of psychology exhibits a lack of agreement on the most basic elements of the mental" (Crawford, 2008, p. 66). The lack of agreement on the basic taxonomies of the mind undermines the project of localization of particular taxonomies.

The varying approaches of psychiatry, cognitive science, and behavioral neurology utilize distinct and non-overlapping conceptual categories to encapsulate human behavior. Within psychiatry, there are taxonomies of a person's mental features (divided into disorders of personality, mood, and thought) as well as into individual syndromic classifications (such as the five subtypes of schizophrenia that include the Paranoid type, Catatonic type, Disorganized type, etc). The evolving taxonomies of behavior are nowhere more evident than in the successive editions of the DSM, which continues to refine definitions and classifications of psychiatric disorders (APA, 2000). "Ideally, the phenomenological work of arriving at a taxonomy of the mental would be accomplished prior to the effort to tie mental functions to brain regions,…" (Crawford, 2008, p 67).

The proposed strategy, although reasonable, ignores the continued and bidirectional interaction between the sciences. It is not just that psychologists aim to differentiate the basic processes, while neuroscientists localize them in the brain, but the localization of particular cognitive functions is seen as evidence for a particular taxonomy. The justification of the various enterprises relies circularly on each other. Modularity and the establishment of particular taxonomies justify the project of localization of discrete functions in the brain, but the localization itself is seen as support for the taxonomy being localized. The more realistic picture is that neither field is isolated from the other and is not likely to be set antecedently to the development in the other fields.

Irrespective of the evolving definitions of behavioral science, functional neuroimaging depicts, in something approximating real-time, *that* particular areas of the brain are working, albeit not *how*. Functional imaging is still in its exploratory phase – it is yet to truly make good on its promise of correlations and offer predictive power beyond allowing neuroscientists to know which areas of the brain are likely to show demonstrable activity when given a particular task. It would be false to extrapolate from these early, pioneering studies that we can extrapolate individual experience from a neuroscience perspective.

ETHICAL IMPLICATIONS

The Impact on Free Will

The localization of mental process is often cited as having vast implications for ethics. Most of the ethical turmoil depends on further developments in neuroscience and parallel developments in brain technology, so ethical discussions on this topic are often in the conditional form. We will continue in the tradition and attempt a reevaluation of proposed ethical implications.

It was hinted earlier that one of the calamitous consequences of mental reduction would be the elimination of free will. To explain the impending threat, we should mention that free will is often thought to be constitutive of our ability to be moral. Consider a moral transgression like embezzling money from a company. Most of us would think that the embezzlers should be held responsible for their actions. Our judgment of personal responsibility in this case rests on the assumption that the moral transgressors could have done otherwise. We would not accept a defense citing that they could not help but steal. Our judgment of their action is supported by our belief that there are various things a person can do when faced with certain environmental circumstances, no matter how tempting.

Consider now that we can achieve complete reduction of all our psychological faculties, including those that underlay our ability to be moral. Our moral faculties would become part of the physical universe, subject to deterministic physical laws. Determinists argue that all physical states are predetermined by the initial state of the universe and the workings of natural laws. If the universe is deterministic in that way, then anything in the physical universe is predetermined, including brain activity. If psychological processes – including those needed for moral reasoning and action – are part of the physical universe, then deterministic laws regulate them as well. In this view there is no freedom, and the embezzlers, whose actions we considered, are not responsible for stealing.

The new developments in brain science may be instrumental when it comes to the attainment of a physical explanation of psychological states. The threats to free will, however, are not new. Thinkers who long predate the development of brain technology were cognizant of the threat that determinism posed for free will. From the inception of scientific explanations, philosophers recognized that if our mental features could be reduced to physical states, our purported ability to be moral might be affected. Some have attempted to carve out a space for morality outside of the physical universe (Kant, 2008). Some have argued that determinism and free will are compat-

ible. Others yet, argued that the universe is not deterministic (Kane, 2002).

Since the idea that "determinism threatens morality" is not new, the current trepidations about the moral implications of determinism, we think, stem from the popularization of brain science. Furthermore, the acceptance within philosophy of naturalistic views about the mind has diminished the uniqueness of the mental realm. It was possible to salvage our moral abilities by characterizing them as mental, but nowadays the argument that mental states are not physical states appears more and more obsolete.

Does neuroscience prove that the universe is determinist?

No: neuroscience will remain silent on this matter. The picture that neuroscience has yielded so far is one of mechanisms infused with indeterministic or stochastic (random or probabilistic) processes. Whether or not a neuron will fire, what pattern of action potentials it generates, or how many synaptic vesicles are released have all been characterized as stochastic phenomena in our current best models. (Roskies, 2006, p.420)

It is unclear whether the indeterminism suggested by the current best models is a feature of the brain or a failure of those models to capture its deterministic nature. Either way, the apparent indeterminism at the level of neurons can be compatible with the assumption of determinism at a more fundamental physical level (Roskies, 2006). Determinism at those levels is not in need of further supporting evidence and neuroscience ought not to be conceived as collecting further evidence for determinism. "Moreover, although scientific successes are evidence that behavior is driven by biological mechanisms rather than 'the soul' neuroscientific results cannot prove that we are nothing more than mechanisms" (Roskies, 2006, p.421).

Roskies argues that it is perhaps not the theoretical conflict between free will and determinism that seems to be the problem; rather it is our perception of the problem. There seems to be a strict conflict between free will and determinism because we cannot intuitively conceive that the two could be compatible. One cannot be both free and determined. She further argues that determinism cannot be the real threat to moral responsibility because our intuitive notions of moral responsibility are robust and not controlled by theoretical commitments to determinism.

Although determinism might not be the problem, she argues, reductivism might be. According to studies cited by Roskies, people seem to be very much affected by deterministic accounts of deliberation and decision-making. We are not worried, then, about determinism at a fundamental physical level, but we are worried about the reductivist views of our psychological processes. We prefer the idea that we are in control of our decisions. In conclusion, Roskies argues that our views about moral responsibility might develop to accommodate scientific views and avoid the incompatibility inherent in the idea that we cannot be in control in a determinist universe (Roskies, 2006). Reduction, however, is the notion that higher levels of explanation, such as biological or psychological, can be reduced to more fundamental physical explanations, such as neuroscience and physics. Consequently, the worry about reductivism can be construed as the worry about determinism.

The prediction that our current conception of moral responsibility is likely to change as a result of scientific evidence seems warranted. The ethical worries associated with the development of brain technology are evidence that science is seeping into our conceptions of moral responsibility. That our current commonsense ideas are malleable in response to science is evidence that they change in general. Common sense is in development, and any characterization of our intuitive views about moral responsibility can provide only a temporary glimpse into common sense. Roskies (2006) argues that our concern about incompat-ibility of free will and determinism is intuitive and not informed by theoretical concerns about determinism. We would argue that the prediction that intuition will change as a result of scientific developments shows that theories, in this case scientific, influence the formation of our common sense. There is not a clear distinction between intuitive and theoretical views. It might be useful to know what our intuitive notions about moral responsibility are, but speculations about the current state of our intuition ought not to be used to characterize moral problems.

In conclusion, there is enough evidence to claim that developments in neuroscience cannot uniquely affect issues of free will. As Roskies argues (2006), the development of neuroscience does not provide any additional evidence for or against determinism. Furthermore, the argument that determinism and free will are incompatible is not the result of advancement in neuroscience; as we cited, a long philosophical tradition exists on that conflict.

Brain Imaging, Mind Reading, and Privacy

One of the most widely discussed future uses of functional neuroimaging technology (including fMRI) is its introduction into the interrogation room by way of mind reading and lie detection. Indeed, there are several commercial fMRI enterprises that offer high-tech lie detection services based on research comparing neuronal activation patterns of liars and truth-tellers (Fenton et al., 2008). This would appear contrary to the limitations of fMRI as providing information as to neural correlates of cognitive processes, but not the *content* of mental states. As with the Owen et al. (2006) paper that reported how fMRI could be used to know that a subject is imagining "walking through her house," no window of insight into the actual contents of her thoughts could be inferred. We may be able to state with certainty that she was thinking about "walking through the rooms in her house," but one could not know from the data obtained in her fMRI what, in fact, her house looked like. The technique of fMRI lie detection is not, however, based on imaging the truth or falsehood of a thought itself, but rather functional imaging of a thought process required for deception. The finding that more fMRI activation is seen in the prefrontal and anterior cingulate regions in the "lie condition" relative to the "truth condition" in an experimental setting is the basis of fMRI lie detection.

Although the specifics may vary considerably with the circumstances, to lie always requires the intent to deceive. Deception involves knowing (or at least believing something to be) the truth, and saying or implying the opposite, and it necessarily involves judgments about the beliefs and knowledge of the audience (Pardo & Patterson, in press). Brain-scan lie detection is predicated on the idea that lying requires more cognitive effort, and therefore more oxygenated blood, than truth-telling. Particular areas of the brain are said to be deciding when and whether to lie, and then engaging in the processes to carry out this decision (Pardo & Patterson, in press). The message put forth in the popular media is that brain scanning promises to show us directly what the polygraph showed us obliquely (Talbot, 2007). But as with traditional polygraphs, neuroscience research is looking for a correlation between deceptive behavior and some other, objectively measurable phenomena. With polygraphs it was increased heart rates, breathing, and perspiring; with functional neuroimaging it is increased blood flow to certain regions of the brain. But as we have seen, these too are highly abstracted surrogate markers for actual thought.

A central problem with research on lying is whether research participants understand their speech acts as lies (rather than, say, as role playing in a game that involves misleading an interlocutor). A concomitant worry is whether the behaviors of research participants in test situations properly qualify as lying (Fenton et al., 2008). The limita-tions on applications of neuroimaging technology are further exacerbated by the need for cooperation on the part of the individual being imaged, and the need to rely on first-person reporting. In Fenton et al.'s view, the anticipated breakthroughs in "brain reading" (i.e., imaging and interpreting brain activity) in the service of "mind reading" (i.e., ascribing specific beliefs, desires, thoughts, and intentions) imply an independence from the cooperation of the imaged individual that is unrealistic (Fenton et al., 2008). Functional neuroimaging indeed cannot be accomplished without the extraordinary cooperation and patience on the part of the subject. Such willing participants in fMRI research projects, having consented to participate in research knowing that their thoughts are being analyzed with a brain scan, would appear to have opposite goals (utilizing different mental functions, presumably with different neurological substrates) than people in real-world situations legitimately attempting to conceal the truth.

And of course, real-world situations are as manifold in their variations as experiments in the laboratory are tightly controlled. Even the necessary "intention to deceive" may not serve as a unifying characteristic amenable to neurologic localization at all. Margaret Talbot, in her 2007 article in *The New Yorker* on the changing state of lie detection technology summarizes the scope of what can be considered deception:

Small, polite lies; big, brazen, self-aggrandizing lies; lies to protect or enchant our children; lies that we don't really acknowledge to ourselves as lies; complicated alibis that we spend days rehearsing. Certainly, it's hard to imagine that all these lies will bear the identical neural signature. In their degrees of sophistication and detail, their moral weight, their emotional valence, lies are as varied as the people who tell them (Talbot, 2007).

The use of brain imaging technology for the identification of memories or single thoughts might also pose an issue for the right-to-privacy.

We are in some cases used to various compromises when it comes to our privacy. We are used to relinquishing our privacy in the doctor's office, in public places such as security check points at the airport, and we are getting used to the loss of privacy on the Internet. In some of those cases the intrusion of privacy is justified because we value our health or safety more than our privacy and because we have laws, such as HIPAA (The Health Insurance Portability and Accountability Act of 1996) to restrict the use of private information. The threat to our mental privacy, however, seems to be an intrusion of privacy of the worse kind. In the George Orwell novel *Nineteen Eighty Four*, the author describes a totalitarian regime using sophisticated surveillance to encroach upon the right of individuals in order to suppress dissent. In the novel the author describes a regime so oppressive that the government uses surveillance technology to detect even the thoughts of dissent amongst its citizens. "To those who live in free societies, Orwell's Oceania was the ultimate dystopia in which the Thought Police possessed effective means for identifying what was going on inside the minds of individuals based on their overt behavior" (Meegan, 2008, p.14).

There are two issues to be distinguished in the above description. The morally averse aspects of Oceania are first, the infringement on the right-to-privacy, and also that the information about peoples' thoughts falls into the wrong hands. We would argue that the degree of discomfort with mind reading might be correlated with the purpose and future use of the contents of one's thoughts. In that sense the discomfort need not be with mind reading as such.

Ignoring the current state of mind reading technology and all its limitations, and assuming that we could read others' minds: is the infringement on privacy graver, if it involves the mind? To begin, the moral transgression can be condemned only if unwarranted. So there are contexts in which we might all agree that infringements on privacy are justified, by the pursuit of greater good, for instance. In clinical practice people often divulge a large amount of private information in order to facilitate diagnosis and treatment. Although they might dislike relinquishing their privacy, the negatives outweigh the positives of obtaining adequate treatment. Our commitment to privacy strengthens or weakens depending on our other goals. We prioritize health over privacy, so we justify disclosing private information to physicians. The impact on privacy in those cases is abated by the implementations of laws such as HIPAA that restrict the use of personal health information to only those people who need to know it in order to care for the patient. It is our contention that similar regulations will be put in place to restrict the use of private information obtained from fMRIs, if the need arises.

Drawing on our previous arguments, the uniqueness of mental states derives in part from our Cartesian conception of those states. We think that mental states ought to be private because they are defined as essentially subjective and dependent on our personal access to them. Assuming theoretical adjustments in our understanding of mental states, we can establish continuity between mental and bodily states. They are both physical. If that is the case, it is unclear why there would be any further moral quandaries specifically associated with mind reading.

We think that part of the moral discomfort with mind reading comes from the confusion between mental privacy, as a view of the nature of mental states, and the right-to-privacy, the ethical principle. The view about mental privacy is not an implication of the right-to-privacy; rather it is the view that the contents of mental states are inaccessible by any other method besides introspection. If that view is correct, no developments within brain science will affect the privacy of mental states. The right-to-privacy of the mental does not derive from any particular view about the mind; it is a result of a social agreement that our mental and bodily states ought to be disclosed only with our permission.

We come to the second aspect of the Orwellian scenario. Who will be privy to information about our thoughts? One of the proposed applications of the use of fMRI for lie detection is in the realm of criminal justice. The use of this technology in criminal proceedings does not pose any new ethical issues. If this technology is sufficiently developed, it could be used in place of traditional lie detectors. The moral justification for the use of the latter can be extended to the use of fMRIs. We use those in cases where the intrusion of privacy is justified by the goal of convicting criminals, or by the prevention of further harm.

Broader applications of fMRI and their moral justification would have to be decided on a case-by-case basis. In general, if there were provisions that restrict the use of this new technology to only those cases where its use is morally justified, our moral opposition to intrusion on mental privacy might dissipate. In clinical settings, if the use of brain technology can be restricted by the rules of doctor-patient confidentiality, most of the negative consequences of mind reading could be prevented. Thus, as long as we have moral guidelines and legal provisions in place to prevent undue infringement of the right-to-privacy, brain technology will not result in morally negative outcomes.

FUTURE ISSUES

Most of this chapter has focused on the potential ethical impact of brain imaging technology. Obviously, future projects attempting the localization of psychological processes in the brain will have relevance for these issues. In addition, any techniques refining brain imaging technology will affect the role of the brain image in the ratification of reductive theories about the mind, as well as its role in mind reading and lie detection. Proliferation of the use of brain imaging technology will give rise to the need to extend laws governing confidentiality of medical information to include information obtained using such technology.

Currently and for the foreseeable future, cognitive studies using fMRI are designed to compare groups of subjects with a given condition with a group of normal control subjects, while performing behaviors during fMRI experiments. In this way, the neural circuitry associated with a *disorder* can be revealed (Ball & Holland, 2009). As discussed, the fMRI signal is a surrogate marker for neural activity, and it may potentially confuse the opposing contributions of excitation and inhibition (Logothetis, 2008). It is thus suited to revealing issues of mental *processes*, rather than that of an individual's mental *content*. The degree of variability of real-time brain function across the human population precludes drawing any meaningful conclusions about an individual's beliefs, desires, thoughts, and intentions solely from images of brain activity (Fenton et al., 2008). This speaks to a pervasive fallacy in the mis-application of data describing populations: that information about an individual can be extrapolated from them. We can extrapolate from individuals up to populations, but not the reverse. The limitations of fMRI studies thus return to the conceptual limitations that form the foundations for these investigations: that they are intended to look for correlations between neuroimaging and that of reported experiences or observable behaviors, not to reduce or replace our understanding of a particular individual's experiential life.

Further research needs to be done in order to discover more about actual moral deliberation and behavior. Those issues need to be compared with traditional conceptions of morality and ought to produce a reassessment of the approaches on both ends. Philosophical approaches to morality ought to take into account evidence about actual moral deliberation and behavior, while neuroscientists ought to continue to refine their theoretical frameworks in regard to their implications for problems of morality.

REFERENCES

American Psychiatric Association. (2000). *Diagnostic and statistical manual of mental disorders* (4th ed., text revision). Washington, DC: American Psychiatric Association.

Ball, W., & Holland, S. (2009). The fear of new technology: a naturally occurring phenomenon. *The American Journal of Bioethics*, 9(1), 14–16. doi:10.1080/15265160802617977

Block, N. J. (1978). Troubles with functionalism. In C. W. Savage (Ed.) Perception and cognition: Issues in the foundations of psychology (Minnesota Studies in the Philosophy of Science 9,pp. 261-325). Minneapolis, MN: University of Minnesota Press.

Churchland, P. (1981). Eliminative materialism and the propositional attitudes. *The Journal of Philosophy*, 77(2), 67–90. doi:10.2307/2025900

Crawford, M. B. (2008, Winter). The limits of neuro-talk. *New Atlantis (Washington, D.C.)*, (19): 65–78.

Davidson, D. (1970). Mental events. In Rosenthal, D. (Ed.), *The nature of mind* (pp. 247–257). New York: Oxford University Press.

Descartes, R. (1994). *A discourse on method, meditations, and principles* (Veitch, J., Ed.). New York: Everyman.

Eisenberger, N. I., Lieberman, M. D., & Williams, K. D. (2003). Does rejection hurt? An FMRI study of social exclusion. *Science*, 302, 290–292. doi:10.1126/science.1089134

Fenton, A., Meynell, L., & Baylis, F. (2009). Ethical challenges and interpretive difficulties with non-clinical applications of pediatric FMRI. *The American Journal of Bioethics*, 9(1), 3–13. doi:10.1080/15265160802617829

Fins, J. J., Bernat, J. L., Hirsch, J., Illes, J., Laureys, S., & Murphy, E. R. (2008). Neuroimaging and disorders of consciousness: Envisioning an ethical research agenda. *The American Journal of Bioethics*, 8(9), 3–12. doi:10.1080/15265160802318113

Jabbi, M., Keysers, C., Singer, T., & Stephan, K. E. (in press). Response to "Voodoo Correlations in Social Neuroscience" by Vul et al. – summary information for the press. Available at http://www.bcn-nic.nl/replyVul.pdf

Kane, R. (Ed.). (2002). *The Oxford handbook on free will*. New York: Oxford University Press.

Kant, I. (2008). *The groundwork for the metaphysics of morals*. USA: Wilder Publications.

Logothetis, N. K. (2008). What we can do and what we cannot do with fMRI. *Nature*, 453, 869–878. doi:10.1038/nature06976

McCabe, D. P., & Castel, A. D. (2008). Seeing is believing: The effect of brain images on judgments of scientific reasoning. *Cognition*, 107, 343–352. doi:10.1016/j.cognition.2007.07.017

Meegan, D. V. (2008). Neuroimaging techniques for memory detection: Scientific, ethical, and legal issues. *The American Journal of Bioethics*, 8, 9–20. doi:10.1080/15265160701842007

Merikle, P., & Daneman, M. (2000). Conscious vs. unconscious perception. In Gazzaniga, M. (Ed.), *The New Cognitive Neurosciences* (2nd ed.). Cambridge, MA: MIT Press.

Nagel, T. (1974). What is it like to be a bat? *The Philosophical Review*, 83, 435–450. doi:10.2307/2183914

Nandhagopal, R., McKeown, M. J., & Stoessl, A. J. (2008). Functional imaging in Parkinson disease. *Neurology*, 70((16 Pt 2)), 1478–1488. doi:10.1212/01.wnl.0000310432.92489.90

Owen, A. M., Coleman, M. R., Boly, M., Davis, M. H., Laureys, S., & Pickard, J. D. (2006). Detecting awareness in the vegetative state. *Science, 313,* 1402. .doi:10.1126/science.1130197

Pardo, M. S., & Patterson, D. (2009, Feb. 6). *Philosophical foundations of law and neuroscience.* University of Illinois Law Review, 2010; U of Alabama Public Law Research Paper No. 1338763. Available at SSRN: http://ssrn.com/abstract=1338763

Place, U. T. (1956). Is consciousness a brain process? *The British Journal of Psychology, 47*(1), 44–50.

Putnam, H. (1960). Minds and machines. In Hook, S. (Ed.), *Dimensions of mind* (pp. 138–164). New York: New York University Press.

Roskies, A. (2006). Neuroscientific challenges to free will and responsibility. *Trends in Cognitive Sciences, 10,* 419–423. doi:10.1016/j.tics.2006.07.011

Roskies, A. L. (2008). Neuroimaging and inferential distance. *Neuroethics, 1,* 19–30. doi:10.1007/s12152-007-9003-3

Talbot, M. (2007, July). Duped: Can brain scans uncover lies? *The New Yorker.* Retrieved from http://www.newyorker.com/reporting/2007/07/02/070702fa_fact_talbot

Uttal, W. R. (2001). *The new phrenology: the limits of localizing cognitive processes in the brain.* Cambridge, MA: MIT Press.

Vul, E., Harris, C., Winkielman, P., & Pashler, H. (2009). Puzzlingly high correlations in fMRI studies of emotion, personality, and social cognition. (The article was formerly known as "Voodoo correlations in social neuroscience. »). *Perspectives on Psychological Science, 4,* 274–290. doi:10.1111/j.1745-6924.2009.01125.x

Weisberg, D. S., Keil, F. C., Goodstein, J., Rawson, E., & Gray, J. R. (2008). The seductive allure of neuroscience explanations. *Journal of Cognitive Neuroscience, 20*(3), 470–477. doi:10.1162/jocn.2008.20040

Section 6
Future Uses of Technology

Chapter 15
Integrating Supports for Ubiquitous Eldercare

Dario Bottazzi
Guglielmo Marconi Labs, Italy

Rebecca Montanari
University of Bologna, Italy

Tarik Taleb
NEC Research Laboratories, Germany

ABSTRACT

The demographic compression, along with heightened life expectancy and decreases in fertility rates, is dramatically raising the number of older adults in society, thus putting many countries' healthcare systems under significant pressure. Eventual loss of physical and cognitive skills makes it quite difficult for elders to maintain autonomous life-styles and often forces them to move to assisted living environments, with severe emotional and social impacts. The main challenge for the years to come is, therefore, to identify more sustainable approaches to eldercare, capable of improving elders' independence in order to avoid, or at least to delay, hospitalization. Providing suitable support for elders is, indeed, a highly challenging problem. However, recent advancements in pervasive computing enable the development of advanced eldercare services. The main focus of eldercare research to date has been directed towards the development of smart environments capable of assisting elders, for example, in monitoring their psychophysical conditions, and of reminding and facilitating their routine activities. Few research efforts have been directed towards the investigation of solutions capable of improving social engagement for elders living alone, and of facilitating the coordination of care-giving efforts. The chapter provides an overview of the state-of-the-art technology in eldercare research and suggests the extension of available solutions by adopting integrated approaches that aim at addressing both assistance and social/coordination issues stemming from eldercare.

DOI: 10.4018/978-1-61520-733-6.ch015

INTRODUCTION

Healthcare spending accounts for a significant fraction of any nation's budget. In the years to come, the demographic compression will undoubtedly increase the number of older adults in society, thus raising both the number of healthcare beneficiaries and the average cost per healthcare beneficiary (United Nations, 2000). As a consequence, ongoing demographic changes will put many countries' social and welfare systems under tremendous pressure, with the risk of undermining economic sustainability of healthcare institutions.

Finding suitable answers to medium and long term economic sustainability of healthcare systems is a rather challenging task. Wise and long-term welfare-oriented policies that take into account the novel challenges posed by the aging in society are mandatory. However, technology can play a crucial role in compensating effects for the demographic changes in society. The main goal is to provide elders with solutions capable of improving their independence in daily life and of limiting their needs for assistance, thus avoiding the need for hospital care as long as possible, with a positive impact on emotional and social costs (Mann, 2004).

Since the early nineties, the emergence of the Web has forced medical institutions to rethink and to redesign healthcare service provisioning. Today, growing numbers of resources are invested in the development of Internet-based healthcare services that permit users to access their medical records, to schedule clinical tests, to interact with medical staff, or simply to keep in touch with people affected by the same disease/pathology.

Unquestionably, the existing solutions are an important step ahead. However, the widespread diffusion of low-cost portable and embedded devices, and the growing availability of wireless networking solutions, offer unique opportunities to improve healthcare service delivery and to envisage new classes of eldercare applications available anywhere and at anytime, i.e., ubiquitous eldercare service (Bellavista, Bottazzi, Corradi, & Montanari, 2006; Soomro & Cavalcanti, 2007). Ubiquitous computing technologies permit the development of solutions enabling the mitigation of the impact of patients' disabilities (elder patients in particular) by assisting them in everyday life activities and increasing their independence, safety, and quality of life.

However, providing suitable solutions for assisting elders at home is a rather challenging task (Hirsh et al., 2000; Mann, 2004). Aging leads to the decline of vision, hearing, motion, and cognitive skills of individuals. Motion impairment can affect a person's ability to walk, use the hands, and move the trunk or even the neck. Vision impairments pose continuous challenges to safety and autonomy for elders. Hearing impairments reduce elders' abilities to communicate with others, and may lead to dangerous situations, e.g., misunderstanding between elders and caregivers on medical prescriptions. Cognition impairments undermine elders' abilities to meet safety, self-care, household, leisure, social interaction, and vocational needs, and eventually lead them to lose even the ability to perform basic activities such as eating and putting on clothes.

Along with the decline of physical and cognitive skills, elders also tend to reduce social relations with friends and family members (Hirsh et al., 2000; Mann, 2004). As a result, the aging process may lead to physical isolation of seniors that is correlated with late-life depression. It is worth noting that loneliness does not only reduce quality of life of seniors, but it may also have a serious impact on elders' safety. For example, accidental falls may be very dangerous for elders living alone (Doughty, Lewis, & McIntosh, 2000). In fact, it may be quite difficult for an injured elder to ask for or get help. As a consequence, it is essential to promote broad involvement of the elder's friends and family members in eldercare.

Several research efforts have been directed at addressing elders' physical and cognitive impairments, i.e., ubiquitous assistance solutions (Horgas & Abowd, 2004). Ubiquitous assistance solutions tend to recognize the need to populate the environment where the elder lives with sensors and actuators. Information gathered through deployed sensors provides a suitable basis to infer the current situation of the elder and to also react accordingly, e.g., by driving actuators. Studies in the literature tend to focus on addressing a single specific impairment, e.g. vision or cognitive impairment, and to show different characteristics according to the place where the patient lives, e.g., her home, retirement facilities, and so forth (Bellavista et al., 2006).

In recent times, few research studies have investigated technology-oriented solutions capable of facilitating social interaction among elders and caregivers, or aimed at coordinating care activities, i.e., ubiquitous care networking (Bellavista et al., 2006). To facilitate the interaction with the elder and among her caregivers, available ubiquitous care networking proposals tend to be designed around grouping abstractions. Shared data spaces or message-based group communication models are often employed to support inter-personal communication. The places where the elders live, along with their physical conditions, strongly affect the choice of ubiquitous care networking solutions. As a consequence, this chapter will survey solutions not only for individuals living at home (and possibly still able to spend time in outdoor environments), but also for individuals living in retirement communities or some form of long term care facility.

To the best of our knowledge, the eldercare research field is still in its infancy, and available research works are still proof-of-concept prototypes. In particular, the main limitation of available solutions in literature is that they focus on specific aspects of care, either on ubiquitous assistance or on ubiquitous care networking technologies. The chapter moves from these considerations and delineates the need for adopting an integrated eldercare service design approach capable of addressing both assistance and relational aspects of eldercare.

The chapter will present eldercare requirements and a discussion of eldercare service design guidelines and relevant state-of-the-art research efforts in the medical literature. Finally, we will consider integrated approaches to ubiquitous eldercare and present the AssistiNG ELders At Home (ANGELAH) framework, which embodies these ideas (Taleb, Bottazzi, Guizani, & Nait-Charif, 2009).

ELDERCARE REQUIREMENTS AND DESIGN GUIDELINES

Eldercare Requirements

Identifying eldercare requirements precisely is an incredibly challenging task, because it involves improving autonomy and life-quality for elders and requires researchers to address different dimensions of aging, e.g., psychological and physical limitations, difficulties in maintaining a socially-rich life, and so forth. In addition, elders' needs are extremely heterogeneous, vary from person to person, and tend to change when the individual starts the actual aging process (Hirsh et al., 2000; Horgas & Abowd, 2004).

Eldercare technologies must be seamlessly integrated in the living environments of the seniors, should be extremely easy to use, and appropriately composed and customized to fit the actual impairments of the elders (Bellavista et al., 2006; Horgas & Abowd, 2004). In the spirit of ubiquitous computing, the ubiquitous eldercare infrastructure should disappear and its use should not impose any "cognitive load" on the user (Hirsh et al., 2000). User Interfaces (UIs) should allow simple and natural human-computer interactions. Sensors may provide useful information to infer the actual situation that the user is experiencing and present a suitable basis to let the eldercare infrastructure determine what response is best suited to support the elder, and to guide actuators accordingly. For example, a gas sensor may detect dangerous situations, such as an open knob, and should let the ubiquitous eldercare infrastructure react accordingly, e.g., by driving suitable actuators to shut down the knob. Along this line, video and audio sensors may be relevant, as they enable the development of gesture and speech-based UIs that can significantly facilitate the interaction between the elder and deployed assistance services in a natural manner and without any need, at all, for the user to learn how to interact with his/her own computing infrastructure.

In ubiquitous eldercare service provisioning, it is important to identify suitable tradeoffs to balance the mismatch that often exists between elders' actual and perceived psycho-physical skills. It is frequent for elders either to overestimate or underestimate their actual skills. By overestimating his/her abilities, an elder may become exposed to (often severe) domestic injuries that, besides physical implications, may lead to late-life depressions with the eventual lack of autonomy. Similarly, underestimating her skills may lead the elder to reduce her ability to live independently, with a negative impact on her quality of life (Hirsh et al., 2000).

Early research in this field recognized a "purely-medical" definition of care and aimed at mitigating the impact of physical or cognitive disabilities affecting elders. However, the challenge is to provide elders with solutions capable of improving their independence, as well as alleviating their sense of loneliness (Taleb et al., 2009). Eldercare research community circles have reached a broad agreement on the need to provide elders with technology-oriented supports to set them in a rich social context (Keller, Van der Hoog, & Stappers, 2004; Santana, Rodriguez, Gonzalez, Castro, & Andrade, 2005). However, the kind of support needed to achieve this goal should be carefully considered. In fact, it seems necessary to determine appropriate tradeoffs between the elders' independence and engagement.

Technologies excessively relying on external people can make elders feel an important focus of attention, but at the same time, may have negative impacts on elders' abilities to live independently. As a consequence, it seems appropriate to consider eldercare approaches capable of stimulating and promoting an independent and socially rich life-style.

Finally, eldercare service provisioning requires consideration of further challenging aspects. In particular, it is necessary to improve user acceptance of eldercare services. Eldercare solutions should also be designed by taking into account aesthetic considerations, and should impose minor visible changes on elders' living environments (Pirkl & Pulos, 1997). People tend to resist the adoption of technologies stigmatizing their reliance on assistance supports. As a consequence, considerations concerning elders' preferences on look and feel, material, and colors seem to be relevant for successful ubiquitous eldercare service adoption. In addition, it is worth considering that a number of aspects including elders' gender, opinions, tastes, and cultural surroundings seem to affect ubiquitous eldercare service requirements (Hirsh et al., 2000). For instance, recent advances in medical anthropology shed light on the cultural differences that exist in perception, acceptance, and beliefs regarding the concepts of illness and aging. According to these results, it appears that solutions that seem to be appropriate for elders living in one specific cultural setting may be unfit to support elders living in another (Bellavista et al., 2006; Hirsh et al., 2000; Horgas & Abowd, 2004).

Eldercare Design Guidelines

So far, existing eldercare solutions have either aimed at providing ubiquitous assistance or ubiquitous eldercare support to seniors living on their own. Available supports tend to show a high degree of heterogeneity and to display different design guidelines.

Ubiquitous Assistance

Ubiquitous assistance solutions are based upon the "context-awareness" principle. The literature usually defines context as the whole information needed to determine the situation of the user, including her characteristics, attributes, location, and so forth (Dey, 2001). In eldercare realms, context-aware ubiquitous solutions tend to recognize the need to take full advantage of the visibility of various pieces of context information, such as the elder's physical location, gestures, and health status that are needed to determine whether the elder is in need of help. According to the current situation, ubiquitous assistance solutions should identify what kind of help is actually required, and should adopt eldercare service provisioning accordingly. For instance, in the case of an elder with vision impairment, the ubiquitous assistance service may track changes in the home layout and could notify the elder of these changes, e.g., via a speech-based interface, thus reducing (and hopefully avoiding) the risk of accidental falls.

The literature of this field recognizes the need to gather, aggregate, and distribute context information to interested entities. In fact, available solutions tend to assume the possibility of benefiting from a sensor platform, which should be composed according to the elder's requirements, and deployed in the environment where she lives (Helal et al., 2005). At regular time intervals, ubiquitous assistance solutions gather raw measurements from available sensors. The context information, thus gathered, is then aggregated to transform the raw sensed data into a higher degree of abstraction (Dey, 2001). Aggregation of context information permits us to decouple application logic from all technical details of the deployed sensor platform, thus simplifying application development and opening the possibility to run the same application over different sensing platforms. Once context aggregation is accomplished, the context information is distributed to interested entities, e.g., different service components. As a

consequence, it is possible for different eldercare services to benefit from the visibility of the same context information. It should be worth pointing out that the visibility of an entity refers to its access of context information from the system.

Ubiquitous Care Networking

Grouping is the primary issue to address in the design of ubiquitous care networking solutions. The metaphor of group, team, or community, greatly simplifies the need for interactions and coordination in decision-making (Bottazzi, Corradi, & Montanari, 2006). In fact, grouping solutions provide each group member with the full visibility of available collaborating parties and informs individuals on the amount of responsibility that the other takes in eldercare (Mynatt, Rowan, Craighill, & Jacobs, 2001). The main advantage is to provide caregivers, e.g., elder family members, the possibility of sharing caring duties in a fair manner. In addition, grouping abstractions restrict the scope of information dissemination/sharing to only the members of the same group. The metaphor of group can, therefore, significantly simplify the establishment of inter-member interactions and decision-making (Bellavista et al., 2006; Bottazzi et al., 2006).

According to elder conditions and needs, various types of eldercare communities can be formed spontaneously to provide assistance to elders. On the one hand, *a priori* determined communities may be composed of professional care staff, and/or elder relatives and friends (Mynatt et al., 2001; Santana et al., 2005). On the other hand, in the case of an emergency situation, impromptu rescue groups composed of individuals, who are allocated in the physical proximity of the elder and are willing to help, may be dynamically composed. It is worth stressing that unlike *a priori* determined communities where context tends to play a small role, context awareness should be considered in composing and organizing the collaboration infrastructure in the case of impromptu rescue teams (Bardram, 2005; Bottazzi et al., 2006). In fact, in the latter case, context information permits the system to determine whether the elder is in danger, to verify the best suited individuals that should be selected to provide prompt assistance, and so forth.

ELDERCARE SOLUTIONS

The eldercare research field is still in its infancy and several research efforts are currently underway. Available applications in the field are often proof of concept prototypes that only aim at demonstrating technical feasibility and effectiveness of techniques (e.g., vision-based algorithms for emergency detection) and software architectures (e.g., smart environment architectures) tailored for eldercare (Bellavista et al., 2006; Horgas & Abowd, 2004). However, due to the economic relevance of eldercare, a few products are also starting to emerge on the market.

As stated before, available eldercare solutions can be categorized as ubiquitous assistance and ubiquitous care networking supports (Bellavista et al., 2006). However, even within the same category, available systems tend to display a strong degree of heterogeneity, and tend to be focused on addressing specific problems affecting elders, e.g., vision impairments, reduced ability to freely move, and so forth. Despite their differences, available research also demonstrates some common aspects. In particular, the place where the elder lives significantly affects eldercare service design, mainly because, as relevant research recently demonstrated, a strong relation exists between the elder's housing and her psycho-physical conditions (Horgas & Abowd, 2004).

Although people often prefer to continue living in their own homes, with their personal possessions, and their familiar surroundings, there is a number of factors that determine the living environments of senior members in society (Horgas & Abowd, 2004). The ability to perform self-care tasks, such

as bathing, dressing, responding to nature's call, transferring, continence, and feeding, plays a key role in triggering a transition from private housing to an assisted living environment that provides supportive services or total care. In addition, acute illness (such as a stroke), progression of chronic diseases (e.g., Alzheimer's disease), cognitive and mental disorders (e.g., wandering, or aggressive behaviors) and lack of social support may lead to hospitalized care for the elder.

Because ubiquitous eldercare systems should be tailored to suit elder needs and pathologies, it should be of no surprise to expect appreciable differences in goals and design principles between solutions intended to support elders living in their own private homes and in assisted environments (e.g., nursing homes or hospitals), respectively (Horgas & Abowd, 2004). As a consequence, we consider a fine-grained classification for ubiquitous eldercare solutions next. In particular, we classify available proposals not only as ubiquitous assistance or ubiquitous care networking solution, but also, we further distinguish between solutions for aging "in place" and solutions for assisted living environments.

Ubiquitous Assistance Solutions

In the first category, there has been a plethora of research work addressing various aspects of telemedicine (Soomro & Cavalcanti, 2007). The scope of this research ranges from standardization activities for telemedicine deployment (Choi, Krause, Seo, Capitan, & Chung, 2006), privacy and security solutions (Xiao, Shen, Sun, & Cai, 2006), up to the whole realization of a system (Garawi, Istepanian, & Abu-Rghef, 2006; Hodgins et al., 2008; Poon, Zhang, & Bao, 2006). The main concerns of these solutions consist of assisting elders in their routine life activities, in constant monitoring of their health conditions, and in promptly alerting involved authorities under emergency situations.

Solutions for Aging in Place

Ubiquitous assistance solutions for aging in place aim at empowering elders and at improving their abilities to live independently. Meeting this goal is a particularly difficult endeavor, and requires identification and support of elders' activities. In addition effective solutions should also detect possibly dangerous situations and should enforce all actions needed for avoiding (or at least mitigating the impact of) possibly occurring problems (Tabar, Keshavarz, & Aghajan, 2004).

For example, in McKenna, Maruis-Faulkes, Gregor, and Newell (2003), a computer vision-based system is proposed to support people with severe vision impairments. The system enables safe navigation of a particular environment by generating alert messages via a speech output interface whenever a change occurs in the layout of the environment. This makes people, who live in that environment and are constrained with vision deficiency, aware of such changes. In Mihailidis, Carmichael, and Boger (2004), artificial intelligence (AI) learning and planning techniques are used to define proper steps of basic activities of daily living (e.g., hand-washing). The resultant system provides visual or verbal instructions to a person with dementia on how to perform a particular daily activity. The system consists of three components, namely, tracking, planning, and prompting modules. The tracking module employs computer vision to monitor the user's actions by determining the spatial coordinates of the person's body and hands within the environment. Upon obtaining these coordinates, the planning module determines what step the user is performing and whether that particular step is correct. If the system detects that the user has made an error, such as completing a step out of sequence or missing a step altogether, the prompting module selects and plays a prompt message. In Pollack et al. (2003), a cognitive orthotic system, called auto-minder, was proposed that tracks the daily plans of an individual and decides when and where to remind

the person of the execution of those plans. The developed techniques are deployed on a mobile robot, as part of the Nursebot project's "Initiative on Personal Robotic Assistance of the Elderly." Lo et al., in their UbiSense system, used embedded smart vision techniques to detect changes in posture, gait, and activities. In addition to monitoring normal daily activities and detecting potential adverse events such as falls, the system aims at capturing signs of deterioration of the patients by analyzing subtle changes in posture and gait (Lo, Wang, & Yang, 2005).

Solutions for Assisted Living Environments

Systems tailored for ubiquitous assistance in assisted living environments do not typically stress the need for improving elder independence, as elders are assumed to already rely on professional care. As a consequence, available solutions for assisted living environments are more focused on monitoring the degradation of elders' physical and cognitive skills. Monitoring of the psychological and physical condition for elders is an important aspect to consider in assisted living environments, because it permits tailoring of the provision of elder assistance according to their actual needs. In addition, monitoring of elder conditions also facilitates diagnosis of diseases that frequently affect older adults. For example, sensors deployed in an elder's bed can monitor his/her particular sleeping pattern. The prompt detection of sleeping disorders is a useful indicator to diagnose various illnesses, such as late-life depression or infection from a urinary apparatus that forces the elder to frequently go to the bathroom.

Following the relevant and pioneering experiences matured at Elite Care (Elite Care, 2009), a few ubiquitous assistance solutions are starting to appear. A notable example of a ubiquitous system for assisted living environment is the Vigil Platform (Vigil Health Solutions, 2009) that continually monitors resident rooms to detect unexpected behaviors such as extended time out of bed or in the bathroom, leaving the room, even incontinence. In addition, the Vigil Platform also integrated a wireless personal transmitter that permits the elder to call for help by pressing a button. Incidents are automatically reported to the appropriate caregiver via silent pager or wireless phone calls, and the elder can be located within the assisted healthcare institution by using a location tracking system. Further solutions aim at analyzing videos to detect anomalies in the posture and gait of the monitored individuals, and to promptly detect tremors characterizing Parkinson disease, thus providing medical staff the opportunity to plan and adopt suitable actions in the early stages of the disorder.

Ubiquitous Care Networking Solutions

The research and development efforts in ubiquitous care networking are still quite immature with only a few solutions proposed. The primary objective of ubiquitous care networking is to promote social interactions among elders and their family/friends. In addition, work is beginning in the investigation and development of support solutions capable of facilitating care coordination between all involved stakeholders, i.e., elder family members and professional care staff.

Solutions for Aging in Place

Research for ubiquitous care networking attempts to reinforce the emotional ties between elders and family members who live apart. These systems are particularly relevant for elders who are living at home, with poor (or even without) professional assistance. In fact, systems of this class not only permit improvement in the social life of older adults, but also grant peace of mind to elder family members (Keller et al., 2004).

For example, Gust of Presence provides an easy-to-use point-to-point communication support for enabling "affective interactions" between distant family members (Keller et al., 2004). Gust of Presence notifies family members when the elder is at home and able to interact through video streaming, thus improving the sense of connectedness between elders and their relatives. Further research investigating web-based collaboration lets elders distribute personal information to their family members (Santana et al., 2005), in the form of a "senior-friendly" web-log. Such frameworks allow the elders and their respective family members to easily share pictures, videos, and short stories. Collected experimental evidence demonstrates that these web-based supports can be an important aid in maintaining strong relationships between elders and the rest of their family.

Further research work is aimed at facilitating the coordination of assistance activities among all stakeholders involved in eldercare. Along this line, the Digital Family Portrait provides awareness on the activities and needs of the elders to their family members, thus promoting broad involvement in eldercare activities. The basic idea is to support various forms of coordination between elder family members and to propagate visibility of care activities that can be divided among involved individuals. For example, a shared agenda reminds the elders' relatives and friends about relevant care tasks, e.g., taking the elder to the doctor, and allows distribution of caring duties (Mynatt et al., 2001).

More recently, a few research efforts have started to investigate how to take full advantage of ubiquitous technologies for eldercare even in outdoor environments (Bottazzi et al., 2006). A notable example of systems of this class is AGAPE which promotes and supports impromptu collaboration between users allocated in proximity with the elder, in case of emergency events, such as strokes and so forth. The basic idea is not only to consider doctors and family members to play their roles in eldercare, but also to involve individuals allocated in the elder's physical proximity, who may occasionally be able to help the elder in emergency situations (Bottazzi et al., 2006). This approach is particularly well suited for non-individualistic cultures, e.g., Asian cultures, or for particular countries (e.g., Italy), where regulations impose upon all citizens the obligation to provide assistance in emergency situations.

Solutions for Assisted Living Environments

The research on ubiquitous care networking in assisted living environments tends to be focused on providing professional caregivers with advanced tools that facilitate and improve the coordination of caring activities. This permits caring institutions to improve the quality of provided services, e.g., by promptly reacting to emergency situations and by reducing the risk of mistakes in eldercare, for instance by reducing the risk of giving the wrong medication to an elder.

Systems of this class provide timely notification of members' availability and often support different forms of communication. For example, in Munoz, Rodriguez, Favela, Martinez-Garcia, and Gonzales (2003) an instant messenger has been extended to provide each group member with the full visibility of all potential collaborators available. Coordination of users is supported via their access to shared resources within the group. Coordination is based on user roles, e.g., physician, nurse, and so forth. This is a relevant aspect to consider, as professionals involved in care follow precise work-shifts and may change at any time. Another notable example of ubiquitous care networking solution for assisted living recently appeared in Bardram, 2005. This research not only recognizes the need to consider caregivers' availability and roles, but also takes into account the activities they are currently involved in. This means care providers will not be distracted by information that is deemed unnecessary for the time being. For example, a doctor who is visiting a patient should be interrupted by a colleague only in the case of an emergency, whereas currently irrelevant information should be presented to the doctor at a later time.

INTEGRATING SUPPORTS FOR UBIQUITOUS ELDERCARE

So far, most of the available literature has described either ubiquitous assistance or ubiquitous care networking support for different elder housing. However, providing suitable answers to the issues stemming from eldercare requires healthcare researchers to provide a rich support that integrates both ubiquitous assistance and care networking features. Despite the relevance of the issue, it is technically difficult to develop integrated eldercare solutions. In fact, to the best of our knowledge, none of the available solutions and research prototypes has been able to present a comprehensive framework for supporting the design, development, and deployment of any-time, anywhere healthcare services (Taleb et al., 2009). In addition, the vast majority of studies is built on top of the network layer and tends to provide dedicated support for specific applications. However, this approach is not without its shortcomings. First, application designers can hardly customize applications to follow changes in elders' requirements and needs. Second, it is rather difficult to reuse implemented supports in different application scenarios, e.g., to address different pathologies. Consequently, it is necessary to design and develop a new support system from scratch whenever it is necessary to implement a new application. Let us finally stress that building healthcare applications on top of the network layer can be tedious and error-prone because it is necessary to deal explicitly with all the issues related to users and device mobility, intermittent connectivity, sensor data acquisition and processing, and so forth (Bottazzi et al., 2006).

Middleware-level solutions for health care may offer interesting opportunities to master the complexity of health care (Bottazzi et al., 2006).

Middleware solutions could, for example, provide support for different service management details, such as user location detection and tracking, user profiling, acquisition of bio-signals from sensors, and so forth. In addition, middleware-level solutions also integrate developed solutions and can consider several challenging integration aspects, including data interoperability, coordination protocols, and so forth. The main advantage of adopting a middleware approach is to provide application developers with adequate support that permits them to focus only on design and development of the application logic, without the need for implementing low-level features. This significantly simplifies and accelerates application development. Designers may use the same middleware-level support in different ubiquitous eldercare applications, thus encouraging interoperation between different applications and their rapid prototyping.

THE ANGELAH MIDDLEWARE

ANGELAH is a context-aware middleware solution that promotes and supports the development of healthcare applications for pervasive computing environments (Taleb et al., 2009). ANGELAH is tailored to respond to detected emergency scenarios that may endanger the resident elder(s). This peculiarity/distinction makes ANGELAH well suited to support a broad range of in-house safety applications.

A further relevant contribution of ANGELAH is to demonstrate the feasibility of integrated approaches between ubiquitous assistance and ubiquitous care networking solutions. In fact, the ANGELAH framework provides a set of basic facilities for integrating these two aspects. In particular, ANGELAH provides various support facilities that gather context information from sensors deployed in the environment where the elder lives, aggregates context information, and detects situations where the elder is in need of as-

sistance. In addition, ANGELAH also integrates a groupware collaboration management support to compose and manage groups of volunteers willing to help the elder in emergency situations.

THE ANGELAH MODEL

As depicted in Figure 1, ANGELAH identifies different management roles with different responsibilities, namely the Sensing Entity (SE), the Actuator Entity (AE), the Home Manager (HM), the Surveillance Center (SC), the Locality Manager (LM), and the Local Responder (LR) roles.

The Home Manager (HM) role operates as a central server and is in charge of gathering available context information from deployed sensors, i.e., Sensing Entities (SEs), aggregate this information and detect whether the elder is in need of help. According to the current situation, HM also triggers the execution of safety-related actions that typically involve the coordination among different actuators, i.e., Actuator Entities (AEs). Upon detecting an emergency situation, the HM notifies the Surveillance Center (SC) of the event via an emergency notification message, referred to as SOS, followed by some context information that may help a SC agent to understand the kind of support that is required by the elder.

The SC is in charge of coordinating prompt response in emergency situations. When SC receives an SOS message from an elder's HM, it first obtains the visibility of all Locality Responders (LRs) allocated in the proximity of the elder's home. LRs represent individuals willing to provide prompt help to elders when an emergency situation occurs. LRs are statically subscribed to the ANGELAH service. They can be family members of the elder, his friends, relatives living in his immediate surroundings, or simply passers-by allocated in physical proximity with the elder, neighborhood community representatives, and paid help, such as professional caregivers, doctors, pharmacists, and so forth. Each LR is

Figure 1. The ANGELAH model

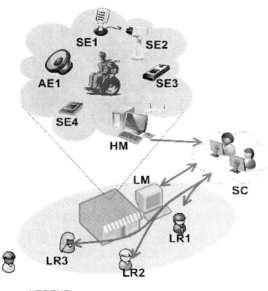

LEGEND

SE: Sensing Entity   **SC**: Surveillance Center
AE: Actuator Entity   **LM**: Locality Manager
HM: Home Manager   **LR**: Local Responder

characterized by a unique User IDentifer (UID) and a profile describing his characteristics such as his identity, current physical location, medical expertise, track record, and skills in providing assistance within the ANGELAH framework, and the trust SC associates with him.

Once the LR's profile information is obtained, the SC promotes the formation of a support group composed of the best suited LRs willing to assist the elder. In particular, upon receiving an SOS message, the SC defines the emergency type from the context information analysis. In addition, SC forwards a "Call For Assistance" (CFA) message to LRs that are currently in the proximity of the elder's home. CFA messages may include information such as the elder's personal information (e.g., age, gender), his physical and cognitive characteristics, the kind of assistance he is in need of, along with additional information (if available) describing the current conditions of the elder (e.g., heart-pulse). In response to the CFA message, each LR willing to help sends back

an "Acceptance Notification" (AN) message to the SC that contains personal information of this particular volunteer (e.g., his UID), his current location, and the estimated time it may take him to get to the location of the elder in need of help. After receiving AN messages from an adequate number of LRs, the SC then runs an algorithm to select the most adequate LRs. Once the adequate LRs are sorted out, the SC notifies them and provides them with information on how to access the elder's residence and with instructions on how to assist him/her.

It is worth noting that composing a response group is a rather difficult problem. ANGELAH is based on the locality concept both to mitigate the complexity of the group formation problem and to reduce responders' intervention time. ANGELAH defines a locality as the set of all LRs located within the area covered by the same network access point, i.e., the same wireless cell. ANGELAH associates a LM to each locality that is in charge of monitoring the availability and maintaining a list of co-located LRs. In addition to responders' locations, different criteria such as LRs' medical skills, the elder's pathologies, and so forth are taken into account for formulating the *ad hoc* rescue group. As a consequence, it seems appropriate to adopt a Multi-Attribute Decision Making (MADM) approach (elaborated later in this section) for the selection of best-suited LRs to join the response group.

Once the SC selects a set of adequate individuals willing to provide assistance to the elder, it notifies them, and provides them with instructions on how to assist the elder. In ANGELAH, each elder support group is uniquely identified by a Group IDentifer (GID) and a profile that includes information on the elder's identity, his pathologies, his contact information and home address, and so forth.

The ANGELAH Architecture

Figure 2 depicts the ANGELAH middleware architecture implemented on top of the Java Virtual Machine. As Figure 2 portrays, the modular ANGELAH architecture is composed of three main layers, namely the Monitoring and Assistance, the Response Management, and the Group Collaboration layers.

Monitoring and Assistance Layer

The Monitoring and Assistance Layer is in charge of integrating and managing all available sensors and actuators deployed in the elder's home; of gathering, aggregating, and distributing the whole sensed context information; of detecting emergency situations for the elder; of reacting accordingly, e.g., by driving actuators and/or by alerting the surveillance center. The monitoring and assistance layer is implemented on top of the OSGi middleware that facilitates deployment, update, and management of all software

entities that compose the assistance services for the elder.

This layer has a number of components as depicted in Figure 2. First, the Context Gathering Service (CGS) module gathers the sensed data from the deployed sensors. The CGS requires context information at regular time intervals, and the time between consecutive requests depends on the technical characteristics of the sensors. In ANGELAH, each sensor is statically associated with a Sensor Proxy (SP) that is basically a software entity that operates beneath its corresponding sensor. As a consequence, ANGELAH decouples context gathering logic from sensor-specific technical details, thus simplifying the context information collecting process. The CGS forwards the obtained context information both to Context Repository Service (CRS) and Context Aggregation Service (CAS) modules. The CRS records the whole context information to facilitate the diagnosis of elder's pathologies or conditions. The CAS aggregates context information obtained from different context sources and detects possibly

Figure 2. The ANGELAH architecture

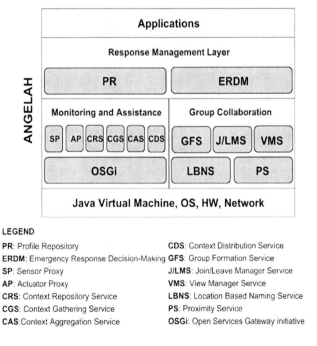

LEGEND

PR: Profile Repository
ERDM: Emergency Response Decision-Making
SP: Sensor Proxy
AP: Actuator Proxy
CRS: Context Repository Service
CGS: Context Gathering Service
CAS:Context Aggregation Service

CDS: Context Distribution Service
GFS: Group Formation Service
J/LMS: Join/Leave Manager Service
VMS: View Manager Service
LBNS: Location Based Naming Service
PS: Proximity Service
OSGi: Open Services Gateway initiative

dangerous situations. Finally, the CAS forwards the aggregated context information to the Context Distribution Service (CDS) module. Then, the CDS distributes the aggregated context data to the interested entities. In particular, in case of emergency situations, CDS sends a SOS message to the Emergency Response Decision Making (ERDM) instance deployed at the SC. Each SOS message includes the complete information required to dynamically compose an elder rescue group, e.g., elder's home address, elder's identity, and emergency type.

Response Management Layer

Upon reception of an emergency notification message from an elder's HM, the Response Management Layer triggers the ERDM instance to form groups composed of individuals willing to provide assistance to the elder. In particular, the ERDM coordinates with the Proximity Service, installed at the LM of the locality where the elder resides, and requests the visibility of all nearby LRs. By coordinating with the Profile Repository (PR) at SC, ERDM can obtain further information on available helpers, such as their medical expertise, their history records, and skills in providing assistance. On the basis of available information, ERDM solves a MADM problem to compose a response group comprising the best suited individuals willing to help the elder. Then, the ERDM coordinates with the Group Formation Service (GFS) to promote the newly formed group and invite all selected individuals to join it.

Group Collaboration Layer

The Group Collaboration Layer provides the basic facilities needed to compose and manage emergency response groups in wireless environments. When an emergency situation occurs, the GFS instance, installed at LM, promotes the creation of a new response group. For this purpose, the GFS coordinates with the Location-Based Naming Ser-

vice (LBNS) that randomly generates and assigns GIDs (and Profile IDs (PIDs)) by exploiting the Universally Unique Identifier (UUID) naming approach. The GFS also requests ERDM for the elder profile information (e.g., elder's identity, address, pathologies, emergency level, and so forth) and for the list of selected helpers that should form the new emergency response group. Following this, the GFS coordinates with the Join/Leave Manager Service (J/LMS) installed on the helpers' devices to invite them to join the group.

At regular time intervals, the View Manager Service (VMS) creates, maintains, and disseminates views to ANGELAH group members. A view contains the context-dependent information comprising the list of co-located group members along with their profiles. Each view entry includes several data, namely group members' PID/IP addresses obtained from the PS, and also their identities and medical skills obtained from the PR. In addition, to cope with mobility-induced changes in group membership, the VMS coordinates with the PS for the notification of arrival, departure, and disconnection events of a group member entity, and accordingly updates the views. It is worth pointing out that the PS instance, installed at LM, monitors responders' availability using periodic advertisement messages from LRs. When the latency between consecutive advertisement messages from a LR exceeds a threshold value, the LR is assumed to be disconnected.

INSIGHTS ON ERDM (EMERGENCY RESPONSE DECISION MAKING) IMPLEMENTATION

In emergency situations, ERDM selects available responders by solving the MADM problem. Indeed, in ANGELAH, the PR instance at SC maintains profiles of each LR; already subscribed to the ANGELAH service. For each subscriber, a set of attributes is associated. In particular, the attributes represent (1) the expertise and skills of

LRs; (2) their history in providing assistance; and (3) the trust level SC associates with them. These attributes are constantly updated and maintained by SC.

In ANGELAH, we assume that there are M *a priori* defined emergency levels. For each emergency level and each attribute, SC defines a weight to differentiate the relevance of the attributes in group-formation decision-making. Additionally, with each emergency level, three parameters are associated:

- **Action time:** the minimum amount of time within which assistance should be provided to the elder.
- **Waiting timeout:** the maximum time SC should wait for receiving AN messages from LRs.
- **Acceptance threshold:** the threshold for selecting LRs.

These three parameters should be carefully set by the SC. For example, in case of a life-threatening event (e.g., heart attack), both action time and waiting timeout should be set to small values. In case of a bone fracture due to a fall, expertise and skills become more important so that the system may set the acceptance threshold to higher values with a particular focus on the skills-related attribute, whereas action time and timeout can also be set to relatively high values. Upon receiving an SOS message, the agent in charge (at SC) first defines the corresponding emergency level based on two things, namely the type of the emergency event and the profile of the elder. The event type (e.g., fall, faintness, heart attack) can be determined by coordinating with CDS to obtain various pieces of context information, e.g., captured video. The profile of the senior (comprising his physical and cognitive characteristics) is assumed to be available at the PR instance. For a finite amount of time, ERDM waits for responses from LRs. After either the system has received enough replies or the wait-

ing timeout has expired, ERDM sorts out the LRs based on information available in their response messages. A response message includes various data such as the user's will to help, his identity, physical proximity with the elder, and so forth. Out of the sorted LRs, those with attributes that suit best with the current incident are chosen. In case the number of LRs available for helping the elder exceeds the current needs, only a restricted group of LRs are requested to assist and are provided with information on how to access the senior's residence along with instructions corresponding to the determined emergency level. This avoids the bystander apathy problem (Darley, 2000) in which people around a person in apparent need of help usually voluntarily intervene. The bystander apathy problem states that help is surprisingly less likely to be provided when more people are present. In some cases, a large group of bystanders may indeed fail to assist a person who is in obvious need of help.

CONCLUSION

The growing percentage of seniors in the society requires a rethinking and reshaping of current practice in eldercare. Cost effective solutions are essential to improve the quality of eldercare and to promote independent life-styles even among seniors living alone. Given the impossibility of significantly increasing professional care to elders in a sustainable manner, it seems necessary to investigate innovative technology solutions for eldercare. The emerging pervasive computing field can offer relevant opportunities for the development of advanced supports capable of providing different forms of assistance and of facilitating social engagement for older adults, anytime and anywhere.

Despite the scientific relevance of available research in the literature, much work is still required to turn early research prototypes into robust and reliable product-level solutions. In fact, available proposals are still investigating foundational aspects of eldercare and seem to focus on precise techniques to solve specific (indeed challenging) problems, e.g., how to detect user location, activities, and so forth. The chapter advocates the need to further extend the scope of eldercare research to investigate middleware-level solutions able of integrating different and heterogeneous elder assistance tools and technologies, ranging from monitoring solutions, assistance platforms, collaborative supports, and so forth. The main advantage of the proposed approach is the possibility to customize eldercare infrastructures according to elders' needs, to merge and orchestrate heterogeneous services, and to provide application developers with a uniform framework upon which to develop their applications. Along this line, the chapter presents the ANGELAH framework, a middleware-level solution that incarnates these ideas.

Despite the great research interest, several issues are still open and should be considered in future research. Our early experiences suggest considering solutions that minimize the need to rely upon technical support. In particular, we advocate that novel solutions should be able to autonomously configure, reconfigure, heal, and maintain themselves without the need for continuous human intervention. This aspect is of paramount importance both because eldercare application domains require cost effective solutions, and also because it is impossible to assume the availability of technical staff capable of maintaining the eldercare support infrastructure, anywhere and anytime. In addition, privacy concerns are further important aspects that need investigation. In eldercare systems design, it is important to identify a tradeoff between elder privacy and the availability of monitored, sensitive, and health-related information to caregivers and others.

ACKNOWLEDGMENT

Work partially supported by the FIRB TOCAI Project "Tecnologie Orientate alla Conoscenza per Aggregazioni di Imprese in Internet".

REFERENCES

Bardram, J. E. (2005). Activity-based computing: Support for mobility and collaboration in ubiquitous computing. *Personal and Ubiquitous Computing, 9*(5), 312–322. doi:10.1007/s00779-004-0335-2

Bellavista, P., Bottazzi, D., Corradi, A., & Montanari, R. (2006). Challenges, opportunities and solutions for ubiquitous eldercare. In Al-Hakim, L. (Ed.), *Web mobile-based applications for healthcare management* (pp. 142–165). Hershey, PA: Idea Group.

Bottazzi, D., Corradi, A., & Montanari, R. (2006). Context-aware middleware solutions for anytime and anywhere emergency assistance to elderly people. *IEEE Communications Magazine, 44*(4), 82–90. doi:10.1109/MCOM.2006.1632653

Choi, Y. B., Krause, J. S., Seo, H., Capitan, K. E., & Chung, K. (2006). Telemedicine in the USA: Standardization through information management and technical applications. *IEEE Communications Magazine, 44*(4), 41–48. doi:10.1109/MCOM.2006.1632648

Darley, J. M. (2000). Bystander phenomenon. In Kazden, A. (Ed.), *Encyclopedia of Psychology* (*Vol. 1*, pp. 493–495). Washington, DC: American Psychological Association Press. doi:10.1037/10516-195

Dey, A. K. (2001). Understanding and using context. *Personal and Ubiquitous Computing Journal, 5*(1), 4–7. doi:10.1007/s007790170019

Doughty, K., Lewis, R., & McIntosh, A. (2000). The design of a practical and reliable fall detector for community and institutional telecare. *Journal of Telemedicine and Telecare, 6*(1), (supplement), 150-154.

Elite Care. (2009). Web Site: http://www.elite-care.com.

Garawi, S., Istepanian, R. S. H., & Abu-Rghef, M. A. (2006). 3G wireless communications for mobile robotic tele-ultrasonography systems. *IEEE Communications Magazine, 44*(4), 91–96. doi:10.1109/MCOM.2006.1632654

Health Solutions, V. I. G. I. L. *Inc.* (2009). Retrieved from http://www.vigil.com

Helal, S., Mann, W., El-Zabadani, H., King, J., Kaddoura, Y., & Jansen, E. (2005). The Gator Tech Smart House: A programmable pervasive space. *IEEE Computer Magazine, 38*(3), 50–60.

Hirsh, T., Forlizzi, J., Hyder, E., Goetz, J., Kurtz, C., & Stroback, J. (2000). The ELDer project: Social, emotional, and environmental factors in the design of eldercare technologies. In *Proceedings of the ACM Conference on Universal Usability (CUU 2000)*, (pp. 72-79). Arlington, VA: ACM Press.

Hodgins, D., Bertsch, A., Post, N., Frischholz, M., Volckaerts, B., & Spensley, J. (2008). Healthy aims: Developing new medical implants and diagnostic equipment. *IEEE Pervasive Computing Magazine, 7*(1), 14–21. doi:10.1109/MPRV.2008.8

Horgas, A., & Abowd, G. (2004). The impact of technology on living environments for older adults. In Pew, R. W., & Van Hemel, S. B. (Eds.), *Technology for adaptive aging* (pp. 230–252). Washington, DC: National Academy Press.

Keller, I., Van der Hoog, W., & Stappers, P. J. (2004). Gust of Me: Reconnecting mother and son. *IEEE Pervasive Computing Magazine, 3*(1), 22–28. doi:10.1109/MPRV.2004.1269125

Lo, B. P., Wang, J. L., & Yang, G. Z. (2005). From imaging networks to behavior profiling: Ubiquitous sensing for managed homecare of the elderly. In *Proceedings of the 3rd International Conference on Pervasive Computing (Pervasive 2005)*, (pp. 101-104). Munich, Germany: IEEE Press.

Mann, W. C. (2004). The aging population and its needs. *IEEE Pervasive Computing Magazine, 3*(2), 12–14. doi:10.1109/MPRV.2004.1316812

McKenna, S. J., Marquis-Faulkes, F., Gregor, P., & Newell, A. F. (2003). Scenario-based drama as a tool for investigating user requirements with application to home monitoring for elderly people. In *Proceedings of the 10th International Conference on Human - Computer Interaction (HCI 2003)*, (pp. 512-516). Crete, Greece: ACM Press.

Mihailidis, A., Carmichael, B., & Boger, J. (2004). The use of computer vision in an intelligent environment to support aging-in-place, safety, and independence in the home. *IEEE Transactions on Information Technology in Biomedicine, 8*(3), 238–247. doi:10.1109/TITB.2004.834386

Munoz, M. A., Rodriguez, M., Favela, J., Martinez-Garcia, A. I., & Gonzales, V. M. (2003). Context-aware mobile communication in hospitals. *IEEE Computer Magazine, 36*(9), 38–46.

Mynatt, E. D., Rowan, J., Craighill, S., & Jacobs, A. (2001). Digital family portraits: Providing peace of mind for extended family members. In *Proceedings of the 2001 ACM Conference on Human Factors in Computing Systems (CHI 2001)*, (pp. 333-340). Seattle, WA: ACM Press.

Pirkl, J., & Pulos, A. (1997). *Transgenerational design: Products for an aging population*. New York: James Wiley & Sons.

Pollack, M. E., Brown, L., Colbry, D., McCarthy, C. E., Orosz, C., & Peintner, B. (2003). Autominder: An intelligent cognitive orthotic system for people with memory impairment. *Robotics and Autonomous Systems, 44*(3-4), 273–282. doi:10.1016/S0921-8890(03)00077-0

Poon, C. Y., Zhang, Y., & Bao, S. (2006). A novel biometrics method to secure wireless body area sensor networks for telemedicine and M-Health. *IEEE Communications Magazine, 44*(4), 73–81. doi:10.1109/MCOM.2006.1632652

Santana, P. C. Rodríguez, M. D., González, V. M., Castro, L. A., & Andrade, A. G. (2005). Supporting emotional ties among Mexican elders and their families living abroad. In *Proceedings of the Conference on Human Factors in Computing Systems (CHI 05),* (pp. 2099-2103). Portland, OR: ACM Press.

Soomro, A., & Cavalcanti, D. (2007). Opportunities and challenges in using WPAN and WLAN technologies in medical environments. *IEEE Communications Magazine, 45*(2), 114–122. doi:10.1109/MCOM.2007.313404

Tabar, A. M., Keshavarz, A., & Aghajan, H. (2006). Smart Home care network using sensor fusion and distributed vision-based reasoning. In *Proceedings of the 4th ACM International Workshop on Video Surveillance and Sensor Network (VSSN 2004),* (pp. 145-154). Santa Barbara, CA: ACM Press.

Taleb, T., Bottazzi, D., Guizani, M., & Nait-Charif, H. (2009). ANGELAH: A framework for assisting elders at home. *IEEE Journal on Selected Areas in Communications, 27*(4), 480–495. doi:10.1109/JSAC.2009.090511

United Nations Population Division. (2000). *World population prospects: The 2000 revision.* Retrieved from http://www.un.org/esa/population/publications/wpp2000/wpp2000_volume3.htm

Xiao, Y., Shen, X., Sun, B., & Cai, L. (2006). Security and privacy in RFID and applications in telemedicine. *IEEE Communications Magazine, 44*(4), 64–72. doi:10.1109/MCOM.2006.1632651

Chapter 16
Implications of Web 2.0 Technology on Healthcare:
A Biomedical Semantic Blog Case Study

Jinan Fiaidhi
Lakehead University, Canada

Sabah Mohammed
Lakehead University, Canada

Yuan Wei
Lakehead University, Canada

ABSTRACT

Now that the health and medical sector is slowly but surely beginning to embrace Web 2.0 technologies and tactics such as social networking, blogging, and sharing health information, such usage may become an everyday occurrence. This new trend is emerging under the Health 2.0 umbrella where it has important effects on the future of medicine. This chapter introduces some important Health 2.0 concepts and discusses their advantages for health care and medical practice. In addition, this chapter provides a case study for building a Semantic Blog for Gene Annotation and Searching (GAS) among social network users. The GAS Blog enables users to syndicate and aggregate gene case studies via the RSS protocol, annotate gene case studies with the ability to add new tags (folksonomy), and search for/navigate gene case studies among a group or cross-groups based on FOAF, GO, and SCORM metadata. The GAS Blog is built upon an open source toolkit (WordPress) and further programmed via PHP. The GAS Blog is found to be very effective for annotation and navigation when compared with the traditional gene annotation and navigation systems, as well as with traditional search engines such as XPath.

INTRODUCTION

Recently, a new wave of web technology and interactive tools in medicine and health care has been called Health 2.0. Unlike traditional eHealth technologies, that only allow web users to accept information passively, Health 2.0 provides web users with the ability to actively modify web information. Health 2.0 services, applications, and tools are defined as "participatory health care characterized by the ability to rapidly share, classify and summarize individual

DOI: 10.4018/978-1-61520-733-6.ch016

health information with the goals of improving health care systems, experiences and outcomes via integration of patients and stakeholders" (Furst, 2008, p.2). Such tools enable (1) social networking; (2) participation; (3) openness; and (4) collaboration within and between user groups (Eysenbach, 2008). Actually, Health 2.0 tools are built on the new vision of the future of the Web or what is known as the "Web 2.0" initiative. Web 2.0 aims to enhance creativity, secure information sharing, collaboration, and functionality of the web. Web 2.0 concepts have led to the development and evolution of web-based communities and their hosted services, such as social-networking sites, video sharing sites, wikis, blogs, and folksonomies. The term became notable after the first O'Reilly Media Web 2.0 conference in 2004 (O'Reilly, 2005). What seems clear is that Web 2.0 brings people together in a more dynamic and interactive space.

The vast implications of Health 2.0 are now beginning to appear. Many sectors in the healthcare industry are rethinking their fundamental business model; and many health care organizations are investing in information technology and implementing e-Health programs. Additionally, e-Health initiatives, such as Web 2.0, have the potential for significant improvement of the health status in rural communities. Giustini (2007) provided a summary of useful Web 2.0 applications in medicine (e.g., Ves Dimov's Clinical Cases and Images Blog; Ask Dr. Wiki; Ganfyd; and PubDrug). MacManus (2008) provided the top ten Web 2.0 applications in medicine (e.g., Patients-LikeMe; Sermo; DoubleCheckMD; Vitals.com; Carol.com; and MyMedLab). Besides various medical websites and portals offering different medical and health services, there are various kinds of e-health systems focusing on:

1. *Health related web sites or portals* offering health related information for patients or health professionals.

2. *Virtual communities and online support groups* where people share experiences and information about their disease and provide emotional support to each other.

3. *Electronic Health Records (EHR)* used in the clinical environment by health professionals and online Personal Health Records (PHR) where the individual is the owner of his/her medical records.

4. *Home care and chronic disease management systems* used to monitor chronic diseases at home, to monitor elderly people or to communicate with professionals from home.

5. *Telemedicine and teleconsultation applications* in areas such as dermatology, ophthalmology, radiology, and psychiatry, enabling collaboration between health professionals and communication with patients.

Figure 1 illustrates some of the Web 2.0 applications in health care.

Web 2.0 is successful in supporting some of these major e-health applications; however, blogging and tweeting are the most popular Health 2.0 applications as they have made it possible for ordinary users to publish on the Web, and thus become content producers instead of content consumers. A number of blogging and tweeting platforms such as Blogger, WordPress, Twitter, TypePad, or Movable Type allow users to publish almost any kind of data on the web. Blog authors manage their own content in their own blog, structure it through time in the form of discrete blog entries, and are able to categorize these entries (Möller, Breslin, & Decker, 2005). It is also possible to comment on other people's entries or refer to them through links (trackbacks, pingbacks). Most blogs provide a so-called newsfeed that acts as a syndicated table of contents. These feeds are usually published alongside the blog at a separate URL and can contain various kinds of metadata for each entry (e.g., a title, short description, date, author, link). Feeds are used by blog or newsread-

Figure 1. Applications of web 2.0 in health care and medicine

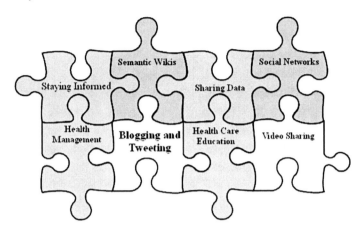

ers and aggregators to allow subscription to, and aggregation of, different blogs. Various kinds of dialects for newsfeeds are currently in use, the most prominent being the RSS (Really Simple Syndication) family of feed languages. Table 1 provides some examples of health care blogs for different types of health care users.

The mission of this chapter is to explain how Health 2.0 services are playing an important role in the future of health care and how they are going to change the way medicine is practiced and health care is delivered. We use one case study to explain the differences between traditional eHealth, based on Web 1.0, and the new Health 2.0 techniques, based on Web 2.0. This case study uses the notion of Semantic Blogging

for the annotation and navigation of biomedical information. Central to the notion of semantic blogging is the application of ideas, techniques, and tools from the Semantic Web paradigm as applied in blogging. Semantic principles are applied to enrich and extend the blogging metaphor by providing machine-understandable metadata as well as mechanisms to search, discover, link, and navigate based on these metadata. The added semantic is structured in a way to provide flexible usage of the provided services.

Figure 2 illustrates the levels of semantics introduced on top of the usual blogging primitives. The first and most general semantics level is the SCORM metadata, which identifies, in our example, the gene case studies as learning objects

Table 1. Example of blogs used in health care paradigm

User Type	Blog Purpose and Examples
PHYSICIAN	http://www.docnotes.net - Occasional notes from a family physician http://www.kevinmd.com/blog - A practicing primary-care physician tells it like it is.
NURSE	http://www.emergiblog.com - The life and times of an ER nurse
STUDENT	http://blog.vitummedicinus.com - A fourth year medical student reflects upon his journey through medicine (a "vitum medicinus" or a life of medicine). http://casesblog.blogspot.com - Clinical Cases and Images
LIBRARIAN	http://davidrothman.net - Exploring medical librarianship
PATIENTS	http://www.thecancerblog.com - about cancer; http://mykidney.com/blog - about hemodialysis; http://www.diabetesmine.com - about diabetes.

and enables users to catalogue them and search for their availability at the Blog repository. SCORM (Sharable Content Object Reference Model) is a collection of standards and specifications for web-based e-learning (see http://www.scorm.com/). SCORM introduces an idea called sequencing, which is a set of rules that specifies the order in which a learner may experience content objects. In simple terms, they constrain a learner to a fixed set of paths through the training material and permit the learner to "bookmark" their progress when taking breaks. The second semantics level is used to identify collaborating groups and define their interests with FOAF (Friend of a Friend) metadata (see http://www.foaf-project.org/). The third semantics level is based on RSS (Really Simple Syndication- http://www.whatisrss.com/) metadata that allows collaborators to syndicate their gene learning feeds in order to register their interest in specific areas, as well as applying a sequence of aggregators that allows downloading automatically the required gene learning contents. The final semantics level is the gene ontology (GO) that provides the global metadata for categorizing gene case studies and, with the availability of its huge gene open source datasets (http://www.geneontology.org/), we can establish an effective repository for gene learning objects. The use of this hierarchy of semantics has been tested by developing a semantic blog prototype called GAS (Gene Annotation/navigation System) (Wei, 2008).

Ultimately, Health 2.0 can create for healthcare users a vibrant, dynamic, and challenging informal environment in which to contribute, share, and learn. Such environments go beyond the traditional boundaries of the clinical and healthcare environments, and travel into areas that are yet to be fully explored, raising interesting questions for health care users to address and answer. One thing is certain – the popularity of Health 2.0 on the Internet will continue to grow as more users begin to exploit the potential to generate their own meaning and construct their own personal-

ized learning experiences. The implications of using Health 2.0 on the future of medicine can be summarized as follows (Giustini, 2007; Spivack, 2006):

- Will enable the transformation of the Web from a network of separately siloed applications and content repositories to a seamless and interoperable whole;
- Will be based on ubiquitous connectivity, broadband adoption, mobile Internet access, and mobile devices;
- Utilizes network computing, software-as-a-service business model, Web services interoperability, distributed computing, grid computing, and cloud computing;
- Will be constructed with open technologies and standards, open APIs and protocols, open data formats, open-source software platforms, and open data (e.g. Creative Commons, Open Data License);
- Utilizes open identity, OpenID, open reputation, roaming portable identity and personal data, single sign-on (SSO);
- Incorporates intelligence and semantic Web technologies based on standard ontology formats (e.g. RDF, OWL, SWRL, SPARQL, GRDDL) that incorporate

Figure 2. The blog enriched with four semantic levels

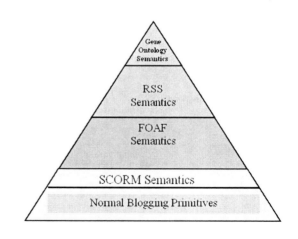

medical ontologies, natural language processing, machine learning, machine reasoning, autonomous agents; and

- Enables interfacing of distributed databases by semantic Web technologies.

The pros or advantages of such future trends for health care are obvious as it helps in (Mohammed, Fiaidhi, & Yang 2004):

- Reducing transcription errors by letting nurses transcribe notes and order medications right from the patients' bedside to improve accuracy and quality of care.;
- Improving scheduling since caregivers can bring computing wherever they go. They can more easily arrange and rearrange scheduling of tests than if they were to have to wait for a terminal to be available;
- Reducing physical and space restraints in normally cramped hospital spaces. Health 2.0 technologies are ubiquitous and hence can be installed easily and unobtrusively;
- **Mobility:** Doctors and nurses are always on the go, wireless and ubiquitous technologies gives them the ability to communicate wherever, whenever they wish;
- Data accessibility by improving physician access to data by providing rounds information, order entry, and immediate clinical alerts in almost any setting of care;
- **Speeding consultations:** Ubiquitous and social networking technologies speed the process of consultations among doctors and specialists;
- **Enabling social connectivity:** A person diagnosed with a rare illness can find hundreds of other people across the world who can recommend doctors or provide firsthand information about treatments;
- Reducing training and support costs;
- Providing a collaborative framework for patients, caregivers, and clinicians to collaborate more closely. Patients managing

their own health information; clinicians communicating, sharing knowledge and experience more efficiently; getting relevant research information quickly.

However, the cons or disadvantages of adopting Web 2.0 can be summarized as follows:

- Anyone can make changes due to the lack of authoritative control over the content; this process builds a degree of vulnerability into the end product, so it can be difficult to gauge the reliability and accuracy of such resources;
- Cultural and ethical chaos due to the risk of plagiarism and intellectual property theft;
- Vast amount of information which is often scattered and disorganized: users may suffer "information overload";
- **Privacy and confidentiality:** personal data could be captured and misused.

Therefore, in adopting Health 2.0, healthcare institutions need to protect patient's safety and adopt proven standards and techniques that guarantee interoperability.

DEVELOPING A SMART PLATFORM OF PARTICIPATION = RIA + WEB 3.0

The concept of the "web as platform of participation or Web 2.0" (O'Reilly, 2005) is positioned to have a most interesting impact on e-health and e-Medicine. Physicians, nurses, medical students, and health researchers who consume web media can actively participate in the creation and distribution of content, helping to customize information and technology for their own purposes. The term Web 2.0 does not refer to new technical standards, but to new ways of using the Internet as a platform for interactive and collaborative applications. A distinguishing characteristic of Web 2.0 is the concept of online social networking — the use of Internet technologies to create value through mass user participation. These technologies are characterized by constant development and enrichment (evolution) because of user interactions. Those who use these services assist with their development and are part of the "collective intelligence" that is harnessed to make the services better and more responsive. If Web 1.0 connects people to web servers, then we can imagine Web 2.0 as a forum for connecting people to other people through the Internet and allowing people to collaborate with each other by exchanging knowledge and resources. One of the most significant features of Web 2.0 that contributes to the smart platform of participation is the use of Rich Internet Applications (RIA). The key difference between RIAs and other Internet applications is the amount of interaction in the interface. In a traditional page-based Internet application, interaction is limited to a small set of standard controls such as checkboxes, radio buttons, form fields, and buttons. This severely limits the ability to create usable and engaging applications, and most Internet applications have been clumsier and more difficult to use than their desktop counterparts. An RIA can use a wider and better range of controls to improve the users' interaction with the interface, allowing efficient interactions, better error management, feedback, and overall user experience. The key features of RIA applications include:

- The user interacts directly with page elements using inline editing and drag-and-drop primitives;
- Part of a page is updated instead of reloading;
- More detailed information is available on the same page instead of on a new page;
- Feedback, confirmation, and error messages are provided within the page.

These rich features are also those that provide the greatest challenge for designers who wish to

ensure applications are highly usable. Figure 3 illustrates the contributing programming elements of any RIA.

This means that in an RIA environment, the client is capable of doing more than just rendering pages. The client is able to perform computations, send and retrieve data in the background asynchronously from the user's requests, redraw sections of a screen, use audio and video in a tightly integrated manner, and so forth, independently of the server or back end to which it is connected. Because of their architecture and capabilities, RIAs have the potential to fundamentally change the way blogs are designed and programmed. There are many technologies that can help in building RIA applications such as AJAX, Adobe's Flex, Microsoft's Silverlight, and Sun's JavaFX. The decision to adopt one of these RIA enabling technologies depends on the type of user interface we would like to have (see Figure 4).

Since most health care applications require a ubiquitous user interface (UI), AJAX becomes the most common choice for most RIA applications. Actually, AJAX is neither a product nor a new technology, but a new branding for RIA technology that is based on JavaScript, XML, and

Figure 3. Contributing technologies to rich internet applications (RIA)

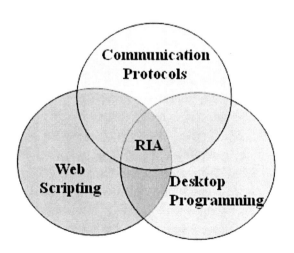

other technologies. To enable Ajax-based Web applications at the client's end, an "Ajax engine" is needed, which is already found in most web browsers. This additional layer provides a means to enable "partial" web page refresh that improves the responsiveness of the web application. However, more enabling technologies can contribute to RIAs such as the concept of Software-as-a-Service (SaaS). SaaS is a business model to deliver software to the end user as a service instead of as packaged software that requires local installation. SaaS is often referred to as Software-on-Demand or Application-on- Demand. Furthermore, to construct more intelligent RIA applications one needs to incorporate reasoning mechanisms that are based on certain levels of semantics. The introduction of intelligence requires the use of what is currently termed as Web 3.0 tools (Markoff, 2006). Thus, a semantic blog is a platform of participation

Figure 4. Selecting an RIA supporting technology decision tree

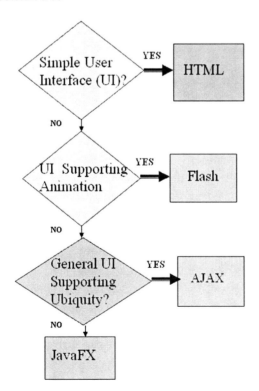

that supports interoperability, decentralization, ubiquity, and intelligence, based on concepts and techniques from Web 1, Web 2.0, and Web 3.0. Figure 5 illustrates this view.

BUILDING A BIOMEDICAL SMART PLATFORM OF PARTICIPATION

As stated earlier, a smart platform of participation can be built by extending the functionalities of the regular blog (Möller et al., 2005). Among the most important extensions is the issue of adding semantics. By adding semantics the smart platform of participation is called a semantic blog. The semantic blog that we are going to describe here deals with gene searching and annotation. We experimented with building this semantic blog as a case study to show the effectiveness of Health 2.0. Current gene searching and annotation systems such as Blast2GO (http://www.blast2go.org/), gProfiler (http://biit.cs.ut.ee/gprofiler/), Gene-Tools (http://www.genetools.microarray.ntnu. no/common/intro.php), GoAnna (http://agbase. msstate.edu/GOAnna.html), GoAnnotator (http:// xldb.fc.ul.pt/biotools/rebil/goa/), GoPubMed (http://gopubmed.org/), DYNGO (http://gauss. dbb.georgetown.edu/liblab/dyngo.html), and AmiGO (http://amigo.geneontology.org/cgi-bin/ amigo/go.cgi) are all Web 1.0 applications suffering from the following disadvantages:

- they do not allow users to collaborate with each other;
- gene information is in a silo structure;
- annotations can only be published as extension codes that are stored in another silo;
- it is difficult for users to find the latest annotations to existing genes; and
- the gene search mechanism is inefficient.

To solve these disadvantages, a semantic blog system for gene annotation and searching was developed. The new semantic blog is called "Gene

Figure 5. Elements of a smart platform of participation

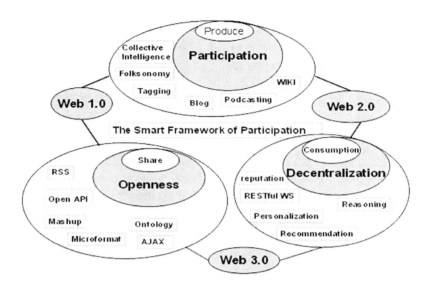

Annotation Semantic blog or GAS". The GAS Blog is built on a regular open source blog system (WordPress) with additional semantic features for enhancing searching, navigation, and annotation of genes. The main additions that the GAS Blog brings over the traditional blog features involve: (1) the use of gene ontology for cataloguing and searching genes and their annotations; (2) linking collaborating users in groups; (3) updating users when a new annotation has been filed for a gene that exists in their profile; (4) cataloguing related sequences of genes and their annotations in relevant learning objects; and (5) updating the gene ontology when users provide new concepts that are not available at the original gene ontology through ontology maturing. Figure 6 illustrates the main features of the GAS Blog.

Selecting a Programming Framework for the GAS Blog

Because adding the semantic features required some degree of server programming, the right server-side programming technology needed to be chosen. Blog developers today benefit from a range of server-side technologies that function as the middle layer between a Web server and the database, including JavaServer Pages (JSP), Active Server Pages (ASP) and PHP. The following are brief descriptions of each of these programming middleware applications.

Active Server Pages (ASP)

Active Server Pages (ASP) is Microsoft's first server-side script engine for dynamically-generated web pages. It was initially marketed as an add-on to Internet Information Services (IIS) via the Windows NT 4.0 Option Pack, but has been included as a free component of the Windows Server since the initial release of Windows 2000 Server. Programming ASP websites is made easier by various built-in objects. Each object corresponds to a group of frequently used functions useful for creating dynamic web pages. Mixing traditional ASP and Microsoft's .NET technology, ASP.NET allows web applications to be more intelligent and complicated. Most ASP pages are written in VBScript, but any other Active Scripting engine can be selected such as Jscript (Microsoft's

Figure 6. The main highlights of the GAS blog

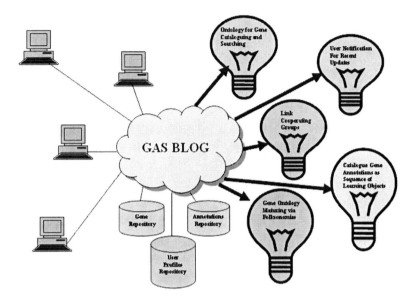

implementation of ECMAScript) and PerlScript (a derivative of Perl), and other third-party installable Active Scripting engines.

Java Server Pages (JSP)

JavaServer Pages (JSP) is a technology for developing web pages that include dynamic content. Unlike a plain HTML page that contains static content that always remains the same, a JSP page can change its content based on any number of variable items, including the identity of the user, the user's browser type, information provided by the user, and selections made by the user (Bergsten, 2001). Unlike ASP, JSP can run on servers with various operating systems. However, the disadvantage of JSP is that it is a heavy weight framework, and costly on hosting.

PHP

PHP is a widely used general-purpose scripting language that is especially suited for web development and can be embedded into HTML. It generally runs on a web server, taking PHP code as its input and creating web pages as output. It can be deployed on most web servers and on almost every operating system and platform free of charge. Like JSP, PHP is system-independent; it runs on servers of different operating systems. The big difference between JSP and PHP is that PHP is a lightweight, open source framework.

Based on the above brief description of each framework, cross system compatibility, and especially server ownership issues ASP is not a good choice for the GAS Blog. JSP meets the requirements for developing the GAS Blog; however, the hosting service cost should also be of concern and the heavyweight framework may cost more development effort than the PHP lightweight framework. Thus, we decided that PHP was the best choice for the GAS Blog.

Selecting a Weblog Platform for the GAS Blog

After selecting the blog programming environment, we also needed to select the Web 2.0 blog development platform that matched the programming environment. The reason for selecting a Web

2.0 development platform is that we did not want to build our semantic blog from scratch. Having a blog development platform provided us with the basic primitives required for blogging (i.e. enabling users to create new postings, to preview new posts, and to notify users of results). Since PHP was the programming medium that we found suitable, we needed to find a blog development platform that also was PHP open-source that could be used for adding the semantics levels required for our GAS blog. There are several popular blogging development platforms available on the Internet (Pingdon, 2009) and the most popular, WordPress, TypePad, Blogsmith, and Movable Type have been summarized.

WordPress

WordPress, written in PHP and supported by MySQL database, is a state-of-the-art semantic personal publishing platform with a focus on web standards and usability (WordPress.org). As a weblog platform, it has all the features of other regular blog systems - blogging, entries management, weblog theme template, archiving, commenting, plug-in support, etc. From the users' viewpoint, it is very similar to Movable Type. They are comparably similar in most fields except Movable Type is partially written in PHP and WordPress is built on pure PHP. Different from ExpressionEngine, WordPress is a blog-only lightweight system that would save some development efforts compared to ExpressionEngine. WordPress meets all the requirements for selecting a blog platform for GAS Blog: open source, written in PHP, and a lightweight system. It is easy to install and configure. WordPress is popular, with detailed development documentation and free support from many other developers all over the world. These two advantages are especially important for modifying open source during the implementation of the GAS Blog. Therefore, it was the best choice for the weblog platform for building the GAS Blog.

TypePad

Depending on the TypePad package you buy, there a different number of features available. With all packages, at least one author is able to write posts, upload photos, and include some form of advertising on their blogs. Packages that are more expensive provide more customization options, more space, and the ability to create more than one blog on a single account. One of the key benefits of choosing TypePad as your blogging software and host is the fact that even the most novice blogger can easily get a new blog up and running very quickly. The software is very intuitive, and customer support is excellent. TypePad blogs are hosted by TypePad. That means blogs will include the ".typepad.com" extension after the blog's domain name that some readers might perceive as a reflection of an amateur site. It is possible to map a personal domain to the blog as well. TypePad is a great choice for novice bloggers who want more flexibility than other blogging software such as Blogger.com offers, but want to avoid the technical side of blogging. However, it is important to remember that there is a cost associated with TypePad, and unlike blogging software such as WordPress, TypePad is limited in the number of features, add-ins, and plug-ins that are available for it. Therefore, TypePad may not be the best choice for power bloggers.

Blogsmith

Blogsmith is the custom blogger software from AOL. With Blogsmith you have the option to have your own domain, but not the option to download code as you can with WordPress for adding semantic features.

Movable Type

Movable Type is a free weblog publishing system. As a weblog platform, it has all the features of other regular blog systems, i.e. blogging, entries management, weblog theme template, archiving, commenting, plug-in support, etc. It is system-independent and can be installed on servers with various operating systems. Since Movable Type is written in both Perl and PHP, communication between two languages may cause some problems, and standard PHP does not support the interaction with Perl code; in this situation, additional libraries need to be installed. As discussed in the section on ASP, web hosting service providers, especially free or low cost providers, do not always have additional libraries installed. For organizations without their own servers, this may cause other problems when they are looking for a web hosting service in the future.

Comparing each weblog platform, no legal access to source code makes TypePad and Blogsmith not good choices for the GAS Blog. As for Moveable Type, it is a similar platform to WordPress in

most respects, however, being coded in Perl makes it not a good choice for system owners who do not have their own servers due to its requirement for installing additional libraries, and standard PHP does not support Perl. For these reasons WordPress was the most suitable blogging platform for developing our GAS blog.

INTRODUCING SEMANTICS TO THE GAS SYSTEM

The primary purpose of the GAS Blog is to enable gene annotation and searching. The general block diagram of the GAS architecture is illustrated in Figure 7.

The main functionality of each GAS building block (see Figure 8) is described below:

Figure 7. The general architecture of the GAS Blog

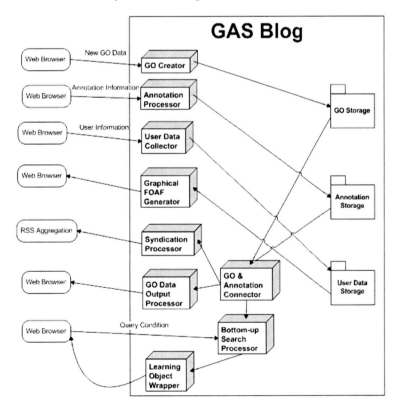

Figure 8. GAS UML class diagram

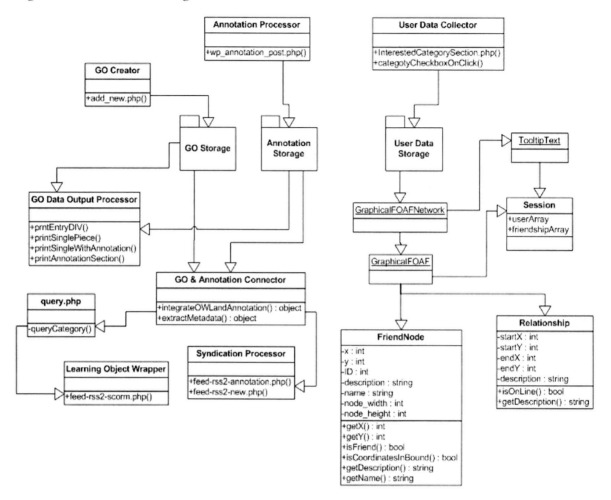

- **GO Creator:** creates a new gene ontology according to data retrieved from users' web browser.
- **Annotation Processor:** annotates to gene ontology according to data retrieved from users' web browser.
- **User Data Collector:** collects user information from users such as user name, email, interested gene ontology categories, groups willing to join, etc.
- **Graphical FOAF Generator:** An AJAX engine that generates and renders the FOAF network information.
- **GO & Annotation Connector:** prepares data for Bottom-up search Processor by

combining the information of gene ontology, annotation, and FOAF network.
- **Syndication Processor:** gets the well-wrapped data from Learning Object Wrapper and generates syndication for RSS aggregation.
- **GO Data Output Processor:** gets the data from gene ontology and annotation, and displays them on web page.
- **Learning Object Wrapper:** gets the gene ontology and annotation data and wraps them as learning objects.
- **Bottom-up Search Processor:** searches through gene ontology, annotation, and FOAF network using bottom-up search

Figure 9. The GAS user interface for browsing a gene term

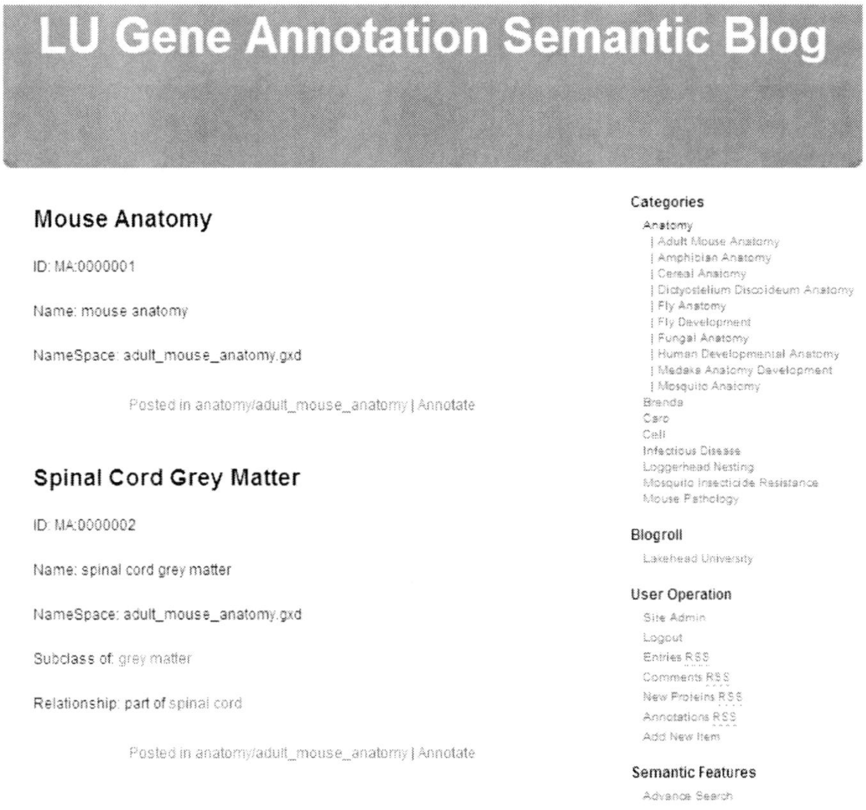

mechanism basing on data prepared by Data Combination Module.

As shown in Figure 8, all the data in the GAS Blog are stored in GO storage, annotation storage, and user data storage. Both the GO storage and annotation are databases expressed as XML files. However, the user data storage is expressed as a MySQL database. The GO Creator, Annotation Processor, User Data Collector, and FOAF Information Collector provide inputs to the GAS Blog. They collect data input from users and store them into related storage for other modules to use. The GO & Annotation Connector is an intermediate module between data storage and output modules; it prepares the data from storage for output purposes. The Graphical FOAF Generator, Syndication Processor, GO Data Output Processor, and Learning Object Wrapper produce the different GAS outputs. They make use of data prepared by the GO & Annotation Connector and deliver them to users.

When a user calls the GAS Blog it loads first the Gene Ontology from an OBO_XML file into web pages for blog users to view in their browsers. Gene Ontology is categorized by a list and users can choose a category to view by clicking the link to the category (see Figure 9).

Based on the GAS Blog interface, the user can do the following:

- Add a new gene ontology term
- Annotate a gene ontology term
- Create a user group
- Join a user group
- Add friends
- Syndicate a new gene term
- Aggregate a gene term
- Search and Navigate for gene terms.

However, one of the most important GAS design issues is the way semantics is added on top of the primitive blogging functionalities. The first type of semantics that we needed to add to any blogging platform like WordPress was gene ontology (GO). The objective of GO is to provide controlled vocabularies for the description of the molecular function, biological process, and cellular component of gene products. The name and definition for each GO term and the parent-child relationships between terms are defined by the members of the GO Consortium (http://www.geneontology.org/). This combination of a controlled vocabulary of defined terms with a structure of relationships between items is referred to as Gene Ontology (GO). Note that the Gene Ontologies themselves contain only information about terms in the ontology and their relationships to other terms. They do not contain gene products of any specific organism. Every Gene Ontology term consists of the following information:

- **id:** a unique numerical identifier of the form. For example: "GO: 0004437" is the id for a GO in the category of Molecular Function;
- **name:** GO term name (e.g. inositol);
- **synonym:** other names of the GO term (e.g. phosphatidylinositol phosphatase activity) ; and relationship (e.g. is-a catalytic activity).

GO terms are linked together by a relationship. There are three different kind of relationship among GO terms:

- is_a: defines a class to subclass relationship, where A is_a B means that A is a subclass of B; for example, nuclear chromosome is_a chromosome.
- part_of: The part_of relationship is slightly more complex; C part_of D means that whenever C is present, it is always a part of

D, but C does not always have to be present. An example would be periplasmic flagellum part_of periplasmic space.
- positively regulates and negatively regulates: These relationships describe interactions between biological processes and other biological processes, molecular functions, or biological qualities. When a biological process E regulates a function or a process F, it modulates the occurrence of F. If F is a biological quality, then E modulates the value of F. An example of the regulation of a biological process would be the term regulation of transcription. When regulation of transcription occurs, it always alters the rate, extent, or frequency at which a gene is transcribed.

There are two major types of Gene Ontology formats:

1. OBO, a plain text format, and
2. XML based formats such as GO RDF-XML, OBO_XML, and OWL.

Between the formats above, plain text format OBO is deprecated. It is difficult to query, troublesome to find out the latest change to the file, and it is not a standard format for storing or displaying data on web pages. Thus, the GAS Blog uses an XML-based format Gene Ontology called OBO_XML that is generated by Perl script from the OBO format. In an OBO_XML file, GO terms are defined as an XML node <term> with the following children:

- id – a unique identity for the term;
- name – name of term;
- def – term definition;
- relationship – term relationship with other terms;
- namespace – a namespace refers to the file in which the term should be stored.

A sample term is described as follows:

```
<term>
  <id>CARO:0000014</id>
  <name>cell component</name>
  <def>
    <defstr>Anatomical structure that is
a direct part of the cell.</defstr>
    <dbxref>
      <acc>MAH</acc>
      <dbname>CARO</dbname>
    </dbxref>
  </def>
  <is_a>CARO:0000003</is_a>
  <relationship>
    <type>part_of</type>
    <to>CARO:0000013</to>
  </relationship>
  <namespace>caro</namespace>
</term>
```

After identifying the required gene terms and format, we can introduce the gene semantics that can be used for annotation and searching. Annotation is the process of assigning GO terms to gene products. Each annotation of Gene Ontology must include an evidence code to indicate how the annotation to a particular term is supported. The available evidence codes are:

1. *Experimental Evidence Codes:*
   EXP: Inferred from Experiment
   IDA: Inferred from Direct Assay
   IPI: Inferred from Physical Interaction
   IMP: Inferred from Mutant Phenotype
   IGI: Inferred from Genetic Interaction
   IEP: Inferred from Expression Pattern
2. *Computational Analysis Evidence Codes:*
   ISS: Inferred from Sequence or Structural
       Similarity
   ISO: Inferred from Sequence Orthology
   ISA: Inferred from Sequence Alignment
   ISM: Inferred from Sequence Model
   IGC: Inferred from Genomic Context

   RCA: inferred from Reviewed Computational
       Analysis
3. *Author Statement Evidence Codes:*
   TAS: Traceable Author Statement
   NAS: Non-traceable Author Statement
4. *Curator Statement Evidence Codes:*
   IC: Inferred by Curator
   ND: No biological Data available
5. *Automatically-Assigned Evidence Codes:*
   IEA: Inferred from Electronic Annotation
6. *Obsolete Evidence Codes:*
   NR: Not Recorded

In our GAS system, the annotation information is stored in separate XML files with the same file base name and a different extension. To connect a GO annotation with a GO term, the GAS Blog system uses XPointer to identify the original GO file location and id of the GO term to which the annotation is assigned. An annotation node contains attributes XPointer type and reference (href) to point to a GO term as well as to the children that may follow. A sample GO annotation is given below.

```
<annotation type="simple" href="http://
localhost/wordpress/wp-content/owl/caro.
obo_xml#CARO:0000000">
  <evidence_code>TAS</evidence_code>
  <content>a sample annotation</content>
  <foaf>
    <author id="1">admin</author>
    <groups>
      <group id="6">Group 1</group>
    </groups>
  </foaf>
  <timestamp time="1210639289">Mon May 12
20:41:29 EDT 2008</timestamp>
</annotation>
```

Adding SCORM Semantics to the GAS Blog

We use SCORM to enhance the GAS blog searching abilities. Based on SCORM we define the gene metadata that is used to describe elements of a content package in its manifest file. Metadata allows gene learning resources to be found when stored in a content package or in a repository. When a learning resource is intended to be searchable and reusable (by adding annotations), it is a best practice to describe it with metadata. Describing learning objects with metadata facilitates their search and discovery across systems. The GAS Blog uses the SCORM standard to syndicate Gene Ontology terms that are wrapped as Learning Objects that can be shared by users. In SCORM, Learning Objects are described by a manifest file. The manifest file is an XML-based file that describes the learning objects' package and its contents. It includes information about the identifier, version, schema, resources, and organization. The manifest node contains the following children to carry Learning Objects information: metadata. The SCORM manifest standard is used in Gene Ontology Navigation for displaying search results. A sample metadata of SCORM manifest is listed below.

```
<?xml version="1.0" encoding="UTF-8" ?>
<manifest identifier="MANIFEST_IDENTI-
FIER" version="1.0"
    xmlns="http://www.imsglobal.org/xsd/
imscp_v1p1"
    xmlns:adlcp="http://www.adlnet.org/
xsd/adlcp_v1p3"
    xmlns:adlnav="http://www.adlnet.org/
xsd/adlnav_v1p3"
    xmlns:adlseq="http://www.adlnet.org/
xsd/adlseq_v1p3"
    xmlns:imsss="http://www.imsglobal.
org/xsd/imsss"
    xmlns:lom="http://ltsc.ieee.org/xsd/
LOM"
    xmlns:xsi="http://www.w3.org/2001/
XMLSchema-instance"
    xsi:schemaLocation="http://www.ims-
global.org/xsd/imscp_v1p1
    imscp_v1p1.xsd http://www.adlnet.org/
xsd/adlcp_v1p3 adlcp_v1p3.xsd
    http://www.adlnet.org/xsd/adlnav_v1p3
adlnav_v1p3.xsd
    http://www.adlnet.org/xsd/adlseq_v1p3
adlseq_v1p3.xsd http://www.imsglobal.org/
xsd/imsss
    imsss_v1p0.xsd http://ltsc.ieee.org/
xsd/LOM lom.xsd"
    xmlns:xlink="http://www.w3.org/1999/
xlink">
  <metadata>
    <schema>ADL SCORM</schema>
    <schemaversion>CAM 1.3</schemaversion>
  </metadata>
  <organizations default="ORG-CARO">
    <organization identifier="ORG-CARO"
structure="hierarchical">
      <title>Activity Tree</title>
      <item identifier="ACT-CARO:0000000"
identifierref="RES-CARO:0000000">
        <title>Anatomical Entity</title>
      </item>
    </organization>
  </organizations>
  <resources>
    <resource identifier="RES-CA-
RO:0000000" type="webcontent"
adlcp:scormType="sco" href="http://lo-
calhost/wordpress/wp-includes/single.
php?category=/caro&ID=CARO:0000000">
      <metadata>
        <lom:lom>
          <lom:general>
            <lom:title>
              <lom:string language=
"en">Anatomical Entity</lom:string>
            </lom:title>
            <lom:language>en</lom:language>
            <lom:description>
              <lom:string language="en">
```

```
Biological entity that is either an indi-
vidual member of a biological species or
constitutes the structural organization
of an individual member of a biological
species.</lom:string>
            </lom:description>
            <lom:keyword>
             <lom:string>TAS</lom:string>
            </lom:keyword>
            <lom:structure>
             <lom:source>LOMv1.0</
lom:source>
             <lom:value>hierarchical</
lom:value>
            </lom:structure>
            <lom:annotation>sample anno-
tation</lom:annotation>
         </lom:general>
       </lom:lom>
     </metadata>
     <file href="http://localhost/word-
press/wp-content/upload/1211166773.gif" />
   </resource>
  </resources>
</manifest>
```

In the GAS Blog, each entry is a Learning Object. However, the syndication feed standard does not carry any information specifically for Learning Objects since the standard RSS only contains metadata of channels and does not carry Learning Object Metadata (LOM) which is necessary for other Learning Management Systems (LMS) to read Learning Objects. To make RSS carry LOM, it should be extended with the LOM schema. A RSS format for Learning Object Metadata (RSS-LOM) is defined by Stephen Downes (Downes, 2003). This format enables RSS to exchange LOM on a network. This format (RSS-LOM) makes it possible to distribute learning objects to courses without having to depend on the content libraries provided by a learning management system; it also will allow authors to distribute learning objects without having to work through an intermediary

such as a publisher (Harrsch, 2003). RSS-LOM includes metadata in the following categories:

- **General Metadata:** LO identifier, language, title, description, keyword, coverage, structure, and aggregation level.
- **Lifecycle Metadata:** RSS version, status, and contribute; metadata such as Metadata identifier, schema, contribute, and language.
- **Technical Metadata:** RSS format, size, location, operation system and browser requirement, installation remarks, other platform requirements, and duration.
- **LO educational Metadata:** interactivity type, learning resource type, interactivity level, semantic density, intended end user role, context, typical age range, difficulty, typical learning time, description, language.
- **LO Rights:** cost, copyright and other restrictions, and description.
- **Relation Metadata:** relation.
- **Annotation Metadata:** annotation.
- **Classification Metadata:** LO classification, prerequisite, educational objective, accessibility restrictions, educational level, skill level, security level, and competency.

Adding FOAF Semantics to the GAS Blog

Friend of a Friend (FOAF) is a machine-readable ontology describing persons, their activities, and their relations to other people and objects. Anyone can use FOAF to describe him or herself. FOAF allows groups of people to describe social networks without the need for a centralized database (Ernst, 2005). In the GAS Blog, FOAF is embedded into the annotation XML fragment as a child to carry annotators' information. Each FOAF node contains the information of annotator/author id, annotator/author name, and group(s) the annotator/author joined.

Similar to integrating Learning Object metadata with RSS, RSS-FOAF was introduced by Johannes Ernst to allow RSS to carry FOAF metadata (Ernst, 2005). The following tags are extended by RSS-FOAF (Ernst 2005):

- rss-foaf:type: this tag indicates that an RSS item should be treated as representing a Person or other entity with whom the individual exporting the extended RSS feed has a relationship;
- rss-foaf:group: this tag indicates that an RSS item should be treated as representing a social group, as seen from the perspective of the individual exporting the extended RSS feed ;
- rss-foaf:rel: this tag may be contained by RSS items that represent a Person or other entity with whom the individual has a relationship.

GAS Blog Navigation

Traditionally, a Gene Ontology query like AmiGO is completely based on database searching primitives. After users fill in a search form, the search engine goes through the database and returns all the matched results. Among these returned results, users can also go through a category systematically to narrow down the number of results and get what they are looking for. This search process can be considered as a blind search that is guided by a top-down search mechanism. Unlike the usual methods of searching, GAS uses a Gene Ontology Navigation (GON) engine that is based on Web 2.0 technologies and the semantic web. Instead of querying through database tables, it relies on metadata extracted dynamically from Gene Ontologies and their annotations (Fiaidhi, Mohammed, Jaam, & Hasnah, 2003). Other than that, GON uses some tag magnet and spelling correction to improve search result accuracy and relevance. The Gene Ontology Navigation in the GAS Blog system consists of two sub-navigation services: Collaborative Navigation and Generic Navigation. The former searches Gene Ontology and annotation information inside a group and the latter searches Gene Ontology and annotation information across all GAS Blog user groups.

Gene Ontology Navigation consists of three modules: Category Redirection, Collaborative Navigation, and Generic Navigation. Among them, Category Redirection is the module shared by Collaborative and Generic Navigation module (see Figure 10).

- Category Redirection: a module that narrows down the query result into a certain

Figure 10. Gene ontology navigation architecture

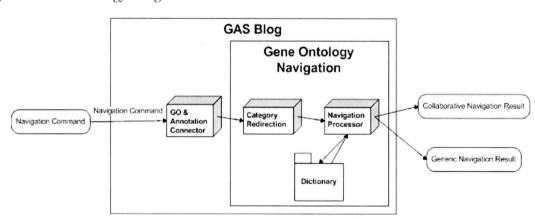

gene ontology category in order to decrease the amount of un-useful information.

- Navigation Processor: used to fill the matched navigation query result redirected from Category Redirection module into the SCORM manifest format based on navigation types – Collaborative or Generic.
- Metadata Extractor: a module to extract metadata dynamically from Gene Ontology annotation description with support of the dictionary.

Collaborative Navigation

Collaborative Navigation is a group-wise navigation. It allows users to search Gene Ontologies or their annotation based on a specific navigation condition only in the groups they joined, under the guide and assistance of the FOAF feature of the GAS Blog. Collaborative Navigation is only available to registered GAS Blog users, and users have to login before using this feature. To use Collaborative Navigation for browsing Gene Ontology, users can find the link of "Group-wise Metadata Search" on the first page of the GAS Blog system.

Generic Navigation

By contrast, to the Collaborative Navigation, Generic Navigation is a cross-group search. It allows users to search Gene Ontologies and their annotation

based on a specific navigation condition all through the GAS Blog under the guide and assistance of the FOAF feature of the GAS Blog.

CONCLUSION

This chapter introduces the notion of a Semantic Blog and describes the development of a prototype for Gene Annotation and Navigation (GAS). The GAS prototype has four levels of semantics that can help in promoting collaboration/annotation and navigation/searching for gene terms. However, the success of such a semantic blog needs to be tested and compared to traditional techniques. On one hand, our experiments for annotations show the type of collaborations as guided by GO, FOAF, and SCORM are superior to the traditional annotation techniques where all the gene terms and their annotations are stored in one silo. The details of such comparisons were given by Wei (2008). However, one needs to specify some criteria for comparison. The following are some criteria for comparison:

- *Number of comparisons*: A measure that counts number of comparisons used to find the required term.
- *Number of results returned*: A measure that counts the number of hits found when searching for a term.

Figure 11. The advantage of using GAS over a traditional search engine such as XPATH in number of comparisons

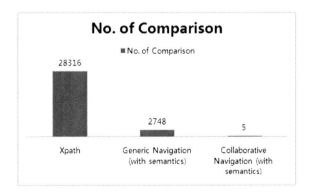

Figure 11 illustrates one of the findings of the GAS navigation when we search for something such as "Adult Mouse Anatomy". In our analysis the GO dataset considered for the purpose of searching for a gene term (under "adult mouse anatomy") was 28,316 gene terms. As displayed in Figure 11 the plain XPATH search engine will go through all the dataset entries (28,316) as there is no semantics to guide its search, while if we use GAS there are two types of navigation. When the user profile is used and the search is restricted to the group of people with whom the user has a relation, the navigation finds only 5 matching terms (this is our collaborative navigation that has found five gene ontologies that are annotated by users in the same group). However when GAS is used but the navigation is not restricted to the user group (i.e., FOAF is not part of the semantics), then the navigation is only guided by SCORM and GO, and in this particular example finds 2,748 term matches to the original query. Thus by adding semantics we can reduce the number of comparisons and save much of the navigation time even with the availability of annotation.

In summary, this chapter presented a Semantic Blog for Gene Annotation and Searching: a Web 2.0 application. The development methodology involves several Semantic Web technologies (e.g. FOAF and GO ontologies), Learning Objects technologies (e.g. SCORM) and Web 2.0 technologies (e.g. RSS, WordPress Blogging). These technologies have been employed to create a new personal learning environment for gene annotation, searching, and navigation where clients can collaborate, annotate existing gene learning objects, as well as search for gene learning objects in specialized group or cross groups.

REFERENCES

Anderson, P. (2007). What is Web 2.0? Ideas, technologies and implications for education. *JISC Technology and Standards Watch, Feb*. Retrieved from http://www.jisc.ac.uk/media/documents/techwatch/tsw0701b.pdf

Bergsten, H. (2001). *JavaServer Pages* (3rd ed.). Sebastopol, CA: O'Reilly.

Desisto, R. P., & Pring, B. L'heureux, B., & Karamouzis, F. (2006). SaaS delivery challenges on-premise software. *Gartner Research,* 26 September 2006. ID Number: G00143160, see http://www.gartner.com

Downes, S. (2003, May 10). RDF *Site Summary 1.0 Modules: Learning object metadata.* Retrieved January 22, 2008, from Stephen's Web: http://www.downes.ca/xml/RSS_LOM.htm

Ernst, J. (2005, September 27). *Embedding FOAF information in RSS*. Retrieved January 22, 2008, from Johannes Ernst's Blog: http://netmesh.info/jernst/Big_Picture/foaf-in-rss.html

Eysenbach, G. (2008). Medicine 2.0: Social networking, collaboration, participation, apomediation, and openness. *Journal of Medical Internet Research, 10*(3), e22. <URL: http://www.jmir.org/2008/3/e22/>

Fiaidhi, J., Mohammed, S., Jaam, J., & Hasnah, A. (2003). A standard framework for search hosting via ontology based query expansion. *Journal of Information Technology, 2*, 66–70.

Furst, I. (2008). *Wait time and delayed care*. Retrieved from http://waittimes.blogspot.com

Giustini, D. (2007). Web 3.0 and medicine: Make way for the semantic web. *British Medical Journal, 335*, 1273–1274. doi:10.1136/bmj.39428.494236.BE

Hardman, L., & Troncy, R. (2008).*A semantic multimedia web: Create, annotate, present and share your media*. Tutorial presented at the 3rd International Conference on Semantic and Digital Media Technologies. Koblenz-Germany, December 3-5, 2008. Retrieved from http://www.cwi.nl/~media/samt08/

Harrsch, M. (2003). RSS: The next killer app for education. *Illinois Computing Educators Computer Update Bulletin for Educators, 4*, 10.

MacManus, R. (2008, February). Top Health 2.0 web apps. *ReadWriteWeb Online Journal*, February 21, 2008. Retrieved from http://www.readwriteweb.com/archives/top_health_20_web_apps.php

Markoff, J. (2006, November 12). Entrepreneurs see a web guided by common sense. *New York Times*, November 11, 2006. Retrieved from http://www.nytimes.com/2006/11/12/business/12web.html?pagewanted=1&ei=5088&en=254d697964cedc62&ex=1320987600

Meng, P. (2005, March). *Podcasting and vodcasting*. White paper, University of Missouri, Columbia, MO. Available online at http://edmarketing.apple.com

Mohammed, S., Fiaidhi, J., & Yang, L. (2004). Developing multitier lightweight techniques for protecting medical images within ubiquitous environments. *IEEE 2nd Communications, Networks and Service Research Conference (CNSR04)*. Fredericton, Canada, May 19-21, 2004.

Möller, K., Breslin, J., & Decker, S. (2005). SemiBlog – semantic publishing of desktop data. In *14th Conference on Information Systems Development (ISD2005)*. Karlstad, Sweden, August 2005, (pp. 855-866).

O'Reilly, T. (2005, September). *What is Web 2.0: Design patterns and business models for the next generation of software*. O'Reilly Net, 09/30/2005: Available online at http://www.oreillynet.com/pub/a/oreilly/tim/news/2005/09/30/what-is-web-20.html

Pingdom. (2009, January 15th). The blog platforms of choice among the top 100 blogs. Retrieved from http://royal.pingdom.com/2009/01/15/the-blog-platforms-of-choice-among-the-top-100-blogs/

Spivack, N. (2006). The third-generation web is coming. *KurzweilAI.net*, December 17, 2006. http://www.kurzweilai.net/meme/frame.html?main=/articles/art0689.html?m%3D3

Wei, Y. (2008). *Building a semantic blog support system for gene learning objects on Web 2.0 environment*. MSc Thesis, September 2008, Department of Computer Science, Lakehead University.

Chapter 17

Technology Transforming Healthcare:
Tipping Points, Strange Attractors, and a Singularity

Emmett Davis
More Information, USA

ABSTRACT

Information and knowledge technologies, both alone and embedded in other advancing technologies, will transform health care. These technologies become part of health care because they bring efficiencies until they reach a tipping point where health care cannot function without them. These technologies add to the complexity of health care further creating a complex adaptive system. They function as strange attractors, or focal points, for intense, persistent, and accelerating change, which transforms the culture and control mechanisms of health care. Such smart technologies as artificial intelligence combined with genomic and nanotechnologies may bring about such a radical change that we could not return to today's health care system. For the transformation to be optimal, health care needs to address such issues as quality improvement processes, more intelligent electronic security, new control mechanisms, redefinition of the boundaries of health care enterprises, and a change from operating in discrete to continuous information flows.

INTRODUCTION

Technology, especially information and knowledge technology, will continue to exponentially transform health care. Health care is vulnerable to this transformation as it is a loosely coupled, distributed system spanning a wide range of enterprises and settings with their own decision makers: clinics, health facilities, public health offices, in-home chronic disability and aging services, insurance and health maintenance organizations, and behavioral health services integrated with medical and dental services. In all these settings, the focus of health care is the health of individuals and communities.

Information and knowledge technology, as traditionally expressed in software applications and also as expressed embedded in genomic and nanotechnology forms, is in the forefront of this

DOI: 10.4018/978-1-61520-733-6.ch017

transformation. Information and knowledge technology is also embedded in new logistics and telecommunications, in new materials and biochemistry, in smart buildings and efforts to be green, in evidence based and actuarial driven design, and in other parallel advances.

While health care has an understanding of information technology in the wide range of applications from word processors with spell checkers and electronic records systems to payroll and ERP – enterprise resource planning – systems, knowledge technology is less widely understood. Partly this is because knowledge based systems and artificial intelligence are often used to quietly enhance existing information systems.

TRANSFORMATION DRIVERS

In health care's drive to be explicit about best practice, to thoroughly document services and results within taxonomies, to improve processes with evidence-based design, to strive for consistency and quality through reviews of services, health care personnel have extracted and made explicit vast amounts of specialized knowledge. Increasingly this knowledge is represented in forms that fulfill a precondition that will increasingly allow computers to reason over this information. If health care provides knowledge systems with access to information and data, these knowledge systems can apply the represented knowledge to the information, and draw conclusions and inferences that will provide advice to humans. Given both real time access to information and control of appropriate physical systems, these knowledge systems can be cybernetic, developing feedback loops, and can act as thermostats do in regulating a building's consistent temperature.

While technology is visible in transforming health care, the persistent drivers of change come from the economy and society. These drivers are complex and exponential: cost, underserved populations, the coming demographic tsunami, and globalization.

Cost containment is more than just reducing expenditures. Cost containment also includes increasing the value or utility ratio to cost. In an industry where technology change is so rapid and both extends health care's capacity and raises expectations of increased competence, cost containment is not being applied to a static system. While health care might reduce personnel costs in a hospital cancer unit by thousands, the cost of the newest cancer pharmaceuticals increases by tens and hundreds of thousands. Still society strives to contain health care costs (Moroney, 2003).

Underserved populations and a coming demographic tsunami of an aging population increase the pressure to serve all, and early, while containing costs. These populations adapt to health care information technology. "The most common factor influencing the successful use of the interactive technology by these specific populations was that the consumers' perceived a benefit from using the system" (AHRQ, 2008, p. v).

Ever closer global neighbors are becoming relevant to each nation's health care system. Poor health and epidemics in once far away lands are no longer far away. Thus, among other examples, Canada's Global Public Health Intelligence Network (GPHIN) searches the Internet for advance warning of outbreaks of, for example, SARS (Mykhalovskiv & Weir, 2006).

The choice is not between the cold inhumanity of technological health care or human-intense health care. The choice is between optimal health care or less-than-optimal health care. Technology alone is not sufficient for adequate health care. Technology is only a part of the solution. Technology must be a part of the solution.

INTELLIGENCE

The question is often stated as how much technology? A better question is rather how much intelligence. Consider two guidelines that I use to know how much intelligence is needed. One: always the most appropriate intelligence first, human intelligence. Two: if human intelligence is not available, then the second most appropriate intelligence should be present, technological intelligence. These guidelines are my own; consider if they work for you.

Each year in the United States, over 30 infants are accidently left vulnerable in vehicles while the weather is too hot or too cold. The total number of United States hyperthermia deaths of children left in cars in 2008 was 43 and for 2009 up through August 12, 2009 was 26 (Null, 2009). The adult driver too busy and distracted leaves the vehicle and forgets the infant in a car seat in the rear. In the closed vehicle, the child tragically dies of exposure to too much heat or cold.

Infants should always have the most appropriate intelligence available, human intelligence. If human intelligence is not available, then the second most appropriate intelligence should be available, technological intelligence. But the infant should never be without some guardian intelligence.

Imagine cars that are intelligent enough to be aware that an infant is in danger all alone in a parked car with the temperature rising or falling dangerously. Imagine a car that intervenes by calling 911 and emergency services, blowing the car's horn, turning on the car and its heater or air conditioner, and calling for nearby humans to intervene. Imagine 30 plus infants not dying by accident each year because adult humans were absent (Null, 2009).

In November 1999 the Institute of Medicine, which is a component of the National Academy of Sciences published the report, *To Err is Human: Building a Safer Health System*, about how:

Heath care in the United States is not as safe as it should be – can be. At least 44,000 people, and perhaps as many as 98,000 people, die in hospitals each year as a result of medical errors that could have been prevented, according to estimates from two major studies. Even using the lower estimate, preventable medical errors in hospitals exceed attributable deaths to such feared threats as motor-vehicle wrecks, breast cancer, and AIDS. (Institute of Medicine, 1999, p. 1)

Ten years later, the nonprofit Consumers Union reports that there has been little or no progress in preventing these preventable deaths due to human error (Consumers Union, 2009).

For this discussion, we must emphasize that these annual deaths are preventable. They are caused by characteristics of the health care system. Again from *To Err is Human*:

One of the report's main conclusions is that the majority of medical errors do not result from individual recklessness or the actions of a particular group--this is not a "bad apple" problem. More commonly, errors are caused by faulty systems, processes, and conditions that lead people to make mistakes or fail to prevent them. For example, stocking patient-care units in hospitals with certain full-strength drugs, even though they are toxic unless diluted, has resulted in deadly mistakes.

Thus, mistakes can best be prevented by designing the health system at all levels to make it safer--to make it harder for people to do something wrong and easier for them to do it right. Of course, this does not mean that individuals can be careless. People still must be vigilant and held responsible for their actions. But when an error occurs, blaming an individual does little to make the system safer and prevent someone else from committing the same error. (Institute of Medicine, 1999)

Imagine then a health care facility never mistakenly implanting the wrong organ into a patient, never giving the wrong dose of medicine, or the wrong blood product. Imagine each clinic or pharmacy always being open and useful even if there is no human medical staff locally available.

Technological change, persistently driven by interrelated forces, adds to the complexity and speed of health care's transformation. Health care is a complex adaptive system. Intelligent systems can assist with managing the complex adaptive system of health care.

While the health care instance is a more complex form than maintaining the stable temperature of a building, stability in certain dynamic systems is the "trick" of the thermostat. It is the trick of having consistent and stable temperatures inside a building while day time, night time, and seasonal temperatures vary widely. The trick is in a cybernetic design of feedback loops of information to and from intelligent regulators. For health care the simple primitiveness of a single attribute (e.g. temperature) regulator of the furnace is not sufficient. Now the trick is to find simplicity within multiple attributes interacting with each other. Now we need complex adaptive systems with tipping points, strange attractors, and singularities.

TIPPING POINTS

Increasing technology with accompanying micro transformations gets technology in the door by bringing value and utility with its efficiencies. Especially where the technology is invisible, but systemic, even those opposed to new technologies find value in just-in-time inventory and logistics (Schonberger, 1984). The cost burden of a full inventory of supplies has become too great. The temporal and spatial logics of just-in-time logistics reduce the cost of inventory, while heightening the risk of sensitivity to logistical disruptions.

In health care, a labor-intensive industry, resource allocation improves by using technology substitutes. Hospital rooms have buzzers for patients and intercom speakers for nurses and patients to communicate without the nurse always having to enter the room.

Information and knowledge technologies get in the door because of the efficiencies they bring by squeezing temporal and spatial costs from transactions. Information and knowledge technologies improve service quality by supporting consistency and management of localized complexity. The integration of information and knowledge technology into health care will reach a tipping point after which health care decision makers will be unable to easily do without these technologies.

Consider the systems that today we consider essential. We find essential systems that gather data continuously and automatically. We find essential systems that ease and speed up our ability to interpret, that is, extract what would be invisible information. We find essential systems that provide complex therapy. Consider laboratory systems and radiology systems. Consider physiological monitoring systems and glucometers. Consider dialysis.

With cost containment and continued quality service, technology assists in reducing some risk triggers. Smart systems, that parallel and twice-think the care of hospital patients, lead to fewer deaths and better quality health care. Such systems reason with knowledge using real-time data about the patient and their care by multiple actors. Thus a smart system can warn an actor of negative interactions arising from potential mistakes. For example, McKesson Corporation's Horizon Med Manager "helps to reduce medication errors through integration with First DataBank's knowledge bases for compliance monitoring, drug-dose checking, patient consultations, allergy screening, drug-interaction screening, therapeutic duplication and drug-disease interactions" (McKesson Corporation, 2009b). Intelligent systems assist with managing local complexities.

The power of these new technologies is that they work on the improvement of all three of project management's conceptual golden triangle where a reduction in one of three usually devastates the other two: time, resources, and quality (Project Management Institute, 2008). Information and knowledge services uniquely allow for improved quality of health care globally and locally while reducing resources and time delays.

Smart systems can lessen transaction costs, especially the costs due to errors (McKesson Corporation, 2009a). Reducing transaction costs certainly is a plus for reaching the goals of cost containment (Rada, 2008). The reduction in the cost of transactions will become significant enough to invoke Coase's Law, the insight of Ronald Coase (1937) and transform the organizational size and architecture of health care. A transaction cost is the cost of making an economic exchange, including search costs of finding who has what one wants, communication costs getting in touch with that party, negotiation costs for settling on the price and terms of the exchange, logistics costs (including time delays) in obtaining what you want, performance and monitoring costs, and payment transaction costs to compensate everyone involved. This is all especially true when information is asymmetrical, and not equally available to all actors.

Enterprises can either outsource or bring inside transactions. When the transaction costs for the firm/enterprise of outsourced economic exchanges is higher than for internal transactions, the firm or enterprise will grow by building resources internally to perform those functions internally (Coase, 1937).

A form of bringing transactions inside an enterprise is vertical integration. The Ford Motor Company's 1930's River Rouge Complex is an extreme example. Located in Dearborn, Michigan, along the Rouge River, the River Rouge Complex when it was completed in 1928, had become the largest integrated factory in the world.

There were ore docks, steel furnaces, coke ovens, rolling mills, glass furnaces and plate-glass rollers. Buildings included a tire-making plant, stamping plant, engine casting plant, frame and assembly plant, transmission plant, radiator plant, tool and die plant, and, at one time, even a paper mill. A massive power plant produced enough

electricity to light a city the size of nearby Detroit, and a soybean conversion plant turned soybeans into plastic auto parts. ...

It was a city without residents. At its peak in the 1930s, more than 100,000 people worked at the Rouge. To accommodate them required a multi-station fire department, a modern police force, a fully staffed hospital and a maintenance crew 5,000 strong. One new car rolled off the line every 49 seconds. Each day, workers smelted more than 1,500 tons of iron and made 500 tons of glass, and every month 3,500 mop heads had to be replaced to keep the complex clean.

Henry Ford's ultimate goal was to achieve total self-sufficiency by owning, operating and co-ordinating all the resources needed to produce complete automobiles. (Ford Motor Company, 2009, p. 1)

If the internal costs are higher, the enterprise will downsize and outsource transactions. The economist, Ronald Coase, began to discuss these concepts in his 1937 work, *The Nature of the Firm*.

While economists debate the reality of the hype, information technology, when implemented properly including with enabling technologies, can reduce transaction costs. Consider Google.com and other Internet search engines which reduce search transaction costs.

A difficulty is that information technology increases the amount of information available and needing to be managed. Antonio Cordella and Kai A. Simon (1997) call the cost of processing this information coordination costs. While Cordella questions whether *Does Information Technology Always Lead to Lower Transaction Costs?* (Cordella, 2001) and *Does IT Add Up?* (Cordella, 2006), the cure for reducing coordination costs is often more and improved information technology coupled with business process improvements. Disintermediation is one such process, whereby layers of processes and workflow are eliminated or automated.

In economics, disintermediation is the removal of intermediaries in a supply chain: "cutting out the middleman." Instead of going through traditional distribution channels, that had some type of intermediate (distributor, wholesaler, broker, or agent), companies may now deal with each customer directly.

Disintermediation initiated by consumers is often the result of high market transparency, in that buyers are aware of supply prices direct from the manufacturer. Buyers bypass the middlemen (wholesalers and retailers) in order to buy directly from the manufacturer and thereby pay less. Buyers can alternatively elect to purchase from wholesalers. Often, a B2C [Business to Customer] company functions as the bridge between buyer and manufacturer (Disintermediation, 2009).

Consider the transactional costs of physician orders where staff record, transmit, record, approve, record, implement, record, and review these orders. Consider the transactional costs in each service in the health care value chain as each service is implemented.

Smart systems allow for busy staff to communicate with each other about their decisions by communicating into smart systems both to record and cause the implementation of the decision, as well as to trigger the system to reason over the effects of acting or not acting.

A health care enterprise operates consistently under best practices designed and reviewed by enterprise decision makers. Who is the enterprise? Thomas Friedman (2005) in his book, *The World Is Flat: A Brief History of the Twenty-first Century*, writes about physicians in India reading North American X-rays during their day and our night. When a health facility uses such services, where are the boundaries of the health facility and of the regulators and licensing agencies that monitor the health facility? The question concerning

health care enterprise boundaries today is about where the complexity is located in the value chain and who has necessary and sufficient knowledge to handle this complexity for the benefit of the patient and all stakeholders.

Complexities continually increase in number and in the severity of their impact. Complexities come in both local and global flavors. The need at all levels for specialists increases. But how do we support specialists in a team environment with many players (generalists and specialists in other fields) in a distributed health care system? Smart technologies must be a part of the solution space. Smart technologies, in particular knowledge technologies, overlay information and communication technologies. How can we ensure that these technologies will better enable the specialist to focus, but not become isolated? (Yolles, 2005).

Fortunately, the creation of smart systems will be driven by behaviors health care has already developed in evolving best practice, such as, value-based design and evidence-based design. This iterative and incremental approach to reaching perfection will prove essential (Petroski, 1992).

STRANGE ATTRACTORS

We can design information and knowledge technology to provide an increase in access points to the appropriate level for each situation. Atlantic Health hopes to increase communication with patients and between health care professionals. In part, they will do this by making many processes visible, by quantifying them and making that information available to appropriate actors, including knowledge bases (McKesson Corporation, 2009a). These technologies will lower the cost of communicating with many stakeholders at the appropriate level. Doing so they in reality increase the number of access points for both disseminating meaningful information, and therefore the likelihood each stakeholder can act based on being more fully informed.

This access to information and knowledge will further transform the architecture and culture of health care. Much of health care is appropriately cautious toward broad, unrestricted, HIPAA-violating communication among all stakeholders. The United States Health Insurance Portability and Accountability Act of 1996, which regulates the privacy and use of patient's health information, is known by its acronym, HIPAA. HIPAA, specialized terms and knowledge, time intense processes, and other constraints too often cause health care to forego optimal communication with the members of each individual's continuum of care, the value chain of health care, including appropriate family members and other specialists and generalists.

In the field of information technology, Fred Brooks (1975) in his book *The Mythical Man-Month* realized the exponential cost of increasing an operation's human resources and gave us Brook's Law. Communication overhead exponentially increases as the number of people increase. The number of different communication channels increases along with the square of the number of people; doubling the number of people results in four times as many different conversations. Communication tends to a hypercube. Everyone working on dependent tasks needs to keep in sync, so as more people are added, they spend more time trying to find out what others are doing. Brook's Law is a rough, empirical description of how, when we add humans to a process, we are exponentially increasing communication costs.

Will then smart technology collapse under its own weight as it expands and includes more active players, as we turn consumers of information at the end of essentially one way communication channels into stakeholders able to widely communicate in multiple directions and contribute information and knowledge? Perhaps not, since Brook's Law is founded on a point-to-point communication architecture.

Smart technologies can be designed to replace point-to-point communication designs with more efficient structures, such as blackboard structures, where information is communicated to a central hub for software agents to read.

A blackboard system is an artificial intelligence application based on the blackboard architectural model, where a common knowledge base, the "blackboard", is iteratively updated by a diverse group of specialist knowledge sources, starting with a problem specification and ending with a solution. Each knowledge source updates the blackboard with a partial solution when its internal constraints match the blackboard state. In this way, the specialists work together to solve the problem. The blackboard model was originally designed as a way to handle complex, ill-defined problems. (Blackboard, 2009)

Also hybrid human and intelligent technology communication architectures could be designed as small world networks under a power law as opposed to a normal distribution. That is, a few nodes might bear the largest burden of communicating to appropriate members (Barabasi, 2003; Watts, 2003).

Walls become permeable boundaries with smart technologies. Smart systems that are aware of each stakeholder in a continuum of care and the information and knowledge that can be displayed for each stakeholder can, without violating HIPAA and other such privacy and intellectual property rules, facilitate and create more effective and efficient communication, including monitoring alerts for coming due or overdue tasks.

This distributed and decentralized pattern of networks for the flow of information and knowledge parallels the architecture of the software itself. Software increasingly will be composed of *ad hoc* chains of software services. A software service needing other services invokes those services that can be provided by software agents and automated processes.

A less appreciated and parallel impact of intelligent technology is that they are beginning to change the access points into health care inputs, processes, and outputs. These technologies are transforming the architecture and control culture of health care delivery. Static walls are becoming permeable boundaries busy with information, knowledge, service flows, and new actors in a variety of modalities.

As stand-alone applications in information and knowledge technologies dissolve into a service-oriented architecture, so health care services also will dissolve from a chain of stand-alone, large-organization bordered systems into intertwined systems of systems. The services will still encapsulate functional modules with independent actors who influence each other. But the services are no longer restricted to within this or that organization. Thus laboratory work has migrated from in-house hospital labs into independent organizations that serve several hospitals. How much further can this outsourcing extend?

For this increased complexity and faster rate of change to optimally function, all participants will need to become fully active as both consumers and as wikinomics prosumers - consumers who produce value, adding to our store of information and knowledge (Tapscott & Williams, 2008). The end of passive roles will support trust in health care in a variety of settings, stretching from India's Comprehensive Rural Health Project based in Jamkhed (2009) that uses village health workers to American Well (2009), the online Internet service where patients "see" an individual doctor, and on to smart houses where vulnerable individuals including seniors living alone in their house or in nursing homes are no longer isolated when their situation deteriorates (Home Automation, 2009).

Increasingly a health care worker will be defined, not by what they know, but by what they can learn and translate into meaningful and productive results. Just-in-time learning will not only occur when a worker in a clinical situation needs to use an upgraded medical tool they have not used for over a year, but will also include higher levels of abstraction, of knowledge transfers so that a worker can recognize a pattern occurring in their service community.

The movement and development of information and knowledge will soon occur automatically within systems of systems. Health care will soon become more aware of strange attractors creating patterns within this complex chaos.

SINGULARITY

A futurist, Ray Kurzweil (2005), describes his future projections of the degree of the radical change by borrowing a concept from physics about the behavior of black holes. As matter approaches the event horizon, or boundary, where the black hole's extraordinary gravity takes hold, matter cannot return back out of the black hole. That point is a singularity. Using this concept as a metaphor, Kurzweil describes how by 2045 the change to our information world will have been so radical that a singularity will occur. The degree of changes will be such that we will not be able to return to today's conditions.

Ray Kurzweil (2005) in his book, *The Singularity Is Near*, uses Twentieth Century historical data and charts to support his insight that Moore's Law of exponential growth in the number of transistors on a computer chip applies to multiple areas of information technology. He projects that exponential growth will continue out to and beyond 2045 when we will have

the singularity – representing a profound and disruptive transformation in human capability -- ... The nonbiological intelligence created in that year will be one billion times more powerful than all human intelligence today (Kurzweil, 2005, p. 137).

Ray Kurzweil is part of a tradition of technology futurists that includes Vernor Vinge who wrote *The*

Coming Technological Singularity (1993). On the other hand, Judith V. Grabiner is part of a parallel tradition that points out where the super-optimists supporting Artificial Intelligence have failed to make their case (Garbiner, 1988). Kurzweil points out that the parallel growth of hard artificial intelligence in robots, nanotechnology, and genomics, one growth curve layering on the other, will lead to great medical and other advances. Proponents of a technology singularity might be labeled as utopian. It is not necessary to agree with a full or partial utopian interpretation of their arguments to find value in what they are saying.

This is particularly true given that parallel proponents of technological change, if not progress, support Kurzweil's and his colleagues' position. Consider Don Tapscott and Anthony D. Williams (2008), co-authors of *Wikinomics: How Mass Collaboration Changes Everything,* a book about the open network architecture of the Internet and its services.

One of the Internet's services is the online encyclopedia written by anyone who wants to contribute, the Wikipedia. Wikinomics is about the pattern of turning consumers of a one-directional communication architecture (such as of the Encyclopedia Britannia.com) into "prosumers," consumers who also produce value and information (Tapscott & Williams, 2008). This pattern, this use of existing software, itself, contributes to the increases in productivity parallel to the hardware based productivity upon which Gordon Moore (1965) based his insights.

Some observers question how valuable this "wikinomics" information is since it may be severely flawed and inaccurate in some cases depending on who contributes. This is an ongoing concern. However, given the great utility of this type of media for distributing information, perhaps our focus should be on improving the accuracy of this type of media as we do information legacy formats.

It is reasonable to throw metaphorical stones at these artesian fountains of information, bubbling progress at the bottom of oceans of information. Are smart technologies not just more noise? Again smart technologies by their very nature provide both floods of information and knowledge and an increasing sensitivity to relevance and recall. These terms of *relevance* and *recall* are from the field of information retrieval. Relevance is a measure of whether the records retrieved are useful in answering the intent of the query. There should be, ideally, no noise. Recall is a measure of whether all the relevant records in the store have been retrieved. Recall and relevance are roughly equivalent to sensitivity and specificity, or in statistics to type 1 and type 2 errors.

There should be, ideally, no relevant information left behind. In practice, information retrieval systems often need to have a balance. Depending on the sensitivity and needs of the user asking the query, they will either be hungry for all the relevant items (because what they have is insufficient) and are willing to tolerate some irrelevant records, or the user has a sufficiency of information and will tend to be intolerant of "obviously" irrelevant retrieved records. Health care is especially interested in increases in recall with minimal additional noise when common, in-the-box thinking and information has been exhausted without a satisfactory solution.

While health care is deploying basic information systems, particularly enterprise resource planning systems (ERP), knowledge systems are beginning to appear that will allow health care to more fully obey Moore's Law of exponential growth in productivity. Knowledge based systems will reason over the content of integrated information systems with models that lead to exponential results (Kurzweil, 2005).

For health care professionals the question is what of what Ray Kurzweil describes is true? What if even just a part of what he describes is true? Health care professionals would be prudent to at least partially follow Ray Kurzweil's insights about how the combination of nanotechnology, genomic technology, and knowledge based or artificial intelligence technologies will lead to progress.

FUTURE DIRECTIONS: ON THE WAY TO THE SINGULARITY

What is the Enterprise's Boundary?

In the first paragraph of this chapter, the last sentence is, "In all these settings, the focus of health care is the health of individuals and communities." If the center of health care is the health of individuals and communities, then are the boundaries of health care enterprises different than that of other businesses and commercial organizations?

If the cost of transactions will substantially change in the near future, will the boundaries of health care enterprises change? In Friedman's (2005) book the *World Is Flat*, he discusses examples of turning work into information and accomplishing the work at the other end of a telephone wire. A health care example of his is around X-ray images taken in North America at night when the local expert who interprets the images is not working those hours. The images are then transmitted to, in this case, India where an expert during local South Asian business hours interprets the images. This immediate, though geographically distant interpretation, avoids a temporal disruption in local therapeutic processes. But these processes do open issues of training, liability, licensing, and compensation.

Has the Boundary of Health Care Enterprises Changed?

Consider an example that we will bring to your attention below where hundreds of individual doctor's offices now have their record systems feed public health analysis systems. Has the enterprise defining boundary of each of these doctor's offices just changed? If this has not changed their enterprise defining boundaries, what would change

the boundaries? If the boundaries are changed, consider what would be the impact.

A dyed-in-the-wool organization man, every working day in a white shirt and tie, instinctively believes in a narrow organization or enterprise. Still the walls are becoming so permeable that the enterprise may become larger than the firm. The concept of ERP – enterprise resource planning – software systems integrating across an organization's silos may now be limiting if one considers the enterprise to be larger and no longer coequal to the corporate organization, the firm. Even given the need for continuing competition and local innovation, still the definition of the enterprise may exceed any organization, if not industry. While once an academic question beyond the reach of known software, this is no longer true.

Health care information and knowledge is now represented in explicit forms able to be reasoned over by rule and semantic net engines and able to be transferred from one rule base to another anywhere in the world. E-health medical records will follow the individual wherever they go in the world. Software services, that is, independent modules of software functions, are able to be assembled on demand throughout the world. These and other developments allow health care managers to re-conceive of health care enterprise boundaries as extending out geographically globally and extending down to each patient and their communities wherever they receive services.

The technology that once could not support the dreams of visionaries is now able to offer functions that even health care visionaries are not sure they want. Consider that rates for many health care services are standardized within networks. Consider if all rates, in and out of network, in fact globally, were the same. Consider if there was no longer an in network or out of network difference in transaction rates. Imagine if an insured person could go anywhere at any time. Imagine if all the information and knowledge and best practices before any visit anywhere was available to the health care staff at that visit plus any new information from that visit is added to that individual's medical record. What would be the impact of such new definitions of the enterprise?

Health care's enterprise boundaries would be more than just universal access, health care would emerge from independent health care processes as they occur. Health care would continue being event driven, as the architecture of many computer systems are becoming. Given this option, why are the boundaries of the health care enterprise where they are? Of the functions of the enterprise, why are these functions performed within the enterprise and not outsourced? Will health facilities coordinate billing and payment for services not performed within their enterprise, but only contracted for a patient? Will health facilities provide a physical in-patient platform for services, but not employ the staff performing those services? What changes might occur that would cause reasonable people to move one or more of these functions outside of the enterprise, to the marketplace?

What technology changes, especially information and knowledge technology changes would move functions outside of an organization? Would move outside of the health care industry? Will Microsoft and Google determine the boundaries of health care enterprises?

Quality Improvement Processes

Health care has embedded in its processes multiple and successful quality assurance processes. Health care workers and managers, advocates, regulators, as well as patients and their continuum of care members, actively contribute to improving the quality of health care. Still in the transformation of health care that is occurring due to technology, health care stakeholders will need to redouble their efforts and enhance the quality assurance models they use.

The increased complexity and the speed of change require this new effort. We will need a quality improvement program similar to the following.

The TQRADS program uses a cascade of increasingly sophisticated series of quality awareness processes: Testing, Quality, Risk, Architecture, Design, and Scale. The program initially stresses just testing a product or service, a classic and common, bounded domain of testing.

Then it also focuses on the quality of processes that generates the product or service. The analytical assumption is that a root cause of error is in the processes that generate the product or service. Because there is too much to test, we then use risk analysis and risk management to focus our testing resources on where the most severe or common errors are likely to be.

Architectural awareness allows the testers to compensate for the effects of reuse and deployment. Then we use design to understand the utility (or not) of the product or service. Finally we consider scale for increases in complexity and quantity that cause otherwise hidden errors to arise. Stress testing is a common form of this aspect of testing.

At a day to day level, all health care participants will need to extend current quality assurance processes. We will continue to test product and service, and to use quality techniques to probe the source of defects within the processes that created these products and services. Unable to test everything, we will use risk techniques to assist us to focus our attention where most needed. We will understand the architecture of our systems to discover where modules are reused and where deployment processes mangle blue prints and designs (thus regression testing). We will return to understand design in order to ask if a system has optimal utility for the people it serves. Finally we will understand how our systems scale for both complexity (algorithmic and not, centralized or distributed) and quantity growth.

No Human Error

No human error may be an exaggeration. But far, far fewer preventable human errors would be worth achieving.

The strangest details will mark the new transformed health care. No human worker will be alone and going wrong because of a lack of knowledge. Imagine no "newbies." Nor will the workers drop calls, forget tasks, or inadvertently act inconsistently. Deaths and damage due to these slips will disappear. Instead we will dwell in complexity arising from simple embedded rules with a variety of intelligent resources: swarming, cooperative, and problem solving.

Consider what human error is in health care. A type of human error is a loss of focus and attention, an absence of necessary knowledge, a miscalculation in a hurried and complex situation, and inconsistent fine motor control. What are the strengths of technological intelligence: inhuman focus and attention; vast stores of knowledge; rapid and repeatable computed calculations no matter the hurry or haste; and consistent control. Thus, we have spell checkers in our word processors, calculators for adding numbers, robots in pharmacies filling prescriptions, and human-assisting robots in surgery.

What a partnership!

New Security

This transformation requires that information and knowledge security be redesigned. HIPAA and proprietary intellectual property are simple compared to the security architecture yet to come. The current awareness within information technology security focuses on the source of information and knowledge. To this we will add the receiver where data will be transported and the entities represented. Security will add an awareness of the relationship of all actors; the value of the service; feedback on how to improve the service; and the trajectory or intent of use of data, information, and knowledge. The implementation of security will migrate from the source system to the data, information, and knowledge itself whether in the source system or elsewhere.

Current data security architecture will need to be redesigned for an agent based world. Data is protected within databases that we conceive of as static fortresses, as opposed to mobile agents. A database understands itself to be a source of data and that authorized entities may request, insert, delete, or maintain its data.

What the database does not have is a social awareness of all the actors interested in itself. Nor does each instance of datum in the database have a sense of the value of its services for other agents. Hence each instance of datum can neither request nor process feedback about how to improve its services or utility. This would involve each instance of datum being aware of its trajectory and intent of its use. The very grammar of this paragraph seems incorrect when we discuss what was until now such a primitive and passive entity as data compared with data having the intelligence of software agents.

In the May 2001 issue of *Scientific American*, Tim Berners-Lee, James Hendler, and Ora Lassila (2001) described "The Semantic Web" and the revolution of new possibilities it may bring. The semantic web depends on two situations: information meaningful to computers as well as persistent and personalized software agents. The increasing digitization of medical information (such as medical records and data gathered by electronic medical devices) within a taxonomy or schema of meta-data that describes the meaning of that information makes that data meaningful to computers. Persistent and personalized software agents are intelligent programs that are always available. These types of software agents have yet to be perfected. When these conditions are met, the following becomes possible:

At the doctor's office, Lucy instructed her Semantic Web agent through her handheld Web browser. The agent promptly retrieved information about Mom's prescribed treatment from the doctor's agent, looked up several lists of providers, and checked for the ones in-plan for Mom's insurance within a 20-mile radius of her home and with a rating of excellent or very good on trusted rating services. It then began trying to find a match between available appointment times (supplied by the agents of individual providers through their Web sites) and Pete's and Lucy's busy schedules.

In a few minutes the agent presented them with a plan. Pete didn't like it: University Hospital was all the way across town from Mom's place, and he'd be driving back in the middle of rush hour. He set his own agent to redo the search with stricter preferences about location and time. Lucy's agent, having complete trust in Pete's agent in the context of the present task, automatically assisted by supplying access certificates and shortcuts to the data it had already sorted through. (Berners-Lee, 2001, pp. 1-2)

In the last paragraph above, the authors use the phrase "complete trust." "Lucy's agent, having complete trust in Pete's agent in the context of the present task …" is extraordinarily challenging. How will Lucy's consent be handled? Especially if, in fact, Lucy may not know what possible uses the data/information will be used for? While part of this challenge must be met by technical professionals, health care professionals with others must also contribute by defining the possible "contexts" in which health information and care may possibly be used. There is much work yet to be done.

Change from Discrete to Continuous

The transformation in health care will increasingly be marked by changes that, while insubstantial, will be intense enough to feel as a tactile sensation. Up to now the information age has been remarkable for an overabundance of information. Going forward, the flow of information will increase exponentially.

In fact, the flow of information will literally flow and change from discrete and frequent amounts of information to a continuous flow. While we ingest discrete amounts of food, we prosper within a flow of air and oxygen, as well as light. We do not feel that a flow of air or light is overwhelming. So we will not feel that the change from receiving information in discrete amounts with frequency to continuous will be overwhelming. Partly this will be because we will develop new ways to manage and make sense of this flow of information. From calculus we will learn to monitor flows of data and information with derivatives, whose slope will meaningfully tell us about changes in the flow of information.

Also we will change from having a single focus toward information with implied multiple meanings to multiple foci with multiple levels of granularity (cell to system to ecological community). So much of the information our body takes in is relegated to involuntary systems that do not need our conscious attention. Thus we can walk and chew gum as well as multi-process many other marvelous and necessary tasks. Even my heart knows enough to pump faster when my muscles need more oxygen when I exert myself.

At a more subtle level, we will change from diagnosis as model-confirming and searching for a best-fit model to model improving. We will change to continuous user driven design (Davis, Davis, & Hawkins, 2008). We will change to evaluating using probabilities. Certainty will no longer be the pretended goal. Consider the outlier situations that arise as less than optimal outcomes using today's diagnostic methods. Consider the complexity of the outliers with their dual and multiple diagnoses.

Control Goes Puff!

Not only will certainty no longer be the pretended goal, but the brave new world coming will also change what we control. If anyone has ever felt in control, and surgeons may have, control will likely go puff! The new technologies, while giving health care workers new tools of control, will open up current processes to more stakeholders.

Health care processes will have more technology and, through that technology, more insight and oversight by others. Mayor Bloomberg of New York City urged the small, private physicians of New York to computerize their paper based patient records.

About 1,000 primary-care physicians ... collect the smallest details of their patients' lives in a database as part of a $60 million city health department project. Experts say it is the most ambitious government effort nationwide to harness electronic data for public-health goals like monitoring disease frequency, cancer screening and substance abuse. ... And echoing the city's cash-incentive experiments in the school system, the health department will soon start offering doctors bonuses of perhaps $100 for each patient who hits specified targets like controlling blood pressure or cholesterol, up to $20,000 for each doctor (Hartocollis, 2008).

The act of recording in electronic systems designed to ease the harvest of value goes many places quickly. In the above New York City case, medical information becomes immediate public health information.

Health care may want to defend areas of control where the psychological comfort of the workers needs it. Health care certainly will want to defend control where it is needed. The Twentieth Century, with increasingly educated non-physician populations, saw the physician–patient relationship change from slight and shallow explanations to further ensure compliance with a prescribed therapy to ever more lengthy and meaningful explanations. The Internet transforms bibliotherapy through small patient libraries into targeted medical education (Tapscott & Williams, 2008).

The barriers to fuller participation by patients in diagnosis-therapy processes are for patients to understand the meaning of the technical, medical information pouring from this cornucopia and also to have the experience of knowing how things happen in different types of people. While it sometimes appears that health care legitimately like medieval craft guilds is protecting income-earning, proprietary information, the complexities of medical, biomedical, genomic, biochemical, statistical, and other layers of new developments and fields impedes health care from reaching its goal of providing individuals with fully informed options.

As individual consumers receive their own individual software agents and as their discourse communities receive more and more knowledge and information sources and technologies, individuals will themselves acquire larger and larger amounts of medical knowledge and information, including basic competencies for early prevention. Health care will then seem, as it does now, even more distributed.

CONCLUSION

For the transformation of health care to be optimal, health care needs to more actively address issues of quality improvement processes, more intelligent security, new control mechanisms, to redefine the boundaries of health care enterprises, and change from operating in discrete to continuous information flows.

When Thomas Edison, the inventor of applied electricity, died some wanted to salute his accomplishments by shutting down the electrical grids for five minutes. But we could not afford to do so; the World could no longer do without that, which but short decades earlier, it did not have. So too, today we do without independent software agents, semantic webs, and other knowledge based technologies, that soon we will not be able to disconnect for five minutes without catastrophic results.

REFERENCES

AHRQ (Agency for Health Care Research and Quality). (2008) *Barriers and drivers of health information technology use for the elderly, chronically ill, and underserved.* Structured Abstract. November 2008. Agency for Health care Research and Quality (AHRQ), Rockville, MD. Retrieved August 10, 2009 from http://www.ahrq.gov/clinic/tp/hitbartp.htm.

American Well. (2009). *American Well: The next generation of health communication.* Retrieved on January 30, 2009 from http://www.american-well.com/

Armour, P. G. (2009). The ontology of paper. *Communications of the ACM, 52*(1), 23–24. doi:10.1145/1435417.1435427

Barabasi, A.-L. (2003). *Linked: how everything is connected to everything else and what it means for business, science, and everyday life.* New York: Plume.

Berners-Lee, T., Hendler, J., & Lassila, O. (2001, May). The Semantic Web. *Scientific American.* Retrieved on August 12, 2009 from http://www.si.umich.edu/~rfrost/courses/si110/readings/in_out_and_beyond/semantic_web.pdf

Blackboard. (2009). In *Wikipedia, the free encyclopedia.* Retrieved on August 12, 2009 from http://en.wikipedia.org/wiki/Blackboard_(computing)

Brooks, F. (1995). *The mythical man month* (2nd ed.). Boston: Addison-Wesley Professional.

Coase, R. H. (1937). The nature of the firm. *Economica, N.S., 4*(16), 386-405.

Coase, R. H. (1960). The problem of social cost. *The Journal of Law & Economics, 3*, 1–44. doi:10.1086/466560

Consumers Union. (2009). *U.S health care system fails to protect patients from deadly medical errors: Consumers Union assesses lack of progress ten years after Institute of Medicine found up to 98,000 die from preventable errors.* Issued on May 19, 2009. Retrieved on August 12, 2009 from http://www.consumersunion.org/pub/core_health_care/011324.html

Cordella, A. (2001). *Does information technology always lead to lower transaction costs?* Presented at The 9th European Conference on Information Systems, Bled, Slovenia, June 27-29, 2001.

Cordella, A. (2006). Transaction costs and information systems: Does IT add up? *Journal of Information Technology, 21*, 195–202. doi:10.1057/palgrave.jit.2000066

Cordella, A., & Simon, K. A. (1997). *The impact of information technology on transaction and coordination cost.* Presented at Conference on Information Systems Research in Scandinavia (IRIS 20), Oslo, Norway, August 9-12, 1997.

Davis, E., Davis, J., & Hawkins, B. (2008). *Citizen driven design selects among multiple communication channels.* Presented at the 7th International EGOV Conference 2008, September 1-4, 2008, Turin, Italy.

Disintermediation. (2009). In *Wikipedia, the free encyclopedia.* Retrieved on August 12, 2009 from http://en.wikipedia.org/wiki/Disintermediation.

Ford Motor Company. (2009). *Ford Rouge Factory Tour: History of the Rouge.* Retrieved on August 12, 2009 from http://www.thehenryford.org/rouge/historyofrouge.aspx

Friedman, T. L. (2005). *The world is flat: A brief history of the twenty-first century.* New York: Farrar, Straus and Giroux.

Grabiner, J. V. (1988). Partisans and critics of a new science: The case of Artificial Intelligence and some historical parallels. In Aspray, W., & Kitcher, P. (Eds.), *History and philosophy of modern Mathematics*. Minneapolis, MN: University of Minnesota Press.

Hartocollis, A. (2008, December 29). Looking to private records for public health goals: Doctors to get cash payments from city to contribute to a vast medical database. *New York Times*, A18 - A19. Retrieved on January 30, 2009 from http://labs.daylife.com/journalist/anemona_hartocollis and http://www.nytimes.com/2008/12/30/nyregion/30records.html

Home Automation. (2009). In *Wikipedia, the free encyclopedia*. Retrieved on January 30, 2009 from Wikipedia at http://en.wikipedia.org/wiki/Home_automation_for_the_elderly_and_disabled

Institute of Medicine. (1999). *To err Is human: Building a safer health system.* L. T. Kohn, J. M. Corrigan, & M. S. Donaldson (Eds). Washington, DC: National Academy Press. Retrieved on August 12, 2009 from http://www.iom.edu/Object.File/Master/4/117/ToErr-8pager.pdf

Jamkhed. (2009). *Jamkhed: Comprehensive rural health project*. Retrieved on January 30, 2009 from http://www.jamkhed.org.

Kurzweil, R. (2005). *The singularity is near: When humans transcend biology*. New York: Penguin.

McKesson Corporation. (2009a). *Atlantic Health creates a fully integrated electronic health record with advanced technologies*. Retrieved on August 12, 2009 from http://www.mckesson.com/static_files/McKesson.com/MPT/Documents/AtlanticHealth_PRT387.pdf

McKesson Corporation. (2009b). *Horizon Meds Manager*. Retrieved on August 12, 2009 from http://www.mckesson.com/en_us/McKesson.com/For+Healthcare+Providers/Hospitals/Interdisciplinary+Care+Solutions/Horizon+Meds+Manager.html

McKesson Corporation. (2009c). *McKesson as your partner for patient safety*. Retrieved on August 12, 2009 from http://www.mckesson.com/static_files/McKesson.com/MPT/Documents/McKessonasYourPartnerforPatientSafety_WHT273.pdf

Moore, G. E. (1965, April 18). Cramming more components onto integrated circuits. *Electronics Magazine, 38* (8). Retrieved on August 12, 2009 from ftp://download.intel.com/museum/Moores_Law/Articles-Press_Releases/Gordon_Moore_1965_Article.pdf.

Moroney, S. D. (2003). *Understanding health care cost drivers*. National Institute of Health Policy. Retrieved on August 12, 2009 from http://www.bluecrossmn.com/bc/wcs/groups/bcbsmn/@mbc_bluecrossmn/documents/public/mbc1_health care_cost_drivers.pdf

Mykhalovskiv, E., & Weir, L. (2006). The Global Public Health Intelligence Network and early warning outbreak detection: a Canadian contribution to global public health. *Canadian Journal of Public Health, 97,* 42-44. Retrieved on January 30, 2009 from National Center for Biotechnology Information's database at http://www.ncbi.nlm.nih.gov/pubmed/16512327

Null, J. (2009). *Hyperthermia deaths of children in vehicles.* Updated August 12, 2009. Retrieved on August 13, 2009 from http://ggweather.com/heat/

Petroski, H. (1992). *To engineer is human: The role of failure in successful design*. New York: Vintage Books.

Project Management Institute. (2008). *A Guide to the Project Management Body of Knowledge* (4th ed.). Newtown Square, PA: Project Management Institute.

Rada, R. (2007). *Information systems and health care enterprises*. Hershey, PA: IGI Publishing.

Schonberger, R. J. (1984). Just-in-time production systems: Replacing complexity with simplicity in manufacturing management. *Industrial Engineering (American Institute of Industrial Engineers)*, *18*(10), 52–63.

Tapscott, D., & Williams, A. D. (2008). *Wikinomics: How mass collaboration changes everything, (Expanded Edition)*. New York: Portfolio.

Vinge, V. (1993). *The coming technological singularity: How to survive in the post-human era.* VISION-21 Symposium sponsored by NASA Lewis Research Center and the Ohio Aerospace Institute, March 30-31, 1993. Retrieved on August 14, 2009 from http://www.rohan.sdsu.edu/faculty/vinge/misc/singularity.html

Watts, D. J. (2003). *Six degrees: The science of a connect age*. New York: Norton.

Yolles, M. (2005). Knowledge cycles and sharing: Considerations for health care management. In Bali, R. K. (Ed.), *Clinical knowledge management: Opportunities and challenges*. Hershey, PA: Idea Group.

Compilation of References

Aarts, J., Ash, J., & Berg, M. (2007). Extending the understanding of computerized physician order entry: Implications for professional collaboration, workflow and quality of care. *International Journal of Medical Informatics*, *76*(Suppl 1), 4–13. doi:10.1016/j.ijmedinf.2006.05.009

Aarts, J., Doorewaard, H., & Berg, M. (2004). Understanding implementation: the case of a computerized physician order entry system in a large Dutch university medical center. *Journal of the American Medical Informatics Association*, *11*(3), 207–216. doi:10.1197/jamia.M1372

Abel-Smith, B. (1989). Health economies in developing countries. *The Journal of Tropical Medicine and Hygiene*, *92*, 229–241.

Ackoff, R. L. (1989). From data to wisdom. *Journal of Applied Statistics*, *16*, 3–9.

Adato, M., & Meinzen-Dick, R. (2002). Assessing the impact of agricultural research on poverty using the sustainable livelihoods framework. *International Food Policy Research Institute (IFPRI)*. Retrieved from http://www.ifpri.org/sites/default/files/publications/eptdp89.pdf

Afford, C. W. (2003). *Corrosive reform: failing health systems in Eastern Europe.* Geneva: International Labour Office. Available at http://www.ilo.org/public/english/protection/ses/download/docs/corrosive.pdf

AHIMA. (2003, July 10). *American Health Information Management Association (AHIMA) Statement on the Privacy, Confidentiality, and Security of Health Records.* Available at http://library.ahima.org/xpedio/groups/public/documents/ahima/bok1_019923.hcsp?dDocName=bok1_019923

AHRQ (Agency for Health Care Research and Quality). (2008) *Barriers and drivers of health information technology use for the elderly, chronically ill, and underserved.* Structured Abstract. November 2008. Agency for Health care Research and Quality (AHRQ), Rockville, MD. Retrieved August 10, 2009 from http://www.ahrq.gov/clinic/tp/hitbartp.htm.

Aiken, T. D., & Catalano, J. T. (1994). *Legal, ethical, and political issues in nursing.* Philadelphia: F.A. Davis.

Akematsu, Y., & Tsuji, M. (2009). An empirical analysis of the reduction in medical expenditure by e-health users. *Journal of Telemedicine and Telecare*, *15*, 109–111. doi:10.1258/jtt.2009.003001

Akesson, K. M., Saveman, B. I., & Nilsson, G. (2007). Health care consumers' experiences of information communication technology- a summary of literature. *International Journal of Medical Informatics*, *76*(9), 633–645. doi:10.1016/j.ijmedinf.2006.07.001

Akhtar, R. (1991). *Health care patterns and planning in developing countries.* New York: Greenwood Press.

Albert, K. M. (2006). Open access: implications for scholarly publishing and medical libraries. *Journal of the Medical Library Association*, *94*(3), 253–262.

Alberts, D. S., Gartska, J. J., & Stein, F. P. (1999). *Network centric warfare: Developing and leveraging information superiority* (pp. 193–197). Washington, DC: CCRP Publication Series.

Alliance, T. M. (2004). *Telemedicine 2010: Visions for a personal medical network*. Retrieved January 14, 2009, from http://www.euro.who.int/eprise/main/who/progs/tme/about/20021009_1

Aloisio, G., Barba, M. C., Biasi, E., Cafaro, M., Fiore, S., & Mirto, M. (2005). A web service-based Grid portal for Edgebreaker compression. *Methods of Information in Medicine, 44*(2), 233–238.

Al-Rousan, M., Al-Ali, A. R., & Eberlein, A. (2006). Remote patient monitoring and information system. *International Journal of Electronic Healthcare, 2*(3), 231–249.

Amarasingham, R., Plantinga, L., Diener-West, M., Gaskin, D. J., & Powe, N. R. (2009). Clinical information technologies and inpatient outcomes: a multiple hospital study. *Archives of Internal Medicine, 169*(2), 108–114. doi:10.1001/archinternmed.2008.520

American Psychiatric Association. (2000). *Diagnostic and statistical manual of mental disorders* (4th ed., text revision). Washington, DC: American Psychiatric Association.

American Well. (2009). *American Well: The next generation of health communication.* Retrieved on January 30, 2009 from http://www.americanwell.com/

Anderson, G. F., & Steinberg, E. P. (1984). Hospital readmissions in the Medicare population. *The New England Journal of Medicine, 311*(21), 1349–1353.

Anderson, P. (2007). What is Web 2.0? Ideas, technologies and implications for education. *JISC Technology and Standards Watch, Feb*. Retrieved from http://www.jisc.ac.uk/media/documents/techwatch/tsw0701b.pdf

Anderson, P. (2007). *What is Web 2.0? Ideas, technologies and implications for education*. Retrieved from http://www.jisc.ac.uk/media/documents/techwatch/tsw0701b.pdf

Andrews, L. (2005). Harnessing the benefits of biobanks. *The Journal of Law, Medicine & Ethics, 33*, 22–30. doi:10.1111/j.1748-720X.2005.tb00207.x

Andronico, G., Barbera, R., Falzone, A., Lo Re, G., Pulvirenti, A., & Rodolico, A. (2005). The GENIUS web portal – an easy way to access the Grid. *Methods of Information in Medicine, 44*(2), 215–220.

Anoto Group AB. (2009). *Protecting children – Digital pen and paper enables caseworkers to spend more time in the field*. Retrieved August 11, 2009, from http://www.anoto.com/filearchive/1/14709/pendatasolutions_children_090626.pdf

Arar, N. H., Wen, L., McGrath, J., Steinbach, R., & Pugh, J. A. (2005). Communicating about medications during primary care outpatient visits: the role of electronic medical records. *Informatics in Primary Care, 13*(1), 13–22.

Armour, P. G. (2009). The ontology of paper. *Communications of the ACM, 52*(1), 23–24. doi:10.1145/1435417.1435427

Arveson, P. (1998). *The emerging field of management engineering*. Retrieved March 31, 2008, from http://www.balancedscorecard.org/ManagementEngineering/tabid/134/Default.aspx

Asaro, P. V., Sheldahl, A. L., & Char, D. M. (2006). Embedded guideline information without patient specificity in a commercial emergency department computerized order-entry system. *Academic Emergency Medicine, 13*(4), 452–458. doi:10.1111/j.1553-2712.2006.tb00325.x

Ash, J. S., & Bates, D. W. (2005). Factors and forces affecting EHR adoption: Report of a 2004 ACMI discussion. *Journal of the American Medical Informatics Association, 12*(1), 8–12. doi:10.1197/jamia.M1684

Ash, J. S., Berg, M., & Coiera, E. (2004). Some unintended consequences of information technology in health care: the nature of patient care information system-related errors. *Journal of the American Medical Informatics Association, 11*(2), 104–112. doi:10.1197/jamia.M1471

Associated Press. (2006). Global warming causing disease to rise: Malaria, dengue fever increasing as temperature heats up, experts warn. *MSNBC*. Retrieved from http://www.msnbc.msn.com/id/15717706/

Attaran, A. (2004). Where did it go wrong? *Nature, 430*, 2–3. doi:10.1038/430932a

Auf der Heide, E. (2006). The importance of evidence-based disaster planning. *Annals of Emergency Medicine, 1*, 34–49. doi:10.1016/j.annemergmed.2005.05.009

Australian Institute of Health and Welfare (AIHW). (2008). *Rural, regional and remote health: Indicators of health status and determinants of health, (cat. no. PHE 97)*. Canberra, Australia: Australian Institute of Health and Welfare.

Baba, M. L. (1999). Dangerous liaisons: Trust, distrust, and information technology in American work organizations. *Human Organization, 58,* 331–346. Retrieved from http://findarticles.com/p/articles/mi_qa3800/is_199910/ai_n8856547/?tag=content;col1.

Baker, L., Wagner, T. H., Singer, S., & Bundorf, M. K. (2003). Use of the Internet and e-mail for health care information: Results from a national survey. *Journal of the American Medical Association, 289*, 2400–2406. doi:10.1001/jama.289.18.2400

Ball, M. J., & Gold, J. (2006). Banking on health: Personal records and information exchange. *Journal of Healthcare Information Management, 20*(2), 71–83.

Ball, M. J., & Lillis, J. C. (2000). Health information systems: challenges for 21st century. *AACN Clinical Issues, 11*(3), 386–395. doi:10.1097/00044067-200008000-00006

Ball, W., & Holland, S. (2009). The fear of new technology: a naturally occurring phenomenon. *The American Journal of Bioethics, 9*(1), 14–16. doi:10.1080/15265160802617977

Ballester, F., Michelozzi, P., & Iñiguez, C. (2003). Editorial: Weather, climate, and public health. *Journal of Epidemiology and Community Health, 57,* 759–760. doi:10.1136/jech.57.10.759

Barabasi, A.-L. (2003). *Linked: how everything is connected to everything else and what it means for business, science, and everyday life.* New York: Plume.

Bardram, J. E. (2005). Activity-based computing: Support for mobility and collaboration in ubiquitous computing. *Personal and Ubiquitous Computing, 9*(5), 312–322. doi:10.1007/s00779-004-0335-2

Barnett, T. P. M. (2004). *The Pentagon's new map.* New York: Putnam & Sons.

Batalden, P. B., Nelson, E. C., Edwards, W. H., Godfrey, M. M., & Mohr, J. J. (2003). Microsystems in health care, Part 9. Developing small clinical units to attain peak performance. *Joint Commission Journal on Quality and Safety, 29*(11), 575–585.

Bates, D. W. (2005). Physicians and ambulatory electronic health records. *Health Affairs, 24*(5), 1180–1189. doi:10.1377/hlthaff.24.5.1180

Bates, D. W. (2009). The effects of health information technology on inpatient care. *Archives of Internal Medicine, 169*(2), 105–107. doi:10.1001/archinternmed.2008.542

Bates, D. W., & Gawande, A. A. (2003). Improving safety with information technology. *The New England Journal of Medicine, 348*, 2526–2534. doi:10.1056/NEJMsa020847

Bates, D. W., Boyle, D. L., Rittenberg, E., & Kuperman, G. J., Ma'Luf, N., Menkin, V. et al. (1998). What proportion of common diagnostic tests appear redundant? *The American Journal of Medicine, 104*(4), 361–368. doi:10.1016/S0002-9343(98)00063-1

Bates, D. W., O'Neil, A. C., Boyle, D., Teich, J., Chertow, G. M., Komaroff, A. L., & Brennan, T. A. (1994). Potential identifiability and preventability of adverse events using information systems. *Journal of the American Medical Informatics Association, 1*(5), 404–411.

Bates, D. W., Spell, N., Cullen, D. J., Burdick, E., Laird, N., & Petersen, L. A. (1997). The costs of adverse drug events in hospitalized patients. Adverse Drug Events Prevention Study Group. *Journal of the American Medical Association, 277*(4), 307–311. doi:10.1001/jama.277.4.307

Bates, D. W., Teich, J. M., Lee, J., Seger, D., & Kuperman, G. J., Ma'Luf, N. et al. (1999). The impact of computerized physician order entry on medication error prevention.

Journal of the American Medical Informatics Association, 6(4), 313–321.

Bauer, S., Percevic, R., & Kordy, H. (2004). *The use of short message service (SMS) in the aftercare treatment for patients with Bulimia Nervosa.* Paper presented at Med-e-Tel 2004, Luxembourg, D.G. of Luxembourg. Retrieved December 15, 2008 from http://www.mede-tel.lu/download/2004/parallel_sessions/abstract/0422/THE_USE_OF_SHORT_MESSAGE_SERVICE.doc

Bazell, R. (2007). Global healthcare is fashionable, but falls short. *MSNBC*. Retrieved from http://www.msnbc.msn.com/id/18274808/

Beck, T. (2007). *Regional need analysis questionnaire survey for analyzing the acceptance & awareness of e-health in 5 European countries Germany, Sweden, Finland, Poland, Lithuania.* Presented at Cross-border e-health in the Baltic Sea region. Stockholm, Sweden. Retrieved December 15, 2008 from http://www.e-health-conference.info/Presentations/b_thorsten_beck.pdf

Bell, G. B., & Sethi, A. (2001). Matching Records in a National Medical Patient Index. *Communications of the ACM, 44*(9), 83–88. doi:10.1145/383694.383711

Bellavista, P., Bottazzi, D., Corradi, A., & Montanari, R. (2006). Challenges, opportunities and solutions for ubiquitous eldercare. In Al-Hakim, L. (Ed.), *Web mobile-based applications for healthcare management* (pp. 142–165). Hershey, PA: Idea Group.

Belson, D. (2007). *Improving efficiency, management engineering comes to the safety net.* Retrieved March 30, 2008, from http://www.chcf.org/documents/hospitals/ManagementEngineering.pdf

Benbassat, J., & Taragin, M. (2000). Hospital readmissions as a measure of quality of health care: advantages and limitations. *Archives of Internal Medicine, 160*(8), 1074–1081. doi:10.1001/archinte.160.8.1074

Bensink, M., Wootton, R., Irving, H., Hallahan, A., Theodoros, D., Russell, T., et al. (2007). Investigating the cost-effectiveness of video telephone based support for newly diagnosed paediatric oncology patients and their families: design of a randomized controlled trial.

BioMed Central Health Services Research, 7(38). Retrieved January 3, 2009 from http://www.biomedcentral.com/1472-6963/7/38

Beresford, E. B. (1991, Jul. - Aug.). Uncertainty and the shaping of medical decisions. *The Hastings Center Report, 21*(4), 6–11. doi:10.2307/3562993

Berg, M. (1998). Medical work and the computer-based patient record: a sociological perspective. *Methods of Information in Medicine, 37*(3), 294–301.

Berg, M. (1999). Accumulation and coordinating: occasions for information technologies in medical work. *Computer Supported Cooperative Work, 8*, 373–401. doi:10.1023/A:1008757115404

Bergsten, H. (2001). *JavaServer Pages* (3rd ed.). Sebastopol, CA: O'Reilly.

Berland, G. K., Elliot, M. N., Morales, L. S., Algazy, J. I., Kravitz, R. L., & Broder, M. S. (2001). Health information on the Internet: accessibility, quality, and readability in English and Spanish. *Journal of the American Medical Association, 285*, 2612–2621. doi:10.1001/jama.285.20.2612

Bernardini, A. L., Chiari, G., & Vanelli, M. (2008). Telephone hotline service (THS) for children and adolescents with type 1 diabetes as a strategy to reduce diabetes-related emergencies and costs for admittance. *Global Telemedicine / e-health Updates.* Luxembourg: Publ. Luxexpo. *Knowledge Resources, 1*, 26–29.

Berners-Lee, T., & Hendler, J. (2001). Publishing on the semantic Web. *Nature, 410*, 1023–1024. doi:10.1038/35074206

Berners-Lee, T., Hendler, J., & Lassila, O. (2001, May). The Semantic Web. *Scientific American.* Retrieved on August 12, 2009 from http://www.si.umich.edu/~rfrost/courses/si110/readings/in_out_and_beyond/semantic_web.pdf

Bhargava, A., & Chatterjee, B. (2007). Chikungunya fever, falciparum malaria, dengue fever, Japanese encephalitis...are we listening to the warning signs for public health in India? *Indian Journal of Medical Ethics, 4*(1), 18–23.

Binns, P. (2004). The impact of the electronic health record on patient safety: an Alberta perspective. *Healthcare Papers*, *5*(3), 47–51.

Birnsteel, L. (2008). *E-health 2.0: Web 2.0 in the health sector: Industry review with UK perspective. E-health Media Ltd.* Retrieved September 17, 2009 from http://www.e-health-insider.com/img/ehi_reports0332/EHI-ehealth_20_research_report_2008_Exec_Summary.pdf

Bishop, L., Holmes, B. J., & Kelley, C. M. (2005). *National Consumer Health Privacy Survey 2005 California HealthCare Foundation*. CHCF.

Bissio, R. (2008). Rights in the time of crisis. In *Rights is the answer. Social Watch Report 2008,* (pp. 1-3). Retrieved from http://www.socialwatch.org/sites/default/files/pdf/en/bangladeshoverview2008_eng.pdf

Blackboard. (2009). In *Wikipedia, the free encyclopedia.* Retrieved on August 12, 2009 from http://en.wikipedia.org/wiki/Blackboard_(computing)

Blakely, T., & Salmond, C. (2002). Probabilistic record linkage and a method to calculate the positive predictive value. *International Journal of Epidemiology, 31*(6), 1246–1252. doi:10.1093/ije/31.6.1246

Blanchard, B. S., & Fabrycky, W. J. (2005). *Systems engineering and analysis.* Upper Saddle River, NJ: Prentice Hall.

Blignaut, P. J. (1999). Software for primary healthcare in a developing country: Background and problem statement. *Computers in Nursing, 17*(6), 291–296.

Blobel, B. (2004). Advanced EHR architectures – promises or reality. In B. Blobel, G. Gell, C. Hildebrand, & R. Engelbrecht, (Eds.), *Contribution of Medical Informatics to Health, Proceedings of MIE 2004 Special Topics Conference,* (pp. 73-78). Amsterdam: IOS Press.

Block, N. J. (1978). Troubles with functionalism. In C. W. Savage (Ed.) Perception and cognition: Issues in the foundations of psychology (Minnesota Studies in the Philosophy of Science 9, pp. 261-325). Minneapolis, MN: University of Minnesota Press.

Blum, B. J. (1986). *Clinical Information Systems.* New York: Springer-Verlag.

Boaden, R., & Joyce, P. (2006). Developing the electronic record: what about patient safety. *Health Services Management Research, 19*(2), 94–104. doi:10.1258/095148406776829103

Boddington, P. & Räisänen, U. (2006, August 24). *Attributions of responsibility within health care policy: Sharing our responsibility within a situation of inequality.* Presented at European Society of Philosophy and Medicine, Helsinki, Finland.

Booth, N., Robinson, P., & Kohannejad, J. (2004). Identification of high-quality consultation practice in primary care: the effects of computer use on doctor-patient rapport. *Informatics in Primary Care, 12*(2), 75–83.

Born, A. P., Sparenberg, A., Russomano, T., Timm, R., Soares, E., & Schaun, T. (2008). Eight years of a tele-ECG system in southern Brazil: a multidisciplinary analysis regarding the degree of satisfaction. In Jordanova, M., & Lievens, F. (Eds.), *Global Telemedicine / e-health Updates: Knowledge Resources* (*Vol. 1*, pp. 203–204). Luxembourg: Luxexpo.

Börve, A., & Molina-Martinez, R. (2008). 24-hour anonymous medical information service using the mobile telephone in Sweden: A pilot study during the summer of 2008. In Jordanova, M., & Lievens, F. (Eds.), *Global Telemedicine/e-health Updates: Knowledge Resources* (*Vol. 2*, pp. 181–185). Luxembourg: Luxexpo.

Botsis, T., Paraskeva, P., & Syrigos, K. N. (2006). *Implementation of computerized information systems in oncology unit.* Paper presented at Med-e-Tel 2006. Retrieved August 10, 2009 from http://www.medetel.eu/download/2006/parallel_sessions/presentation/0406/Botsis.pdf

Bottazzi, D., Corradi, A., & Montanari, R. (2006). Context-aware middleware solutions for anytime and anywhere emergency assistance to elderly people. *IEEE Communications Magazine, 44*(4), 82–90. doi:10.1109/MCOM.2006.1632653

Bouchama, A. (2005). The 2003 European heat wave. *Intensive Care Medicine, 30*(1), 1–3. doi:10.1007/s00134-003-2062-y

Boulos, M. N. K., & Wheeler, S. (2007). The emerging Web 2.0 social software: an enabling suite of sociable technologies in health and health care education. *Health Information and Libraries Journal, 24*, 2–23. doi:10.1111/j.1471-1842.2007.00701.x

Boulos, M. N., Marimba, I., & Wheeler, S. (2006). Wikis, blogs and podcasts: a new generation of Web-based tools for virtual collaborative clinical practice and education. *BMC Medical Education, 6*, 41–49. doi:10.1186/1472-6920-6-41

Boyle, A. (2006). Five-tech forecast. *Cosmic Log, MSN-BC*. Retrieved September 18, 2009 from http://cosmiclog.msnbc.msn.com/archive/2006/12/28/23418.aspx

Bradford, Z. B., & Brown, F. J. (2008). America's army: A model for interagency effectiveness. Westport, CN: Praeger Security International.

Bradley, C. J., Given, C. W., Luo, Z., Roberts, C., Copel, G., & Virnig, B. A. (2007). Medicaid, Medicare, and the Michigan tumor registry: A linkage strategy. *Medical Decision Making, 27*(4), 352–363. doi:10.1177/0272989X07302129

Braithwaite, J., Westbrook, M. T., Hindle, D., Iedema, R. A., & Black, D. A. (2006). Does restructuring hospitals result in greater efficiency?--An empirical test using diachronic data. *Health Services Management Research, 19*(1), 1–12. doi:10.1258/095148406775322016

Brandeau, M. L. (2004). Allocating resources to control infectious diseases. In Brandeau, M. L., Sainfort, F., & Pierskalla, W. P. (Eds.), *Operations research and health care, A handbook of methods and applications* (pp. 443–464). Boston: Kluwer Academic Publishers.

Braslow, A., Brennan, R. T., Newman, M. M., Bircher, N. G., Batcheller, A. M., & Kaye, W. (1997). CPR training without an instructor: development and evaluation of a video self-instructional system for effective performance of cardiopulmonary resuscitation. *Resuscitation, 34*, 207–220. doi:10.1016/S0300-9572(97)01096-4

Brennan, P. F. (2007). CPOE: sufficient, but not perfect, evidence for taking action. *Journal of the American Medical Informatics Association, 14*(1), 130–131. doi:10.1197/jamia.M2303

Brennan, R. J., & Nandy, R. (2001). Complex humanitarian emergencies: a major global challenge. *Emergency Medicine, 13*(2), 147–156.

Brennan, T. A., Leape, L. L., Laird, N. M., Hebert, L., Localio, A. R., & Lawthers, A. G. (1991). Incidence of adverse events and negligence in hospitalized patients. Results of the Harvard Medical Practice Study I. *The New England Journal of Medicine, 324*, 370–376.

Brewin, B. (2008, November 13). Adoption of e-health records depends on consolidation of systems. *NextGov*. Retrieved from http://www.nextgov.com/nextgov/ng_20081113_1406.php

Brickley, K. F. (1995). *Corporate and white collar crime. Cases and materials* (2nd ed.). Boston: Little, Brown and Company.

Brooks, F. (1995). *The mythical man month* (2nd ed.). Boston: Addison-Wesley Professional.

Brown, F. J. (2002). Imperatives for tomorrow. *Military Review, 85*, 81–91.

Brown, F.J. (2008). *Designing of ToL pilots*. Unpublished working document (author's permission 12/31/08).

Brown, F.J. (2008). *Institutionalizing EUR ToL*. Unpublished working document (author's permission 12/31/08).

Brown, J. R., & Goolsbee, A. (2002). Does the Internet make markets more competitive? Evidence from the life insurance industry. *The Journal of Political Economy, 110*, 481–507. doi:10.1086/339714

Bryant, D., & Colgrave, O. (2006). Knowledge and informatics within home medicine (KIM): the role of a home health hub. *International Journal of Healthcare Technology and Management, 7*(5), 335–347.

Brynjolfsson, E. (1993). The productivity paradox of information technology. *Communications of the ACM, 36*(12), 67–77. doi:10.1145/163298.163309

Buchan, J. (2004). What difference does ("good") HRM make? *Human Resources for Health, 2,* 1–7. doi:10.1186/1478-4491-2-6

Buck, D. A., Trainor, J. E., & Aguirre, B. E. (2006). A critical evaluation of Incident Command System and NIMS. *Journal of Homeland Security and Emergency Management, 3*(3), 1–27. doi:10.2202/1547-7355.1252

Bujnowska-Fedak, M., Staniszewski, A., Steciwko, A., & Puchala, E. (2000). System of telemedicine services designed for family doctors' practices. *Telemedicine Journal and e-Health, 6*(4), 449–452. doi:10.1089/15305620050503933

Butler, J., Speroff, T., Arbogast, P. G., Newton, M., Waitman, L. R., & Stiles, R. (2006). Improved compliance with quality measures at hospital discharge with a computerized physician order entry system. *American Heart Journal, 151*(3), 643–653. doi:10.1016/j.ahj.2005.05.007

California HealthCare Foundation. (1999, January). *Medical privacy and confidentiality survey.* CHCF Organization. Available at http://www.chcf.org/topics/view.cfm?itemID=12500

California HealthCare Foundation. (2005, November). *National consumer health privacy survey 2005.* CHCF Organization. Available at: http://www.chcf.org/topics/view.cfm?itemID=115694

Callen, J. L., Buyankhishig, B., & McIntosh, J. H. (2008). Clinical information sources used by hospital doctors in Mongolia. *International Journal of Medical Informatics, 77*(4), 249–255. doi:10.1016/j.ijmedinf.2007.06.003

Callison, R. C., & Leira, E. C. (2008). Strategies to improve acute stroke care of patients in rural and other geographically dispersed areas. *Current Treatment Options in Neurology, 10*(6), 450–454. doi:10.1007/s11940-008-0047-4

Campana, B. A., Jarvis-Selinger, S., Ho, K., Evans, W. L., & Zwimpfer, T. J. (2004). Use of telemedicine for an emergency craniotomy in a pediatric trauma. *Canadian Medical Association Journal, 171,* 444–446. doi:10.1503/cmaj.1040006

Campbell, E. M., Guappone, K. P., Sittig, D. F., Dykstra, R. H., & Ash, J. S. (2009). Computerized provider order entry adoption: implications for clinical workflow. *Journal of General Internal Medicine, 24*(1), 21–26. doi:10.1007/s11606-008-0857-9

Campbell, E. M., Sittig, D. F., Ash, J. S., Guappone, K. P., & Dykstra, R. H. (2006). Types of unintended consequences related to computerized provider order entry. *Journal of the American Medical Informatics Association, 13*(5), 547–556. doi:10.1197/jamia.M2042

Campbell, K. M. (2008). Record linkage software in the public domain: a comparison of Link Plus, the Link King, and a `basic' deterministic algorithm. *Health Informatics Journal, 14*(1), 5–15. doi:10.1177/1460458208088855

Canada Health Infoway. (2006). *Electronic health record privacy and security: conceptual architecture.* Ottawa, Canada: CHI.

Canada Health Infoway. (2007, March). *White paper on information governance of the interoperable electronic health record (EHR).* Ottawa, Canada: CHI.

Canadian Health Information Management Association. (2004). *A toolkit for privacy and access & disclosure of personal & health information.* London, Canada: CHIMA.

Canadian Health Information Management Association. (2007). Health data access, use, and control for secondary uses. *Professional Practice Brief: PPB – 0003.07.*

Canadian Health Information Management Association. (2009). *Fundamentals in health information management.* Ottawa, Canada: CHA Press.

Canadian Institutes of Health Research (CIHR). (2002, November). *Secondary use of personal information in health research: case studies.* Available at http://www.cihr-irsc.gc.ca/e/6827.html

Canadian Institutes of Health Research (CIHR). (2005). *CIHR best practices for protecting privacy in health research - September 2005.* Ottawa, Canada: Public Works and Government Services Canada. Available at http://www.cihr-irsc.gc.ca/e/documents/et_pbp_nov05_sept2005_e.pdf

Canadian Institutes of Health Research (CIHR). (2006). *Harmonizing research & privacy: Standards for a collaborative future. Executive Summary: Privacy Best Practices for Secondary Data Use (SDU).* Ottawa, ON: CIHR.

Canadian Medical Association. (1998). *CMA health information privacy code.* Available online at http://www.cma.ca/index.cfm/ci_id/3216/la_id/1.htm

Canadian Standards Association. (1996). *Model code for the protection of personal health information.* Can be accessed online at http://www.csa.ca/standards/privacy/code/Default.asp?language=english

Carr, D. (2004). Improving the health of the world's poorest people. [Washington, DC: Population Reference Bureau. Retrieved from http://www.prb.org/pdf/ImprovingtheHealthWorld_Eng.pdf]. *Health Bulletin, 1.*

Carter, M. J. (2008, December 30). Global agenda increasingly disease driven. *Inter Press Service (IPS).* Retrieved from http://www.ipsnews.net/news.asp?idnews=43619

Castelli; D., Schlachta-Fairchild, L. & Pyke, R. (2008). Telenursing panel: telenursing implementation strategies and success factors. In M. Jordanova & F. Lievens (Eds.), *Global telemedicine / e-health updates: Knowledge resources,* (Vol. 1, pp. 409-414). Luxembourg: Publ. Luxexpo.

Cavalier, J. C., & Klein, J. D. (1998). Effects of cooperative versus individual learning and orienting activities during computer-based instruction. *Educational Technology Research and Development, 46*(1), 5–17. doi:10.1007/BF02299826

Cavanagh, K., Shapiro, D. A., Van Den Berg, S., Swain, S., Barkham, M., & Proudfoot, J. (2006). The effectiveness of computerized cognitive behavioural therapy in routine care. *The British Journal of Clinical Psychology, 45*(Pt 4), 499–514. doi:10.1348/014466505X84782

Cavoukian, A. (2009). *Privacy by design: The 7 foundational principles.* Toronto, ON: Office of the Information and Privacy Commissioner of Ontario. Available at http://www.ipc.on.ca/images/Resources/7foundationalprinciples.pdf

Cayton, H. (2006). Information governance in the Department of Health and the NHS. UK: National Health Service (No. 3349).

Chaplin: E., Mailey, M., Crosby, R., Gorman, D., Holland, X., Hippe, C. et al. (1999). Using quality function deployment to capture the voice of the customer and translate it into the voice of the provider. *Joint Commission Journal on Quality Improvement, 25*(6), 300–315.

Charette, R. (2008, May 19). E-health needs better design. *NextGov.* Retrieved from http://techinsider.nextgov.com/2008/05/ehealth_needs_better_design.php

Chassin: M. (1998). Is healthcare ready for Six Sigma quality? *The Milbank Quarterly, 76*(4), 565–591.

Chaudhry, B., Wang, J., Wu, S., Maglione, M., Mojica, W., & Roth, E. (2006). Systematic review: impact of health information technology on quality, efficiency, and costs of medical care. *Annals of Internal Medicine, 144*(10), 742–752.

Chen, L., Evans, T., Anand, S., Boufford, J. I., Brown, H., & Chowdhury, M. (2004). Human resources for health: overcoming the crisis. *Lancet, 364,* 1984–1990. doi:10.1016/S0140-6736(04)17482-5

Chhanabhai, P., & Holt, A. (2007). Consumers are ready to accept the transition to online and electronic records if they can be assured of the security measures. *Medscape General Medicine, 9*(1), 8.

Choi, Y. B., Krause, J. S., Seo, H., Capitan, K. E., & Chung, K. (2006). Telemedicine in the USA: Standardization through information management and technical applications. *IEEE Communications Magazine, 44*(4), 41–48. doi:10.1109/MCOM.2006.1632648

Chou, W. L., & Wang, Z. (2009). Regional inequality in China's health care expenditure. *Health Economics, 18*(Suppl 2), S137–S146.

Churchland, P. (1981). Eliminative materialism and the propositional attitudes. *The Journal of Philosophy, 77*(2), 67–90. doi:10.2307/2025900

Chused, A., Kuperman, G. J., & Stetson, P. D. (2008). Alert override reasons: a failure to communicate. *AMIA Annual Symposium Proceedings*, 111-115.

Ciborra, C. (2002). *The labyrinths of information, challenging the wisdom of systems*. Oxford, UK: Oxford University Press.

Cintron, A., Phillips, R., & Hamel, M. B. (2006). The effect of a web-based, patient-directed intervention on knowledge, discussion, and completion of a health care proxy. *Journal of Palliative Medicine*, 9(6), 1320–1328. doi:10.1089/jpm.2006.9.1320

Clark, D. E. (2004). Practical introduction to record linkage for injury research. *Injury Prevention*, 10(3), 186–191. doi:10.1136/ip.2003.004580

Clark, R. A., Inglis, S. C., McAlister, F., Cleland, J. G. F., & Stewart, S. (2007). Telemonitoring or structured telephone support programmes for patients with chronic heart failure: systematic review and metaanalysis. *British Medical Journal*, 334, 942–953. doi:10.1136/bmj.39156.536968.55

Clarke, K., Hartswood, M., Procter, R., Rouncefield, M., & Slack, R. (2003). Trusting the record. *Methods of Information in Medicine*, 42(4), 345–352.

Clement, F. M., Ghali, W. A., Donaldson, C., & Manns, B. J. (2009). The impact of using different costing methods on the results of an economic evaluation of cardiac care: Microcosting vs gross-costing approaches. *Health Economics*, 18, 377–388. doi:10.1002/hec.1363

Cline, R. J. W., & Haynes, K. M. (2001). Consumer health information seeking on the Internet: The state of the art. *Health Education Research*, 16, 671–692. doi:10.1093/her/16.6.671

COACH. (2009). *Guidelines for the protection of health information*. COACH (Canada's Health Informatics Association). Available through http://coachorg.com

Coase, R. H. (1937). The nature of the firm. *Economica, N.S.*, 4(16), 386-405.

Coase, R. H. (1960). The problem of social cost. *The Journal of Law & Economics*, 3, 1–44. doi:10.1086/466560

Coiera, E. (2003). *Guide to Health Informatics* (2nd ed.). New York: Oxford University Press.

Colgan, A. L. (2002). Hazardous health: the World Bank and IMF in Africa: Africa Action position paper. *Africa Action*. Retrieved from http://www.africaaction.org/action/sap0204.htm

Colleran, K. M., Richards, A., & Shafer, K. (2007). Disparities in cardiovascular disease risk and treatment: demographic comparison. *Journal of Investigative Medicine*, 55(8), 415–422. doi:10.2310/6650.2007.00028

Consumers Union. (2009). *U.S health care system fails to protect patients from deadly medical errors: Consumers Union assesses lack of progress ten years after Institute of Medicine found up to 98,000 die from preventable errors*. Issued on May 19, 2009. Retrieved on August 12, 2009 from http://www.consumersunion.org/pub/core_health_care/011324.html

Cook, G., Depares, J., Singh, M., & McElduff, P. (2006). Readmission after hysterectomy and prophylactic low molecular weight heparin: retrospective case-control study. *British Medical Journal*, 332, 819–820. doi:10.1136/bmj.38783.624444.55

Cook, R. I., & McDonald, J. S. R. & Smalhout, R. (1989). Human error in the operating room, Identifying cognitive lock up. *Cognitive Systems Engineering Laboratory Technical Report 89-TR-07*. Columbus, OH: Department of Industrial and Systems Engineering, Ohio State University.

Cook, R. I., Woods, D. D., & Miller, C. (1998). *A tale of two stories: contrasting views of patient safety*. Chicago: National Patient Safety Foundation.

Cooke, F. (2001). Email health support service is already operating in Africa. *British Medical Journal*, 322, 51. doi:10.1136/bmj.322.7277.51

Cooper, C., & Block, R. (2006). *Disaster: Hurricane Katrina and the failure of homeland security*. New York: Times Books/Henry Holt and Company.

Cordella, A. (2001). *Does information technology always lead to lower transaction costs?* Presented at The 9th

European Conference on Information Systems, Bled, Slovenia, June 27-29, 2001.

Cordella, A. (2006). Transaction costs and information systems: Does IT add up? *Journal of Information Technology*, *21*, 195–202. doi:10.1057/palgrave.jit.2000066

Cordella, A., & Simon, K. A. (1997). *The impact of information technology on transaction and coordination cost*. Presented at Conference on Information Systems Research in Scandinavia (IRIS 20), Oslo, Norway, August 9-12, 1997.

Cosgrave, C. M. (2008, February). Preparing your organization for E-discovery, Part 2. *HHN's Most Wired online magazine.* February 13, 2008. Available at: http://www.hhnmostwired.com/hhnmostwired_app/jsp/articledisplay.jsp?dcrpath=HHNMOSTWIRED/Article/data/Winter2008/080213MW_Online_Cosgrave&domain=HHNMOSTWIRED

Cotton, S. R., & Gupta, S. S. (2004). Characteristics of online and offline health information seekers and factors that discriminate between them. *Social Science & Medicine*, *59*, 1795–1806. doi:10.1016/j.socscimed.2004.02.020

Coulter, A., & Ham, C. (2002). *The global challenge of health care rationing*. Buckingham, UK: Open University Press.

Council for International Organizations of Medical Sciences. (2002). *International ethical guidelines for biomedical research involving human subjects*. Retrieved from CIOMS Web Site http://www.cioms.ch/frame_guidelines_nov_2002.htm

Covvey, H. D., Zitner, D., & Bernstein, R. M. (2001, March). Pointing the way: Competencies and curricula in health informatics. *H/IT Advisors*. Available online at http://www.informatics-review.com/thoughts/pointing.html

Covvey, H. D., Zitner, D., Bernstein, R., & MacNeill, J. E. (2001). The development of model curricula for health informatics. In V.L. Patel, R. Rogers, & R. Haux (Eds.), *Medinfo 2001, Proceedings of the 10ᵗʰ World Congress on Medical Informatics*, (pp. 1009-1113). Amsterdam: IOS Press.

Crane, A. B. (2007). Management engineers: A scientific approach to pinpoint a hospital's problems and find common-sense solutions. *Hospitals & Health Networks*, *4*, 50–54.

Crawford, M. B. (2008, Winter). The limits of neuro-talk. *New Atlantis (Washington, D.C.)*, (19): 65–78.

Creighton, H. (1986). *Law every nurse should know* (5th ed.). Philadelphia: W.B. Saunders.

Crosson, J. C., Ohman-Strickland, P. A., Hahn, K. A., DiCicco-Bloom, B., Shaw, E., Orzano, A. J., & Crabtree, B. F. (2007). Electronic medical records and diabetes quality of care: results from a sample of family medicine practices. *Annals of Family Medicine*, *5*(3), 209–215. doi:10.1370/afm.696

Culver, J. D., Gerr, F., & Frumkin, H. (1997). Medical information on the internet: A study of an electronic bulletin board. *Journal of General Internal Medicine*, *12*(8), 466–470. doi:10.1046/j.1525-1497.1997.00084.x

Curry, A., & Knowles, G. (2005). Strategic information management in health care – myth or reality? *Health Services Management Research*, *18*(1), 53–62. doi:10.1258/0951484053051942

Czajka, J. L. (1997, March 20-21) Linking administrative records over time: Lessons from the panels of tax returns. In Record Linkage Techniques - 1997: Proceedings of an International Workshop and Exposition (pp. 49-56), Arlington, VA. Washington, DC: National Academy Press.

Daft, R. L., Lengel, R. H., & Trevino, L. K. (1987). Message Equivocality, Media Selection, and Manager Performance - Implications for Information-Systems. *Management Information Systems Quarterly*, *11*(3), 355–366. doi:10.2307/248682

Dalton, R. (2002). Tribe blasts 'exploitation' of blood samples. *Nature*, *420*, 111. doi:10.1038/420111a

Daly, B. J., Douglas, S. L., Kelley, C. G., O'Toole, E., & Montenegro, H. (2005). Trial of a disease management program to reduce hospital readmissions of the chronically critically ill. *Chest*, *128*(2), 507–517. doi:10.1378/chest.128.2.507

Darley, J. M. (2000). Bystander phenomenon. In Kazden, A. (Ed.), *Encyclopedia of Psychology* (*Vol. 1*, pp. 493–495). Washington, DC: American Psychological Association Press. doi:10.1037/10516-195

Dashtseren, I. F. A., Saligumba, I., & Khoja, S. (2009). Improving maternal health care services by using ICTs for remote consultation and education. In Jordanova, M., & Lievens, F. (Eds.), *Global Telemedicine/e-health Updates: Knowledge Resources* (*Vol. 2*, pp. 505–507). Luxembourg: Luxexpo.

Datar, A., & Sood, N. (2006). Impact of postpartum hospital-stay legislation on newborn length of stay, readmission, and mortality in California. *Pediatrics, 118*, 63–72. doi:10.1542/peds.2005-3044

Davenport, T. H., & Harris, J. C. (2007). *Competing on analytics: The new science of winning*. Boston: Harvard Business School Press.

Davidson, D. (1970). Mental events. In Rosenthal, D. (Ed.), *The nature of mind* (pp. 247–257). New York: Oxford University Press.

Davis, D. A., & Taylor-Vaisey, A. (1997). Translating guidelines into practice. A systematic review of theoretic concepts, practical experience and research evidence in the adoption of clinical practice guidelines. *Canadian Medical Association Journal, 157*, 408–416.

Davis, E., Davis, J., & Hawkins, B. (2008). *Citizen driven design selects among multiple communication channels*. Presented at the 7th International EGOV Conference 2008, September 1-4, 2008, Turin, Italy.

Davis, K., Doty, M. M., Shea, K., & Stremikis, K. (2009). Health information technology and physician perceptions of quality of care and satisfaction. *Health Policy (Amsterdam), 90*(2-3), 239–246. doi:10.1016/j.healthpol.2008.10.002

Day, C. (1997). A checklist for evaluating record linkage software. In: Record Linkage Techniques - 1997: Proceedings of an International Workshop and Exposition (pp. 483-488). Arlington, VA. March 20-21, 1997. Washington, DC: National Academy Press.

Deirdre, H. A., Gloria, G., Sven, C., Lene, M., Martha, L., & Hans-Olof, A. (2003). Mortality and cancer incidence among individuals with Down Syndrome. *Archives of Internal Medicine, 163*(6), 705–711. doi:10.1001/archinte.163.6.705

Del Beccaro, M. A., Jeffries, H. E., Eisenberg, M. A., & Harry, E. D. (2006). Computerized provider order entry implementation: no association with increased mortality rates in an intensive care unit. *Pediatrics, 118*(1), 290–295. doi:10.1542/peds.2006-0367

DeLone, W. H., & McLean, E. R. (1992). Information systems success: the quest for the dependent variable. *Information Systems Research, 3*(1), 60–95. doi:10.1287/isre.3.1.60

DeLone, W. H., & McLean, E. R. (2003). The DeLone and McLean model of information systems success: a ten-year update. *Journal of Management Information Systems, 19*(4), 9–30.

Demartines, N., Mutter, D., Vix, M., Leroy, J., Glatz, D., & Rösel, F. (2000). Assessment of telemedicine in surgical education and patient care. *Annals of Surgery, 231*, 282–291. doi:10.1097/00000658-200002000-00019

Deng, L., Poole, M., Brown, H., & Miller, C. (2005). Learning through telemedicine: Case study of a wound care network. *International Journal of Healthcare Technology and Management, 6*, 4–6. doi:10.1504/IJHTM.2005.007005

Descartes, R. (1994). *A discourse on method, meditations, and principles* (Veitch, J., Ed.). New York: Everyman.

Deshpande, A., & Jadad, A. R. (2006). Web 2.0: Could it help move the health system into the 21st century? *Journal of Men's Health & Gender, 3*(4), 332–336. doi:10.1016/j.jmhg.2006.09.004

Desisto, R. P., & Pring, B. L'heureux, B., & Karamouzis, F. (2006). SaaS delivery challenges on-premise software. *Gartner Research*, 26 September 2006. ID Number: G00143160, see http://www.gartner.com

Devitt, N., & Murphy, J. (2004). A survey of the information management and technology training needs of doctors in an acute NHS trust in the United Kingdom. *Health Information and Libraries Journal, 21*(3), 164–172. doi:10.1111/j.1471-1842.2004.00492.x

Dexter, P. R., Perkins, S. M., Maharry, K. S., Jones, K., & McDonald, C. J. (2004). Inpatient computer-based standing orders vs physician reminders to increase influenza and pneumococcal vaccination rates: a randomized trial. *Journal of the American Medical Association, 292*(19), 2366–2371. doi:10.1001/jama.292.19.2366

Dey, A. K. (2001). Understanding and using context. *Personal and Ubiquitous Computing Journal, 5*(1), 4–7. doi:10.1007/s007790170019

Dey, D., Sarkar, S., & De, P. (1998). A probabilistic decision model for entity matching in heterogeneous databases. *Management Science, 44*(10), 1379–1395. doi:10.1287/mnsc.44.10.1379

Diaz, J. A., Griffith, R. A., Ng, J. J., Reinert, S. E., Friedmann, P. D., & Moulton, A. W. (2002). Patients' use of the Internet for medical information. *Journal of General Internal Medicine, 17*, 180–185. doi:10.1046/j.1525-1497.2002.10603.x

Dick, R. S., Steen, E. B., & Detmer, D. E. (Eds.). (1997). *The computer-based patient record* (Rev. ed.). Washington, DC: National Academy Press.

Dinkelbach, W. (1990). Operational research modeling. In Grochla, E. V. (Ed.), *Handbook of German Business Management* (pp. 1564–1575). Stuttgart, Germany: Poeschel/Springer.

Disintermediation. (2009). In *Wikipedia, the free encyclopedia.* Retrieved on August 12, 2009 from http://en.wikipedia.org/wiki/Disintermediation.

Dixon, N. M., Allen, N., Burgess, T., Kilner, P., & Schweitzer, S. (2005). *CompanyCommand: Unleashing the power of the army profession.* West Point, NY: Center for the Advancement of Leader Development & Organizational Learning.

Dols, V. (2001). Challenges faced by e-health comparative data warehouses. *Journal of Healthcare Information Management, 15*(2), 183–188.

Doughty, K., Lewis, R., & McIntosh, A. (2000). The design of a practical and reliable fall detector for community and institutional telecare. *Journal of Telemedicine and Telecare, 6*(1), (supplement), 150-154.

Dovey, S., Weitzman, M., Fryer, G., Green, L., Yawn, B., Lanier, D., & Phillips, R. (2003). The ecology of medical care for children in the United States. *Pediatrics, 111*, 1024–1029. doi:10.1542/peds.111.5.1024

Downes, S. (2003, May 10). RDF *Site Summary 1.0 Modules: Learning object metadata.* Retrieved January 22, 2008, from Stephen's Web: http://www.downes.ca/xml/RSS_LOM.htm

Dubay, L., Holahan, J., & Cook, A. (2006). The uninsured and the affordability of health insurance coverage. *Health Affairs, 26*(1), w22–w30..doi:10.1377/hlthaff.26.1.w22

Dugdale, D. C., Epstein, R., & Pantilat, S. Z. (1999). Time and the patient-physician relationship. *Journal of General Internal Medicine, 14*(1), 34–40. doi:10.1046/j.1525-1497.1999.00263.x

Dunn, H. L. (1946). Record linkage. *American Journal of Public Health, 36*(12), 1412–1416. doi:10.2105/AJPH.36.12.1412

Durbak, C. K., & Strauss, C. M. (2005). Securing a healthier world. In Dodds, F., & Pippard, T. (Eds.), *Human and environmental security: An agenda for change.* London: Earthscan.

Economist. (2003, April 5). After the outbreak; SARS. *The Economist.* Retrieved from http://www.economist.com/world/asia/displaystory.cfm?story_id=E1_TGRPRNP

Eddrippulige, S., Marasinghe, R. B., Smith, A. C., Fujisawa, Y., Herath, W. B., Jiffry, M. T., & Wootton, R. (2007). Medical students' knowledge and perception of e-health: results of a study in Sri Lanka. *Medinfo, 12*(Pt.2), 1406–1409.

Edirippulige, S., & Wootton, R. (2006). Telehealth and communication. In Conrick, M. (Ed.), *Health informatics, transforming health care with technology* (pp. 266–278). Melbourne, Australia: Thomson.

Edmondson, A. C., Winslow, A. B., Bohmer, R. M. J., & Pisano, G. P. (2003). Learning how and learning what: effects of tacit and codified knowledge on performance improvement following technology adoption. *Decision Sciences, 34*(2), 197–223. doi:10.1111/1540-5915.02316

Eich, H. P., Ohmann, C., & Lang, K. (1997). Decision support in acute abdominal pain using an expert system for different knowledge bases. In *Proceedings of 10th IEEE Symposium on Computer-Based Medical Systems (CBMS'97)*. Available online at http://csdl2.computer.org/persagen/DLAbsToc.jsp?resourcePath=/dl/proceedings/cbms/&toc=http://csdl2.computer.org/comp/proceedings/cbms/1997/7928/00/7928toc.xml&DOI=10.1109/CBMS.1997.596400

Einthoven, W. (1906). Le telecardiogramme. *Archives Internationales de Physiologie, 4*, 132.

Eisenberger, N. I., Lieberman, M. D., & Williams, K. D. (2003). Does rejection hurt? An FMRI study of social exclusion. *Science, 302*, 290–292. doi:10.1126/science.1089134

EKOS Research Associates. (2007, August). *Electronic health information and privacy survey: What Canadians think — 2007.* Submitted to Canada Health Infoway, Health Canada, and the Office of the Privacy Commissioner of Canada, Ottawa.

Elite Care. (2009). Web Site: http://www.elitecare.com.

Ellingsen, G., & Monteiro, E. (2008). The organizing vision of integrated health information systems. *Health Informatics Journal, 14*(3), 223–236. doi:10.1177/1081180X08093333

Emery, J., & Hayflick, S. (2001). The challenge of integrating genetic medicine into primary care. *British Medical Journal, 322*, 1027–1030. doi:10.1136/bmj.322.7293.1027

Emery, J., Lucassen, A., & Murphy, M. (2001). Common hereditary cancers and implications for primary care. *Lancet, 358*, 56–63. doi:10.1016/S0140-6736(00)05257-0

England, R. S. (2007). *The physician's role in rising health care costs: Perspectives on the high and rising cost of physician compensation.* Retrieved March 17, 2008, from http://64.233.167.104/search?q=cache,p9wh2ciGLA8J,www.age-usa.org/docs/Robert_England_Paper_on_MDs_and_Health_Costs.doc%3FPHPSESSID%3D6219db4f036f9151c3b77607dd56eb85+The+Physician%E2%80%99s+Role+in+Rising+Health+Care+Costs&hl=en&ct=clnk&cd=1&gl=us&client=firefox-a

Ericson, P. (2009). *Improving patient care through real-time electronic data capture with digital pen and paper.* Paper Presented at Med-e-Tel 2009. Retrieved August 11, 2009 from http://www.medetel.eu/download/2009/parallel_sessions/presentation/day2/improving_patient_care.pdf

Ernst, J. (2005, September 27). *Embedding FOAF information in RSS.* Retrieved January 22, 2008, from Johannes Ernst's Blog: http://netmesh.info/jernst/Big_Picture/foaf-in-rss.html

Escobar, G., Greene, J., Hulac, P., Kincannon, E., Bischoff, K., & Gardner, M. (2005). Rehospitalization after birth hospitalization: patterns among infants of all gestations. *Archives of Disease in Childhood, 90*, 125–131. doi:10.1136/adc.2003.039974

Eslami, S., Keizer, N. F., & Abu-Hanna, A. (2007). The impact of computerized physician medication order entry in hospitalized patients-A systematic review. *International Journal of Medical Informatics.* doi:.doi:10.1016/j.ijmedinf.2007.10.001

Ethical, Legal and Social Issues [ELSI] Symposium on Biobanking. (2006). *Reexamining the ELSI implications of biobanking: A cross cultural perspective.* Presented at ELSI Symposium, Taiwan, September 17-18, 2006.

European Institute of Medicine. (2003). *Health is wealth: Strategic Vision for European healthcare at the beginning of the 21st century.* Salzburg, Austria: European Academy of Arts and Sciences.

European Ministers of Education. (1999). *Bologna Declaration.* Retrieved from http://www.bologna-bergen2005.no/Docs/00-Main_doc/990719BOLOGNA_DECLARATION.PDF

European Policy Center. (2008). *International Perspective Report.* Retrieved from http://www.epc.eu/en/er.asp?AI=439&LV= 293&PG= ER/EN/detail&TYP=ER&see=y&t=2

Evans, G. (1993). Health and security in the global village. *World Health Forum, 14,* 133–135.

Evans, R. S., Pestotnik, S. L., Classen, D. C., Clemmer, T. P., Weaver, L. K., & Orme, J. F. Jr,... Burke, J. P. (1998). A computer-assisted management program for antibiotics and other antiinfective agents. *The New England Journal of Medicine, 338,* 232–238. doi:10.1056/NEJM199801223380406

Ewusi-Mensah, K. (2003). *Software development failures.* Cambridge, MA: The MIT Press.

Eysenbach, G. (2001). What is e-health? *Journal of Medical Internet Research, 3*(2). Retrieved January 28, 2009, from http://www.jmir.org/2001/2/e20/

Eysenbach, G. (2006). *Home Page.* Retrieved August 10, 2008 from http://yi.com/home/EysenbachGunther/

Eysenbach, G. (2008). Medicine 2.0: Social networking, collaboration, participation, apomediation, and openness. *Journal of Medical Internet Research, 10*(3), e22. <URL: http://www.jmir.org/2008/3/e22/>

Fair, M. E. (1995). An overview of record linkage in Canada. In *Proceedings of the Social Statistics Section of the American Statistical Association,* (pp.25-33), Alexandria, VA.

Fair, M. E. (1997, March 20-21). Record linkage in an information age society. In Proceedings of an International Workshop and Exposition (pp. 427-441), Arlington, VA. Washington, DC: National Academy Press.

Farley, D., Damberg, C., Berry, S., Sorbero, M., Teleki, S., Ricc, K., & Pollock, N. (2005). *Assessment of the National patient Safety Initiative.* Context and Baseline Evaluation Report 1. Rand Corporation, United States. Agency for Healthcare Research and Quality.

Fayyad, U., Piatetsky-Shapiro, G., & Smyth, P. (1996, Fall). From data mining to knowledge discovery in dDatabases. *AI Magazine,* (pp. 37-54). Retrieved on December 17, 2008 from http://borg.cs.bilgi.edu.tr/aimag-kdd-overview-1996-Fayyad.pdf

FederalCommittee on Statistical Methodology. (n.d.). Retrieved January 29, 2009, from http://www.fcsm.gov/working-papers/charlesday.pdf

Feistritzer, N. R., & Keck, B. R. (2000). Perioperative supply chain management. *Seminars for Nurse Managers, 8*(3), 151–157.

Feld, C. S., & Stoddard, D. B. (2004). Getting IT right. *Harvard Business Review, 82*(2), 72–79.

Feldstein, A., Elmer, P. J., Smith, D. H., Herson, M., Orwoll, E., & Chen, C.,... Swain, M. C. (2006). Electronic medical record reminder improves osteoporosis management after a fracture: a randomized, controlled trial. *Journal of the American Geriatrics Society, 54*(3), 450–457. doi:10.1111/j.1532-5415.2005.00618.x

Fellegi, I. P. (1997, March 20-21). Record linkage and public policy – A dynamic evolution. In: Record Linkage Techniques - 1997: Proceedings of an International Workshop and Exposition (pp. 3-12), Arlington, VA. Washington, DC: National Academy Press.

Fellegi, I. P., & Sunter, A. B. (1969). A theory for record linkage. *Journal of the American Statistical Association, 69*(6), 1183–1210. doi:10.2307/2286061

Fenton, A., Meynell, L., & Baylis, F. (2009). Ethical challenges and interpretive difficulties with non-clinical applications of pediatric FMRI. *The American Journal of Bioethics, 9*(1), 3–13. doi:10.1080/15265160802617829

Ferguson, T. (2000). Online patient-helpers and physicians working together: A new partnership for high quality health care. *British Medical Journal, 321,* 1129–1132. doi:10.1136/bmj.321.7269.1129

Ferguson, T. (2002). From patients to end users. *British Medical Journal, 324,* 555–556. doi:10.1136/bmj.324.7337.555

Fernandez, I. (2002). Global battle cry: Health is a right, not a commodity. *Canadian HIV/AIDS Policy & Law Review, 7,* 80–84.

Fiaidhi, J., Mohammed, S., Jaam, J., & Hasnah, A. (2003). A standard framework for search hosting via ontology based query expansion. *Journal of Information Technology, 2*, 66–70.

Figueira, R. M., Alkmim, M. B. M., Ribeiro, A. L. P., Pena, M., & Campos, F. E. (2008). Implementation and maintenance costs for a tele-health system in Brazil. In Jordanova, M., & Lievens, F. (Eds.), *Global telemedicine / e-health updates: Knowledge resources* (*Vol. 1*, pp. 354–359). Luxembourg: Luxexpo.

Finkelstein, M. O., & Levin, B. (1990). *Statistics for lawyers* (pp. 153–155, 489–490). New York: Springer-Verlag.

Fins, J. J., Bernat, J. L., Hirsch, J., Illes, J., Laureys, S., & Murphy, E. R. (2008). Neuroimaging and disorders of consciousness: Envisioning an ethical research agenda. *The American Journal of Bioethics, 8*(9), 3–12. doi:10.1080/15265160802318113

Fisher, E., Goodman, D., Skinner, J., & Bronner, K. (2009). *Health care spending, quality, and outcomes: More isn't always better.* A Dartmouth Atlas Project Topic Brief. Available at: http://www.dartmouthatlas.org/atlases/Spending_Brief_022709.pdf

Flegel, K. (2008). Getting to the electronic medical record. *Canadian Medical Association Journal, 178*(5), 531. doi:10.1503/cmaj.080139

Flood, C. M. (2001). *Profiles of six health care systems: Canada, Australia, the Netherlands, New Zealand, the UK, and the US.* A Report for the Standing Senate Committee on Social Affairs, Science and Technology. Available at: http://www.parl.gc.ca/37/1/parlbus/commbus/senate/Com-e/soci-e/rep-e/volume3ver1-e.pdf

Fogarty, K. (2006). Stitching up health records, privacy compliance lags. *eWeek.* Retrieved August 10, 2009 from http://www.eweek.com/article2/0,1896,1949646,00.asp

Folland, S., Goodman, A. C., & Stano, M. (2004). *The economics of health and health care* (4th ed., pp. 311–313). Upper Saddle River: Pearson Education, Inc.

Fonkwo, P. N. (2008, July). Pricing infectious disease. The economic and health implications of infectious diseases. *EMBO Reports, 9*(Suppl 1), S13–S17. doi:10.1038/embor.2008.110

Ford Motor Company. (2009). *Ford Rouge Factory Tour: History of the Rouge.* Retrieved on August 12, 2009 from http://www.thehenryford.org/rouge/historyofrouge.aspx

Ford, E. W., Menachemi, N., Peterson, L. T., & Huerta, T. R. (2009). Resistance is futile: but it is slowing the pace of EHR adoption nonetheless. *Journal of the American Medical Informatics Association, 16*(3), 274–281. doi:10.1197/jamia.M3042

Fordyce, A. M., Chen, F. M., Doescher, M. P., & Hart, L. G. (2007). 2005 physician supply and distribution in rural areas of the United States. *Final Report # 116.* Seattle, WA: WWAMI Rural Health Research Center, University of Washington.

Frankel, R., Altschuler, A., George, S., Kinsman, J., Jimison, H., Robertson, N. R., & Hsu, J. (2005). Effects of exam-room computing on clinician-patient communication: a longitudinal qualitative study. *Journal of General Internal Medicine, 20*(8), 677–682. doi:10.1111/j.1525-1497.2005.0163.x

Friedman, C. P., Altman, R. B., Kohane, I. S., McCormick, K. A., Miller, P. L., & Ozbolt, J. O. (2004). Training the next generation of informaticians: The impact of "BISTI" and bioinformatics – A report from the American College of Medical Informatics. *Journal of the American Medical Informatics Association, 11*(3), 167–172. doi:10.1197/jamia.M1520

Friedman, T. L. (2005). *The world is flat: A brief history of the twenty-first century.* New York: Farrar, Straus and Giroux.

Fries, J. F. (1994). Can prevention lower health costs by reducing demand? Yes. *Hospitals & Health Networks, 68*(3), 10.

Friman, O., Borga, M., Lundberg, M., Tylén, U., & Knutsson, H. (2002, August). Recognizing emphysema: A neural network approach. In *ICPR'02 Proceedings of*

16th International Conference on Pattern Recognition. Available online at http://www.imt.liu.se/mi/Publications/Publications/PaperInfo/fbltk02.html

Fukuyama, F. (2004). Nation Building 101. *Atlantic Monthly, 293*(1), 159–162. Retrieved from http://www.esiweb.org/pdf/esi_europeanraj_reactions_id_27.pdf.

Furst, I. (2008). *Wait time and delayed care.* Retrieved from http://waittimes.blogspot.com

Galanter, W. L., Polikaitis, A., & DiDomenico, R. J. (2004). A trial of automated safety alerts for inpatient digoxin use with computerized physician order entry. *Journal of the American Medical Informatics Association, 11*(4), 270–277. doi:10.1197/jamia.M1500

Gans, D., Kralewski, J., Hammons, T., & Dowd, B. (2005). Medical groups' adoption of electronic health records and information systems. *Health Affairs (Project Hope), 24*(5), 1323–1333. doi:10.1377/hlthaff.24.5.1323

GAO. (2004). *Emerging infectious diseases: Review of state and federal disease surveillance efforts (GAO 04-877), I-IV* (pp. 1–64). Washington, DC: Government Accounting Office.

Garawi, S., Istepanian, R. S. H., & Abu-Rghef, M. A. (2006). 3G wireless communications for mobile robotic tele-ultrasonography systems. *IEEE Communications Magazine, 44*(4), 91–96. doi:10.1109/MCOM.2006.1632654

Gardner, P., & Schaffner, W. (1993). Immunization of adults. *The New England Journal of Medicine, 328,* 1252–1258. doi:10.1056/NEJM199304293281708

Garg, A. X., Adhikari, N. K., McDonald, H., Rosas-Arellano, M. P., Devereaux, P. J., & Beyene, J. (2005). Effects of computerized clinical decision support systems on practitioner performance and patient outcomes: a systematic review. *Journal of the American Medical Association, 293*(10), 1223–1238. doi:10.1001/jama.293.10.1223

Garrett, L. (1994). *The coming plague: newly emerging diseases in the world out of balance.* New York: Penguin.

Garrett, L. (2001, Winter). Responding to the nightmare of bioterrorism. *The Responsive Community, 12*(1), 88–93.

Garrett, L. (2007, January/February). Midway in the journey. From "marvelous momentum" to healthcare for all: success is possible with the right programs. *Foreign Affairs.* Retrieved from

Garrett, L. (2007, January/February). The challenge of global health. *Foreign Affairs.* Retrieved from http://www.foreignaffairs.org/20070101faessay86103/laurie-garrett/the-challenge-of-global-health.html?mode=print

Garrido, T., Jamieson, L., Zhou, Y., Wiesenthal, A., & Liang, L. (2005). Effect of electronic health records in ambulatory care: retrospective, serial, cross sectional study. *British Medical Journal, 330,* 581–585. doi:10.1136/bmj.330.7491.581

Gaskell, G., Einsiedel, E., Hallman, W., Hornig Priest, S., Jackson, J., & Olsthoorn, J. (2005). Social values and the governance of science. *Science, 310,* 1908–1909. doi:10.1126/science.1119444

Gearon, C.J., Barrett, M., Flatley Brennan, P., Kibbe, D., Lansky, D., Nobel, J., & Sands, D. (2007, June). Perspective on the future of the personal health record. *California Health Care Foundation iHealth Report.*

Gertz, R. (2007). *An electronic health record for Scotland: Legal problems regarding access and maintenance.* Paper Presented at Med-e-Tel 2007. Retrieved August 11, 2009 from http://www.medetel.eu/download/2007/parallel_sessions/presentation/0420/An_Electronic_Health_Record.pdf

Gesler, W. M., & Webb, J. L. (1983). Patterns of mortality in Freetown, Sierra Leone. *Singapore Journal of Tropical Geography, 4*(2), 99–118. doi:10.1111/j.1467-9493.1983.tb00136.x

Getting, B. (2007). *Basic definitions: Web 1.0, Web 2.0, Web 3.0. Practical ecommerce: insights for online merchants.* Retrieved September 14, 2009 from http://www.practicalecommerce.com/articles/464-Basic-Definitions-Web-1-0-Web-2-0-Web-3-0

Girosi, F., Meili, R., & Scoville, R. (2005). *Extrapolating evidence of health information technology and costs.* Santa Monica, CA: RAND Corporation.

Giustini, D. (2007). Web 3.0 and medicine: Make way for the semantic web. *British Medical Journal, 335,* 1273–1274. doi:10.1136/bmj.39428.494236.BE

Glaser, B. (2002). *Efficiency versus sustainability in dynamic decision making, Advances in intertemporal compromising.* New York: Springer-Verlag.

Glaser, J., Henley, D. E., Downing, G., & Brinner, K. M. (2008). Personalized Health Care Workgroup of the American Health Information Community. Advancing personalized health care through health information technology: an update from the American Health Information Community's Personalized Health Care Workgroup. *Journal of the American Medical Informatics Association, 15,* 391–396. doi:10.1197/jamia.M2718

Gluck, C. (2005, July 4). Taiwan's aborigines find new voice. *BBC News.* Retrieved from http://news.bbc.co.uk/2/hi/asia-pacific/4649257.stm

Godfrey, M. M., Nelson, E. C., Wasson, J. H., Mohr, J. J., & Batalden, P. B. (2003). Microsystems in health care, Part 3. Planning patient-centered services. *Joint Commission Journal on Quality and Safety, 29*(4), 159–170.

Goiser, K., & Christen, P. (2006). Towards automated record linkage. In *Proceedings of the Fifth Australasian Conference on Data Mining and Analytics,* (pp. 23-31).

Gokhale, A. A. (1995). Collaborative learning enhances critical thinking. *Journal of Technology Education, 7*(1), 22–30.

Goldacre, M. J., Abisgold, J. D., Yeates, D. G. R., & Seagroatt, V. (2006). Risk of multiple sclerosis after head injury: record linkage study. *Journal of Neurology, Neurosurgery, and Psychiatry, 77,* 351–353. doi:10.1136/jnnp.2005.077693

Goldstein, J. (2006, September 29). Readmissions up, but deaths down. *Philadelphia Inquirer,* (pp. A01).

Goldzweig, C. L., Towfigh, A., Maglione, M., & Shekelle, P. G. (2009). Costs and benefits of health information technology: new trends from the literature. *Health Affairs (Project Hope), 28*(2), w282–w293. doi:10.1377/hlthaff.28.2.w282

Gong, Y. (2009). An Intelligent Medical Incident Reporting System [Kuala Lumpur.]. *HiMSS AsiaPac, 09*(Feb), 24–27.

Gong, Y., Richardson, J., Luan, Z., Alafaireet, P., & Yoo, I. (2008). *Analyzing Voluntary Medical Incident Reports,* AMIA Annual Symposium.

Government of Newfoundland and Labrador. (2007). *New legislation to protect personal health information.* Retrieved February 1, 2009 from http://www.releases.gov.nl.ca/releases/2008/health/0520n03.htm

Government of Ontario. (2004). *Personal Health Information Protection Act (PHIPA), 2004.* Retrieved February 1, 2009 from http://www.e-laws.gov.on.ca/html/statutes/english/elaws_statutes_04p03_e.htm

Grabiner, J. V. (1988). Partisans and critics of a new science: The case of Artificial Intelligence and some historical parallels. In Aspray, W., & Kitcher, P. (Eds.), *History and philosophy of modern Mathematics.* Minneapolis, MN: University of Minnesota Press.

Grad, R. M., Pluye, P., Mercer, J., Marlow, B., Beauchamp, M. E., & Shulha, M. (2008). Impact of research-based synopses delivered as daily e-mail: a prospective observational study. *Journal of the American Medical Informatics Association, 15,* 240–245. doi:10.1197/jamia.M2563

Grady, J. L., & Schlachta-Fairchild, L. (2005). *The 2004 international telenursing role survey executive summary.* Retrieved September 20, 2009 from http://www.mtaloy.edu/tele-health/educational_research/04_05survey/IntlTelenursingSurveyExecSummary.pdf

Grant, R. W., & Middleton, B. (2009). Improving primary care for patients with complex chronic diseases: can health information technology play a role? *Canadian Medical Association Journal, 181,* 17–18. doi:10.1503/cmaj.091101

Gray, C. S. (2006). Clausewitz, history, and the future strategic world. In Murray, W., & Sinnreich, R. H. (Eds.),

The past as prologue: the importance of history to the military profession (pp. 111–132). Cambridge, UK: Cambridge University Press.

Green, L. A., Fryer, G. E., Yawn, B. P., Lanier, D., & Dovey, S. M. (2001). The ecology of medical care revisited. *The New England Journal of Medicine, 344*, 2021–2025. doi:10.1056/NEJM200106283442611

Green, L. V. (2004). Hospital capacity planning and management. In Brandeau, M. L., Sainfort, F., & Pierskalla, W. P. (Eds.), *Operations Research and Health Care: A Handbook of Methods and Applications* (pp. 15–42). Boston: Kluwer Academic Publishers.

Greenough, A., & Graham, H. (2004). Protecting and using patient information: the role of the Caldicott Guardian. *Clinical Medicine, 4*(3), 246–249.

Grime, P. R. (2004). Computerized cognitive behavioural therapy at work: a randomized controlled trial in employees with recent stress-related absenteeism. *Occupational Medicine (Oxford, England), 54*(5), 353–359. doi:10.1093/occmed/kqh077

Grizzle, A. J., Mahmood, M. H., Ko, Y., Murphy, J. E., Armstrong, E. P., & Skrepnek, G. H. (2007). Reasons provided by prescribers when overriding drug-drug interaction alerts. *The American Journal of Managed Care, 13*(10), 573–578.

Gruskin, S., & Tarantola, D. (2002). Health and human rights. In Detels, R., McEwan, J., Beaglehole, R., & Tanaka, H. (Eds.), *The Oxford textbook of public health* (pp. 311–336). New York: Oxford University Press.

Gundim, R. S., & Padilha, R. Q. (2008). Research project: a remote oncology nursing support, hospital Sírio Libanês, São Paulo, Brazil. In Jordanova, M., & Lievens, F. (Eds.), *Global telemedicine / e-health updates: Knowledge resources* (Vol. 1, pp. 406–408). Luxembourg: Luxexpo.

Gyertson, K. (2006). *Doc@Hand - The answer to patient recruitment.* Paper Presented at Med-e-Tel 2006. Retrieved August 11, 2009 from http://www.medetel.eu/download/2006/parallel_sessions/presentation/0406/Doc@Hand_the_answer.pdf

Haddad, A. E., Alkmim, M. B. M., Wen, C. L., & Roschkes, S. (2008). The implementation experience of the National Tele-health Program in Brazil. In Jordanova, M., & Lievens, F. (Eds.), *Global telemedicine / e-health updates: Knowledge resources* (Vol. 1, pp. 365–369). Luxembourg: Luxexpo.

Hadley, F., Graham, K., & Flannery, M. (2005). Workforce management objective A: Assess use, compliance and efficacy: Nursing workload measurement tools. Ottawa, ON: Canadian Nurses Association. Retrieved from http://www.cna-aiic.ca/CNA/documents/pdf/publications/Workload_Measurement_Tools_e.pdf

Hagland, M. (2008). Turning data into improved care: a number of healthcare facilities are working to transform terabytes of raw data into a guide for better care. *Healthcare Informatics, 25*(8), 58–66.

Han, Y. Y., Carcillo, J. A., Venkataraman, S. T., Clark, R. S., Watson, R. S., & Nguyen, T. C. (2005). Unexpected increased mortality after implementation of a commercially sold computerized physician order entry system. *Pediatrics, 116*(6), 1506–1512. doi:10.1542/peds.2005-1287

Hansen, J. I., & Thompson, C. A. (2002). Knowledge management: When people, process, and technology converge. *LIMRA's MarketFacts Quarterly, 21*(2), 14–21.

Hansson, M. (2005). Building on relationships of trust in biobank research. *Journal of Medical Ethics, 31*(7), 415–418. doi:10.1136/jme.2004.009456

Hansson, M., Dillner, J., Bartram, C., Carlson, J., & Helgesson, C. (2006). Should donors be allowed to give broad consent to future biobank research? *The Lancet Oncology, 7*, 266–269. doi:10.1016/S1470-2045(06)70618-0

Hardman, L., & Troncy, R. (2008). *A semantic multimedia web: Create, annotate, present and share your media.* Tutorial presented at the 3rd International Conference on Semantic and Digital Media Technologies. Koblenz-Germany, December 3-5, 2008. Retrieved from http://www.cwi.nl/~media/samt08/

Harpole, L. H., Khorasani, R., Fiskio, J., Kuperman, G. J., & Bates, D. W. (1997). Automated evidence-based critiquing of orders for abdominal radiographs: impact on utilization and appropriateness. *Journal of the American Medical Informatics Association, 4*(6), 511–521.

Harrington, C. (2003, May). Health care costs on the rise. *Journal of Accountancy, 195*(5), 59–63.

Harrsch, M. (2003). RSS: The next killer app for education. *Illinois Computing Educators Computer Update Bulletin for Educators, 4*, 10.

Harry, D., & Kanehe, L. (2005, Winter). Genetic research: Collecting blood to preserve culture? *Cultural Survival Quarterly, 29*(4). Retrieved from http://www.culturalsurvival.org/ourpublications/csq/article/genetic-research-collecting-blood-preserve-culture.

Harry, M. J. (1988). *The nature of six sigma quality.* Schaumburg, IL: Motorola University Press.

Hart, J. T. (1995). Clinical and economical consequences of patients as producers. *Journal of Public Health, 17*, 383–386.

Hartocollis, A. (2008, December 29). Looking to private records for public health goals: Doctors to get cash payments from city to contribute to a vast medical database. *New York Times*, A18 - A19. Retrieved on January 30, 2009 from http://labs.daylife.com/journalist/anemona_hartocollis and http://www.nytimes.com/2008/12/30/nyregion/30records.html

Harville, D. S., & Moore, R. A. (1999). Determining record linkage parameters using an iterative logistic regression approach. In *Proceedings of the Survey Research Methods Section of the American Statistical Association* (pp. 689-694), Alexandria, VA.

Hauser, J. R., & Clausing, D. (1988). The house of quality. *Harvard Business Review, 3*, 63–73.

Haux, R. (2006). Health information systems – past, present, and future. *International Journal of Medical Informatics, 75*(3), 268–281. doi:10.1016/j.ijmedinf.2005.08.002

Havenstein, H. (2005, October). Regional health exchanges slowly start to share data. *Computerworld.* Retrieved from http://www.computerworld.com

Hawn, C. (2009). Take two aspirin and tweet me in the morning: How Twitter, Facebook and other social media are reshaping medicine. *Health Affairs, 28*(2), 361–368. doi:10.1377/hlthaff.28.2.361

Hayrinen, K., Saranto, K., & Nykanen, P. (2008). Definition, structure, use and impacts of electronic health records: a review of the research literature. *International Journal of Medical Informatics, 77*(5), 291–304. doi:10.1016/j.ijmedinf.2007.09.001

Health Canada. (January 2001). *Toward electronic health records.* Ottawa: Office of Health and the Information Highway, Health Canada.

Health Care in Urban and Rural Areas. Combined Years 2004-2006. (2006). *Update of Content in MEPS Chartbook No. 13.* Rockville, MD: Agency for Health Care Policy and Research. Retrieved from http://www.ahrq.gov/data/meps/chbook13up.htm

Health informatics (2009, November 13). In *Wikipedia, the free encyclopedia.* Retrieved November 22, 2009 from http://en.wikipedia.org/wiki/Health_informatics

Health Information and Management Systems Society (HIMSS). (2008). E-Health SIG White Paper, *Health Information and Management Systems Society News, 13* (7: 12). Retrieved December 16, 2008 from www.himss.org/content/files/e-health_whitepaper.pdf

Health Solutions, V. I. G. I. L. *Inc.* (2009). Retrieved from http://www.vigil.com

Healthcare Information and Management Systems Society (HIMSS). (2007). *Management engineering and process improvement.* Retrieved March 28, 2008 from http://www.himss.org/ASP/topics_managementProcess.asp

Hebbar, S., Pasupathy, K., & Williamson, M. (2008). Determinants of patient satisfaction. In *Proceedings of the 3rd INFORMS Workshop on Data Mining and Health Informatics,* Washington, DC.

Helal, S., Mann, W., El-Zabadani, H., King, J., Kaddoura, Y., & Jansen, E. (2005). The Gator Tech Smart House: A programmable pervasive space. *IEEE Computer Magazine, 38*(3), 50–60.

Hempel, P. S. (2004). Preparing the HR profession for technology and information work. *Human Resource Management, 43*(2/3), 163–177. doi:10.1002/hrm.20013

Hendy, J., Reeves, B. C., Fulop, N., Hutchings, A., & Masseria, C. (2005). Challenges to implementing the national programme for information technology (NPfIT): a qualitative study. *British Medical Journal, 331*, 331–336. doi:10.1136/bmj.331.7512.331

Hersh, W. (2002). Medical informatics – improving health care through information. *Journal of the American Medical Association, 288*, 1955–1958. doi:10.1001/jama.288.16.1955

Hersh, W. (2006). Who are the informaticians? What we know and should know. *Journal of the American Medical Informatics Association, 13*, 166–170. doi:10.1197/jamia.M1912

Hersh, W. (2008). Health and biomedical informatics: Opportunities and challenges for a twenty-first century profession and its education. In Geissbuhler, A., & Kulikowski, C. (Eds.), *IMIA Yearbook of Medical Informatics 2008* (pp. 138–145). Stuttgart, Germany: Schattauer.

Hersh, W. (2008). *Information retrieval: A health and biomedical perspective* (3rd ed.). New York: Springer.

Hershey, J., Pierskalla, W., & Wandel, S. (1981). Nurse staffing management. In Boldy, D. (Ed.), *Operational research applied to health services* (pp. 189–220). London: Croom-Helm Ltd.

Herzog, T. N., & Eilerman, W. J. (1997). Linking records on federal housing administration single-family mortgages. In Record Linkage Techniques - 1997: Proceedings of an International Workshop and Exposition (pp. 279-291). Arlington, VA. March 20-21, 1997. Washington, DC: National Academy Press.

Herzog, T. N., Scheuren, F. J., & Winkler, W. E. (2007). *Data quality and record linkage techniques.* Washington, DC: Springer.

Hetzel, B. (1993). *Making software measurement work: Building an effective measurement program.* Boston: QED Publishing Group.

Heymann, D. (2003). Evolving infectious disease threats to national and global security. In Chen, L., Leaning, J., Narasimhan, V., & de Waal, A. (Eds.), *Global health challenges for human security.* Cambridge, MA: Harvard University Press.

Hillestad, R., Bigelow, J. H., Chaudhry, B., Dreyer, P., Greenberg, M. D., & Meili, R. C. (2008). *Identity crisis: An examination of the costs and benefits of a unique patient identifier for the U.S. health care system.* Santa Monica, CA: RAND Corporation.

Hinman, A. R., & Davidson, A. J. (2009). Linking children's health information systems: Clinical care, public health, emergency medical systems, and schools. *Pediatrics, 123*, S67–S73. doi:10.1542/peds.2008-1755D

HIPAA. (1996, August). *Public Law 104-191: Health Insurance Portability and Accountability Act of 1996.* Available in brief at Administration Simplification, Department of Health and Human Services at http://aspe.hhs.gov/admnsimp/pl104191.htm. Full content available at http://frwebgate.access.gpo.gov/cgi-bin/getdoc.cgi?dbname=104_cong_public_laws&docid=f:publ191.104.pdf

Hirsh, T., Forlizzi, J., Hyder, E., Goetz, J., Kurtz, C., & Stroback, J. (2000). The ELDer project: Social, emotional, and environmental factors in the design of eldercare technologies. In *Proceedings of the ACM Conference on Universal Usability (CUU 2000)*, (pp. 72-79). Arlington, VA: ACM Press.

Ho, K. (2008). Technology enabled knowledge translation: Using information and communication technologies to accelerate evidence based health practices. In: A.W. Kushniruk, & E.M. Borycki, (Ed.) Human, Social, and Organizational Aspects of Health Information Systems, (pp. pp. 301-313). Hershey, PA: Medical Information Science Reference.

Ho, P. M., Peterson, P. N., & Masoudi, F. A. (2008). Evaluating the evidence: Is there a hierarchy. *Circulation, 118*(16), 1675–1684. doi:10.1161/CIRCULATIONAHA.107.721357

Hodgins, D., Bertsch, A., Post, N., Frischholz, M., Volckaerts, B., & Spensley, J. (2008). Healthy aims: Developing new medical implants and diagnostic equipment. *IEEE Pervasive Computing Magazine, 7*(1), 14–21. doi:10.1109/MPRV.2008.8

Hofmann-Wellenhof, R., Salmhofer, W., Binder, B., Okcu, A., Kerl, H., & Soyer, H. (2006). Feasibility and acceptance of telemedicine for wound care in patients with chronic leg ulcers. *Journal of Telemedicine and Telecare, 12*(1), 15–17. doi:10.1258/135763306777978407

Holland, S. (2001). Beyond the embryo: A feminist appraisal of the embryonic stem cell debate. In Holland, S., Lebacqz, K., & Zoloth, L. (Eds.), *The human embryonic stem cell debate* (pp. 73–86). Cambridge, MA: The MIT Press.

Home Automation. (2009). In *Wikipedia, the free encyclopedia*. Retrieved on January 30, 2009 from Wikipedia at http://en.wikipedia.org/wiki/Home_automation_for_the_elderly_and_disabled

Honeywell HomMed. (2007). *MedPartner Medication Reminder*. Retrieved August 11, 2009 from http://www.hommed.com/Products/MedPartner.asp

Honoré, R. (2009). *Survival: How a culture of preparedness can save you and your family from disaster*. New York: Simon and Schuster.

Hopp, F., Whitten, P., Subramanian, U., Woodbridge, P., Mackert, M., & Lowery, J. (2006). Perspectives from the Veterans Health Administration about opportunities and barriers in telemedicine. *Journal of Telemedicine and Telecare, 12*, 404–409. doi:10.1258/135763306779378717

Horgas, A., & Abowd, G. (2004). The impact of technology on living environments for older adults. In Pew, R. W., & Van Hemel, S. B. (Eds.), *Technology for adaptive aging* (pp. 230–252). Washington, DC: National Academy Press.

Houston, T. K., Sands, D. Z., Jenckes, M. W., & Ford, D. E. (2004). Experiences of patients who were early adopters of electronic communication with their physician: satisfaction, benefits, and concerns. *The American Journal of Managed Care, 10*, 601–608.

Hsieh, T. C., Kuperman, G. J., Jaggi, T., Hojnowski-Diaz, P., Fiskio, J., & Williams, D. H. (2004). Characteristics and consequences of drug allergy alert overrides in a computerized physician order entry system. *Journal of the American Medical Informatics Association, 11*(6), 482–491. doi:10.1197/jamia.M1556

Hsu, J., Huang, J., Fung, V., Robertson, N., Jimison, H., & Frankel, R. (2005). Health information technology and physician-patient interactions: impact of computers on communication during outpatient primary care visits. *Journal of the American Medical Informatics Association, 12*(4), 474–480. doi:10.1197/jamia.M1741

Hubbard, T. (2002). Biological information: making it accessible and integrated (and trying to make sense of it). *Bioinformatics (Oxford, England), 18*(Suppl. 2), S140.

Hudson, H. (2005). Rural telemedicine: Lessons from Alaska for developing regions. *Telemedicine and e-Health, 11*(4), 460 -467.

Humphreys, J. S. (1990). Super-clinics or a country practice? Contrasts in rural life and health service provision in northern NSW. In D.J. Walmsley (Ed.), Change and adjustment in Northern NSW, (pp. 73-84). Armidale: University of New England.

Hussain, I. (2001). Impact of globalization on poverty in Pakistan. *Mahbub ul Haq Human. Developmental Review, 1*, 23–31. Retrieved from http://www.sbp.org.pk/about/speech/2001/ Impact_of_globalization_Mahboobul_Haq.pdf.

Iakovidis, I. (1998). From electronic medical record to personal health records: present situation and trends in European Union in the area of electronic healthcare records. *Studies in health technology and informatics, 52*(Pt 1: suppl), 18-22.

Ichikawa, K., Date, S., Kaishima, T., & Shimojo, S. (2005). A framework supporting the development of a Grid portal for analysis based on ROI. *Methods of Information in Medicine, 44*(2), 265–269.

Imwinkelried, E. J. (2002). *Evidentiary foundations* (5th ed.). Newark, NJ: LexisNexis.

Indigenous Peoples Council on Biocolonialism. (2005, April 13). *Indigenous peoples oppose National Geographic & IBM genetic research project that seeks indigenous peoples' DNA*. Retrieved from http://www.ipcb.org/issues/human_genetics/htmls/geno_pr.html

Indigenous Peoples Council on Biocolonialism. (2005, April 13). *IPCB action alert to oppose the genographic project*. Retrieved from http://www.ipcb.org/issues/human_genetics/htmls/action_geno.html

Indigenous Peoples Council on Biocolonialism. (2006, May 15). *Collective statement of indigenous organizations opposing "The Genographic Project"Agenda Item 4*. Retrieved from http://www.ipcb.org/issues/human_genetics/htmls/unpf5_collstate.html

Institute for Healthcare Communication. (2008). Retrieved August 11, 2009, from http://www.healthcarecomm.org/index.php?sec=courses&sub=faculty&course=3

Institute of Medicine. (1999). *To err Is human: Building a safer health system*. L. T. Kohn, J. M. Corrigan, & M. S. Donaldson (Eds). Washington, DC: National Academy Press. Retrieved on August 12, 2009 from http://www.iom.edu/Object.File/Master/4/117/ToErr-8pager.pdf

Institute of Medicine. (2001). *Crossing the quality chasm: A new health system for the 21st Century*. Washington, DC: National Academy Press.

International Indian Treaty Council. (9 March 2008). *The UN declaration on the rights of indigenous peoples, treaties and the right to free, prior, and informed consent: The framework for a new mechanism for reparations, restitution and redress*. Retrieved from http://www.treatycouncil.org/PDFs/FPIC%20Treaties%20and%20the%20UN%20Dec%20UNPFII%203508.pdf

International Work Group for Indigenous Affairs. (2007, July). *Indigenous peoples in Argentina*. Retrieved from http://www.iwgia.org/sw17294.asp

Jabbi, M., Keysers, C., Singer, T., & Stephan, K. E. (in press). Response to "Voodoo Correlations in Social Neuroscience" by Vul et al. – summary information for the press. Available at http://www.bcn-nic.nl/replyVul.pdf

Jacklin, P., Roberts, J., Wallace, P., Haines, A., Harrison, R., & Barber, J. (2003). The virtual outreach project group: economic evaluation of joint teleconsultations for patients referred by their general practitioner for a specialist opinion. *British Medical Journal, 327*, 84. doi:10.1136/bmj.327.7406.84

Jacobi, C., Morris, L., Beckers, C., Bronisch-Holtze, J., Winter, J., Winzelberg, A. J., & Taylor, C. B. (2007). Maintenance of internet-based prevention: a randomized controlled trial. *The International Journal of Eating Disorders, 40*(2), 114–119. doi:10.1002/eat.20344

Jain, S. H. (2009). Practicing medicine in the age of Facebook. *The New England Journal of Medicine, 361*(7), 649–651. doi:10.1056/NEJMp0901277

Jakubowski, E., & Busse, R. (1998). *European Parliament Report: Healthcare systems in the EU: A comparative study*. Luxembourg: European Parliament. Retrieved from http://www.europarl.europa.eu/workingpapers/saco/pdf/101_en.pdf

James, B.C. (1989). Improving quality can reduce costs. *QA Review: quality assurance and news, 1*(1), 4.

Jamkhed. (2009). *Jamkhed: Comprehensive rural health project*. Retrieved on January 30, 2009 from http://www.jamkhed.org.

Jaro, M. A. (1989). Advances in record-linkage methodology as applied to matching the 1985 census of Tampa, Florida. *Journal of the American Statistical Society, 84*(406), 414–420.

Jarvis, C. W. (2009). Investigate funding alternatives to support successful EHR implementation. *The Journal of Medical Practice Management, 24*(6), 335–338.

Jha, A. K., Doolan, D., Grandt, D., Scott, T., & Bates, D. W. (2008). The use of health information technology in seven nations. *International Journal of Medical Informatics, 77*(12), 848–854. doi:10.1016/j.ijmedinf.2008.06.007

Jha, A. K., Ferris, T. G., Donelan, K., DesRoches, C., Shields, A., Rosenbaum, S., & Blumenthal, D. (2006). How common are electronic health records in the United States? A summary of the evidence. *Health Affairs, 25*(6), w496–w507. doi:10.1377/hlthaff.25.w496

Jiang, H. J., Andrews, R., Stryer, D., & Friedman, B. (2005). Racial/ethnic disparities in potentially preventable readmissions: The case of diabetes. *American Journal of Public Health*, 95, 1561–1567. doi:10.2105/AJPH.2004.044222

Jiang, Z., Sarkar, S., De, P., & Dey, D. (2007). A framework for reconciling attribute values from multiple data sources. *Management Science*, 53(12), 1946–1963. doi:10.1287/mnsc.1070.0745

Johns, R. J., & Blum, B. I. (1979). The use of clinical information systems to control cost as well as to improve care. *Transactions of the American Clinical and Climatological Association*, 90, 140–152.

Johnson, A. C., & Warkentin, M. (2008). Information privacy compliance in the healthcare industry. *Information Management & Computer Security*, 16(1), 5–19. doi:10.1108/09685220810862715

Joint Commission on Accreditation of Healthcare Organizations (JCAHO). (2005). *2004 General public quality report user guide*. Retrieved from http://www.jointcommission.org.

Joint Commission on Accreditation of Healthcare Organizations (JCAHO). (2009). *Federal deemed status and state recognition: Facts about federal deemed status and state recognition*. Retrieved on October 12, 2009 from http://www.jointcommission.org/StateFederal/deemed_status.htm

Jordanova, M. (2005). e-health: From space medicine to civil healthcare. In *Proceedings of 2nd International Conference on Recent Advances in Space Technologies*, Turkey, (pp. 739-743).

Jordanova, M. (2009). Telemedicine or e-health. In M. Jordanova, L. Vasileva, M. Rasheva & R. Bojinova. Telepsychology as a part of e-health. (pp. 7-36). Bulgaria: Academic Publishing House "M. Drinov."

Jordanova, M., Vasileva, L., Rasheva, M., & Bojinova, R. (2008). Tele-psychology: Users' demands. In Jordanova, M., & Lievens, F. (Eds.), *Global telemedicine / e-health updates: Knowledge resources* (*Vol. 1*, pp. 266–269). Luxembourg: Luxexpo.

Joshi, S. (2008). HIPPA, HIPPA, Hooray? Current challenges and initiatives in health informatics in the United States. *Medical Informatics Insights, 1*, 45-56. Retrieved from http://www.la-press.com/hipaa-hipaa-hooray-current-challenges-and-initiatives-in-health-i-a1198

Joshipura, M. K. (2008). Trauma care in India: current scenario. *World Journal of Surgery*, 32(8), 1613–1617. doi:10.1007/s00268-008-9634-5

Judd, F., & Humphreys, J. (2001). Mental health issues for rural and remote Australia. *The Australian Journal of Rural Health*, 6(5), 254–258. doi:10.1046/j.1440-1584.2001.00417.x

Juengst, E. (2003). Community engagement in genetic research: The "slow code" of research ethics? In Knopper, B. (Ed.), *Populations and genetics: Legal and socioethical perspectives* (p. 182). Leiden, The Netherlands: Brill Academic Publishers.

Justo, R., Smith, A. C., Williams, M., Westhuyzen, J. V., & der,., Murray, J., Sciuto, G., & Wootton, R. (2004). Paediatric telecardiology services in Queensland: a review of three years' experience. *Journal of Telemedicine and Telecare*, 10(Suppl 1), 57–60. doi:10.1258/1357633042614258

Kachhal, S. K., & Schramm, W. R. (1995). Changing roles of IEs in healthcare. *IIE Solutions*, 27(9), 26–30.

Kaiser Family Foundation. (2008). *The uninsured: A primer. Key facts about Americans without health insurance*. Washington, DC: Kaiser Family Foundation. Retrieved from http://www.kff.org/uninsured/upload/7451-04.pdf

Kalawsky, R.S., Nee, S.P., Holmes, I., & Coveney, P.V. (2005) A grid-enabled lightweight computational steering client: a.NET PDA implementation. *Philosophical transactions. Series A, Mathematical, physical, and engineering sciences, 363*(1833), 1885-1894.

Kalawsky, R.S., O'Brien, J. & Coveney, P.V. (2005) Improving scientists' interaction with complex computational-visualization environments based on a distributed grid infrastructure. *Philosophical transactions. Series*

A, Mathematical, physical, and engineering sciences, 363(1833), 1867-1884.

Kamel Boulos, M. N., & Wheeler, S. (2007). The emerging Web 2.0 social software: an enabling suite of sociable technologies in health and health care education. *Health Information and Libraries Journal, 24*(1), 2–23. doi:10.1111/j.1471-1842.2007.00701.x

Kane, R. (Ed.). (2002). *The Oxford handbook on free will.* New York: Oxford University Press.

Kant, I. (2008). *The groundwork for the metaphysics of morals.* USA: Wilder Publications.

Kaplan, R. S., & Norton, D. P. (1992). The balanced scorecard – measures that drive performance. *Harvard Business Review, 70*, 71–79.

Kaplan, R. S., & Norton, D. P. (1996). *The balanced scorecard-translating strategy into action.* Boston: Harvard Business School Press.

Kaplan, R. S., & Norton, D. P. (1996, Fall). Linking the balanced scorecard to strategy. *California Management Review, 4*, 53–79.

Karasawas, K. A., Baldock, R., & Burger, A. (2004). Bioinformaticsatics integration and agent technology. *Journal of Biomedical Informatics, 37*(3), 205–219. doi:10.1016/j.jbi.2004.04.003

Kasimov, O., Karchenova, E., & Tuchin, V. (2009). Role of nurses in different directions of the telemedicine activity in Saratov Railway Clinic. In Jordanova, M., & Lievens, F. (Eds.), *Global Telemedicine/e-health Updates: Knowledge Resources* (*Vol. 2*, pp. 207–209). Luxembourg: Luxexpo.

Kaushal, R., Jha, A. K., Franz, C., Glaser, J., Shetty, K. D., & Jaggi, T. (2006). Return on investment for a computerized physician order entry system. *Journal of the American Medical Informatics Association, 13*(3), 261–266. doi:10.1197/jamia.M1984

Keller, I., Van der Hoog, W., & Stappers, P. J. (2004). Gust of Me: Reconnecting mother and son. *IEEE Pervasive Computing Magazine, 3*(1), 22–28. doi:10.1109/MPRV.2004.1269125

Kemper, A. R., Kennedy, E. J., Dechert, R. E., & Saint, S. (2005). Hospital readmission for bronchiolitis. *Clinical Pediatrics, 44*, 509–513. doi:10.1177/000992280504400607

Kemper, A. R., Uren, R. L., & Clark, S. J. (2006). Adoption of electronic health records in primary care pediatric practices. *Pediatrics, 118*(1), e20–e24. doi:10.1542/peds.2005-3000

Kersten, H. B., Thompson, E. D., & Frohna, J. G. (2008). The use of evidence-based medicine in pediatrics: Past, present, and future. *Current Opinion in Pediatrics, 20*(3), 326–331. doi:10.1097/MOP.0b013e3283005843

Khatri, N. (2006a). Building HR capability in health care organizations. *Health Care Management Review, 31*(1), 45–54.

Khatri, N. (2006b). Building IT capability in health care organizations. *Health Services Management Research, 19*(2), 73–79. doi:10.1258/095148406776829095

Kim, D., Labkoff, S., & Holliday, S. H. (2008). Opportunities for electronic health record data to support business functions in the pharmaceutical industry—A case study from Pfizer, Inc. *Journal of the American Medical Informatics Association, 15*(5), 581–584. doi:10.1197/jamia.M2605

Kisely, S., Smith, M., Lawrence, D., & Maaten, S. (2005). Mortality in individuals who have had psychiatric treatment - Population-based study in Nova Scotia. *The British Journal of Psychiatry, 18*(6), 552–558. doi:10.1192/bjp.187.6.552

Kladiashvili, E. (in press). *Grid Technologies for eHealth: Applications for Telemedicine Services and Delivery.* Hershey, PA. *IGI Press.*

Klein, H. A., & Isaacson, J. J. (2003). Making medication instructions usable. *Ergonomics in Design, 11*, 7–11.

Klein, H. A., & Meininger, A. R. (2004). Self-management of medication and diabetes, cognitive control. *IEEE Transactions on Systems, Man, and Cybernetics. Part A, Systems and Humans, 34*(6), 718–725. doi:10.1109/TSMCA.2004.836791

Kohn, L. T., Corrigan, J. M., & Donaldson, M. S. (Eds.). (2000). *To err is human: building a safer health system. Committee on Quality of Health Care in America, Institute of Medicine*. Washington, DC: National Academy Press.

Koppel, R., & Kreda, D. (2009). Health care information technology vendors' "hold harmless" clause: Implications for patients and clinicians. *Journal of the American Medical Association, 301*, 1276–1278. doi:10.1001/jama.2009.398

Koppel, R., Metlay, J. P., Cohen, A., Abaluck, B., Localio, A. R., Kimmel, S. E., & Strom, B. L. (2005). Role of computerized physician order entry systems in facilitating medication errors. *Journal of the American Medical Association, 293*(10), 1197–1203. doi:10.1001/jama.293.10.1197

Koppel, R., Wetterneck, T., Telles, J. L., & Karsh, B. T. (2008). Workarounds to barcode medication administration systems: their occurrences, causes, and threats to patient safety. *Journal of the American Medical Informatics Association, 15*(4), 408–423. doi:10.1197/jamia.M2616

Korb, H. (2008). Telemonitoring – the intelligent solution for chronic patient care. In Jordanova, M., & Lievens, F. (Eds.), *Electronic Proceedings Med-e-Tel: The international educational and networking forum for e-health, telemedicine and health ICT* (pp. 9–15). Luxembourg: Luxexpo.

Korukonda, A. R., & Korukonda, S. (2006). From buzzword to business strategy. *International Journal of Electronic Healthcare, 2*(4), 362–377.

Krulwich, B. (1996). The BargainFinder agent: Comparison price shopping on the Internet. In Williams, J. (Ed.), *Bots, and Other Internet Beasties*. Indianapolis, IN: Macmillan Computer Publishing.

Kulkarni, R., & Nathanson, L. A. (2005). Medical informatics in medicine. *E-Medicine*. Retrieved from http://www.emedicine.com/emerg/topic879.htm

Kun, L. G. (2001). Telehealth and the global health network in the 21st century: From homecare to public health informatics. *Computer Methods and Programs in Biomedicine, 64*(3), 155–167. doi:10.1016/S0169-2607(00)00135-8

Kuo, G. M., Mullen, P. D., McQueen, A., Swank, P. R., & Rogers, J. C. (2007). Cross-sectional comparison of electronic and paper medical records on medication counseling in primary care clinics: a Southern Primary-Care Urban Research Network (SPUR-Net) study. *Journal of the American Board of Family Medicine, 20*(2), 164–173. doi:10.3122/jabfm.2007.02.060113

Kurstedt, H. A. (2000). *Management systems theory, applications, and design*. Blacksburg, VA: Manuscript, Virginia Tech.

Kurzweil, R. (2005). *The singularity is near: When humans transcend biology*. New York: Penguin.

Kwankam, Y. (2008). *e-health and health system development: WHO priority areas*. Paper presented at 11th STI Symposium, April 22, 2008, Basel, Switzerland. Retrieved September 18, 2009 from http://www.sti.ch/fileadmin/user_upload/Bilder/Symposium/Yunkap_Kwankam__11_STI_Sysmposium_2008_WHO_proirity_areas.pdf

Kyle, R., & Murray, B. (2008). *Clinical simulation: Operations, engineering, and management*. Amsterdam: Elsevier Press.

Lacher, D., Nelson, E., Bylsma, W., & Spena, R. (2000). Computer use needs of internists: A survey of members of the American College of Physicians-American Society of Internal Medicine. In *Proceedings of the AMIA Symposium*, (pp. 453-456). Philadelphia, PA: American College of Physicians-American Society of Internal Medicine.

Landauer, T. K. (1995). *The trouble with computers: usefulness, usability, and productivity*. Cambridge, MA: MIT Press.

Lanfranco, A. R., Castellanos, A. E., Desai, J. P., & Meyers, W. C. (2004). Robotic surgery: A current perspective. *Annals of Surgery, 239*(1), 14–21. doi:10.1097/01.sla.0000103020.19595.7d

Langley, G. L., Nolan, K. M., Nolan, T. W., Norman, C. L., & Provost, L. P. (2009). *The improvement guide: A practical approach to enhancing organizational performance* (2nd edition). San Francisco: Jossey-Bass, A Wiley Imprint. Retrieved August 24, 2009 from http://www.ihi.org/IHI/Topics/Improvement/ImprovementMethods/HowToImprove/

Lapane, K. L., Waring, M. E., Schneider, K. L., Dube, C., & Quilliam, B. J. (2008). A mixed method study of the merits of e-prescribing drug alerts in primary care. *Journal of General Internal Medicine, 23*(4), 442–446. doi:10.1007/s11606-008-0505-4

Lattimer, V., Brailsford, S., Turnbull, J., Tarnaras, P., Smith, H., & George, S. (2004). Reviewing emergency care systems. I: Insights from system dynamics modeling. *Emergency Medicine Journal, 21,* 685–691. doi:10.1136/emj.2002.003673

Leach, A. J. (1999). Otitis media in Australian Aboriginal children: An overview. *International Journal of Otorhinolaryngology, 49*(Suppl 1), S173–S178. doi:10.1016/S0165-5876(99)00156-1

Leape, L. L., & Berwick, D. M. (2005). Five years after *To Err Is Human*: What have we learned? *Journal of the American Medical Association, 293*(19), 2384–2390. doi:10.1001/jama.293.19.2384

Lee, J. W., & McKibbin, W. J. (2003). Globalization and disease: The case of SARS. *The Brookings Institution.* Retrieved from http://www.brookings.edu/dybdocroot/views/papers/mckibbin/20030520.pdf

Lee, M. Y., Albright, S. A., Alkasab, T., Damassa, D. A., Wang, P. J., & Eaton, E. K. (2003). Tufts Health Sciences Database: lessons, issues, and opportunities. *Academic Medicine, 78,* 254–264.

Leeder, S., Raymond, S., Greenberg, H., Liu, H., & Esson, K. (2004). A race against time: The challenge of cardiovascular disease in developing countries. *The Earth Institute at Columbia University, May 2004.* Retrieved from http://www.earthinstitute.columbia.edu/news/2004/images/raceagainsttime_FINAL_051104.pdf

Lehmann, H. P., & Shortliffe, E. H. (2003). Information technology support of clinical research: An introduction. *Information Systems Frontiers, 5*(4), 415–419. doi:10.1023/B:ISFI.0000005654.91278.5a

Leira, E. C., Hess, D. C., Torner, J. C., & Adams, H. P. Jr. (2008). Rural-urban differences in acute stroke management practices: a modifiable disparity. *Archives of Neurology, 65*(7), 887–891. doi:10.1001/archneur.65.7.887

Lemaire, E. D., Boudrias, Y., & Greene, G. (2001). Low-bandwidth Internet-based videoconferencing for physical rehabilitation consultations. *Journal of Telemedicine and Telecare, 7*(2), 82–89. doi:10.1258/1357633011936200

Lester, W. T., Grant, R. W., Barnett, G. O., & Chueh, H. C. (2006). Randomized controlled trial of an informatics-based intervention to increase statin prescription for secondary prevention of coronary disease. *Journal of General Internal Medicine, 21*(1), 22–29. doi:10.1111/j.1525-1497.2005.00268.x

Lewis, W. W. (2006). *The power of productivity: Wealth, poverty, and the threat to global stability.* Chicago, IL: Chicago University Press.

Li, L. C., Grimshaw, J. M., Nielson, C., Judd, M., Coyte, P. C., & Graham, I. D. (2009). Use of communities of practice in business and health care sectors: a systematic review. *Implementation Science; IS, 17*(4), 27. doi:10.1186/1748-5908-4-27

Li, M., & Eastman, C. J. (2003). Working with funding agencies in the delivery of healthcare in the Asia Pacific region. *The Medical Journal of Australia, 178,* 13–16.

Lievens, F., & Jordanova, M. (2004). *An approach to the global vision about telemedicine/e-health.* Keynote presentation at Med-e-Tel, Luxembourg, G. D. of Luxembourg. Retrieved December 20, 2008 from http://www.medetel.lu/index.php?rub=educational_program&page=opening_session_2004

Lievens, F., & Jordanova, M. (2007). Telemedicine and medical informatics: The global approach. *Proceedings of World Academy of Science. Engineering and Technology, 31,* 258–262.

Lindberg, D. A. B., & Humphreys, B. L. (1998). Medicine and health on the Internet: The good, the bad, and the ugly. *Journal of the American Medical Association, 280,* 1303–1304. doi:10.1001/jama.280.15.1303

Linder, J. A., Ma, J., Bates, D. W., Middleton, B., & Stafford, R. S. (2007). Electronic health record use and the quality of ambulatory care in the United States. *Archives of Internal Medicine, 167*(13), 1400–1405. doi:10.1001/archinte.167.13.1400

Lipnack, J., Stamps, J., Prevou, M., & Hannah, M. (2010). *Teams of Leaders Handbook.* Leavenworth, KS: Battle Command Knowledge System Combined Arms Center - Knowledge.

Liu, H. (2009, August). *In the name of "UK Biobank Model"—The myth of the governance of Taiwan Biobank.* Powerpoint presented at European Society of Philosophy and Medicine, Helsinki, Finland.

Liu, S., Heaman, M., Joseph, K.S., Liston, R.M., Huang, L., Sauve, R., & Kramer, M.S. (for the Maternal Health Study Group of the Canadian Perinatal Surveillance System). (2005). Risk of maternal postpartum readmission associated with mode of delivery. *Obstetrics and Gynecology, 105,* 836–842.

Lo, B. P., Wang, J. L., & Yang, G. Z. (2005). From imaging networks to behavior profiling: Ubiquitous sensing for managed homecare of the elderly. In *Proceedings of the 3rd International Conference on Pervasive Computing (Pervasive 2005),* (pp. 101-104). Munich, Germany: IEEE Press.

Logothetis, N. K. (2008). What we can do and what we cannot do with fMRI. *Nature, 453,* 869–878. doi:10.1038/nature06976

Lou, Y. (2001). Small group and individual learning with technology. *Review of Educational Research, 71*(3), 449–521. doi:10.3102/00346543071003449

Love, D., Rudolph, B., & Shah, G. H. (2008). Lessons learned in using hospital discharge data for state and national public health surveillance: Implications for Centers for Disease Control and Prevention tracking program. *Journal of Public Health Management and Practice, 14*(6), 533–542.

Lucas, H. C. Jr. (1975). *Why information systems fail.* New York: Columbia University Press.

Lundberg, C., Warren, J., Brokel, J., Bulechek, G., Butcher, H., McCloskey Dochterman, J., et al. (2008). Selecting a standardized terminology for the electronic health record that reveals the impact of nursing on patient care. *Online Journal of Nursing Informatics (OJNI), 12*(2). Available at http://ojni.org/12_2/lundberg.pdf

Lupianez-Villanueva, F., Mayer, M. A., & Torrent, J. (n.d.). Opportunities and challenges of Web 2.0 within the health care systems: an empirical exploration. *Informatics for Health & Social Care, 34*(3), 117–126. doi:10.1080/17538150903102265

Lusignan, S., & Weel, C. (2006). The use of routinely collected computer data for research in primary care: opportunities and challenges. *Family Practice, 23*(2), 253–263. doi:10.1093/fampra/cmi106

Lyman, P., & Varian, H. R. (2003). *How much information.* Retrieved on December 17, 2008 from http://www.sims.berkeley.edu/how-much-info-2003

Lyon, D. (1994). *The electronic eye: The rise of surveillance society.* Minneapolis, MN: University of Minnesota Press.

Ma'ayeh, S. (1999, October 26) US-funded $ 40m primary healthcare initiative gets under way. *Jordan Times.* Retrieved from http://www.jordanembassyus.org/102699005.htm

MacManus, R. (2008, February). Top Health 2.0 web apps. *ReadWriteWeb Online Journal,* February 21, 2008. Retrieved from http://www.readwriteweb.com/archives/top_health_20_web_apps.php

Mair, F., & Whitten, P. (2000). Systematic review of studies of patient satisfaction with telemedicine. *British Medical Journal, 320,* 1517–1520. doi:10.1136/bmj.320.7248.1517

Mair, F., Goldstein, P., Shiels, C., Roberts, C., Angus, R., & O'Connor, J. (2006). Recruitment difficulties in a home telecare trial. *Journal of Telemedicine and Telecare*, *12*(Suppl 1), 26–28. doi:10.1258/135763306777978371

Makoul, G., Curry, R. H., & Tang, P. C. (2001). The use of electronic medical records: communication patterns in outpatient encounters. *Journal of the American Medical Informatics Association*, *8*(6), 610–615.

Mandl, D. K., Szolovits, P., & Kohane, S. I. (2001). Public standards and patients' control: How to keep electronic medical records accessible but private. *British Medical Journal*, *322*, 283–287. doi:10.1136/bmj.322.7281.283

Mann, W. C. (2004). The aging population and its needs. *IEEE Pervasive Computing Magazine*, *3*(2), 12–14. doi:10.1109/MPRV.2004.1316812

Mantas, J. (2002). Electronic health record. *Studies in Health Technology and Informatics*, *65*, 250–257.

Margalit, R. S., Roter, D., Dunevant, M. A., Larson, S., & Reis, S. (2006). Electronic medical record use and physician-patient communication: An observational study of Israeli primary care encounters. *Patient Education and Counseling*, *61*(1), 134–141. doi:10.1016/j.pec.2005.03.004

Markoff, J. (2006, November 12). Entrepreneurs see a web guided by common sense. *New York Times*, November 11, 2006. Retrieved from http://www.nytimes.com/2006/11/12/business/12web.html?pagewanted=1&ei=5088&en=254d697964cedc62&ex=1320987600

Martínez, A., Villarroel, V., Seoane, J., & del Pozo, F. (2004). A study of a rural telemedicine system in the Amazon region of Peru. *Journal of Telemedicine and Telecare*, *10*(4), 219–225. doi:10.1258/1357633041424412

Mathur, S., Shanti, N., Brkaric, M., Sood, V., Kubeck, J., Paulino, C., & Merola, A. A. (2005). Surfing for scoliosis: the quality of information available on the Internet. *Spine*, *30*, 2695–2700. doi:10.1097/01.brs.0000188266.22041.c2

Mattocks, K., Lalime, K., Tate, J. P., Giannotti, T. E., Carr, K., & Carrabba, A. (2007). The state of physician office-based health information technology in Connecticut: current use, barriers and future plans. *Connecticut Medicine*, *71*(1), 27–31.

McCabe, D. P., & Castel, A. D. (2008). Seeing is believing: The effect of brain images on judgments of scientific reasoning. *Cognition*, *107*, 343–352. doi:10.1016/j.cognition.2007.07.017

McCarthy, V. (1997). Strike it rich! *Datamation*, *43*(2), 44–50.

McClanahan, K. (2008). Balancing good intentions: Protecting the privacy of electronic health information. *Bulletin of Science, Technology & Society*, *28*(1), 69–79. doi:10.1177/0270467607311485

McClure Wasko, M., & Faraj, S. (2000). "It is what one does": why people help others in electronic communities of practice. *The Journal of Strategic Information Systems*, *9*(2-3), 155–173. doi:10.1016/S0963-8687(00)00045-7

McCoy, S., Galleta, D., Everard, A., & Polak, P. (2004, December 10-11). *A study of the effects of online advertising: A focus on pop-up and in-line ads*. Paper presented at the Third Annual Workshop on HCI Research in MIS, Washington, D.C.

McDermott, R. (1999). Why information technology inspired but cannot deliver knowledge management. *California Management Review*, *41*(4), 103–117.

McDonald, C. J. (1976). Protocol-based computer reminders, the quality of care and the non-perfectability of man. *The New England Journal of Medicine*, *295*(24), 1351–1355.

McEntire, D. A. (1999). Issues in disaster relief: progress, perpetual problems and prospective solutions. *Disaster Prevention and Management*, *8*(5), 351–361. doi:10.1108/09653569910298279

McGlynn, E. A., Ash, S. M., Adams, J., Keesey, J., Hicks, J., DeCristoforo, A., & Kerr, E. A. (2003). The quality of health care delivered to adults in the United States. *The New England Journal of Medicine*, *348*, 2635–2645. doi:10.1056/NEJMsa022615

McIntyre, K. M. (1983). Medicolegal aspects of cardiopulmonary resuscitation (CPR) and emergency cardiac care. In McIntrye, K. M., & Lewis, A. J. (Eds.), *Textbook of advanced cardiac life support*. Dallas, TX: American Heart Association.

McKenna, S. J., Marquis-Faulkes, F., Gregor, P., & Newell, A. F. (2003). Scenario-based drama as a tool for investigating user requirements with application to home monitoring for elderly people. In *Proceedings of the 10th International Conference on Human-Computer Interaction (HCI 2003)*, (pp. 512-516). Crete, Greece: ACM Press.

McKesson Corporation. (2009). *Atlantic Health creates a fully integrated electronic health record with advanced technologies*. Retrieved on August 12, 2009 from http://www.mckesson.com/static_files/McKesson.com/MPT/Documents/AtlanticHealth_PRT387.pdf

McKesson Corporation. (2009). *Horizon Meds Manager*. Retrieved on August 12, 2009 from http://www.mckesson.com/en_us/McKesson.com/For+Healthcare+Providers/Hospitals/Interdisciplinary+Care+Solutions/Horizon+Meds+Manager.html

McKesson Corporation. (2009). *McKesson as your partner for patient safety*. Retrieved on August 12, 2009 from http://www.mckesson.com/static_files/McKesson.com/MPT/Documents/McKessonasYourPartnerforPatientSafety_WHT273.pdf

McLaughlin. D. B. & Hays, J. M. (2008). Healthcare operations management. Chicago: Health Administration Press.

McMahon, G. T., Gomes, H. E., Hickson Hohne, S., Hu, T. M., Levine, B. A., & Conlin, P. R. (2005). Web-based care management in patients with poorly controlled diabetes. *Diabetes Care, 28*(7), 1624–1629. doi:10.2337/diacare.28.7.1624

McNeil, I., Wales, J., & Azarmina, P. (2008). Satisfaction: the effect of a telephone based care management service on patient outcomes in the UK. In Jordanova, M., & Lievens, F. (Eds.), *Electronic proceedings Med-e-Tel: The international educational and networking forum for e-health, telemedicine and health ICT* (pp. 415–420). Luxembourg: Luxexpo.

Medina-Borja, A., & Pasupathy, K. (2007, August). Uncovering complex relationships in system dynamics modeling: Exploring the use of CHAID and CART. In *Proceedings of the System Dynamics Conference,* Boston.

Medina-Borja, A., Pasupathy, K., & Triantis, K. (2007). Large scale data envelopment analysis (DEA) implementation: A strategic performance management approach. *The Journal of the Operational Research Society, 58*(8), 1084–1098. doi:10.1057/palgrave.jors.2602200

Medscape Today. (2008). Editorial: Rotavirus Surveillance – Worldwide, 2002 – 2008. *Medscape.* Retrieved from http://www.medscape.com/viewarticle/584676_1

Meegan, D. V. (2008). Neuroimaging techniques for memory detection: Scientific, ethical, and legal issues. *The American Journal of Bioethics, 8*, 9–20. doi:10.1080/15265160701842007

Mekhjian, H. S., Kumar, R. R., Kuehn, L., Bentley, T. D., Teater, P., & Thomas, A. (2002). Immediate benefits realized following implementation of physician order entry at an academic medical center. *Journal of the American Medical Informatics Association, 9*(5), 529–539. doi:10.1197/jamia.M1038

Melville, N., Kraemer, K., & Gurbaxani, V. (2004). Information technology and organizational performance: An integrative model of IT business value. *Management Information Systems Quarterly, 28*(2), 283–322.

Meng, P. (2005, March). *Podcasting and vodcasting.* White paper, University of Missouri, Columbia, MO. Available online at http://edmarketing.apple.com

Meric, F., Bernstam, E. V., Mirza, N. Q., Hunt, K. K., Ames, F. C., & Ross, M. I. (2002). Breast cancer on the World Wide Web: Cross sectional survey of quality of information and popularity of websites. *British Medical Journal, 324*, 577–581. doi:10.1136/bmj.324.7337.577

Merikle, P., & Daneman, M. (2000). Conscious vs. unconscious perception. In Gazzaniga, M. (Ed.), *The New Cognitive Neurosciences* (2nd ed.). Cambridge, MA: MIT Press.

Meyer, S. (1997, March 20-21). Using MS Access to perform exact record linkages. In: Record Linkage Techniques - 1997: Proceedings of an International

Workshop and Exposition (pp. 280-286), Arlington, VA. Washington, DC: National Academy Press.

Michelon, T., Magne, P., & Simon-Delavell, F. (2005). Lessons of the 2003 heat-wave in France and action taken to limit the effects of future heat waves. In Kirch, W., Bertollini, R., & Menne, B. (Eds.), *Extreme weather events and public health response* (pp. 131–140). Berlin, Heidelberg: Springer. doi:10.1007/3-540-28862-7_13

Mihailidis, A., Carmichael, B., & Boger, J. (2004). The use of computer vision in an intelligent environment to support aging-in-place, safety, and independence in the home. *IEEE Transactions on Information Technology in Biomedicine, 8*(3), 238–247. doi:10.1109/TITB.2004.834386

Mikhailov, A.I., Chernyl, A.I., & Gilyarevskii, R.S. (1966). Informatika – novoe nazvanie teorii naučnoj informacii. *Naučno tehničeskaja informacija, 12,* 35–39.

Mili, F., Khoury, M. J., Flanders, D. W., & Greenberg, R. S. (1993). Risk of childhood cancer for infants with birth defects: A record linkage study. Atlanta, Georgia, 1968-1988. *American Journal of Epidemiology, 137*(6), 629–638.

Milisen, K., Abraham, I., Siebens, K., Darras, E., & Dierckx de Casterle, B. (representing the BELIMAGE group). (2006). Work environment and workforce problems: A cross-sectional questionnaire survey of hospital nurses in Belgium. *International Journal of Nursing Studies, 43,* 745-754. Available at: http://www.scribd.com/doc/15107961/Autonomy-in-Nurses

Miller, A. R., & Tucker, C. (2009). Privacy protection and technology diffusion: the case of electronic medical records. *Management Science, 55*(7), 1077–1093. doi:10.1287/mnsc.1090.1014

Miller, E. (1997, March 20-21). Record linkage of progress towards meeting the New Jersey high school proficiency testing requirements. In: Record Linkage Techniques - 1997: Proceedings of an International Workshop and Exposition, (pp. 227-234), Arlington, VA. Washington, DC: National Academy Press.

Miller, R. A., Pople, H. E., & Myers, J. D. (1982). INTERNIST-1, an experimental computer-based diagnostic consultant for general internal medicine. *The New England Journal of Medicine, 307,* 468–476.

Miller, R. H., West, C., Brown, T. M., Sim, I., & Ganchoff, C. (2005). The value of electronic health records in solo or small group practices. *Health Affairs (Project Hope), 24*(5), 1127–1137. doi:10.1377/hlthaff.24.5.1127

Minard, A. (2005, March 24). UA scientist named in two suits by Havasupai tribe members. *Arizona Daily Star.* Retrieved from: http://www.nathpo.org

Mishra, R. C. (2003). *Information technology and poverty reduction in South Asia.* Delhi, India: Authors Press.

MIT Open Courseware. (n.d.). Retrieved August 24, 2009 from http://ocw.mit.edu/OcwWeb/Web/home/home/index.htm

Mitchell, T. M. (1997). Does machine learning really work? *AI Magazine, 18*(3), 11–20.

Mohammed, S., Fiaidhi, J., & Yang, L. (2004). Developing multitier lightweight techniques for protecting medical images within ubiquitous environments. *IEEE 2nd Communications, Networks and Service Research Conference (CNSR04).* Fredericton, Canada, May 19-21, 2004.

Molina, G., & Medina-Borja, A. (2006). Are we teaching our students to think systematically? Systems thinking in engineering education. *International Conference on Engineering Education,* San Juan, PR.

Möller, K., Breslin, J., & Decker, S. (2005). SemiBlog – semantic publishing of desktop data. In *14th Conference on Information Systems Development (ISD2005).* Karlstad, Sweden, August 2005, (pp. 855-866).

Monden, Y. (1983). *Toyota production system, practical approach to production management.* Norcross, GA: Industrial Engineering and Management Press, Institute of Industrial Engineers.

Moody, L. E., Slocumb, E., Berg, B., & Jackson, D. (2004). Electronic health records documentation in nursing: Nurses' perceptions, attitudes, and preferences. *Computers, informatics, nursing. CIN, 22*(6), 337–344.

Moore, G. E. (1965, April 18). Cramming more components onto integrated circuits. *Electronics Magazine, 38* (8). Retrieved on August 12, 2009 from ftp://download. intel.com/museum/Moores_Law/Articles-Press_Releases/Gordon_Moore_1965_Article.pdf.

Moroney, S. D. (2003). *Understanding health care cost drivers*. National Institute of Health Policy. Retrieved on August 12, 2009 from http://www.bluecrossmn.com/bc/wcs/groups/bcbsmn/@mbc_bluecrossmn/documents/public/mbc1_health care_cost_drivers.pdf

Mucic, D. (2007). Telepsychiatry in Denmark: Mental health care in rural and remote areas. *Journal of e-health Technology and Application, 5*(3), 277-282.

Mucic, D. (2008). International telepsychiatry, patient acceptability. In Jordanova, M., & Lievens, F. (Eds.), *Global telemedicine / e-health updates: Knowledge resources* (*Vol. 1*, pp. 383–384). Luxembourg: Luxexpo.

Mulholland, H. C., Casey, F., Brown, D., Corrigan, N., & Quinn, M., McCord, B.et al. (1999). Application of a low cost telemedicine link to the diagnosis of neonatal congenital heart defects by remote consultation. *Heart (British Cardiac Society), 82*, 217–221.

Mullett, C. J., Evans, R. S., Christenson, J. C., & Dean, J. M. (2001). Development and impact of a computerized pediatric antiinfective decision support program. *Pediatrics, 108*(4), E75. doi:10.1542/peds.108.4.e75

Mullinax, C., & Lawley, M. (2002). Assigning patients to nurses in neonatal intensive care. *The Journal of the Operational Research Society, 53*(1), 25–35. doi:10.1057/palgrave/jors/2601265

Munoz, M. A., Rodriguez, M., Favela, J., Martinez-Garcia, A. I., & Gonzales, V. M. (2003). Context-aware mobile communication in hospitals. *IEEE Computer Magazine, 36*(9), 38–46.

Murray, M. D., Harris, L. E., Overhage, J. M., Zhou, X. H., Eckert, G. J., & Smith, F. E. (2004). Failure of computerized treatment suggestions to improve health outcomes of outpatients with uncomplicated hypertension: results of a randomized controlled trial. *Pharmacotherapy, 24*(3), 324–337. doi:10.1592/phco.24.4.324.33173

Murray, M., & Berwick, D. M. (2003). Advanced access, reducing waiting and delays in primary care. *Journal of the American Medical Association, 289*(8), 1035–1040. doi:10.1001/jama.289.8.1035

Musen, M. A., Shahar, Y., & Shortliffe, E. H. (2006). Clinical decision support systems. In Shortliffe, E. H., & Cimino, J. J. (Eds.), *Biomedical informatics: computer applications in health care and biomedicine* (3rd ed.). New York: Springer.

Myers, J., Frieden, T. R., Bherwani, K. M., & Henning, K. J. (2008). Ethics in public health research: Privacy and public health at risk: Public health confidentiality in the digital age. *American Journal of Public Health, 98*, 793–800. doi:10.2105/AJPH.2006.107706

Mykhalovskiv, E., & Weir, L. (2006). The Global Public Health Intelligence Network and early warning outbreak detection: a Canadian contribution to global public health. *Canadian Journal of Public Health, 97*, 42-44. Retrieved on January 30, 2009 from National Center for Biotechnology Information's database at http://www.ncbi.nlm.nih.gov/pubmed/16512327

Mynatt, E. D., Rowan, J., Craighill, S., & Jacobs, A. (2001). Digital family portraits: Providing peace of mind for extended family members. In *Proceedings of the 2001 ACM Conference on Human Factors in Computing Systems (CHI 2001)*, (pp. 333-340). Seattle, WA: ACM Press.

Naditz, A. (2005). Telemedicine at the VA: VistA, MyHealtheVet, and other VA programs. *Telemedicine Journal and e-Health, 14*(4), 330–332. doi:10.1089/tmj.2008.9973

Nagel, T. (1974). What is it like to be a bat? *The Philosophical Review, 83*, 435–450. doi:10.2307/2183914

Nagle, L. M. (2007). Informatics: Emerging concepts and issues. *Electronic Healthcare, 5*(4), 1–2.

Nandhagopal, R., McKeown, M. J., & Stoessl, A. J. (2008). Functional imaging in Parkinson disease. *Neurology, 70*((16 Pt 2)), 1478–1488. doi:10.1212/01.wnl.0000310432.92489.90

Nash, D. B., & Quigley, G. D. (2008). Looking forward to the end of autonomy. *Headache*, *48*(5), 719–726. doi:10.1111/j.1526-4610.2008.01113.x

National Alliance for Health Information Technology (NAHIT). (2008). *Report to the Office of the National Coordinator for Health Information Technology on defining key health information technology terms.* Retrieved October 15, 2009 from http://healthit.hhs.gov/portal/server.pt/gateway/PTARGS_0_10741_848133_0_0_18/10_2_hit_terms.pdf

National Coalition on Healthcare. (2004). *Building a better health: Specifications for reform.* Washington DC: National Coalition on Healthcare. Accessed 11/14/2009 at http://www.kaisernetwork.org/health_cast/uploaded_files/072004_nchc_healthcare_transcript.pdf

National Institute of Standards and Technology (NIST). (2009). *Baldrige National Quality Program.* Available online at: http://www.quality.nist.gov

Nayeemuddin, M., Majeed, M. A., Muneer, A., & Misra, A. (2007). *An out-patient survey of plastic surgery patients.* Paper presented at Med-e-Tel 2007, Luxembourg, G.D. of Luxembourg. Retrieved January 21, 2009, from http://www.medetel.lu/download/2007/parallel_sessions/presentation/0418/An_Out-Patient_Survey.pdf

Nazi, K. M., & Woods, S. S. (2008). MyHealtheVet PHR: A description of users and patient portal use. *American Medical Informatics Association Annual Symposium Proceedings, Nov 6*, 1182.

Nebeker, J. R., Hoffman, J. M., Weir, C. R., Bennett, C. L., & Hurdle, J. F. (2005). High rates of adverse drug events in a highly computerized hospital. *Archives of Internal Medicine*, *165*(10), 1111–1116. doi:10.1001/archinte.165.10.1111

Neelamkavil, F. (1987). *Computer simulation and modelling.* New York: Wiley.

Neerincx, P. B. T., & Leunissen, J. A. M. (2005). Evolution of web services in bioinformatics. *Briefings in Bioinformatics*, *6*(2), 178–188. doi:10.1093/bib/6.2.178

Nelson, R. & Joos, I. (1989). On language in nursing: From data to wisdom. *PLN Visions, 6.*

Nemeth, C., & Cook, R. (2005). Hiding in plain sight: What Koppel et al. tell us about healthcare IT. *Journal of Biomedical Informatics*, *38*(4), 262-263. doi:10.1016/j.jbi.2005.05.010

NeSmith. N.P. (1997). Record linkage and genealogical files. In: Record Linkage Techniques - 1997: Proceedings of an International Workshop and Exposition (pp. 358-361). Arlington, VA. March 20-21, 1997. Washington, DC: National Academy Press.

Ness, R. M., Klein, R. W., & Dittus, R. S. (2003). The cost-effectiveness of fecal DNA testing for colorectal cancer. *Gastrointestinal Endoscopy*, *57*(5), AB94–AB94.

Newcombe, H. B. (1994). Cohorts and privacy. *Cancer Causes & Control*, *5*, 287–292. doi:10.1007/BF01830251

Newcombe, H. B., Kennedy, J. M., Axford, S. L., & James, A. P. (1959). Automatic linkage of vital records. *Science*, *130*, 954–959. doi:10.1126/science.130.3381.954

Niazkhani, Z., Pirnejad, H., Berg, M., & Aarts, J. (2009). The impact of computerized provider order entry systems on inpatient clinical workflow: a literature review. *Journal of the American Medical Informatics Association*, *16*(4), 539–549. doi:10.1197/jamia.M2419

Nielsen//Netratings. (2004). *Web surfers comparison shop online for Mother's Day gifts, according to Nielson//NetRatings, Inc.* Retrieved from http://www.nielsen-online.com/pr/pr_040507.pdf

Noji, E. K. (2005). Disasters: introduction and state of the art. *Epidemiologic Reviews*, *27*(1), 3–8. doi:10.1093/epirev/mxi007

Noor, A. K. (2007). Re-engineering healthcare. *Mechanical Engineering (New York, N.Y.)*, *11*, 22–27.

Norris, T. E., Hart, G. L., Larson, E. H., Tarczy-Hornoch, P., Masuda, D. L., & Fuller, S. S. (2002). Low-bandwidth, low-cost telemedicine consultations in rural family practice. *The Journal of the American Board of Family Practice*, *15*(2), 123–127.

Null, J. (2009). *Hyperthermia deaths of children in vehicles.* Updated August 12, 2009. Retrieved on August 13, 2009 from http://ggweather.com/heat/

Nunn, S., & Hamburg, M. (2003, May 26). Op-ed: Diseases gaining ground: SARS exposes gaps in system that should be addressed. *Atlanta Journal-Constitution.* Retrieved from http://www.nti.org/c_press/ oped_sars_052603.pdf

O'Brien-Pallas, L., Tomblin Murphy, G., & Shamian, J. (2008 September). *Final report. Understanding the costs and outcomes of nurses' turnover in Canadian hospitals.* Nursing Health Services Research Unit. Available at: http://www.hhrchair.ca/images/CMSImages/ TOS_Final%20Report.pdf

O'Connor, A.M., Bennett, C.L., Stacey, D., Barry, M., Col, N.F., Eden, K.B., et al. (2006). Decision aids for people facing health treatment or screening decisions. *Cochrane Database of Systematic Reviews, 3.* Retrieved from Art. No.: CD001431. DOI: 10.1002/14651858. CD001431.pub2

O'Donnell, H. C., Kaushal, R., Barron, Y., Callahan, M. A., Adelman, R. D., & Siegler, E. L. (2009). Physicians' attitudes towards copy and pasting in electronic note writing. *Journal of General Internal Medicine, 24*(1), 63–68. doi:10.1007/s11606-008-0843-2

O'Keefe, R. M. (1985). Investigating outpatient departments, implementable policies and qualitative approaches. *The Journal of the Operational Research Society, 36*(8), 705–712.

O'Neill, L., & Dexter, F. (2004). Evaluating the efficiency of hospitals' perioperative services using DEA. In Brandeau, M. L., Sainfort, F., & Pierskalla, W. P. (Eds.), *Operations research and health care: A handbook of methods and applications* (pp. 147–168). Boston: Kluwer Academic Publishers.

O'Neill, L., & Klepack, W. (2007). Electronic medical records for a rural family practice: a case study in systems development. *Journal of Medical Systems, 31*(1), 25–33. doi:10.1007/s10916-006-9040-1

O'Reilly, T. (2005, September). *What is Web 2.0: Design patterns and business models for the next generation of software.* O'Reilly Net, 09/30/2005: Available online at http://www.oreillynet.com/pub/a/oreilly/tim/ news/2005/09/30/what-is-web-20.html

Oddie, S. J., Hammal, D., Richmond, S., & Parker, L. (2005). Early discharge and readmission to hospital in the first month of life in the Northern Region of the UK during 1998: a case cohort study. *Archives of Disease in Childhood, 90*(2), 119–124. doi:10.1136/adc.2003.040766

OECD (Organization for Economic Co-operation and Development). (2004). *OECD Health Data 2004.* OECD. Retrieved from www.oecd.org/health/healthdata

OECD. (2009). *OECD Health Data 2009.* Accessed on August 7, 2009 from http://www.oecd.org/ dataoecd/46/2/38980580.pdf

Office of the Privacy Commissioner of Canada. (n.d.). *Fact Sheet: Privacy Impact Assessments.* Retrieved January 26, 2009 from http://www.privcom.gc.ca/pia-efvp/index_e.asp

Oh, H., Rizo, C., Enkin, M., & Jadad, A. (2005). What is e-health (3): A systematic review of published definitions. *Journal of Medical Internet Research, 7*(1), e1. Retrieved February 24, 2008 from www.jmir.org/2005/1/e1/

Olive, M., Rahmouni, H., & Solomonides, T. (2008). SHARE the journey: a European Healthgrid Roadmap. *EU Commission: Information Society and Media.* Retrieved from http://ec.europa.eu/information_society/activities/health/docs/publications/200810share-roadmap.pdf

Olive, M., Rahmouni, H., Solomonides, T., Breton, V., Legré, Y., Blanquer, I., & Hernandez, V. (2008). SHARE, from vision to road map: technical steps. *Studies in Health Technology and Informatics, 129*(Pt.2), 1149–1153.

Oliveira, I. C., Oliveira, J. L., Lopéz-Alonso, V., Martin-Sanchez, F., Maojo, V., & Sousa Pereira, A. (2005). Grid requirements for the integration of biomedical information resources for health applications. *Methods of Information in Medicine, 44*(2), 161–167.

Onen, C. L. (2004). Medicine in resource-poor settings: time for a paradigm shift? *Clinical Medicine, 4,* 355–360.

Orland, L. (1995). *Corporate and white collar crime: An anthology.* Newark, NJ: LexisNexis Anderson Publishing.

Orszag, P. R. (2008). *Evidence on the costs and benefits of health information technology.* Washington, DC: The Office of the National Coordinator of Health Information Technology.

Orszag, P. R., & Ellis, P. (2007). The challenge of rising health care costs--a view from the Congressional Budget Office. *The New England Journal of Medicine, 357*(18), 1793–1795. doi:10.1056/NEJMp078190

Osheroff, J. A., Teich, J. M., Middleton, B. F., Steen, E. B., Wright, A., & Detmer, D. E. (2006). A roadmap for national action on clinical decision support (No. HHSP233200500877P). Bethesda, MD.

Oster, S., Langella, S., Hastings, S., Ervin, D., Madduri, R., Phillips, J. ... Saltz, J. (2008). caGrid 1.0: An enterprise grid infrastructure for biomedical research. *Journal of the American Medical Informatics Association, 15(2),* 138-149.

Osterholm, M., & Branswell, H. (2005). Emerging pandemic: Costs and consequences of an avian influenza outbreak. *Global Health Initiative/Woodrow Wilson International Center for Scholars.* Retrieved from http://www.wilsoncenter.org/index.cfm?event_id=142787&fuseaction=topics.event_summary&topic_id=116811

Overby, S. (2004). *Iceland court ruling stalls medical database.* Retrieved from http://www. mis-asia.com

Owen, A. M., Coleman, M. R., Boly, M., Davis, M. H., Laureys, S., & Pickard, J. D. (2006). Detecting awareness in the vegetative state. *Science, 313,* 1402..doi:10.1126/science.1130197

Ozcan, Y. A. Merwln: E., Lee, K., & Morrissey, J. P. (2004). State of the art applications in benchmarking using DEA: The case of mental health organizations. In

M.L. Brandeau (Ed.), Operations Research and Health Care: A Handbook of Methods and Applications, (pp. 169–190). Boston: Kluwer Academic Publishers.

Ozdas, A., Speroff, T., Waitman, L. R., Ozbolt, J., Butler, J., & Miller, R. A. (2006). Integrating "best of care" protocols into clinicians' workflow via care provider order entry: impact on quality-of-care indicators for acute myocardial infarction. *Journal of the American Medical Informatics Association, 13*(2), 188–196. doi:10.1197/jamia.M1656

Pagliari, C. (2005). *Welcome and introduction.* Retrieved December 8, 2008, from http://www.e-health.ed.ac.uk/presentations/may2005/Claudia%20Pagliari.ppt

Pal, S. K., & Mittal, B. (2004). Fight against cancer in countries with limited resources: The post the post genomic era scenario. *Asian Pacific Journal of Cancer Prevention, 5,* 328–333.

Palen, T. E., Raebel, M., Lyons, E., & Magid, D. M. (2006). Evaluation of laboratory monitoring alerts within a computerized physician order entry system for medication orders. *The American Journal of Managed Care, 12*(7), 389–395.

Pan, W.T. (2004, November 18 - 19). *Health information technology 2004: improving chronic disease care in California. California HealthCare Foundation.* San Francisco, CA: SBC Park.

PandemicFlu.gov. (n.d.). Retrieved from http://www.pandemicflu.gov/global/index.html

Panton, R. L., Downie, R., Truong, T., Mackeen, L., Kabene, S., & Yi, Q. L. (2008). A visual approach to providing prognostic information to parents of children with retinoblastoma. *Psycho-Oncology, 18*(3), 300–304. doi:10.1002/pon.1397

Paradiso, R., Belloc, C., Loriga, G., & Taccini, N. (2005). Wearable healthcare systems, new frontiers of e-textile. In Nugent, C., McCullagh, P., McAdams, E., & Lymberis, A. (Eds.), *Personalised Health Management Systems: The Integration of Innovative Sensing, Textile, Information and Communication Technologies* (pp. 9–17). Amsterdam, The Netherlands: IOS Press.

Pardo, M. S., & Patterson, D. (2009, Feb. 6). *Philosophical foundations of law and neuroscience.* University of Illinois Law Review, 2010; U of Alabama Public Law Research Paper No. 1338763. Available at SSRN: http://ssrn.com/abstract=1338763

Pare, G. (2002). Implementing clinical information systems: a multiple-case study within a US Hospital. *Health Services Management Research, 15,* 71–92. doi:10.1258/0951484021912851

Pare, G., Jaana, M., & Sicotte, C. (2007). Systematic review of home telemonitoring for chronic diseases the evidence base. *Journal of the American Medical Informatics Association, 14,* 269–277. doi:10.1197/jamia.M2270

Pasupathy, K., & Medina-Borja, A. (2008). Integrating Excel, Access, and Visual BASIC to deploy performance measurement and evaluation at the American Red Cross. *Interfaces, 38*(4), 324–337. doi:10.1287/inte.1080.0366

Pasupathy, K., & Triantis, K. (2007). A framework to evaluate service operations: Dynamic service-profit chain. *Quality Management Journal, 14*(3), 36–49.

Pasupathy, K., & Triantis, K. (2007). Investments in operational attributes and impact on outcomes in training services. In *Proceedings of the System Dynamics Conference,* Boston.

Pasupathy, K., Gong, Y., Vest, S., Cole, N., & Jackson-Thompson, J. (2008). Quality-oriented establishment of characteristics for central cancer registry software systems. *Journal of Registry Management, 35*(2), 81–89.

Pasupathy, K., Medina-Borja, A., & Triantis, K. (2008). Performance Measurement and Evaluation System, Intellectual Property, VTIP09-034, http://vtip.org/availableTech/technology.php?id=284982.

Patel, V. L., Kushniruk, A. W., Yang, S., & Yale, J. F. (2000). Impact of a computer-based patient record system on data collection, knowledge organization, and reasoning. *Journal of the American Medical Informatics Association, 7*(6), 569–585.

Paterno, M. D., Maviglia, S. M., Gorman, P. N., Seger, D. L., Yoshida, E., & Seger, A. C. (2009). Tiering drug-drug interaction alerts by severity increases compliance rates. *Journal of the American Medical Informatics Association, 16*(1), 40–46. doi:10.1197/jamia.M2808

Patterson, E. S., Cook, R. I., Woods, D. D., Chow, R., & Gomes, J. O. (2004). Hand-off strategies in settings with high consequences for failure: lessons for health care operations. *International Journal for Quality in Health Care, 16*(2), 125–132. doi:10.1093/intqhc/mzh026

Pearce, C., Dwan, K., Arnold, M., Phillips, C., & Trumble, S. (2009). Doctor, patient and computer--a framework for the new consultation. *International Journal of Medical Informatics, 78*(1), 32–38. doi:10.1016/j.ijmedinf.2008.07.002

Pearce, C., Trumble, S., Arnold, M., Dwan, K., & Phillips, C. (2008). Computers in the new consultation: within the first minute. *Family Practice, 25*(3), 202–208. doi:10.1093/fampra/cmn018

Pearce, C., Walker, H., & O'Shea, C. (2008). A visual study of computers on doctors' desks. *Informatics in Primary Care, 16*(2), 111–117.

Pearlson, K. E. (2001). *Managing and using information systems: A strategic approach.* New York: Wiley.

Pennsylvania Health Care Cost Containment Council (PHC4). (June 2009). *An Annual Report on the Financial Health of Pennsylvania's Hospitals.* Financial Analysis: Volume One General Acute Care Hospitals. Available at: http://www.phc4.org/reports/fin/08/docs/fin2008report_volumeone.pdf

Perreault, L., & Metzger, J. (1993). A pragmatic framework for understanding clinical decision support. *Journal of Healthcare Information Management, 13*(2), 5–21.

Perry, M. (2006). Humanitarian relief challenges in the wake of South East Asian tsunami disaster. *Department of Management Working Paper Series, Monash University.* Retrieved from http://www.buseco.monash.edu.au/mgt/research/working-papers/2006/wp16-06.pdf

Petroski, H. (1992). *To engineer is human: The role of failure in successful design.* New York: Vintage Books.

Pingdom. (2009, January 15th). The blog platforms of choice among the top 100 blogs. Retrieved from http://royal.pingdom.com/2009/01/15/the-blog-platforms-of-choice-among-the-top-100-blogs/

PIPED Act (2000, update 2006). *Personal Information Protection and Electronic Documents Act.* Department of Justice, Canada. Full text available at http://laws.justice.gc.ca/en/P-8.6/text.html

Pirkl, J., & Pulos, A. (1997). *Transgenerational design: Products for an aging population.* New York: James Wiley & Sons.

Pizziferri, L., Kittler, A. F., Volk, L. A., Honour, M. M., Gupta, S., & Wang, S. (2005). Primary care physician time utilization before and after implementation of an electronic health record: a time-motion study. *Journal of Biomedical Informatics, 38*(3), 176–188. doi:10.1016/j.jbi.2004.11.009

Place, U. T. (1956). Is consciousness a brain process? *The British Journal of Psychology, 47*(1), 44–50.

Platt, R. (2009). Opportunity knocks: the electronic (public health) medical record. *Epidemiology (Cambridge, Mass.), 20*(5), 662–663. doi:10.1097/EDE.0b013e3181b0fb78

Plitch, P. (2002, September 16). E-Commerce (A special report): The rules --- Law: Are bots legal? --- Comparison-shopping sites say they make the Web manageable; Critics say they trespass. *Wall Street Journal,* p. R13.

Poissant, L., Pereira, J., Tamblyn, R., & Kawasumi, Y. (2005). The impact of electronic health records on time efficiency of physicians and nurses: a systematic review. *Journal of the American Medical Informatics Association, 12*(5), 505–516. doi:10.1197/jamia.M1700

Pollack, A. (2006, August 16). Monsanto buys delta and pine land, top supplier of cotton seeds in America. *The New York Times.* Retrieved from http://www.nytimes.com/2006/08/16/business/16seed.html

Pollack, M. E., Brown, L., Colbry, D., McCarthy, C. E., Orosz, C., & Peintner, B. (2003). Autominder: An intelligent cognitive orthotic system for people with memory impairment. *Robotics and Autonomous Systems, 44*(3-4), 273–282. doi:10.1016/S0921-8890(03)00077-0

Pomfret, J., & Nelson, D. (2000, December 20). An isolated region's genetic mother lode. *Washington Post,* A1.

Poon, C. Y., Zhang, Y., & Bao, S. (2006). A novel biometrics method to secure wireless body area sensor networks for telemedicine and M-Health. *IEEE Communications Magazine, 44*(4), 73–81. doi:10.1109/MCOM.2006.1632652

Potts, A. L., Barr, F. E., Gregory, D. F., Wright, L., & Patel, N. R. (2004). Computerized physician order entry and medication errors in a pediatric critical care unit. *Pediatrics, 113*(Pt 1), 59–63. doi:10.1542/peds.113.1.59

Priest, D. (2004). *The mission: waging war and keeping peace with American military.* New York: Norton.

Probert, A., Semenciw, R., Mao, Y., & Gentleman, J. F. (1997, March 20-21). Analysis of immigration data: 1980-1994. In Record Linkage Techniques - 1997: Proceedings of an International Workshop and Exposition (pp. 287-291), Arlington, VA. Washington, DC: National Academy Press.

Project Management Institute. (2008). *A Guide to the Project Management Body of Knowledge* (4th ed.). Newtown Square, PA: Project Management Institute.

Protti, D. J. (1995). The synergism of health/medical informatics revisited. *Methods of Information in Medicine, 34,* 441–445.

Proudfoot, J., Ryden, C., Everitt, B., Shapiro, D. A., Goldberg, D., & Mann, A. (2004). Clinical efficacy of computerised cognitive-behavioural therapy for anxiety and depression in primary care: randomised controlled trial. *The British Journal of Psychiatry, 185,* 46–54. doi:10.1192/bjp.185.1.46

Purcell, G. P., Wilson, P., & Delamothe, T. (2002). The quality of health information on the Internet. *British Medical Journal, 324,* 557–558. doi:10.1136/bmj.324.7337.557

Putnam, H. (1960). Minds and machines. In Hook, S. (Ed.), *Dimensions of mind* (pp. 138–164). New York: New York University Press.

Qiu, R. (1992, February). Asian perspectives: Tension between modern values and Chinese culture. In Z. Bankowski, & R. J. Levine (Eds.), *Ethics and research on human subjects: International Guidelines,* (pp. 188-197). Presented at The XXVIth CIOMS Conference, Geneva, Switzerland.

Qiu, R. (1999, September). A concern for the collective good. From *Is China's law eugenic?* Retrieved from: http://www.unesco.org/courier/1999_09/uk/dossier/txt07.htm

Qiu, R. (2001, April). *Protecting human genome and safeguarding human rights.* Presented at UNESCO's Workshop related to Ethical Issues on Biotechnology and Biosafety, Hangzhou, Peoples Republic of China.

Quass, D., & Starkey, P. (2003, August 24-27). Record linkage for genealogical databases. In *ACM SIGKDD 03 Workshop on Data Cleaning, Record Linkage, and Object Consolidation,* (pp. 40-42), Washington, DC.

Queensland Health. (2008). *Queensland Health Annual Report 2007-2008.* Brisbane, Australia: Queensland Government. Available at http://www.health.qld.gov.au/publications/corporate/annual_reports/annualreport2008/default.asp

Qui, R. (2008, March). Personal communication.

Rada, R. (2007). *Information systems and health care enterprises.* Hershey, PA: IGI Publishing.

Radetzky, U., Leser, U., Schultze-Rauschenbach, S. C., Zimmermann, J., Lüssem, J., Bode, T., & Cremers, A. B. (2006). Adapters, shims, and glue – services interoperability for in silico experiments. *Bioinformatics (Oxford, England), 22*(9), 1137–1143. doi:10.1093/bioinformatics/btl054

Rawls, J. (1971). *A theory of justice.* Cambridge, MA: The Belknap Press of Harvard University.

Ray, W. A., Murray, K. T., Meredith, S., Narasimhulu, S. S., Hall, K., & Stein, C. M. (2004). Oral erythromycin and the risk of sudden death from cardiac causes. *The New England Journal of Medicine, 351,* 1089–1096. doi:10.1056/NEJMoa040582

Reid, P. P., Compton, W. D., Grossman, J. H., & Fanjiang, G. (Eds.). (2005). *Building a better delivery system: a new engineering/health care partnership. Committee on Engineering and the Health Care System, Institute of Medicine and National Academy of Engineering.* Washington, DC: National Academy Press.

Resmini, F., Tavares, A. P., Sparenberg, A., Russomano, T., Bainy, S., & Timm, R. (2008). Telepsychiatry: A new tool for remodeling mental health assistance in South Brazil. In Jordanova, M., & Lievens, F. (Eds.), *Global telemedicine / e-health updates: Knowledge resources* (*Vol. 1,* pp. 395–397). Luxembourg: Luxexpo.

Rice, R. E. (2006). Influences, usage and outcomes of Internet health information searching: Multivariate results from the pew surveys. *International Journal of Medical Informatics, 75,* 8–28. doi:10.1016/j.ijmedinf.2005.07.032

Rifkin, J. (2001). *The age of access.* New York: Tarcher/Putnam.

Rind, D. M., Kohane, I. S., Szolovits, P., Safran, C., Chueh, H. C., & Barnett, G. O. (1997). Maintaining the confidentiality of medical records shared over the Internet and the World Wide Web. *Annals of Internal Medicine, 127,* 138–141.

Rindfleisch, T. C. (1997). Privacy, information technology, and health care. *Communications of the ACM, 40*(8), 92–100. doi:10.1145/257874.257896

Ring, I., & Brown, N. (2003). The health status of indigenous peoples and others. *British Medical Journal, 327,* 404–405. doi:10.1136/bmj.327.7412.404

Rinkus, S. M., & Chitwood, A. (2002). Cognitive analyses of a paper medical record and electronic medical record on the documentation of two nursing tasks: patient education and adherence assessment of insulin administration. In *AMIA 2002 Annual Symposium Proceedings, Proc AMIA Symp,* (pp. 657-661).

Rodas, E. B., & Mora, F. Tamariz, Vicuna, A., Merrell, R. C., & Rodas, E. (2006 a). Telemedicine applications in mobile surgery. In M. Jordanova & F. Lievens (Eds.), e-Health: Proceedings of Med-e-Tel 2006, The international trade event and conference for e-health, telemedicine and health ICT, (pp. 307-309). Luxembourg: Publ. Luxexpo.

Rodas, E. B., & Mora, F. Tamariz, Vicuna, A., Merrell, R. C., Rodas, E. (2006 b). River health: Description of an integral healthcare program in a remote river basin of Ecuador. In M. Jordanova & F. Lievens (Eds.), e-Health: Proceedings of Med-e-Tel 2006, The international trade event and conference for e-health, telemedicine and health ICT, (pp. 311-313). Luxembourg: Publ. Luxexpo.

Roosevelt, F. (1937, January). *Second inaugural address*. Retrieved from: http://www.bartleby.com/124/pres50.html

Rosenberg, C. E. (1995). *The care of strangers: the rise of America's hospital system*. Baltimore, MD: The John Hopkins University Press.

Roskies, A. (2006). Neuroscientific challenges to free will and responsibility. *Trends in Cognitive Sciences*, *10*, 419–423. doi:10.1016/j.tics.2006.07.011

Roskies, A. L. (2008). Neuroimaging and inferential distance. *Neuroethics*, *1*, 19–30. doi:10.1007/s12152-007-9003-3

Rothkopf, D. (2008). *Superclass: The global power elite and the world they are making*. New York: Farrar, Straus and Giroux.

Rothschild, J. M., Federico, F. A., Gandhi, T. K., Kaushal, R., Williams, D. H., & Bates, D. W. (2002). Analysis of medication-related malpractice claims: causes, preventability, and costs. *Archives of Internal Medicine*, *162*(21), 2414–2420. doi:10.1001/archinte.162.21.2414

Rothschild, J. M., McGurk, S., Honour, M., Lu, L., McClendon, A. A., & Srivastava, P. (2007). Assessment of education and computerized decision support interventions for improving transfusion practice. *Transfusion*, *47*(2), 228–239. doi:10.1111/j.1537-2995.2007.01093.x

Roumie, C. L., Elasy, T. A., Greevy, R., Griffin, M. R., Liu, X., & Stone, W. J. (2006). Improving blood pressure control through provider education, provider alerts, and patient education: a cluster randomized trial. *Annals of Internal Medicine*, *145*(3), 165–175.

Royal College of Nursing (RCN). (2008). *RCN e-Health Programme Policy Statement. Nursing content of electronic patient /client records*. Retrieved from http://www.rcn.org.uk/__data/assets/pdf_file/0010/176860/ndc_Briefing_June_08.pdf

Royall, J., van Schayk, I., Bennett, M., Kamau, N., & Alilio, M. (2005). Crossing the digital divide: The contribution of information technology to the professional performance of malaria researchers in Africa. *African Health Sciences*, *5*(3), 246–254.

Sachs, J. D. (2001). *Microeconomics and health: Investing in health for economic development*. Geneva: WHO.

Sachs, J. D. (2007, January). Beware false tradeoffs. *Foreign Affairs*. Retrieved from http://www.foreignaffairs.org/special/global_health/sachs

Safran, C. (1999). Editorial. *International Journal of Medical Informatics*, *54*(3), 155–156. doi:10.1016/S1386-5056(99)00003-9

Safran, C., Bloomrosen, M., Hammond, E., Labkoff, S., Markel-Fox, S., Tang, P. C., & Detmer, D. E. (2007). Toward a national framework for the secondary use of health data: An American Medical Informatics Association White Paper. *Journal of the American Medical Informatics Association*, *14*, 1–9. doi:10.1197/jamia.M2273

Saligumba, F., Raza, S., Soegijoko, S., & Khoja, S. (2009). Community based e-health promotion for safe motherhood: Linking community maternal health needs with health services system. In Jordanova, M., & Lievens, F. (Eds.), *Global Telemedicine/e-health Updates: Knowledge Resources* (*Vol. 2*, pp. 489–490). Luxembourg: Luxexpo.

Saltz, J., Hastings, S., Langella, S., Oster, S., Kurc, T., & Payne, P. (2008). The roadmap for caGrid, an enterprise Grid architecture for biomedical research. *Studies in Health Technology and Informatics*, *138*, 224–237.

Sands, D. Z. (1999). Electronic patient-centered communication: managing risks, managing opportunities, managing care. *The American Journal of Managed Care, 5*(12), 1569–1571.

Santana, P. C. Rodríguez, M. D., González, V. M., Castro, L. A., & Andrade, A. G. (2005). Supporting emotional ties among Mexican elders and their families living abroad. In *Proceedings of the Conference on Human Factors in Computing Systems (CHI 05),* (pp. 2099-2103). Portland, OR: ACM Press.

Sapirstein, A., Lone, N., Latif, A., Fackler, J., & Pronovost, P. J. (2009). Best practice & research. *Clinical anaesthesiolog, 23*(1), 115-126.

Sarathy, R., & Muralidhar, K. (2006). Secure and useful data sharing. *Decision Support Systems, 42,* 204–220. doi:10.1016/j.dss.2004.10.013

Sato, H. (2004). Social consensus on medical technology policy; ethical issues and citizen participation. *Eiseigaku Zasshi Nippon,* (. *Japanese Journal of Hygiene, 59*(1), 12–22.

Schaefer, A. J., Bailey, M. D., Shechter, S. M., & Roberts, M. S. (2004). Medical treatment decisions using Markov decision processes. In Brandeau, M. L., Sainfort, F., & Pierskalla, W. P. (Eds.), *Operations research and health care: A handbook of methods and applications* (pp. 595–614). Boston: Kluwer Academic Publishers.

Scheetz, L. J., Zhang, J., Kolassa, J. E., Allen, P., & Allen, M. (2008). Evaluation of injury databases as a preliminary step to developing a triage decision rule. *Journal of Nursing Scholarship, 40*(2), 144–150. doi:10.1111/j.1547-5069.2008.00219.x

Scheffler, R. M., Liu, J. X., Kinfu, J., & Dal Poz, M. L. (2008). Forecasting the global shortage of physicians: an economic- and needs-based approach. *Bulletin of the World Health Organization, 86*(7), 516–523..doi:10.2471/BLT.07.046474

Schlachta-Fairchild, L., Castelli, D., & Pyke, R. (2008). International telenursing: A strategic tool for nursing shortage and access to nursing care. In M. Jordanova & F. Lievens (Eds.), Global telemedicine / e-health updates:

Knowledge resources (Vol. 1, pp. 399-405). Luxembourg: Publ. Luxexpo.

Schonberger, R. J. (1984). Just-in-time production systems: Replacing complexity with simplicity in manufacturing management. *Industrial Engineering (American Institute of Industrial Engineers), 18*(10), 52–63.

Schumacher, S. (2007, August). Probabilistic record linkage. Paper presented at *2007 CDC Assessment Initiative Annual Conference*, Atlanta, GA.

Seely Brown, J., & Duguid, P. (1991). Organizational learning and communities of practice: toward a unified view of working, learning, and innovation [Special Issue]. *Organization Science, 2*(1), 40–57. doi:10.1287/orsc.2.1.40

Seers, K. (2007). Evaluating complex interventions. *Worldviews on Evidence-Based Nursing, 4*(2), 67–68. doi:10.1111/j.1741-6787.2007.00083.x

Sel`kov, A. I., Stolyar, V. L., Atkov, O. U., Sel`kova, E. A., & Chueva, N. V. (2008). Development conception of E-Diagnosis departments of small towns and villages clinics for developing regions and countries. In M. Jordanova & F. Lievens (Eds.), Electronic proceedings Med-e-Tel 2008: The international educational and networking forum for e-health, telemedicine and health ICT (pp. 395-414). Luxembourg: Publ. Luxexpo.

Sel`kov, A. I., Stolyar, V. L., Atkov, O. U., Sel`kova, E. A., & Chueva, N. V. (2007). Telemedicine experience to serve e-clinics. In M. Jordanova & F. Lievens (Eds.), Electronic proceedings Med-e-Tel 2007: The international educational and networking forum for e-health, telemedicine and health ICT, (pp. 211-217). Luxembourg: Publ. Luxexpo.

Selkov, A., Stolyar, V., Selkova, E., Atkov, O., & Chueva, N. (2005). Nine-years experience in telemedicine for rural & remote districts of Russia. *Ukrainian Journal of Telemedicine and Medical Telematics, 3*(2), 141–147.

Sequist, T. D., Gandhi, T. K., Karson, A. S., Fiskio, J. M., Bugbee, D., & Sperling, M. (2005). A randomized trial of electronic clinical reminders to improve quality of care for diabetes and coronary artery disease. *Journal of the American Medical Informatics Association, 12*(4), 431–437. doi:10.1197/jamia.M1788

Shachak, A., & Reis, S. (2009). The impact of electronic medical records on patient-doctor communication during consultation: a narrative literature review. *Journal of Evaluation in Clinical Practice, 15,* 641–649. doi:10.1111/j.1365-2753.2008.01065.x

Shachak, A., Hadas-Dayagi, M., Ziv, A., & Reis, S. (2009). Primary care physicians' use of an electronic medical record system: A cognitive task analysis. *Journal of General Internal Medicine, 24*(3), 341–348. doi:10.1007/s11606-008-0892-6

Shah, G. H. (2007). *Application of record linkage in public health: A review of software packages and purposes of linkage.* Poster presented at National Association of Health Data Organizations' Annual Meeting, October 18 – 20, 2007, San Diego, CA.

Shah, G. H. (2007). *Tracking hospital readmissions: Business case, and future directions.* Presented at 2007 CDC Assessment Initiative Annual Conference, Atlanta, GA.

Shah, G. H., Clarkson-Freeman, P. A., Ahmad, S. R., Varner, M., & Xu, W. (2008). Episiotomy and obstetric trauma in Utah: Evidence from linked hospital discharge and birth data. *Utah's Health. An Annual Review, 13,* 44–52.

Shah, G. H., Clarkson-Freeman, P. A., Cofrin, K., & Xu, W. (2007). Cesarean deliveries and newborn injuries: Evidence from linked Utah birth certificate and inpatient discharge data. *Utah's Health. An Annual Review, 12,* 10–24.

Shah, G. H., Fatima, F., & McBride, S. (2007). A *critical assessment of record linkage software used in public health.* National Association of Health Data Organizations (NAHDO) White Paper, 2008. Retrieved Jan 28, 2009 from http://nahdo.org/cs/media/p/124/download.aspx

Shah, G. H., Greenway, J. A., & Yang, W. (2007). Episiotomy and obstetric trauma in Nevada: Evidence from linked hospital discharge and birth data. *Nevada Public Health Association Journal, 4*(1), 1–10.

Shah, N. R., Seger, A. C., Seger, D. L., Fiskio, J. M., Kuperman, G. J., Blumenfeld, B., et al. (2005). Improving override rates for computerized prescribing alerts in ambulatory care. *AMIA Annual Symposium Proceedings,* (pp. 1110).

Shah, S., Kapoor, A., Ding, J., Guion, P., Petrisor, P., & Karanian, J. (2008). Surgical robotics, instrumentation and navigation. *International Journal of Computer Assisted Radiology and Surgery, 3*(1), 119–125. doi:10.1007/s11548-008-0181-1

Shao-hua, L. (29 August 2000). Genes, ethics, and Aborigines. *Taipei Times.* Retrieved from http://www.taipeitimes.com/news/2000/08/29/print/0000050974

Sharma, M. (2005). Information and communication technology for poverty reduction. *Turkish On-Line Journal of Distance Education, 6*(2). Retrieved from http://tojde.anadolu.edu.tr/tojde18/ notes_for_editor/note2.htm

Shea, S. (2007). The informatics for diabetes and education telemedicine (IDEATel) project. *Transactions of the American Clinical and Climatological Association, 118,* 289–304.

Shefter, S. M. (2006). Workflow technology: the new frontier. How to overcome the barriers and join the future. *Lippincott's Case Management, 11*(1), 25–34.

Shieber, S. M. (2009). Equity for open-access journal publishing. *PLoS Biology, 7*(8), e1000165. doi:10.1371/journal.pbio.1000165

Shortliffe, E. H. (2005). Strategic action in health information technology: Why the obvious has taken so long. *Health Affairs, 24*(5), 1222–1233. doi:10.1377/hlthaff.24.5.1222

Shulman, R., Singer, M., Goldstone, J., & Bellingan, G. (2005). Medication errors: a prospective cohort study of hand-written and computerised physician order entry in the intensive care unit. *Critical Care (London, England), 9*(5), R516–R521. doi:10.1186/cc3793

Sidorov, J. (2006). It ain't necessarily so: The electronic health record and the unlikely prospect of reducing health care costs. *Health Affairs, 25*(4), 1079–1085. doi:10.1377/hlthaff.25.4.1079

Sidoti, M. S., Asfendis, P. E., & Etish, S. J. (2009). *Case Law Update: A discussion of key federal court decisions involving electronic discovery from 2008 to present.* Available at http://www.gibbonslaw.com/news_publications/articles.php?action=display_publication&publication_id=2718&practice_id=76

Silber, D. (2003). *The case for e-health.* Paper presented at the European Commission's first high-level conference on e-health. Brussels, Belgium.

Silenas, R., Waller, S.G., D'Amore, A.R., & Carlton, P.K. (2008). US Armed Forces medical operations other than war. *International journal of risk assessment and management, 9*(4), 367-375.

Silipec, S. (1988). Making the switch from manufacturing to health care. *Industrial Engineering (American Institute of Industrial Engineers), 20*(10), 76–77.

Silver, J., Zhang, B., & Pasupathy, K. (2010) Interruptions in Pharmacy: Classification and Error Estimation. *Proceedings of the 2010 Industrial Engineering Research Conference,* Cancun, Mexico.

Silvert, W. (2001). Modeling as a discipline. *International Journal of General Systems, 30*(3), 261–282. doi:10.1080/03081070108960709

Simpson, L., Robinson, P., Fletcher, M., & Wilson, R. (2005). e-Communication skills. Oxford, UK: Radcliff.

Slack, W. V. (2001). *Cybermedicine: how computing empowers doctors and patients for better care.* San Francisco, CA: Jossey-Bass.

Slaughter, A. M. (2009, January-February). America's edge: power in the networked century. *Foreign Affairs.* Retrieved from http://www.foreignaffairs.org/20090101faessay88107-p0/anne-marie-slaughter/america-s-edge.html

Sleeboom, M. (2005). The Harvard case of Xu Xiping: Exploitation of the people, scientific advance, or genetic theft? *New Genetics & Society, 24*(1), 57–78. doi:10.1080/14636770500037776

Smalley, H. E. (1982). *Hospital management engineering.* New Jersey: Prentice-Hall, Inc.

Smith, A. C., & Gray, L. (2009). Telemedicine across the ages. *The Medical Journal of Australia, 190*(1), 15–19.

Smith, A. C., Batch, J., Lang, E., & Wootton, R. (2003). The use of online health techniques to assist with the delivery of specialist paediatric diabetes services in Queensland. *Journal of Telemedicine and Telecare, 9*(Suppl 2), 54–57. doi:10.1258/135763303322596273

Smith, A. C., Coulthard, M., Clark, R., Armfield, N., Taylor, S., & Goffe, R. (2005). Wireless telemedicine for the delivery of specialist paediatric services to the bedside. *Journal of Telemedicine and Telecare, 11*(Suppl. 2), 81–85. doi:10.1258/135763305775124669

Smith, A. C., Scuffham, P., & Wootton, R. (2007). The cost and potential savings of a novel telepaediatric service in Queensland. *BMC Health Services Research, 7,* 35. doi:10.1186/1472-6963-7-35

Smith, A. C., Youngberry, K., Christie, F., Isles, A., McCrossin, R., & Williams, M. (2003). The family costs of attending hospital outpatient appointments via videoconference and in person. *Journal of Telemedicine and Telecare, 9*(Suppl 2), 58–61. doi:10.1258/135763303322596282

Smith, A. C., Youngberry, K., Mill, J., Kimble, R., & Wootton, R. (2004). A review of three years experience using email and videoconferencing for delivery of post-acute burns care to children in Queensland. *Burns, 30*(3), 248–252. doi:10.1016/j.burns.2003.11.003

Smith, A., Scuffham, P., & Wootton, R. (2007). The costs and potential savings of a novel telepaediatric service in Queensland. *BioMed Central Health Services Research, 7,* 35..doi:10.1186/1472-6963-7-35

Smith, D. H., Perrin, N., Feldstein, A., Yang, X., Kuang, D., & Simon, S. R. (2006). The impact of prescribing safety alerts for elderly persons in an electronic medical record: an interrupted time series evaluation. *Archives of Internal Medicine, 166*(10), 1098–1104. doi:10.1001/archinte.166.10.1098

Smith, P. (2007). *The utility of force: The art of war in the modern world*. New York: Knopf.

Smith, R. (2000). Getting closer to patients and their families. *British Medical Journal, 321*. Retrieved from http://www.bmj.com.proxy1.lib.uwo.ca:2048/cgi/reprint/321/7275/0.

Social Watch. (2007). *In Dignity and Rights.* Uruguay: Montevideo. Retrieved from http://www.socialwatch.org/en/informeImpreso/overview2007.htm

Social Watch. (2008). *Rights is the Answer.* Uruguay: Montevideo. Retrieved from http://www.socialwatch.org/en/informeImpreso/index.htm

Soomro, A., & Cavalcanti, D. (2007). Opportunities and challenges in using WPAN and WLAN technologies in medical environments. *IEEE Communications Magazine, 45*(2), 114–122. doi:10.1109/MCOM.2007.313404

Sorrells-Jones, J., Tschirch, P., & Liong, M. (2006). Nursing and tele-health: Opportunities for nurse leaders to shape the future. *Nurse Leader, 4*(5), 42–58. doi:10.1016/j.mnl.2006.07.008

Soyer, H. P., Hofmann-Wellenhof, R., Massone, C., Gabler, G., Dong, H., Ozdemir, F., & Argenziano, G. (2005). telederm.org: Freely available online consultations in dermatology. *Public Library of Science Medicine (PLoS Med), 2*(4), e87. Retrieved January 5, 2009 from http://medicine.plosjournals.org/perlserv/?request=get-document&doi=10.1371%2Fjournal.pmed.0020087&ct=1

Space medicine. (2008). *The Columbia Encyclopedia,* (6th ed.). New York: Columbia University Press. Retrieved January 28, 2009, from http://www.encyclopedia.com/doc/1E1-spacemed.html

Spear, S. J., & Bowen, H. K. (1999). Decoding the DNA of the Toyota production system. *Harvard Business Review, 77*(5), 96–106.

Speicher, C. D. S.J.J. (1983). Choosing Effective Laboratory Tests, W.B. Saunders, (Ed.). Philadelphia, PA: W.B.Saunders.

Spivack, N. (2006). The third-generation web is coming. *KurzweilAI.net*, December 17, 2006. http://www.kurzweilai.net/meme/frame.html?main=/articles/art0689.html?m%3D3

Steel, P. M., & Konschnik, C. A. (1997, March 20-21). Post-matching administrative record linkage between sole proprietorship tax returns and the standard statistical establishment list. In Record Linkage Techniques - 1997: Proceedings of an International Workshop and Exposition (pp. 179-189). Arlington, VA. Washington, DC: National Academy Press.

Steele, A. W., Eisert, S., Witter, J., Lyons, P., Jones, M. A., Gabow, P., & Ortiz, E. (2005). The effect of automated alerts on provider ordering behavior in an outpatient setting. *PLoS Medicine, 2*(9), e255. Retrieved from Doi: 10.1371/journal.pmed.0020255

Steinman, M. (2009). Under the pretence of autonomy: Contradictions in the guidelines for human tissue donation. *Medicine, Health Care, and Philosophy, 12*, 281–28. doi:10.1007/s11019-009-9181-3

Sterman, J. D. (2000). *Business dynamics, system thinking and modeling for a complex world*. New York: Irwin McGraw-Hill.

Sterman, J. D. (2002). All models are wrong: reflections on becoming a systems scientist. *System Dynamics Review, 18*, 501–531. doi:10.1002/sdr.261

Stojakovic, M. (2008). Posttraumatic stress disorder and telepsychiatry. In Jordanova, M., & Lievens, F. (Eds.), *Global telemedicine / e-health updates: Knowledge resources (Vol. 1*, pp. 385–388). Luxembourg: Luxexpo.

Strehle, E. M., & Shabde, N. (2006). One hundred years of telemedicine: Does this new technology have a place in paediatrics? *Archives of Disease in Childhood, 91*, 956–959. doi:10.1136/adc.2006.099622

Stuckler, D., King, L. P., & Basu, S. (2008). International monetary fund programs and tuberculosis outcomes in post-communist countries. *PLoS Medicine, 5*(7), e143.. doi:10.1371/journal.pmed.0050143

Studdert, D. M., Mello, M. M., Gawande, A. A., Gandhi, T. K., Kachalia, A, & Yoon, C.,... Brennan, T.A. (2006). Claims, errors, and compensation payments in medical malpractice litigation. *The New England Journal of Medicine, 354*, 2024–2033. doi:10.1056/NEJMsa054479

Sujith, E. (2008, June 24). Cloud computing in healthcare. *Frost & Sullivan.* Retrieved from http://www.frost.com/prod/servlet/market-insight-top.pag?docid=135578323

Sullivan, L. P. (1986). Quality function deployment. *Quality Progress, 19*(6), 39–50.

Sullivan, L. P. (1988). Policy management through quality function deployment. *Quality Progress, 21*(6), 18–20.

Sum, K., Zheng, Y. P., & Mak, A. F. (2005). In Nugent, C., McCullagh, P., McAdams, E., & Lymberis, A. (Eds.), *Personalised Health Management Systems: The Integration of Innovative Sensing, Textile, Information and Communication Technologies* (pp. 43–50). Amsterdam, The Netherlands: IOS Press.

Sweeney, L. B., & Sterman, J. D. (2000, Winter). Bathtub dynamics, initial results of a systems thinking inventory. *System Dynamics Review, 16*, 249–286. doi:10.1002/sdr.198

Tabar, A. M., Keshavarz, A., & Aghajan, H. (2006). Smart Home care network using sensor fusion and distributed vision-based reasoning. In *Proceedings of the 4th ACM International Workshop on Video Surveillance and Sensor Network (VSSN 2004),* (pp. 145-154). Santa Barbara, CA: ACM Press.

Talbot, M. (2007, July). Duped: Can brain scans uncover lies? *The New Yorker.* Retrieved from http://www.newyorker.com/reporting/2007/07/02/070702fa_fact_talbot

Taleb, T., Bottazzi, D., Guizani, M., & Nait-Charif, H. (2009). ANGELAH: A framework for assisting elders at home. *IEEE Journal on Selected Areas in Communications, 27*(4), 480–495. doi:10.1109/JSAC.2009.090511

Tamblyn, R., Huang, A., Perreault, R., Jacques, A., Roy, D., & Hanley, J. (2003). The medical office of the 21st century (MOXXI): effectiveness of computerized decision-making support in reducing inappropriate pre-

scribing in primary care. *Canadian Medical Association Journal, 169*(6), 549–556.

Tang, P. C., Ash, J. W., Bates, D. W., Overhage, M., & Sands, D. Z. (2006). Personal health records: Definitions, benefits, and strategies for overcoming barriers to adoption. *Journal of the American Medical Informatics Association, 13*, 121–126. doi:10.1197/jamia.M2025

Tang, P. C., LaRosa, M. P., Newcomb, C., & Gorden, S. M. (1999). Measuring the effects of reminders for outpatient influenza immunizations at the point of clinical opportunity. *Journal of the American Medical Informatics Association, 6*, 115–121.

Tapscott, D., & Williams, A. D. (2006). *Wikinomics: How mass collaboration changes everything.* New York: Penguin Group Inc.

Tapscott, D., & Williams, A. D. (2008). *Wikinomics: How mass collaboration changes everything, (Expanded Edition).* New York: Portfolio.

Taylor, K., & Dangerfield, B. (2005). Modelling the feedback effects of reconfiguring health services. *The Journal of the Operational Research Society, 56*, 659–675. doi:10.1057/palgrave.jors.2601862

Taylor, S. (2003). Protecting privacy in Canada's private sector. *Information Management Journal, 37*, 33–39.

Taylor-Gooby, P. (2006). Trust, risk, and healthcare reform. *Health Risk & Society, 8*(2), 97–103. doi:10.1080/13698570600677092

Teerlink, C. C., Hegewald, M. J., & Cannon-Albright, L. A. (2007). A genealogical assessment of heritable predisposition to asthma mortality. *American Journal of Respiratory and Critical Care Medicine, 176*, 865–870. doi:10.1164/rccm.200703-448OC

The Wellcome Trust. (2000, July 23). *Ethical aspects and public consultation. Public perceptions of the collection of human biological samples.* Retrieved from http://www.wellcome.ac.uk/en/1/biovenpopethepub.html

Thede, L. (2008 August). Informatics: The electronic health record: Will nursing be on board when the ship leaves? *Online Journal of Nursing Informatics, 13* (3).

Available at www.nursingworld.org/MainMenuCategories/ANAMarketplace/ANAPeriodicals/OJIN/Columns/Informatics/ElectronicHealthRecord.aspx

Thielke, S., Hammond, K., & Helbig, S. (2007). Copying and pasting of examinations within the electronic medical record. *International Journal of Medical Informatics, 76*(Suppl 1), S122–S128. doi:10.1016/j.ijmedinf.2006.06.004

Thomas, J. A., Martin, V., & Frank, S. (2000). Improving pharmacy supplychain management in the operating room. *Healthcare Financial Management, 54*(12), 58–61.

Tierney, K. J. (2006). Testimony on needed emergency management reforms. *Journal of Homeland Security and Disaster Management, 4*(3), 15.

Tierney, W. M., Overhage, J. M., Murray, M. D., Harris, L. E., Zhou, X. H., & Eckert, G. J. (2005). Can computer-generated evidence-based care suggestions enhance evidence-based management of asthma and chronic obstructive pulmonary disease? A randomized, controlled trial. *Health Services Research, 40*(2), 477–497. doi:10.1111/j.1475-6773.2005.0t369.x

Tierney, W. M., Rotich, J. K., Hannan, T. J., Siika, A. M., Biondich, P. G., & Mamlin, B. W. (2007). The AMPATH medical record system: creating, implementing, and sustaining an electronic medical record system to support HIV/AIDS care in western Kenya. *Studies in Health Technology and Informatics, 129*(Pt 1), 372–376.

Toledo, V. (2006). Indigenous peoples and biodiversity. In Levin, S. (Ed.), *Encyclopedia of biodiversity*. Princeton, NJ: Academic Press.

Toth-Pal, E., Nilsson, G. H., & Furhoff, A. K. (2004). Clinical effect of computer generated physician reminders in health screening in primary health care--a controlled clinical trial of preventive services among the elderly. *International Journal of Medical Informatics, 73*(9-10), 695–703. doi:10.1016/j.ijmedinf.2004.05.007

Tsay, A. A., & Nahmias, S. (1998). Modeling supply chain contracts: A review. In Tayur, S., Magazine, M., & Ganeshan, R. (Eds.), *Quantitative models for supply chain management* (pp. 299–336). Boston: Kluwer Academic Publishers.

Tsitlakidis, C., Mylonakis, J., & Niakas, D. (2005). Economic evaluation of telemedicine for a remotely located population: the case of two Greek islands. *International Journal of Electronic Healthcare, 1*(3), 243–260. doi:10.1504/IJEH.2005.006473

Tsuji, M., Akematsu, Y., & Taoka, F. (2007). *How much can e-health systems save medical expenditures?* Paper Presented at 21st Pacific Science Congress Okinawa, Asia Pacific telemedicine Initiative, June 15-16, Okinawa, 2007.

Tuchman Matthews, J. (1989 Spring). Redefining security. *Foreign Affairs*. Retrieved from http://www.foreignaffairs.org/19890301faessay5953/jessica-tuchman-mathews/redefining-security.html

UNESCO. (2005). *Towards knowledge societies.* Paris: UNESCO Publishing. Retrieved from http://unesdoc.unesco.org/images/0014/001418/141843e.pdf

United Nations Educational, Scientific and Cultural Organization (UNESCO). (2003). *International declaration on human genetic data.* Retrieved from http://portal.unesco.org/en/ev.php-URL_ID=17720&URL_DO=DO_TOPIC&URL_SECTION=201.html

United Nations Population Division. (2000). *World population prospects: The 2000 revision.* Retrieved from http://www.un.org/esa/population/publications/wpp2000/wpp2000_volume3.htm

United States Embassy Beijing. (2000). *Human research subject protection in China: Implications for U.S. collaborators.*

Unruh, L. (2008). Nurse staffing: Key to good patient, nurse, and financial outcomes. Presentation at *136 Annual APHA Meeting*, San Diego, CA, October 26-29, 2008. Available at http://www.dpeaflcio.org/programs/DPE_and_Professional_Associations/docs/APHA_2008_Nurse_staffing_and_outcomes.pdf

US Census Bureau. (2008). *Income, poverty, and health insurance coverage in the United States: 2007.* Washington, DC: US Census Bureau. Retrieved from http://www.census.gov/prod/2008pubs/p60-235.pdf

US Government. (2008). *Federal guidance to assist states in improving state-level pandemic influenza operating plans.* Washington, DC: US Government: Retrieved from http://www.flu.gov/news/guidance031108.pdf

US Mission to the UN. (2002). *Release 65: USAI leads public and private partners to improve health and save lives through food fortification.* New York: USUN. Retrieved from http://www.un.int.usa/02_065.htm

US National Intelligence Council. (2008). *Strategic implications of global health.* Washington, DC: Office of the Director of National Intelligence.

Uttal, W. R. (2001). *The new phrenology: the limits of localizing cognitive processes in the brain.* Cambridge, MA: MIT Press.

Utter, D. (1997, March 20-21). Use of probabilistic linkage for an analysis of the effectiveness of safety belts and helmets. In: Record Linkage Techniques - 1997: Proceedings of an International Workshop and Exposition (pp. 67-70), Arlington, VA. Washington, DC: National Academy Press.

Vallat, B. (2007, July 11). *Avian influenza epizootie: where do we stand in 2007.* [Snowdon Lecture]. Retrieved from http://www.csiro.au/multimedia/SnowdonLecture2007Ch2.html

van der Sijs, H., Aarts, J., Vulto, A., & Berg, M. (2006). Overriding of drug safety alerts in computerized physician order entry. *Journal of the American Medical Informatics Association, 13*(2), 138–147. doi:10.1197/jamia.M1809

VanSuch, M., Naessens, J. M., Stroebel, R. J., Huddleston, J. M., & Williams, A. R. (2006). Effect of discharge instructions on readmission of hospitalised patients with heart failure: Do all of the Joint Commission on Accreditation of Healthcare Organizations heart failure core measures reflect better care? *Quality & Safety in Health Care, 15,* 414–417. doi:10.1136/qshc.2005.017640

Ventres, W., Kooienga, S., & Marlin, R. (2006). EHRs in the exam room: tips on patient-centered care. *Family Practice Management, 13*(3), 45–47.

Ventres, W., Kooienga, S., Marlin, R., Vuckovic, N., & Stewart, V. (2005). Clinician style and examination room computers: a video ethnography. *Family Medicine, 37*(4), 276–281.

Ventres, W., Kooienga, S., Vuckovic, N., Marlin, R., Nygren, P., & Stewart, V. (2006). Physicians, Patients, and the Electronic Health Record: An Ethnographic Analysis. *Annals of Family Medicine, 4*(2), 124–131. doi:10.1370/afm.425

Vinge, V. (1993). *The coming technological singularity: How to survive in the post-human era.* VISION-21 Symposium sponsored by NASA Lewis Research Center and the Ohio Aerospace Institute, March 30-31, 1993. Retrieved on August 14, 2009 from http://www.rohan.sdsu.edu/faculty/vinge/misc/singularity.html

Virapongse, A., Bates, D. W., Shi, P., Jenter, C. A., Volk, L. A., Kleinman, K. et al. (2008). Electronic health records and malpractice claims in office practice. *Archives of Internal Medicine, 168*(21), 2362-7.

Von Clausewitz, C. (1976). On War (M. Howard & P. Paret Trans.). In Howard, M., & Paret, P. (Eds.), *On War.* New York: Knopf.

von Lubitz, D. K. J. E. (2008). Medical readiness for operations other than war: Boyd's OODA Loop and training using advanced distributed simulation technology. *International Journal of Risk Assessment and Management, 9*(4), 409–432. doi:10.1504/IJRAM.2008.020417

von Lubitz, D. K. J. E. (in press). The Teams of Leaders (ToL) concept: the grid, the mesh, and the people in the world of information and knowledge-based global healthcare. In Kladiashvili, E. (Ed.), *Grid Technologies for eHealth: Applications for Telemedicine Services and Delivery.* Hershey, PA: IGI Press.

von Lubitz, D. K. J. E., & Beakley, J. (2009). "Teams of Leaders" concept in homeland security and disaster management operations. *International Journal of*

Homeland Security and Emergency Management, 5(1), 25. doi:.doi:10.2202/1547-7355.1458

von Lubitz, D. K. J. E., & Patricelli, F. (2006). Network-centric healthcare operations; Data warehousing and the associated telecommunication platforms. *International Journal of Services and Standards, 3*(1), 97–119. doi:10.1504/IJSS.2007.011830

von Lubitz, D. K. J. E., & Patricelli, F. (2008). Telecommunications infrastructure for worldwide network-centric healthcare operations and the associated information system. *The International Journal of Business and Systems Research, 2*(1), 34–51. doi:10.1504/IJBSR.2008.018119

von Lubitz, D. K. J. E., & Wickramasinghe, N. (2006a). Healthcare and technology: the doctrine of network-centric healthcare. *International Journal of Electronic Healthcare, 4*, 322–344.

von Lubitz, D. K. J. E., & Wickramasinghe, N. (2006b). Networkcentric healthcare: outline of entry portal concept. *International Journal of Electronic Business Management, 4*(1), 16–28.

von Lubitz, D. K. J. E., Beakley, J., & Patricelli, F. (2008). "All hazards approach" to network-centric disaster management: the role of information and knowledge management, and Boyd's OODA Loop in disaster leadership. *The Journal of Disaster Study, Policy and Management.* DOI:10.1111/j.0361-3666.2008.01060.x Retrieved from http://www.blackwell-synergy.com/ toc/disa/0/0

von Lubitz, D. K. J. E., Beakley, J., & Patricelli, F. (2008). Disaster management: The structure, function, and significance of network-centric operations. *Journal of Homeland Security and Emergency Management, 11*(5). Retrieved from http://www.bepress.com/jhsem/vol5/iss1/1.

von Lubitz, D. K. J. E., Levine, H., & Wolf, E. (2002). The goose, the gander, or the Strasbourg paté for all: Medical education, world, and the Internet. In Chin, W., Patricelli, F., & Milutinovic, V. (Eds.), *Electronic business and education: Recent advances in Internet infrastructures* (pp. 189–210). Boston: Kluwer Academic Publishers.

von Lubitz, D. K. J. E., Levine, H., Patricelli, F., & Richir, S. (2008). Distributed simulation-based medical training: Going beyond the obvious. In Kyle, R., & Murray, B. (Eds.), *Clinical Simulation: Operations, Engineering, and Management* (pp. 591–625). Amsterdam: Elsevier Press.

von Lubitz, D. K. J. E., Wickramasinghe, N., & Yanovsky, G. (2006). Networkcentric healthcare operations: the telecommunications structure. *International Journal of Networking and Virtual Organisations, 3*(1), 60–85. doi:10.1504/IJNVO.2006.008785

von Niman, B. (2007). *User experience guidelines for e-health telecare services - ETSI Industry consensus workshop.* Paper presented at Med-e-Tel 2007, Luxembourg, G.D. of Luxembourg. Retrieved January 21, 2009, from http://www.medetel.lu/download/2007/parallel_sessions/presentation/0418/ETSI.pdf

Vontetsianos, T., Giovas, P., Milsis, A., Katsaras, T., Rigopoulou, A., Mpofos, D., & Giaboudakis, P. (2009). Clinical use of wearable technologies for chronic patients' early hospital discharge. In Jordanova, M., & Lievens, F. (Eds.), *Global telemedicine / e-health updates: Knowledge resources* (*Vol. 2*, pp. 186–190). Luxembourg: Luxexpo.

Vul, E., Harris, C., Winkielman, P., & Pashler, H. (2009). Puzzlingly high correlations in fMRI studies of emotion, personality, and social cognition. (The article was formerly known as "Voodoo correlations in social neuroscience.»). *Perspectives on Psychological Science, 4*, 274–290. doi:10.1111/j.1745-6924.2009.01125.x

Wagner, B., Knaevelsrud, C., & Maercker, A. (2006). Internet-based cognitive-behavioral therapy for complicated grief: a randomized controlled trial. *Death Studies, 30*(5), 429–453. doi:10.1080/07481180600614385

Wagner, D., Bear, M., & Sander, J. (2009). Turning simulation into reality: increasing student competence and confidence. *The Journal of Nursing Education, 48*(8), 465–467. doi:10.3928/01484834-20090518-07

Wahl, J. B. (1997 March 20-21). Linking federal estate tax records. In: Record Linkage Techniques - 1997: Proceedings of an International Workshop and Exposition (pp. 171-178), Arlington, VA. Washington, DC: National Academy Press.

Wald, H. S., Dube, C. E., & Anthony, D. C. (2007). Untangling the web – the impact of Internet use on health care and the physician-patient relationship. *Patient Education and Counseling, 68*(3), 218–224. doi:10.1016/j.pec.2007.05.016

Walker, J., Pan, E., Johnston, D., Adler-Milstein, J., Bates, D. W., & Middleton, B. (2005). The value of health care information exchange and interoperability. *Health Affairs (Project Hope)*, (Suppl Web Exclusives), W5-10–W15-18.

Ward, R., & Wamsley, G. (2007). From a painful past to an uncertain future. In Rubin, C. (Ed.), *Emergency management: The American experience 1900-2005* (pp. 207–242). Fairfax, VA: PERI.

Ward, R., Stevens, C., Brentnall, P., & Briddon, J. (2008). The attitudes of health care staff to information technology: a comprehensive review of the research literature. *Health Information and Libraries Journal, 25*(2), 81–97. doi:10.1111/j.1471-1842.2008.00777.x

Watts, D. J. (2003). *Six degrees: The science of a connect age*. New York: Norton.

Wei, J. S., Greer, B. T., Westermann, F., Steinberg, S. M., Son, C. G., & Chen, Q. R. (2004). Prediction of clinical outcome using gene expression profiling and artificial neural networks for patients with neuroblastoma. *Cancer Research, 64*(19), 6883–6891. doi:10.1158/0008-5472.CAN-04-0695

Wei, Y. (2008). *Building a semantic blog support system for gene learning objects on Web 2.0 environment*. MSc Thesis, September 2008, Department of Computer Science, Lakehead University.

Weick, K. E. (1990). The vulnerable system - an analysis of the Tenerife air disaster. *Journal of Management, 16*(3), 571–596. doi:10.1177/014920639001600304

Weiner, J. P., Kfuri, T., Chan, K., & Fowles, J. B. (2007). "e-Iatrogenesis": the most critical unintended consequence of CPOE and other HIT. *Journal of the American Medical Informatics Association, 14*(3), 387–388, discussion 389. doi:10.1197/jamia.M2338

Weiner, M., & Biondich, P. (2006). The influence of information technology on patient-physician relationships. *Journal of General Internal Medicine, 21*(Suppl 1), S35–S39. doi:10.1111/j.1525-1497.2006.00307.x

Weingart, S. N., Toth, M., Sands, D. Z., Aronson, M. D., Davis, R. B., & Phillips, R. S. (2003). Physicians' decisions to override computerized drug alerts in primary care. *Archives of Internal Medicine, 163*(21), 2625–2631. doi:10.1001/archinte.163.21.2625

Weisberg, D. S., Keil, F. C., Goodstein, J., Rawson, E., & Gray, J. R. (2008). The seductive allure of neuroscience explanations. *Journal of Cognitive Neuroscience, 20*(3), 470–477. doi:10.1162/jocn.2008.20040

Wells, C. (1999). The millennium bug and corporate criminal liability. *The Journal of Information, Law and Technology (JILT), 2*. Available at http://www2.warwick.ac.uk/fac/soc/law/elj/jilt/1999_2/wells

Wen, H. J., & Tan, J. (2005). Mapping e-health strategies: Thinking outside the traditional healthcare box. *International Journal of Electronic Healthcare, 1*(3), 261–276. doi:10.1504/IJEH.2005.006474

Westin, A. F. (2007). *How the public views privacy and health research*. Washington, DC: National Academy of Sciences.

Westwood, M. A., Flett, A. S., Riding, P., & Moon, J. C. (2009). How to Webcast lectures and conferences. *British Medical Journal, 338*, b31. doi:10.1136/bmj.b31

Wheatley, T., & Wegner, D. M. (2001). Automaticity of action, psychology of. In Smelser, N. J., & Baltes, P. B. (Eds.), *International encyclopedia of the social & behavioral sciences* (pp. 991–993). Oxford, UK: Pergamon.

Wheelwright, J. (2005). Native America's alleles. *Discover, 26*(5), 3. Retrieved from http://discovermagazine.com/2005/may/native-americas-alleles.

White, D. A. (1997, March 20-21). Review of the statistics of record linkage for genealogical research, record linkage techniques. In Record Linkage Techniques - 1997: Proceedings of an International Workshop and Exposition (pp. 362-373), Arlington, VA. Washington, DC: National Academy Press.

White, K. L., Williams, T. F., & Greenberg, B. G. (1961). The ecology of medical care. *The New England Journal of Medicine, 265*, 885–892.

Whitten, P. S, Bergman, A., Meese, M., Bridwell, K., & Jule, K. (2009). St. Vincent's home tele-health for congestive heart failure patients. *Journal of Telemedicine and e-Health, 15*, 148-153.

Whitten, P. S., & Mackert, M. S. (2005). Addressing tele-health's foremost barrier: Provider as initial gatekeeper. *International Journal of Technology Assessment in Health Care, 21*, 517–521. doi:10.1017/S0266462305050725

Whitten, P. S., Mair, F. S., Haycox, A., May, C. R., Williams, T. L., & Hellmich, S. (2002). Systematic review of cost effectiveness studies of telemedicine interventions. *British Medical Journal, 324*, 1434–1437. doi:10.1136/bmj.324.7351.1434

Whitten, P., & Buis, L. (2007). Private payer reimbursement for telemedicine services in the United States. *Telemedicine Journal and e-Health, 13*, 15–23. doi:10.1089/tmj.2006.0028

Whitten, P., Buis, L., & Mackert, M. (2007). Factors impacting providers' perceptions regarding a midwestern university-based EMR. *Telemedicine Journal and e-Health, 13*, 391–397. doi:10.1089/tmj.2006.0057

Whitten. P., Johannessen, L.,K., Soerensen, T., Gammon, D., & Mackert, M. (2007). A systematic review of research methodology in telemedicine studies. *Journal of Telemedicine and Telecare, 13*, 230-235.

WHO. (2002). Integrated chronic disease prevention and control, Retrieved January 2, 2009, from http://www.who.int/chp/about/integrated_cd/en/index.html

WHO. (2003). Mental health in WHO's European Region 2001. Retrieved September 20, 2009 from http://www.euro.who.int/document/rc53/edoc07.pdf

WHO. (2005). World Health Assembly resolution on e-health, WHA 58.28, May 2005, Retrieved August 10, 2009, from http://www.euro.who.int/telemed/20060713_1

WHO. (2006). Chronic diseases and their common risk factor. Retrieved August 10, 2009, from http://www.who.int/chp/chronic_disease_report/media/Factsheet1.pdf

Wickramasinghe, N., & Schaffer, J. L. (2006). Creating knowledge-driven healthcare processes with the Intelligence Continuum. *International Journal of Electronic Healthcare, 2*(2), 164–174.

Wigand, R. T., Picot, A., & Reichwald, R. (1997). *Information, organization and management: Expanding markets and corporate boundaries*. Hoboken, NJ: Wiley & Sons.

Wiljer, D., Urowitz, S., Apatu, E., DeLenardo, C., Eysenbach, G, Harth, et al. & Canadian Committee for Patient Accessible Health Records. (2008). Patient accessible electronic health records: Exploring recommendations for successful implementation strategies. *Journal of Medical Internet Research, 10*(4), Retrieved from e34. doi:10.2196/jmir.1061

Williamson, J. W., Goldschmidt, P. G., & Jillson, I. A. (1979). Medical Practice Information Demonstration Project: Final Report. Baltimore, MD: Policy Research Inc. Office of the Assistant Secretary of Health, Department of Health, Education, and Welfare, contract 28277-0068GS.

Winkler, W. E. (1999). *The state of record linkage and current research problems. Technical report, Statistical Research Division, U*. Washington, DC: S. Census Bureau.

Winner, R. I., Pennell, J. P., Bertrand, H. E., & Slusarczuk, M. M. G. (1988). *The role of concurrent engineering in weapons system acquisition*. IDA Report R-338. Alexandria, VA: Institute for Defense Analysis.

Wong, J. G. (1996). Efficiency and effectiveness in the urgent care clinic. *Postgraduate Medicine, 99*(4), 161–166.

Wootton, R., & Tahir, M. S. M. (2004). Challenges in launching a Malaysian teleconsulting network. In Whitten, P., & Cook, D. (Eds.), *Understanding health communication technologies* (1st ed., pp. 11–18). San Francisco: John Wiley and Sons, Inc.

World Economic Forum. (2002). *Eurasia economic summit 2002: health and the future of business.* The Global Health Initiative of the World Economic Forum, 8 August.

World Health Organisation (WHO). (2008). Australia's disturbing health disparities set Aboriginals apart. *Bulletin of the WHO, 86*(4), 241-320. Retrieved December 15, 2008, from http://www.who.int/bulletin/volumes/86/4/08-020408/en/index.html

World Health Organization (WHO). (1998). *Proposed international guidelines on ethical issues in medical genetics and genetic services.* Retrieved from http://whqlibdoc.who.int/hq/1998/WHO_HGN_GL_ETH_98.1.pdf

World Health Organization (WHO). (2003). *Guideline for obtaining informed consent for the procurement and use of human tissues, cells, and fluids in research.* Retrieved from http://www.who.int/reproductivehealth/topics/ethics/human_tissue_use.pdf

World Health Organization (WHO). (2004). *The World Health Report: Changing history.* Geneva: World Health Organization.

World Health Organization (WHO). (2006). *Constitution of the World Health Organization.* Retrieved from http://www.who.int/governance/eb/who_constitution_en.pdf

World Health Organization (WHO). (2008). *Closing the gap in a generation: Health equity through action on the social determinants of health. Commission on Social Determinants of Health Final Report.* Geneva: World Health Organization.

World Health Statistics. (2008). *World Health Statistics Report.* Geneva: World Health Organization. Retrieved from http://www.who.int/whosis/whostat/en

Wu, B., Hicks, L., Jang, W., Savage, G., Pasupathy, K., Klein, C., et al. (2007). Conceptual framework of healthcare systems engineering and pilot curriculum development. In *Conference of American Society of Engineering Education*, Hawaii.

Wu, J. H., Huang, A. S., Hisa, T. L., & Tsai, H. T. (2006). Revolution or evolution? An analysis of E-health innovation and impact using a hypercube model. *International Journal of Electronic Healthcare, 2*(1), 12–34. doi:10.1504/IJEH.2006.008688

Wynn, B. O., & Scott, M. (2007). *Evaluation of severity-adjusted DRG systems. Addendum to the Interim Report.* Santa Monica, CA: RAND Health. Available at http://www.rand.org/pubs/working_papers/2007/RAND_WR434.1.pdf

Xiao, Y., Shen, X., Sun, B., & Cai, L. (2006). Security and privacy in RFID and applications in telemedicine. *IEEE Communications Magazine, 44*(4), 64–72. doi:10.1109/MCOM.2006.1632651

Yee, K. C. (2007). Bermuda Triangle or three to tango: generation Y, e-health and knowledge management. *Studies in Health Technology and Informatics, 129*(Pt.2), 1184–1188.

Yellowlees, P. (2006). Successfully developing a telemedicine system. In Wootton, R., Craig, J., & Patterson, V. (Eds.), *Introduction to telemedicine.* London: Royal Society of Medicine Press.

Yolles, M. (2005). Knowledge cycles and sharing: Considerations for health care management. In Bali, R. K. (Ed.), *Clinical knowledge management: Opportunities and challenges.* Hershey, PA: Idea Group.

Young, T., & Ireson, C. (2003). Effectiveness of school-based tele-health care in urban and rural elementary schools. *Pediatrics, 112*, 1088–1094. doi:10.1542/peds.112.5.1088

Zhang, B., & Pasupathy, K. (2009). *Pharmacy System Informatics: Data Mining using Data Envelopment Analysis to Improve Performance.* San Diego, CA: Data Mining System Informatics Workshop.

Zilinskas, R. A., & Chapman, R. C. (2007, January). *Security and public health: how and why do public health emergencies affect the security of a country.* Available as an NTI: Issue Brief at http://www.nti.org/e_research/ e3_84.html

Zupan, J. (2003). Perinatal mortality and morbidity in developing countries: A global view. *Medecine Tropicale, 63*, 366–368.

Candace J Gibson, PhD, CHIM is an Associate Professor in the Department of Pathology at the Schulich School of Medicine and Dentistry, the University of Western Ontario, in London, ON. She has been involved in medical research, teaching to undergraduate baccalaureate, medical, nursing and dental students, and administration in the department's graduate and undergraduate degree programs. Over the past decade she has been actively engaged in the introduction of teaching in health informatics as a medical school elective and in the health information management program in the Faculty of Health Sciences. In the latter program she teaches courses in pathology, health informatics, and health information management. Her current interests include the development of effective e-learning tools, HI and HIM curriculum development, and the introduction and use of the electronic health record.

Nada Gligorov completed her PhD in philosophy from the Graduate Center of City University of New York. Her two areas of specialization are philosophy of mind and bioethics. She has been a bioethics fellow from 2002-2007 at the Mount Sinai School of Medicine, where she has remained on the faculty as Assistant Professor of Medical Education and Assistant Director of Bioethics Education. She teaches both research and clinical ethics for the Mount Sinai--Union Graduate College Bioethics program. Her professional interests include neuroethics, advanced directives and the personal identity problem, consciousness, and the distinction between commonsense and scientific theories.

Terry John Hannan M.B.B.S FRACP, FACHI, FACMI, is a Consultant Physician in Internal Medicine at the Launceston General Hospital in Tasmania, Australia. He is an inaugural Fellow of the Australian College of Health Informatics and was its President from 2007 to 2009. His initial work in informatics was the international transfer and implementation of the Johns Hopkins Oncology computerized medical record system in a major teaching hospital in New South Wales. In 2000 he was invited to cofound the Mosoriot Medical Record System (MMRS) in Kenya that became the fore runner of the AMPATH (Academic Model for the Provision and Treatment of Health Care) which is based on the OpenMRS record project. He is a current member of the AMIA International Affairs Committee.

Kendall Ho, MD, FRCPC, is a practicing emergency medicine specialist and Associate Professor in the Department of Emergency Medicine at the University of British Columbia. He is the founding Director, eHealth Strategy Office, University of British Columbia Faculty of Medicine. He was the immediate past Associate Dean of the Division of Continuing Professional Development and Knowledge Translation (UBC CPD-KT). He is the executive director of the Technology Enabled Knowledge Translation Investigative Centre (TEKTIC) interdisciplinary research team in B.C. Dr. Ho's academic and research interests fall into the domain of technology enabled knowledge translation (TEKT) – the use of information technologies to accelerate the incorporation of latest health evidence into routine practice. Specific directions within TEKT include telehealth, information and communication technologies (ICT) and patient safety, ICT and public engagement, and evidence based policy translation in eHealth. He is a recipient of a number of provincial, national, and international research grants in eHealth and eLearning, and has published related papers and textbook chapters in these subjects.

Malina Jordanova, MD, Ph.D. received her medical degree in 1984, Ph.D. in neuropsychology in 1990, and subsequently a post-doctoral position at the Max-Planck Institute for Human Development and Education, Germany in 1994-1995. Dr. Jordanova is author and co-author of over 120 papers and more than 100 conference presentations; Vice-Rapporteur for Question 14/2 of International Telecom-

About the Contributors

Stefane M. Kabene, MPs, PhD, is a faculty member in the Aubrey Dan Program in Management and Organizational Studies with a cross appointment in the Faculty of Health Science at the University of Western Ontario, London, Ontario, Canada. His primary interests are in health care, information and communication technology and human resources for health. His focus is on interprofessional collaborative practice, knowledge transfer, quality of care and patient involvement in clinical decision making. The future of health care lies in health professionals' capacity and willingness to develop new ways of working together for the benefit of the patient. Knowledge and power sharing, role valuing, use of information and communication technology and patients' participation in decision making are only a few of the variables we need to better understand. Dr. Kabene is involved in research projects with the Schulich School of Medicine and Dentistry, the School of Nursing, and the Faculty of Social Sciences.

* * *

Jos Aarts is a research scientist at the Institute of Health Policy and Management and the Department of Medical Informatics of Erasmus University, Rotterdam in the Netherlands. His scientific interest is the impact of information technology on clinical work practices. His PhD thesis was on the implementation of computerized physician order entry systems in Dutch and American hospitals. His research papers on CPOE appeared in Health Affairs, the Journal of American Medical Informatics Association, the International Journal of Medical Informatics and Methods of Information in Medicine. Dr. Aarts has been a visiting scientist at the Oregon Health and Science University in the USA, and the University of New South Wales and the University of Sydney in Australia. Currently he is also a visiting research fellow at the University of Pennsylvania in the USA. He is chair of the Working Group on Human and Organizational Factors of Medical Informatics of the European Federation for Medical Informatics.

Kelly J. Abrams, MPA, CHIM, is Vice President of Education and Professional Practice for the Canadian Health Information Management Association (CHIMA). She has a diploma in Health Information Technology, an undergraduate degree in Health Administration, and a Masters degree in Public Administration (Public Policy). Kelly has over 25 years experience as a certified HIM Professional and has been involved in coding classification, data analysis, risk management, privacy, telehealth, teaching and management. She was awarded the CIHI/CHIMA Joady Murray Memorial Award in 2008.

Anteneh Ayanso is an Associate Professor of Information Systems at Brock University. He received his Ph.D. in Information Systems from the University of Connecticut and an MBA from Syracuse University. He teaches Data Management, Data Mining Techniques & Applications, Data Analysis & Business

Modelling, and Management of Information Systems & Technology. His research interests include data management, information retrieval, electronic business, and quantitative modelling in supply chains. His articles are published in Communications of the AIS, European Journal of Operational Research, Decision Support Systems, International Journal of Electronic Commerce, Journal of Computer Information Systems, Journal of Database Management, and in proceedings of major international conferences in information systems. His research has been funded by the Natural Sciences and Engineering Research Council of Canada (NSERC).

Robert J. Barnet M.D., M.A., FACP, FACC is a Senior Scholar in Residence at the Center for Clinical Bioethics at Georgetown University, Washington, DC. Dr. Barnet is a graduate of the University of Notre Dame and Loyola University School of Medicine (Chicago). Dr. Barnet practiced Cardiology for over 25 years in Reno, Nevada. Dr. Barnet received an M.A. in History from the University of Nevada (1986) and an M.A. in Philosophy from the University of Notre Dame (1988). He was a visiting scholar at the University of Notre Dame in 1989-90 (Theology: Ethics and Health Policy) and 1996-1997 (Philosophy). Dr. Barnet has been involved in medical ethics since 1982. He has lectured internationally and published more than 65 articles, on both cardiology and ethics, including on AIDS, end of life issues, health policy and the philosophy of medicine.

Nicholas G. Bircher is Associate Professor of Anesthesiology, University of Pittsburgh, from 1996-present; A.B., Chemistry and Physics, Harvard, 1977; M.D., University of Pittsburgh, 1981; Chair, Bylaws and Procedures Committee, 2007- present, Faculty Representative, Budget Committee of the Board of Trustees, 2005-present; President, University Senate 2003-2005; Co-Chair, American College of Critical Care Medicine Task Force on Glycemic Control, 2005-present; Scientist Emeritus, 2009-present, Senior Clinician Scientist, 2001-2009, and Associate Director, 1989-2001, Safar Center for Resuscitation Research; Co-Director, Neurovascular Intensive Care Unit, Presbyterian University Hospital, 2001-2007; Program Director, Anesthesiology Critical Care Medicine Fellowship, 2001-2007; Chairman, School of Medicine Planning and Budgeting Committee, 1993-2001; Senior Vice Chancellor Health Sciences Planning and Budgeting Committee, 1995-2001; Member, Faculty Assembly, 1997-2006, 2007-present; Faculty Representative, Health Sciences Committee of the Board of Trustees, 1997-2001; Member, Council, Faculty Association of the School of Medicine, 1998-present; Member, Ad Hoc University of Pittsburgh Physicians Faculty Oversight Committee, 1998-1999.

Dario Bottazzi PhD is currently working as a senior researcher at Guglielmo Marconi Labs SpA, Pontecchio (BO), Italy. Prior to his current position, he was research fellow in the Department of Electronic and Information Systems at the University of Bologna. His research interests include middleware solutions for collaborative applications in mobile environments, social computing, and pervasive computing technologies. He received his PhD in computer science engineering from the University of Bologna.

Emmett Davis, as an information worker in compliance with Moore's Law, was a librarian for one decade. For over two decades, he has innovated in information technology within local government Human Services. Emmett creates, consults, and authors on knowledge and information systems, including diffuse systems, artificial intelligence, quality, the synergy of technology and business processes, and e-government. Miracle materials are wonderful. But a culture, which continually builds brick walls, needs new ideas to also build arches in those walls for doors and windows.

Sisira Edirippulige PhD (Moscow), PhD (Auckland), MSc (Moscow), GradCe is Coordinator of Graduate Programs in e-Health care at the University of Queens line Health, Australia. Dr Edirippulige's main responsibilities involve teaching and undergraduate and graduate programs in e-healthcare. His research interests inclu promotion, and integration of telehealth education and telemedicine applications in tor. Before joining the University of Queensland, Dr Edirippulige taught at Kobe C Japan and at the University of Auckland in New Zealand. He has extensive experie studies working in a number of countries including Russia, Sri Lanka, South Afr Zealand.

Henry Ergas is a Canberra based economist. He was an economist at the OECL where he headed the Secretary-General's Task Force on Structural Adjustment (1 subsequently Counsellor for Structural Policy in the Economics Department. Sinc in 1993, Henry's work has focused on competition policy and regulatory econo closely involved in dealing with regulatory issues in a range of industries, includi tions, electricity, aviation, surface transport, and financial services. He chaired the I and Competition Policy Review Committee for the Australian Government in 19 member of the Prime Minister's Export Infrastructure Task Force in 2005 and of th Consultative Group in 2006. He has taught at a number of universities, including de la Statistique et de L'administration Economique (Paris), the Kennedy Schoo Harvard, Monash University in Melbourne and the University of Auckland.

Susan Evans-Mueller is a Project Director for HCA Shared Services Group, I ceived her MAIS from University of Houston, Victoria and has a BAAS from Tex – Kingsville.

Jinan Fiaidhi is Full Professor of Computer Science at Lakehead University. Sh Research Professor with the University of Western Ontario. She received a Ph.D. in Science from Brunel University in 1986, a Postgraduate Diploma in Microprocessors Essex University in 1983 and a Diploma in Production Engineering from the Univers 1978. Her research interest involves Collaborative Learning, Telemedical Education Environments, Virtual Multimedia Learning Objects, Mobile Learning, Collaborat Enterprise Level and at the Web, Applications of Mashups and Rich Internet Applic Developing Learning Infrastructures (e.g. P2P, Mobile, Wireless, Grid, Web 2.0), L and Folksonomies, and Learning Reasoners. Dr. Fiaidhi has a long research and tea she has held various academic positions including being a chairperson of the Depar Science-University of Technology, the postgraduate organizer of the Department ence, Sultan Qaboos University. Dr. Fiaidhi's research is fully supported by NSER(and Engineering Research Council) and CFI (Canada Foundation for Innovation) r Fiaidhi has authored four books, five chapters in books and over 100 refereed article journals and conference proceedings. Dr. Fiaidhi has had several notable research include Virtual SceneBeans, DICOM Based Mobile Infrastructure for Telemedical Le Semantic Blog, and Ontology Extracting Agent for Telemedical Blogging. Dr. Fiaid Software Engineer of Ontario (PEng), member of IEEE, CIPS, ACM and the BCS.

munication Union, Switzerland. Currently she is focusing on eHealth and ICT applications in health care. At present she coordinates a project devoted to telepsychology, funded by the Bulgarian National Science Fund. Since 2002 she has coordinated the annual Educational program of Med-e-Tel (The International eHealth, Telemedicine and Health ICT Forum for Education, Networking and Business, http://www.medetel.eu) and with F. Lievens is editor of the series "Global Telemedicine and eHealth Updates: Knowledge Resources". Volumes 1 & 2 were published in 2008 and 2009.

Stephen Krieger, MD completed his Neurology residency training at Mount Sinai in 2006. He received a Fellowship in clinical research from the National Multiple Sclerosis Society 2006, and completed a two-year fellowship training in Multiple Sclerosis at Mount Sinai in 2008. He graduated from Columbia College, and received his MD degree from Yale University. In addition to his clinical work at the MS Center, he has an academic appointment as Assistant Professor of Neurology at the Mount Sinai School of Medicine, where he is a member of the Education Committee and runs the Brain and Behavior seminar series for the medical school. His professional interests include MS, behavioral neurology, and modern MRI techniques.

Kaveepan Lertwachara is an Associate Professor of Information Systems at the Orfalea College of Business, California Polytechnic State University. He received his PhD in Information Systems from The University of Connecticut. His industry background is in health care information systems, public health, and health care quality. Dr. Lertwachara's research interest includes healthcare informatics, electronic commerce, online data retrieval, and economics of information systems. His research has been published in leading academic journals such as Communications of the Association for Information Systems, Decision Support Systems, International Journal of Human-Computer Studies, Journal of Computer Information Systems, Journal of Law and Economics, Journal of Management Information Systems, and Management Science.

Sabah Mohammed joined Glasgow University in 1979 for his graduate studies where he obtained his Post-Graduate Diploma and Masters in Computing Science. He continued his PhD graduate studies in Computer Science at Brunel University, London, UK where his PhD thesis was about developing an intelligent system for designing adaptive computer architectures. Subsequently, Dr. Mohammed joined several academic institutions as Assistant/Associate Professor of Computer Science (BU, Amman University, Philadelphia University, Applied Science University and HCT). During that time (1986-2001) Dr. Mohammed chaired several Computer Science and Information Systems departments including those at Philadelphia University, Applied Science University, HCT. Since late 2001, Dr. Mohammed has been a Professor of Computer Science at Lakehead University, Ontario, Canada. Dr. Mohammed also served as a Visiting Professor at Laurentian University, Department of Math and Computer Science during winter 2007. Currently Dr. Mohammed is also an Adjunct Research Professor at the University of Western Ontario (2009-2012). Dr. Mohammed has co-authored four text books on Compilers, Artificial Intelligence, Java Programming and Applied Image Processing. Dr. has published over 90 refereed publications and supervised numerous graduate students and has received research support from a variety of governmental and industrial organizations. Dr. Mohammed organized two international conferences as well as chairing several conference sessions and has been an IPC member of several notable conferences. Dr. Mohammed is the coordinator of the Northern Ontario Web Intelligence research group established in 2003. His research interests include Web Intelligence, Ubiquitous Computing,

Web-Oriented Architectures, Ambient and Mobile Computing, Image Processing for Ubiquitous Images and Medical Informatics. Dr. Mohammed is the Editor-in-Chief of the Journal of Emerging Technologies in Web Intelligence. Dr. Mohammed is also on the editorial boards of several other journals (e.g. Computer Aided Engineering and Technology, Journal of Universal Computing, International Journal of Computing and Information Sciences, International Journal of Network Security, International Journal of Pattern Recognition and Machine Intelligence and Journal of Computer Science). Dr. Mohammed is a member of the British Computer Society, Professional Software Engineer of Ontario, and a professional member of the ACM, CIPS and IEEE.

Rebecca Montanari PhD is an associate professor of computer engineering in the Department of Electronic and Information Systems at the University of Bologna. Her research interests include policy-based networking and systems/service management, mobile agent systems, security management mechanisms, and tools in both traditional and mobile systems. She received her PhD in computer science engineering from the University of Bologna. She is a member of the IEEE and AICA.

Francesco Paolucci (1977) is a health economist and research fellow at the Australian Centre for Economic Research on Health at the Australian National University. Prior to taking up his current post in 2007, he worked for five years as a researcher at the Institute of Health Policy and Management, Erasmus University of Rotterdam, where he wrote his PhD thesis entitled "The design of basic and supplementary healthcare financing schemes: implications for affordability and efficiency". Since leaving Erasmus, Francesco's work and research have focused on the economic analysis of healthcare governance in Australia, risk adjustment and managed competition, long-term care and aged-care, and on the economics of health information technology. His previous and current appointments include: Coordinator/lecturer of the course in "Competition policy in the health care sector" at Erasmus University Rotterdam (2007); Coordinator/lecturer of the course in "Health Insurance and Financing" at the Australian National University (2007); member of the iHEA Scientific Committee (2005); member of the risk adjustment network (2009).

Kalyan Sunder Pasupathy is an Assistant Professor in Health Management & Informatics in the School of Medicine at the University of Missouri. Dr. Pasupathy has a PhD in Industrial & Systems Engineering from Virginia Tech. Prior to joining University of Missouri, he worked for the American Red Cross, national headquarters in Washington DC for four years, where he was part of the operations research & analysis unit in corporate strategy. His work has been published in refereed journals and peer reviewed conference proceedings, and his research has been funded by various organizations. Along with his colleagues, he was awarded the Goodeve Medal in 2008 by the Operations Research Society at the Royal Society in London, UK for the development and implementation of a data envelopment analysis-based performance management system. He has also been recognized as a New Face of Engineering by the National Engineers' Week Foundation in 2009.

Shmuel Reis, MD, MHPE, is a family physician to a stable patient population in Northern Israel within a regional integrated health and social services health center pioneered over 31 years ago. He is presently the Chairperson of the Division of Family Medicine and immediate past-chair of Medical Education in the Technion [Israel Institute of Technology] Rappaport Faculty of Medicine, Haifa, Israel. He also coordinated the Galil Center for Medical Informatics and Telemedicine in the same faculty.

About the Contributors

Stefane M. Kabene, MPs, PhD, is a faculty member in the Aubrey Dan Program in Management and Organizational Studies with a cross appointment in the Faculty of Health Science at the University of Western Ontario, London, Ontario, Canada. His primary interests are in health care, information and communication technology and human resources for health. His focus is on interprofessional collaborative practice, knowledge transfer, quality of care and patient involvement in clinical decision making. The future of health care lies in health professionals' capacity and willingness to develop new ways of working together for the benefit of the patient. Knowledge and power sharing, role valuing, use of information and communication technology and patients' participation in decision making are only a few of the variables we need to better understand. Dr. Kabene is involved in research projects with the Schulich School of Medicine and Dentistry, the School of Nursing, and the Faculty of Social Sciences.

* * *

Jos Aarts is a research scientist at the Institute of Health Policy and Management and the Department of Medical Informatics of Erasmus University, Rotterdam in the Netherlands. His scientific interest is the impact of information technology on clinical work practices. His PhD thesis was on the implementation of computerized physician order entry systems in Dutch and American hospitals. His research papers on CPOE appeared in Health Affairs, the Journal of American Medical Informatics Association, the International Journal of Medical Informatics and Methods of Information in Medicine. Dr. Aarts has been a visiting scientist at the Oregon Health and Science University in the USA, and the University of New South Wales and the University of Sydney in Australia. Currently he is also a visiting research fellow at the University of Pennsylvania in the USA. He is chair of the Working Group on Human and Organizational Factors of Medical Informatics of the European Federation for Medical Informatics.

Kelly J. Abrams, MPA, CHIM, is Vice President of Education and Professional Practice for the Canadian Health Information Management Association (CHIMA). She has a diploma in Health Information Technology, an undergraduate degree in Health Administration, and a Masters degree in Public Administration (Public Policy). Kelly has over 25 years experience as a certified HIM Professional and has been involved in coding classification, data analysis, risk management, privacy, telehealth, teaching and management. She was awarded the CIHI/CHIMA Joady Murray Memorial Award in 2008.

Anteneh Ayanso is an Associate Professor of Information Systems at Brock University. He received his Ph.D. in Information Systems from the University of Connecticut and an MBA from Syracuse University. He teaches Data Management, Data Mining Techniques & Applications, Data Analysis & Business

Modelling, and Management of Information Systems & Technology. His research interests include data management, information retrieval, electronic business, and quantitative modelling in supply chains. His articles are published in Communications of the AIS, European Journal of Operational Research, Decision Support Systems, International Journal of Electronic Commerce, Journal of Computer Information Systems, Journal of Database Management, and in proceedings of major international conferences in information systems. His research has been funded by the Natural Sciences and Engineering Research Council of Canada (NSERC).

Robert J. Barnet M.D., M.A., FACP, FACC is a Senior Scholar in Residence at the Center for Clinical Bioethics at Georgetown University, Washington, DC. Dr. Barnet is a graduate of the University of Notre Dame and Loyola University School of Medicine (Chicago). Dr. Barnet practiced Cardiology for over 25 years in Reno, Nevada. Dr. Barnet received an M.A. in History from the University of Nevada (1986) and an M.A. in Philosophy from the University of Notre Dame (1988). He was a visiting scholar at the University of Notre Dame in 1989-90 (Theology: Ethics and Health Policy) and 1996-1997 (Philosophy). Dr. Barnet has been involved in medical ethics since 1982. He has lectured internationally and published more than 65 articles, on both cardiology and ethics, including on AIDS, end of life issues, health policy and the philosophy of medicine.

Nicholas G. Bircher is Associate Professor of Anesthesiology, University of Pittsburgh, from 1996-present; A.B., Chemistry and Physics, Harvard, 1977; M.D., University of Pittsburgh, 1981; Chair, Bylaws and Procedures Committee, 2007- present, Faculty Representative, Budget Committee of the Board of Trustees, 2005-present; President, University Senate 2003-2005; Co-Chair, American College of Critical Care Medicine Task Force on Glycemic Control, 2005-present; Scientist Emeritus, 2009-present, Senior Clinician Scientist, 2001-2009, and Associate Director, 1989-2001, Safar Center for Resuscitation Research; Co-Director, Neurovascular Intensive Care Unit, Presbyterian University Hospital, 2001-2007; Program Director, Anesthesiology Critical Care Medicine Fellowship, 2001-2007; Chairman, School of Medicine Planning and Budgeting Committee, 1993-2001; Senior Vice Chancellor Health Sciences Planning and Budgeting Committee, 1995-2001; Member, Faculty Assembly, 1997-2006, 2007-present; Faculty Representative, Health Sciences Committee of the Board of Trustees, 1997-2001; Member, Council, Faculty Association of the School of Medicine, 1998-present; Member, Ad Hoc University of Pittsburgh Physicians Faculty Oversight Committee, 1998-1999.

Dario Bottazzi PhD is currently working as a senior researcher at Guglielmo Marconi Labs SpA, Pontecchio (BO), Italy. Prior to his current position, he was research fellow in the Department of Electronic and Information Systems at the University of Bologna. His research interests include middleware solutions for collaborative applications in mobile environments, social computing, and pervasive computing technologies. He received his PhD in computer science engineering from the University of Bologna.

Emmett Davis, as an information worker in compliance with Moore's Law, was a librarian for one decade. For over two decades, he has innovated in information technology within local government Human Services. Emmett creates, consults, and authors on knowledge and information systems, including diffuse systems, artificial intelligence, quality, the synergy of technology and business processes, and e-government. Miracle materials are wonderful. But a culture, which continually builds brick walls, needs new ideas to also build arches in those walls for doors and windows.

Sisira Edirippulige PhD (Moscow), PhD (Auckland), MSc (Moscow), GradCert in Health Sc (UQ) is Coordinator of Graduate Programs in e-Health care at the University of Queensland, Centre for On-line Health, Australia. Dr Edirippulige's main responsibilities involve teaching and the coordination of undergraduate and graduate programs in e-healthcare. His research interests include the development, promotion, and integration of telehealth education and telemedicine applications in the health care sector. Before joining the University of Queensland, Dr Edirippulige taught at Kobe Gakuin University in Japan and at the University of Auckland in New Zealand. He has extensive experience in development studies working in a number of countries including Russia, Sri Lanka, South Africa, Japan and New Zealand.

Henry Ergas is a Canberra based economist. He was an economist at the OECD from 1978 to 1993, where he headed the Secretary-General's Task Force on Structural Adjustment (1984-1987), and was subsequently Counsellor for Structural Policy in the Economics Department. Since leaving the OECD in 1993, Henry's work has focused on competition policy and regulatory economics. He has been closely involved in dealing with regulatory issues in a range of industries, including telecommunications, electricity, aviation, surface transport, and financial services. He chaired the Intellectual Property and Competition Policy Review Committee for the Australian Government in 1999-2000, and was a member of the Prime Minister's Export Infrastructure Task Force in 2005 and of the Defence Industry Consultative Group in 2006. He has taught at a number of universities, including the Ecole Nationale de la Statistique et de L'administration Economique (Paris), the Kennedy School of Government at Harvard, Monash University in Melbourne and the University of Auckland.

Susan Evans-Mueller is a Project Director for HCA Shared Services Group, Houston. Susan received her MAIS from University of Houston, Victoria and has a BAAS from Texas A&M University – Kingsville.

Jinan Fiaidhi is Full Professor of Computer Science at Lakehead University. She is also an Adjunct Research Professor with the University of Western Ontario. She received a Ph.D. degree in Computer Science from Brunel University in 1986, a Postgraduate Diploma in Microprocessors Programming from Essex University in 1983 and a Diploma in Production Engineering from the University of Technology in 1978. Her research interest involves Collaborative Learning, Telemedical Education, Personal Learning Environments, Virtual Multimedia Learning Objects, Mobile Learning, Collaborative Learning at the Enterprise Level and at the Web, Applications of Mashups and Rich Internet Applications in Learning, Developing Learning Infrastructures (e.g. P2P, Mobile, Wireless, Grid, Web 2.0), Learning Ontologies and Folksonomies, and Learning Reasoners. Dr. Fiaidhi has a long research and teaching experience as she has held various academic positions including being a chairperson of the Department of Computer Science-University of Technology, the postgraduate organizer of the Department of Computer Science, Sultan Qaboos University. Dr. Fiaidhi's research is fully supported by NSERC (National Science and Engineering Research Council) and CFI (Canada Foundation for Innovation) research grants. Dr. Fiaidhi has authored four books, five chapters in books and over 100 refereed articles in highly reputed journals and conference proceedings. Dr. Fiaidhi has had several notable research achievements that include Virtual SceneBeans, DICOM Based Mobile Infrastructure for Telemedical Learning, Biomedical Semantic Blog, and Ontology Extracting Agent for Telemedical Blogging. Dr. Fiaidhi is a Professional Software Engineer of Ontario (PEng), member of IEEE, CIPS, ACM and the BCS.

Candace J Gibson, PhD, CHIM is an Associate Professor in the Department of Pathology at the Schulich School of Medicine and Dentistry, the University of Western Ontario, in London, ON. She has been involved in medical research, teaching to undergraduate baccalaureate, medical, nursing and dental students, and administration in the department's graduate and undergraduate degree programs. Over the past decade she has been actively engaged in the introduction of teaching in health informatics as a medical school elective and in the health information management program in the Faculty of Health Sciences. In the latter program she teaches courses in pathology, health informatics, and health information management. Her current interests include the development of effective e-learning tools, HI and HIM curriculum development, and the introduction and use of the electronic health record.

Nada Gligorov completed her PhD in philosophy from the Graduate Center of City University of New York. Her two areas of specialization are philosophy of mind and bioethics. She has been a bioethics fellow from 2002-2007 at the Mount Sinai School of Medicine, where she has remained on the faculty as Assistant Professor of Medical Education and Assistant Director of Bioethics Education. She teaches both research and clinical ethics for the Mount Sinai--Union Graduate College Bioethics Program. Her professional interests include neuroethics, advanced directives and the personal identity problem, consciousness, and the distinction between commonsense and scientific theories.

Terry John Hannan M.B.B.S FRACP, FACHI, FACMI, is a Consultant Physician in Internal Medicine at the Launceston General Hospital in Tasmania, Australia. He is an inaugural Fellow of the Australian College of Health Informatics and was its President from 2007 to 2009. His initial work in informatics was the international transfer and implementation of the Johns Hopkins Oncology computerized medical record system in a major teaching hospital in New South Wales. In 2000 he was invited to cofound the Mosoriot Medical Record System (MMRS) in Kenya that became the fore runner of the AMPATH (Academic Model for the Provision and Treatment of Health Care) which is based on the OpenMRS record project. He is a current member of the AMIA International Affairs Committee.

Kendall Ho, MD, FRCPC, is a practicing emergency medicine specialist and Associate Professor in the Department of Emergency Medicine at the University of British Columbia. He is the founding Director, eHealth Strategy Office, University of British Columbia Faculty of Medicine. He was the immediate past Associate Dean of the Division of Continuing Professional Development and Knowledge Translation (UBC CPD-KT). He is the executive director of the Technology Enabled Knowledge Translation Investigative Centre (TEKTIC) interdisciplinary research team in B.C. Dr. Ho's academic and research interests fall into the domain of technology enabled knowledge translation (TEKT) – the use of information technologies to accelerate the incorporation of latest health evidence into routine practice. Specific directions within TEKT include telehealth, information and communication technologies (ICT) and patient safety, ICT and public engagement, and evidence based policy translation in eHealth. He is a recipient of a number of provincial, national, and international research grants in eHealth and eLearning, and has published related papers and textbook chapters in these subjects.

Malina Jordanova, MD, Ph.D. received her medical degree in 1984, Ph.D. in neuropsychology in 1990, and subsequently a post-doctoral position at the Max-Planck Institute for Human Development and Education, Germany in 1994-1995. Dr. Jordanova is author and co-author of over 120 papers and more than 100 conference presentations; Vice-Rapporteur for Question 14/2 of International Telecommunication Union, Switzerland. Currently she is focusing on eHealth and ICT applications in health care. At present she coordinates a project devoted to telepsychology, funded by the Bulgarian National Science Fund. Since 2002 she has coordinated the annual Educational program of Med-e-Tel (The International eHealth, Telemedicine and Health ICT Forum for Education, Networking and Business, http://www.medetel.eu) and with F. Lievens is editor of the series "Global Telemedicine and eHealth Updates: Knowledge Resources". Volumes 1 & 2 were published in 2008 and 2009.

Stephen Krieger, MD completed his Neurology residency training at Mount Sinai in 2006. He received a Fellowship in clinical research from the National Multiple Sclerosis Society 2006, and completed a two-year fellowship training in Multiple Sclerosis at Mount Sinai in 2008. He graduated from Columbia College, and received his MD degree from Yale University. In addition to his clinical work at the MS Center, he has an academic appointment as Assistant Professor of Neurology at the Mount Sinai School of Medicine, where he is a member of the Education Committee and runs the Brain and Behavior seminar series for the medical school. His professional interests include MS, behavioral neurology, and modern MRI techniques.

Kaveepan Lertwachara is an Associate Professor of Information Systems at the Orfalea College of Business, California Polytechnic State University. He received his PhD in Information Systems from The University of Connecticut. His industry background is in health care information systems, public health, and health care quality. Dr. Lertwachara's research interest includes healthcare informatics, electronic commerce, online data retrieval, and economics of information systems. His research has been published in leading academic journals such as Communications of the Association for Information Systems, Decision Support Systems, International Journal of Human-Computer Studies, Journal of Computer Information Systems, Journal of Law and Economics, Journal of Management Information Systems, and Management Science.

Sabah Mohammed joined Glasgow University in 1979 for his graduate studies where he obtained his Post-Graduate Diploma and Masters in Computing Science. He continued his PhD graduate studies in Computer Science at Brunel University, London, UK where his PhD thesis was about developing an intelligent system for designing adaptive computer architectures. Subsequently, Dr. Mohammed joined several academic institutions as Assistant/Associate Professor of Computer Science (BU, Amman University, Philadelphia University, Applied Science University and HCT). During that time (1986-2001) Dr. Mohammed chaired several Computer Science and Information Systems departments including those at Philadelphia University, Applied Science University, HCT. Since late 2001, Dr. Mohammed has been a Professor of Computer Science at Lakehead University, Ontario, Canada. Dr. Mohammed also served as a Visiting Professor at Laurentian University, Department of Math and Computer Science during winter 2007. Currently Dr. Mohammed is also an Adjunct Research Professor at the University of Western Ontario (2009-2012). Dr. Mohammed has co-authored four text books on Compilers, Artificial Intelligence, Java Programming and Applied Image Processing. Dr. has published over 90 refereed publications and supervised numerous graduate students and has received research support from a variety of governmental and industrial organizations. Dr. Mohammed organized two international conferences as well as chairing several conference sessions and has been an IPC member of several notable conferences. Dr. Mohammed is the coordinator of the Northern Ontario Web Intelligence research group established in 2003. His research interests include Web Intelligence, Ubiquitous Computing,

Web-Oriented Architectures, Ambient and Mobile Computing, Image Processing for Ubiquitous Images and Medical Informatics. Dr. Mohammed is the Editor-in-Chief of the Journal of Emerging Technologies in Web Intelligence. Dr. Mohammed is also on the editorial boards of several other journals (e.g. Computer Aided Engineering and Technology, Journal of Universal Computing, International Journal of Computing and Information Sciences, International Journal of Network Security, International Journal of Pattern Recognition and Machine Intelligence and Journal of Computer Science). Dr. Mohammed is a member of the British Computer Society, Professional Software Engineer of Ontario, and a professional member of the ACM, CIPS and IEEE.

Rebecca Montanari PhD is an associate professor of computer engineering in the Department of Electronic and Information Systems at the University of Bologna. Her research interests include policy-based networking and systems/service management, mobile agent systems, security management mechanisms, and tools in both traditional and mobile systems. She received her PhD in computer science engineering from the University of Bologna. She is a member of the IEEE and AICA.

Francesco Paolucci (1977) is a health economist and research fellow at the Australian Centre for Economic Research on Health at the Australian National University. Prior to taking up his current post in 2007, he worked for five years as a researcher at the Institute of Health Policy and Management, Erasmus University of Rotterdam, where he wrote his PhD thesis entitled "The design of basic and supplementary healthcare financing schemes: implications for affordability and efficiency". Since leaving Erasmus, Francesco's work and research have focused on the economic analysis of healthcare governance in Australia, risk adjustment and managed competition, long-term care and aged-care, and on the economics of health information technology. His previous and current appointments include: Coordinator/lecturer of the course in "Competition policy in the health care sector" at Erasmus University Rotterdam (2007); Coordinator/lecturer of the course in "Health Insurance and Financing" at the Australian National University (2007); member of the iHEA Scientific Committee (2005); member of the risk adjustment network (2009).

Kalyan Sunder Pasupathy is an Assistant Professor in Health Management & Informatics in the School of Medicine at the University of Missouri. Dr. Pasupathy has a PhD in Industrial & Systems Engineering from Virginia Tech. Prior to joining University of Missouri, he worked for the American Red Cross, national headquarters in Washington DC for four years, where he was part of the operations research & analysis unit in corporate strategy. His work has been published in refereed journals and peer reviewed conference proceedings, and his research has been funded by various organizations. Along with his colleagues, he was awarded the Goodeve Medal in 2008 by the Operations Research Society at the Royal Society in London, UK for the development and implementation of a data envelopment analysis-based performance management system. He has also been recognized as a New Face of Engineering by the National Engineers' Week Foundation in 2009.

Shmuel Reis, MD, MHPE, is a family physician to a stable patient population in Northern Israel within a regional integrated health and social services health center pioneered over 31 years ago. He is presently the Chairperson of the Division of Family Medicine and immediate past-chair of Medical Education in the Technion [Israel Institute of Technology] Rappaport Faculty of Medicine, Haifa, Israel. He also coordinated the Galil Center for Medical Informatics and Telemedicine in the same faculty.

He is teaching and mentoring at all levels from student to practitioners in CME. He co-edited: *Patients and Doctors: Life-Changing Stories From Primary Care* (1999), and is the PI for an instruction and assessment of primary care physicians' communication skills in the computerized environment research project, conducted in the Israeli National Simulation Center.

Aviv Shachak holds a Ph.D. in Information Science from Bar-Ilan University, Israel. Following a post-doctoral fellowship at Galil Center for Medical Informatics, Telemedicine and Personalized Medicine at the Technion-Israel Institute of Technology, he is now Assistant Professor in University of Toronto's Department of Health Policy, Management and Evaluation (Faculty of Medicine) and Faculty of Information. His main research focus is the implementation and use of information systems in health care and biomedicine; in particular the organizational factors that influence the deployment and use of electronic medical records (EMRs) in primary care, the cognitive factors involved in their use during consultations, and their impact on communication and decision making processes. His work has been published in medical, health informatics, and information science journals including the Journal of General Internal Medicine, the International Journal of Medical Informatics and the Journal of the American Society for Information Science and Technology.

Gulzar H. Shah is a Senior Research and Evaluation Analyst, at the National Association of County and City Health Officials (NACCHO), and an adjunct Professorial Lecturer at the Department of Health Policy, George Washington University. Dr. Shah has an interdisciplinary training with bachelor's degree in Mathematics, Masters in Statistics, another Masters Degree in Social Sciences and PhD in Sociology with Medical Sociology and Demography as areas of emphasis. His research interests include ways to address issues surrounding health data integration, analysis, reporting, and dissemination; measuring and reporting healthcare quality, safety and performance; reproductive health; gender issues; healthcare disparities, statistical methods in healthcare and public health research; and probabilistic record linkage of large healthcare data. Dr. Shah's publications have appeared in top international journals, including Obstetrics and Gynecology, Population Research and Policy Review, Euro-Asian Journal of Applied Sciences, Journal of Public Health Management and Practice JPHMP, and European Journal of Scientific Research. In May of 2005, Dr. Shah was awarded a recognition Shield of "Distinguished Scholar for Outstanding Academic Research" by the European Journal of Scientific Research.

Anthony C Smith PhD, MEd (Adult & Workplace Training), BNurs., RN, is Deputy Director at the University of Queensland Centre for Online Health. Dr Smith is the Senior Research Fellow in Telemedicine at the Centre for Online Health. He completed a doctoral degree in the field of medicine in 2004 examining the feasibility and cost-effectiveness of a novel telepediatric service in Queensland. His principal role in the Centre for Online Health includes the management, coordination, and evaluation of telepediatric services. Dr Smith has made a substantial contribution to the literature on telepediatrics publishing numerous articles in peer-reviewed journals and book chapters on the subject. Dr Smith assists in the supervision of a broad range of telemedicine projects and teaching programs in the Centre for Online Health and also provides consultancy services to other university departments and external organisations.

Tarik Taleb is currently working as Senior Researcher at NEC Europe Ltd, Heidelberg, Germany. Prior to his current position, he worked as assistant professor at Tohoku University, Japan. He received his MSc and PhD degrees in Information Sciences from Tohoku University. His research interests lie in the field of architectural enhancements to 3GPP networks, mobile multimedia streaming, wireless networking, inter-vehicular communications, satellite and space communications. He is on the editorial board of the IEEE Transactions on Vehicular Technology, IEEE Communications Surveys & Tutorials, and a number of Wiley journals.

Dag von Lubitz, Ph.D, M.D.(Sc.) describes himself as a generalist and conceptualist; he is recently retired from the posts of Chairman of the Board and Chief Scientist at MedSMART, Inc. Prior to his nearly decade-long affiliation with the business industry, Dr. von Lubitz had a distinguished academic career at several leading universities and research institutions of Europe and the US resulting in over 220 papers, book chapters, and books spanning medicine, molecular neuropharmacology, IT, leadership, and homeland defense and security. Laureate of the Smithsonian Institution Award, winner of the Laval Prize, and holder of several other national and international scientific awards, Dr. von Lubitz works currently as a consultant in the US and EU concentrating on global healthcare, decision-making and leadership in crises and disasters, and homeland defence and security. An avid mondialist, von Lubitz specializes in developing effective collaboration and cooperation based on combined people-technology approaches (including network-centricity and social networks) in worldwide affairs of civil society, business, politics, and health care.

Yun Wan, PhD is an Assistant Professor in computer information systems and Director of the graduate program at the University of Houston, Victoria. His research interests include decision support systems, especially software agents, and e-commerce. Wan received his Ph.D. in Management Information Systems from the University of Illinois at Chicago. He has a BS in management and a BE in computer science from the University of Science and Technology of China.

Yuan Wei graduated with a BSc in Computer Science from China in 2006. She completed her MSc in Computer Science in August 2008 under the supervision of both Dr. Jinan Fiaidhi and Dr. Sabah Mohammed.

Melody Wolfe is currently a psychology student at the University of Western Ontario specializing in Cognitive and Behavioural Neuroscience and a research assistant to Dr. Stefane Kabene. She is currently examining the association between psychopathology and creativity, specifically, how traits commonly coupled with psychopathic behaviour are correlated with the expression of creativity in artists. Prior research includes the effect of semantic priming on memory, and the cognitive processes involved with discriminating between concrete and abstract concepts. Ms. Wolfe is also involved with volunteer programs at Sunnybrook Hospital in Toronto, ON, and the Epilepsy Support Centre in London, ON. She recently spent a summer in Tacloban City, Philippines providing free health care services to underprivileged communities. Her remaining free time is spent volunteering for a variety of on-campus organizations and writing freelance articles for newspapers in both Toronto and London, Ontario.

Index

A

actionable information 145, 163
actionable knowledge 145, 151, 157, 158,
    160, 163, 164, 165
actionable understanding 158, 161, 163, 165
active server pages (ASP) 276, 277, 279
actuator entity (AE) 261
adaptive systems 127, 136
adverse drug events (ADE) 14, 16, 17
affective interactions 259
alert fatigue 76
ambivalent 222
annotation processor 280
ANOTO 44
APACHE 89, 95
a priori 256, 265
artificial intelligence (AI) 258
AssistiNG ELders At Home (ANGELAH)
    254, 261, 262, 263, 264, 265, 266,
    268
asynchronous 103, 104
avionics 85, 93

B

backbone network 120
background noise 239
balanced scorecard 130, 140
BargainFinder 117, 121
best guess 90
bidirectional 86
biobanking 216, 217, 218, 219, 220, 226,
    227, 229, 230
biocolonialism 223, 224, 231
bioethical 224

bioethicists 234
biotech 217, 221
bio-terrorism 41
blocking 201, 207, 208
blocking variables 207, 208
blood-oxygen-level dependent (BOLD)
    233, 237, 238, 239
bottom-up 145, 160, 163, 164, 165, 227
brain-drain 147
business-to-consumer (B2C) 117

C

call for assistance (CFA) 262
cardiovascular disease (CVD) 147
caregiver 259
Centers for Medicare and Medicaid Services
    (CMS) 116, 117, 126, 209
Centre for Online Health (COH)
    101, 105, 106, 107, 108
change agent 63
chronic obstructive pulmonary disease (COPD)
    24
civil monetary penalties (CMP) 95
clinical complexity 18
clinical decision making (CDM) 15, 16
clinical decision support system (CDSS)
    73, 74, 148
clinical informaticians 17
Club Penguin 4
co-creation 6, 8
code record 86
cognitive gap 150
cognitive load 76, 254
cognitive science 233, 243
common good 218

Breinigsville, PA USA
27 October 2010
248036BV00003BD/6/P

9 781615 207336